PENGUIN ENGLISH LIBRARY

Selections from *The Tatler* and *The Spectator*

Angus Ross is Reader in English at the University of Sussex. The author of a study of Swift's *Gulliver's Travels*, he has also edited Daniel Defoe's *Robinson Crusoe* and Tobias Smollett's *The Expedition of Humphry Clinker* for the Penguin English Library, and a number of eighteenth-century texts and anthologies.

Selections from

THE TATLER

and

THE SPECTATOR

of Steele and Addison

Edited with an Introduction and Notes by
ANGUS ROSS

PENGUIN BOOKS

Penguin Books Ltd, Harmondsworth, Middlesex, England
Penguin Books, 625 Madison Avenue, New York, New York 10022, U.S.A.
Penguin Books Australia Ltd, Ringwood, Victoria, Australia
Penguin Books Canada Ltd, 2801 John Street, Markham, Ontario, Canada L3R 1B4
Penguin Books (N.Z.) Ltd, 182–190 Wairau Road, Auckland 10, New Zealand

Published in Penguin English Library 1982

Made and printed in Great Britain by
Hazell Watson & Viney Ltd, Aylesbury, Bucks
Set in Garamond

To
John Ross and Agnes Simpson

Contents

Essays from THE TATLER

Contents

Essays from *THE SPECTATOR*

I *Form and Framework: Mr Spectator and the Club*

II *Men, Women, Manners*

III *The Town and Daily Life*

IV *Essays in Criticism*

Preface

The aim of this collection of essays from *The Tatler* and *The Spectator* is three-fold. It seeks to present the writing in the two major, eighteenth-century periodicals in such a way as to allow full and enjoyable realization of the great imaginative achievement of Steele and Addison, a success which places each of them high in the ranks of English writers. Secondly, the volume is also arranged to give some idea of the intellectual, social, political and literary life in London in the reign of Queen Anne, a seminal period in our culture. The *Tatler* and *Spectator* essays are almost designed for this. They appeared in periodical papers, the 271 numbers of *The Tatler* thrice-weekly, the 555 numbers of *The Spectator* in its first series, daily. Clearly the pieces had to have an immediacy, topicality and a rapport with a regular purchasing public. Thirdly, of course, the essays have a more lasting worth and appeal. They were immediately sold in collections, even before the runs had finished. The present volume, therefore, is also meant to embody some of the essays that made the collections a shaping force in English writing, as well as in British, and indeed in European, culture generally for the rest of the eighteenth century and later.

The earlier *Tatler* papers, following the original plan, consist of several different pieces, not all of equal interest. Each constituent piece has been treated here as a separate essay, and where appropriate selection has been made among the pieces. Each piece is given an editorial title, within square brackets. This is done sometimes at the expense of a little violence to the text, since even in small-scale constituent parts, Steele often starts with one topic and strolls round a few others. Complete papers and selected pieces, representing thirty-nine numbers of the periodical, are printed in chronological order which will give the reader a flavour of the *farrago nostri libelli*, the hotch-potch of the book, mentioned in the motto to the opening numbers. *The Spectator* is different. Most of the papers consist of single essays, most of them more connected, more substantial than the *Tatler* pieces. Some form series, like Addison's eleven essays on 'The Pleasures of the Imagination'. Seventy-nine *Spectator* papers have been reprinted here, therefore, not in chronological order, but under six headings:

Form and Framework: Mr Spectator and the Club (16 essays)
Men, Women, Manners   (10 essays)
The Town and Daily Life   (9 essays)
Essays in Criticism   (30 essays)
Politics and Public Affairs   (9 essays)
Religion and the Conduct of Life   (15 essays)

Within each section, essays are sometimes grouped together regardless of chronology, like the De Coverley papers, the series on 'The Pleasures of the Imagination' or that on Milton's *Paradise Lost*. The sections are naturally not mutually exclusive, but give an indication of the spread of interests in the periodical as a whole. The numbers of essays within the sections do not indicate the frequency with which such topics appear in the run of the papers. There were in fact two series of *Spectator* papers: the first, appearing daily from March 1711 to December 1712 (nos. 1–555), was conducted jointly by Steele and Addison; the second, a continuation by Addison helped by Eustace Budgell and Thomas Tickell, appeared three times a week from June to November 1714 (nos. 556–635). The papers printed in the present volume are taken only from the first, Steele–Addison, series. Each essay is given an editorial title within square brackets. A list in numerical order with page references of the *Spectator* essays included in this volume will be found on p. 20.

It is often unclear when reference is made to *The Tatler* or to *The Spectator* whether the thrice-weekly and daily papers or the collected essays are meant, and whether the second series of *The Spectator* is also intended. So far as the collected series of essays are concerned, these were first prepared by Steele himself for *The Tatler* and by Steele and Addison themselves for the first series of *The Spectator*. The Note on the Text below (pp. 59–62) gives further details about the relationship between the original papers and the collections, and explains the nature of the text printed in this volume. Since it is the original collected essays of *The Tatler* and *The Spectator* that are used by later readers, an Appendix of papers relating to these collections is included (pp. 485–502).

The *Tatler* and *Spectator* essays may easily be read and enjoyed without explanations, and have been for two and a half centuries. They do, however, contain much matter of entertaining and topical interest to their own readers, which may need a little illustration now; certain aids to the reader have therefore been placed out of the way at the back of this book. There are notes, separately numbered for each essay. To avoid duplication of notes to writing so deeply rooted in a small, cohesive society, a Biographical Index of Contemporaries Mentioned in the Essays has been provided on pp. 566–76, reference to which is made in the notes by the symbol ⟐. Two maps may be found useful, that of operations in the War of the Spanish Succession (p. 577) and that of contemporary London (pp. 578–9). Finally a Glossary of Words and Phrases is given on pp. 580–91; reference to this in the text is by the symbol ° preceding an entry word.

Acknowledgements

All students of early eighteenth-century English literature are greatly in the debt of two scholars: R. P. Bond for his work on the periodical press in general and, even though his long-awaited edition is not yet available, on *The Tatler* in particular; and D. F. Bond for his indispensable edition of *The Spectator*. Direct quotation from their work is noted, but the editor's general debt is also great. All editors of these essays of course draw freely on the hard work of their predecessors, beginning with Bishop Percy and including J. Nichols, Chalmers, Henry Morley, G. Gregory Smith and G. A. Aitken. Grateful thanks for assistance in preparing the volume are also given to Penny Admiraal, Anthea Ross, members of the Burgess Hill W.E.A. English Literature class 1978–9 and, especially, David Woolley.

Abbreviations

S 1	a *Spectator* paper included in this volume
Spectator 5	a *Spectator* paper not included in this volume
T 1	a *Tatler* paper included in this volume
Tatler 7	a *Tatler* paper not included in this volume
◊	preceding a name indicates an entry in the Biographical Index of Contemporaries Mentioned in the Essays (e.g. Alexander ◊ Pope)
°	preceding a word or phrase indicates an entry in the Glossary (e.g. °biters, °Act of Settlement)

List *in* Numerical Order *of* Spectator *Essays in This Volume*

Introduction

On Tuesday, 12 April 1709, the first number of a new periodical was offered to patrons of London coffee-houses and to customers in the bookshops, who no doubt carried it home to readers in their domestic circles. A neat, simple title, *The Tatler*, suggested the tone of the new journal, modest, friendly, disengaged, fashionable and self-deprecatory. It promised to appear three times a week, on Tuesdays, Thursdays and Saturdays. The first four numbers were given free, thereafter the cost was a penny (three half-pence for a copy with a blank sheet of paper for the purchaser's correspondence if it was to be sent down into the country).

The physical appearance of the new paper makes clear several of its links with contemporary periodicals. It is not very well printed on somewhat brown paper (see *T* 101) in the format known as a folio half-sheet, some 8¼ inches wide by 13½ inches long. The text is set in two columns on both sides of the paper, except for the first number which carries on two-thirds of the recto a four-paragraph introduction in italics running across both columns.

The last part of the text consists of a set of 'Advertisements': these comprise editorial intimations, including acknowledgements, *errata*, and the like; notices concerning the publication of *The Tatler*, such as the sale of title pages for readers who were collecting the individual numbers or invitations to subscribe to the collected editions; and finally paid advertisements by a wide range of tradesmen for goods and services. The space at the disposal of the writer or editor of the periodical was fixed, on average 1,600–1,800 words, though the printer could occasionally to a small extent make the text denser (almost 3,000 words) or sparser (almost 1,000). As the 'Advertisements' section became longer, however, with the increasing prosperity of the venture, ranging from a line or two in the first few numbers to a column and a half or more at the end of the series, the text became less extensive.

In appearance and lay-out *The Tatler* resembles a contemporary newspaper or journal. This resemblance, which is strengthened by the inclusion in some sixty-four numbers of a section of news, is not remarkable when it is recalled that 'John Morphew near *Stationers-Hall*', whose name appears at the end of each number as the seller, at the same time as *The Tatler* also published the leading Tory newspaper, Abel Roper's *The Post-Boy* and its *Supplement*, as well as other journals like the *Monthly Miscellany* of 1707 and a *Monthly Amusement* of serialized fiction. It was another well-known stationer, however, John Nutt, who entered the individual *Tatlers* and 'all other volumes whatsoever' in the *Stationers' Register* on 2 May and 5 September 1710, observing the terms of the new Copyright Act. He had been concerned in printing *The Tatler*. The physical context of the original numbers is absent from collected and reprinted essays and so is often neglected, yet several features of the contents and format of both *The Tatler* and *The Spectator* spring as much from the conditions of the original publication as from the authorial intention or literary choice that is the usual subject of rhetorical analysis of the papers.

As well as a physical context, the *Tatler* and *Spectator* essays also have an important background in the periodical literature of the time. From the small beginning in the first decades of the seventeenth century, the London periodical press grew during the Civil War, and thereafter flourished, with ups and downs of censorship and other difficulties. It has been estimated that of newspapers, journals and other serials some seven hundred titles had appeared up to this time. A large number of these, of course, were ephemeral, running for only two or three numbers; some, however, became well established and prospered in the new outburst of journalism that followed the lapse of the Licensing Act in 1695. A torrent of journalism marked in particular the political warfare and literary enterprise of Queen Anne's reign.

It is no exaggeration to say that every form of writing, every topic of discussion or method of circulation (save the issue of collected papers by subscription) characteristic of *The Tatler* and *The Spectator* had been seen in some periodical or other before they appeared. The impact and imaginative authority of these two periodicals was such, however, that for later readers they imposed an order on literary history, turning earlier periodicals into *fore-runners* and later papers into *successors*. This cultural map has its uses, but the actual relation between *The Tatler* and *The Spectator* on the one hand, and the flux of contemporary journalism on the other, is a good deal more complicated than such a scheme implies. The contemporary format of the newspapers, folio half-sheets in double columns with advertisements, had been established by Henry Muddiman's *Oxford Gazette*, later the *London Gazette*, the government newspaper which started on 16 November 1665 and is still running. *Momus Ridens: or, Comical Remarks on the Publick Reports* (no. 1, 29 October 1690 to no. 18, 25 February 1691) contained joke news with date-lines from The Hague, Whitehall and Westminster; *The English Lucian: or, Weekly Discoveries in the Witty Intrigues, Comical Passages and Remarkable Transactions in Town and Country, With Reflections on the Vices of the Times* (no. 1, 18 January to no. 15, 18 April 1698) took the form of facetious news from Whitechapel, Lincoln's Inn Fields, the Old Bailey, Drury Lane, Lombard Street, St James's and 'My Lodgings in Kent Street'. Both of these papers suggest the 'departments' of the early *Tatlers*, as well as drawing attention to the admirable economy of its title. Clearly there are unlikely to be 'influences' from ephemeral publications more than a decade earlier, but this gives some idea of the wealth of experimentation in the contemporary periodical press.

As newspapers multiplied, they became more specialized and spread into the provinces. General or miscellany journals dropped their news sections in response. Examples of periodicals that shed their news paragraphs in this way are Peter Motteux's *The Gentleman's Journal: or, The Monthly Miscellany by way of Letter to a Gentleman in the Country, consisting of News, History, Philosophy, Poetry, Musick* (January 1692 to November 1694); John Dunton's (monthly) *The Post-Angel* (January 1701 to September 1702); and Henry Playford's (weekly) *The Diverting Post: or, The Universal Medley* (no. 1, 28 October 1704 to no. 36, 30 June 1705 and January to February 1706). The abandonment of the news department is one of the changes often commented on in the history of *The Tatler*, but it is part of a wider trend as well as a personal choice on the part of the editor.

Some other features that connect *The Tatler* and *The Spectator*
with other periodicals of the time may be briefly noted as follows.
Nothing is better remembered about *The Spectator* than the
characters of Sir Roger de Coverley, Sir Andrew Freeport and the
other members of their club, like Will Wimble and of course Mr
Spectator himself. An earlier club is introduced in *The Tatler*, the
group meeting at the Trumpet Tavern in Sheer Lane (*T* 132). But
the plan of a club, round which periodical papers could be disposed,
was quite a common one. Aaron Hill's very successful, twice-weekly
The British Apollo: or, Curious Amusements for the Ingenious (13
February 1708 to May 1711) was 'performed by a Society of
Gentlemen'. The familiar device was inserted in *The Tatler* perhaps
as it flagged, and neither there nor in *The Spectator* does it become
the organizing principle. Could it have been held in reserve in case
of a shortage of material, or because it was familiar and comfortable?
The club motif is one of the links between the *Tatler* and *Spectator*
enterprises and one of the most astonishing periodicals of the age,
widely referred to as Daniel Defoe's *Review*. Defoe single-handed
ran this fascinating commentary on the contemporary scene first
twice-weekly, then three times a week, together with supplements
and special editions under three different titles. The most important
of these is the last, *A Review of the State of the English Nation*. The
whole venture ran from 19 February 1704 to 11 June 1713. As a
kind of light relief in the early numbers, a 'club' section followed
his essays on political events, economic and foreign affairs; this
burgeoned into two separate periodicals which Defoe also conducted: *A Supplementary Journal to the Advice from the Scandal Club*
(monthly, September 1704 to January 1705) and *The Little Review:
or, An Inquisition of Scandal; consisting in Answers of Questions and
Doubts, Remarks, Observations and Reflections* (thrice-weekly, no. 1,
6 June to no. 23, 22 August 1705).

Clubs demand talk, and *The Tatler* and *The Spectator* rely on
familiar conversation between fictional speakers or between the
friendly writer and the involved, though silent, reader. The
dialogue was in fact a staple form of presentation in early periodicals
and even newspapers, starting with a famous political sheet,
*Heraclitus Ridens: or, A Discourse between Jest and Earnest, where many
a true Word is spoken in Opposition to all Libellers against the Government*

(no. 1, 1 February 1681 to no. 82, 22 August 1682); other journals employing this mode include Sir Robert L'Estrange's pro-government *The Observator, in Question and Answer* (irregularly, 13 April 1681 to 9 March 1687).

The readership of *The Tatler* and *The Spectator* was involved and socialized by the answering of readers' questions (real or invented) and the printing of readers' contributions (genuine or editorially inspired), again both well-established contemporary operations, as in John Dunton's *The Athenian Gazette* (later *Mercury*): *or, Casuistical Mercury, Resolving all the most Nice and Curious Questions Proposed by the Ingenious* (no. 1, 17 March 1690 to no. 600, 14 June 1697). It has been calculated that letters make up eleven per cent of the contents of *The Tatler* and twenty-five per cent of the first series of *The Spectator*.

Many of the other forms and topics found in *The Tatler* and *The Spectator* might be traced in other papers, such as dream visions (like the essay on the Bank of England in *S* 3), or characters which were the staple of many popular sheets, or fiction; but enough has perhaps been said to show how inextricably *The Tatler* and *The Spectator* are rooted in the flourishing periodical publishing of the time. One final point, however, is worth noting. While *The Tatler* was in progress, Thomas Baker started *The Female Tatler* (no. 1, 18 July 1709 to no. 115, 2 January 1711). Baker was clearly helping himself to a successful title, but it is in the light of the success enjoyed in turn by Baker's form of a single essay per number, though Defoe and other journalists had employed this form, that the change in format in *The Tatler* itself ought to be considered, a change away from a group of pieces to a single piece, a form which is the hall-mark of *The Spectator*.

The Tatler offered itself as the 'Lucubrations' of '*Isaac Bickerstaff* Esq.' and by this joke draws attention to one of the reasons for its great success and the influence which it attracted, even though many of its modes and topics were familiar and well tried. This was its tone, and in this it was followed by its successor, *The Spectator*. The name of Bickerstaff, taken from 'a Sign over a House where a Locksmith dwelt' in Long Acre, goes back to the best April Fool joke and one of the happiest cluster of satirical pieces created by Jonathan Swift. At the end of February 1708, he published

Predictions for the Year 1708 . . ., 'Written to prevent the People of *England* from being further impos'd on by vulgar Almanack-makers. By Isaac Bickerstaff Esq.'. Embedded in this is the spring of the jest: 'My first Prediction is but a Trifle . . . It relates to *Partrige* the Almanack-Maker; I have consulted the Star of his Nativity by my own Rules; and find he will infallibly die upon the 29th of *March* next, about eleven at Night, of a raging Fever: Therefore I advise him to consider of it, and settle his Affairs in Time.' On 29 March, the unlucky ◊ Partridge heard the street-hawkers selling an anonymous verse broadside, also by Swift, 'An Elegy on Mr. Partrige, the Almanak-maker, who Died on the 29th of this Instant March, 1708'. On the last day of the month, in time for April Fool's Day, Swift assumed the guise of one formerly 'employed in the Revenue', like several of the subscribers to the later collected volumes of *Tatlers* and *Spectators* (see pp. 487–502); in 'A Letter to a Person of Honour', a small four-page 4to pamphlet, he circumstantially gave *The Accomplishment of the First of Mr. Bickerstaff's Predictions*.

Swift returned to the joke in the following year. In February he printed a half-sheet with a wood-cut, *A Famous Prediction of Merlin, the British Wizard; written above a Thousand Years ago, and relating to this present Year*. The ten rhyming couplets in black-letter are surrounded 'With Explanatory Notes by T. N. Philomath', which among other things make the link with the Bickerstaff–Partridge joke. Swift's April Fool piece for 1709, just twelve days before the first appearance of *The Tatler*, is a small eight-page 8vo pamphlet, *A Vindication of Isaac Bickerstaff Esq; against What is objected to Him by Mr. Partridge, in his Almanack for the Present Year* 1709. 'By the said Isaac Bickerstaff Esq.' The *Prediction of Merlin* and *A Vindication* brought back the name of Bickerstaff to public notice; the dates, and the fact that John Morphew, the publisher of *The Tatler*, also published the original *Predictions for the Year* 1708, all emphasize the connection between *The Tatler* and Swift's wit and satire. As well as attacking the imposture of astrologers and quacks, Swift was also satirizing the nonsense, the tone and the mischief inherent in the most lucrative contemporary periodicals of all, the annual almanacs. These not only contained the calendar with astronomical information, astrological notes, weather forecasts and predictions, but also additional material that varied from publication to publication, and which attracted its particular readership to each of some thirty titles. Political writing could be included in the associated matter, gardening hints, interest tables, patent medicine advertisements and a host of other things. Partridge's almanac, *Merlinus Liberatus*, with a circulation of about 20,000 copies, was the leading title; it specialized in low-church anti-Tory verse. Swift's attack was perhaps really fuelled by his scorn of the complacent tone and the shameless cheek of the almanac-writers. His operation is a joke within a joke, which depends on a reader's witty perception for its full effect. Bickerstaff is put up as a 'genuine' astrologer, a really learned 'philomath'. He is meant to be seen through by any wary and perceptive imagination on the same wavelength as his creator.

Readers of *The Tatler* are also meant to see through that particular 'Isaac Bickerstaff' to a witty creator; they are given the same feeling of being party to an in-joke. The wit of the periodical is less incisive than Swift's, however, less unpredictable and the texture of the prose less brilliant; therefore a very large contemporary audience enjoyed it, and as it became fashionable wished to be seen enjoying it. When the possibilities of Isaac Bickerstaff were exhausted, since after all an old bachelor and philomath could not credibly have an interest in everything his fashionable editor wished to talk about, the time came for a new, more supple, more shadowy speaker, and thus Isaac vanished and Mr Spectator took his bow.

As will be seen from a glance at the subscription lists for the collected *Tatlers* and *Spectators* (pp. 487–502), the former periodical was, so far as subscriptions at least were concerned, the up-market publication, a pointer to the tone and wit deployed in it. The writers of both periodicals carefully sought to establish themselves and keep themselves as more than the social equals of any of their readership, and in this endeavour somewhat transparent 'masks' were of great assistance. Swift had placed *his* Bickerstaff higher than the other astrologers, those 'mean, illiterate Traders between us and the Stars', the 'sottish Pretenders to Astrology' who 'with an old paultry Cant, and a few Pot-hooks for Planets' amused the vulgar; Bickerstaff's fortune placed him 'above the little Regard of Writing for a few Pence'. The tone of Swift's satire is easy and lofty.

To the same end, *The Tatler* constantly derided the news-writers (e.g. T18; T178) and dropped its own news paragraphs. Both *The Tatler* and *The Spectator* incessantly if politely remind their readers that they are conducted by independent gentlemen far above 'honest Ichabod ⟨⟩ Dawks', Daniel Defoe or Abel Roper or any of their fellow journalists. It is now time to consider who those independent and trim gentlemen were.

The writer and editor of *The Tatler*, the man behind Isaac Bickerstaff, was Richard Steele. At thirty-nine, with a 'dusky' round face, powerful torso running to fat, black wig and fine clothes, he was a well-known figure in the coffee-houses of the fashionable end of London which provide the date-lines for the *Tatler* essays, as well as in the theatres, and in the taverns in and around St James's and Covent Garden. He had been born in Ireland, a penniless orphan descended from an immigrant family of protestant landowners founded by a remarkable merchant, traveller and courtier of Charles I. Like Swift, also born of an English family in the Irish periphery, Steele set much store by his later, stylish, metropolitan success. Steele's family connections were able to place him in the Charterhouse school in London through the patronage of the Duke of Ormonde, and in 1689 to send him to Oxford, where he was entered at Christ Church, moving to Merton College in 1691. In 1694, however, leaving Oxford without a degree, he began a very varied career which gave him the wide experience of life that underlies his essay-writing. He enlisted as a 'private gentleman' in the second troop of Life Guards, fortunately commanded by Ormonde, his family's patron.

The time was auspicious for military advancement, since King William, having disposed of James II and the civil war in Ireland, was free again to turn his attention to his life's work, the great European war against Louis XIV's expansionist France. Throughout his career, Steele's finances were insufficient for his expectations, life-style, plans and projects. He constantly sought preferment and his enlistment in the royal body-guard was the start of a quest for military advancement. He and his connections could not, however, make a strong enough call on the Irish duke, and in 1695, after a campaign in Flanders, he transferred into the Coldstream Guards, first as an ensign, moving up to a captaincy through the grudging and very hard-earned patronage of Lord Cutts, 'the Salamander', a hard-bitten army commander whom he served as secretary.

Steele's service in the Second Foot Guards gave him a good deal of opportunity for moving in London society, for starting his career as a wit and writer, and also provided him with his title and social position as Captain Steele. In 1700, he nearly killed Henry Kelly of the Queen's Regiment of Dragoons in a duel, and in April of the following year he published his first successful book. It was a surprising production for a young Irish army officer. Entitled *The Christian Hero: or, An Argument Proving that no Principles but those of Religion are Sufficient to make a Great Man*, this manual of piety was somewhat incongruously dedicated to Lord Cutts and shows the straightforward, preaching side of Steele's character that contrasts rather violently with his bohemian, ill-regulated life. The contrast was a gift to his enemies, who made savage fun of his strong urge to rationalize his own sins and errors and reform those of others. United with his literary talent, though, it is also a powerful combination for successful journalism. In this year too, he wrote and published his first successful play, a competent good-natured comedy, *The Funeral: or, Grief à la Mode*; with a strong cast including Colley Cibber and Anne Oldfield, it did well at Drury Lane.

Steele's military duty took him not into active service, but to command a dull garrison at Landguard Fort, an outlier of the defences of the port and packet-station of Harwich in Suffolk. He clearly lacked the resources, and the influence, to engineer a lucrative future in the army, so having written another comedy, *The Lying Lover*, which despite a reasonable six-night run at Drury Lane in December 1703 was, he said, finally 'damn'd for its Piety', he turned his attention in 1704 from the military life to politics. He left the army in 1705 and married his first wife, Margaret Stretch, who brought him an estate in Barbados. He remained in financial difficulties, since overseas investments might be useful as securities for loans but were difficult to turn into ready income. Steele engaged in a number of unsuccessful projects to make money, including an alchemical speculation, but the party warfare of the time offered him more reliable prospects. His connections were now with the Whig Junto, the politicians who provided the

parliamentary support for the war ministry of the Duke of
Marlborough and Lord Treasurer Godolphin. Another comedy, *The
Tender Husband: or, The Accomplished Fool*, opened in April 1705
rather weakly, though it is the best of his plays and long held the
stage. Steele's comedies show in practice the sentimentalizing of
this form which he commended in his essays (e.g. *T*3; *S*65); in this
strong urge, the emotional parallel of his sermonizing, he heralded
the relaxation of the tough fibre of the Restoration comedy of
masters such as Wycherley and Etherege.

   In common with all men in his position at this time, Steele
incessantly canvassed his political patrons for civil employments,
at court or in the administration. His efforts received their first
reward in August 1706, when he was appointed a Gentleman
°Waiter to the Queen's husband, Prince George of Denmark. This
minor place, worth £100 a year, involved attendance at court and
gave him place and status, invaluable to him and useful to his
political associates for gathering intelligence. In the spring of 1707
he was given the quite important post of Gazetteer, the government
news-writer. This was an arduous job, demanding political and
literary skill, with a newly increased yearly salary of £300. The
Gazetteer worked in the Cockpit in Whitehall, the office of the
Secretaries of State, and he had some access to ambassadors' reports
and ministerial discussions; Steele's chief was the Earl of ◊
Sunderland.

   His first wife had died in 1706, and in September 1707, a month
after his new preferment, Steele married Mary Scurlock, the 'Dear
Prue' of the amusing and vivid series of notes that have been
preserved from the years of his life with her. These letters give us,
better than any other series of documents, a sense of what life was
like for this man of the first two decades of the eighteenth century,
a very modern feeling of domestic emotion, work, hope, disappointment and personal activity. His sentiment and carelessness,
his euphoric hope and gloomy despair are all brilliantly rendered in
short bursts of private communication. 'Dear Prue,' he writes from
Lord Sunderland's office on 19 May 1708 at 11 a.m.,

I desire of You to gett the Coach and your Self ready as soon as You can
conveniently and call for Me here from Whence We will go and Spend

some time together in the fresh Air in free Conference. Let my best Periwigg be put in the Coach Box and my New Shoes for 'tis a Comfort to [be] well dress'd in agreeable Company.

You are Vitall Life to
Your Oblig'd Affectionate Husband and Humble Servant
Richd Steele.

A month after *The Tatler* was begun, he writes on 7 May 1709, 'Dear Prue, I am just drinking a pint of wine and will come home forthwith . . .' On 28 July he sends a promise, 'Dear Prue, I enclose two Guinneas and will come home exactly at seven, Yours tenderly, Richd Steele.' On 7 April 1710, a hurried postscript from the Gazetteer asks for her help: 'There are papers in the parlour window, dated from Hamburgh and other places, which I want.' At 'Half Hour after 9' some time in August 1710, as his friends were being driven from power, 'R.S.' tells his wife that he is 'invited to Supper to Mr. ☼ Boyle's' and adds, 'Dear Prue, Don't send after Me for I shall be ridiculous. I send you Word to put you out of Frights.'

From his comedy-writing, Steele brought to his essays a good ear for living speech and a witty way of setting it down, as in 'Things are come to this pass' from *T*12 or 'Voices' from *T*37. His emotional, sincere but not too demanding sense of religious duty could be drawn on for acceptable admonition in a good-tempered piece, or in a campaign against some social abuse of which he had vivid experience, such as 'Against duelling' from *T*25 and 'More against duelling' from *T*31. His military past and political partisanship made Marlborough a hero to him (for example in the Dedication to the fourth volume of collected *Spectators*), and led to fulsome praise of the Whig Junto and their policies, as in 'The glory of the present age' from *T*130. Steele's warm and convivial nature, as well as his domesticity which struggled so hard against other calls on him, made his pieces on family life, the relations between the sexes or friendship, persuasive and credible. His journalistic experience, hard work, need for money and wide acquaintance all worked towards giving his writing in *The Tatler* and *The Spectator* a success and solidity the reader feels to be justly deserved.

Richard Steele was known to be the writer and editor of *The*

Tatler at first only to a few with their ears to the ground, but at length quite widely in London society. In the last issue of the periodical, however, in which he bids his readers farewell as Isaac Bickerstaff (*T*271), he generously if with some exaggeration says 'that the most approved Pieces in it were written by others' and makes particular mention of 'a Person who is too fondly my Friend ever to own' the pieces he contributed; he adds without being on oath that he is in his friend's debt for 'the finest Strokes of Wit and Humour in all Mr. Bickerstaff's Lucubrations'. At the same time, in his Preface to *The Tatler*, first printed in the fourth volume of the first collected edition, he makes further generous acknowledgement to 'one Gentleman' for 'frequent Assistance' and continues in lavish compliment, 'I was undone by my Auxiliary; when I had once called him in, I could not subsist without Dependance on him' (see below, p. 485). Such is Steele's public statement of his collaboration with Joseph Addison, a collaboration which was resumed in *The Spectator* with Addison this time as the dominant partner. Of the 271 *Tatler* papers, allowing for some uncertainty and argument about attributions, Steele was responsible for just over 180 complete papers, and about a further twenty or so in collaboration with others; Addison seems to have written about forty-seven complete papers and to have collaborated with Steele or others in a further twenty-two. (For a convenient summary of the evidence for this allocation, see F. W. Bateson, 'The Errata in *The Tatler*', *Review of English Studies*, vol. 5 (1929), no. 18.)

Joseph Addison was born on 1 May 1672, in the same year as Steele, but six weeks his junior. Addison's character, career and achievements partly complement, partly parallel and partly run counter to those of his friend and collaborator. His father, Dr Launcelot Addison, was an ardent supporter of the monarchy in the last years of the Protectorate, and in 1683, after a spell in Tangier as the governor's chaplain followed by service as rector in a remote Wiltshire parish, his enthusiasms and sympathies were rewarded with the Deanery of Lichfield. On the accession of King William, though, he could not accommodate his impulsive high-church politics to the Revolution, so despite his early promise and a creditable record of publication he received no further promotion in the Church, and in Lichfield he remained until his death in 1703.

His eldest son steadfastly professed Revolution principles, first engaging himself to King William, and afterwards, particularly during the period when *The Tatler* and *The Spectator* were being published, to the Whig Junto. In quiet but unrelenting pursuit of political preferment, he made few false steps and suffered the minimum of ill luck, so that his unusual success and profit might serve as a model for this struggle in which so many of his contemporaries failed. He became a close friend of Steele's at the Charterhouse school, and in 1687 he too went up to Oxford, to Queen's College, and afterwards to Magdalen. Unlike Steele, Addison made a career in the university. The channel through which he sought distinction, first as a tutor at Magdalen and, somewhat surprisingly to our eyes, later in the London literary and political world, was in the writing of polished Latin verse. He became acquainted with Dryden at Will's coffee-house and developed his own minor but genuine talent for writing English verse by contributing to Tonson's third and fourth volumes of *Miscellany Poems*, edited by the great poet. Admitted a fellow of Magdalen in 1698, Addison had so far gained acceptance by Whig politicians that the next year he obtained a Treasury grant of £200 to finance a tour of Europe, as a preparation for some diplomatic or other civil preferment. He was able to retain his fellowship, which in fact he did not resign until 1711, though remaining non-resident. More important, he was able to avoid the requirement of taking Holy Orders, the latter a beckoning option to many able but poor university men, which if taken then became, as in the case of Swift, a barrier to advancement outside the Church.

For the next four years he stayed some time in France, learning the language, and travelled through Italy, Switzerland, Austria, Germany and the Low Countries. During this time he did not neglect to keep his political lines open, and naturally visited the Electoral court in Hanover to make himself known to the family nominated by Parliament to succeed the childless Stuart, Queen Anne. On his return to London, at the beginning of 1704, Addison did not go back to Oxford, but though poor and as yet unplaced set himself up in London, becoming a member of the Whig Kit-Cat

Club of writers and grandees. His opportunity was not long in coming.

In May 1702, while he was travelling in Europe, Queen Anne had joined her allies in declaring war on Louis XIV and his second grandson, Philip of Anjou, who by the will of Charles II the late King of Spain had succeeded to the crown of that country and its vast empire. Thus began the War of the Spanish Succession, the great, bloody and expensive European drama that dominated the next decade. On 13 August 1704, the Duke of Marlborough won his great battle of Blenheim in Upper Germany. The ministers in London badly needed some worthy and persuasive literary celebration of this famous, if costly, victory. Addison was suggested as the man to supply the necessary article, and responding to a ministerial commission, on 14 December he published a poem, the most celebrated in his own day of his sets of verses, *The Campaign: a Poem to His Grace the Duke of Marlborough*. Though now forgotten, it was an immediate success, even claimed by Voltaire to be '*monument plus durable que le palais de Blenheim*'. It was paid for by an appointment as a Commissioner of Appeal in the Excise.

Thereafter Addison pursued two separate careers, as a writer and as an administrator and public appointee, but of the two the latter was the more important to him. In 1705, he published *Remarks on Several Parts of Italy etc.*, which with *A Letter from Italy* (1703) in couplets, represented the literary fruits of his travels, and showed him to be observant and, though far more tolerant of foreign ways than he had been before his tour, certainly no cosmopolitan, both important strands in the imagination and experience he brought to bear in his periodical essays. He helped Steele with his comedy, *The Tender Husband* (1705), contributing also a prologue; in 1707 he wrote the libretto of an unsuccessful, 'British' opera, *Rosamund*, set to music by an incompetent English composer, his friend Thomas Clayton (see *S*18, *n*1, p. 538). This enterprise may be judged as a product of Addison's literary approach to the stage and lack of feeling for performance or non-literary skill; he saw music as an embellishment or decoration to the all-important text.

As the Whig Junto strengthened their grip on the administration in 1705, Addison was further rewarded for his support by a very considerable promotion to Under-Secretary of State for the Southern

Department, first under Sir Charles Hedges, then from the autumn of 1706 under the Earl of ◊ Sunderland. The Junto had finally succeeded in forcing the latter into office against the Queen's strong disinclination, because Lord Treasurer Godolphin badly needed their electoral support. Addison's masterly performance in an important executive position became the basis of his later claims for further advancement in the government machine. In the spring of 1706, he accompanied Lord Halifax on a ceremonial government mission to Hanover, made with the clear political purpose of attaching the future King as closely as possible to the Whig interest, but which also afforded Addison the opportunity of strengthening by personal contact links he had made with European writers and scholars, such as Pierre Bayle, the author of an encyclopedic *Historical and Critical Dictionary*. This was first published in French in 1697, reprinted with additions in 1702, and several times later, and translated into English from 1710; Addison drew quite heavily on the mingled learning of Bayle's work, in meeting the stress of finding material for daily *Spectators*. As Gazetteer, from 1707 Steele worked under Sunderland with Addison, who was responsible for the day to day running of the official newspaper. There is evidence to show that on occasions Addison put complete editions of *The Gazette* to press, and he lived in some intimacy with Steele for the next few years.

In 1707, too, Addison joined the ranks of government place-men important enough to be provided with a seat in Parliament, though he never became a significant parliamentarian. He was first elected to the Commons for the Cornish borough of Lostwithiel in an expensive and disputed election, but from 1709 until his death he sat as one of the members for Malmesbury in Wiltshire, one of the boroughs managed by the leading Junto electioneer, the Earl of Wharton. In 1708, it was Wharton's turn to benefit from the Junto's increasing power; he was appointed to the lucrative Lord Lieutenancy of Ireland and in turn nominated Addison as his Secretary, a position that made him virtually the executive head of the Irish government. With this post went membership of the Irish Privy Council and, of course, a seat in the Irish House of Commons.

When *The Tatler* started, Addison was in Ireland with Wharton,

and there is a tradition that he knew Steele to be the editor only
when he read in *Tatler* 6 a comment on Virgil that he himself had
made in conversation. It seems very unlikely, however, that he
knew nothing before he left the country about his friend's important
new proposal. Addison returned to England in September 1709,
and from the following January his contributions became frequent.
With the failure of the ministry to make anything of French peace
proposals, and an equally severe error of judgement in impeaching
Dr Sacheverell, an inflammatory, popular preacher of extreme
high-church, Tory views, the Whig Junto became identified as a
war party and lost widespread political support; then political
control began to slip from them, bringing down the Lord Treasurer.
Among the rest, Wharton fell with Sunderland and Godolphin,
and Addison lost his secretaryship. He found himself free for the
next two years for literary efforts, including contributions to the
last numbers of *The Tatler*, and to the paper that replaced it, *The
Spectator*.

The new periodical was directed by Addison, out of office and,
though politically engaged, keeping a low profile. Steele, who had
discontinued *The Tatler* partly because of a tendency to introduce
open political controversy in it, worked closely with him. Their
first *Spectator* series ran daily from March 1711 to December 1712
(nos. 1–555). Steele tells us (pp. 213–14) that the papers signed C,
L, I or O were by Addison; clearly, those signed R and T are by
himself; two unsigned papers (*Spectators* 237 and 538) are printed
by Thomas ♭ Tickell in his posthumous edition of Addison's *Works*
(1721). Thus, both men were responsible for 251 papers each;
Addison's are in the form of single, solid, compact essays; Steele's
are more heterogeneous and use much material from correspondents.
A further twenty-nine papers were written by Eustace ♭ Budgell
and six by ♭ Hughes. Eighteen papers remain to be assigned by
deduction, nine signed Z, one signed Q and eight unsigned (see
Spectator, ed. Bond, vol. I, pp. xiv ff.). The thrice-weekly continuation of *The Spectator* ran from June to December 1714 (nos.
556–635) and was wholly by Addison with Budgell's assistance.
Although it contains good papers, the second series was not as
popular as the first, and like most continuations shows some
relaxation of energy.

The daily *Spectator* papers had the same format as the *Tatlers*, a double-columned, folio half-sheet with advertisements. The periodical was published by Samuel Buckley, who also published in the same format the first English daily newspaper, *The Daily Courant*. Both papers were sold by Mrs Baldwin at her shop in Warwick Lane, between Ludgate Hill and Newgate, where the advertisements were taken in. Advertisements were also accepted by Charles Lillie, perfumer, who had formerly sold *The Tatler*, 'at the Corner of Beaufort-Buildings in the Strand' (from *Spectator* 16 onwards). From *Spectator* 499, 2 October 1712, Jacob Tonson, the younger, son of the Jacob Tonson who founded the Kit-Cat Club, and who was Addison's publisher, joined Buckley in publishing *The Spectator*. Buckley and Tonson were also the printers of the collected volumes as well as the daily *Spectator* papers. From the beginning, each *Spectator* contained a single essay, though there were also contributions, chiefly in more than half of Steele's numbers, from correspondents (see e.g. *S*50, *n*1, p. 558).

In discussing the contents of *The Tatler* and *The Spectator*, it is convenient to look at them together, because the very differences between Steele and Addison in character, outlook, interests and style of writing defined the nature of the papers. *The Spectator* grew out of *The Tatler*; many of the journalistic modes, the preoccupations, the purposes of the later publication are found in the earlier, and it is no longer necessary at this date to try to deal exact justice between Steele and Addison. *The Tatler* has more of the tone of the coffee-house, even of the tavern. It appealed, and was designed to appeal, more to the fashionable world than *The Spectator*. The latter, as befitted the character of its silent and retiring 'writer', Mr Spectator, was addressed more to the morning tea-table, to the reflective hours of the civil servants and merchants represented in its subscription list. There was naturally overlap, and Steele's papers in *The Spectator* pulled sometimes towards his *Tatler* interests, while Addison's *Tatler* contributions sometimes reflected the more reserved tone of his *Spectator*. Addison himself was to a degree *The Spectator*. The aims of the periodical are to be found set out in *S*1, *S*4, *S*10 and *Spectator* 16, all papers that he wrote. Both Steele and Addison, though, also shared certain important interests and convictions, political, social and literary, which together give

The Tatler with *The Spectator* a certain homogeneous and powerful presence in English literature.

Form and Framework

Steele's adoption of 'Isaac Bickerstaff' as the transparent mask for writing *The Tatler* has been commented on above. The whimsicality of an old astrologer, of a superior sort, is congenial to Steele's liking for surprising juxtapositions, and a number of associated features keep the arrangement going, such as Isaac Bickerstaff's guardian angel in *Tatler* 13. In *T*89, Steele mingles autobiography, fancy and seriousness in justifying Isaac Bickerstaff's labours: 'As for my Labours, which he is pleased to enquire after, if they can but wear one Impertinence out of human Life, destroy a single Vice, or give a Morning's Chearfulness to an honest Mind . . . I shall not think my Pains, or indeed my Life, to have been spent in vain.' The whole passage, including its somewhat full-blown sentiment and repetitive writing, shows how Steele moves backwards and forwards out of Bickerstaff. It also illustrates Steele's habit of straight, sometimes clumsy moralizing, which reads quaintly now but was clearly no disadvantage to his contemporary popularity. The syntax is of the loose kind (he can write much better) that later provoked Swift with his fastidious sensibility to prose performance, terse and neat or lax and scrambling, to say of another of Steele's sentences: 'If I have ill interpreted him, it is his own fault, for studying cadence instead of propriety, and filling up niches with words before he has adjusted his conceptions to them.' Bickerstaff can accommodate the sermonizing Captain's *penchant* for the solemn paragraph.

   Mr Spectator reads like Addison's idea; Addison it is who introduces him in *S*1 and adds more details in *S*4. The subtlety of the idea suits his wit and comic feeling, as well as his keen sense of social propriety. There is more flexibility and usefulness in the *persona* of 'Mr Spectator' than that of 'Bickerstaff'. The latter is pushed out of character when introduced in unlikely *milieux*, or given feelings too vivid and real, as in 'An hour or two sacred to sorrow' in *T*181. Mr Spectator is more a fictional character, and the familiarity which later English readers reached with the *Spectator* papers must have had a considerable effect on their expectations of any novel framed as the narrative of a fictitious teller. A taste for extraneous and self-deprecatory reflections on the novelist's part may have been strengthened, leading to pieces like 'the Author's' thoughts in *Joseph Andrews* or *Tom Jones*; and the perception of a fiction as something episodic, furnished with occasional essays like those Fielding provides, may be traced to this influential source. Mr Spectator has travelled, thus accommodating Addison's own travels in Europe, though the silent observer's visit to the Great Pyramid is an exotic experience of purely imaginative use. His taciturnity and camouflaged existence is a perfect preparation for any variety of scenes, characters, opinions and situations that the two writers may wish to deploy in the course of their publication. His birth and education are an idealized version of the nurture of both Steele and Addison, particularly his possession from an early age of a small hereditary estate that gave him independence. His wide reading, in 'the Learned or the Modern Tongues', is more plausible and pointed than the learning of Bickerstaff, and of course he, like Bickerstaff, is a Londoner through and through.

Mr Spectator's club has a fore-runner in *The Tatler*, introduced in 'The club at the Trumpet' (*T*132), but is given more space, though it never reached the organizing part it was obviously designed to play. The *Tatler* club is a group of almost Dickensian caricatures; the *Spectator* group carries the earlier sketch into a more developed form. Sir Roger de Coverley is first presented by Steele in *S*2, but Addison takes delight in elaborating this superb creation, and in the elaboration introducing a lightly touched but strong and damaging political slant. Sir Roger is a Tory squire, lovable, generous to a fault, but ineffectual, unbusinesslike, even in his good qualities heedless and possibly dangerous. He is old, a figure from the past, a past that has to be put to rest, so goes the scheme, by the anti-Tory, anti-Jacobite, efficient present. A collaborative piece by Addison and Steele in *The Tatler*, 'A visit of ceremony' (from *T*86), sets out the same scenario. A Whig interest is represented by Sir Andrew Freeport, the merchant, but ironically he never floats into the region of a living, imagined character. The careful political placing of Sir Roger tends to be forgotten by the modern reader, who enjoys the eccentricities, the humour, the details of a figure that has real life and movement, to a degree somewhat aside perhaps from the line indicated by the creators. The values Sir Roger stands for, family honour, hierarchical ostentation, the country interest, sportsmanship in hunting, are not exactly attacked, but glanced at, hinted down, quietly sabotaged. 'Sir Roger at the Country-Assizes' (S 122), by Addison, is a good example of the process. As a principal landowner and ancient country gentleman, Sir Roger could command very considerable local power, but he is temperamentally unfitted to do so, and also disabled by his education. The piece is quite carefully put together. Sir Roger's ceremonial appearance in court is sandwiched between a presentation of the evils of country litigation over land-rights and a tactful piece of commonsense on Sir Roger's part in maintaining his prestige by preventing his head being displayed on an inn-sign. He does this, of course, without offending the well-meaning publican. Mr Spectator, though, retains the last touch, which underlines Sir Roger's naïvety and his own poise based on a wider and stronger experience.

Sir Andrew Freeport possesses the great personal quality most highly valued in both *The Tatler* and *The Spectator*, personal probity, variously embodied according to the possessor's role as giving others the personal respect due to them, credit-worthiness, keeping a bargain, reliability in service. Sir Andrew is not introduced by Steele in S 2 without irony, and in 'Sir Andrew Freeport defends commerce' (S 174), Addison also gives him a few foibles; but in the latter 'debate' with Sir Roger, hereditary baronet *versus* self-made knight, Sir Andrew is clearly meant to have the best of it. As a monied man, he gives the baronet a businesslike rebuke, "Tis the Misfortune of many other Gentlemen to turn out of the Seats of the Ancestors, to make Way for such new Masters as have been more exact in their Accompts than themselves . . .' As he dispersed the Club before ending *The Spectator*, Addison does indeed dismiss Sir Andrew, who now 'thinks he has enough', to a country estate (*Spectator* 549), 'a considerable Purchase' doubtless acquired in this way. The 'Substantial Acres and Tenements' are, however, invested with moral good and Sir Andrew's 'more thoughtful kind of Life' in his retirement is set out in some detail. The persuasive statement in *The Spectator* of this business ethic based on personal honesty, foresight, prudence, assertion of independence, and fair play for personal merit is an important underlying theme. It is exactly the kind of structural emphasis that gave the essays as a collection a wide circulation and appeal for a very long time.

Men, Women, Manners

Both Steele and Addison are moralists who pay particular attention to domestic existence. The essays of *The Tatler* and *The Spectator* offer a criticism of what they considered the abuses, the cruelties, the barbarisms in contemporary families and in turn suggested, as they thought, better behaviour, nobler aspirations, more civilized conventions than the life of former times. In all this the social role of women receives much attention, though there are clear differences of opinion, conscious and unconscious, between Steele and Addison on this point. Both are rather patronizing to women, Addison more so than Steele. Yet their essays must have seemed to many at the time they first appeared, however they may be judged now, as the first general publications sympathetically aimed at a female readership. They printed letters from women; Addison directed his essays at the 'Tea-table', the only theatre in which fashionable women at that time presided. The number of independent women subscribers to the collected *Tatlers* and *Spectators* suggests that there was a lively feminine response to the volumes as they appeared.

Of the two writers, Steele in a sentimental mode is also more natural, more open in his attitude to women, even though the reader feels that he is likely to be, in the fashion of the time, more predatory. His views may be studied in pieces like 'A short story: Pastorella's Aunt' (from *T*9), 'Love-letters' (from *T*30) and 'Ill-natured husbands' (*T* 149). Steele is also more forthright and more realistic in discussing sexual mores as in two remarkable papers, 'Seduction' (*S*182) and 'Poor and publick whores' (*S*266). The latter, as might be expected, landed him in some trouble from that ever-green correspondent 'Disgusted Reader', but he not too apologetically made capital out of such objections in 'Responses to *S* 266' (*S*276).

Addison's attitude to women, 'the fair Sex', is at once more prim and more nervous. 'I consider Woman as a beautiful Romantick Animal, that may be adorned with Furs and Feathers, Pearls and Diamonds, Ores and Silks,' he writes in *Tatler* 116, and he seems fascinated by his female audience, by the details of their dress and ornaments, while at the same time having some sharp aversion to women as living, thinking members of society.

Naturally, in an age which set great store by the decorum of dress and behaviour, there is a great deal of satirical comment by both Steele and Addison on women's fashions, their social behaviour and their vices, but it is the positive interest in the relations between men and women, between lovers, husbands and wives, fathers and daughters, brothers and sisters that is more interesting. Addison's paper 'Male and female roles' (S 57) and Steele's 'The education of girls' (S 66) are instances of this interest.

Some of this preoccupation with family life and with the moral implications of the conventions and manners of familiar society is given significant life in the short pieces of fiction which form an important characteristic of both periodicals. Steele's piece 'A short story: Pastorella's Aunt' from T 9 has already been mentioned, and he has indeed a good touch in this kind of story. His predilection for fictional accounts of sentiment, sensibility, psychology set in domestic circumstances is responsible for a substantial group of influential pieces like 'The serjeant's letter' (T 87), 'The unhappy end of Mr Eustace' (T 172; see n 1, p. 519) and the famous 'Male hypocrisy: the story of Inkle and Yarico' (S 11).

Both Steele and Addison adopted a strongly didactic tone in writing on manners. Steele by presenting Bickerstaff as the 'Censor of Great Britain' disarmed his readers but kept his purpose, as in 'Taking snuff' from T 35. Addison's comic sense often ostensibly seized on small, amusing trends and habits, but the seriousness of his underlying intentions is also clear; 'Manners in Town and in the country' (S 119) is a good example. Such papers appealed to a wide audience. Their teaching, their commitment to moderation, to gradual change, to commonsense in social life are all part of the strong tide of feeling in the first years of the eighteenth century that the 'past age', the age of Charles II's court, had been, however glittering, more than a little barbarous and oppressive. Beau Nash at this very time in Bath was also establishing a benevolent dictatorship over manners, dedicated to more ease, more equality and more decorum in the social round; stiff enough though his ideas seemed to yet later generations. A small instance of the power of *The Tatler* and *The Spectator* in this shift in social perception is to be found in a passage from the *Autobiography* of Dr Alexander 'Jupiter' Carlyle, who was born in 1722, the son of the minister of Prestonpans, near Edinburgh. Writing of his boyhood, he says:

I was very fond of dancing, in which I was a great proficient, having been taught at two different periods in the country, though the manners were then so strict that I was not allowed to exercise my talent at penny-weddings, or any balls but those of the dancing-school. Even this would have been denied me, as it was to Robertson and Witherspoon, and other clergymen's sons, at the time, had it not been for the persuasion of those aunts of mine who had been bred in England, and for some papers in the *Spectator* which were pointed out to my father, which seemed to convince him that dancing would make me a more accomplished preacher, if ever I had the honour to mount the pulpit.

The Town and Daily Life

The Tatler and *The Spectator* both celebrate London, the 'dear, distracting Town'. By far the largest centre of population in England, the city was beginning to feel itself an imperial capital in the wake of the prestige and visible power gained as the country took the economic lead in the war against France. The seat of 'great Anna, whom three Realms obey', it had been given added importance in 1707 by the parliamentary union with Scotland; and the wide dissemination, influence and assured tone of the two periodicals strengthened the sense of London as the cultural capital of the whole island. Half a century later, James Boswell, a refugee at least in his own eyes from the cultural sub-capital of Edinburgh, amusingly exemplifies this sense in his *London Journal*:

Saturday, 8 January 1763: Mrs Gould and Mrs Douglas and I went in the Colonel's Chariot to the Haymarket. As we drove along and spoke good English, I was full of rich imagination of London ideas suggested by the Spectator . . . My blood glows and my mind is agitated with felicity.

The richness of London, its great new public buildings, the teeming variety of its life are suggested by countless touches in the essays and particularly in such pieces as 'Show-business' (from $T4$), 'Sharpers' (from $T56$), 'Will Rosin, the fiddler from Wapping' (from $T105$), 'The Description of a City Shower' ($T238$), 'A visit to Spring-Garden with Sir Roger' (S 383), 'The Indian kings in London' (S 50) and 'The Royal Exchange' (S 69). The various London date-lines of the departments in the early *Tatlers* give a similar feeling of richness and activity. Of course, London is also the sink of iniquity, and Steele and Addison exercise their satirical skill on the unfavourable sides of city life, such as the activities of the upper-class bully-boys known as Mohawks (S 324); but throughout there is a very powerful sense of enjoyment, engagement and admiration. The streets, street signs, street cries, coffee-houses, theatres, taverns are familiarly detailed and brought alive to the audience's imagination. At the risk of boring the reader, the notes to these essays have been made pretty full, since these pieces offer an unrivalled record of contemporary London, and an unparalleled body of richly imagined city-scapes.

Steele's paper 'Twenty-four hours in London' (S 454) is one of the best of his essays, and indeed perhaps he excels Addison in writing on the tide of life in the streets of London. He is acutely sensitive to the way in which the interstices of the city's streets accommodate different levels of people, of how the 'Hours of the Day and Night are taken up in the Cities of *London* and *Westminster* by People as different from each other as those who are Born in different Centuries. Men of Six-a-Clock give Way to those of Nine, they of Nine to the Generation of Twelve, and they of Twelve disappear, and make Room for the fashionable World, who have made Two-a-Clock the Noon of the Day.' Such an urban world, which controls the natural rhythms, is the ancestor of much later fiction, of the London universe of Dickens, and of the city-scene in American art. The coach-chase sequence, Steele in pursuit of 'a young Lady', is also ancestral, with many descendants in cinema and T V narrative, not to mention the conspiratorial 'hackies' reminiscent of Raymond Chandler or Erle Stanley Gardner. 'The industrious part of mankind' (S 552) is a more straightforward account by Steele of the useful activity that seemed to him characteristic of his great city.

Essays in Criticism

No papers in *The Tatler* and *The Spectator* were more influential than the large number that dealt in some way with the criticism of drama, poetry and with the imagination in general. At its lowest, this is probably an instance of the public's liking for being told how to judge, what to read, what to admire, and best of all what to condemn. These essays also, however, form an extensive and sustained body of careful thought, one of the areas in which Steele, and to a greater extent Addison, in the latter's words, 'brought Philosophy out of Closets and Libraries, Schools and Colleges, to dwell in Clubs and Assemblies, at Tea-Tables and in Coffee-Houses' (S 10). The very first *Tatler* contains a piece date-lined from Will's coffee-house, the heading for 'Poetry'. It starts with the actor Thomas ⟡ Betterton's Benefit Night, and goes on to talk of the present social situation at Will's, formerly the haunt of Dryden and other wits and poets.

Steele's critical papers on plays are written by a man of the theatre. He is interested in acting; he knows the players and managers and is involved in theatrical politics, as he shows in 'Show-business' (from *T* 4), or 'Etherege's *The Man of Mode: or, Sir Fopling Flutter*' (S 65). He is also a good reporter of the social place of critical discussion in 'A critic and a wit' (from *T* 29). Addison's papers are more complex. Although he was the author of a successful comedy, and in *Cato* of the most successful tragedy of the time, his view of the drama is that of a literary man, a writer who sees actors, the stage, even perhaps play-goers as regrettable necessities in realizing the meaning of the text; this is notable in his series on English tragedy (S 39, S 40, S 42, S 44). Similarly, though he had written an opera libretto, Addison looks down on the music as a lower form of expression, mere entertainment, unlike the poetry which carries the burden of the didactic purpose of art ('The Italian opera', S 18; see *n* 1, p. 540). In all this he speaks for a very powerful text-bound form of interpretation, which seems somewhat characteristic of British culture, though perhaps now to a lesser extent than formerly. On the other hand, Addison also brings to his critical writing several valuable abilities and interests, apart from his neat and acceptable style.

Both Steele and Addison were well-read, in the classics as well as in English literature. But Addison's reading in Latin poetry as well as in classical criticism was, as we have noted, that of a professional scholar; he was more accomplished in the poetry than the criticism, however, and true to his disdain for pedantry he uses his reading cautiously. He was also quite well read in the works of the French neo-classic critics such as Boileau, Bouhours and the Daciers (see e.g. *S*44, *n* 4, p. 541; *S*409, *n* 3, p. 548). This made his essays acceptable to later European readers, but Addison uses this reading for his own purposes. He was equally well read in the philosophy of Locke. He is poised at the point where the static, neo-classic, genre-based criticism, the discussion based on classification of works, was slowly giving way to a more 'psychological' criticism, a discussion directed to the *process* of creation (in the artist) and the *process* of appreciation (in the reader or viewer). Such an affective criticism receives powerful impetus from Locke's epistemology based on sense-impressions.

In all this, Addison is not an absolute pioneer, but he certainly gave the new trend wide publicity, and by his authority and tone endowed these ideas with a *cachet* that made them fashionable. Thus, he handles the 'rules' of the earlier critics respectfully, but in the style of a gentleman, a man of taste. His free and undogmatic treatment of 'poetic justice', for instance, follows on from Dryden (see 'English tragedy: poetic justice', *S*40). He had the innovative energy to present several *series* of essays in which he could set out his ideas at some length, yet relatively informally, and he had the skill to make these series of disquisitions popular. As a student of Locke's *Essay on the Human Understanding* – see for example 'Qualities necessary for a just critic of *Paradise Lost*' (*S*291) – Addison devoted some care to his account of the imagination, a power he believed to be inherent in the mind, adapted for the arrangement of experience.

His twelve essays on 'The Pleasures of the Imagination' start from a Lockean concept of *taste*, a product of the natural constitution of the mind together with its individual total of experiences (see *n**, p. 548). Addison is not a technical philosopher, and he holds an eclectic body of ideas in balance by his urbane tone of friendly detachment. One of his achievements, however, was to accustom a large, un-professional audience to a series of reasonably rigorous arguments about aesthetics, based on considerable reading and wide experience. This is one of the fields in which he shows himself first among the ranks of the great popularizers, a distinguished group that includes Walter Scott, Macaulay, Thomas Carlyle, John Ruskin and Bertrand Russell. Like all successful popularizers, whose considerable art is undervalued, he later attracted the hostile attention of real innovators.

He showed further originality in successfully devoting a series of eighteen periodical essays to one great work of literature, and that not a classical work by Homer or Virgil, but a poem in English, Milton's *Paradise Lost* (see *n**, p. 554). Here he showed by example that an English work was worth a substantial, systematic critique of a kind hitherto almost reserved for classical literature or the Bible. His reading of the great poem formed public sensibility for some time, though it is a partial account of Milton's masterpiece, stressing certain 'classical' features at the expense of what some readers have regarded as powerful baroque discontinuities. In particular Addison is out of touch with Milton's political and some of his religious doctrines, yet he shows an admirable sense of the life in Milton's poetry, and of the great scope of the work as a whole. Steele also knew Milton's work well; and his critical essays on diverse topics, though fewer in number and simpler than Addison's, are an important feature of the total effect of the two periodicals.

One small component of the socio-literary culture of *The Tatler* and *The Spectator* worth drawing attention to is the motto at the head of each paper. For the first forty *Tatlers*, the same quotation from Juvenal's first *Satire* is used. Thereafter, and for each *Spectator*, a different fragment appears, without translation, sometimes straight, sometimes amusingly adapted to the tone and subject of the paper, as a 'title' or starting point for an essay. This running joke started while Addison was in Ireland, though it is very much in his manner and he obviously kept it going in *The Spectator*. Steele, however, was clearly competent to take his part in it. Many of these quotations are brief, well-known tags from stock texts like Horace's *Ars Poetica*, which would have been familiar, to many male readers at least, from school reading. Others, however, are more complicated pieces, like the lines from one of Horace's *Odes* in *S*66. Some of the readership must have been unable to follow these, and from the 1744 edition of the collected papers, transla-

tions of the mottos were often provided, to place the following
essay in a more widely accessible literary context.

Politics and Public Affairs

Mention has already been made of the sections of news that
appeared in some sixty-two numbers of *The Tatler*, a feature that
dropped out, and never appeared in *The Spectator*. Three of these
sections are included (from T_1, T_9, T_{55}), to give some idea of the
national situation when *The Tatler* began in 1709, at the climax of
a great war in which Britain was in a coalition against France. From
November to April, when the great armies in Flanders rested
between campaigns, the coffee-houses and taverns of London were
full of officers awaiting a chance to join the fashionable social scene,
and for some of them to attend the parliamentary session. The two
great public questions, about which the political warfare of the
time raged, were how to end the war, and what was to happen to
the crown when the ailing, childless Queen died. Or, put another
way, the struggling political groups in the country polarized round
these two major public questions.

Although after the disappearance of the news paragraphs there
are few direct references in both periodicals to public events as they
happened, there is plenty of oblique reference to them; and as the
discussion above of Sir Roger de Coverley and Sir Andrew Freeport
has indicated, there is plenty of political comment, despite editorial
disclaimers of open political arguments and abuse.

Marlborough and Godolphin were the technocrats of the war, the
one military, the other financial, but to maintain a political base for
their operations, they had been forced to ally themselves more and
more exclusively with the Whig Junto, who controlled a parliamentary majority. In 1709, as has already been said, the ministry, for
some complex of reasons not entirely clear, totally rejected peace-
feelers from the French government, which was struggling against
military defeat, economic collapse and sinking public morale. The
situation is a classic one. Marlborough's military advice was that
another year, a larger army, a greater effort would lead to a successful
invasion of France and 'unconditional surrender'. The strain on the
British economy, however, was also very severe. Government expenditure on the navy, the army, subsidies to the allies and servicing and

repaying a huge debt was running at well over eight million pounds a year, an astronomical sum for that time, the largest burden the country had ever borne. The stress of raising funds was fundamentally altering the whole financial, economic and political structure. Country gentlemen like Sir Roger were jibbing at the exactions of the land tax. The monied men like Sir Andrew were not taxed in the same way, and were of course able to increase their income by lending funds to the government, as well as taking part in the vast naval and military contracts which were in operation.

A vigorous and hotly resented press was in force to raise recruits for the navy and armies. From late 1709, the Whig Junto were slipping from power in face of popular discontent, the Queen's dislike and court intrigue. Steele, an admirer of Marlborough, a client of his son-in-law, the Earl of Sunderland, and an office-holder, was more apt than Addison to be stung into straight political comment, as in his orotund piece 'The glory of the present age' (from *T*130), though Addison probably helped him with another apologia for the administration as it was actually collapsing, 'Political change' (*T*214).

Godolphin was replaced as chief minister in August 1710 by Robert Harley, who relied on a Tory majority in the new House of Commons. Harley immediately committed himself by secret and informal diplomacy to peace with France, either by securing the consent of the Allies or unilaterally by exercising English economic power. But unilateral peace moves meant maintaining government credit against much opposition from the monied men and the institution they controlled, the Bank of England. A great political significance may be seen, therefore, in Addison's essay at the start of the *Spectator*'s run 'The Bank of England: a vision' (*S*3). By that time Steele and Addison were both out of office and supporting the opposition's campaign against the peace. One prong of this sought to incriminate the new ministry as Jacobites, supporters of the Queen's brother, the Roman Catholic, legitimist heir to the crown, specifically excluded by the Act of Settlement and supported by Louis XIV. The Junto and their followers were successful in establishing themselves with the protestant Electoral family of Hanover, descended from James I's daughter Elizabeth, as their reliable supporters in terms of the Act, and reaped their reward after 1714.

Such is the background to a naughty piece of direct political controversy, Steele's paper 'A bold stroke in the party war' (S284). As the government forced a peace on its allies, and crammed this policy through Parliament, by making the Queen create twelve new peers to give them a majority in the Lords, the political uproar grew greater. This was naturally a constant topic in *The Spectator*. Addison adopts a moderate tone, but his sympathies are clear in such essays as 'Party among women' (S81) and 'The rage of party' (S125). The ministers finally sought to cool the situation by introducing a device to control the press. This was censorship by a tax on newspapers and periodicals, and Addison amusingly discusses it in 'The Stamp Act' (S445). It is interesting that *The Spectator* was popular enough to maintain its viability even when it had to double its price.

By the end of 1712, both Steele and Addison wished to take a more direct part in the public argument, and this may have contributed a great deal to the ending of *The Spectator*. Steele went on to publish two anti-Tory periodicals, *The Guardian*, with Addison's help (12 March to 1 October 1713) and *The Englishman* (6 October 1713 to 14 February 1714), and several controversial pamphlets, as well as fighting his disputed election to Parliament from which the Tory majority expelled him. Both men were recompensed by preferment after the Queen's death in August 1714. Addison did best. He was appointed Secretary to the Regents who took over until George I landed in England; fell back to his old office as Secretary to the Lord Lieutenant of Ireland; but after a disappointing wait reached home ground in 1715 as a Commissioner of Trade and finally, in 1717, as Secretary of State for the Southern Department. Over-work and the ill-health that dogged him all his life forced his resignation a year later, and he died a year after that. Steele, who had under Godolphin never moved higher than Commissioner in the Stamp Office, was given part of the patent to manage Drury Lane Theatre in October 1714, knighted the next year and made Surveyor of the Royal Stables. He lived through a turbulent and rather unhappy period of politics in the theatre and in Parliament, until in 1725 he retired to a small estate in Wales where he died four years later.

Religion and the Conduct of Life

Boswell records in *The Journal of a Tour in the Hebrides,* 1773 that on 31 August he and Dr Johnson

> came to a house [inn] in Glenmoriston kept by one Macqueen. Our landlord was a sensible fellow. He had learned his [Latin] grammar . . . There was some books here: a treatise against drunkenness, translated from the French, a volume of the *Spectator*, a volume of Prideaux's *Connexion, Cyrus's Travels*. Macqueen said he had more volumes, and his pride seemed to be much picqued that we were surprised at his having books.

This is not only an interesting record of the popularity of the *Spectator* essays, comparable with Coleridge's discovery of a copy of Thomson's *Seasons* on a cottage window-sill. It places the essays in a literary context. The two other books Boswell mentions by title were both very popular religious works. Humphrey Prideaux, Dean of Norwich, published in two volumes *The Old and New Testament connected in the History of the Jews* (1716–18); at least fifteen editions had been published by mid-century. *The Travels of Cyrus* by the quietist, Chevalier Andrew Ramsay, a disciple of Fénelon, was even more popular, one of the most widely read books of the first half of the eighteenth century. First published in French in 1727, it was immediately translated into English, and thereafter published in both tongues in many editions. It is a set of 'philosophical' travels, loosely based on ancient history, which examines the spiritual and moral essentials of education.

Contemporary and later eighteenth-century readers valued *The Tatler*, and more especially *The Spectator*, for the religious pieces they printed, and for their advice on personal conduct. Steele's sentimental theory of comedy as a magazine of exemplary heroes and heroines, good men and women, is related to a strong religious streak in his nature, as is his humanitarianism, his opposition to duelling, his interest in education. His first book, *The Christian Hero* (1701), is an overtly religious work. Addison, the grandson of a parson, the son of a Dean and the nephew of a Bishop, who as a student had set out to make a career at the university, had a more professional interest in religion, and may indeed have gone pretty far in the reading necessary for ordination in the church. His

religious writing in *The Spectator* is characterized by the rational
piety which commended itself to readers during the following
century and later. This particular kind of reflective essay, it may be
conceded, will not be the pieces most popular with modern readers.
No selection from the periodicals, however, would be adequate
without some representation of this strand of thought, of profound
and passionate, if calm, interest to past generations. The revolution
in habits and manners which *The Tatler* and *The Spectator* helped to
bring about and to confirm is nowhere more obvious than in the
way that the demonstrative religious fervour and violent rhetoric of
the mid seventeenth century has modulated, at least in the
publications read by the polite world, to such meditations as *S* 264
and *S* 385, two of the graver papers Addison supplied on Saturdays
for reading in preparation for Sundays.

Before turning to the influence and effect of *The Tatler* and *The
Spectator*, something should be said about the financing and
circulation of the papers. No documents survive that give any
information of this nature directly, such as account books or
printing-house records. It is possible, however, to make certain
deductions.

The Tatler probably started after the four free numbers with a
modest print run, but after a time, increasing success made three or
four settings of earlier numbers necessary for readers who wished to
make up sets. A press printed on one day about 2,000–2,500 folio
half-sheets, so that up to *Tatler* 117 the sale of papers was probably
less than 2,500. It has been shown that from *Tatler* 118 to the end of
the series, two settings of each number on two separate presses were
called for (see p. 60). This implies a sale of 3,000–4,000. The
figure would clearly fluctuate, and may have declined towards the
end. It should be remembered that each paper was read by several
people, especially the papers in coffee-houses and taverns, so that a
readership of 10,000 or more would not be out of the way. Swift
assumes in writing to his ladies in Dublin, in the letters known as the
Journal to Stella, that they were reading the paper, so that it clearly
had a wide geographical circulation too. The costs of printing and
distributing the paper are uncertain. Steele's *Gazette*, a comparable
publication, in 1710 cost 15 shillings, in paper and press-work, to

print 1,000 copies. 9,000 *Tatlers* (3×3,000) in a week, on this reckoning, would cost £7 4 shillings, with unknown other costs. Sold at 1 penny each, they would bring in £37 10 shillings. In addition, there was a considerable advertising revenue. Addison in 'Advertisements' (*T*224) says that the Spirit of Lavender advertisement was sent for insertion with 5 shillings. This is of course a joke, but it must have had some relation to fact, though it is not known how advertising rates were related to circulation or size and frequency of entry. There are more than 2,000 advertisement entries in *The Tatler*, which at a reasonable guess of 2s 6d each would have brought in £250. How the total income was split between Steele and the publisher is also not known.

As for *The Spectator*, Addison boasts in *S*10 that 'my Publisher tells me, that there are already Three thousand of them distributed every Day'. In *Spectator* 124 he is saying that 'the Demand for these my Papers increases daily', and at the end of 1711 further claims that 'the Demand . . . has increased every Month since their Appearance in the World'. The introduction of the Stamp Tax in August 1712 immediately halved the numbers sold, but then they increased again (Steele in *S*555). Steele's statement goes on to say that the Tax brought in 'one Week with another above 20*l* a Week', implying a print run of 1,600–1,700 a number after the tax, 3,200–3,400 before it (see *n* 7, p. 527). Specific numbers had higher sales. Bishop ◊ Fleetwood claimed more than 14,000 for 'A bold stroke in the party war' (*S*384; *see n* 1, p. 561), though they might have been printed and sold over several days.

The volumes of collected papers of both *The Tatler* and *The Spectator* appeared in innumerable editions throughout the eighteenth and nineteenth centuries, as well as in many selections such as *The Beauties of the Spectators, Tatlers and Guardians* (1753 etc.), *Histories, Fables, Allegories and Characters selected from the Spectator and the Guardian* (1753 etc.). The *Tatler* papers were translated into French (1724–5, etc.); into Dutch (1733–52); into German (1756). *The Spectator* was translated into French (1714–26 etc.); into Dutch (1720–44); into German (1739–43); into Italian (selections, 1753).

The later printing history of the *Tatler* and *Spectator* essays is evidence enough of the influence the periodicals had by being

constantly available, studied, and admired. Robert Burns mentions
in a letter that one of the earliest compositions that he remembered
reading with pleasure was 'Human life and eternity: the vision of
Mirzah' (S159). Walter Scott, born in 1771, in his edition of the
Works of Swift published in 1814, refers to 'The *Tatler*, the first
of those excellent periodical publications, which are almost peculiar
to our nation, and have had no small effect in fixing and refining
its character'.

Thirty years earlier, Dr Johnson in his 'Life of Addison' had
elaborated this kind of appreciation of the cultural importance of
both *The Tatler* and *The Spectator* in establishing 'the minuter
decencies and inferior duties', in regulating 'the practice of daily
conversation'. Johnson correctly linked the essays, viewed in this
way, with Renaissance conduct books like Castiglione's *The Courtier*,
though in this case for the middle class, merchants and other people
of substance in town and country, clergymen, small landowners,
superior farmers, as well as their wives and daughters. Johnson goes
on to say that 'Before the Tatlers and Spectators, if the writers for
the theatre are excepted, England had no masters of common life.
No writers had yet undertaken to reform either the savageness of
neglect, or the impertinence of civility.' Steele and Addison helped
to introduce the era of the primacy of middle-class civilized
behaviour, in which the insolence and tyranny of rank and hierarchy
was more and more replaced by an agreed set of rules based for the
greater part on personal merit. The code of honour of the
restoration, with its duels, its licensed *machismo*, its peremptory
humiliations, at least began to be replaced and to be laughed out
of existence.

The essays stand at an important point of social, personal and
intellectual change. All the change perhaps was not for the best.
In a famous remark, C. S. Lewis somewhat defensively commented:
'That sober code of manners under which we still live to-day, in so
far as we have any code at all, and which foreigners call hypocrisy,
is in some important degree a legacy from the *Tatler* and the
Spectator.' So it seemed thirty-five years ago. We may now be living
through another of the periodic shifts in social and personal life. If
so, the *Tatler* and *Spectator* papers have something to interest us,
well presented and forcibly expressed. It is in the literary expression

of manners and morals, personal living and social existence that the essays excel.

The prose of Addison in particular was for decades the model for imitation. One of the features of his writing is that, unlike the astonishing art of his friend and contemporary Swift, it can be imitated. Hugh Blair, in his influential *Lectures on Rhetoric and Belles Lettres*, 1783 (lecture 19, 'General Characters of Style'), advised his students that Addison's prose was 'the highest, most correct and ornamented degree of the simple manner . . . and . . . on the whole, the best model for imitation'. Blair continues, stressing that the construction of his sentences is 'easy, agreeable, and commonly very musical', that 'there is not the least affectation in his manner . . . no marks of labour; nothing forced or constrained'.

There were many imitations of *The Tatler* and *The Spectator*; almost every English writer, it seems, for more than a century tried an essay or two in that manner. Eighteenth-century German writers were enthusiastic imitators of *The Spectator* and published many satirical journals in this vein. A similar fashion is found to a lesser extent in France, Denmark, Poland and other European countries, though it is in French that the most distinguished work of this kind appeared, in Marivaux's brilliantly written papers, *Le Spectateur Français* (1722–3), *L'Indigent Philosophe* (1727), *Le Cabinet du Philosophe* (1734). In mid-century, literary periodicals appeared in Russia, and the first of these *Monthly Papers for Profit and Entertainment* (1757–62) contained translations of some twenty *Spectator* pieces. This was followed by other journals, and in *The Amazing Philosopher* (1766) by a book devoted to translations of essays by Addison, Steele, Swift and other periodical writers, on which imitators drew heavily.

The most important legacy of the two periodicals of Richard Steele and Joseph Addison, however, is moral, personal, intellectual and social awareness united with literary expression of genius. This union is the matrix in which the novel and short story developed, and the novel and short story are the modern forms of this earlier art. It is hoped that the present selection of essays puts the achievement of two important and formative writers in some perspective, and offers the reader a substantial basis for enjoying their success and judging their merit.

Further Reading

See also the Note on the Text (p. 59)

The Periodical Press

R. P. Bond, ed., *Contemporaries of the Tatler and Spectator* (Augustan Reprint Society, Los Angeles, Calif., 1954).

—, *Studies in the Early English Periodical* (U. of North Carolina P., 1957).

R. S. Crane and F. B. Kaye, *A Census of British Newspapers and Periodicals: 1620–1800* (U. of North Carolina P., 1927; 1967).

Walter Graham, *The Beginnings of the English Literary Periodicals: A Study of Periodical Literature, 1665–1715* (O.U.P., 1926). With a useful bibliography.

—, *English Literary Periodicals* (1930).

L. Hanson, *The Government and the Press, 1695–1763* (1936). Gives an account of censorship and the Stamp Act.

Stephen Parks, 'John Dunton and *The Works of the Learned*', *The Library*, 5th ser. 23 (1968). Supplements Graham.

H. L. Snyder, 'The Circulation of Newspapers in the Reign of Queen Anne', *The Library*, 5th ser. 23 (1968).

J. R. Sutherland, 'The Circulation of Newspapers and Literary Periodicals, 1700–1730', *The Library*, 4th ser. 15 (1934).

The Tatler

G. A. Aitken, ed., *The Tatler*, 4 vols. (1898–9). Pending the appearance of R. P. Bond's edition, this is the only complete set of the essays with fairly modern annotation.

R. P. Bond, *New Letters to the Tatler and Spectator* (Austin, Texas, 1959).

—, *The Tatler: The Making of a Literary Journal* (Harvard U.P., Cambridge, Mass., 1971). An indispensable and careful study.

The Spectator

D. F. Bond, ed., *The Spectator*, 5 vols. (O.U.P., 1965). The definitive edition of all the papers of both the first and second series, together with a comprehensive introduction, full textual apparatus, extensive notes and most useful index. Other editions, which are still to be met with in second-hand bookshops, are not always without textual problems, but sometimes have helpful notes: G. A. Aitken, ed., 8 vols. (1898; 1905); H. Morley, ed., 3 vols. (1868; 1883); G. Gregory Smith, ed., 8 vols. (1897–8); the 8 vols. in 4 (Everyman's Library, 1907; 1945).

L. Lewis, *The Advertisements of the Spectator* (Boston, Mass., 1910).

M. R. Watson, 'The Spectator Tradition and the Development of the Familiar Essay', *E.L.H.*, 13 (1946).

Richard Steele

C. Winton, *Captain Steele: The Early Career of Richard Steele* (up to 1714) (Johns Hopkins U.P., 1964). The most useful modern life, with good documentation and sections on *The Tatler* and *The Spectator*.

——, *Sir Richard Steele, M.P.: The Later Career* (Johns Hopkins U.P., 1970).

G. A. Aitken, *Richard Steele*, 2 vols. (1889). Still worth reading.

R. Blanchard, ed., *The Correspondence of Richard Steele* (O.U.P., 1941; 1968).

J. Loftis, *The Politics of Drama in Augustan England* (O.U.P., 1963). Contains material on Steele and Addison.

Joseph Addison

Peter Smithers, *The Life of Joseph Addison* (O.U.P., 1956; 2nd edn rev., 1968).

L. A. Elioseff, *The Cultural Milieu of Addison's Criticism* (Austin, Texas, 1963). With a most useful bibliography.

J. Lannering, *Studies in the Prose Style of Joseph Addison* (Uppsala, 1951).

Note on the Text

The text of the *Tatler* and *Spectator* essays presents complex and separate problems, which have been skilfully discussed in the following pieces, to which the present editor is greatly indebted:

(a)

F. W. Bateson, 'The *Errata* in *The Tatler*', *Review of English Studies*, 5 (1929), 155–66;

R. P. Bond, *The Tatler: The Making of a Literary Journal* (Harvard U.P., Cambridge, Mass., 1971), *passim*;

W. B. Todd, 'Early Editions of *The Tatler*', *Studies in Bibliography*, 15 (1962), 121–33;

(b)

D. F. Bond, 'The First Printing of the *Spectator*', *Modern Philology*, 47 (1950), 164–77;

——, 'The Text of the *Spectator*', *Studies in Bibliography*, 5 (1953), 109–28;

——, ed., *The Spectator*, in Introduction, pp. xx–xxix, vol. 1 (Oxford, 1965).

The present volume is a selection from both periodicals and by its nature cannot serve as a basis for studying these problems. It has been decided, therefore, to present a clear text without an apparatus of variants, which will nevertheless offer a reliable basis for reading essays from *The Tatler* as well as *The Spectator* in a form that substantially represents the authors' intentions and the prose with which their contemporaries were familiar.

After the author's manuscript had been sent to the publisher, the text first saw the light of day in the folio half-sheet of the original periodical. Here, however, the first set of difficulties arise. Since *The Tatler* developed swift, unexpected and at first somewhat unmanageable popularity, reprints of the first thirty-two half-sheets were called for at an early stage, before the runs could be adjusted to meet the demand. From *Tatler* 33, John Morphew the publisher was able to produce in one printing enough *Tatlers* to satisfy the public. Then from *Tatler* 118 to *Tatler* 271, increased demand for each issue led to runs approximately equal in numbers being set up and printed off in two different shops; these were issued simultaneously, though one issue was set up from the other. At the same time, *errata* were being supplied by Steele (and more systematically by Addison) for past numbers, and further authorial revision of misprints took place during the printing. To add to the confusion, the author in making these corrections was using some numbers of one setting and some of another. Any individual folio *Tatler*, therefore, already presents a bibliographical problem.

The folio half-sheets of *The Spectator* do not offer this complexity of relationship. The experience of printing *The Tatler* was assimilated; also, since *The Spectator* appeared daily, instead of *The Tatler's* three times a week, arrangements were made at the outset to print in more or less regular alternation between the two shops of Samuel Buckley and Jacob Tonson, the younger. Large enough runs of the first numbers were printed to allow the advertisement and sale of sets of back numbers from the end of the first month of publication, as the new periodical established its great popularity. Fifty-five rather unsystematic lists of *errata* were included in the 555 folio half-sheets of the first-series *Spectator*; some correct misprints and other errors; some are stylistic improvements and alterations.

The advertisement, and publication on 4 July 1710, of Henry Hills' 12mo two-volume piracy of *Tatlers* 1–100 (see *T* 101, *n* 1, p. 515) prompted the first authentic collected edition of the *Tatler* essays – the four-volume 12mo set with *errata* lists in each volume, stating on the title page that it was 'Revised and Corrected by the Author'. Volumes I and II were published on 10 July 1710; volumes III and IV came out with III and IV of the 8vo edition (see below). From this 12mo edition comes the 8vo subscription edition incorporating most of the *errata*. It is the latter text which is the basis of the present edition. Volumes I and II of the 8vo subscription set were proposed in January 1710, but only volume I appeared with the first two volumes of the 12mo edition; volume II was delayed until 1 September; III and IV came out on 2 January and 17 April 1711. Later printings of both 8vo and 12mo sets give a small number of relatively unimportant improvements and revisions.

The success of the *Tatler* collected editions, as well as the continued popularity of *The Spectator*, necessitated a collected *Spectator*. Tonson organized a subscription edition. Volumes I and II of this were announced in *Spectator* 269 (8 January 1712) as ready; and in *Spectator* 278 (18 January), volumes I and II of a 12mo set were advertised. Volumes III and IV in both 8vo and 12mo were published in November 1712. The publication of the collected first-series *Spectators* was completed with the appearance of V, VI and VII (8vo and 12mo) on 11 April 1713. In the case of the *Spectator* (as of the *Tatler*), the relationship between the folio half-sheets, the 8vo books and the 12mo sets is not straightforward, or uniform throughout the series of numbers. The folios, the 8vo text and the 12mo text of *The Spectator* each have independent validity at different points. To construct a definitive text, so far as this may be done, the text of the folios should be used as a copy text, and the *errata*, alterations and improvements of the successive collected editions scrutinized and adopted or rejected, with an apparatus to indicate editorial choice. Such has been the procedure of D. F. Bond in his edition of *The Spectator*. Further, there is a later edition of Addison's papers on *Paradise Lost* (see *n**, p. 554), which incorporates authorial alterations. In the present selection, however, to preserve uniformity between the *Tatler* and *Spectator* texts, and to avoid the necessity of an apparatus, the 8vo subscription volumes of both periodicals have been used as the copy text, at the risk of a little dubiety and a few false notes. The text presented here is basically that offered to the subscribers listed on pp. 489–502, to readers like the Duchess of Marlborough and Sir Isaac Newton. The mistakes and errors cited by scholars in favour of a more elaborate textual procedure are after all minor and, in a tract of prose of such dimensions, relatively unimportant for the ordinary reader. Those interested in the systematic investigation of printing practice, linguistic usage, authorial habit must in any case use a complete text of each periodical.

In the present text a few obvious typographical errors have been silently corrected. When the 8vo text does not make sense, other editions (folio, 12mo, modern) have been consulted and editorial adjustment is indicated by square brackets. In some cases authorial revision and preferable text from other sources are also incorporated in this way. An 'old-spelling' text has been adopted. The 8vo *Tatler* and *Spectator* pages are easily readable to the modern eye, but they are not modern, and the accretion of modernizations in successive reprintings falsifies the text. This is especially true in formalizing the relative informality of the original punctuation and spelling; the old style aids the establishment of an easy tone as well as the rapid and flexible modulations from narrative to indirect speech to direct speech and back, all features of good essay writing. In the interest of comfortable reading, certain printers' conventions have been modified to signals more familiar to the modern eye, but which, however, are also found in other places in the text. Quotation marks down the left-hand margin at the beginning of each line in long quotations have been replaced by marks at the beginning and end only. Forms like 'seem'd' or 'liken'd' have been normalized to 'seemed' or 'likened' throughout, except in verse. Capitals in words at the start of paragraphs have been reduced to lower case.

Essays from
THE TATLER

The TATLER.

By *Isaac Bickerstaff* Esq;

Quicquid agunt Homines nostri Farrago Libelli.

Tuesday, April 12. 1709.

THO' the other *Papers* which are publish'd for the *Use* of the good People of England have certainly very wholesome *Effects*, and are landable in their particular Kinds, they do not seem to come up to the main *Design* of such *Narrations*, which, I humbly presume, should be principally intended for the *Use* of *Politick Persons*, who are so publick-spirited as to neglect their own *Affairs* to look into *Transactions* of State *Non these Gentlemen*, for the most Part, being *Persons of strong Zeal and weak Intellects*, It is both a Charitable and Necessary Work to offer something, whereby such worthy and well-affected Members of the Commonwealth may b. instructed, after their Reading, what to think: Which shall be the End and Purpose of this my Paper, wherein I shall from Time to Time Report and Consider all Matters of what Kind soever that shall occur to Me, and publish such my *Advices* and *Reflections* every Tuesday, Thursday, and Saturday, in the Week, for the Convenience of the Post. It is also resolv'd by me to have something which may be of Entertainment to the Fair Sex, in Honour of whom I have taken the Title of this Paper. I therefore earnestly desire all Persons, without Distinction, to take it for the present Gratis, and hereafter at the Price of one Penny, forbidding all Hawkers to take more for it at their Peril. And I desire all Persons to consider, that I am at a very great Charge for proper Materials for this Work, as well as that before I resolv'd upon it, I had settled a *Correspondence* in all Parts of the Known and Knowing World; and forasmuch as this Globe is not trodden upon by meer *Drudges* of Business only, but that Men of Spirit and Genius are justly to be esteem'd as considerable *Agents* in it, we shall not upon a *Dearth* of News present you with musty *Forein Edicts*, or dull *Proclamations*, but shall divide our Relation of the *Passages* which occur in *Action* or *Discourse* throughout this Town, as well as depending...... of ...... p.... of *Places* ...... prepare you for the Matter you are to expect, in the following Manner:

All Accounts of Gallantry, Pleasure, and Entertainment, shall be under the Article of White's Chocolate-house; Poetry, under that of Will's Coffee-house; Learning, under the Title of *Grecian*; Foreign and Domestick News, you will have from St. James's Coffee-house; and what else I shall on any other Subject offer, shall be dated from my own Apartment.

I once more desire my Reader to consider, That as I cannot keep an Ingenious Man to go daily to Will's, under Two-pence each Day merely for his Charges; to White's, under Sixpence; nor to the *Grecian*, without allowing him some Plain Spanish, to be as able as others at the Learned Table; and that a good Observer cannot speak with even Kidney at St. James's without clean Linnen. I say, these Considerations will, I hope, make all Persons willing to comply with my Humble Request (when my Gratis Stock is exhausted) of a Penny a Piece; especially since they are sure of some Proper Amusement, and that it is impossible for me to want Means to entertain 'em, having, besides the Helps of my own Parts, the Power of Divination, and that I can, by casting a Figure, tell you all that will happen before it comes to pass.

But this last Faculty I shall use very sparingly, and not speak of any Thing 'till it is pass'd, for fear of divulging Matters which may offend our Superiors.

White's Chocolate-house, April 7.

THE deplorable Condition of a very pretty Gentleman, who walks here at the Hours when Men of Quality first appear, is what is very much lamented. His History is, That on the 9th of *September*, 1705. being in his One and twentieth Year, he was washing his Teeth at a Tavern Window in *Pall-Mall*, when a fine Equipage pass'd by, and in it a young Lady who look'd up at him; away goes the Coach, and the young Gentleman pull'd off his Night-Cap, and instead of rubbing his Gums, as he ought to do, out of the Window till about Four a Clock, he sits him down, and spoke not a Word till Twelve at Night; after which, he began to enquire, If any Body knew the Lady — The Company ask'd, What Lady? But he said no more, till they broke up at Six in the Morning. All the ensuing Winter he went from Church to Church every Sunday, and from Playhouse to Play-house all the Week, but could never find the Original of the Picture which dwelt in his Bosom. In a Word, his Attention to any Thing, but his Passion, was utterly gone. He has lost all the Money he ever play'd for, and been confuted in every Argument he has enter'd upon since the Moment he first saw her. He is of a Noble Family, has naturally a very good Air, is of a frank, honest Temper: But this Passion has so extremely maul'd him, that his Features are set and uninform'd, and his whole Visage is deaden'd by a long Absence of Thought. He never appears in any Alacrity, but when rais'd by Wine; at which Time he is sure to come hither, and throw away a great deal of Wit on Fellows, who have no Sense further than just to observe, That our poor Lover has most Understanding

[The plan of *The Tatler*]
Tuesday, 12 April 1709

Quicquid agunt Homines nostri Farrago Libelli.[1]

Tho' the other Papers which are published for the Use of the good People of England have certainly very wholesom Effects, and are laudable in their particular Kinds, they do not seem to come up to the main Design of such Narrations, which, I humbly presume, should be principally intended for the Use of Politick Persons, who are so publick-spirited as to neglect their own Affairs to look into Transactions of State. Now these Gentlemen, for the most Part, being Persons of strong Zeal and weak Intellects, It is both a Charitable and Necessary Work to offer something, whereby such worthy and well-affected Members of the Commonwealth may be instructed, after their Reading, what to think: *Which shall be the End and Purpose of this my Paper, wherein I shall from Time to Time Report and Consider all Matters of what Kind soever that shall occur to Me, and publish such my Advices and Reflections every* Tuesday, Thursday, *and* Saturday, *in the Week, for the Convenience of the Post.*[2] *I resolve also to have something which may be of Entertainment to the Fair Sex, in Honour of whom I have invented the Title of this Paper. I therefore earnestly desire all Persons, without Distinction, to take it in for the present* Gratis, *and hereafter at the Price of one Penny, forbidding all Hawkers to take more for it at their Peril. And I desire all Persons to consider, that I am at a very great Charge for proper Materials for this Work, as well as that before I resolved upon it I had settled a Correspondence in all Parts of the Known and Knowing World. And forasmuch as this Globe is not trodden upon by mere Drudges of Business only, but that Men of Spirit and Genius are justly to be esteemed as considerable Agents in it, we shall not upon a Dearth of News present you with musty Foreign Edicts, or dull Proclamations, but shall divide our Relation of the Passages which occur in Action or Discourse throughout this Town, as well as elsewhere, under such Dates of Places as may prepare you for the Matter you are to expect, in the following Manner:*

All Accounts of Gallantry, Pleasure, *and* Entertainment, *shall be under the Article of* White's Chocolate-house; Poetry, *under that of* Will's Coffee-house; Learning *under the Title of* Græcian; Foreign *and* Domestick News, *you will have from St.* James's Coffee-house;[3]

*and what else I have to offer on any other Subject, shall be dated from my
own* Apartment.

*I once more desire my Reader to consider, That as I cannot keep an
Ingenious Man to go daily to* Will's, *under Twopence each Day merely for
his Charges; to* White's, *under Sixpence; nor to the* Græcian, *without
allowing him some Plain* °Spanish, *to be as able as others at the Learned
Table; and that a good Observer cannot speak with even* Kidney *at St.*
James's *without clean Linnen: I say, these Considerations will, I hope,
make all Persons willing to comply with my Humble Request (when my
Gratis Stock is exhausted) of a Penny a Piece; especially since they are sure
of some Proper Amusement, and that it is impossible for me to want Means
to entertain 'em, having, besides the Force of my own Parts, the Power of
Divination, and that I can, by* °casting a Figure, *tell you all that will
happen before it comes to pass.*

*But this last Faculty I shall use very sparingly, and speak but of few
Things 'till they are passed, for fear of divulging Matters which may
offend our Superiors.*[4]

[The deplorable condition of a very pretty gentleman]
White's Chocolate-house, April 7.

The deplorable Condition of a very pretty Gentleman, who walks
here at the Hours when Men of Quality first appear, is what is very
much lamented. His History is, That on the 9th of *September*, 1705,
being in his One and twentieth Year, he was washing his Teeth at
a Tavern Window in *Pall-Mall*, when a fine Equipage passed by,
and in it a young Lady who looked up at him; away goes the Coach,
and the young Gentleman pulled off his Night-Cap, and instead of
rubbing his Gums, as he ought to do, out of the Window, 'till
about Four a Clock sits him down, and spoke not a Word 'till
Twelve at Night; after which, he began to enquire, If any Body
knew the Lady . . . The Company asked, What Lady? But he said
no more, 'till they broke up at Six in the Morning. All the ensuing
Winter he went from Church to Church every Sunday, and from
Play-house to Play-house every Night in the Week, but could never
find the Original of the Picture which dwelt in his Bosom. In a
Word, his Attention to any Thing, but his Passion, was utterly
gone. He has lost all the Money he ever played for, and been
confuted in every Argument he has entered upon since the Moment

he first saw her. He is of a Noble Family, has naturally a very good Air, is of a frank, honest Temper: But this Passion has so extreamly mauled him, that his Features are set and uninformed, and his whole Visage is deadened by a long Absence of Thought. He never appears in any Alacrity, but when raised by Wine; at which Time he is sure to come hither, and throw away a great deal of Wit on Fellows, who have no Sense further than just to observe, That our poor Lover has most Understanding when he is drunk, and is least in his Senses when he is sober.

[Mr Betterton's benefit night][5]
Will's Coffee-house, April 8.

On *Thursday* last was acted, for the Benefit of Mr. *Betterton*, the Celebrated Comedy, called *Love for Love*. Those exellent Players, Mrs. *Barry*, Mrs. *Bracegirdle*, and Mr. *Dogget*, tho' not at present concerned in the House, acted on that Occasion. There has not been known so great a Concourse of Persons of Distinction as at that Time; the Stage it self was covered with Gentlemen and Ladies, and when the Curtain was drawn, it discovered even there a very splendid Audience. This unusual Encouragement, which was given to a Play for the Advantage of so great an Actor, gives an undeniable Instance, That the true Relish for manly Entertainments and Rational Pleasures is not wholly lost. All the Parts were acted to Perfection; the Actors were careful of their Carriage, and no one was guilty of the Affectation to insert Witticisms of his own, but a due Respect was had to the Audience, for encouraging this accomplished Player. It is not now doubted but Plays will revive, and take their usual Place in the Opinion of Persons of Wit and Merit, notwithstanding their late Apostacy in Favour of Dress and Sound. This Place is very much altered since Mr. *Dryden* frequented it; where you used to see *Songs, Epigrams*, and *Satyrs*, in the Hands of every Man you met, you have now only a Pack of Cards; and instead of the Cavils about the Turn of the Expression, the Elegance of the Style, and the like, the Learned now dispute only about the Truth of the Game. But however, the Company is altered, all have shewn a great Respect for Mr. *Betterton:* And the very Gaming Part of this House have been so much touched with a Sense of the Uncertainty of Human Affairs, (which alter with themselves every

Moment) that in this Gentleman, they pitied *Mark Anthony* of *Rome*, *Hamlett* of *Denmark*, *Mithridates* of *Pontus*, *Theodosius* of *Greece*,[6] and *Henry* the Eighth of *England*. It is well known, he has been in the Condition of each of those illustrious Personages for several Hours together, and behaved himself in those high Stations, in all the Changes of the Scene, with suitable Dignity. For these Reasons, we intend to repeat this Favour to him on a proper Occasion, lest he who can instruct us so well in personating Feigned Sorrows, should be lost to us by suffering under Real Ones. The Town is at present in very great Expectation of seeing a Comedy now in Rehearsal, which is the 25th Production of my Honoured Friend Mr. *Thomas D'Urfey*; who, besides his great Abilities in the Dramatick, has a peculiar Talent in the Lyrick Way of Writing, and that with a Manner wholly new and unknown to the Antient *Greeks* and *Romans*, wherein he is but faintly imitated in the Translations of the Modern *Italian* Operas.[7]

[News][8]
St. James's Coffee-house, April 11

Letters from the *Hague* of the 16th say, That Major General *Cadogan* was gone to *Brussels*, with Orders to disperse proper Instructions for assembling the whole Force of the Allies in *Flanders* in the Beginning of the next Month. The late Offers concerning Peace, were made in the Style of Persons who think themselves upon equal Terms: But the Allies have so just a Sense of their present Advantages, that they will not admit of a Treaty, except *France* offers what is more suitable to her present Condition. At the same Time we make Preparations, as if we were alarmed by a greater Force than that which we are carrying into the Field. Thus this Point seems now to be argued Sword in Hand. This was what a Great General alluded to, when being asked the Names of those who were to be Plenipotentiaries for the ensuing Peace; answered, with a serious Air, *There are about an Hundred thousand of us*. Mr. *Kidney*, who has the Ear of the greatest Politicians that come hither, tells me, There is a Mail come in to Day with Letters, dated *Hague*, *April* 19. °*N.S.* which say, a Design of bringing Part of our Troops into the Field at the latter End of this Month, is now altered to a Resolution of marching towards the Camp about the 20th of the next. There happened t'other Day, in the °Road of *Scheveling*, an Engagement between a Privateer of *Zealand* and one of *Dunkirk*. The *Dunkirker*, carrying 33 Pieces of Cannon, was taken and brought into the *Texel*. It is said, the Courier of Monsieur *Rouille* is returned to him from the Court of *France*. Monsieur *Vendosme* being reinstated in the Favour of the Dutchess of *Burgundy*, is to command in *Flanders*.

Mr. *Kidney* added, That there were Letters of the 17th from *Ghent*, which give an Account, that the Enemy had formed a Design to surprize two Battalions of the Allies which lay at *Alost*; but those Battalions received Advice of their March, and retired to *Dendermond*. Lieutenant General *Wood* appeared on this Occasion at the Head of 5000 Foot, and 1000 Horse, upon which the Enemy withdrew, without making any further Attempt.

[The death of Mr Partridge]⁹
From my own Apartment

I am sorry I am obliged to trouble the Publick with so much Discourse upon a Matter which I at the very first mentioned as a Trifle, *viz*. the Death of Mr. *Partridge*, under whose Name there is an *Almanack* come out for the Year 1709. In one Page of which it is asserted by the said *John Partridge*, That he is still living, and not only so, but that he was also living some Time before, and even at the Instant when I writ of his Death. I have in another Place, and in a Paper by itself, sufficiently convinced this Man that he is dead, and if he has any Shame, I don't doubt but that by this Time he owns it to all his Acquaintance: For tho' the Legs and Arms, and whole Body of that Man may still appear and perform their animal Functions; yet since, as I have elsewhere observed, his Art is gone, the Man is gone. I am, as I said, concerned, that this little Matter should make so much Noise; but since I am engaged, I take my self obliged in Honour to go on in my Lucubrations, and by the Help of these Arts of which I am Master, as well as my Skill in Astrological Speculations, I shall, as I see Occasion, proceed to confute other dead Men, who pretend to be in Being, that they are actually deceased. I therefore give all Men fair Warning to mend their Manners, for I shall from Time to Time print Bills of Mortality; and I beg the Pardon of all such who shall be named therein, if they who are good for Nothing shall find themselves in the Number of the Deceased.

No. 3 [STEELE]
Thursday, 14 April to Saturday, 16 April 1709

[Thoughts on seeing *The Country Wife*][1]
Will's Coffee-house, April 14.

This Evening, the Comedy, called *The Country Wife*, was acted in *Drury-Lane*, for the Benefit of Mrs. *Bignall*. The Part which gives Name to the Play was performed by her self. Through the whole Action, she made a very pretty Figure, and exactly entered into the Nature of the Part. Her Husband, in the *Drama*, is represented to be one of those Debauchees who run through the Vices of the Town, and believe when they think fit they can marry and settle at their Ease. His own Knowledge of the Iniquity of the Age, makes him chuse a Wife wholly ignorant of it, and place his Security in her Want of Skill how to abuse him. The Poet, on many Occasions, where the Propriety of the Character will admit of it, insinuates, That there is no Defence against Vice, but the Contempt of it: And has, in the Natural Ideas of an Untainted Innocent, shown the gradual Steps to Ruin and Destruction, which Persons of Condition run into, without the Help of a good Education how to form their Conduct. The Torment of a Jealous Coxcomb, which arises from his own False Maxims, and the Aggravation of his Pain, by the very Words in which he sees her Innocence, makes a very pleasant and instructive Satyr. The Character of *Horner*, and the Design of it, is a good Representation of the Age in which that Comedy was written; at which Time Love and Wenching were the Business of Life, and the Gallant Manner of pursuing Women was the best Recommendation at Court. To which only it is to be imputed, that a Gentleman of Mr. *Wicherley's* Character and Sense, condescends to represent the Insults done to the Honour of the Bed, without just Reproof; but to have drawn a Man of Probity with Regard to such Considerations, had been a Monster, and a Poet had at that Time discovered his Want of knowing the Manners of the Court he lived in, by a Virtuous Character in his fine Gentleman, as he would show his Ignorance, by drawing a Vicious One to please the present Audience. Mrs. *Bignall* did her Part very happily, and had a certain Grace in her Rusticity, which gave us Hopes of seeing her a very Skilful Player, and in some Parts, supply our Loss of Mrs. *Verbruggen*. I cannot be of the same Opinion with my Friends and Fellow-Labourers, the °*Reformers of Manners*, in their Severity towards Plays, but must allow, that a good Play, acted before a well-bred Audience, must raise very proper Incitements to good Behaviour, and be the most quick and most prevailing Method of giving Young People a Turn of Sense and Breeding. But as I have set up for a Weekly Historian, I resolve to be a Faithful One; and therefore take this publick Occasion, to admonish a Young Nobleman, who came °flustered into the Box last Night, and let him know, how much all his Friends were out of Countenance for him. The Women sate in Terror of hearing something that should shock their Modesty, and all the gentlemen in as much Pain, out of Compassion to the Ladies, and perhaps Resentment for the Indignity which was offered in coming into their Presence in so disrespectful a Manner. Wine made him say Nothing that was Rude, therefore he is forgiven, upon Condition he will never hazard his offending more in this Kind. As I just now hinted, I own my self of the Society for *Reformation of Manners*. We have lower Instruments than those of the Family of *Bickerstaff*, for punishing great Crimes, and exposing the Abandoned. Therefore, as I design to have Notices from all Publick Assemblies, I shall take upon me only Indecorums, Improprieties, and Negligences, in such as should give us better Examples. After this Declaration, if a Fine Lady thinks fit to giggle at Church, or a Great Beau come in drunk to a Play, either shall be sure to hear of it in my ensuing Paper: For meerly as a well-bred Man, I cannot bear these Enormities.

After the Play, we naturally stroll to this Coffee-house, in Hopes of meeting some new Poem, or other Entertainment, among the Men of Wit and Pleasure, where there is a Dearth at present. But it is wonderful there should be so few Writers, when the Art is become meerly Mechanick, and Men may make themselves Great that Way, by as certain and infallible Rules, as you may be a Joiner or a Mason. There happens a good Instance of this, in what the Hawker just now has offered to Sale; to wit, *Instructions to*

Vanderbank; A Sequel to the Advice to the Poets; A Poem, occasioned by the Glorious Success of her Majesty's Arms, under the Command of the Duke of Marlborough, *the last Year in* Flanders.[2] Here you are to understand, that the Author finding the Poets would not take his Advice, he troubles himself no more about 'em; but has met with one *Vanderbank*, who works in Arras, and makes very good Tapestry Hangings: Therefore, in order to celebrate the Hero of the Age, he claps me together all that can be said of a Man that makes Hangings: As,

> *Then, Artist, who dost Nature's Face express*
> *In Silk and Gold, and Scenes of Action dress;*
> *Dost figured Arras animated leave,*
> *Spin a Bright Story, or a passion weave*
> *By mingling Threads; canst mingle Shade and Light,*
> *Delineate Triumphs, or describe a Fight?*

Well, what shall this Workman do? Why? To show how great an Hero the Poet intends, he provides him a very good Horse:

> *Champing his Foam, and bounding on the Plain,*
> *Arch his High Neck, and Graceful spread his Mane.*

Now as to the Intrepidity, the calm Courage, the constant Application of the Hero, it is not necessary to take that upon yourself; you may, in the Lump, bid him you employ raise him as High as he can, and if he does it not, let him answer for disobeying Orders.

> *Let Fame and Victory in inferior Sky,*
> *Hover with balanc'd Wings, and smiling fly*
> *Above his Head,* &c.

A whole Poem of this Kind may be ready against an ensuing Campagne, as well as a Space left in the Canvas of a Piece of Tapestry for the principal Figure, while the Under-Parts are working. So that in Effect, the Adviser copies after the Man he pretends to direct. This Method should, methinks, encourage young Beginners: For the Invention is so fitted to all Capacities, that by the Help of it a Man may make a °Receipt for a Poem, A young Man may observe, that the °Gigg of the Thing is, as I said,

finding out all that can be said of his Way you employ to set forth
your Worthy. *Waller* and *Denham* had worn out the Expedient of
Advice to a Painter.[3] This Author has transferred the Work, and
sent his *Advice to the Poets*; that is to say, to the *Turners of Verse*, as
he calls 'em. Well, that Thought is worn out also, therefore he
directs his Genius to the Loom, and will have a new Set of Hangings
in Honour of the last Year in *Flanders*. I must own to you, I approve
extreamly this Invention, and it might be improved for the Benefit
of Manufactury: As, suppose an Ingenious Gentleman should write
a Poem of Advice to a Callico-Printer; Do you think there is a Girl
in *England*, that would wear any Thing but *The Taking of* Lisle, or
The Battle of Oudenarde? They would certainly be all the Fashion,
till the Heroes Abroad had cut out some more Patterns. I should
fancy small Skirmishes might do for Under-Petticoats, provided
they had a Siege for the Upper. If our Adviser were well imitated,
many Industrious People might be put to Work. Little Mr. *Dactile*,
now in the Room, who formerly writ a Song and a Half, is a Week
gone in a very pretty Work, upon this Hint: He is writing an
Epigram to a young Virgin who knits very well ('tis a Thousand
Pities he is a *Jacobite*): But his Epigram is by Way of Advice to this
Damsel, to knit all the Actions of the *Pretender* and the Duke of
Burgundy last Campagne in the °Clock of a Stocking.[4] It were
endless to enumerate the many Hands and Trades that may be
employed by Poets, of so useful a Turn as this Adviser's. I shall
think of it; and in this Time of Taxes, shall consult a great Critick
employed in the Custom-house, in order to propose what Tax may
be proper to put upon Knives, Seals, Rings, Hangings, °Wrought-
Beds, Gowns and Petticoats, where any of those Commodities bear
Motto[e]s, or are worked upon Poetical Grounds.

[News]
St. James's Coffee-house, April 15.

Letters from *Turin* of the 3rd Instant, °*N.S.* inform us, That his
Royal Highness[5] employs all his Address in alarming the Enemy,
and perplexing their Speculations concerning his real Designs the
ensuing Campaign. Contracts are entered into with the Merchants
of *Milan*, for a great Number of Mules to transport his Provisions
and Ammunition. His Royal Highness has ordered the Train of

Artillery to be conveyed to *Susa* before the 20th of the next Month.
In the mean Time, all Accounts agree, That the Enemy are very
backward in their Preparations, and almost incapable of defending
themselves against an Invasion, by reason of the general Murmurs
of their own People; which, they find, are no way to be quieted,
but by giving them Hopes of a speedy Peace. When these Letters
were dispatched, the Marshal *de Thesse* was arrived at *Genoa*, where
he has taken much Pains to keep the Correspondents of the
Merchants of *France* in Hopes, that Measures will be found out to
support the Credit and Commerce between that State and *Lyons*.
But the late Declaration of the Agents of Monsieur *Bernard*, that
they cannot discharge the Demands made upon them, has quite
dispirited all those who are engaged in the Remittances of *France*.

[A benefit performance tonight]
From my own Apartment, April 15.

It is a very natural Passion in all good Members of the Common-
wealth, to take what Care they can of their Families. Therefore I
hope the Reader will forgive me, that I desire he would go to the
Play, called the *Stratagem*,[6] this Evening, which is to be acted for
the Benefit of my near Kinsman Mr. *John Bickerstaff*. I protest to
you, the Gentleman has not spoken to me to desire this Favour; but
I have a Respect for him, as well in Regard to Consanguinity, as
that he is an intimate Friend of that Famous and Heroick Actor,
Mr. *George Powell*, who formerly played *Alexander the Great* in all
Places, though he is lately grown so reserved, as to act it only on
the Stage.[7]

from No. 4 [STEELE]
Saturday, 16 April to Tuesday, 19 April 1709

[Show-business][1]
Will's Coffee-house, April 18.

Letters from the *Hay-market* inform us, That on *Saturday* Night
last the Opera of *Pyrrhus* and *Demetrius* was performed with great
Applause.[2] This Intelligence is not very acceptable to us Friends of
the Theatre; for the Stage being an Entertainment of the Reason

and all our Faculties, this Way of being pleased with the Suspence of 'em for Three Hours together, and being given up to the shallow Satisfaction of the Eyes and Ears only, seems to arise rather from the Degeneracy of our Understanding, than an Improvement of our Diversions. That the Understanding has no Part in the Pleasure is evident, from what these Letters very positively assert, to wit, That a great Part of the Performance was done in *Italian:* And a great Critick fell into Fits in the Gallery, at seeing, not only Time and Place, but Languages and Nations confused in the most incorrigible Manner.³ His Spleen is so extremely moved on this Occasion, that he is going to publish a Treatise against Operas, which, he thinks, have already inclined us to Thoughts of Peace, and if tolerated, must infallibly dispirit us from carrying on the War. He has communicated his Scheme to the whole Room, and declared in what manner Things of this Kind were first introduced. He has upon this Occasion considered the Nature of Sounds in general, and made a very elaborate Digression upon the *London Cries*, wherein he has shown from Reason and Philosophy, why Oysters are cried, °Cardmatches sung, and Turneps and all other Vegetables neither cried, sung, nor said, but sold, with an Accent and Tone neither natural to Man or Beast. This Piece seems to be taken from the Model of that excellent Discourse of Mrs. *Manly* the School-Mistress, concerning Samplers.⁴ Advices from the upper End of *Piccadilly* say, That °*May-Fair* is utterly abolished; and we hear, Mr. *Pinkethman* has removed his ingenious Company of Strollers to *Greenwich:*⁵ But other Letters from *Deptford* say, the Company is only making thither, and not yet settled; but that several Heathen Gods and Goddesses, which are to descend in °Machines, landed at the *King's-Head-Stairs* last *Saturday. Venus* and *Cupid* went on Foot from thence to *Greenwich*; *Mars* got drunk in the Town, and broke his Landlord's Head; for which sat in the Stocks the whole Evening; but Mr. *Pinkethman* giving Security that he should do nothing this ensuing Summer, he was set at Liberty. The most melancholy Part of all, was, that *Diana* was taken in the Act of Fornication with a Boatman, and committed by Justice *Wrathful*, which has, it seems, put a Stop to the Diversions of the Theatre of *Black-Heath*. But there goes down another *Diana* and a *Patient Grissel* next Tide from *Billingsgate*.

from No. 5 [STEELE]
Tuesday, 19 April to Thursday, 21 April 1709

[A Project for the Advancement of Religion][1]
Will's Coffee-house, April 20.

This Week being Sacred to Holy Things, and no Publick Diversions
allowed, there has been taken Notice of, even here, a little Treatise,
called, *A Project for the Advancement of Religion; Dedicated to the
Countess of* Berkeley. The Title was so uncommon, and promised so
peculiar a Way of Thinking, that every Man here has read it, and
as many as have done so, have approved it. It is written with the
Spirit of one, who has seen the World enough to undervalue it with
good Breeding. The Author must certainly be a Man of Wisdom,
as well as Piety, and have spent much Time in the Exercise of both.
The Real Causes of the Decay of the Interest of Religion, are set
forth in a clear and lively Manner, without unseasonable Passions;
and the whole Air of the Book, as to the Language, the Sentiments,
and the Reasonings, show it was written by one whose Virtue sits
easie about him, and to whom Vice is throughly contemptible. It
was said by one of this Company, alluding to that Knowledge of
the World the Author seems to have, the Man writes much like a
Gentleman, and goes to Heaven with a very good Mien.

from No. 9 [STEELE with SWIFT]
Thursday, 28 April to Saturday, 30 April 1709

['A Description of the Morning']
Will's Coffee-house, April 28.

This Evening we were entertained with *The Old Batchelor*, a Comedy
of deserved Reputation.[1] In the Character which gives Name to the
Play, there is excellently represented the Reluctance of a battered
Debauchee to come into the Trammels of Order and Decency: He
neither languishes nor burns, but frets for Love. The Gentlemen of
more regular Behaviour, are drawn with much Spirit and Wit, and
the *Drama* introduced by the Dialogue of the first Scene with
uncommon, yet natural Conversation. The Part of *Fondlewife* is a
lively Image of the unseasonable Fondness of Age and Impotence.

But instead of such agreeable Works as these, the Town has this half Age been tormented with Insects, called *Easie Writers*, whose Abilities Mr. *Wycherly* one Day described excellently well in one Word: *That*, said he, *among these Fellows is called* Easy Writing, *which any one may easily write*. Such Jantie Scribblers are so justly laughed at for their Sonnets on *Phillis* and *Chloris*, and Fantastical Descriptions in 'em, that an ingenious Kinsman of mine,[2] of the Family of the *Staffs*, Mr. *Humphrey Wagstaff* by Name, has, to avoid their Strain, run into a Way perfectly new, and described Things exactly as they happen: He never forms Fields, or Nymphs, or Groves, where they are not, but makes the Incidents just as they really appear. For an Example of it; I stole out of his Manuscript the following Lines: They are a Description of the Morning, but of the Morning in Town; nay, of the Morning at this End of the Town, where my Kinsman at present lodges.

> *Now hardly here and there an Hackney-Coach*
> *Appearing, show'd the Ruddy Morn's Approach.*
> *Now Betty from her Master's Bed had flown,*
> *And softly stole to discompose her own.*
> *The Slipshod 'Prentice from his Master's Door,*
> *Had par'd the Street, and sprinkled round the Floor.*
> *Now Moll had whirl'd her Mop with dext'rous Airs,*
> *Prepar'd to scrub the Entry and the Stairs.*
> *The Youth with broomy Stumps began to trace*
> *The Kennel Edge, where Wheels had worn the Place.*
> *The Smallcoal-Man was heard with Cadence deep,*
> *Till drown'd in shriller Notes of Chimney-sweep.*
> *Duns at his Lordship's Gate began to meet;*
> *And Brickdust Moll had scream'd through half a Street.*
> *The Turnkey now his Flock returning sees,*
> *Duly let out a'Nights to steal for Fees.*
> *The watchful Bailiffs take their silent Stands;*
> *And School-boys lag with Satchels in their Hands.*

All that I apprehend is, that Dear °*Numps* will be angry I have published these Lines; not that he has any Reason to be ashamed of 'em, but for Fear of those Rogues, the Bane to all excellent Performances, the *Imitators*. Therefore, before-hand, I bar all

Descriptions of the Evening; as, a Medley of Verses signifying,
Grey-Peas are now cried warm: That Wenches now begin to amble
round the Passages of the Play-house: Or of Noon; as, That fine
Ladies and great Beaus are just yawning out of their Beds and
Windows in *Pall-Mall*, and so forth. I forewarn also all Persons
from encouraging any Draughts after my Cousin; and foretell any
Man who shall go about to imitate him, that he will be very insipid.
The Family Stock is embarked in this Design, and we will not
admit of Counterfeits: Dr. *Anderson* and his Heirs enjoy his Pills,
Sir *William Read* has the Cure of Eyes, and Monsieur *Roselli* can
only cure the Gout.[3] We pretend to none of these Things; but to
examine who and who are together, to tell any mistaken Man he is
not what he believes he is, to distinguish Merit, and expose false
Pretences to it, is a Liberty our Family has by Law in 'em, from an
Inter-marriage with a Daughter of Mr. *Scoggin* the famous Droll of
the last Century.[4] This Right I design to make use of; but will not
encroach upon the above-mentioned Adepts, or any other . . .

[A short story: Pastorella's Aunt]
White's Chocolate-house, April 29.

It is Matter of much Speculation among the Beaus and Oglers,
what it is that can have made so sudden a Change, as has been of
late observed, in the whole Behaviour of *Pastorella*, who never sate
still a Moment till she was Eighteen, which she has now exceeded
by Two Months. Her Aunt, who has the Care of her, has not been
always so rigid as she is at this present Date; but has so good a
Sense of the Frailty of Woman, and Falshood of Man, that she
resolved on all Manner of Methods to keep *Pastorella*, if possible,
in Safety, against her self, and all her Admirers. At the same Time
the good Lady knew by long Experience, that a gay Inclination,
curbed too rashly, would but run to the greater Excess for that
Restraint: Therefore intended to watch her, and take some
Opportunity of ingaging her insensibly in her own Interests,
without the Anguish of an Admonition. You are to know then,
That Miss, with all her Flirting and Ogling, had also naturally a
strong Curiosity in her, and was the greatest Eaves-Dropper
breathing. *Parisatis* (for so her prudent Aunt is called) observed
this Humour, and retires one Day to her Closet, into which she

knew *Pastorella* would peep, and listen to know how she was
employed. It happened accordingly, and the young Lady saw her
good Governante on her Knees, and after a mental Behaviour,
break into these Words: *As for the dear Child committed to my Care,
let her Sobriety of Carriage, and Severity of Behaviour, be such, as may
make that Noble Lord, who is taken with her Beauty, turn his Designs to
such as are honourable.* Here *Parisatis* heard her Neece nestle closer
to the Key-Hole: She then goes on: *Make her the joyful Mother of a
numerous and wealthy Offspring, and let her Carriage be such, as may
make this Noble Youth expect the Blessings of an happy Marriage, from
the Singularity of her Life, in this loose and censorious Age.* Miss having
heard enough, sneaks off for Fear of Discovery, and immediately,
at her Glass, alters the Sitting of her Head; then pulls up her
°Tucker, and forms her self into the exact Manner of *Lindamira*: In
a Word, becomes a sincere Convert to every Thing that's com-
mendable in a fine young Lady; and Two or Three such Matches as
her Aunt feigned in her Devotions, are at this Day in her Choice.
This is the History and Original Cause of *Pastorella's* Conversion
from Coquettry. The Prudence in the Management of this Young
Lady's Temper, and good Judgment of it, is hardly to be exceeded.
I scarce remember a greater Instance of Forbearance of the usual
peevish Way with which the Aged treat the Young, than this,
except that of our famous *Noy*,[5] whose good Nature went so far, as
to make him put off his Admonitions to his Son, even till after his
Death; and did not give him his Thoughts of him, till he came to
read that memorable Passage in his Will: *All the rest of my Estate*,
says he, *I leave to my Son* Edward *(who is Executor to this my Will) to
be squandered as he shall think fit: I leave it him for that Purpose, and
hope no better from him.* A generous Disdain and Reflection, upon
how little he deserved from so excellent a Father, reformed the
young Man, and made *Edward*, from an errant Rake, become a fine
Gentleman.

from No. 12 [STEELE]
Thursday, 5 May to Saturday, 7 May 1709

[Things are come to this pass]
May 5.

When a Man has engaged to keep a Stage-Coach, he is obliged, whether he has Passengers or not, to set out: Thus it fares with us Weekly Historians; but indeed, for my Particular, I hope I shall soon have little more to do in this Work, than to publish what is sent me from such as have Leisure and Capacity for giving Delight, and being pleased in an elegant manner. The present Grandeur of the *British* Nation might make us expect, that we should rise in our Publick Diversions, and Manner of enjoying Life, in Proportion to our Advancement in Glory and Power. Instead of that, take and survey this Town, and you'll find, Rakes and Debauchees are your Men of Pleasure; Thoughtless Atheists, and Illiterate Drunkards, call themselves Free Thinkers; and Gamesters, Banterers, °Biters, Swearers, and Twenty new-born Insects more, are, in their several Species, the Modern Men of Wit. Hence it is, that a Man who has been out of Town but one half Year, has lost the Language, and must have some Friend to stand by him, and keep him in Countenance for talking common Sense. To Day I saw a short Interlude at *White*'s of this Nature, which I took Notes of, and put together as well as I could in a Publick Place. The Persons of the *Drama* are, °*Pip*, the last Gentleman that has been made so at Cards; *Trimmer*, a Person half undone at 'em, and is now between a Cheat and a Gentleman; *Acorn*, an honest *English* Man, of good plain Sense and Meaning; and Mr. *Friendly*, a reasonable Man of the Town.

White's Chocolate-house, May 5.

Enter *Pip, Trim.* and *Acorn.*

Ac. What's the Matter, Gentlemen? What? Take no Notice of an old Friend?

Pip. Pox on it! don't talk to me, I am °Vowel'd by the Count, and cursedly out of Humour.

Ac. Vowel'd! Prithee, *Trimmer,* What does he mean by that?

Trim. Have a Care, *Harry*, speak softly; don't show your
Ignorance: – If you do, they'll Bite you where-e're they meet you;
they are such cursed Curs, – the present Wits.

Ac. Bite me! What do you mean?

Pip. Why! Don't you know what Biting is? Nay, you are in the
Right on't. However, one would learn it only to defend ones self
against Men of Wit, as one would know the Tricks of Play, to be
secure against the Cheats. But don't you hear, *Acorn*, that Report,
That some Potentates of the Alliance have taken Care of themselves,
exclusive of us?

Ac. How! Heav'n forbid! After all our Glorious Victories; all this
Expence of Blood and Treasure!

Pip. Bite –

Ac. Bite? How?

Trim. Nay, he has Bit you fairly enough; that's certain.

Ac. Pox! I don't feel it – How? Where?

Exit Pip, and Trimmer, laughing.

Ac. Ho! Mr. *Friendly*, your most humble Servant; you heard
what passed between those fine Gentlemen and me. *Pip* complained
to me, That he has been °Vowel'd; and they tell me, I am Bit.

Friend. You are to understand, Sir, That Simplicity of Behaviour,
which is the Perfection of good Breeding and good Sense, is utterly
lost in the World; and in the Room of it, there are started a
Thousand little Inventions, which Men, barren of better Things,
take up in the Place of it. Thus, for every Character in Conversation
that used to please, there is an Impostor put upon you. Him whom
we allowed formerly for a certain pleasant Subtilty, and natural
Way of giving you an unexpected Hit, called a *Droll*, is now
mimicked by a *Biter*, who is a dull Fellow, that tells you a Lye with
a grave Face, and laughs at you for knowing him no better than to
believe him. Instead of that Sort of Companion, who could rally
you, and keep his Countenance, 'till he made you fall into some
little Inconsistency of Behaviour, at which you your self could laugh
with him, you have the Sneerer, who will keep you Company from
Morning to Night, to gather your Follies of the Day, (which
perhaps you commit out of Confidence in him) and expose you in
the Evening to all the Scorners in Town. For your Man of Sense and
free Spirit, whose Set of Thoughts were built upon Learning,

Reason, and Experience, you have now an impudent Creature made up of Vice only, who supports his Ignorance by his Courage, and Want of Learning by Comtempt of it.

Ac. Dear Sir, hold: What you have told me already of this Change in Conversation, is too miserable to be heard with any Delight; but, methinks, as these new Creatures appear in the World, it might give an excellent Field to Writers for the Stage, to divert us with the Representation of them there.

Friend. No, No: As you say, there might be some Hopes of Redress of these Grievances, if there were proper Care taken of the Theatre; but the History of that is yet more lamentable, than that of the Decay of Conversation I gave you.

Ac. Pray, Sir, a little: I han't been in Town these Six Years, till within this Fortnight.

Friend. It is now some Years, since several Revolutions in the Gay World had made the Empire of the Stage subject to very fatal Convulsions, which were too dangerous to be cured by the Skill of little King *Oberon*,[1] who then sate in the Throne of it. The Laziness of this Prince threw him upon the Choice of a Person who was fit to spend his Life in Contentions, an able and profound Attorney, to whom he mortgaged his whole Empire. This *Divito* is the most skilful of all Politicians[2]: He has a perfect Art in being unintelligible in Discourse, and uncomeatable in Business. But he having no Understanding in this polite Way, brought in upon us, to get in his Money, °Ladder-dancers, °Rope-dancers, Jugglers, and Mountebanks, to strut in the Place of *Shakespear*'s Heroes, and *Johnson*'s Humourists. When the Seat of Wit was thus mortgaged, without Equity of Redemption, an Architect arose, who has built the Muse a new Palace, but secured her no Retinue; so that instead of Action there, we have been put off by Song and Dance.[3] This latter Help of Sound has also began to fail for Want of Voices; therefore the Palace has since been put into the Hands of a Surgeon,[4] who cuts any Foreign Fellow into an Eunuch, and passes him upon us for a Singer of *Italy*.

Ac. I'll go out of Town to Morrow.

Trim. Things are come to this Pass; and yet the World will not understand, that the Theatre has much the same Effect on the Manners of the Age as the Bank on the Credit of the Nation. Wit

and Spirit, Humour and good Sense, can never be revived, but
under the Government of those who are Judges of such Talents,
who know, that whatever is put up in their Stead, is but a short
and trifling Expedient, to support the Appearance of 'em for a
Season. It is possible, a Peace will give Leisure to put these Matters
under new Regulations; but at present, all the Assistance we can
see towards our Recovery, is as far from giving us Help, as a
Poultice is from performing what can be done only by the °Grand
Elixir.

from No. 18 [STEELE and ADDISON]
Thursday, 19 May to Saturday, 21 May 1709

[Peace stares news-writers in the face]
St. James's Coffee-house, May 20.

This Day a Mail arrived from *Holland*, by which there are Advices
from *Paris*, That the Kingdom of *France* is in the utmost Misery
and Distraction. The Merchants of *Lions* have been at Court, to
remonstrate their great Sufferings by the Failure of their Publick
Credit; but have received no other Satisfaction, than Promises of a
sudden Peace; and that their Debts will be made good by Funds
out of the Revenue, which will not answer, but in case of the Peace
which is promised. In the mean Time, the Cries of the Common
People are loud for Want of Bread, the Gentry have lost all Spirit
and Zeal for their Country, and the King himself seems to languish
under the Anxiety of the pressing Calamities of the Nation, and
retires from hearing those Grievances, which he hath not Power to
redress. Instead of Preparations for War, and the Defence of their
Country, there is nothing to be seen but evident Marks of a general
Despair. Processions, Fastings, Publick Mournings, and Humiliations, are become the sole Employments of a People, who were
lately the most vain and gay of any in the Universe.

The Pope has written to the *French* King on the Subject of a
Peace, and his Majesty has answered in the lowliest Terms, That
he entirely submits his Affairs to Divine Providence, and shall soon
show the World, that he prefers the Tranquility of his People to the
Glory of his Arms, and Extent of his Conquests.

Letters from the *Hague* of the 24th say, That his Excellency the Lord *Townshend* delivered his Credentials on that Day to the States-General, as Plenipotentiary from the Queen of *Great-Britain*; as did also Count *Zinzendorf*, who bears the same Character from the Emperor.

Prince *Eugene* intended to set out the next day for *Brussels*, and his Grace the Duke of *Marlborough* on the *Tuesday* following. The Marquis *de Torcy* talks daily of going, but still continues here. The Army of the Allies is to assemble on the 7th of the next Month at *Helchin*; though 'tis generally believed, that the Preliminaries to a Treaty are fully adjusted.

The Approach of a Peace[1] strikes a Pannick thro' our Armies, tho' that of a Battle could never do it, and they almost repent of their Bravery, that made such haste to humble themselves and the *French* King. The Duke of *Marlborough*, tho' otherwise the greatest General of the Age, has plainly shown himself unacquainted with the Arts of Husbanding a War. He might have grown as old as the Duke of *Alva*, or Prince *Waldeck*, in the *Low-Countries*,[2] and yet have got Reputation enough every Year for any reasonable Man: For the Command of General in *Flanders* hath been ever looked upon as a Provision for Life. For my Part, I can't see how his Grace can answer it to the World, for the great Eagerness he hath shown to send a Hundred Thousand of the bravest Fellows in *Europe* a begging. But the private Gentlemen of the Infantry will be able to shift for themselves; a brave Man can never starve in a Country stocked with Hen-roosts. *There is not a Yard of Linnen*, says my honoured Progenitor, Sir *John Falstaff, in my whole Company; but as for that*, says this worthy Knight, *I am in no great Pain, we shall find Shirts on every Hedge*.[3] There is another Sort of Gentlemen whom I am much more concerned for, and that is, the Ingenious Fraternity of which I have the Honour to be an unworthy Member; I mean the *News-Writers* of *Great Britain*, whether *Post-Men* or *Post-Boys*,[4] or by what other Name or Title soever dignified or distinguished. The Case of these Gentlemen is, I think, more hard than that of the Soldiers, considering that they have taken more Towns, and fought more Battels. They have been upon Parties and Skirmishes, when our Armies have lain still; and given the General Assault to many a Place, when the Besiegers were quiet in their Trenches. They

have made us Masters of several strong Towns many Weeks before
our Generals could do it; and compleated Victories, when our
greatest Captains have been glad to come off with a drawn Battle.
Where Prince *Eugene* had slain his Thousands, *Boyer* has slain his
Ten Thousands. This Gentleman can indeed be never enough
commended for his Courage and Intrepidity during this whole
War: He has laid about him with an inexpressible Fury, and like
the offended *Marius* of Ancient *Rome*,⁵ made such Havock among
his Countrymen, as must be the Work of two or three Ages to
repair. It must be confessed, the Redoubted Mr *Buckley* has shed as
much Blood as the former; but I cannot forbear saying, (and I hope
it will not look like Envy) that we regard our Brother *Buckley* as a
kind of °*Drawcansir*, who spares neither Friend or Foe. But generally
kills as many of his own Side as the Enemy's. It is impossible for
this ingenious Sort of Men to subsist after a Peace: Every one
remembers the Shifts they were driven to in the Reign of King
Charles the Second, when they could not furnish out a single Paper
of News, without lighting up a Comet in *Germany*, or a Fire in
Moscow. There scarce appeared a Letter without a Paragraph on an
Earthquake. Prodigies were grown so familiar, that they had lost
their Name, as a great Poet of that Age has it. I remember Mr.
Dyer, who is justly looked upon by all the Fox-hunters in the
Nation as the greatest Statesman our Country has produced, was
particularly famous for dealing in Whales; insomuch that in Five
Months Time (for I had the Curiosity to examine his Letters on that
Occasion) he brought Three into the Mouth of the River *Thames*,
besides Two °Porpusses and a Sturgeon. The judicious and wary
Mr. *I. Dawks* hath all along been the Rival of this greater Writer,
and got himself a Reputation from Plagues and Famines, by which,
in those Days, he destroyed as great Multitudes, as he has lately
done by the Sword. In every Dearth of News, *Grand Cairo* was sure
to be unpeopled.

It being therefore visible, that our Society will be greater Sufferers
by the Peace than the Soldiery it self; insomuch that the *Daily
Courant* is in Danger of being broken, my Friend *Dyer* of being
reformed, and the very best of the whole Band of being reduced to
Half-Pay; Might I presume to offer any Thing in the Behalf of my
distressed Brethren, I would humbly move, That an Appendix of

proper Apartments furnished with Pen, Ink, and Paper, and other
Necessaries of Life, should be added to the Hospital of *Chelsea*, for
the Relief of such decayed News-Writers as have served their
Country in the Wars; and that for their Exercise, they should
compile the Annals of their Brother Veterans, who have been
engaged in the same Service, and are still obliged to do Duty after
the same Manner.

I cannot be thought to speak this out of an Eye to any private
Interest; for, as my chief Scenes of Action are Coffee-houses, Play-
houses, and my own Apartment, I am in no need of Camps,
Fortifications, and Fields of Battle, to support me; I don't call out
for Heroes and Generals to my Assistance. Tho' the Officers are
broken, and the Armies disbanded, I shall still be safe as long as
there are Men or Women, or Politicians, or Lovers, or Poets, or
Nymphs, or Swains, or °Cits, or Courtiers in Being.

from No. 25 [STEELE]
Saturday, 4 June to Tuesday, 7 June 1709

[Against duelling]
White's Chocolate-house, June 6.

A letter from a young Lady, written in the most passionate Terms,
wherein she laments the Misfortune of a Gentleman, her Lover,
who was lately wounded in a Duel, has turned my Thoughts to that
Subject, and enclined me to examine into the Causes which
precipitate Men into so fatal a Folly. And as it has been proposed
to treat of Subjects of Gallantry in the Article from hence, and no
one Point in Nature is more proper to be considered by the
Company who frequent this Place, than that of Duels, it is worth
our Consideration to examine into this Chimærical groundless
Humour, and to lay every other Thought aside, till we have
strip[pe]d it of all its false Pretences to Credit and Reputation
amongst Men.

But I must confess, when I consider what I am going about, and
run over in my Imagination all the endless Crowd of Men of Honour
who will be offended at such a Discourse; I am undertaking,
methinks, a Work worthy an invulnerable Hero in Romance, rather

than a private Gentleman with a single Rapier: But as I am pretty well acquainted by great Opportunities with the Nature of Man, and know of a Truth, that all Men fight *against their Will*, the Danger vanishes, and Resolution rises upon this Subject. For this Reason I shall talk very freely on a Custom which all Men wish exploded, tho' no Man has Courage enough to resist it.

But there is one unintelligible Word which I fear will extremely perplex my Dissertation; and I confess to you I find very hard to explain, which is, the Term *Satisfaction*. An honest Country Gentleman had the Misfortune to fall into Company with Two or Three modern Men of Honour, where he happened to be very ill treated; and one of the Company being conscious of his Offence, sends a Note to him in the Morning, and tells him, He was ready to give him Satisfaction. This is fine Doing (says the plain Fellow): Last Night he sent me away cursedly out of Humour, and this Morning he fancies it would be a Satisfaction to be run through the Body.

As the Matter at present stands, it is not to do handsome Actions denominates a Man of Honour; it is enough if he dares to defend ill Ones. Thus you often see a common Sharper in Competition with a Gentleman of the first Rank; tho' all Mankind is convinced, that a fighting Gamester is only a Pick-pocket with the Courage of an Highway-Man. One cannot with any Patience reflect on the unaccountable Jumble of Persons and Things in this Town and Nation, which occasions very frequently, that a brave Man falls by a Hand below that of the common Hangman, and yet his Executioner escapes the Clutches of the Hangman for doing it. I shall therefore hereafter consider, how the bravest Men in other Ages and Nations have behaved themselves upon such Incidents as we decide by Combat; and show, from their Practice, that this Resentment neither has its Foundation from true Reason, or solid Fame; but is an Imposture, made up of Cowardice, Falshood, and Want of Understanding. For this Work, a good History of Quarrels would be very edifying to the Publick, and I apply my self to the Town for Particulars and Circumstances within their Knowledge, which may serve to embellish the Dissertation with proper Cuts. Most of the Quarrels I have ever known, have proceeded from some valiant Coxcomb's persisting in the Wrong, to defend some prevailing Folly, and preserve himself from the Ingenuity of owning a Mistake.

By this Means it is called, *Giving a Man Satisfaction*, to urge your Offence against him with your Sword; which puts me in Mind of *Peter*'s Order to the Keeper, in *The Tale of a Tub*: *If you neglect to do all this, damn you and your Generation for ever; and so we bid you heartily farewel.*[1] If the Contradiction in the very Terms of one of our Challenges were as well explained, and turned into downright *English*, would it not run after this Manner?

SIR,

Your extraordinary Behaviour last Night, and the Liberty you were pleased to take with me, makes me this Morning give you this, to tell you, because you are an ill-bred Puppy, I will meet you in Hide-Park *an Hour hence; and because you want both Breeding and Humanity, I desire you would come with a Pistol in your Hand, on Horseback, and endeavour to shoot me through the Head; to teach you more Manners. If you fail of doing me this Pleasure, I shall say, You are a Rascal °on every Post in Town: and so, Sir, if you will not injure me more, I shall never forgive what you have done already. Pray Sir, do not fail of getting every Thing ready, and you will infinitely oblige,*

SIR,
Your most Obedient,
Humble Servant, &c.

from No. 29 [STEELE]
Tuesday, 14 June to Thursday, 16 June 1709

[A critick and a wit]
From my own Apartment, June 14.

I am just come hither at Ten at Night, and have ever since Six been in the most celebrated, tho' most nauseous, Company in Town: The two Leaders of the Society were a Critick and a Wit. These two Gentlemen are great Opponents upon all Occasions, not discerning that they are the nearest each other in Temper and Talents of any two Classes of Men in the World; for to profess Judgment, and to profess Wit, both arise from the same Failure, which is Want of

Judgment. The Poverty of the Critick this Way proceeds from the Abuse of his Faculty; that of the Wit from the Neglect of it. It's a particular Observation I have always made, That of all Mortals, a Critick is the silliest; for by inuring himself to examine all Things, whether they are of Consequence or not, he never looks upon any Thing but with a Design of passing Sentence upon it; by which Means, he is never a Companion, but always a Censor. This makes him earnest upon Trifles; and dispute on the most indifferent Occasions with Vehemence. If he offers to speak or write, that Talent which should approve the Work of the other Faculties, prevents their Operation. He comes upon Action in Armour; but without Weapons: He stands in Safety; but can gain no Glory. The Wit on the other Hand has been hurried so long away by Imagination only, that Judgment seems not to have ever been one of his natural Faculties. This Gentleman takes himself to be as much obliged to be merry, as the other to be grave. A thorough Critick is a Sort of Puritan in the polite World. As an °Enthusiast in Religion stumbles at the ordinary Occurrences of Life, if he cannot quote Scripture Examples on the Occasion; so the Critick is never safe in his Speech or Writing, without he has among the celebrated Writers an Authority for the Truth of his Sentence. You will believe we had a very good Time with these Brethren, who were so far out of the Dress of their native Country, and so lost to its Dialect, that they were as much Strangers themselves, as to their Relation to each other. They took up the whole Discourse; sometimes the Critick grew passionate, and when reprimanded by the Wit for any Trip or Hesitation in his Voice, he would answer, Mr. *Dryden* makes such a Character on such an Occasion break off in the same manner; so that the Stop was according to Nature, and as a Man in a Passion should do. The Wit, who is as far gone in Letters as himself, seems [to] be at a Loss to answer such an Apology; and concludes only, that though his Anger is justly vented, it wants Fire in the Utterance. If Wit is to be measured by the Circumstances of Time and Place, there is no Man has generally so little of that Talent, as he who is a Wit by Profession. What he says, instead of arising from the Occasion, has an Occasion invented to bring it in. Thus he is new for no other Reason, but that he talks like no Body else; but has taken up a Method of his own, without

Commerce of Dialogue with other People. The lively *Jasper Dactyle* is one of this Character. He seems to have made a Vow to be witty to his Life's End. When you meet him, 'What do you think,' says he, 'I have been entertaining my self with?' Then out comes a premeditated Turn; to which 'tis to no Purpose to answer, for he goes on in the same Strain of Thought he designed without your speaking. Therefore I have a general Answer to all he can say; as, *Sure there never was any Creature had so much Fire! Spondee*, who is a Critick, is seldom out of this fine Man's Company. They have no Manner of Affection for each other, but keep together, like *Novell* and *Oldfox* in the *Plain-Dealer*, because they show each other.[1] I know several of Sense who can be diverted with this Couple; but I see no Curiosity in the Thing, except it be, that *Spondee* is dull, and seems dull; but *Dactyle* is heavy with a brisk Face. It must be owned also, that *Dactyle* has almost Vigour enough to be a Coxcomb; But *Spondee*, by the Lowness of his Constitution, is only a Blockhead.

from No. 30 [STEELE]
Thursday, 16 June to Saturday, 18 June 1709

[Love-letters]
Will's Coffee-house, June 17.

The Suspension of the Playhouse[1] has made me have nothing to send you from hence; but calling here this Evening, I found the Party I usually sit with, upon the Business of Writing, and examining what was the handsomest Style in which to address Women, and write Letters of Gallantry. Many were the Opinions which were immediately declared on this Subject: Some were for a certain Softness; some for I know not what Delicacy; others for something inexpressibly Tender: When it came to me, I said there was no Rule in the World to be made for writing Letters, but that of being as near what you speak Face to Face as you can; which is so great a Truth, that I am of Opinion Writing has lost more Mistresses than any one Mistake in the whole Legend of Love. For when you write to a Lady for whom you have a solid and honourable Passion, the great Idea you have of her, joined to a quick Sense of her Absence, fills your Mind with a Sort of Tenderness, that gives your Language too much the Air of Complaint, which is seldom successful. For a Man may flatter himself as he pleases, but he will find, that the Women have more Understanding in their own Affairs than we have, and Women of Spirit are not to be won by Mourners. He that can keep handsomely within Rules, and support the Carriage of a Companion to his Mistress, is much more likely to prevail, than he who lets her see, the whole Relish of his Life depends upon her. If possible therefore divert your Mistress, rather than sigh to her. The pleasant Man she will desire for her own Sake; but the languishing Lover has nothing to hope from but her Pity. To show the Difference, I produced two Letters a Lady gave me, which had been writ by two Gentlemen who pretended to her, but were both killed the next Day after the Date at the Battle of *Almanza*.[2] One of them was a mercurial gay-humoured Man; the other a Man of a serious, but a great and gallant Spirit. Poor *Jack Careless!* This is his Letter: You see how it is folded: The Air of it is so negligent, one might have read half of it by peeping into it, without breaking it open. He had no Exactness.

MADAM,

It is a very pleasant Circumstance I am in, that while I should be thinking of the good Company we are to meet within a Day or two, where we shall go to °Loggerheads, my Thoughts are running upon a Fair Enemy in England. *I was in Hopes I had left you there; but you follow the Camp, tho' I have endeavoured to make some of our Leaguer Ladies drive you out of the Field. All my Comfort is, you are more troublesome to my Colonel than my self: I permit you to visit me only now and then; but he downright keeps you. I laugh at his Honour as far as his Gravity will allow me; but I know him to be a Man of too much Merit to succeed with a Woman. Therefore defend your Heart as well as you can, I shall come Home this Winter irresistibly dressed, and with quite a new Foreign Air. And so I had like to say, I rest, but alass! I remain,*

Madam,
Your most Obedient,
Most Humble Servant,

John Careless.

Now for Colonel *Constant*'s Epistle: you see it is folded and directed with the utmost Care.

MADAM,
I do my self the Honour to write to you this Evening, because I believe to Morrow will be a Day of Battle, and something forebodes in my Breast that I shall fall in it. If it proves so, I hope you will hear, I have done nothing below a Man who had the Love of his Country, quickened by a Passion for a Woman of Honour. If there be any Thing noble in going to a certain Death; if there be any Merit, that I meet it with Pleasure, by promising my self a Place in your Esteem; if your Applause, when I am no more, is preferable to the most glorious Life without you: I say, Madam, If any of these Considerations can have Weight with you, you will give me a kind Place in your Memory, which I prefer to the Glory of Cæsar. I hope, this will be read, as it is writ, with Tears.

The beloved Lady is a Woman of a sensible Mind; but she has confessed to me, that after all her true and solid Value for *Constant*, she had much more Concern for the Loss of *Careless*. Those noble and serious Spirits have something equal to the Adversities they meet with, and consequently lessen the Objects of Pity. Great Accidents seem not cut out so much for Men of familiar Characters, which makes them more easily pitied, and soon after beloved. Add to this, that the Sort of Love which generally succeeds, is a Stranger to Awe and Distance. I asked *Romana*, Whether of the Two she should have chosen had they survived? She said, She knew she ought to have taken *Constant*; but believed, she should have chosen *Careless*.

Mr. Bickerstaff *gives Notice to all Persons that dress themselves as they please, without Regard to Decorum, (as with blue and red Stockings in Mourning;* °*tucked Cravats, and* °*Nightcap-Wigs, before People of the First Quality) That he has yet received no Fine for indulging them in that Liberty, and that he expects their Compliance with this Demand, or that they go Home immediately and shift themselves. This is farther to acquaint the Town, That the Report of the Hosiers,* °*Toymen, and Milleners, having compounded with Mr.* Bickerstaff *for tolerating such Enormities, is utterly false and scandalous.*

from No. 31   [STEELE and SWIFT]
Saturday, 18 June to Tuesday, 21 June 1709

[More against duelling]
Grecian Coffee-house, June 18.

In my Dissertation against the Custom of Single Combat, it has
been objected, that there is not Learning, or much Reading, shown
therein, which is the very Life and Soul of all Treatises; for which
Reason, being always easy to receive Admonitions, and reform my
Errors, I thought fit to consult this learned Board on the Subject.
Upon proposing some Doubts, and desiring their Assistance, a
very hopeful young Gentleman, my Relation, who is to be called
to the Bar within a Year and an half at farthest, told me, That he
had, ever since I first mentioned Duelling, turned his Head that
Way; and that he was principally moved thereto, because he
designed to follow the Circuits in the North of *England* and South
of *Scotland*, and to reside mostly at his own Estate at *Landbadernawz*[1]
in *Cardiganshire*. The Northern *Britains* and the Southern *Scots* are
a warm People, and the *Welsh a Nation of Gentlemen*; so that it
behoved him to understand well the Science of Quarrelling. The
young Gentleman proceeded admirably well, and gave the Board
an Account, that he had read *Fitzherbert's Grand Abridgment*,[2] and
had found, that Duelling is a very ancient Part of the Law: For
when a Man is sued, be it for his Life or his Land, the Person that
joins the Issue, whether Plaintiff or Defendant, may put the Tryal
upon the Duel. Further he argued, under Favour of the Court, that
when the Issue is joined by the Duel in Treason or other Capital
Crimes, the Parties accused and Accuser must fight in their own
proper Persons: But if the Dispute be for Lands, you may hire a
Champion at °*Hockley in the Hole*, or any where else. This Part of
the Law we had from the *Saxons*; and they had it, as also the Trial
by *Ordeal*, from the *Laplanders*. It is indeed agreed, said he, the
Southern and Eastern Nations never knew any Thing of it; for
though the ancient *Romans* would scold, and call Names filthily,
yet there is not an Example of a Challenge that ever passed among
them.

His quoting the Eastern Nations, put another Gentleman in
Mind of an Account he had from a Boatswain of an *East-India* Man;

which was, that a *Chinese* had tricked and °bubbled him, and that when he came to demand Satisfaction the next Morning, and like a true Tar of Honour called him Son of a Whore, Lyar, Dog, and other rough Appellatives used by Persons conversant with Winds and Waves; the *Chinese*, with great Tranquility, desired him not to come abroad fasting, nor put himself in a Heat, for it would prejudice his Health. Thus the East knows nothing of this Gallantry.

There sat at the Left of the Table a Person of a venerable Aspect, who asserted, That half the Impositions which are put upon these Ages, have been transmitted by Writers who have given too great Pomp and Magnificence to the Exploits of the ancient *Bear-Garden*, and made their Gladiators, by fabulous Tradition, greater than *Gorman* and others of *Great Britain*.[3] He informed the Company, that he had searched Authorities for what he said, and that a learned Antiquary, *Humphrey Scarecrow* Esq; of *Hockley in the Hole*, Recorder to the *Bear-Garden*, was then writing a Discourse on the Subject. It appears by the best Accounts, says this Gentleman, that the high Names which are used among us with so great Veneration, were no other than Stage-fighters, and Worthies of the ancient *Bear-Garden*. The renowned *Hercules* always carried a Quarter-staff, and was from thence called *Claviger*. A learned Chronologist is about proving what Wood this Staff was made of, whether Oak, Ash, or Crab-Tree. The first Trial of Skill he ever performed, was with one *Cacus*, a Dear-Stealer; the next was with *Typhonus*, a Giant of forty Foot four Inches. Indeed it was unhappily recorded, that meeting at last with a Sailor's Wife, she made his Staff of Prowess serve her own Use, and dwindle away to a Distaff: She clapt him on an old °Tar-Jacket of her Husband's; so that this great Hero drooped like a Scabbed Sheep. Him his Contemporary *Theseus* succeeded in the *Bear-Garden*, which Honour he held for many Years: This grand Duellist went to Hell, and was the only one of that Sort that ever came back again. As for *Achilles* and *Hector*, (as the Ballads of those Times mention) they were pretty Smart Fellows; they fought at Sword and Buckler; but the former had much the better of it; his Mother, who was an Oyster-Woman,[4] having got a Black-Smith of *Lemnos* to make her Son's Weapons. There's a Pair of trusty *Trojans* in a Song of *Virgil*'s, that were famous for handling their Gauntlets,

Dares, and *Entellus*; and indeed it does appear, they fought no °Sham-Prize.[5] What Arms the Great *Alexander* used, is uncertain; however, the Historian mentions, when he attacked *Thalestris*, it was only at Single Rapier; but the Weapon soon failed; for it was always observed, that the *Amazons* had a Sort of Enchantment about them, which made the Blade of the Weapon, tho' of never so good Metal, at every home Push lose its Edge and grow feeble.

The *Roman Bear-Garden* was abundantly more magnificent than any Thing *Greece* could boast of; it flourished most under those Delights of Mankind, *Nero*, and *Domitian:* At one Time it's recorded 400 Senators entered the List, and thought it an Honour to be cudgelled and quarterstaffed.[6] I observe, the °*Lanistæ* were the People chiefly employed, which makes me imagine our *Bear-Garden* copied much after this, the Butchers being the greatest Men in it.

Thus far the Glory and Honour of the *Bear-Garden* stood secure, till Fate, that irresistible Ruler of Sublunary Things, in that universal Ruin of Arts and politer Learning, by those savage People the *Goths* and *Vandals*, destroyed and levelled it to the Ground. Then fell the Grandeur and Bravery of the *Roman* State, till at last the Warlike Genius (but accompanied with more Courtesie) revived in the Christian World under those puissant Champions, St. *George*, St. *Dennis*, and other dignified Heroes: One killed his Dragon, another his Lion, and were all afterwards canonized for it, having °red Letters before them to illustrate their Martial Temper. The *Spanish* Nation it must be owned, were devoted to Gallantry and Chivalry above the rest of the World. What a great Figure does that great Name, Don *Quixot*, make in History? How shines this glorious Star in the *Western* World? O renowned Hero! O Mirror of Knighthood!

> *Thy brandished* °*Winyard all the World defies,*
> *And kills as sure as* del Tobosa's *Eyes.*

— I am forced to break off abruptly, being sent for in Haste, with my Rule, to measure the Degree of an Affront, before the two Gentlemen (who are now in their °Breeches and Pumps ready to engage behind *Mountague*-House) have made a Pass.

[A mortifying letter from the country]
From my own Apartment, June 18.

It is an unreasonable Objection I find against my Labours, that my
Stock is not all my own, and therefore the kind Reception I have
met with, is not so deserved as it ought to be. But, I hope, tho' it
be never so true, that I am obliged to my Friends for laying their
Cash in my Hands, since I give it them again when they please,
and leave them at their Liberty to call it Home, it will not hurt me
with my gentle Readers. Ask all the Merchants who °act upon
Consignments, Where is the Necessity (if they answer readily what
their Correspondents draw) of their being wealthy themselves? Ask
the greatest Bankers, If all the men they deal with were to draw at
once, what would be the Consequence? But indeed a Country
Friend has writ me a Letter which gives me great Mortification;
wherein I find I am so far from expecting a Supply from thence,
that some have not heard of me, and the rest do not understand
me. His Epistle is as follows:

Dear Cousin,

'I thought when I left the Town to have raised your Fame here, and
helped you to support it by Intelligence from hence; but alas! they
had never heard of the *Tatler* 'till I brought down a Set. I lent them
from House to House; but they asked me what they meant. I began
to enlighten them, by telling who and who were supposed to be
intended by the Characters drawn. I said for Instance, *Chloe* and
Clarissa are two eminent Toasts. A Gentleman (who keeps his
Greyhound and Gun, and one would think might know better)
told me, he supposed they were Papishes, for their Names were not
English: Then, said he, Why do you call live-People Toasts? I
answered, That was a new Name found out by the Wits, to make
a Lady have the same Effect as °Burridge in the Glass when a Man
is drinking. But, says I, Sir, I perceive this is to you all
bamboozling; why you look as if you were °*Don Diegoed* to the Tune
of a Thousand Pounds. All this good Language was lost upon him:
He only stared, though he is as good a Scholar as any Layman in the
Town, except the Barber. Thus, Cousin, you must be content with
London for the Center of your Wealth and Fame; we have no Relish
for you. Wit must describe its proper Circumference, and not go

beyond it, lest (like little Boys, when they straggle out of their own Parish) it may wander to Places where it is not known, and be lost. Since it is so, you must excuse me that I am forced, at a Visit to sit silent, and only lay up what excellent Things pass at such Conversations.

'This Evening I was with a Couple of young Ladies; one of them has the Character of the prettiest Company, yet really I thought her but silly; the other, who talked a great deal less, I observed to have Understanding. The Lady who is reckoned such a Companion among her Acquaintance, has only, with a very brisk Air, a Knack of saying the commonest Things: The other, with a sly serious one, says home Things enough. The first (Mistress *Giddy*) is very quick; but the second (Mrs. *Slim*) fell into *Giddy*'s own Style, and was as good Company as she. *Giddy* happens to drop her Glove; *Slim* reaches it to her: Madam (says *Giddy*) I hope you'll have a better Office. Upon which *Slim* immediately repartees, and sits in her Lap, and cries, Are you not sorry for my Heaviness? This sly Wench pleased me to see how she hit her Height of Understanding so well. We sat down to Supper. Says *Giddy*, mighty prettily, Two Hands in a Dish, and One in a Purse: Says *Slim*, Ay, Madam, the More the Merrier; but the Fewer the Better Chear. I quickly took the Hint, and was as witty and talkative as they. Says I,

> He that will not when he may,
> When he will he shall have Nay;

And so helped my self. *Giddy* turns about, What have you found your Tongue? Yes, (says I) 'tis Manners to speak when I am spoken to; but your greatest Talkers are the least Doers, and the still Sow eats up all the Broth. Ha! Ha! says *Giddy*, One would think he had nothing in him, and do you hear how he talks when he pleases. I grew immediately roguish and pleasant to a Degree in the same Strain. *Slim*, who knew how good Company we had been, cried, You'll certainly print this bright Conversation.'

from No. 35 [STEELE]
Tuesday, 28 June to Thursday, 30 June 1709

[Taking snuff]
Grecian Coffee-house, 28 June.

There is an Habit or Custom which I have put my Patience to the utmost Stretch to have suffered so long, because several of my intimate Friends are in the Guilt; and that is, the Humour of taking Snuff, and looking Dirty about the Mouth by Way of Ornament.

My Method is to dive to the Bottom of a Sore before I pretend to apply a Remedy. For this Reason, I sat by an eminent Story-teller and Politician who takes half an Ounce in five Seconds, and has mortgaged a pretty Tenement near the Town, meerly to improve and dung his Brains with this prolifick Powder. I observed this Gentleman t'other Day in the midst of a Story diverted from it by looking at something at a Distance, and I softly hid his Box. But he returns to his *Tale*, and looking for his Box, he cries, *And so Sir* – Then when he should have taken a Pinch; *As I was saying*, says he, – *Has no Body seen my Box?* His Friend beseeches him to finish his Narration. Then he proceeds; *And so Sir* – *Where can my Box be?* Then turning to me; *Pray Sir, Did you see my Box?* Yes Sir, said I, I took it to see how long you could live without it. He resumes his Tale; and I took Notice, that his Dulness was much more regular and fluent than before. A Pinch supplied the Place of, *As I was saying, And so Sir*; and he went on currently enough in that Style which the Learned call the Insipid.

This Observation easily led me into a Philosophick Reason for taking Snuff, which is done only to supply with Sensations the Want of Reflection. This I take to be an "Ευρηκα, a °*nostrum*; upon which I hope to receive the Thanks of this Board. For as it is natural to lift a Man's Hand to a Sore, when you fear any Thing coming at you; so when a Person feels his Thoughts are run out, and has no more to say, it is as natural to supply his weak Brain with Powder at the nearest Place of Access, *viz.* the Nostrils. This is so evident, that Nature suggests the Use according to the Indigence of the Persons who use this Medicine, without being prepossessed with the Force of Fashion or Custom. For Example;

the Native *Hibernians*, who are reckoned not much unlike the ancient °*Bæotians*, take this Specifick for Emptiness in the Head, in greater Abundance than any other Nation under the Sun. The learned *Sotus*, as sparing as he is in his Words, would be still more silent if it were not for this Powder.

However low and poor the taking Snuff argues a Man to be in his own Stock of Thought, or Means to employ his Brains and his Fingers, yet there is a poorer Creature in the World than He, and this is a Borrower of Snuff; a Fellow that keeps no Box of his own, but is always asking others for a Pinch. Such poor Rogues put me always in Mind of a common Phrase among School-Boys when they are composing their °Exercise, who run to an upper Scholar, and cry, *Pray give me a little Sense.* But of all Things, commend me to the Ladies who are got into this pretty Help to Discourse. I have been this three Years perswading *Sagissa* to leave it off; but she talks so much, and is so Learned, that she is above Contradiction. However, an Accident t'other Day brought that about, which my Eloquence never could accomplish: She had a *very Pretty Fellow* in her Closet, who ran thither to avoid some Company that came to visit her. She made an Excuse to go in to him for some Implement they were talking of. Her eager Gallant snatched a Kiss; but being unused to Snuff, some Grains from off her upper Lip made him sneeze aloud, which alarmed the Visitants, and has made a Discovery, that profound Reading, very much Intelligence, and a general Knowledge of who and who's together, cannot fill up her vacant Hours so much, but that she is sometimes obliged to descend to Entertainments less intellectual.

from No. 37 [STEELE]
Saturday, 2 July to Tuesday, 5 July 1709

[Voices]
White's Chocolate-house, July 2.

By Mrs. Jenny Distaff, *Half-Sister to Mr.* Bickerstaff.

It may be thought very unaccountable, that I who can never be supposed to go to *White*'s, should pretend to talk to you of Matters proper for, or in the Style of, that Place. But tho' I never visit these publick Haunts, I converse with those who do; and for all they °pretend so much to the contrary, they are as talkative as our Sex, and as much at a Loss to entertain the present Company, without sacrificing the last, as we ourselves. This Reflection has led me into the Consideration of the Use of Speech; and made me look over in my Memory all my Acquaintance of both Sexes, to know to which I may more justly impute the Sin of superfluous Discourse, in Regard to Conversation, without entring into it as it respects Religion.

I foresee my Acquaintance will immediately, upon starting this Subject, ask me, How I shall celebrate Mrs. *Alse Copswood*, the *Yorkshire* Huntress, who is come to Town lately, and moves as if she were on her Nag, and going to take a Five-Bar Gate; and is as loud as if she were following her Dogs? I can easily answer that; for she is as soft as *Damon*, in Comparison of her Brother-in-Law *Tom. Bellfrey*, who is the most accomplished Man in this Kingdom for all Gentleman-like Activities and Accomplishments. It is allowed, that he is a professed Enemy to the *Italian* Performers in Musick. But then for our own native Manner, according to the Customs and known Usages of our Island, he is to be preferred, for the Generality of the Pleasure he bestows, much before those Fellows, tho' they sing to full Theatres. For what is a Theatrical Voice to that of a Fox-hunter? I have been at a Musical Entertainment in an open Field, where it amazed me to hear to what Pitches the chief Masters would reach. There was a Meeting near our Seat in *Staffordshire*, and the most Eminent of all the Counties of *England* were at it. How wonderful was the Harmony between Men and Dogs! *Robin Cartail* of *Bucks* was to answer to *Jowler*; Mr. *Tinbreast* of *Cornwal* was appointed to open with *Sweetlips*, and Beau *Slimber*, a *Londoner*,

undertook to keep up with *Trips*, a Whelp just set in: *Tom. Bellfrey*
and *Ringwood* were coupled together, to fill the Cry on all Occasions,
and be in at the Death of the Fox, Hare, or Stag; for which both the
Dog and the Man were excellently suited, and loved one another,
and were as much together as *Banister* and *King*.[1] When *Jowler* first
alarmed the Field, *Cartail* repeated every Note; *Sweetlips*'s Treble
succeeded, and shook the Wood; *Tinbreast* ecchoed a Quarter of a
Mile beyond it. We were soon after all at a Loss, till we rid up, and
found *Trips* and *Slimber* at a Default in Half-Notes: But the Day
and the Tune was recovered by *Tom. Bellfrey* and *Ringwood*, to the
great Joy of us all, tho' they drowned every other Voice: For *Bellfrey*
carries a Note Four Furlongs, Three Rood, and Six Paces, further
than any other in *England*.

I fear the Mention of this will be thought a Digression from my
Purpose about Speech: But I answer, No. Since this is used where
Speech rather should be employed, it may come into Consideration
in the same Chapter: For Mr. *Bellfrey* being at a Visit where I
was, *viz.* his Cousin's (Lady *Dainty*'s) in *Soho*, was asked, What
Entertainments they had in the Country? Now *Bellfrey* is very
ignorant, and much a Clown; but confident withal. In a Word, he
struck up a Fox-Chase: Lady *Dainty*'s Dog, Mr. °*Sippet*, as she
calls him, started and jumped out of his Lady's Lap, and fell a
barking. *Bellfrey* went on and called all the Neighbouring Parishes
into the Square. Never was Woman in such Confusion as that
delicate Lady. But there was no stopping her Kinsman. A Room
full of Ladies fell into the most violent Laughter: My Lady looked
as if she was shrieking; Mr. *Sippet* in the Middle of the Room
breaking his Heart with barking, but all of us unheard. As soon
as *Bellfrey* became silent, up gets my Lady, and takes him by the
Arm to lead him off: *Bellfrey* was in his Boots. As she was
hurrying him away, his Spurs takes hold of her Petticoat; his
Whip throws down a Cabinet of *China*: He cries, *What! Are your
Crocks rotten? Are your Petticoats ragged? A Man can't walk in your
House for Trincums*.

Every County of *Great-Britain* has One Hundred or more of this
Sort of Fellows, who Roar instead of Speaking. Therefore if it be
true, that we Women are also given to greater Fluency of Words
than is necessary, sure she that disturbs but a Room or a Family is

more to be tolerated, than one who draws together Parishes and Counties, and sometimes (with an Estate that might make him the Blessing and Ornament of the World around him) has no other View and Ambition, but to be an Animal above Dogs and Horses, without the Relish of any one Enjoyment, which is peculiar to the Faculties of humane Nature. I know it will here be said, that talking of meer Country 'Squires at this Rate, is, as it were, to write against *Valentine* or *Orson*.[2] To prove any Thing against the Race of Men, you must take 'em as they are adorned with Education, as they live in Courts, or have received Instructions in Colledges.

But I am so full of my late Entertainment by Mr. *Bellfrey*, that I must defer pursuing this Subject to another Day; and wave the proper Observations upon the different Offenders in this Kind, some by profound Eloquence, on small Occasions, others by degrading Speech upon great Circumstances. Expect therefore to hear of the Whisperer without Business, the Laugher without Wit, the Complainer without receiving Injuries, and a very large Crowd, which I shall not forestall, who are common (tho' not commonly observed) Impertinents, whose Tongues are too voluble for their Brains, and are the general Despisers of us Women, tho' we have their Superiors, the Men of Sense, for our Servants.

No. 55 [STEELE]
Saturday, 13 August to Tuesday, 16 August 1709

[A blind young man gains his sight][1]
White's Chocolate-house, August 5.

Paulo Majora canamus[2]

While others are busied in Relations which concern the Interests of Princes, the Peace of Nations, and the Revolutions of Empire, I think (tho' these are very great Subjects) my Theme of Discourse is sometimes to be of Matters of a yet higher Consideration. The slow Steps of Providence and Nature, and strange Events which are brought about in an Instant, are what, as they come within our View and Observation, shall be given to the Publick. Such Things are not accompanied with Show and Noise, and therefore seldom draw the Eyes of the unattentive Part of Mankind; but are very proper at once to exercise our Humanity, please our Imaginations, and improve our Judgments. It may not therefore be unuseful to relate many Circumstances, which were observable upon a late Cure done upon a young Gentleman who was born Blind, and on the 29th of *June* last received his Sight at the Age of Twenty Years, by the Operation of an Oculist. This happened no farther off than *Newington*, and the Work was prepared for in the following Manner. The Operator, Mr. *Grant*, having observed the Eyes of his Patient, and convinced his Friends and Relations, among others the Reverend Mr. *Caswell*[3] Minister of the Place, that it was highly probable he should remove the Obstacle which prevented the Use of his Sight; all his Acquaintance, who had any Regard for the young Man, or Curiosity to be present when one of full Age and Understanding received a new Sense, assembled themselves on this Occasion. Mr. *Caswell* being a Gentleman particularly curious, desired the whole Company, in case the Blindness should be cured, to keep Silence, and let the Patient make his own Observations, without the Direction of any Thing he had received by his other Senses, or the Advantage of discovering his Friends, by their Voices. Among several others, the Mother, Brethren, Sisters, and a young Gentlewoman for whom he had a Passion, were present. The Work was performed with great Skill and Dexterity. When the Patient first received the Dawn of Light, there appeared such an Extacy in his Action, that he seemed ready to swoon away in the Surprize of Joy and Wonder. The Surgeon stood before him with his Instruments in his Hand. The young Man observed him from Head to Foot; after which he surveyed himself as carefully, and seemed to compare him to himself; and observing both their Hands, seemed to think they were exactly alike, except the Instruments, which he took for Parts of his Hands. When he had continued in this Amazement some Time, his Mother could not longer bear the Agitations of so many Passions as thronged upon her, but fell upon his Neck, crying out, My Son! My Son! The Youth knew her Voice, and could speak no more than, Oh me! Are you my Mother? and fainted. The whole Room, you will easily conceive, were very affectionately employed in recovering him; but above all, the young Gentlewoman who loved him, and whom he loved, shreiked in the loudest Manner. That Voice seemed to have a sudden Effect upon him as he recovered, and he showed a double Curiosity in observing her as she spoke and called to him; till at last he broke out, What has been done to me? Whither am I carried? Is all this about me, the Thing I have heard so often of? Is this the Light? Is this Seeing? Were you always thus happy, when you said you were glad to see each other? Where is *Tom*, who used to lead me? But I could now, methinks, go any where without him. He offered to move, but seemed afraid of every Thing around him. When they saw his Difficulty, they told him, till he became better acquainted with his new Being, he must let the Servant still lead him. The Boy was called for, and presented to him. Mr. *Caswell* asked him, What Sort of Thing he took *Tom* to be before he had seen him. He answered, He believed there was not so much of him as of himself; but he fancied him the same Sort of Creature. The Noise of this sudden Change made all the Neighbourhood throng to the Place where he was. As he saw the Crowd thickening, he desired Mr. *Caswell* to tell him, how many there were in all to be seen. The Gentleman, smiling, answered him, That it would be very proper for him to return to his late Condition, and suffer his Eyes to be covered, till they had received Strength; for he might remember well enough, that by Degrees he had from little and little come to the Strength he had at present in his Ability of Walking and Moving; and that it was the same Thing with his Eyes, which, he said, would lose the Power of continuing to him that wonderful Transport he was now in, except he would be contented to lay aside the Use of them, till they were strong enough to bear the Light without so much Feeling, as he knew he underwent at present. With much Reluctance he was prevailed upon to have his Eyes bound, in which Condition they kept him in a dark Room, till it was proper to let the Organ receive its Objects without farther Precaution. During the Time of this Darkness, he bewailed himself in the most distressed Manner, and accused all his Friends, complaining, that some Incantation had been wrought upon him, and some strange Magick used to deceive him into an Opinion, that he had enjoyed what they called Sight. He added, That the Impressions then let in upon his Soul would certainly distract him, if he were

not so at that present. At another Time he would strive to name
the Persons he had seen among the Crowd after he was °couched,
and would pretend to speak (in perplexed Terms of his own
making) of what he in that short Time observed. But on the 6th
Instant it was thought fit to unbind his Head, and the young
Woman whom he loved was instructed to open his Eyes accordingly, as well to indear her self to him by such a Circumstance,
as to moderate his Extasies by the Perswasion of a Voice, which
had so much Power over him as hers ever had. When this beloved
young Woman began to take off the Binding of his Eyes, she
talked to him as follows:

'Mr. *William*, I am now taking the Binding off, though when I
consider what I am doing, I tremble with the Apprehension, that
(tho' I have from my very Childhood loved you, dark as you were,
and tho' you had conceived so strong a Love for me, yet) you will
find there is such a Thing as Beauty, which may ensnare you into
a Thousand Passions of which you now are innocent, and take you
from me for ever. But before I put my self to that Hazard, tell me
in what Manner that Love you always professed to me entered into
your Heart; for its usual Admission is at the Eyes.'

The young Man answered, 'Dear *Lidia*, If I am to lose by Sight
the soft Pantings which I have always felt when I heard your Voice;
If I am no more to distinguish the Step of her I love when she
approaches me, but to change that sweet and frequent Pleasure for
such an Amazement as I knew the little Time I lately saw; Or if I
am to have any Thing besides, which may take from me the Sense
I have of what appeared most pleasing to me at that Time (which
Apparition it seems was you): Pull out these Eyes, before they lead
me to be ungrateful to you, or undo my self. I wished for them but
to see you; pull them out, if they are to make me forget you.'

Lidia was extremely satisfied with these Assurances; and pleased
her self with playing with his Perplexities. In all his Talk to her,
he shewed but very feint Ideas of any Thing which had not been
received at the Ear; and closed his Protestation to her by saying,
That if he were to see *Valentia* and *Barcelona*, whom he supposed
the most esteemed of all Women, by the Quarrel there was about
them, he would never like any but *Lidia*.

[Charles XII of Sweden defeated at Poltava; Tournai besieged][4]
St. James's Coffee-house, August 15.

We have repeated Advices of the entire Defeat of the *Swedish* Army near *Pultowa* on the 27th of *June*, °*O. S.* And Letters from *Berlin* give the following Account of the Remains of the *Swedish* Army since the Battle: Prince *Menzikoff* being ordered to pursue the Victory, came up with the *Swedish* Army (which was left to the Command of General *Lewenhaupt*) on the 30th of *June, O. S.* on the Banks of the *Boristhenes*; whereupon he sent General *Lewenhaupt* a Summons to submit to his present Fortune: *Lewenhaupt* immediately dispatched Three General Officers to that Prince, to treat about a Capitulation; but the *Swedes*, tho' they consisted of 15000 Men, were in so great Want of Provision and Ammunition, that they were obliged to surrender themselves at Discretion. His Czarish Majesty dispatched an Express to General *Goltz* with an Account of these Particulars, and also with Instructions to send out Detachments of his Cavalry to prevent the King of *Sweden*'s joining his Army in *Poland.* That Prince made his Escape with a small Party, by swimming over the *Boristhenes.* The last Letters from the Duke of *Marlborough*'s Camp at *Orchies* of the 19th Instant advise, That Monsieur *Ravignan* being returned from the *French* Court with an Account, That the King of *France* refused to ratify the Capitulation for the Surrender of the Citadel of *Tournay*, the Approaches have been carried on with great Vigour and Success: Our Miners have discovered several of the Enemy's Mines, who have sprung divers others, which did little Execution; but for the better Security of the Troops, both Assaults are carried on by the cautious Way of Sapping. On the 18th, the Confederate Army made a general Forage without any Loss. Marshal *Villars* continues in his former Camp, and applies himself with great Diligence in casting up new Lines behind the old on the *Scarp.* The Duke of *Marlborough* and Prince *Eugene* designed to begin a General Review of the Army on the 20th.

from No. 56 [STEELE]
Tuesday, 16 August to Thursday, 18 August 1709

[Sharpers]
White's Chocolate-house, August 17.

There is a young Foreigner committed to my Care, who puzzles me extremely in the Questions he asks about the Persons of Figure we meet in Publick Places. He has but very little of our Language, and therefore I am mightily at a Loss to express to him Things, for which they have no Word in that Tongue to which he was born. It has been often my Answer, upon his asking, Who such a fine Gentleman is? That he is what we call a *Sharper*, and he wants my Explication. I thought it would be very unjust to tell him, he is the same the *French* call *Coquin*; the *Latins*, *Nebulo*; or the *Greeks*, Ρασκαλ[1]. For as Custom is the most powerful of all Laws, and that the Order of Men we call *Sharpers* are received amongst us, not only with Permission, but Favour, I thought it unjust to use them like Persons upon no Establishment. Besides that, it would be an unpardonable Dishonour to our Country, to let him leave us with an Opinion, that our Nobility and Gentry kept Company with common Thiefs and Cheats; I told him, they were a Sort of tame °Hussars that were allowed in our Cities, like the wild Ones in our Camp, who had all the Privileges belonging to us, but at the same Time were not tied to our Discipline or Laws. *Aletheus*, who is a Gentleman of too much Virtue for the Age he lives in, would not let this Matter be thus palliated, but told my Pupil, That he was to understand, that Distinction, Quality, Merit, and Industry, were laid aside amongst us by the Incursions of these civil Hussars, who had got so much Countenance, that the Breeding and Fashion of the Age turned their Way to the Ruin of Order and °Occonomy in all Places where they are admitted. But *Sophronius*, who never falls into Heat upon any Subject, but applies proper Language, Temper, and Skill, with which the Thing in Debate is to be treated, told the Youth, that Gentleman had spoken nothing but what was literally true, but fell upon it with too much Earnestness to give a true Idea of that Sort of People he was declaiming against, or to remedy the Evil which he bewailed: For the Acceptance of these Men being an Ill which hath crept into the Conversation-part of our Lives, and not into our Constitution it self, it must be corrected where it began, and consequently is to be amended only by bringing Raillery and Derision upon the Persons who are guilty, or those who converse with them. For the *Sharpers* (continued he) at present are not as formerly, under the Acceptation of Pickpockets; but are by Custom erected into a real and venerable Body of Men, and have subdued us to so very particular a Deference to them, that tho' they are known to be Men without Honour or Conscience, no Demand is called a Debt of Honour so indisputably as theirs. You may lose your Honour to them, but they lay none against you: As the Priesthood in Roman-Catholick Countries can purchase what they please for the Church, but they can alienate nothing from it. It is from this Toleration, that *Sharpers* are to be found among all Sorts of Assemblies and Companies, and every Talent amongst Men is made Use of by some one or other of the Society for the Good of their Common Cause: So that an unexperienced young Gentleman is as often ensnared by his Understanding as his Folly: For who could be unmoved, to hear the eloquent *Dromio* explain the Constitution, talk in the Key of *Cato*, with the Severity of one of the ancient Sages, and debate the greatest Question of State in a common Chocolate or Coffee-house; Who could, I say, hear this generous Declamator, without being fired at his noble Zeal, and becoming his professed Follower, if he might be admitted. *Monoculus*'s Gravity would be no less inviting to a Beginner in Conversation, and the Snare of his Eloquence would equally catch one who had never seen an old Gentleman so very wise, and yet so little severe. Many other Instances of extraordinary Men among the Brotherhood might be produced; but every Man who knows the Town, can supply himself with such Examples without their being named. *Will. Vafer*, who is skilful at finding out the ridiculous Side of a Thing, and placing it in a new and proper light, (tho' he very seldom talks) thought fit to enter into this Subject. He has lately lost certain loose Sums, which half the Income of his Estate will bring in within seven Years: Besides which, he proposes to marry to set all right. He was therefore indolent enough to speak of this Matter with great Impartiality. 'When I look round me,' said this easy Gentleman, 'and consider in a just Ballance us °Bubbles, Elder Brothers, whose

Support our dull Fathers contrived to depend upon certain Acres; with the Rooks, whose Ancestors left them the wild World; I cannot but admire their Fraternity, and contemn my own. Is not *Jack Heyday* much to be preferred to the Knight he has bubbled? *Jack* has his Equipage, his Wenches, and his Followers: The Knight so far from a Retinue, that he is almost one of *Jack's*. However, he is gay, you see, still; a florid Outside – His Habit speaks the Man – And since he must unbutton, he would not be reduced outwardly, but is stripped to his upper Coat. But tho' I have great Temptation to it, I will not at this Time give the History of the losing Side, but speak the Effects of my Thoughts, since the Loss of my Money, upon the gaining People. This ill Fortune makes most Men contemplative, and given to Reading; at least it has happened so to me; and the Rise and Fall of the Family of Sharpers in all Ages has been my Contemplation.'

I find, all Times have had of this People; *Homer*, in his excellent Heroick Poem, calls them *Myrmidons*,[2] who were a Body who kept among themselves, and had nothing to lose; therefore never spared either *Greek* or *Trojan*, when they fell in their Way, upon a Party. But there is a memorable Verse which gives us an Account of what broke that whole Body, and made both *Greeks* and *Trojans* Masters of the Secret of their Warfare and Plunder. There is nothing so pedantick as many Quotations; therefore I shall inform you only, that in this Battalion there were two Officers called *Thersites* and *Pandarus*; they were both less renowned for their Beauty than their Wit; but each had this particular Happiness, that they were plunged over Head and Ears in the same Water, which made *Achilles* invulnerable; and had ever after certain Gifts which the rest of the World were never to enjoy. Among others, they were never to know they were the most dreadful to the Sight of all Mortals, never to be diffident of their own Abilities, never to blush, or ever to be wounded but by each other. Tho' some Historians say, Gaming began among the *Lydians* to divert Hunger, I could cite many Authorities to prove it had its Rise at the Siege of *Troy*; and that *Ulysses* won the Sevenfold Shield at °Hazard. But be that as it may, the Ruin of the Corps of the *Myrmidons* proceeded from a Breach between *Thersites* and *Pandarus*. The First of these was Leader of a Squadron, wherein the latter was but a private Man; but having all the good Qualities necessary for a °Partizan, he was the Favourite of his Officer. But the whole History of the several Changes in the Order of Sharpers, from those *Myrmidons* to our Modern Men of Address and Plunder, will require that we consult some ancient Manuscripts. As we make these Enquiries, we shall diurnally communicate them to the Publick, that the Knights of the Industry may be better understood by the good People of *England*. These Sort of Men in some Ages, were Sycophants and Flatterers only, and were endued with Arts of Life to capacitate them for the Conversation of the Rich and Great; but now the °Bubble courts the Impostor, and pretends at the utmost to be but his Equal. To clear up the Reasons and Causes in such Revolutions, and the different Conduct between Fools and Cheats, shall be one of our Labours for the Good of this Kingdom. How therefore Pimps, Footmen, Fiddlers, and Lacqueys, are elevated into Companions in this present Age, shall be accounted for, from the Influence of the Planet Mercury on this Island; the Ascendency of which Sharper over *Sol*, who is a Patron of the Muses, and all honest Professions, has been noted by the learned *Job Gadbury* to be the Cause, that *Cunning and Trick are more esteemed than Art and Science*. It must be allowed also, to the Memory of Mr. *Partridge*, late of *Cecil-street* in the *Strand*,³ that in his Answer to an °Horary Question, At what Hour of the Night to set a Fox-Trap in *June* 1705? He has largely discussed, under the Character of *Reynard*, the Manner of surprizing all Sharpers as well as him. But of these great Points, after more mature Deliberation.

[Letters acknowledged]
From my own Apartment, August 17.

I am to acknowledge several Letters which I have lately received; among others, one subscribed *Philanthropos*, another *Emilia*, both which shall be honoured. I have a Third from an Officer of the Army, wherein he desires I would do Justice to the many gallant Actions which have been done by Men of private Characters, or Officers of lower Stations, during this long War; that their Families may have the Pleasure of seeing we lived in an Age wherein Men of all Orders had their proper Share in Fame and Glory. There is nothing I should undertake with greater Pleasure than Matters of this Kind: If therefore they who are acquainted with such Facts, would please to communicate them, by Letter directed to me at Mr. *Morphew*'s, no Pains should be spared to put them in a proper and distinguishing Light.

from No. 62 [STEELE]
Tuesday, 30 August to Thursday, 1 September 1709

[Wit: the propriety of words and thoughts]
Will's Coffee-house, August 31.

This Evening was spent at our Table in Discourse of Propriety of Words and Thoughts, which is Mr. *Dryden*'s Definition of Wit[1]; but a very odd Fellow, who would intrude upon us, and has a Briskness of Imagination more like Madness than regular Thought, said, that *Harry Jacks* was the first who told him of the taking of the Citadel of *Tournay*, and (says he) *Harry* deserves a Statue more than the Boy who ran to the Senate with a Thorn in his Foot to tell of a Victory. We were astonished at the Assertion; and *Spondee* asked him, What Affinity is there between that Boy and *Harry*, that you say their Merit resembles so much as you just now told us? Why, (says he) *Harry* you know is in the *French* Interest, and it was more Pain to him to tell the Story of *Tournay*, than to the Boy to run upon a Thorn to relate a Victory which he was glad of. The Gentleman who was in the Chair upon the Subject of Propriety of Words and Thoughts, would by no Means allow, that there was Wit in this Comparison; and urged, that to have any Thing gracefully said, it must be natural; but that whatsoever was introduced to common Discourse with so much Premeditation, was insufferable. That Critick went on: Had Mr. *Jacks* (said he) told him the Citadel was taken, and another had answered, He deserves a Statue as well as the *Roman* Boy, for he told it with as much Pain; it might have passed for a sprightly Expression: But there is a Wit for Discourse, and a Wit for Writing. The Easiness and Familiarity of the first, is not to savour in the least of Study; but the Exactness of the other, is to admit of something like the Freedom of Discourse, especially in Treatises of Humanity, and what regards the *Belles Lettres*. I do not in this allow, that *Bickerstaff*'s *Tatlers*, or

Discourses of Wit by Retail, and for the Penny, should come within the Description of *Writing*. I bowed at his Compliment, and – But he would not let me proceed.

You see in no Place of Conversation the Perfection of Speech so much as in an accomplished Woman. Whether it be, that there is a Partiality irresistible when we judge of that Sex, or whatever it is, you may observe a wonderful Freedom in their Utterance, and an easy Flow of Words, without being distracted (as we often are who read much) in the Choice of Dictions and Phrases. My Lady *Courtly* is an Instance of this: She was talking the other Day of Dress, and did it with so excellent an Air and Gesture, that you would have sworn she had learned her Action from our *Demosthenes*. Besides which, her Words were so particularly well adapted to the Matter she talked of, that tho' Dress was a new Thing to us Men, she avoided the Terms of Art in it, and described an unaffected Garb and Manner in so proper Terms, that she came up to that of *Horace*'s °*Simplex Munditiis*; which, whoever can translate in Two Words, has as much Eloquence as Lady *Courtly*. I took the Liberty to tell her, That all she had said with so much good Grace, was spoken in Two Words in *Horace*, but would not undertake to translate them; upon which she smiled, and told me, She believed me a very great Scholar, and I took my Leave.

from No. 77 [STEELE]
Tuesday, 4 October to Thursday, 6 October 1709

[A burlesque letter]¹
St. James's Coffee-house, October 5.

I have no Manner of News, more than what the whole Town had t'other Day; except that I have the Original Letter of the Mareschal *Boufflers* to the *French* King, after the late Battle of the Woods, which I translate for the Benefit of the *English* Reader.

SIR,
'This is to let your Majesty understand That, to your immortal Honour, and the Destruction of the Confederates, your Troops have lost another Battle. *Artagnan* did Wonders. *Rohan* performed

Miracles, *Guiche* did Wonders, *Gattion* performed Miracles, the whole Army distinguished themselves and every Body did Wonders. And to conclude the Wonders of the Day, I can assure your Majesty, That though you have lost the Field of Battle, you have not lost an Inch of Ground. The Enemy marched behind us with Respect, and we ran away from 'em as bold as Lions.'

Letters have been sent to Mr. Bickerstaff, *relating to the present State of the Town of Bath, wherein the People of that Place have desired him to call Home the Physicians. All Gentlemen therefore of that profession are hereby directed to return forthwith to their Places of Practice; and the Stage-Coaches are required to take them in before other Passengers, until there shall be a Certificate signed by the Mayor, or Mr.* Powel,[2] *that there are but Two Doctors to One Patient left in Town.*

No. 81 [STEELE and ADDISON]
Thursday, 13 *October to Saturday,* 15 *October* 1709

[The Tables of Fame: a vision][1]

Hic Manus ob Patriam pugnando Vulnera passi
Quiq; pii Vates & Phœbo digna locuti,
Inventas aut qui Vitam excoluere per Artes,
Quiq; sui memores alios fecere merendo.   Virg.[2]

From my own Apartment, October 14.

There are two Kinds of Immortality; that which the Soul really enjoys after this Life, and that Imaginary Existence by which Men live in their Fame and Reputation. The best and greatest Actions have proceeded from the Prospect of the one or the other of these; but my Design is to treat only of those who have chiefly proposed to themselves the latter as the principal Reward of their Labours. It was for this Reason that I excluded from my Tables of Fame all the great Founders and Votaries of Religion; and it is for this Reason also that I am more than ordinarily anxious to do Justice to the Persons of whom I am now going to speak; for since Fame was the only End of all their Enterprizes and Studies, a Man cannot be too scrupulous in allotting them their due Proportion of it. It was this Consideration which made me call the whole Body of the Learned to my Assistance; to many of whom I must own my Obligations for the Catalogues of illustrious Persons which they have sent me in upon this Occasion. I Yesterday employed the whole Afternoon in comparing them with each other; which made so strong an Impression upon my Imagination, that they broke my Sleep for the first Part of the following Night, and at length threw me into a very agreeable Vision, which I shall beg Leave to describe in all its Particulars.

I dreamed that I was conveyed into a wide and boundless Plain, that was covered with prodigious Multitudes of People, which no Man could number. In the Midst of it there stood a Mountain, with its Head above the Clouds. The sides were extremely steep, and of such a particular Structure, that no Creature, which was not made in an humane Figure, could possibly ascend it. On a sudden there was heard from the Top of it a Sound like that of a Trumpet; but so exceeding sweet and harmonious, that it filled the Hearts of those who heard it with Raptures, and gave such high and delightful Sensations, as seemed to animate and raise humane Nature above it self. This made me very much amazed to find so very few in that innumerable Multitude, who had Ears fine enough to hear or relish this Musick with Pleasure: But my Wonder abated, when, upon looking round me, I saw most of them attentive to Three Sirens cloathed like Goddesses, and distinguished by the Names of *Sloth, Ignorance*, and *Pleasure*. They were seated on Three Rocks, amidst a beautiful Variety of Groves, Meadows, and Rivulets, that lay on the Borders of the Mountain. While the base and grovelling Multitude of different Nations, Ranks and Ages were listening to these delusive Deities, those of a more erect Aspect, and exalted Spirit separated themselves from the rest, and marched in great Bodies towards the Mountain; from whence they heard the Sound, which still grew sweeter the more they listened to it.

On a sudden, methought this select Band sprang forward, with a Resolution to climb the Ascent, and follow the Call of that Heavenly Musick. Every one took something with him that he thought might be of Assistance to him in his March. Several had their Swords drawn; some carried Rolls of Paper in their Hands; some had Compasses, others Quadrants, other Telescopes, and

others Pencils; some had Lawrels on their Heads, and others
Buskins on their Legs: In short, there was scarce any Instrument of
a Mechanick Art or Liberal Science which was not made Use of on
this Occasion. My good *Dæmon*, who stood at my Right Hand
during the Course of this whole Vision, observing in me a burning
Desire to join that glorious Company, told me, he highly approved
that generous Ardor with which I seemed transported; but at the
same Time advised me to cover my Face with a Mask all the while
I was to labour on the Ascent. I took his Counsel without inquiring
into his Reasons. The whole Body now broke into different Parties,
and began to climb the Precipice by Ten Thousand different Paths.
Several got into little Allies, which did not reach far up the Hill,
before they ended and led no further: And I observed, That most
of the Artizans, which considerably diminished our Number, fell
into these Paths.

We left another considerable Body of Adventurers behind us,
who thought they had discovered By-ways up the Hill, which
proved so very intricate and perplexed, that after having advanced
in them a little, they were quite lost among the several Turns and
Windings; and tho' they were as active as any in their Motions,
they made but little Progress in the Ascent. These, as my Guide
informed me, were Men of subtle Tempers, and puzzled Politicks
who would supply the Place of real Wisdom with Cunning and
Artifice. Among those who were far advanced in their Way, there
were some that by one false Step fell backward, and lost more
Ground in a Moment, than they had gained for many Hours, or
could be ever able to recover. We were now advanced very high,
and observed, That all the different Paths which ran about the
Sides of the Mountain, began to meet in Two great Roads, which
insensibly gathered the whole Multitude of Travellers into Two
great Bodies. At a little Distance from the Entrance of each Road,
there stood an hideous Phantom, that opposed our further Passage.
One of these Apparitions had his Right Hand filled with Darts,
which he brandished in the Face of all who came up that Way.
Crowds ran back at the Appearance of it, and cried out, *Death*. The
Spectre that guarded the other Road, was *Envy*: She was not armed
with Weapons of Destruction like the former; but by dreadful
Hissings, Noises of Reproach, and a horrid distracted Laughter,

she appeared more frightful than Death it self, insomuch that
Abundance of our Company were discouraged from passing any
further, and some appeared ashamed of having come so far. As for
my self, I must confess my Heart shrunk within me at the Sight of
these ghastly Appearances: But on a sudden, the Voice of the
Trumpet came more full upon us, so that we felt a new Resolution
reviving in us; and in Proportion as this Resolution grew, the
Terrors before us seemed to vanish. Most of the Company who had
Swords in their Hands, marched on with great Spirit; and an Air
of Defiance, up the Road that was commanded by Death; while
others, who had Thought and Contemplation in their Looks, went
forward in a more composed Manner up the Road possessed by
Envy. The Way above these Apparitions grew smooth and uniform,
and was so delightful, that the Travellers went on with Pleasure,
and in a little Time arrived at the Top of the Mountain. They here
began to breath a delicious Kind of Æther, and saw all the Fields
about them covered with a kind of Purple Light, that made them
reflect with Satisfaction on their past Toils, and diffused a secret
Joy through the whole Assembly, which shewed it self in every
Look and Feature. In the Midst of these happy Fields, there stood
a Palace of a very glorious Structure: It had Four great folding
Doors, that faced the Four several quarters of the World. On the
Top of it was enthroned the Goddess of the Mountain, who smiled
upon her Votaries, and sounded the silver Trumpet which had
called them up, and cheared them in their Passage to her Palace.
They had now formed themselves into several Divisions, a Band of
Historians taking their Stations at each Door, according to the
Persons whom they were to introduce.

On a sudden the Trumpet, which had hitherto founded only a
March, or a °Point of War, now swelled all its Notes into Triumph
and Exultation: The whole Fabrick shook, and the Doors flew open.
The First who stepped forward, was a beautiful and blooming
Hero, and as I heard by the Murmurs round me, *Alexander the
Great.* He was conducted by a Crowd of Historians. The Person
who immediately walked before him, was remarkable for an
emboidered Garment, who not being well acquainted with the
Place, was conducting him to an Apartment appointed for the
Reception of fabulous Heroes. The Name of this false Guide was

Quintus Curtius. But *Arrian* and *Plutarch*, who knew better the
Avenues of this Palace, conducted him into the great Hall, and
placed him at the upper End of the First Table.[3] My good Dæmon,
that I might see the whole Ceremony, conveyed me to a Corner of
this Room, where I might perceive all that passed without being
seen my self. The next who entered was a charming Virgin, leading
in a venerable old Man that was blind. Under her Left Arm she
bore a Harp, and on her Head a Garland. *Alexander*, who was very
well acquainted with *Homer*, stood up at his Entrance, and placed
him on his Right Hand. The Virgin, who it seems was one of the
Nine Sisters that attended on the Goddess of *Fame*, smiled with an
ineffable Grace at their Meeting, and retired.

Julius Cæsar was now coming forward; and though most of the
Historians offered their Service to introduce him, he left them at
the Door, and would have no Conductor but himself.[4]

The next who advanced, was a Man of homely but chearful
Aspect, and attended by Persons of greater Figure than any that
appeared on this Occasion. *Plato* was on his Right Hand, and
Xenophon on his Left. He bowed to *Homer*, and sat down by him.
It was expected that *Plato* would himself have taken a Place next
to his Master *Socrates*; but on a sudden there was heard a great
Clamour of Disputants at the Door, who appeared with *Aristotle* at
the Head of them. That Philosopher, with some Rudeness, but
great Strength of Reason, convinced the whole Table, that a Title
to the Fifth Place was his Due, and took it accordingly.

He had scarce sat down, when the same beautiful Virgin that
had introduced *Homer* brought in another, who hung back at the
Entrance, and would have excused himself, had not his Modesty
been overcome by the Invitation of all who sat at the Table. His
Guide and Behaviour made me easily conclude it was *Virgil*. *Cicero*
next appeared, and took his place. He had inquired at the Door for
one *Lucceius* to introduce him; but not finding him there, he
contented himself with the Attendance of many other Writers,
who all (except *Sallust*) appeared highly pleased with the Office.[5]

We waited some Time in Expectation of the next Worthy, who
came in with a great Retinue of Historians, whose Names I could
not learn, most of them being Natives of *Carthage*. The Person
thus conducted, who was *Hannibal*, seemed much disturbed, and

could not forbear complaining to the Board of the Affronts he had met with among the *Roman* Historians, who attempted, says he, to carry me into the Subterraneous Apartment; and perhaps would have done it, had it not been for the Impartiality of this Gentleman, pointing to *Polybius*, who was the only Person, except my own Countrymen, that was willing to conduct me hither.[6]

The *Carthaginian* took his Seat, and *Pompey* entered with great Dignity in his own Person, and preceded by several Historians. *Lucan* the Poet was at the Head of them,[7] who observing *Homer* and *Virgil* at the Table, was going to sit down himself, had not the latter whispered him, That whatever Pretence he might otherwise have had, he forfeited his Claim to it, by coming in as one of the Historians. *Lucan* was so exasperated with the Repulse, that he muttered something to himself, and was heard to say, That since he could not have a Seat among them himself, he would bring in one who alone had more Merit than their whole Assembly: Upon which he went to the Door, and brought in *Cato* of *Utica*. That great Man approached the Company with such an Air, that showed he contemned the Honour which he laid a Claim to. Observing the Seat opposite to *Cæsar* was vacant, he took Possession of it; and spoke Two or Three smart Sentences upon the Nature of Precedency, which, according to him, consisted not in Place, but in intrinsick Merit; to which he added, That the most virtuous Man, wherever he was seated, was always at the Upper End of the Table. *Socrates*, who had a great Spirit of Raillery with his Wisdom, could not forbear smiling at a Virtue which took so little Pains to make it self agreeable. *Cicero* took the Occasion to make a long Discourse in Praise of *Cato*, which he uttered with much Vehemence. *Cæsar* answered him with a great Deal of seeming Temper: But as I stood at a great Distance from them, I was not able to hear one Word of what they said. But I could not forbear taking Notice, That in all the Discourse which passed at the Table, a Word or Nod from *Homer* decided the Controversy.

After a short Pause, *Augustus* appeared looking round him with a serene and affable Countenance upon all the Writers of his Age, who strove among themselves which of them should show him the greatest Marks of Gratitude and Respect. *Virgil* rose from the Table to meet him; and though he was an acceptable Guest to all, he appeared more such to the Learned, than the Military Worthies. The next Man astonished the whole Table with his Appearance: He was slow, solemn, and silent in his Behaviour, and wore a Raiment curiously wrought with Hieroglyphicks. As he came into the Middle of the Room, he threw back the Skirt of it, and discovered a Golden Thigh. *Socrates*, at the Sight of it, declared against keeping Company with any who were not made of Flesh and Blood; and therefore desired *Diogenes* the *Laertian* to lead him to the Apartment allotted for Fabulous Heroes, and Worthies of Dubious Existence.[8] At his going out, he told them, That they did not know whom they dismissed; that he was now *Pythagoras*, the First of Philosophers, and that formerly he had been a very brave Man at the Siege of *Troy*. That may be very true, said *Socrates*; but you forget that you have likewise been a very great Harlot in your Time.[9] This Exclusion made Way for *Archimedes*, who came forward with a Scheme of Mathematical Figures in his Hand; among which, I observed a Cone and a Cylinder.

Seeing this Table full, I desired my Guide for Variety to lead me to the Fabulous Apartment, the Roof of which was painted with Gorgons, Chimeras, and Centaurs, with many other Emblematical Figures, which I wanted both Time and Skill to unriddle. The First Table was almost full. At the Upper End sat *Hercules*, leaning an Arm upon his Club. On his Right Hand were *Achilles* and *Ulysses*, and between them *Æneas*. On his left were *Hector*, *Theseus*, and *Jason*. The Lower End had *Orpheus*, *Æsop*, *Phalaris*, and *Musæus*.[10] The Ushers seemed at a Loss for a Twelfth Man, when methought, to my great Joy and Surprize, I heard some at the Lower End of the Table mention *Isaac Bickerstaff*: But those of the Upper End received it with Disdain, and said, If they must have a *British* Worthy, they would have *Robin Hood*.

While I was transported with the Honour that was done me, and burning with Envy against my Competitor, I was awakened by the Noise of the Cannon which were then fired for the taking of *Mons*.[11] I should have been very much troubled at being thrown out of so pleasing a Vision on any other Occasion; but thought it an agreeable Change to have my Thoughts diverted from the greatest among the Dead and Fabulous Heroes, to the most Famous among the Real and the Living.

from No. 86 [ADDISON and STEELE]
Tuesday, 25 *October to Thursday,* 27 *October* 1709

[A visit of ceremony]
From my own Apartment, October 25.

When I came Home last Night, my Servant delivered me the following Letter:

SIR,   *Octob.* 21.
'I have Orders from Sir *Harry Quickset,* of *Staffordshire,* Bar. to acquaint you, That his Honour Sir *Harry* himself, Sir *Giles Wheelbarrow* Kt. *Thomas Rentfree* Esq; Justice of the °*Quorum, Andrew Windmill* Esq; and Mr. *Nicholas Doubt* of the *Inner-Temple,* Sir *Harry*'s Grandson, will wait upon you at the Hour of Nine to Morrow Morning, being *Tuesday* the 25th of *October,* upon Business which Sir *Harry* will impart to you by Word of Mouth. I thought it proper to acquaint you before hand so many Persons of Quality came, that you might not be surprized therewith. Which concludes, tho' by many Years Absence since I saw you at *Stafford,* unknown,
SIR,
Your most humble Servant,
John Thrifty.'

I received this Message with less Surprize than I believe Mr. *Thrifty* imagined; for I knew the good Company too well to feel any Palpitations at their Approach: But I was in very great Concern how I should adjust the Ceremonial, and demean my self to all these great Men, who perhaps had not seen any Thing above themselves for these Twenty Years last past. I am sure that's the Case of Sir *Harry.* Besides which, I was sensible that there was a great Point in adjusting my Behaviour to the simple 'Squire, so as to give him Satisfaction, and not disoblige the Justice of the *Quorum.*

The Hour of Nine was come this Morning, and I had no sooner set Chairs (by the Steward's Letter) and fixed my Tea-Equipage, but I heard a Knock at my Door, which was opened, but no one entered; after which followed a long Silence, which was broke at last by, 'Sir, I beg your Pardon; I think I know better': And another Voice,

'Nay, good Sir *Giles* –.' I looked out from my Window, and saw
the good Company all with their Hats off, and Arms spread,
offering the Door to each other. After many Offers, they entered
with much Solemnity, in the Order Mr. *Thrifty* was so kind as to
name 'em to me. But they are now got to my Chamber-Door, and
I saw my old Friend Sir *Harry* enter. I met him with all the Respect
due to so reverend a Vegetable; for you are to know, that is my
Sense of a Person who remains idle in the same Place for half a
Century. I got him with great Success into his Chair by the Fire,
without throwing down any of my Cups. The Knight-Batchelor
told me, he had a great Respect for my whole Family, and would,
with my Leave, place himself next to Sir *Harry*, at whose Right
Hand he had sat at every Quarter-Sessions this Thirty Years, unless
he was sick. The Steward in the Rear whispered the young Templer,
'That's true to my Knowledge.' I had the Misfortune, as they stood
Cheek by Jole, to desire the 'Squire to sit down before the Justice
of the *Quorum*, to the no small Satisfaction of the former, and
Resentment of the latter: But I saw my Error too late, and got 'em
as soon as I could into their Seats. 'Well,' said I, 'Gentlemen, after
I have told you how glad I am of this great Honour, I am to desire
you to drink a Dish of Tea.' They answered one and all, That they
never drank Tea in a Morning. 'Not in a Morning,' said I! staring
round me. Upon which the pert Jackanapes *Nick Doubt* tipped me
the Wink, and put out his Tongue at his Grandfather. Here
followed a profound Silence, when the Steward in his Boots and
Whip proposed, That we should adjourn to some Publick-House,
where every Body might call for what they pleased, and enter upon
the Business. We all stood up in an Instant, and Sir *Harry* filed off
from the Left very discreetly, counter-marching behind the Chairs
towards the Door: After him, Sir *Giles* in the same Manner. The
simple 'Squire made a sudden Start to follow; but the Justice of the
Quorum whipped between upon the °Stand of the Stairs. A Maid
going up with Coals made us halt, and put us into such Confusion,
that we stood all in a Heap, without any visible Possibility of
recovering our Order: For the young Jackanapes seemed to make
a jest of this Matter, and had so contrived, by pressing amongst us
under Pretence of making way, that his Grandfather was got into
the Middle, and he knew no body was of Quality to stir a Step, till

Sir *Harry* moved first. We were fixed in this Perplexity for some Time, till we heard a very loud Noise in the Street; and Sir *Harry* asking what it was, I, to make 'em move, said it was Fire. Upon this, all ran down as fast as they could, without Order or Ceremony, till we got into the Street, where we drew up in very good Order, and filed off down *Sheer-Lane*, the impertinent Templer driving us before him, as in a String, and pointing to his Acquaintance who passed by.

I must confess, I love to use People according to their own Sense of good Breeding, and therefore whipped in between the Justice and the simple 'Squire. He could not properly take this ill; but I over-heard him whisper the Steward, That he thought it hard that a common °Conjurer should take Place of him, tho' an elder 'Squire. In this Order we marched down *Sheer-Lane*, at the upper End of which I lodge. When we came to *Temple-Bar*, Sir *Harry* and Sir *Giles* got over; but a Run of the Coaches kept the rest of us on this Side of the Street: However we all at last landed, and drew up in very good Order before *Ben. Tooke*'s Shop, who favoured our Rallying with great Humanity. From hence we proceeded again, till we came to *Dick*'s Coffee-house,[1] where I designed to carry 'em. Here we were at our old Difficulty, and took up the Street upon the same Ceremony. We proceeded through the Entry, and were so necessarily kept in Order by the Situation, that we were now got into the Coffee-house itself, where, as soon as we arrived, we repeated our Civilities to each other; after which, we marched up to the high Table, which has an Ascent to it inclosed in the Middle of the Room. The whole House was alarmed at this Entry, made up of Persons of so much State and Rusticity. Sir *Harry* called for a Mug of Ale, and °*Dyer*'s Letter. The Boy brought the Ale in an Instant; but said, they did not take in the Letter. 'No,' says Sir *Harry*! 'Then take back your Mug; we are like indeed to have good Liquor at this House.' Here the Templer tipped me a second Wink, and if I had not looked very grave upon him, I found he was disposed to be very familiar with me. In short, I observed after a long Pause, that the Gentlemen did not care to enter upon Business till after their Morning-Draught, for which Reason I called for a Bottle of °Mum; and finding that had no Effect upon 'em, I ordered a Second, and a Third: After which, Sir *Harry* reached over to me,

and told me in a low Voice, that the Place was too publick for
Business; but he would call upon me again to Morrow Morning at
my own Lodgings, and bring some more Friends with him.

No. 87 [STEELE]
Thursday, 27 October to Saturday, 29 October 1709

[The serjeant's letter]
Will's Coffee-house, Octob. 28.

There is nothing which I contemplate with greater Pleasure than
the Dignity of Humane Nature, which often shows itself in all
Conditions of Life: For notwithstanding the Degeneracy and
Meanness that is crept into it, there are a Thousand Occasions in
which it breaks through its Original Corruption, and shows what
it once was, and what it will be hereafter. I consider the Soul of
Man, as the Ruin of a glorious Pile of Building; where, amidst
great Heaps of Rubbish, you meet with noble Fragments of
Sculpture, broken Pillars and Obelisks, and a Magnificence in
Confusion. Virtue and Wisdom are continually employed in
clearing the Ruins, removing these disorderly Heaps, recovering
the noble Pieces that lie buried under [them], and adjusting
them as well as possible according to their ancient Symmetry and
Beauty. A happy Education, Conversation with the finest Spirits,
looking abroad into the Works of Nature, and Observations upon
Mankind, are the great Assistances to this necessary and glorious
Work. But even among those who have never had the Happiness
of any of these Advantages, there are sometimes such Exertions of
the Greatness that is natural to the Mind of Man, as show Capacities
and Abilities, which only want these Accidental Helps to fetch
them out, and show them in a proper Light. A Plebeian Soul is still
the Ruin of this glorious Edifice, though encumbered with all its
Rubbish. This Reflection rose in me from a Letter which my
Servant drop[pe]d as he was dressing me, and which he told me
was communicated to him as he is an Acquaintance of some of the
Persons mentioned in it. The Epistle is from Serjeant *Hall* of the
Foot-Guards. It is directed, *To Serjeant* Cabe, *in the* Cold-stream

Regiment of Foot-Guards,[1] *at the* Red °Lettice *in the* Butcher-Row *near* Temple-Bar.

I was so pleased with several Touches in it, that I could not forbear shewing it to a Cluster of Criticks, who, instead of considering it in the Light I have done, examined it by the Rules of Epistolary Writing: For as these Gentlemen are seldom Men of any great Genius, they work altogether by Mechanical Rules, and are able to discover no Beauties that are not pointed out by *Bouhours* and *Rapin.*[2] The Letter is as follows:

From the Camp before Mons, Sept. 26

Comrade,

'I Received Yours, and am glad your self and your Wife are in good Health, with all the rest of my Friends. Our Battalion suffered more than I could wish in the Action;[3] but who can withstand Fate? Poor *Richard Stephenson* had his Fate with a great many more: He was killed dead before we entered the Trenches. We had above 200 of our Battalion killed and wounded: We lost 10 Serjeants; 6 are as followeth, *Jenings, Castles, Roach, Sherring, Meyrick,* and my Son *Smith.* The rest are not your Acquaintance. I have received a very bad Shot in my Head my self, but am in Hopes, and please God, I shall recover. I continue in the Field, and lie at my Colonel's Quarters. *Arthur* is very well; but I can give you no Account of *Elms*; he was in the Hospital before I came into the Field. I will not pretend to give you an Account of the Battle, knowing you have a better in the Prints. Pray give my Service to Mrs. *Cook* and her Daughter, to Mr. *Stoffet* and his Wife, and to Mr. *Lyver,* and *Thomas Hogsdon,* and to Mr. *Ragdell,* and to all my Friends and Acquaintance in general who do ask after me: My Love to Mrs. *Stephenson.* I am sorry for the sending such ill News. Her Husband was gathering a little Money together to send to his Wife, and put it into my Hands. I have Seven Shillings and Three Pence, which I shall take Care to send her; wishing your Wife a safe Delivery, and both of you all Happiness, rest

Your assured Friend,
and Comrade,
John Hall.'

'We had but an indifferent Breakfast, but the Mounseers never had such a Dinner in all their Lives.

'My kind Love to my Comrade *Hinton*, and Mrs. *Morgan*, and to *John Brown* and his Wife. I sent Two Shillings, and *Stephenson* Sixpence, to drink with you at Mr. *Cook*'s; but I have heard nothing from him. It was by Mr. *Edgar*.

'Corporal *Hartwell* desires to be remembered to you, and desires you to enquire of *Edgar*, what is become of his Wife *Pegg*; and when you write, to send Word in your Letter what Trade she drives.

'We have here very bad Weather, which I doubt will be a Hindrance to the Siege;⁴ but I am in Hopes we shall be Masters of the Town in a little Time, and then I believe we shall go to Garrison.'

I saw the Criticks prepared to nibble at my Letter; therefore examined it myself, partly in their Way, and partly my own. This is (said I) truly a *Letter*, and an honest Representation of that chearful Heart which accompanies the poor Soldier in his Warfare. Is not there in this all the Topick of submitting to our Destiny as well discussed, as if a greater Man had been placed, like *Brutus* in his Tent at Midnight, reflecting on all the Occurrences of past Life, and saying fine Things on Being it self? What Serjeant *Hall* knows of the Matter, is, that he wishes there had not been so many killed, and he had himself a very bad Shot in the Head, and should recover if it please God. But be that as it will, he takes Care, like a Man of Honour, as he certainly is, to let the Widow *Stephenson* know, that he had Seven and three Pence for her; and that if he lives, he is sure he shall go into Garrison at last. I doubt not but all the good Company at the *Red °Lettice* drank his Health with as much real esteem as we do any of our Friends. All that I am concerned for, is, that Mrs. *Peggy Hartwell* may be offended at showing this Letter, because her Conduct in Mr. *Hartwell*'s Absence is a little enquired into. But I could not sink that Circumstance, because you Criticks would have lost one of the Parts which I doubt not but you have much to say upon, Whether the Familiar Way is well hit in this Style or not? As for my self, I take a very particular Satisfaction in seeing any Letter that is fit only for those to read who are concerned in it, but especially on such a Subject.

If we consider the Heap of an Army, utterly out of all Prospect of Rising and Preferment, as they certainly are, and such great Things executed by them, it is hard to account for the Motive of their Gallantry. But to me, who was a Cadet at the Battle of *Coldstream* in *Scotland*,[5] when *Monk* charged at the Head of the Regiment, now called *Coldstream* from the Victory of that Day; (I remember it as well as if it were Yesterday) I stood on the Left of old West, who I believe is now at *Chelsea*; I say, to me, who know very well this Part of Mankind, I take the Gallantry of private Soldiers to proceed from the same, if not from a nobler, Impulse than that of Gentlemen and Officers. They have the same Taste of being acceptable to their Friends, and go thro' the Difficulties of their Profession by the same irresistible Charm of Fellowship, and the Communication of Joys and Sorrows, which quickens the Relish of Pleasures and abates the Anguish of Pain. Add to this, that they have the same Regard to Fame, though they do not expect so great a Share as Men above them hope for; but I'll engage, Serjeant *Hall* would die Ten Thousand Deaths, rather than a Word should be spoken at the *Red Lettice*, or any Part of the *Butcher-Row*, in Prejudice to his Courage or Honesty. If you will have my Opinion then of the Serjeant's letter, I pronounce the Style to be mixed, but truly Epistolary; the Sentiment relating to his own Wound, is in the Sublime; the Postscript of *Pegg Hartwell*, in the gay; and the Whole, the Picture of the bravest Sort of Men, that is to say, a Man of great Courage, and small Hopes.

From my own Apartment, October 28.

When I came Home this Evening, I found after many Attempts to vary my Thoughts, that my Head still ran upon the Subject of the Discourse to Night at *Will's*. I fell therefore into the Amusement of proportioning the Glory of a Battle among the whole Army, and dividing it into Shares, according to the Method of the °Million-Lottery. In this Bank of Fame, by an exact Calculation, and the Rules of Political Arithmetick, I have allotted Ten hundred thousand Shares; Five hundred thousand of which is the Due of the General, Two hundred thousand I assign to the General Officers, and Two hundred thousand more to all the Commissioned Officers, from Colonels to Ensigns; the remaining Hundred thousand must be distributed among the Non-Commissioned Officers, and private Men: According to which Computation I find Serjeant *Hall* is to have one Share and a Fraction of two Fifths. When I was a Boy at *Oxford*, there was among the Antiquities near the Theatre a great Stone, on which were engraven the Names of all who fell in the Battle of *Marathon*. The generous and knowing People of *Athens* understood the Force of the Desire of Glory, and would not let the meanest Soldier perish in Oblivion. Were the natural Impulse of the *British* Nation animated with such Monuments, What Man would be so mean, as not to hazard his Life for his Ten hundred thousandth Part of the Honour in such a Day as that of *Blenheim* or *Blaregnies*.[6]

from No. 89 [STEELE]
Tuesday, 1 November to Thursday, 3 November 1709

[Isaac Bickerstaff justifies his life and work]

Rura mihi placeant, riguiq; in Vallibus Amnes,
Flumina Arnem Sylvasq; inglorius —[1]

Grecian Coffee-house, November 2.

I have received this short Epistle from an unknown Hand:
   SIR,
'I have no more to trouble you with, than to desire you would in your next help me to some Answer to the Inclosed concerning your self. In the Mean Time I congratulate you upon the Increase of your Fame, which you see has extended it self beyond the Bills of Mortality.'

   SIR,
That the Country is barren of News, has been the Excuse Time out of Mind for dropping a Correspondence with our Friends in London; *as if it were impossible out of a Coffee-house to write an agreeable Letter. I am too ingenuous to endeavour at the covering of my Negligence with so common an Excuse. Doubtless, amongst Friends bred as we have been, to the Knowledge of Books as well as Men, a Letter dated from a Garden, a Grotto, a Fountain, a Wood, a Meadow, or the Banks of a River, may*

be more entertaining, than one from Tom's, Will's, White's, *or St.* James's.[2] *I promise therefore to be frequent for the future in my rural Dates to you: But for fear you should, from what I have said, be induced to believe I shun the Commerce of Men, I must inform you, that there is a fresh Topick of Discourse lately risen amongst the Ingenious in our Part of the World, and is become the more fashionable for the Ladies giving into it. This we owe to* Isaac Bickerstaff, *who is very much censured by some, and as much justified by others. Some criticise his Style, his Humour and his Matter; others admire the whole Man: Some pretend, from the Informations of their Friends in Town, to decipher the Author; and others confess they are lost in their Guesses. For my Part, I must own my self a professed Admirer of the Paper, and desire you to send me a compleat Set, together with your Thoughts of the 'Squire, and his Lucubrations.*

There is no Pleasure like that of receiving Praise from the Praise-worthy; and I own it a very solid Happiness, that these my Lucubrations are approved by a Person of so fine a Taste as the Author of this Letter, who is capable of enjoying the World in the Simplicity of its natural Beauties. This Pastoral Letter, if I may so call it, must be written by a Man who carries his Entertainment wherever he goes, and is undoubtedly one of those happy Men who appear far otherwise to the Vulgar. I dare say, he is not envied by the Vicious, the Vain, the Frolick, and the Loud, but is continually blessed with that strong and serious Delight which flows from a well-taught and liberal Mind. With great Respect to Country Sports, I may say, this Gentleman could pass his Time agreeably, if there were not a Hare or a Fox in his County. That calm and elegant Satisfaction which the Vulgar call Melancholy, is the true and proper Delight of Men of Knowledge and Virtue. What we take for Diversion, which is a kind of forgetting our selves, is but a mean Way of Entertainment, in Comparison of that which is considering, knowing, and enjoying our selves. The Pleasures of ordinary People are in their Passions; but the Seat of this Delight is in the Reason and Understanding. Such a Frame of Mind raises that sweet Enthusiasm which warms the Imagination at the Sight of every Work of Nature, and turns all round you into Picture and Landskip. I shall be ever proud of Advices from this Gentleman;

for I profess writing News from the learned, as well as the busie World.

As for my Labours, which he is pleased to enquire after, if they can but wear one Impertinence out of humane Life, destroy a single Vice, or give a Morning's Chearfulness to an honest Mind: In short, if the World can be but one Virtue the better, or in any Degree less vicious, or receive from them the smallest Addition to their innocent Diversions, I shall not think my Pains, or indeed my Life, to have been spent in vain.

Thus far as to my Studies. It will be expected I should in the next Place give some Account of my Life. I shall therefore, for the Satisfaction of the present Age, and the Benefit of Posterity, present the World with the following Abridgment of it.

It is remarkable, that I was °bred by Hand, and eat nothing but Milk till I was a Twelve-month old; from which Time, to the 8th Year of my Age, I was observed to delight in Pudding and Potatoes; and indeed I retain a Benevolence for that Sort of Food to this Day. I do not remember that I distinguished my self in any Thing at those Years, but by my great Skill at °Taw, for which I was so barbarously used, that it has ever since given me an Aversion to Gaming. In my Twelfth Year, I suffered very much for Two or Three false Concords. At Fifteen, I was sent to the University, and stayed there for some Time; but a Drum passing by, (being a Lover of Musick) I listed my self for a Soldier. As Years came on, I began to examine Things, and grew discontented at the Times. This made me quit the Sword, and take to the Study of the Occult Sciences, in which I was so wrap[pe]d up, that *Oliver Cromwell* had been buried, and taken up again, Five Years before I heard he was dead. This gave me first the Reputation of a °Conjurer, which has been of great Disadvantage to me ever since, and kept me out of all Publick Employments. The greater Part of my later Years has been divided between *Dick*'s Coffee-house, the *Trumpet* in *Sheer-Lane*,[3] and my own Lodgings.

from No. 101 [STEELE and ADDISON]
Tuesday, 29 November to Thursday, 1 December 1709

[A set of wretches we authors call pirates][1]

— *Postquam fregit subsellia versu*
Esurit intactam Paridi nisi vendit Agaven: Juv.[2]

From my own Apartment, November 30.

The Progress of my intended Account of what happened when *Justice* visited Mortals, is at present interrupted by the Observation and Sense of an Injustice against which there is no Remedy, even in a Kingdom more happy in the Care taken of the Liberty and Property of the Subject, than any other Nation upon Earth. This Iniquity is committed by a most impregnable Set of Mortals, Men who are Rogues within the Law; and in the very Commission of what they are guilty of, professedly own, that they forbear no Injury but from the Terror of being punished for it. These Miscreants are a Set of Wretches we Authors call Pirates, who print any Book, Poem, or Sermon, as soon as it appears in the World, in a smaller Volume, and sell it (as all other Thieves do stolen Goods) at a cheaper Rate. I was in my Rage calling them Rascals, Plunderers, Robbers, Highway-men — But they acknowledge all that, and are pleased with those, as well as any other Titles; nay, will print them themselves to turn the Penny.

I am extremely at a Loss how to act against such open Enemies, who have not Shame enough to be touched with our Reproaches, and are as well defended against what we can say, as what we can do. Railing therefore we must turn into Complaint, which I cannot forbear making, when I consider that all the Labours of my long Life may be disappointed by the First Man that pleases to rob me. I had flattered my self, that my Stock of Learning was worth 150 *l. per Annum*, which would very handsomely maintain me and my little Family, who are so happy or so wise as to want only Necessaries. Before Men had come up to his bare-faced Impudence, it was an Estate to have a Competency of Understanding.

An ingenious Drole, who is since dead (and indeed it is well for

him he is so, for he must have starved had he lived to this Day)
used to give me an Account of his good Husbandry in the
Management of his Learning. He was a general Dealer, and had his
Amusements as well comical as serious. The merry Rogue said,
when he wanted a Dinner, he writ a Paragraph of *Table-Talk*, and
his Bookseller upon Sight paid the Reckoning. He was a very good
Judge of what would please the People, and could aptly hit both
the Genius of his Readers, and the Season of the Year in his
Writings. His Brain, which was his Estate, had as regular and
different Produce as other Men's Land. From the Beginning of
November till the Opening of the Campagne, he writ Pamphlets
and Letters to Members of Parliament, or Friends in the Country:
But sometimes he would relieve his ordinary Readers with a
Murder, and lived comfortably a Week or Two upon *strange and
lamentable Accidents*. A little before the Armies took the Field, his
Way was to open your Attention with a Prodigy; and a Monster
well writ, was two Guineas the lowest Price. This prepared his
Readers for *his Great and Bloody News* from *Flanders* in *June* and
July. Poor *Tom!*[3] He is gone — But I observed, he always looked
well after a Battle, and was °apparently fatter in a fighting Year.
Had this honest careless Fellow lived till now, Famine had stared
him in the Face, and interrupted his Merriment; as it must be a
solid Affliction to all those whose Pen is their Portion.

As for my Part, I do not speak wholly for my own Sake in this
Point; for Palmistry and Astrology will bring me in greater Gains
than these my Papers; so that I am only in the Condition of a
Lawyer, who leaves the Bar for °Chamber-Practice. However, I
may be allowed to speak in the Cause of Learning it self, and
lament, that a liberal Education is the only one which a polite
Nation makes unprofitable.[4] All Mechanick Artizans are allowed
to reap the Fruit of their Invention and Ingenuity without invasion;
but he that has separated himself from the rest of Mankind, and
studied the Wonders of the Creation, the Government of his
Passions, and the Revolutions of the World, and has an Ambition
to communicate the Effect of half his Life spent in such noble
Enquiries, has no Property in what he is willing to produce, but is
exposed to Robbery and Want, with this melancholy and just

Reflection, That he is the only Man who is not protected by his Country, at the same Time that he best deserves it.

According to the ordinary Rules of Computation, the greater the Adventure is, the greater ought to be the Profit of those who succeed in it; and by this Measure, none have Pretence of turning their Labours to greater Advantage than Persons brought up to Letters. A learned Education, Passing through great Schools and Universities, is very expensive, and consumes a moderate Fortune, before it is gone through in its proper Forms. The Purchase of an handsome Commission or Employment, which would give a Man a good Figure in another Kind of Life, is to be made at a much cheaper Rate. Now, if we consider this expensive Voyage which is undertaken in the Search of Knowledge, and how few there are who take in any considerable Merchandise, how less frequent it is to be able to turn what Men have gained into Profit; How hard is it, that the very small Number who are distinguished with Abilities to know how to vend their Wares, and have the good Fortune to bring them into Port, should suffer being plundered by Privateers under the very Cannon that should protect them! The most eminent and useful Author of the Age we live in, after having laid out a Princely Revenue in Works of Charity and Beneficence, as became the Greatness of his Mind, and the Sanctity of his Character, would have left the Person in the World who was the dearest to him in a narrow Condition, had not the Sale of his immortal Writings brought her in a very considerable Dowry, tho' it was impossible for it to be equal to their Value. Every one will know, that I here mean the Works of the late Archbishop of *Canterbury*, the Copy of which was sold for 2500 *l.*[5]

I do not speak with Relation to any Party; but it has happened, and may often so happen, that Men of great Learning and Virtue cannot qualify themselves for being employed in Business, or receiving Preferments. In this Case, you cut them off from all Support, if you take from them the Benefit that may arise from their Writings. For my own Part, I have brought my self to consider Things in so unprejudiced a manner, that I esteem more a Man who can live by the Products of his Understanding, than One who does it by the Favour of Great Men.

The Zeal of an Author has transported me thus far, tho' I think my self as much concerned in the Capacity of a Reader. If this Practice goes on, we must never expect to see again a beautiful Edition of a Book in *Great Britain*.

We have already seen the Memoirs of Sir *William Temple* published in the same °Character and Volume with the History of *Tom Thumb*,[6] and the Works of our greatest Poets shrunk into Penny Books and °Garlands. For my own Part, I expect to see my Lucubrations printed on Browner Paper than they are at present[7]; and, if the Humour continues, must be forced to retrench my expensive Way of Living, and not smoke above Two Pipes a Day.

from No. 105 [STEELE]
Thursday, 8 December to Saturday, 10 December 1709

[Will Rosin, the fiddler of Wapping]
Sheer-Lane, December 9.

As soon as my Midnight Studies are finished, I take but a very short Repose, and am again up at an Exercise of another Kind; that is to say, my Fencing. Thus my Life passes away in a restless Pursuit of Fame, and a Preparation to defend myself against such as attack it. This Anxiety in the Point of Reputation is the peculiar Distress of fine Spirits, and makes them liable to a Thousand Inquietudes, from which Men of grosser Understandings are exempt; so that Nothing is more common, than to see one Part of Mankind live at perfect Ease under such Circumstances as would make another Part of them entirely miserable.

This may serve for a Preface to the History of poor *Will. Rosin*, the Fid[d]ler of *Wapping*, who is a Man as much made for Happiness, and a quiet Life, as any one breathing; but has been lately intangled in so many intricate and unreasonable Distresses, as would have made him (had he been a Man of too nice Honour) the most wretched of Mortals. I came to the Knowledge of his Affairs by meer Accident. Several of the narrow End of our Lane having made an Appointment to visit some Friends beyond St. *Katherine*'s, where there was to be a merry Meeting, they would needs take with them the Old Gentleman, as they are pleased to call me. I, who value my Company by their good Will, which naturally has the same Effect as good Breeding, was not too stately, or too wise, to accept of the Invitation. Our Design was to be Spectators of a Sea-Ball; to which I readily consented, provided I might be *incognito*, being naturally pleased with the Survey of humane Life in all its Degrees and Circumstances. In order to this Merriment, *Will. Rosin* (who is the *Corelli* of the *Wapping*-Side, as *Tom. Scrape* is the *Bononcini* of *Redriffe*) was immediately sent for; but to our utter Disappointment, poor *Will.* was under an Arrest, and desired the Assistance of all his kind Masters and Mistresses, or he must go to Gaol. The whole Company received his Message with great Humanity, and very generously threw in their Halfpence apiece in a great Dish, which purchased his Redemption out of the Hands of the Bailiffs. During the Negotiation for his Enlargement, I had an Opportunity of acquainting my self with his History.

Mr. *William Rosin*, of the Parish of St. *Katherine*, is somewhat stricken in Years, and married to a young Widow, who has very much the Ascendant over him: This degenerate Age being so perverted in all Things, that even in the State of Matrimony, the Young pretend to govern their Elders. The Musician is extremely fond of her; but is often obliged to lay by his Fiddle to hear louder Notes of hers, when she is pleased to be angry with him: For you are to know, *Will.* is not of Consequence enough to enjoy her Conversation but when she chides him, or makes use of him to carry on her Amours. For she is a Woman of Stratagem; and even in that Part of the World where one would expect but very little Gallantry, by the Force of natural Genius, she can be sullen, sick, out of Humour, splenatick, want new Clothes, and more Money, as well as if she had been bred in *Cheapside* or *Cornhill*.[1] She was lately under a secret Discontent, upon Account of a Lover she was like to lose by his Marriage: For her Gallant, Mr. *Ezekiel Boniface*, had been twice asked in Church, in order to be joined in Matrimony with Mrs. *Winifred Dimple*, Spinster, of the same Parish. Hereupon Mrs. *Rosin* was far gone in that Distemper which well-governed Husbands know by the Description of, *I am I know not how;* and *Will.* soon understood, that it was his Part to enquire into the Occasion of her Melancholy, or suffer as the Cause of it himself. After much Importunity, all he could get out of her, was, That she was the most unhappy and the most wicked of all Women, and had no Friend in the World to tell her Grief to. Upon this, *Will*. doubled his Importunities; but she said, That she should break her poor Heart, if he did not take a solemn Oath upon a Book, that he would not be angry; and that he would expose the Person who had wronged her to all the World, for the Ease of her Mind, which was no way else to be quieted. The Fiddler was so melted, that he immediately kissed her, and afterwards the Book. When his Oath was taken, she began to lament her self, and revealed to him, that (miserable Woman as she was) she had been false to his Bed. *Will*. was glad to hear it was no worse; but before he could reply, Nay (said she) I will make you all the Atonement I can, and take Shame upon me by proclaiming it to all the World, which is the only Thing that can remove my present Terrors of Mind. This was indeed too true; for her Design was to prevent Mr. *Boniface*'s Marriage, which was all she apprehended. *Will*. was throughly angry, and began to curse and swear, the ordinary Expressions of Passion in Persons of his Condition. Upon which his Wife — Ah *William!* How well you Mind the Oath you have taken, and the Distress of your poor Wife, who can keep nothing from you; I hope you won't be such a perjured Wretch as to forswear your self. The Fiddler answered, That his Oath obliged him only not to be angry at what was passed; but I find you intend to make me laughed at all over *Wapping*. No, no, (replied Mrs. *Rosin*) I see well enough what you would be at, you poor-spirited Cuckold — You are afraid to expose *Boniface*, who has abused your poor Wife, and would fain perswade me still to suffer the Stings of Conscience; but I assure you Sirrah, I won't go to the Devil for you. Poor *Will*. was not made for Contention, and beseeching her to be pacified, desired she would consult the Good of her Soul her own Way, for he would not say her nay in any Thing.

Mrs. *Rosin* was so very loud and publick in her Invectives against *Boniface*, that the Parents of his Mistress forbad the Ban{n}s, and his Match was prevented, which was the whole Design of this deep Stratagem. The Father of *Boniface* brought this Action of Defamation, arrested the Fiddler, and recovered Dammages. This was the Distress from which he was relieved by the Company; and the good Husband's Air, History, and Jollity, upon his Enlargement, gave Occasion to very much Mirth; especially when *Will*. finding he had

Friends to stand by him, proclaimed himself a Cuckold by Way of Insult over the Family of the *Bonifaces*. Here is a Man of Tranquility without reading *Seneca!* What Work had such an Incident made among Persons of Distinction? The Brothers and Kindred of each Side must have been drawn out, and Hereditary Hatred entailed on the Families as long as their very Names remained in the World. Who would believe that *Herod*, *Othello*, and *Will. Rosin*, were of the same Species?

There are quite different Sentiments which reign in the Parlour and the Kitchin; and it is by the Point of Honour, when justly regulated, and inviolably observed, that some Men are superior to others, as much as Mankind in general are to Brutes. This puts me in Mind of a Passage in the admirable Poem called the *Dispensary*, where the Nature of true Honour is artfully described in an Ironical Dispraise of it.

> *But e're we once engage in Honour's Cause,*
> *First know what Honour is, and whence it was.*
> *Scorn'd by the Base, 'tis courted by the Brave,*
> *The Hero's Tyrant, and the Coward's Slave.*
> *Born in the noisy Camp, it lives on Air;*
> *And both exists by Hope, and by Despair.*
> *Angry when e'er a Moment's Ease we gain,*
> *And reconciled at our Returns of Pain.*
> *It lives, when in Death's Arms the Hero lies,*
> *But when his Safety he consults, it dies.*
> *Bigotted to this Idol, we disclaim,*
> *Rest, Health, and Ease, for nothing but a Name.*[2]

No. 112 [STEELE and ?]
Saturday, 24 December to Tuesday, 27 December 1709

[A letter from the country]

*Accedat Suavitas quædam oportet Sermonum, atque Morum, haudquaquam medio-
cre Condimentum Amicitiæ. Tristitia autem, & in omni Re Severitas absit. Habet
illa quidem Gravitatem, sed Amicitia remissior esse debet, & liberior, & dulcior, &
ad omnem Comitatem Facilitatemque proclivior.*   Tull.[1]

Sheer-Lane, December 26.

As I was looking over my Letters this Morning, I chanced to cast
my Eye upon the following one, which came to my Hands about
Two Months ago from an old Friend of mine, who, as I have since
learned, was the Person that writ the agreeable Epistle inserted in
my Paper of the Third of the last Month. It is of the same Turn
with the other, and may be looked upon as a Specimen of *Right
Country Letters.*

SIR,

*This sets out to you from my Summer-House upon the Terras, where I am
enjoying a few Hours Sunshine, the scanty sweet Remains of a fine Autumn.
The Year is almost at the lowest; so that in all Appearance, the rest of my
Letters between this and Spring will be dated from my Parlour-Fire, where
the little fond Prattle of a Wife and Children will so often break in upon
the Connexion of my Thoughts, that you'll easily discover it in my Style.
If this Winter should prove as severe as the last, I can tell you before-hand,
that I am likely to be a very miserable Man, through the perverse Temper
of my eldest Boy. When the Frost was in its Extremity, you must know,
that most of the Black-birds, Robins, and Finches, of the Parish (whose
Musick had entertained me in the Summer) took Refuge under my Roof.
Upon this, my Care was, to rise every Morning before Day to set open my
Windows for the Reception of the Cold and the Hungry, whom at the same
Time I relieved with a very plentiful Alms, by strewing Corn and Seeds
upon the Floors and Shelves. But* Dicky, *without any Regard to the Laws
of Hospitality, considered the Casements as so many Traps, and used every
Bird as a °Prisoner at Discretion. Never did Tyrant exercise more various
Cruelties: Some of the poor Creatures he chased to Death about the Room;
others he drove into the Jaws of a Blood-thirsty Cat; and even in his*

greatest Acts of Mercy, either clipped the Wings, or singed the Tails, of his innocent Captives. You'll laugh, when I tell you I sympathized with every Bird in its Misfortunes; but I believe you'll think me in the Right for bewailing the Child's unlucky Humour. On the other Hand, I am extremely pleased to see his younger Brother carry an universal Benevolence towards every Thing that has Life. When he was between Four and Five Years old, I caught him weeping over a beautiful Butterfly, which he chanced to kill as he was playing with it; and I am informed, that this Morning he has given his Brother Three Halfpence (which was his whole Estate) to spare the Life of a Tom-Tit. These are at present the Matters of greatest Moment within my Observation, and I know are too trifling to be communicated to any but so wise a Man as your self, and from one who has the Happiness to be,

Your most Faithful,
And most Obedient Servant.

The best Critick that ever wrote, speaking of some Passages in *Homer* which appear extravagant or frivolous, says indeed that they are Dreams; but the Dreams of *Jupiter*. My Friend's Letter appears to me in the same Light. One sees him in an idle Hour; but at the same Time in the idle Hour of a wise Man. A great Mind has something in it too severe and forbidding, that is not capable of giving it self such little Relaxations, and of condescending to these agreeable Ways of Trifling. *Tully*, when he celebrates the Friendship of *Scipio* and *Lelius*, who were the greatest, as well as the politest, Men of their Age, represents it as a beautiful Passage in their Retirement, that they used to gather up Shells on the Sea-Shore, and amuse themselves with the Variety of Shape and Colour, which they met with in those little unregarded Works of Nature.[2] The great *Agesilaus* could be a Companion to his own Children, and was surprised by the Ambassadors of *Sparta*, as he was riding among them upon an Hobby-Horse.[3] *Augustus* indeed had no Play-Fellows of his own begetting; but is said to have passed many of his Hours with little *Moorish* Boys at a Game of Marbles, not unlike our modern °Taw. There is (methinks) a Pleasure in seeing great Men thus fall into the °Rank of Mankind, and entertain themselves with Diversions and Amusements that are agreeable to the very weakest of the Species. I must frankly confess, that it is to me a

Beauty in *Cato*'s Character, that he would drink a chearful Bottle with a Friend; and I cannot but own, that I have seen with great Delight one of the most celebrated Authors of the last Age feeding the Ducks in St. *James*'s Park. By Instances of this Nature, the Heroes, the Statesmen, the Philosophers, become as it were familiar with us, and grow the more amiable, the less they endeavour to appear awful. A Man who always acts in the Severity of Wisdom, or the Haughtiness of Quality, seems to move in a personated Part: It looks too Constrained and Theatrical for a Man to be always in that Character which distinguishes him from others. Besides that, the Slackening and Unbending our Minds on some Occasions, makes them exert themselves with greater Vigour and Alacrity, when they return to their proper and natural State.

As this innocent Way of passing a leisure Hour is not only consistent with a great Character, but very graceful in it, so there are Two Sorts of People to whom I would most earnestly recommend it. The First, are those who are uneasy out of Want of Thought; the Second, are those who are so out of a Turbulence of Spirit. The First are the impertinent, and the Second the dangerous Part of Mankind.

It grieves me to the very Heart, when I see several young Gentlemen, descended of honest Parents, run up and down hurrying from one End of the Town to the other, calling in at every Place of Resort, without being able to fix a Quarter of an Hour in any, and in a particular Haste without knowing for what. It would (methinks) be some Consolation, if I could perswade these precipitate young Gentlemen to compose this Restlessness of Mind, and apply themselves to any Amusement, how trivial soever, that might give them Employment, and keep them out of Harm's Way. They cannot imagine how great a Relief it would be to them, if they could grow sedate enough to play for Two or Three Hours at a Game of °Push-pin. But these busie, idle Animals, are only their own Tormentors: The Turbulent and Dangerous are for embroiling Councils, stirring up Seditions, and subverting Constitutions, out of a meer Restlessness of Temper, and an Insensibility of all the Pleasures of Life that are calm and innocent. It is impossible for a Man to be so much employed in any Scene of Action, as to have great and good Affairs enough to fill up his whole Time; there will still be C[h]asms and empty Spaces, in which a working Mind will employ it self to its own Prejudice, or that of others, unless it can be at Ease in the Exercise of such Actions as are in themselves indifferent. How often have I wished, for the Good of the Nation, That several famous Politicians could take any Pleasure in feeding Ducks. I look upon an able Statesman out of Business like a huge Whale, that will endeavour to overturn the Ship, unless he has an empty Cask to play with.

But to return to my good Friend and Correspondent, I am afraid we shall both be laughed at, when I confess, that we have often gone out into the Field to look upon a Bird's-Nest; and have more than once taken an Evening's Walk together on purpose to see the Sun set. I shall conclude with my Answer to his foregoing Letter:

Dear SIR,

I thank you for your obliging Letter, and your Kindness to the Distressed, who will, doubtless, express their Gratitude to you themselves the next Spring. As for Dick the Tyrant, I must desire you will put a Stop to his Proceedings; and at the same Time take Care, that his little Brother be no Loser by his Mercy to the Tom-Tit. For my own Part, I am excluded all Conversation with Animals that delight only in a Country Life, and am therefore forced to entertain my self as well as I can with my little Dog and Cat. They both of 'em sit by my Fire every Night, expecting my coming Home with Impatience; and at my Entrance, never fail of running up to me, and bidding me welcome, each of 'em in his proper Language. As they have been bred up together from their Infancy, and seen no other Company, they have learned each others Manners, so that the Dog often gives himself the Airs of a Cat, and the Cat, in several of her Motions and Gestures, affects the Behaviour of the little Dog. When they are at Play, I often make one with them; and sometimes please my self with considering, how much Reason and Instinct are capable of delighting each other. Thus, you see, I have communicated to you the material Occurrences in my Family, with the same Freedom that you use to me; as I am with the same Sincerity and Affection,

Your most Faithful
Humble Servant,
Isaac Bickerstaff.

from No. 130 [STEELE]
Saturday, 4 February to Tuesday, 7 February 1710

[The glory of the present age]

—*At me*
Cum magnis vixisse invita fatebitur usque
Invidia. –   Hor.[1]

Sheer-Lane, February 6.

I find some of the most polite *Latin* Autors, who wrote at a Time
when *Rome* was in its Glory, speak with a certain noble Vanity of
the Brightness and Splendour of the Age in which they lived. *Pliny*
often compliments his Emperor *Trajan* upon this Head; and when
he would animate him to any Thing great, or disswade him from
any Thing that was improper, he insinuates, that it is befitting or
unbecoming (the *Claritas & Nitor Sæculi*[2]) that Period of Time which
was made illustrious by his Reign. When we cast our Eyes back on
the History of Mankind, and trace them through their several
Successions to their first Original, we sometimes see them breaking
out in great and memorable Actions, and towring up to the utmost
Heights of Virtue and Knowledge; when, perhaps, if we carry our
Observation to a little Distance, we see them sunk into Sloth and
Ignorance, and altogether lost in Darkness and Obscurity. Sometimes the whole Species is asleep for Two or Three Generations,
and then again awakens into Action, flourishes in Heroes, Philosophers, and Poets, who do Honour to humane Nature, and leave
such °Tracts of Glory behind them, as distinguish the Years, in
which they acted their Part, from the ordinary Course of Time.

Methinks a Man cannot, without a secret Satisfaction, consider
the Glory of the present Age, which will shine as bright as any
other in the History of Mankind. It is still big with great Events,
and has already produced Changes and Revolutions which will be
as much admired by Posterity, as any that have happened in the
Days of our Fathers, or in the old Times before them. We have seen
Kingdoms divided and united, Monarchs erected and deposed,
Nations transferred from one Sovereign to another; Conquerors
raised to such a Greatness as has given a Terror to *Europe*, and
thrown down by such a Fall, as has moved their Pity.

But it is still a more pleasing View to an *Englishman*, to see his own Country give the chief Influence to so illustrious an Age, and stand in the strongest Point of Light amidst the diffused Glory that surrounds it.

If we begin with Learned Men, we may observe, to the Honour of our Country, That those who make the greatest Figure in most Arts and Sciences, are universally allowed to be of the *British* Nation; and what is more remarkable, That Men of the greatest Learning are among the Men of the greatest Quality.

A Nation may indeed abound with Persons of such uncommon Parts and Worth, as may make them rather a Misfortune than a Blessing to the Publick. Those who singly might have been of infinite Advantage to the Age they live in, may, by rising up together in the same Crisis of Time, and by interfering in their Pursuits of Honour, rather interrupt than promote the Service of their Country. Of this we have a famous Instance in the Republick of *Rome*, when *Cæsar*, *Pompey*, *Cato*, *Cicero*, and *Brutus*, endeavoured to recommend themselves at the same Time to the Admiration of their Contemporaries. Mankind was not able to provide for so many extraordinary Persons at once, or find out Posts suitable to their Ambition and Abilities. For this Reason, they were all as miserable in their Deaths, as they were famous in their Lives, and occasioned, not only the Ruin of each other, but also that of the Commonwealth.

It is therefore a particular Happiness to a People, when the Men of superior Genius and Character are so justly disposed in the high Places of Honour, that each of them moves in a Sphere which is proper to him, and requires those particular Qualities in which he excels.

[3]If I see a General commanding the Forces of his Country, whose Victories are not to be paralleled in °Story, and who is as famous for his Negotiations as his Victories; and at the same Time see the Management of a Nation's Treasury in the Hands of one who has always distinguished himself by a generous Contempt of his own private Wealth, and an exact Frugality of that which belongs to the Publick; I cannot but think a People under such an Administration may promise themselves Conquest Abroad, and Plenty at Home. If I were to wish for a proper Person to preside over the publick Councils, it should certainly be one as much admired for his

universal Knowledge of Men and Things, as for his Eloquence, Courage and Integrity, in the exerting of such extraordinary Talents.

Who is not pleased to see a Person in the highest Station in the Law, who was the most eminent in his Profession, and the most accomplished Orator at the Bar? Or at the Head of the Fleet a Commander, under whose Conduct the Common Enemy received such a Blow, as he has never been able to recover?

Were we to form to our selves the Idea of one whom we should think proper to govern a distant Kingdom, consisting chiefly of those who differ from us in Religion, and are influenced by foreign Politicks, would it not be such a one as had signalized himself by an uniform and unshaken Zeal for the Protestant Interest, and by his Dexterity in defeating the Skill and Artifice of its Enemies. In short, if we find a great Man popular for his Honesty and Humanity, as well as famed for his Learning and great Skill in all the Languages of *Europe*, or a Person eminent for those Qualifications which make Men shine in publick Assemblies, or for that Steadiness, Constancy, and good Sense, which carry a Man to the desired Point thro' all the Opposition of Tumult and Prejudice, we have the Happiness to behold them all in Posts suitable to their Characters.

Such a Constellation of great Persons, if I may so speak, while they shine out in their own distinct Capacities, reflect a Lustre upon each other, but in a more particular Manner on their Sovereign, who has placed them in those proper Situations, by which their Virtues become so beneficial to all Her Subjects. It is the Anniversary of the Birth-day of this Glorious Queen, which naturally led me into this Field of Contemplation, and instead of joining in the public Exultations that are made on such Occasions, to entertain my Thoughts with the more serious Pleasure of ruminating upon the Glories of her Reign.

While I behold her surrounded with Triumphs, and adorned with all the Prosperity and Success which Heaven ever shed on a Mortal, and still considering herself as such, tho' the Person appears to me exceeding great that has these just Honours paid to her; yet I must confess, she appears much greater in that she receives them with such a glorious Humility, and shows she has no further Regard for them, than as they arise from these great Events which have made her Subjects happy. For my own Part, I must confess, when I see private Virtues in so high a Degree of Perfection, I am not astonished at any extraordinary Success that attends them, but look upon publick Triumphs as the natural Consequences of religious Retirements.

No. 132 [STEELE]

Thursday, 9 February to Saturday, 11 February 1709

[The club at the Trumpet]

Habeo Senectuti magnam Gratiam, quæ mihi Sermonis aviditatem auxit, Potionis & Cibi sustulit.   Tull. de Sen.[1]

Sheer-Lane, February 10.

After having applied my Mind with more than ordinary Attention to my Studies, it is my usual Custom to relax and unbend it in the Conversation of such as are rather easy than shining Companions. This I find particularly necessary for me before I retire to Rest, in order to draw my Slumbers upon me by Degrees, and fall asleep insensibly. This is the particular Use I make of a Set of heavy honest Men, with whom I have passed many Hours with much Indolence, though not with great Pleasure. Their Conversation is a kind of Preparative for Sleep: It takes the Mind down from its Abstractions, leads it into the familiar °Traces of Thought; and lulls it into that State of Tranquility, which is the Condition of a thinking Man when he is but half awake. After this, my Reader will not be surprised to hear the Account which I am about to give of a Club of my own Contemporaries, among whom I pass Two or Three Hours every Evening. This I look upon as taking my first Nap before I go to Bed. The Truth of it is, I should think my self unjust to Posterity, as well as to the Society at the *Trumpet*,[2] of which I am a Member, did not I in some Part of my Writings give an Account of the Persons among whom I have passed almost a Sixth Part of my Time for these last Forty Years. Our Club consisted originally of Fifteen; but partly by the Severity of the Law in arbitrary Times, and partly by the natural

Effects of old Age, we are at present reduced to a Third Part of that Number: In which however we have this Consolation, That the best Company is said to consist of Five Persons. I must confess, besides the afore-mentioned Benefit which I meet with in the Conversation of this select Society, I am not the less pleased with the Company, in that I find my self the greatest Wit among them, and am heard as their Oracle in all Points of Learning and Difficulty.

Sir *Jeoffrey Notch*, who is the oldest of the Club, has been in Possession of the Right-Hand Chair Time out of Mind, and is the only Man among us that has the Liberty of stirring the Fire. This our Foreman is a Gentleman of an ancient Family, that came to a great Estate some Years before he had Discretion, and run it out in Hounds, Horses, and Cock-fighting; for which Reason he looks upon himself as an honest worthy Gentleman who has had Misfortunes in the World, and calls every thriving Man a pitiful Upstart.

Major *Matchlock* is the next Senior, who served in the last Civil Wars, and has all the Battles by Heart. He does not think any Action in *Europe* worth talking of since the Fight of *Marston-Moor*; and every Night tells us of his having been knocked off his Horse at the Rising of the *London* Apprentices; for which he is in great Esteem amongst us.[3]

Honest old *Dick Reptile* is the Third of our Society: He is a good-natured indolent Man, who speaks little himself, but laughs at our Jokes, and brings his young Nephew along with him, a Youth of Eighteen Years old, to show him good Company, and give him a Tast of the World. This young Fellow sits generally silent; but whenever he opens his Mouth, or laughs at any Thing that passes, he is constantly told by his Uncle after a jocular Manner, 'Ay, ay, *Jack*, you young Men think us Fools; but we old Men know you are.'

The greatest Wit of our Company, next to my self, is a Bencher of the neighbouring Inn, who in his Youth frequented the °Ordinaries about *Charing-Cross*, and pretends to have been intimate with *Jack Ogle*.[4] He has about Ten Distichs of *Hudibras* without Book, and never leaves the Club till he has applied them all. If any modern Wit be mentioned, or any Town Frolick spoken of, he shakes his Head at the Dulness of the present Age, and tells us a Story of *Jack Ogle*.

For my own Part, I am esteemed among them, because they see I am something respected by others, though at the same Time I understand by their Behaviour, that I am considered by them as a Man of a great deal of Learning, but no Knowledge of the World; insomuch that the Major sometimes, in the Height of his Military Pride, calls me the Philosopher: And Sir *Jeoffrey* no longer ago than last Night, upon a Dispute what Day of the Month it was then in *Holland*, pulled his Pipe out of his Mouth, and cried, What does the Scholar say to it?

Our Club meets precisely at Six a Clock in the Evening; but I did not come last Night till Half an Hour after Seven, by which Means I escaped the Battle of *Naseby*,[5] which the Major usually begins at about Three Quarters after Six; I found also, that my good Friend the Bencher had already spent Three of his Distichs, and [was] only waiting an Opportunity to hear a Sermon spoken of, that he might introduce the Couplet where *a-Stick* rhimes to *Ecclesiastick*.[6] At my Entrance into the Room, they were naming a red Petticoat and a Cloak, by which I found that the Bencher had been diverting them with a Story of *Jack Ogle*.

I had no sooner taken my Seat, but Sir *Jeoffrey*, to show his good Will towards me, gave me a Pipe of his own Tobacco, and stirred up the Fire. I look upon it as a Point of Morality, to be obliged by those who endeavour to oblige me; and therefore in Requital for his Kindness, and to set the Conversation a going, I took the best Occasion I could to put him upon telling us the Story of old *Gantlett*, which he always does with very particular Concern. He traced up his Descent on both Sides for several Generations, describing his Diet and Manner of Life, with his several Battles, and particularly that in which he fell. This *Gantlett* was a Game-Cock, upon whose Head the Knight in his Youth had won Five Hundred Pounds, and lost Two Thousand. This naturally set the Major upon the Account of *Edgehill* Fight,[7] and ended in a Duel of *Jack Ogle*'s.

Old *Reptile* was extremely attentive to all that was said, though it was the same he had heard every Night for these Twenty Years, and upon all Occasions winked upon his Nephew to mind what passed.

This may suffice to give the World a Tast of our innocent Conversation, which we spun out till about Ten of the Clock, when my Maid came with a Lanthorn to light me Home. I could not but reflect with my self as I was going out upon the talkative Humour of old Men, and the little Figure which that Part of Life makes in one who cannot employ this natural Propensity in Discourses which would make him venerable. I must own, it makes me very melancholy in Company, when I hear a young Man begin a Story; and have often observed, That one of a Quarter of an Hour long in a Man of Five and twenty, gathers Circumstances every Time he tells it, till it grows into a long, *Canterbury* Tale of two Hours by that Time he is Threescore.

The only Way of avoiding such a trifling and frivolous old Age, is, to lay up in our Way to it such Stores of Knowledge and Observation as may make us useful and agreeable in our declining Years. The Mind of Man in a long Life will become a Magazine of Wisdom or Folly, and will consequently discharge itself in something impertinent or improving. For which Reason, as there is nothing more ridiculous than an old trifling Story-Teller, so there is nothing more venerable than one who has turned his Experience to the Entertainment and Advantage of Mankind.

In short, we who are in the last Stage of Life, and are apt to indulge ourselves in Talk, ought to consider, if what we speak be worth being heard, and endeavour to make our Discourse like that of *Nestor*, which *Homer* compares to the Flowing of Honey for its Sweetness.

I am afraid I shall be thought guilty of this Excess I am speaking of, when I cannot conclude without observing, that *Milton* certainly thought of this Passage in *Homer*, when in his Description of an eloquent Spirit, he says, *His Tongue drop[pe]d Manna.* [8]

No. 149 [STEELE]
Tuesday, 21 March to Thursday, 23 March 1710

[Ill-natured husbands]
From my own Apartment, March 22.

It has often been a solid Grief to me, when I have reflected on this glorious Nation, which is the Scene of publick Happiness and Liberty, that there are still Crowds of private Tyrants, against whom there neither is any Law now in Being, nor can there be invented any by the Wit of Man. These cruel Men are ill-natured Husbands. The Commerce in the Conjugal State is so delicate, that it is impossible to prescribe Rules for the Conduct of it, so as to fit Ten Thousand nameless Pleasures and Disquietudes which arise to People in that Condition. But it is in this as in some other nice Cases, where touching upon the Malady tenderly, is half Way to the Cure; and there are some Faults which need only to be observed to be amended. I am put into this Way of Thinking by a late Conversation which I am going to give an Account of.

I made a Visit the other Day to a Family for which I have a great Honour, and found the Father, the Mother, and Two or Three of the younger Children, drop off designedly to leave me alone with the eldest Daughter, who was but a Visitant there as well as my self, and is the Wife of a Gentleman of a very fair Character in the World. As soon as we were alone, I saw her Eyes full of Tears, and methought she had much to say to me, for which she wanted Encouragement. 'Madam,' said I, 'You know I wish you all as well as any Friend you have: Speak freely what I see you are oppressed with, and you may be sure, if I cannot relieve your Distress, you may at least reap so much present Advantage, as safely to give your self the Ease of uttering it.' She immediately assumed the most becoming Composure of Countenance, and spoke as follows: 'It is an Aggravation of Affliction in a marryed Life, that there is a sort of Guilt in communicating it: For which Reason it is, that a Lady of your and my Acquaintance, instead of speaking to you her self, desired me the next Time I saw you, as you are a professed Friend to our Sex, to turn your Thoughts upon the reciprocal Complaisance which is the Duty of a married State.

'My Friend was neither in Fortune, Birth or Education, below the Gentleman whom she has married. Her Person, her Age, and her Character, are also such as he can make no Exception to. But so it is, that from the Moment the Marriage-Ceremony was over, the Obsequiousness of a Lover was turned into the Haughtiness of a Master. All the kind Endeavours which she uses to please him, are at best but so many Instances of her Duty. This Insolence takes away that secret Satisfaction, which does not only excite to Virtue, but also rewards it. It abates the Fire of a free and generous Love, and imbitters all the Pleasures of a Social Life.' The young Lady spoke all this with such an Air of Resentment, as discovered how nearly she was concerned in the Distress.

When I observed she had done speaking, 'Madam,' said I, 'The Affliction you mention is the greatest that can happen in Humane Life, and I know but one Consolation in it, if that be a Consolation, that the Calamity is a pretty general One. There is nothing so common as for Men to enter into Marriage, without so much as expecting to be happy in it. They seem to propose to themselves a few Holidays in the Beginning of it; after which, they are to return at best to the usual Course of their Life; and for ought they know, to constant Misery and Uneasiness. From this false Sense of the State they are going into, proceeds the immediate Coldness and Indifference, or Hatred and Aversion, which attend ordinary Marriages, or rather bargains to cohabit.' Our Conversation was here interrupted by Company which came in upon us.

The Humour of affecting a superior Carriage, generally arises from a false Notion of the Weakness of a Female Understanding in general, or an over-weaning Opinion that we have of our own: For when it proceeds from a natural Ruggedness and Brutality of Temper, it is altogether incorrigible, and not to be amended by Admonition. Sir *Francis Bacon*, as I remember, lays it down as a Maxim, That no Marriage can be happy in which the Wife has no Opinion of her Husband's Wisdom[1]; but without Offence to so great an Authority, I may venture to say, That a sullen-wise Man is as bad as a good-natured Fool. Knowledge, softened with Complacency and good Breeding, will make a Man equally beloved and respected; but when joined with a severe, distant and unsociable Temper, it creates rather Fear than Love. I who am a Batchelor, have no other Notion of Conjugal Tenderness, but what I learn from Books, and shall therefore produce Three Letters of *Pliny*, who was not only one of the greatest, but the most learned Men in the whole *Roman* Empire.[2] At the same Time I am very much ashamed, that on such Occasions I am obliged to have Recourse to Heathen Authors, and shall appeal to my Readers, if they would not think it a Mark of a narrow Education in a Man of Quality to write such passionate Letters to any Woman but a Mistress. They were all Three written at a Time when she was at a Distance from him: The first of them puts me in Mind of a married Friend of Mine, who said, Sickness it self is pleasant to a Man that is attended in it by one whom he dearly loves.

Pliny to Calphurnia.

I never was so much offended at Business, as when it hindered me from going with you into the Country, or following you thither: For I more particularly wish to be with you at present, that I might be sensible of the Progress you make in the Recovery of your Strength and Health; as also of the Entertainment and Diversions you can meet with in your Retirement. Believe me, it is an anxious State of Mind to live in Ignorance of what happens to those whom we passionately love. I am not only in Pain for your Absence, but also for your Indisposition. I am afraid of every-Thing, fancy every Thing, and, as it is the Nature of Men in Fear, I fancy those Things most which I am most afraid of. Let me therefore earnestly desire you to favour me under these my Apprehensions with One Letter every Day, or, if possible, with Two; for I shall be a little at Ease while I am reading your Letters, and grow anxious again as soon as I have read them.

Second Letter.

You tell me, That you are very much afflicted at my Absence, and that you have no Satisfaction in any Thing but my Writings, which you often lay by you upon my Pillow. You oblige me very much in wishing to see me, and making me your Comforter in my Absence. In Return, I must let you know, I am no less pleased with the Letters which you writ to me, and read them over a Thousand Times with new Pleasure. If your Letters are capable of giving me so much Pleasure, what would your Conversation do? Let me beg of you to write to me often; though at the same Time I must confess, your Letters give me Anguish whilst they give me Pleasure.

Third Letter.

It is impossible to conceive how much I languish for you in your Absence; the tender Love I bear you, is the chief Cause of this my Uneasiness, which is still the more insupportable, because Absence is wholly a new Thing to us. I lie awake most Part of the Night in thinking of you, and several Times of the Day go as naturally to your Apartment, as if you were there to receive me; but when I miss you, I come away dejected, out of Humour, and like a Man that had suffered a Repulse. There is but one Part of the Day in which I am relieved from this Anxiety, and that is when I am engaged in Publick Affairs.

You may guess at the uneasy Condition of one who has no Rest but in Business, no Consolation but in Trouble.

I shall conclude this Paper with a beautiful Passage out of *Milton*, and leave it as a Lecture to those of my own Sex, who have a Mind to make their Conversation agreeable as well as instructive, to the Fair Partners who are fallen into their Care. *Eve* having observed, That *Adam* was entring into some deep Disquisitions with the Angel, who was sent to visit him, is described as retiring from their Company, with a Design of learning what should pass there from her Husband.

> *So spake our Sire, and by his Count'nance seem'd*
> *Entring on studious Thoughts abstruse, which* Eve
> *Perceiving where she sat retir'd in Sight,*
> *With Lowliness Majestick from her Seat*
> *[And grace that won who saw to wish her stay,]*
> *Rose, and went forth among her Fruits and Flowers . . .*
> *Yet went she not, as not with such Discourse*
> *Delighted, or not capable her Ear*
> *Of what was high: Such Pleasure she reserv'd,*
> Adam *relating, she sole Auditress;*
> *Her Husband the Relater she preferr'd*
> *Before the Angel, and of him to ask*
> *Chose rather: He, she knew would intermix*

Grateful Digressions, and solve high Dispute
With Conjugal Caresses, from his Lip
Not Words alone pleas'd her. O! When meet now
Such Pairs, in Love and mutual Honour join'd?[3]

No. 155 [ADDISON]
Tuesday, 4 April to Thursday 6 April 1710

[The greatest newsmonger in our quarter]

—*Aliena Negotia curat*
Excussus propriis. —   Hor.[1]

From my own Apartment, April 5.

There lived some Years since within my Neighbourhood a very
grave Person, an Upholsterer, who seemed a Man of more than
ordinary Application to Business. He was a very early Riser, and
was often abroad Two or Three Hours before any of his Neighbours.
He had a particular Carefulness in the knitting of his Brows, and
a kind of impatience in all his Motions, that plainly discovered he
was always intent on Matters of Importance. Upon my Enquiry
into his Life and Conversation, I found him to be the greatest
Newsmonger in our Quarter; that he rose before Day to read the
°*Post-Man*; and that he would take Two or Three Turns to the other
End of the Town before his Neighbours were up, to see if there
were any *Dutch* Mails come in. He had a Wife and several Children;
but was much more inquisitive to know what passed in *Poland* than
in his own Family, and was in greater Pain and Anxiety of Mind for
King *Augustus*'s Welfare than that of his nearest Relations. He
looked extremely thin in a Dearth of News, and never enjoyed
himself in a °Westerly Wind. This indefatigable kind of Life was
the Ruin of his Shop; for about the Time that his Favourite Prince
left the Crown of *Poland*, he °broke and disappeared.

This Man and his Affairs had been long out of my Mind, till
about Three Days ago, as I was walking in St. *James's* Park, I heard
some Body at a Distance hemming after me: And who should it be
but my old Neighbour the Upholsterer? I saw he was reduced to
extreme Poverty, by certain shabby Superfluities in his Dress: For

notwithstanding that it was a very sultry Day for the Time of the Year, he wore a loose great Coat and a Muff, with a long °Campaign-Whig out of Curl; to which he had added the Ornament of a Pair of black Garters buckled under the Knee. Upon his coming up to me, I was going to enquire into his present Circumstances; but was prevented by his asking me, with a Whisper, Whether the last Letters brought any Accounts that one might rely upon from *Bender*? I told him, None that I heard of; and asked him, Whether he had yet married his eldest Daughter? He told me, No. But pray, says he, tell me sincerely, What are your Thoughts of the King of *Sweden*? For though his Wife and Children were starving, I found his chief Concern at present was for this great Monarch.[2] I told him, That I looked upon him as one of the first Heroes of the Age. But pray, says he, do you think there is any Thing in the Story of his Wound? And finding me surprised at the Question, Nay, says he, I only propose it to you. I answered, That I thought there was no Reason to doubt of it. But why in the Heel, says he, more than in any other Part of the Body? Because, says I, the Bullet chanced to light there.

This extraordinary Dialogue was no sooner ended, but he began to launch out into a long Dissertation upon the Affairs of the *North*; and after having spent some Time on them, he told me, He was in a great Perplexity how to reconcile the °*Supplement* with the °*English-Post*, and had been just now examining what the other Papers say upon the same Subject. The °*Daily-Courant*, says he, has these Words, *We have Advices from very good Hands, That a certain Prince has some Matters of great Importance under Consideration*. This is very mysterious; but the °*Post-Boy* leaves us more in the Dark, for he tells us, *That there are private Intimations of Measures taken by a certain Prince, which Time will bring to Light*. Now the *Post-Man*, says he, who uses to be very clear, refers to the same News in these Words; *The late Conduct of a certain Prince affords great Matter of Speculation*. This certain Prince, says the Upholsterer, whom they are all so cautious of naming, I take to be – Upon which, though there was no body near us, he whispered something in my Ear, which I did not hear, or think worth my while to make him repeat.

We were now got to the upper End of the *Mall*, where were Three or Four very odd Fellows sitting together upon the Bench.

These I found were all of them Politicians, who used to Sun themselves in that Place every Day about Dinner-time. Observing them to be Curiosities in their Kind, and my Friend's Acquaintance, I sat down among them.

The chief Politician of the Bench was a great Asserter of Paradoxes. He told us, with a seeming Concern, That by some News he had lately read from *Muscovy*, it appeared to him that there was a Storm gathering in the Black Sea, which might in Time do Hurt to the Naval Forces of this Nation. To this he added, That for his Part, he could not wish to see the Turk driven out of *Europe*, which he believed could not but be prejudicial to our Woollen Manufacture. He then told us, That he looked upon those extraordinary Revolutions which had lately happened in these Parts of the World, to have risen chiefly from Two Persons who were not much talked of; and those, says he, are Prince *Menzikoff*, and the Dutchess of *Mirandola*. He backed his Assertions [with] so many broken Hints, and such a Show of Depth and Wisdom, that we gave our selves up to his Opinions.

The Discourse at length fell upon a Point which seldom escapes a Knot of true-born *Englishmen*, Whether in Case of a Religious War, the Protestants would not be too strong for the Papists? This we unanimously determined on the Protestant Side. One who sat on my Right Hand, and, as I found by his Discourse, had been in the *West-Indies*, assured us, That it would be a very easy Matter for the Protestants to beat the Pope at Sea; and added, That whenever such a War does break out, [it] must turn to the Good of the *Leeward* Islands. Upon this, one who sat at the End of the Bench, and, as I afterwards found, was the Geographer of the Company, said, That in case the Papists should drive the Protestants from these Parts of *Europe*, when the worst came to the worst, it would be impossible to beat them out of *Norway* and *Greenland*, provided the Northern Crowns hold together, and the Czar of *Muscovy* stand Neuter.

He further told us for our Comfort, That there were vast Tracts of Land about the Pole, inhabited neither by Protestants nor Papists, and of greater Extent than all the *Roman* Catholick Dominions in *Europe*.

When we had fully discussed this Point, my Friend the

Upholsterer began to exert himself upon the present Negotiations of Peace, in which he deposed Princes, settled the Bounds of Kingdoms, and ballanced the Power of *Europe*, with great Justice and Impartiality.

I at length took my Leave of the Company, and was going away; but had not been gone Thirty Yards, before the Upholsterer hemmed again after me. Upon his advancing towards me, with a Whisper, I expected to hear some secret Piece of News, which he had not thought fit to communicate to the Bench; but instead of that, he desired me in my Ear to lend him Half a Crown. In Compassion to so needy a Statesman, and to dissipate the Confusion I found he was in, I told him, if he pleased, I would give him Five Shillings, to receive Five Pounds of him when the Great Turk was driven out of *Constantinople*; which he very readily accepted, but not before he had laid down to me the Impossibility of such an Event, as the Affairs of *Europe* now stand.

This Paper I design for the particular Benefit of those worthy Citizens who live more in a Coffee-house than in their Shops, and whose Thoughts are so taken up with the Affairs of the Allies, that they forget their Customers.

No. 172 [STEELE]
Saturday, 13 May to Tuesday, 16 May 1710

[The unhappy end of Mr Eustace][1]

Quod quisque vitet, nunquam Homini satis Cautum est in Horas. —   Hor.[2]

From my own Apartment, May 15.

When a Man is in a serious Mood, and ponders upon his own Make, with a Retrospect to the Actions of his Life, and the many fatal Miscarriages in it, which he owes to ungoverned Passions, he is then apt to say to himself, That Experience has guarded him against such Errors for the future: But Nature often recurs in Spite of his best Resolutions, and it is to the very End of our Days a Struggle between our Reason and our Temper, which shall have the Empire over us. However, this is very much to be helped by

Circumspection, and a constant Alarm against the first Onsets of Passion. As this is in general a necessary Care to make a Man's Life easie and agreeable to himself, so it is more particularly the Duty of such as are engaged in Friendship and more near Commerce with others. Those who have their Joys, have also their Griefs in Proportion, and none can extremely exalt or depress Friends, but Friends. The harsh Things which come from the rest of the World, are received and repulsed with that Spirit which every honest Man bears for his own Vindication; but Unkindness in Words or Actions among Friends, affects us at the first Instant in the inmost Recesses of our Souls. Indifferent People, if I may so say, can wound us only in heterogeneous Parts, maim us in our legs or Arms; but the Friend can make no Pass but at the Heart it self. On the other Side, the most impotent Assistance, the meer well Wishes of a Friend, gives a Man Constancy and Courage against the most prevailing Force of his Enemies. It is here only a Man enjoys and suffers to the Quick. For this Reason, the most gentle Behaviour is absolutely necessary to maintain Friendship in any Degree above the common Level of Acquaintance. But there is a Relation of Life much more near than the most strict and sacred Friendship, that is to say, Marriage. This Union is of too close and delicate a Nature to be easily conceived by those who do not know that Condition by Experience. Here a Man should, if possible, soften his Passions; if not for his own Ease, in Compliance to a Creature formed with a Mind of a quite different Make from his own. I am sure, I do not mean it an Injury to Women, when I say there is a Sort of Sex in Souls. I am tender of offending them, and know it is hard not to do it on this Subject; but I must go on to say, That the Soul of a Man and that of a Woman, are made very unlike, according to the Employments for which they are designed. The Ladies will please to observe, I say, our Minds have different, not superior Qualities to theirs. The Virtues have respectively a Masculine and a Feminine Cast. What we call in Men Wisdom, is in Woman Prudence. It is a Partiality to call one greater than the other. A prudent Woman is in the same Class of Honour as a wise Man, and the Scandals in the Way of both are equally dangerous. But to make this State any Thing but a Burthen, and not hang a Weight upon our very Beings, it is very proper each of the Couple should frequently remember, that there are many Things which grow out of their very Natures that are pardonable, nay, becoming, when considered as such, but without that Reflection must give the quickest Pain and Vexation. To manage well a great Family, is as worthy an Instance of Capacity, as to execute a great Employment; and for the Generality, as Women perform the considerable Part of their Duties, as well as Men do theirs; so in their common Behaviour, those of ordinary Genius are not more trivial than the common Rate of Men; and in my Opinion, the playing of a Fan is every Whit as good an Entertainment as the beating a Snuff-box.

But however I have rambled in this Libertine Manner of Writing by Way of Essay, I now [sit] down with an Intention to represent to my Readers, how pernicious, how sudden, and how fatal, Surprizes of Passion are to the Mind of Man; and that in the most intimate Commerces of Life they are most liable to arise, even in our most sedate and indolent Hours. Occurrences of this Kind have had very terrible Effects; and when one reflects upon 'em, we cannot but tremble to consider what we are capable of being wrought up to against all the Ties of Nature, Love, Honour, Reason, and Religion, though the Man who breaks through them all, had, an Hour before he did so, a lively and virtuous Sense of their Dictates. When unhappy Catastrophes make up Part of the History of Princes, and Persons who act in high Spheres, or are represented in the moving Language, and well wrought Scenes of Tragedians, they do not fail of striking us with Terror; but then they [a]ffect us only in a transient Manner, and pass through our Imaginations, as Incidents in which our Fortunes are too humble to be concerned, or which Writers form for the Ostentation of their own Force, or, at most, as Things fit rather to exercise the Powers of our Minds, than to create new Habits in them. Instead of such high Passages, I was thinking it would be of great Use (if any Body could hit it) to lay before the World such Adventures as befal[l] Persons not exalted above the common Level. This, methought, would better prevail upon the ordinary Race of Men, who are so prepossessed with outward Appearances, that they mistake Fortune for Nature, and believe nothing can relate to them that does not happen to such as live and look like themselves.

The unhappy End of a Gentleman whose Story an Acquaintance

of mine was just now telling me, would be very proper for this End if it could be related with all the Circumstances as I heard it this Evening; for it touched me so much, that I cannot forbear ent[e]ring upon it.

Mr. *Eustace*, a young Gentleman of a good Estate near *Dublin* in *Ireland*, married a Lady of Youth, Beauty, and Modesty, and lived with her in general with much Ease and Tranquility; but was in his secret Temper impatient of Rebuke: She is apt to fall into little Sallies of Passion, yet as suddenly recalled by her own Reflection on her Fault, and the Consideration of her Husband's Temper. It happened, as he, his Wife, and her Sister, were at Supper together about Two Months ago, that in the midst of a careless and familiar Conversation, the Sisters fell into a little Warmth and Contradiction. He, who was one of that Sort of Men who are never unconcerned at what passes before them, fell into an outragious Passion on the Side of the Sister. The Person about whom they disputed was so near, that they were under no Restraint from running into vain Repetitions of past Heats: On which Occasion all the Aggravations of Anger and Distast boiled up, and were repeated with the Bitterness of exasperated Lovers. The Wife observing her Husband extremely moved, began to turn it off, and rally him for interposing between Two People who from their Infancy had been angry and pleased with each other every half Hour. But it descended deeper into his Thoughts, and they broke up with a sullen Silence. The Wife immediately retired to her Chamber, whither her Husband soon after followed. When they were in Bed, he soon dissembled a Sleep, and she, pleased that his Thoughts were composed, fell into a real One. Their Apartment was very distant from the rest of their Family, in a lonely Country House. He now saw his Opportunity, and with a Dagger he had brought to Bed with him, stabbed his Wife in the Side. She awaked in the highest Terror; but immediately imagined it was a Blow designed for her Husband by Ruffians, began to grasp him, and strive to awake and rouze him to defend himself. He still pretended himself sleeping, and gave her a second Wound.

She now drew open the Curtains, and by the Help of Moon-light saw his Hand lifted up to stab her. The Horror disarmed her from further Struggling; and he enraged anew at being discovered, fixed his Poniard in her Bosom. As soon as he believed he had dispatched her, he attempted to escape out of the Window: But she, still alive, called to him not to hurt himself; for she might live. He was so stung with the insupportable Reflection upon her Goodness and his own Villany, that he jumped to the Bed, and wounded her all over with as much Rage as if every Blow was provoked by new Aggravations. In this Fury of Mind he fled away. His Wife had still Strength to go to her Sister's Apartment, and give her an Account of this wonderful Tragedy; but died the next Day. Some Weeks after, an Officer of Justice, in attempting to seize the Criminal, fired upon him, as did the Criminal upon the Officer. Both their Balls took Place, and both immediately expired.

No. 178 [STEELE]
Saturday, 27 May to Tuesday, 30 May 1710

[The dangers of reading newspapers]
Sheer-Lane, May 29.

When we look into the delightful History of the most ingenious *Don Quixot* of the *Mancha*, and consider the Exercises and Manner of Life of that renowned Gentleman, we cannot but admire the exquisite Genius and discerning Spirit of *Michael Cervantes*, who has not only painted his Adventurer with great Majesty in the conspicious Parts of his Story, which relate to Love and Honour, but also intimated in his ordinary Life, Oeconomy and Furniture, the infallible Symptoms he gave of his growing Phrenzy, before he declared himself a Knight-Errant. His Hall was furnished with old Launces, Halbards, and °Morrions; his Food, Lentils; his Dress, amorous. He slept moderately, rose early, and spent his Time in Hunting. When by Watchfulness and Exercise he was thus qualified for the Hardships of his intended Peregrinations, he had nothing more to do but to fall hard to study; and before he should apply himself to the Practical Part, get into the Methods of making Love and War by reading Books of Knighthood. As for raising tender Passion in him, *Cervantes* reports, That he was wonderfully delighted with a smooth intricate Sentence; and when they listened at his Study-Door, they could frequently hear him read aloud, *The*

Reason of the Unreasonableness, which against my Reason is wrought, doth so weaken my Reason, as with all Reason I do justly complain on your Beauty. Again, he would pause till he came to another charming Sentence, and with the most pleasing Accent imaginable be loud at a new Paragraph: *The high Heavens, which, with your Divinity, do fortify you divinely with the Stars, make you Deserveress of the Deserts, that your Greatness deserves.* With these, and other such Passages, (*says my Author*) the poor Gentleman grew distracted, and was breaking his Brains Day and Night to understand and unravel their Sense.

As much as the Case of this distempered Knight is received by all the Readers of his History as the most incurable and ridiculous of all Phrensies, it is very certain we have Crowds among us far gone in as visible a Madness as his, though they are not observed to be in that Condition. As great and useful Discoveries are sometimes made by accidental and small Beginnings, I came to the Knowledge of the most Epidemick Ill of this Sort, by falling into a Coffee-house where I saw my Friend the Upholsterer, whose °Crack towards Politicks I have heretofore mentioned. This Touch in the Brain of the *British* Subject, is as certainly owing to the reading News-Papers, as that of the *Spanish* Worthy above mentioned to the reading Works of Chivalry. My Contemporaries the °Novelists have, for the better spinning out Paragraphs, and working down to the End of the Columns, a most happy Art in Saying and Unsaying, giving Hints of Intelligence, and Interpretations of indifferent Actions, to the great Disturbance of the Brains of ordinary Readers. This Way of going on in the Words, and making no Progress in the Sense, is more particularly the Excellence of my most ingenious and renowned Fellow-Labourer, the °*Post-Man*; and it is to this Talent in him that I impute the Loss of my Upholsterer's Intellects. That unfortunate Tradesman has for Years past been the chief Orator in ragged Assemblies, and the Reader in Alley Coffee-houses. He was Yesterday surrounded by an Audience of that Sort, among whom I sat unobserved through the Favour of a Cloud of Tobacco, and saw him with the *Post-Man* in his Hand, and all the other Papers safe under his Left Elbow. He was intermixing Remarks, and reading the *Paris* Article of *May* 30, which says, *That it is given out that an Express arrived this Day, with*

Advice, that the Armies were so near in the Plain of Lens, *that they cannonaded each other.* (Ay, ay, here we shall have Sport.) *And that it was highly probable the next Express would bring us an Account of an Engagement.* (They are welcome as soon as they please.) *Though some others say, That the same will be put off till the 2d or 3d of* June, *because the Mareschal* Villars *expects some further Reinforcements from* Germany, *and other Parts, before that Time.* (What-a-Pox does he put it off for? Does he think our Horse is not marching up at the same Time? But let us see what he says further.) *They hope, that Monsieur* Albergotti, *being encouraged by the Presence of so great an Army, will make an extraordinary Defence.* (Why then I find, *Albergotti* is one of those that love to have a great many on their Side – Nay, I'll say that for this Paper, he makes the most natural Inferences of any of them all.) *The Elector of* Bavaria *being uneasy to be without any Command, has desired Leave to come to Court to communicate a certain Project to his Majesty – Whatever it be, it is said, that Prince is suddenly expected, and then we shall have a more certain Account of his Project, if this Report has any Foundation.* (Nay, this Paper never imposes upon us; he goes upon sure Grounds; for he won't be positive the Elector has a Project, or that he will come, or if he does come at all; for he doubts, you see, whether the Report has any Foundation.)

What makes this the more lamentable is, that this Way of Writing falls in with the Imagination of the cooler and duller Part of Her Majesty's Subjects. The being kept up with one Line contradicting another, and the whole, after many Sentences of Conjecture, vanishing in a Doubt whether there is any Thing at all in what the Person has been reading, puts an ordinary Head into a Vertigo, which his natural Dulness would have secured him from. Next to the Labours of the *Post-Man*, the Upholsterer took from under his Elbow honest °*Icabod Dawk's* Letter, and there, among other Speculations, the Historian takes upon him to say, *That it is discoursed that there will be a Battel in* Flanders *before the Armies separate, and many will have it to be to Morrow, the great Battel of* [Ramillies] *being fought on a* Whit-Sunday. A Gentleman who was a Wag in this Company laughed at the Expression, and said, By Mr. *Dawks's* Favour, I warrant ye, if we meet them on *Whit-Sunday,* or *Monday,* we shall not stand upon the Day with them, whether it be before or after the Holidays. An Admirer of this Gentleman stood up, and told a Neighbour at a distant Table the Conceit, at which indeed we were all very merry. These Reflections in the Writers of the Transactions of the Times, seize the Noddles of such as were not born to have Thoughts of their own, and consequently lay a Weight upon every Thing which they read in Print. But Mr. *Dawks* concluded his Paper with a courteous Sentence, which was very well taken and applauded by the whole Company. *We wish*, says he, *all our Customers a merry* Whitsuntide, *and many of them*. Honest *Icabod* is as extraordinary a Man as any of our Fraternity, and as particular. His Style is a Dialect between the Familiarity of Talking and Writing, and his Letter such as you cannot distinguish whether Print or Manuscript, which gives us a °Refreshment of the Idea from what has been told us from the Press by others. This wishing a good Tide had its Effect upon us, and he was commended for his Salutation, as showing as well the Capacity of a °Bell-man as an Historian. My distempered old Acquaintance read in the next Place the Account of the Affairs abroad in the °*Courant*; but the Matter was told so distinctly, that these Wanderers thought there was no News in it; this Paper differing from the rest as an History from a Romance. The Tautology, the Contradictions, the Doubts, and Wants of Confirmations are what keep up imaginary Entertainments in empty Heads, and produce Neglect of their own Affairs, Poverty, and Bankruptcy, in many of the Shop-Statesmen; but turn the Imaginations of those of a little higher Orb into Deliriums of Dissatisfaction, which is seen in a continual Fret upon all that touches their Brains, but more particularly upon any Advantage obtained by their Country, where they are considered as Lunaticks, and therefore tolerated in their Ravings.

What I am now warning the People of is, That the News-Papers of this Island are as pernicious to weak Heads in *England* as ever Books of Chivalry to *Spain*; and therefore shall do all that in me lies, with the utmost Care and Vigilance imaginable, to prevent these growing Evils. A flaming Instance of this Malady appeared in my old Acquaintance at this Time, who, after he had done reading all his Papers, ended with a Thoughtful Air, *If we should have a Peace, we should then know for certain whether it was the King of* Sweden *that lately came to* Dunkirk. I whispered him, and desired him to step aside a little with me. When I had Opportunity, I decoyed him into a Coach, in order for his more easy Conveyance to *Moorfields*. The Man went very quietly with me; and by that Time he had brought the *Swede* from the Defeat by the Czar to the *Beristhenes*, we were passing by *Will*'s Coffee-house, where the Man of the House beckoned to us. We made a full Stop and could hear from above a very loud Voice swearing, with some Expressions towards Treason, That the Subject in *France* was as free as in *England*. His Distemper would not let him reflect, that his own Discourse was an Argument of the contrary. They told him, One would speak with him below. He came immediately to our Coach-Side. I whispered him, That I had an Order to carry him to the *Bastile*. He immediately obeyed with great Resignation: For to this Sort of Lunatick, whose Brain is touched for the *French*, the Name of a Gaol in that Kingdom has a more agreeable Sound, than that of a Paternal Seat in this their own Country. It happened a little unluckily bringing these Lunaticks together, for they immediately fell into a Debate concerning the Greatness of their respective Monarchs; one for the King of *Sweden*, the other for the Grand Monarch of *France*. This Gentleman from *Will*'s is now next Door to the Upholsterer, safe in his Apartment in my *Bedlam*, with proper Medicaments, and the °*Mercure Gallant* to sooth his Imagination that he is actually in *France*. If therefore he should escape to *Covent-Garden* again, all Persons are desired to lay hold of him, and deliver him to Mr. *Morphew*, my Overseer. At the same Time, I desire all true Subjects to forbear Discourse with him, any otherwise than when he begins to fight a Battle for *France*, to say, *Sir, I hope to see you in* England.

No. 181 [STEELE]
Saturday, 3 June to Tuesday, 6 June 1710

[An hour or two sacred to sorrow]

—Dies, ni fallor, adest, quem semper acerbum,
Semper honoratum; sic, Dii, voluistis, habebo.   Virg.[1]

From my own Apartment, June 5.

There are those among Mankind, who can enjoy no Relish of their Being, except the World is made acquainted with all that relates to them, and think every Thing lost that passes unobserved; but others find a solid Delight in stealing by the Crowd, and modelling their Life after such a Manner, as is as much above the Approbation as the Practice of the Vulgar. Life being too short to give Instances great enough of true Friendship or Good-Will, some Sages have thought it pious to preserve a certain Reverence for the °Manes of their deceased Friends, and have withdrawn themselves from the rest of the World at certain Seasons, to commemorate in their own Thoughts such of their Acquaintance who have gone before them out of this Life: And indeed, when we are advanced in Years, there is not a more pleasing Entertainment, than to recollect in a gloomy Moment the many we have parted with that have been dear and agreeable to us, and to cast a melancholy Thought or Two after those with whom, perhaps, we have indulged our selves in whole Nights of Mirth and Jollity. With such Inclinations in my Heart I went to my Closet Yesterday in the Evening, and resolved to be sorrowful; upon which Occasion, I could not but look with Disdain upon my self, that though all the Reasons which I had to lament the loss of many of my Friends are now as forcible as at the Moment of their Departure, yet did not my Heart swell with the same Sorrow which I felt at that Time; but I could, without Tears, reflect upon many pleasing Adventures I have had with some who have long been blended with common Earth. Though it is by the Benefit of Nature that Length of Time thus blots out the Violence of Afflictions; yet with Tempers too much given to Pleasure, it is almost necessary to revive the old Places of Grief in our Memory, and ponder Step by Step on past Life, to lead the Mind into that Sobriety of Thought which poises the Heart, and makes it beat with due Time, without being quickened with Desire, or retarded with Despair, from its proper and equal Motion. When we wind up a Clock that is out of Order, to make it go well for the future, we do not immediately set the Hand to the present Instant, but we make it strike the Round of all its Hours, before it can recover the Regularity of its Time. Such, thought I, shall be my Method this Evening; and since it is that Day of the Year which I dedicate to the Memory of such in another Life as I much delighted in when living, an Hour or Two shall be sacred to Sorrow and their Memory, while I run over all the melancholy Circumstances of this Kind which have occurred to me in my whole Life.

The first Sense of Sorrow I ever knew was upon the Death of my Father, at which Time I was not quite Five Years of Age; but was rather amazed at what all the House meant, than possessed with a real Understanding why no Body was willing to play with me. I remember I went into the Room where his Body lay, and my Mother sat weeping alone by it. I had my Battledore in my Hand, and fell a beating the Coffin, and calling Papa; for I know not how I had some slight idea that he was locked up there. My Mother catched me in her Arms, and transported beyond all Patience of the silent Grief she was before in, she almost smothered me in her Embrace, and told me in a Flood of Tears, Papa could not hear me, and would play with me no more, for they were going to put him under Ground, whence he could never come to us again. She was a very beautiful Woman, of a noble Spirit, and there was a Dignity in her Grief amidst all the Wildness of her Transport, which, methought, struck me with an Instinct of Sorrow, which, before I was sensible of what it was to grieve, seized my very Soul, and has made Pity the Weakness of my Heart ever since. The Mind in Infancy is, methinks, like the Body in Embrio, and receives Impressions so forcible, that they are as hard to be removed by Reason, as any Mark with which a Child is born is to be taken away by any future Application. Hence it is, that Good-Nature in me is no Merit; but having been so frequently over-whelmed with her Tears before I knew the Cause of any Affliction, or could draw Defences from my own Judgment, I imbibed Commiseration, Remorse, and an unmanly Gentleness of Mind, which has since insnared me into Ten Thousand Calamities, and from whence I can reap no Advantage, except it be, that in such an Humour as I am now in, I can the better indulge my self in the Softness of Humanity, and enjoy that sweet Anxiety which arises from the Memory of past Afflictions.

We that are very old, are better able to remember Things which befel[l] us in our distant Youth, than the Passages of later Days. For this Reason it is, that the Companions of my strong and vigorous Years present themselves more immediately to me in this Office of Sorrow. Untimely or unhappy Deaths are what we are most apt to lament, so little are we able to make it indifferent when a Thing happens, though we know it must happen. Thus we groan under Life, and bewail those who are relieved from it. Every Object that returns to our Imagination raises different Passions, according to the Circumstances of their Departure. Who can have lived in an Army, and in a serious Hour reflect upon the many gay and agreeable Men that might long have flourished in the Arts of Peace, and not join with the Imprecations of the Fatherless and Widow on the Tyrant to whose Ambition they fell Sacrifices? But gallant Men, who are cut off by the Sword, move rather our Veneration than our Pity, and we gather Relief enough from their own Contempt of Death, to make it no Evil, which was approached with so much Chearfulness, and attended with so much Honour. But when we turn our Thoughts from the great Parts of Life on such Occasions, and instead of lamenting those who stood ready to give Death to those from whom they had the Fortune to receive it; I say, when we let our Thoughts wander from such noble Objects, and consider the Havock which is made among the Tender and the Innocent, Pity enters with an unmixed Softness, and possesses all our Souls at once.

Here (were there Words to express such Sentiments with proper Tenderness) I should record the Beauty, Innocence, and untimely Death, of the first Object my Eyes ever beheld with Love. The beauteous Virgin! How ignorantly did she charm, how carelessly excel? Oh Death! Thou hast Right to the Bold, to the Ambitious, to the High, and to the Haughty; but why this Cruelty to the Humble, to the Meek, to the Undiscerning, to the Thoughtless? Nor Age, nor Business, nor Distress, can erase the dear Image from my Imagination. In the same Week, I saw her dressed for a Ball, and in a Shrowd. How ill did the Habit of Death become the Pretty Trifler? I still behold the smiling Earth – A large Train of Disasters were coming on to my Memory, when my Servant knocked at my Closet Door, and interrupted me with a Letter, attended with a Hamper of Wine, of the same Sort with that which is to be put to Sale on *Thursday* next at *Garraway*'s Coffee-house.[2] Upon the Receipt of it, I sent for Three of my Friends. We are so intimate, that we can be Company in whatever State of Mind we meet, and can entertain each other without expecting always to rejoice. The Wine we found to be generous and warming, but with such an Heat as moved us rather to be chearful than frolicksome. It revived the Spirits without firing the Blood. We commended it till Two of the Clock this Morning, and having to Day met a little before Dinner, we found, that though we drank Two Bottles a Man, we had much more Reason to recollect than forget what had passed the Night before.

from No. 195 [STEELE]
Thursday, 6 July to Saturday 8 July 1710

[A dissatisfied reader]
Grecian Coffee-house, July 7.

The Learned World are very much offended at many of my Ratiocinations, and have but a very mean Opinion of me as a Politician. The Reason of this is, That some erroneously conceive a Talent for Politicks to consist in the Regard to a Man's own Interest; but I am of quite another Mind, and think the first and essential Quality towards being a Statesman, is to have a publick Spirit. One of the Gentlemen who are out of Humour with me, imputes my falling into a Way wherein I am so very awkward to a Barrenness of Invention, and has the Charity to lay new Matter before me for the future. He is at the Bottom my Friend, but is at a Loss to know whether I am a Fool or a Physician, and is pleased to expostulate with me with Relation to the latter. He falls heavy upon °Licentiates, and seems to point more particularly at us who are not regularly of the Faculty. But since he has been so civil to me, as to meddle only with those who are employed no further than about Men's Lives, and not reflected upon me as of the Astrological Sect, who concern our selves about Lives and Fortunes also, I am not so much hurt as to stifle any Part of his fond Letter.

SIR,

'I am afraid there is something in the Suspicions of some People, that you begin to be short of Matter for your Lucubrations. Tho' several of them now and then did appear somewhat dull and insipid to me, I was always charitably inclined to believe the Fault lay in my self, and that I wanted the true Key to uncypher your Mysteries, and remember your Advertisement upon this Account. But since I have seen you fall in an unpardonable Error, yea with a Relapse: I mean, since I have seen you turn Politician in the present unhappy Dissentions, I have begun to stagger, and could not choose but lessen the great Value I had for the Censor of our Isle. How is it possible that a Man, whom Interest did naturally lead to a constant Impartiality in these Matters, and who hath Wit enough to judge, that his Opinion was not like to make many Proselytes? How is it possible, I say, that a little Passion (for I have still too good an Opinion of you to think you was bribed by the Staggering Party[1]) could blind you so far as to offend the very better Half of the Nation, and to lessen off so much the Number of your Friends? Mr. *Morphew* will not have Cause to thank you, unless you give over, and endeavour to regain what you have lost. There is still a great many Themes you have left untouched; such as the ill Managements of Matters relating to Law and Physick, the setting down Rules for knowing the Quacks in both Professions. What a large Field is there left in discovering the Abuses of the College, who had a Charter and Privileges granted them to hinder the creeping in and prevailing of Quacks and °Pretenders; and yet grant Licences to Barbers; and write Letters of Recommendation in the Country Towns, out of the Reach of their Practice, in Favour of meer Boys; valuing the Health and Lives of their Countrymen no farther than they get Money by them. You have said very little or nothing about the Dispensation of Justice in Town and Country, where Clerks are the Counsellors to their Masters.

'But as I can't expect that the Censor of *Great Britain* should publish a Letter, wherein he is censured with too much Reason himself; yet I hope you will be the better for it, and think upon the Themes I have mentioned, which must certainly be of greater Service to the World, your self, and Mr. *Morphew*, than to let us know whether you are a *Wig* or a *Tory*. I am still

Your Admirer and Servant,

Cato Junior.'

No. 214 [STEELE? and ADDISON]
Saturday, 15 August to Tuesday, 22 August 1710

[Political change][1]

— *Soles & aperta Serena Prospicere, & certis poteris cognoscere Signis.* Virg.[2]

From my own Apartment, August 21.

In every Party there are Two Sorts of Men, the *Rigid*, and the *Supple*. The *Rigid* are an intractable Race of Mortals, who act upon Principle, and will not, forsooth, fall into any Measures that are not consistent with their received Notions of Honour. These are Persons of a stubborn, unpliant Morality, that sullenly adhere to their Friends when they are disgraced, and to their Principles though they are exploded. I shall therefore give up this stiff-necked Generation to their own Obstinacy, and turn my Thoughts to the Advantage of the *Supple*, who pay their Homage to Places, and not Persons; and without enslaving themselves to any particular Scheme of Opinions, are as ready to change their Conduct in Point of Sentiment, as of Fashion. The well-disciplined Part of a Court are generally so perfect at their Exercise, that you may see a whole Assembly, from Front to Rear, face about at once to a new Man of Power, though at the same Time they turn their Backs upon him that brought them thither. The great Hardship these complaisant Members of Society are under, seems to be the Want of Warning upon any approaching Change or Revolution; so that they are obliged in a Hurry to tack about with every Wind, and stop short in the Midst of a full Career, to the great Surprize and Derision of their Beholders.

When a Man foresees a decaying Ministry, he has Leisure to grow a Malecontent, reflect upon the present Conduct, and by gradual Murmurs fall off from his Friends into a new Party, by just Steps and Measures. For Want of such Notices, I have formerly known a very well-bred Person refuse to return a Bow of a Man whom he thought in Disgrace, that was next Day made Secretary of State; and another, who after a long Neglect of a Minister, came to his Levee, and made Professions of Zeal for his Service the very Day before he was turned out.

This produces also unavoidable Confusions and Mistakes in the Descriptions of great Men's Parts and Merits. That ancient °Lyrick, Mr. *D'Urfey*, some Years ago writ a Dedication to a certain Lord, in which he celebrated him for the greatest Poet and Critick of that Age, upon a Misinformation in °*Dyer*'s Letter, that his noble Patron was made Lord Chamberlain.[3] In short, innumerable Votes, Speeches, and Sermons, have been thrown away, and turned to no Account, meerly for Want of due, and timely Intelligence. Nay, it has been known, that a Panegyrick has been half printed off, when the Poet, upon the Removal of the Minister, has been forced to alter it into a Satyr.

For the Conduct therefore of such useful Persons as are ready to do their Country Service upon all Occasions, I have an Engine in my Study, which is a Sort of a Political Barometer, or, to speak more intelligibly, a State *Weather-Glass*, that, by the rising and falling of a certain Magical Liquor, pressages all Changes and Revolutions in Government, as the common Glass does those of the Weather. This Weather-Glass is said to have been invented by *Cardan*, and given by him as a Present to his great Countryman and Contemporary *Machiavel*,[4] which (by the Way) may serve to rectify a received Error in Chronology, that places one of these some Years after the other. How or when it came into my Hands, I shall desire to be excused, if I keep to my self; but so it is, that I have walked by it for the better Part of a Century, to my Safety at least, if not to my Advantage; and have among my Papers, a Register of all the Changes that have happened in it from the Middle of Queen *Elizabeth*'s Reign.

In the Time of that Princess, it stood long at *settled Fair*. At the latter End of King *James* the First, it fell to *Cloudy*. It held several Years after at *Stormy*; insomuch that at last despairing of seeing any *Clear* Weather at Home, I followed the Royal Exile, and some

Time after finding my Glass rise, returned to my native Country with the rest of the Loyalists. I was then in Hopes to pass the Remainder of my Days in *settled Fair*: But alas! during the greatest Part of that Reign, the *English* Nation lay in a *dead Calm*, which, as it is usual, was followed by high Winds and Tempests till of late Years: In which, with unspeakable Joy and Satisfaction, I have seen our Political Weather returned to *settled Fair*. I must only observe, that for all this last Summer my Glass has pointed at Changeable. Upon the whole, I often apply to Fortune *Æneas*'s Speech to the Sibyl:

— *Non ulla Laborum,*
O Virgo, nova mi Facies inopinave surgit
Omnia præcepi, atq; Animo mecum ante peregi.[5]

The Advantages which have accrued to those whom I have advised in their Affairs, by Vertue of this Sort of Præscience, have been very considerable. A Nephew of mine, who has never put his Money into the Stocks, or taken it out, without my Advice, has in a few Years raised Five Hundred Pounds to almost so many Thousands. As for my self, who look upon Riches to consist rather in Content than Possessions, and measure the Greatness of the Mind rather by its Tranquillity than its Ambition, I have seldom used my Glass to make my Way in the World, but often to retire from it. This is a By-Path to Happiness, which was first discovered to me by a most pleasing Apothegm of *Pythagoras: When the Winds*, says he, *rise, worship the Eccho*. That great Philosopher (whether to make his Doctrines the more venerable, or to guild his Precepts with the Beauty of Imagination, or to awaken the Curiosity of his Disciples; for I will not suppose what is usually said, that he did it to conceal his Wisdom from the Vulgar) has couched several admirable Precepts in remote Allusions and mysterious Sentences. By the Winds in this Apothegm, are meant State-Hurricanes and popular Tumults. When these arise, says he, worship the Eccho; that is, withdraw your self from the Multitude into Deserts, Woods, Solitudes, or the like Retirements, which are the usual Habitations of the Eccho.

No. 224 [ADDISON]

Tuesday, 1 2 September to Thursday, 1 4 September 1 7 1 0

[Advertisements]

Materiam superabat Opus. – Ovid.[1]

From my own Apartment, September 1 3.

It is my Custom in a Dearth of News, to entertain my self with those Collections of Advertisements that appear at the End of all our publick Prints. These I consider as Accounts of News from the little World, in the same Manner that the foregoing Parts of the Paper are from the great. If in one we hear that a Sovereign Prince is fled from his Capital City, in the other we hear of a Tradesman who hath shut up his Shop, and run away. If in one we find the Victory of a General, in the other we see the Desertion of a private Soldier. I must confess, I have a certain Weakness in my Temper, that is often very much affected by these little Domestick Occurrences, and have frequently been caught with Tears in my Eyes over a melancholy Advertisement.

But to consider this Subject in its most ridiculous Lights, Advertisements are of great Use to the Vulgar: First of all, as they are Instruments of Ambition. A Man that is by no Means big enough for the °*Gazette*, may easily creep into the Advertisements; by which Means we often see an Apothecary in the same Paper of News with a Plenipotentiary, or a Running-Footman with an Ambassador. An Advertisement from *Pickadilly* goes down to Posterity, with an Article from *Madrid*; and *John Bartlett* of *Goodman's Fields*[2] is celebrated in the same Paper with the Emperor of *Germany*. Thus the Fable tells us, That the Wren mounted as high as the Eagle, by getting upon his Back.

A Second Use which this Sort of Writings have been turned to of late Years, has been the Management of Controversy, insomuch that above half the Advertisements one meets with now-a-Days are purely Polemical. The Inventors of *Strops for Razors* have written against one another this Way for several Years,[3] and that with great Bitterness; as the whole Argument *pro* and *con* in the Case of the *Morning Gowns* is still carried on after the same Manner.[4] I need not mention the several Proprietors of Dr. *Anderson*'s Pills;[5] nor take Notice of the many Satyrical Works of this Nature so frequently published by Dr. *Clark* who has had the Confidence to advertise upon that learned Knight, my very worthy Friend, Sir *William Read*[6]: But I shall not interpose in their Quarrel; Sir *William* can give him his own in Advertisements, that, in the Judgement of the Impartial, are as well penned as the Doctor's.

The Third and last Use of these Writings is, to inform the World where they may be furnished with almost every Thing that is necessary for Life. If a Man has Pains in his Head, Cholicks in his Bowels, or Spots in his Clothes, he may here meet with proper Cures and Remedies. If a Man would recover a Wife or a Horse that is stolen or strayed; if he wants new Sermons, °Electuaries, Asses Milk, or any Thing else, either for his Body or his Mind, this is the Place to look for them in.

The great Art in writing Advertisements, is the finding out a proper Method to catch the Reader's Eye; without which a good Thing may pass over unobserved, or be lost among Commissions of Bankrupt. Asterisks and Hands were formerly of great Use for this Purpose. Of late Years, the *N. B.* has been much in Fashion; as also little Cuts and Figures, the Invention of which we must ascribe to the Author of Spring-Trusses. I must not here omit the °blind *Italian* Character, which being scarce legible, always fixes and detains the Eye, and gives the curious Reader something like the Satisfaction of prying into a Secret.

But the great Skill in an Advertiser, is chiefly seen in the Style which he makes Use of. He is to mention *the universal Esteem, or general Reputation*, of Things that were never heard of. If he is a Physician or Astrologer, he must change his Lodgings frequently, and (though he never saw any Body in them besides his own Family) give publick Notice of it, *For the Information of the Nobility and Gentry*. Since I am thus usefully employed in writing Criticisms on the Works of these diminutive Authors, I must not pass over in Silence an Advertisement which has lately made its Appearance, and is written altogether in a *Ciceronian* Manner. It was sent to me, with Five Shillings, to be inserted among my Advertisements; but as it is a Pattern of good Writing in this Way, I shall give it a Place in the Body of my Paper.

The highest compounded Spirit of Lavender, the most glorious (if the Expression may be used) enlivening Scent and Flavour that can possibly be, which so raptures the Spirits, delights the Gust, and gives such Airs to the Countenance, as are not to be imagined but by those that have tried it. The meanest Sort of the Thing is admired by most Gentlemen and Ladies; but this far more, as by far it exceeds it, to the gaining among all a more than common Esteem. It is sold (in neat °Flint Bottles for the Pocket) only at the Golden-Key in Warton's-Court near Holborn-Bars, for 3s. 6d. with Directions.

At the same Time I recommend the several Flowers in which this Spirit of Lavender is wrapped up, (if the Expression may be used) I cannot excuse my Fellow-Labourers for admitting into their Papers several uncleanly Advertisements, not at all proper to appear in the Works of polite Writers. Among these I must reckon the *Carminitive Wind-expelling* Pills. If the Doctor had called them only his °Carminitive Pills, he had been as cleanly as one could have wished; but the Second Word entirely destroys the Decency of the First. There are other Absurdities of this Nature so very gross, that I dare not mention them; and shall therefore dismiss this Subject, with a publick Admonition to *Michael Parrot*, That he do not presume any more to mention a certain Worm he knows of, which, by the Way, has grown Seven Foot in my Memory; for, if I am not much mistaken, it is the same that was but Nine Foot long about Six Months ago.[7]

By the Remarks I have here made, it plainly appears, that a Collection of Advertisements is a Kind of Miscellany; the Writers of which, contrary to all Authors, except Men of Quality, give Money to the Booksellers who publish their Copies. The Genius of the Bookseller is chiefly shown in his Method of ranging and digesting these little Tracts. The last Paper I took up in my Hands, places them in the following Order:

The true Spanish Blacking for Shoes, &c.
The Beautifying Cream for the Face, &c.
Pease and Plaisters, &c.
Nectar and Ambrosia, &c.
Four Freehold Tenements of 15 l. per Annum, &c.

*₊*The Present State of England, &c.
†↓†Annotations upon the Tatler, &c.

A Commission of Bankrupt being awarded against B. L. Bookseller, &c.[8]

No. 230 [SWIFT]
Tuesday, 26 September to Thursday, 28 September 1710

[The continual corruption of our English tongue][1]
From my own Apartment, Sept. 27.

The following Letter has laid before me many great and manifest Evils in the World of Letters which I had overlooked; but they open to me a very busy Scene, and it will require no small Care and Application to amend Errors which are become so universal. The Affectation of Politeness is exposed in this Epistle with a great deal of Wit and Discernment; so that whatever Discourses I may fall into hereafter upon the Subjects the Writer treats of, I shall at present lay the Matter before the World without the least Alteration from the Words of my Correspondent.

To Isaac Bickerstaff *Esq*;

SIR,

'There are some Abuses among us of great Consequence, the Reformation of which is properly your Province; though as far as I have been conversant in your Papers, you have not yet considered them. These are the deplorable Ignorance that for some Years hath reigned among our *English* Writers, the great Depravity of our Tast, and the continual Corruption of our Style. I say nothing here of those who handle particular Sciences, Divinity, Law, Physick, and the like; I mean the Traders in History and Politicks, and the *Belles Lettres*; together with those by whom Books are not Translated, but (as the common Expressions are) *Done out of French, Latin*, or other Language, and *Made English*. I cannot but observe to you, that till of late Years, a *Grubstreet* Book was always bound in Sheepskin, with suitable Print and Paper, the Price never above a Shilling, and taken off wholly by common Tradesmen or Country

Pedlars; but now they appear in all Sizes and Shapes, and in all Places: They are handed about from Lap-fulls in every Coffee-house to Persons of Quality; are shewn in *Westminster-Hall* and the °Court of Requests. You may see them gilt and in Royal Paper of Five or Six Hundred Pages, and rated accordingly. I would engage to furnish you with a Catalogue of *English* Books published within the Compass of Seven Years past, which at the first Hand would cost you a Hundred Pounds, wherein you shall not be able to find Ten Lines together of common Grammar or common Sense.

'These two Evils, Ignorance and Want of Tast, have produced a Third; I mean the continual Corruption of our *English* Tongue, which, without some timely Remedy, will suffer more by the false Refinements of Twenty Years past, than it hath been improved in the foregoing Hundred. And this is what I design chiefly to enlarge upon, leaving the former Evils to your Animadversion.

'But instead of giving you a List of the late Refinements crept into our Language, I here send you the Copy of a Letter I received some Time ago from a most accomplished Person in this Way of Writing; upon which I shall make some Remarks. It is in these Terms:

> *SIR,*
> 'I *Cou'd n't* get the Things you sent for all *about Town* — I *thôt* to *ha'* come down myself, and then *I'd h' brôt 'um*; but I *ha'n't don't*, and I believe I *can't do't*, that's °*Pozz* — *Tom* begins to *gi'mself* Airs, because *he's* going with the °*Plenipo's* — 'Tis said, the *French* King will *bamboozl' us agen*, which *causes many Speculations*. The °*Jacks* and others of that *Kidney* are very *uppish*, and *alert upon't*, as you may see by their °*Phizz's* — *Will Hazzard* has got the °*Hipps*, having lost *to the Tune of* Five Hundr'd Pound, *thô* he understands Play very well, *no body better*. He has promis't me upon °*Rep*, to leave off Play; but you know 'tis a Weakness *he's* too apt to *give into, thô* he has as much Wit as any Man, *no body more*. He has lain *incog* ever since — The °*Mobb's* very quiet with us now — I believe you *thôt* I *banter'd* you in my last like a °*Country Put* — I *sha'n't* leave Town this Month, *&c.*'

'This Letter is in every Point an admirable Pattern of the present polite Way of Writing, nor is it of less Authority for being an Epistle: You may gather every Flower in it, with a Thousand more of equal Sweetness, from the Books, Pamphlets, and single Papers, offered us every Day in the Coffee-houses: And these are the Beauties introduced to supply the Want of Wit, Sense, Humour, and Learning, which formerly were looked upon as Qualifications for a Writer. If a Man of Wit, who died Forty Years ago, were to rise from the Grave on Purpose, How would he be able to read this Letter? And after he had got through that Difficulty, How would he be able to understand it? The first Thing that strikes your Eye, is the *Breaks* at the End of almost every Sentence, of which I know not the Use, only that it is a Refinement, and very frequently practised. Then you will observe the Abbreviations and Elisions, by which Consonants of most obdurate Sound are joined together, without one softening Vowel to intervene; and all this only to make One Syllable of Two, directly contrary to the Example of the *Greeks* and *Romans*, altogether of the *Gothick* Strain, and a natural Tendency towards relapsing into Barbarity, which delights in Monosyllables, and uniting of mute Consonants, as it is observable in all the Northern Languages. And this is still more visible in the next Refinement, which consists in pronouncing the first Syllable in a Word that has many, and dismissing the rest; such as °*Phizz*, °*Hipps*, °*Mobb*, °*Pozz*, °*Rep*, and many more, when we are already overloaded with Monosyllables, which are the Disgrace of our Language. Thus we cram one Syllable, and cut off the rest, as the Owl fattened her Mice after she had bit off their Legs, to prevent them from running away; and if ours be the same Reason for maiming our Words, it will certainly answer the End, for I am sure no other Nation will desire to borrow them. Some Words are hitherto but fairly split, and therefore only in their Way to Perfection; as *Incog*, and °*Plenipo*: But in a short Time, 'tis to be hoped, they will be further docked to *Inc*, and *Plen*. This Reflection has made me of late Years very impatient for a Peace, which I believe would save the Lives of many brave Words, as well as Men. The War has introduced abundance of Polysyllables, which will never be able to live many more Campaigns. *Speculations, Operations, Preliminaries, Ambassadors, Pallisadoes, Communication, Circumvallation, Battalions*, as numerous as they are, if they attack us too frequently in our Coffee-houses, we shall certainly put them to Flight, and cut off the Rear.

'The Third Refinement observable in the Letter I send you, consists in the Choice of certain Words invented by some *pretty Fellows*, such as *Banter, Bamboozle,* °*Country Put*, and *Kidney*, as it is there applied, some of which are now struggling for the Vogue, and others are in Possession of it. I have done my utmost for some Years past to stop the Progress of *Mobb* and *Banter*, but have been plainly born down by Numbers, and betrayed by those who promised to assist me.

'In the last Place, you are to take Notice of certain choice Phrases scattered through the Letter, some of them tolerable enough, till they were worn to Rags by servile Imitators. You might easily find them, though they were not in a different Print, and therefore I need not disturb them.

'These are the false Refinements in our Style which you ought to correct: First, by Argument and fair Means; but if those fail, I think you are to make Use of your Authority as Censor, and by an Annual *Index Expurgatorius* expunge all Words and Phrases that are offensive to good Sense, and condemn those barbarous Mutilations of Vowels and Syllables. In this last Point, the usual Pretence is, That they spell as they speak: A noble Standard for Language! To depend upon the Caprice of every Coxcomb, who because Words are the Cloathing of our Thoughts, cuts them out and shapes them as he pleases, and changes them of[te]ner than his Dress. I believe all reasonable People would be content that such Refiners were more sparing in their Words, and liberal in their Syllables: And upon this Head, I should be glad you would bestow some Advice upon several young Readers in our Churches, who coming up from the University [full fraught] with Admiration of our Town Politeness, will needs correct the Style of their Prayer-Books. In reading the Absolution, they are very careful to say *Pardons* and *Absolves*; and in the Prayer for the Royal Family, it must be, *Endue 'um, enrich 'um, prosper 'um*, and *bring 'um*. Then in their Sermons they use all the modern Terms of Art, *Sham, Banter,* °*Mob,* °*Bubble,* °*Bully,* °*Cutting, Shuffling,* and *Palming*; all which, and many more of the like Stamp, as I have heard them often in the Pulpit from such young °*Sophisters*, so I have read them in some of *those Sermons that have made most Noise of late.* The Design, it seems, is to avoid the dreadful Imputation of Pedantry; to shew us, that they know the Town, understand Men and Manners, and have not been poring upon old unfashionable Books in the University.

'I should be glad to see you the Instrument of introducing into our Style that Simplicity which is the best and truest Ornament of most Things in Life, which the politer Ages always aimed at in their Building and Dress, (°*Simplex Munditiis*) as well as their Productions of Wit. 'Tis manifest, that all new affected Modes of Speech, whether borrowed from the Court, the Town, or the Theatre, are the first perishing Parts in any Language; and, as I could prove by many Hundred Instances, have been so in ours. The Writings of *Hooker*, who was a Country Clergyman,[2] and of *Parsons* the Jesuit,[3] both in the reign of Queen *Elizabeth*, are in a Style that, with very few Allowances, would not offend any present Reader; much more clear and intelligible than those of Sir *H. Wotton*, Sir *Rob. Naunton, Osborn, Daniel* the Historian,[4] and several others who writ later; but being Men of the Court, and affecting the Phrases then in Fashion, they are often either not to be understood, or appear perfectly ridiculous.

'What Remedies are to be applied to these Evils, I have not Room to consider, having, I fear already taken up most of your Paper. Besides, I think it is our Office only to represent Abuses, and yours to redress them. I am with great Respect,

SIR,
Your, &c.'

No. 238 {SWIFT with STEELE}
Saturday, 14 October to Tuesday, 17 October 1710

['The Description of a City Shower'][1]

— *Poetica surgit*
Tempestas —   Juv.[2]

From my own Apartment, October 16.

Storms at Sea are so frequently described by the ancient Poets, and copied by the Moderns, that whenever I find the Winds begin to rise in a new Heroick Poem, I generally skip a Leaf or two till I come into Fair Weather. *Virgil*'s *Tempest* is a Master-piece in this

Kind, and is indeed so naturally drawn, that one who has made a Voyage can scarce read it without being Sea-sick.

Land-Showers are no less frequent among the Poets than the former, but I remember none of them which have not fallen in the Country; for which Reason they are generally filled with the Lowings of Oxen, and the Bleatings of Sheep, and very often embellished with a Rainbow.

Virgil's Land-Shower is likewise the best in its Kind: It is indeed a °Shower of Consequence, and contributes to the main Design of the Poem, by cutting off a tedious Ceremonial, and bringing Matters to a speedy Conclusion between Two Potentates of different Sexes. My ingenious Kinsman Mr. *Humphrey Wagstaff*, who treats of every Subject after a Manner that no other Author has done, and better than any other can do, has sent me the Description of a City Shower. I do not question but the Reader remembers my Cousin's Description of the Morning as it breaks in Town, which is printed in the 9th *Tatler*, and is another exquisite Piece of this Local Poetry:

> *Careful Observers may foretel the Hour*
> *(By sure Prognosticks) when to dread a Show'r:*
> *While Rain depends, the pensive Cat gives o'er*
> *Her Frolicks, and pursues her Tail no more.*
> *Returning Home at Night, you'll find the Sink*
> *Strike your offended Sense with double Stink.*
> *If you be wife, then go not far to dine,*
> *You'll spend in Coach-hire more than save in Wine.*
> *A coming Show'r your shooting Corns presage,*
> *Old Aches³ throb, your hollow Tooth will rage.*
> *Sauntring in Coffee-house is* Dulman *seen;*
> *He damns the Climate, and complains of Spleen.*
>
> *Mean while the South rising with dabbled Wings,*
> *A Sable Cloud athwart the Welkin flings,*
> *That swill'd more Liquor than it could contain,*
> *And like a Drunkard gives it up again.*
> *Brisk Susan whips her Linen from the Rope,*
> *While the first drizzling Show'r is born aslope.*
> *Such is that Sprinkling which some careless Quean*
> *Flirts on you from her Mop, but not so clean.*

You fly, invoke the Gods; then turning, stop
To rail; she singing, still whirls on her Mop.
Not yet, the Dust had shun'd th'unequal Strife,
But aided by the Wind, fought still for Life;
And wafted with its Foe by violent Gust,
'Twas doubtful which was Rain, and which was Dust.
Ah! where must needy Poet seek for Aid,
When Dust and Rain at once his Coat invade;
His only Coat, where Dust confus'd with Rain
Roughen the Nap, and leave a mingled Stain.

   Now in contiguous Drops the Flood comes down,
Threat'ning with Deluge this °devoted Town.
To Shops in Crowds the daggled Females fly,
Pretend to cheapen Goods, but nothing buy.
The Templer spruce, while ev'ry Spout's a-broach,
Stays till 'tis fair, yet seems to call a Coach.
The tuck'd-up Sempstress walks with hasty Strides,
While Streams run down her oil'd Umbrella's Sides.
Here various Kinds by various Fortunes led,
Commence Acquaintance underneath a Shed.
Triumphant Tories, and desponding Whigs,
Forget their Fewds, and join to save their Wigs.
Box'd in a Chair the Beau impatient sits,
While Spouts run clatt'ring o'er the Roof by Fits;
And ever and anon with frightful Din
The Leather sounds, he trembles from within.
So when Troy Chair-men bore the Wooden Steed,
Pregnant with Greeks, impatient to be freed.
(Those Bully Greeks, who, as the Moderns do,
Instead of paying Chair-men, run them thro'.)
Laoco'n struck the Outside with his Spear,
And each imprison'd Hero quak'd for Fear.

   Now from all Parts the swelling Kennels flow,
And bear their Trophies with them as they go:
Filth of all Hues and Odours seem to tell
What Street they sail'd from, by their Sight and Smell.
They, as each Torrent drives, with rapid Force,

From Smithfield *or St.* Pulchre*'s shape their Course,*
And in huge Confluent join'd at Snow-Hill *Ridge,*
Fall from the Conduit *prone to* Holborn-Bridge.
Sweepings from Butchers Stalls, Dung, Guts, and Blood,
Drown'd Puppies, stinking Sprats, all drench'd in Mud,
Dead Cats, and Turnip-Tops come tumbling down the Flood.

No. 242 [STEELE]
Tuesday, 24 *October to Thursday,* 26 *October* 1710

[Satire]

—Quis iniquæ
Tam patiens Urbis, tam ferreus ut teneat se? Juv.[1]

From my own Apartment, October 25.

It was with very great Displeasure I heard this Day a Man say of a Companion of his with an Air of Approbation, *You know* Tom *never fails of saying a spightful Thing.* He has a great deal of Wit, but Satyr is his particular Talent. *Did you mind how he put the young Fellow out of Countenance that pretended to talk to him?* Such impertinent Applauses, which one meets with every Day, put me upon considering what true Raillery and Satyr were in themselves; and this, methought, occurred to me from Reflection upon the great and excellent Persons that were admired for Talents this Way. When I had [run] over several such in my Thoughts, I concluded, (however unaccountable the Assertion might appear at first Sight) that good Nature was an essential Quality in a Satyrist, and that all the Sentiments which are beautiful in this Way of Writing must proceed from that Quality in the Author. Good Nature produces a Disdain of all Baseness, Vice, and Folly, which prompts [satirists] to express themselves with Smartness against the Errors of Men, without Bitterness towards their Persons. This Quality keeps the Mind in Equanimity, and never lets an Offence unreasonably throw a Man out of his Character. When *Virgil* said, He that did not hate *Bavius* might love *Mævius*,[2] he was in perfect good Humour and was not so much moved at their Absurdities, as passionately to call them Sots or Blockheads in a direct Invective, but laughed at them with a Delicacy of Scorn, without any Mixture of Anger.

The best good Man, with the worst-natured Muse, was the Character among us of a Gentleman as famous for his Humanity as his Wit.[3]

The ordinary Subjects for Satyr are such as incite the greatest Indignation in the best Tempers, and consequently Men of such a Make are the best qualified for speaking of the Offences in Humane Life. These Men can behold Vice and Folly when they injure Persons to whom they are wholly unacquainted, with the same Severity as others resent the Ills they do themselves. A good-natured Man cannot see an over-bearing Fellow put a bashful Man of Merit out of Countenance, or outstrip him in the Pursuit of any Advantage; but he is on Fire to succour the Oppressed, to produce the Merit of the one, and confront the Impudence of the other.

The Men of the greatest Character in this Kind were *Horace* and *Juvenal*. There is not, that I remember, one ill-natured Expression in all their Writings, not one Sentence of Severity which does not apparently proceed from the contrary Disposition. Whoever reads them, will, I believe, be of this Mind; and if they were read with this View, it may possibly perswade our young Fellows, that they may be very witty Men without speaking ill of any but those who deserve it: But in the Perusal of these Writers it may not be unnecessary to consider, that they lived in very different Times. *Horace* was intimate with a Prince of the greatest Goodness and Humanity imaginable, and his Court was formed after his Example: Therefore the Faults that Poet falls upon were little Inconsistencies in Behaviour, false Pretences to Politeness, or impertinent Affectations of what Men were not fit for. Vices of a coarser Sort could not come under his Consideration, or enter the Palace of *Augustus*. *Juvenal* on the other Hand lived under *Domitian*, in whose Reign every Thing that was great and noble was banished the Habitations of the Men in Power. Therefore he attacks Vice as it passes by in Triumph, not as it breaks into Conversation. The Fall of Empire, Contempt of Glory, and a general Degeneracy of Manners, are before his Eyes in all his Writings. In the Days of *Augustus*, to have talked like *Juvenal* had been Madness, or in those of *Domitian* like *Horace*. Morality and Virtue are every where recommended in *Horace*, as became a Man in a polite Court, from the Beauty, the

Propriety, the Convenience, of pursuing them. Vice and Corruption are attacked by *Juvenal* in a Style which denotes, he fears he shall not be heard without he calls to them in their own Language with a bare-faced Mention of the Villanies and Obscenities of his Contemporaries.

This accidental Talk of these Two great Men runs me from my Design, which was, to tell some Coxcombs that run about this Town with the Name of Smart Satyrical Fellows, that they are by no Means qualified for the Characters they pretend to, of being severe upon other Men, for they want good Nature. There is no Foundation in them for arriving at what they aim at; and they may as well pretend to flatter, as rail agreeably, without being good-natured.

There is a certain Impartiality necessary to make what a Man says bear any Weight with those he speaks to. This Quality, with Respect to Men's Errors and Vices, is never seen but in good-natured Men. They have ever such a Frankness of Mind, and Benevolence to all Men, that they cannot receive Impressions of Unkindness without mature Deliberation; and writing or speaking ill of a Man upon Personal Considerations, is so irreparable and mean an Injury, that no one possessed of this Quality is capable of doing it: But in all Ages there have been Interpreters to Authors when living, of the same Genius with the Commentators, into whose Hands they fall when dead. I dare say, it is impossible for any Man of more Wit than one of these to take any of the Four and twenty Letters, and form out of them a Name to describe the Character of a Vicious Man with greater Life, but one of these would immediately cry, Mr. such a One is meant in that Place. But the Truth of it is, Satyrists describe the Age, and Backbiters assign their Descriptions to private Men.

In all Terms of Reproof, when the Sentence appears to arise from Personal Hatred or Passion, it is not then made the Cause of Mankind, but a Misunderstanding between Two Persons. For this Reason, the Representations of a good-natured Man bear a Pleasantry in them, which shows there is no Malignity at Heart, and by Consequence are attended to by his Hearers or Readers because they are unprejudiced. This Deference is only what is due to him; for no Man thoroughly nettled can say a Thing general enough to pass off with the air of an Opinion declared, and not a Passion gratified. I remember a humorous Fellow at *Oxford*, when he heard any one had spoken ill of him, used to say, *I won't take my Revenge on him till I have forgiven him.* What he meant by this, was, That he would not enter upon this Subject, till it was grown as indifferent to him as any other; and I have, by this Rule, seen him more than once triumph over his Adversary with an inimitable Spirit and Humour; for he came to the Assault against a Man full of sore Places, and he himself invulnerable.

There is no Possibility of succeeding in a Satyrical Way of Writing or Speaking, except a Man throws himself quite out of the Question. It is great Vanity to think any one will attend a Thing because it is your Quarrel. You must make your Satyr the Concern of Society in general, if you would have it regarded. When it is so, the good Nature of a Man of Wit will prompt him to many brisk and disdainful Sentiments and Replies, to which all the Malice in the World will not be able to °repartee.

No. 249 [STEELE]
Thursday, 9 November to Saturday, 11 November 1710

[The life and adventures of a shilling][1]

Per varios Casus, per tot Discrimina Rerum, Tendimus.   – Virg.[2]

From my own Apartment, November 10.

I was last Night visited by a Friend of mine who has an inexhaustible Fund of Discourse, and never fails to entertain his Company with a Variety of Thoughts and Hints that are altogether new and uncommon. Whether it were in Complaisance to my Way of Living, or his real Opinion, he advanced the following Paradox, That it required much greater Talents to fill up and become a retired Life, than a Life of Business. Upon this Occasion he rallied very agreeably the busie Men of the Age, who only valued themselves for being in Motion, and passing through a Series of trifling and insignificant Actions. In the Heat of his Discourse, seeing a Piece of Money lying on my Table, I defie (says he) any of these active Persons to produce half the Adventures that this

Twelvepenny-Piece has been engaged in, were it possible for him to give us an Account of his Life.

My Friend's Talk made so odd an Impression upon my Mind, that soon after I was a-Bed I fell insensibly into a most unaccountable *Resverie*, that had neither Moral nor Design in it, and cannot be so properly called a Dream as a Delirium.

Methoughts the Shilling that lay upon the Table reared it self upon its Edge, and turning the Face towards me, opened its Mouth, and in a soft Silver Sound gave me the following Account of his Life and Adventures:

I was born, says he, on the Side of a Mountain, near a little Village of *Peru*, and made a Voyage to *England* in a Ingot, under the Convoy of Sir *Francis Drake*. I was, soon after my Arrival, taken out of my *Indian* Habit, refined, naturalized, and put into the *British* Mode, with the Face of Queen *Elizabeth* on one Side, and the Arms of the Country on the other. Being thus equipped, I found in me a wonderful Inclination to ramble, and visit all the Parts of the new World into which I was brought. The People very much favoured my natural Disposition, and shifted me so fast from Hand to Hand, that before I was Five Years old, I had travelled into almost every Corner of the Nation. But in the Beginning of my Sixth Year, to my unspeakable Grief, I fell into the Hands of a miserable old Fellow, who clapped me into an Iron Chest, where I found Five Hundred more of my own Quality who lay under the same Confinement. The only Relief we had, was to be taken out and counted over in the fresh Air every Morning and Evening. After an Imprisonment of several Years, we heard some Body knocking at our Chest, and breaking it open with an Hammer. This we found was the old Man's Heir, who, as his Father lay a dying, was so good as to come to our Release: He separated us that very Day. What was the Fate of my Companions I know not: As for my self, I was sent to the Apothecary's Shop for a Pint of °Sack. The Apothecary gave me to an Herb-Woman, the Herb-Woman to a Butcher, the Butcher to a Brewer, and the Brewer to his Wife, who made a Present of me to a Nonconformist Preacher. After this Manner I made my Way merrily through the World; for, as I told you before, we Shillings love nothing so much as travelling. I sometimes fetched in a Shoulder of Mutton, sometimes a Play-

Book, and often had the Satisfaction to treat a Templer at a Twelvepenny °Ordinary, or carry him with Three Friends to *Westminster-Hall*.

In the Midst of this pleasant Progress which I made from Place to Place, I was arrested by a superstitious old Woman, who shut me up in a greasy Purse, in Pursuance of a foolish Saying, That while she kept a Queen *Elizabeth*'s Shilling about her, she should never be without Money. I continued here a close Prisoner for many Months, till at last I was exchanged for Eight and Forty Farthings.

I thus rambled from Pocket to Pocket till the Beginning of the Civil Wars, when, to my Shame be it spoken, I was employed in raising Soldiers against the King: For being of a very tempting Breadth, a Serjeant made Use of me to inveigle Country Fellows, and list them in the Service of the Parliament.

As soon as he had made one Man sure, his Way was to oblige him to take a Shilling of a more homely Figure, and then practise the same Trick upon another. Thus I continued doing great Mischief to the Crown, till my Officer chancing one Morning to walk Abroad earlier than ordinary, sacrificed me to his Pleasures, and made Use of me to seduce a Milk-Maid. This Wench bent me, and gave me to her Sweetheart, applying more properly than she intended the usual Form of, *To my Love and from my Love*. This ungenerous Gallant marrying her within few Days after, pawned me for a Dram of Brandy, and drinking me out next Day, I was beaten flat with an Hammer, and again set a running.

After many Adventures, which it would be tedious to relate, I was sent to a young Spendthrift, in Company with the Will of his deceased Father. The young Fellow, who I found was very extravagant, gave great Demonstrations of Joy at the receiving the Will; but opening it, he found himself disinherited and cut off from the Possession of a fair Estate, by Vertue of my being made a Present to him. This put him into such a Passion, that after having taken me in his Hand, and cursed me, he °squirred me away from him as far as he could fling me. I chanced to light in an unfrequented Place under a dead Wall, where I lay undiscovered and useless, during the Usurpation of *Oliver Cromwell*.

About a Year after the King's Return, a poor Cavalier that was walking there about Dinner-time fortunately cast his Eye upon me, and, to the great Joy of us both, carried me to a Cook's Shop, where he dined upon me, and drank the King's Health. When I came again into the World, I found that I had been happier in my Retirement than I thought, having probably by that Means escaped wearing a monstrous Pair of Breeches.[3]

Being now of great Credit and Antiquity, I was rather looked upon as a Medal than an ordinary Coin; for which Reason a Gamester laid hold of me, and converted me to a Counter, having got together some Dozens of us for that Use. We led a melancholy Life in his Possession, being busy at those Hours wherein Current Coin is at rest, and partaking the Fate of our Master, being in a few Moments valued at a Crown, a Pound, or a Sixpence, according to the Situation in which the Fortune of the Cards placed us. I had at length the good Luck to see my Master °break, by which Means I was again sent Abroad under my primitive Denomination of a Shilling.

I shall pass over many other Accidents of less Moment, and hasten to that fatal Catastrophe when I fell into the Hands of an °Artist who conveyed me under Ground, and with an unmerciful Pair of Sheers cut off my °Titles, clipped my °Brims, retrenched my Shape, rubbed me to my inmost Ring, and, in short, so spoiled and pillaged me, that he did not leave me worth a Groat. You may think what a Confusion I was in to see my self thus curtailed and disfigured. I should have been ashamed to have shown my Head, had not all my old Acquaintance been reduced to the same shameful Figure, excepting some few that were punched through the Belly. In the midst of this general Calamity, when every Body thought our Misfortune irretrievable, and our Case desperate, we were thrown into the Furnace together, and (as it often happens with Cities rising out of a Fire) appeared with greater Beauty and Lustre than we could ever boast of before. What has happened to me since this Change of Sex[4] which you now see, I shall take some other Opportunity to relate. In the mean Time I shall only repeat Two Adventures, as being very extraordinary, and neither of them having ever happened to me above once in my Life. The First was, my being in a Poet's Pocket, who was so taken with the Brightness and Novelty of my Appearance, that it gave Occasion to the finest Burlesque Poem in the *British* Language, entituled from me, *The*

Splendid Shilling.[5] The Second Adventure, which I must not omit, happened to me in the Year 1703, when I was given away in Charity to a blind Man; but indeed this was by a Mistake, the Person who gave me having heedlessly thrown me into the Hat among a Pennyworth of Farthings.

No. 271 [STEELE]
Saturday, 30 December 1710 to Tuesday, 2 January 1711

[Richard Steele bids his readers farewell as Isaac Bickerstaff]

The Printer having informed me, that there are as many of these Papers printed as will make Four Volumes, I am now come to the End of my Ambition in this Matter, and have nothing further to say to the World under the Character of *Isaac Bickerstaff*. This Work has indeed for some Time been disagreeable to me, and the Purpose of it wholly lost by my being so long understood as the Author. I never designed in it to give any Man any secret Wound by my Concealment, but spoke in the Character of an old Man, a Philosopher, an Humorist, an Astrologer, and a Censor, to allure my Reader with the Variety of my Subjects, and insinuate, if I could, the Weight of Reason with the Agreeableness of Wit. The general Purpose of the whole has been to recommend Truth, Innocence, Honour, and Virtue, as the chief Ornaments of Life; but I considered, that Severity of Manners was absolutely necessary to him who would censure others, and for that Reason, and that only, chose to talk in a Mask. I shall not carry my Humility so far as to call my self a vicious Man; but at the same Time must confess, my Life is at best but pardonable. And with no greater Character than this, a Man would make but an indifferent Progress in attacking prevailing and fashionable Vices, which Mr. *Bickerstaff* has done with a Freedom of Spirit that would have lost both its Beauty and Efficacy, had it been pretended to by Mr. *Steele*.

As to the Work it self, the Acceptance it has met with is the best Proof of its Value; but I should err against that Candour which an honest Man should always carry about him, if I did not own, that the most approved Pieces in it were written by others, and those which have been most excepted against by my self. The Hand that has assisted me in those noble Discourses upon the Immortality of the Soul, the glorious Prospects of another Life, and the most sublime Idea's of Religion and Virtue, is a Person who is too fondly my Friend ever to own them; but I should little deserve to be his, if I usurped the Glory of them. I must acknowledge at the same Time, that I think the finest Strokes of Wit and Humour in all Mr. *Bickerstaff*'s Lucubrations are those for which he is also beholden to him.[1]

As for the Satyrical Parts of these Writings, those against the Gentlemen who profess Gaming are the most licentious; but the main of them I take to come from losing Gamesters, as Invectives against the Fortunate; for in very many of them, I was very little else but the Transcriber. If any have been more particularly °marked at, such Persons may impute it to their own Behaviour, (before they were touched upon) in publickly speaking their Resentment against the Author, and professing they would support any Man who should insult him. When I mention this Subject, I hope Major-General *Davenport*, Brigadier *Bisset*, and my Lord *Forbes*, will accept of my Thanks for their frequent good Offices, in professing their Readiness to partake any Danger that should befall me in so just an Undertaking, as the Endeavour to banish Fraud and °Couzenage from the Presence and Conversation of Gentlemen.

But what I find is the least excusable Part of all this Work, is, That I have, in some Places in it, touched upon Matters which concern both the Church and State. All I shall say for this is, That the Points I alluded to are such as concerned every Christian and Freeholder in *England*; and I could not be cold enough to conceal my Opinion on Subjects which related to either of those Characters. But Politicks apart, I must confess, it has been a most exquisite Pleasure to me to frame Characters of Domestick Life, and put those Parts of it which are least observed into an agreeable View; to enquire into the Seeds of Vanity and Affectation, to lay before my Readers the Emptiness of Ambition: In a Word, to trace Humane Life through all its Mazes and Recesses, and show much shorter Methods than Men ordinarily practise, to be happy, agreeable, and great.

But to enquire into Men's Faults and Weaknesses has something in it so unwelcome, that I have often seen People in Pain to act before me, whose Modesty only make[s] them think themselves liable to Censure. This, and a Thousand other nameless Things, have made it an irksome Task to me to personate Mr. *Bickerstaff* any longer; and I believe it does not often happen, that the Reader is delighted where the Author is displeased.

All I can now do for the further Gratification of the Town, is to give them a faithful Index and Explication of Passages and Allusions, and sometimes of Persons intended in the several scattered Parts of the Work. At the same Time, the succeeding Volumes shall discover which of the whole have been written by me, and which by others, and by whom, as far as I am able, or permitted.[2]

Thus I have voluntarily done what I think all Authors should do when called upon. I have published my Name to my Writings, and given my self up to the Mercy of the Town (as *Shakespear* expresses it) with all my Imperfections on my Head.[3] The indulgent Reader's

> *Most Obliged,*
> *Most Obedient*
> *Humble Servant,*
> Richard Steele.

Advertisements

☞ The THIRD Volume of these LUCUBRATIONS being just finished, on a large Letter in Octavo, such as please to subscribe for it on a Royal Paper, to keep up their Sets, are desired to send their Names to Charles Lillie, Perfumer, at the Corner of Beauford-Buildings in the Strand, or John Morphew near Stationers Hall. Where the First and Second Volumes are to be delivered.

⁂ Bibliotheca Cotterelliana; or, A Catalogue of the Library of the late eminent and learned Sir Charles Cotterell, consisting of a large Collection of the most valuable Authors in Gr. Lat. Spanish, Italian, French, and English, the best Editions, and well bound; will begin to be sold by Auction on Monday January 8, at Exeter-Change in the Strand, from 5 to 8 every Evening till all are sold: By Edm. Curll, Bookseller, against St. Dunstan's Church, Fleetstreet; where Catalogues are to be delivered Gratis: Also by J. Harding at the Post-house in St. Martin's-lane, R. Parker under the Royal Exchange, H. Clements in St. Paul's Church-yard, B. Barker in Westminster Hall, and at the Place of Sale.

⁂ For the further Improvement of Dancing, A Treatise of CHOROGRAPHY, or the Art of dancing Country Dances after a new Character; in which the Figures, Steps, and Manner of Performing, are described, and the Rules demonstrated in an easie Method, adapted to the meanest Capacity. Translated from the French of Mons. Feuillet, and improved with many Additions; all fairly engraved on Copper Plates: And a new Collection of Country Dances, described in the same Character. By John Essex. To which is now published; Six new Country Dances, and Twelve new Minuets and Rigadoons, by the same Author, which may either be had singly at 1s. each or else with the aforesaid Book at the former Price of 5s. Sold by J. Walsh, Musical Instrument Maker in Ordinary to Her Majesty, and P. Randall, at the Harp and Hautboy in Katherine-street in the Strand; J. Hare at the Viol and Flute in Cornhill; and J. Collins at the Buck without Temple-Bar.

⁂ On a Sheet of Imperial Paper; The Young Accomptant's Remembrancer; directing him to find the proper Debtors and Creditors in the most usual Transactions and Occurrences of Trade; with the Method of Ballancing Accounts, and Transferring them into a new Leidger. (The 4th Edition.) by Tho. Mercer of the Bank. Sold by John Lyons in Philpot-lane near Fenchurch-street, who carefully teaches a Scheme of Merchants Accompts by a new Method, purposely composed by the said Author, to exemplify the Remembrancer. He likewise continues to teach Writing and Arithmetick, as formerly.

⁂ The London new Method and Art of teaching Children to Spell and Read, so as they may, without the Help of any other Books, read the Bible in less than 12 Months. This Way of Teaching is approved by most Schoolmasters, &c. Price bound 6d. with good Allowance to such as (sell or) give them to Charity-Schools, &c. Sold by Edm. Parker at the Bible and Crown in Lombard-street near Stocks-market.

THE Sale of the Rich BED and HANGINGS, which was seen at Westminster and Drapers Hall, will be drawn the 10th of this Instant January. All Persons that design to become Adventurers, are desired to take out their Tickets speedily, which are to be had at One Guinea apiece, with new Proposals, at St. James's and Young Man's Coffee-houses; at Mr. Lillie's, Perfumer, at Beauford-Buildings, Mrs. Betly's in Bow-street, Covent-Garden; Mr. Fleming's, Goldsmith, against St. Dunstan's Church; Mr. Motteaux in Leadenhall-street, Mr. Nath. Carpenter's, Merchant, in St. Clement's-lane, Lombard-street, (who stands Security for the fair Performance) and at the other Places mentioned in the Proposals. Part of the Goods may be seen at the said Mr. Carpenter's and Mrs. Betly's.

At the Golden Sugar-Loaf right against the Horse at Charing-Cross, is sold Morning-Gowns for Men and Women, of rich golden Sattins, fine japan'd and stained Silks, Thread Sattins, flowered Silks, Stuffs, and Callicoes, being really the Goods of Shop-keepers that have lately broke. To be sold a great Pennyworth, the lowest Prizes being set on each Gown, being the right old Gown Shop.

⁂ A Book entitled, Physico-Mechanical Experiments on various Subjects; or, An Account of several surprising Phenomena touching Light and Electricity produceable on the Attrition of Bodies. Together with new Observations on the Ascent of Liquids between the nearly contiguous Surfaces of different Bodies, the Pressure and Retraction of Air, the different Densities of that Element, from the greatest Degree of Heat to that of Cold in this Climate; the Propagation of Sound; and on divers other Heads not before taken Notice of. To which are added, the Explana-

tions of all the Machines, (the Figures of which are done from Copper curiously engraved) and other Apparatus used in making the Experiments. Sold by J. Knapton, H. Clements, R. Smith, Booksellers; and in Hind-court against Water-lane, Fleetstreet, by the Author F. Hauksbee, F. R. S. 4to. Price bound 6s.

ALL Persons who for themselves or Friends, having red and grey Hairs, would have 'em dyed and turned black or dark-brown Colour, will find entire Satisfaction, as a great many have already, in the Use of a clear Water found out by Mr. Michon, and is to be sold at the said Mr. Michon's, Goldsmith, at the Crown and Pearl in Grafton-street; at P. Varenne's, Bookseller, at Seneca's-Head near Somerset-House in the Strand; at the Rainbow Coffee-house beyond the Royal-Exchange in Cornhill; at Hen. Ribbotteau's at the Crown over-against Exeter-Exchange in the Strand; and A. Bell at the Cross-Keys and Bible in Cornhill.

AIR Pumps, both single and double Barrels, with Apparatus for the many Experiments, demonstrating the several Properties of the Air; Machines for condensing Air; small Air Pumps, with Glasses for the new and most approved Way of Cupping; Scarrificators, one of which at once makes 10, another 13, another 16, effectual Incisions; Syphons, and Blow-pipes with Valves for Anatomical Injections; Hydrostatical Ballances for finding the specifick Gravities of Liquids and Solids, with Ease and Accuracy: All which, according to their latest Improvements, with Directions how to use and order them on all Occasions, are sold only in Hind-court against Water-lane, Fleetstreet, by F. Hauksbee, Author of them.

FOR Sale by the Candle, on Thursday next the 4th Instant, at Lloyd's Coffee-house in Lombard-street, at 5 in the Afternoon, 54 Pipes of new excellent Canary Wines, neat, (only one Cask in a Lot) racy, and of a delicate Flavour, compleating the Cargo of the Martin Galley, just landed; and 4 Pipes of new Zant White-Wine, of a very fine Flavour, neat, in a Cellar in the Gate-way of Buttolph-Wharf, and up two Pair of Stairs on the said Wharf fronting the Thames, between London-Bridge and Billingsgate. Also 15 Pipes and 16 Hhds of Red-Wine, fit for Draught, 1 Hhd of White-Wine, 1 Pipe and 1 Hhd of Maderas, 1 Ullage Butt of White Bottoms, 1 Aum of Red ditto, and 300 Flasks of Florence Wine; in Vaults under the House of the Widow Hinchman in Buttolph-Lane near the Queen's Weigh-house. All the aforesaid Wines to be seen and tasted all Day to Morrow, and Thursday till the Time of Sale. To be sold by Tho. Tomkins, Broker, in Seething-lane, between Tower-street and Crouched-Fryars.

FOR Sale by the Candle, on Wednesday the 10th Instant, at Lloyd's Coffee-house in Lombard-street, at 9 in the Forenoon, about 36 Tuns of new excellent French (Prize) Claret, fresh, deep, bright, and of a most curious Flavour, of the best Growths, and of the very last Vintage; 5 Puncheons of French (Prize) Brandy, 4 Tuns of new French (Prize) White Wine, extraordinary good; 28 Barrels of new superfine Pruants, and 22 Chests of very good Soap; the entire Cargoes of two French

Prizes brought into Dartmouth by Capt. Daniel Nastell of Guernsey, now in the Custody of Mr. Tho. Plumley, Merchant, in Dartmouth aforesaid. And there shall be exposed to View and Tast the aforementioned Wines, Brandy, Pruants, and Soap, till the Time of Sale. Catalogues shall be timely dispersed. To be sold by Thomas Tomkins, Broker, in Seething-lane.

THE Late Right Hon. the Lord Brooks's Houshold-Goods, Plate, Linen, Pewter, Brass, fine India japan'd Cabinets, Screens, China, &c. will be sold by Auction at his Lordship's late Dwelling House in Arlington-street near St. James's, on Tuesday the 9th Instant. The Goods, &c. to be seen on Friday, Saturday, and Monday next, before the Sale. The Sale to begin at Ten in the Morning, and to continue till all are sold. Catalogues to be had at the Place of Sale.

THE Sale of Goods at Mr. Stocton's not being yet full, Notice is hereby given, That it is, by the Consent of the Adventurers, defer'd till the 20th Instant, when it will most certainly be drawn, or the Money return'd; 2s. each Ticket, 773 Prizes, one at 100 l. one at 50 l. two at 30 l. &c. 12 Blanks to one Lot. Tickets to be had at the said Mr. Stocton's at the Bell in Henrietta-street, Covent-Garden; at Mr. Amson's at the Gold Ring the Corner of Salisbury Court; where Satisfaction may be had of the Value of the Goods, and the Goods seen, there being only a just and living Profit received; and at Mrs. Davis's, a Milliner in the Strand, near Hungerford-Market. Note, This is the very last Sale of Goods in this Manner.

Essays from
THE SPECTATOR

The SPECTATOR.

Non fumum ex fulgore, fed ex fumo dare lucem
Cogitat, ut fpeciofa dehinc miracula promat. Hor.

To be Continued every Day.

Thurfday, March 1. 1711.

I Have obferved, that a Reader feldom perufes a Book with Pleafure 'till he knows whether the Writer of it be a black or a fair Man, of a mild or cholerick Difpofition, Married or a Batchelor, with other Particulars of the like nature, that conduce very much to the right Underftanding of an Author. To gratify this Curiofity, which is fo natural to a Reader, I defign this Paper, and my next, as Prefatory Difcourfes to my following Writings, and fhall give fome Account in them of the feveral Perfons that are engaged in this Work. As the chief Trouble of Compiling, Digefting and Correcting will fall to my Share, I muft do my felf the Juftice to open the Work with my own Hiftory.

I was born to a fmall Hereditary Eftate, which I find, by the Writings of the Family, was bounded by the fame Hedges and Ditches in *William* the Conqueror's Time that it is at prefent, and has been delivered down from Father to Son whole and entire, without the Lofs or Acquifition of a fingle Field or Meadow, during the Space of fix hundred Years. There goes a Story in the Family, that when my Mother was gone with Child of me about three Months, fhe dreamt that fhe was brought to Bed of a Judge: Whether this might proceed from a Law-Suit which was then depending in the Family, or my Father's being a Juftice of the Peace, I cannot determine; for I am not fo vain as to think it prefaged any Dignity that I fhould arrive at in my future Life, though that was the Interpretation which the Neighbourhood put upon it. The Gravity of my Behaviour at my very firft Appearance in the World, and all the Time that I fucked, feemed to favour my Mother's Dream: For, as fhe has often told me, I threw away my Rattle before I was two Months old, and would not make ufe of my Coral 'till they had taken away the Bells from it.

As for the reft of my Infancy, there being nothing in it remarkable, I fhall pafs it over in Silence. I find, that, during my Nonage, I had the Reputation of a very fullen Youth, but was always a Favourite of my School-Mafter, who ufed to fay, *that my Parts were folid and would wear well.* I had not been long at the Univerfity, before I diftinguifhed my felf by a moft profound Silence: For during the Space of eight Years, excepting in the publick Exercifes of the College, I fcarce uttered the Quantity of an hundred Words; and indeed do not remember that I ever fpoke three Sentences together in my whole Life. Whilft I was in this Learned Body I applied my felf with fo much Diligence to my Studies, that there are very few celebrated Books, either in the Learned or the Modern Tongues, which I am not acquainted with.

Upon the Death of my Father I was refolved to travel into Foreign Countries, and therefore left the Univerfity, with the Character of an odd unaccountable Fellow, that had a great deal of Learning, if I would but fhow it. An infatiable Thirft after Knowledge carried me into all the Countries of *Europe*, where there was any thing new or ftrange to be feen; nay, to fuch a Degree was my Curiofity raifed, that having read the Controverfies of fome great Men concerning the Antiquities of *Egypt*, I made a Voyage to *Grand Cairo*, on purpofe to take the Meafure of a Pyramid; and as foon as I had fet my felf right in that Particular, returned to my Native Country with great Satisfaction.

I have paffed my latter Years in this City, where I am frequently feen in moft publick Places, tho' there are not above half a dozen of my felect Friends that know me; of whom my next Paper fhall give a more particular Account. There is no Place of Publick Refort, wherein I do not often make my Appearance; fometimes I am feen thrufting my Head into a Round of Politicians at *Will's*, and liftning with great Attention to the Narratives that are made in thofe little Circular Audiences. Sometimes I fmoak a Pipe at *Child's*; and whilft I feem attentive to nothing but the *Poft-Man*, over-hear the Converfation of every Table in the Room. I appear on *Sunday* Nights at St. *James's* Coffee-Houfe, and fometimes join the little Committee of Politicks in the inner-Room, as one who comes there to hear and improve. My Face is likewife very well known at the *Grecian*, the *Cocoa-Tree*, and in the Theaters both of *Drury-Lane*, and the *Hay-Market*. I have been taken for a Merchant upon

I Form and Framework:
Mr Spectator and the Club

No. 1 [ADDISON]

[Mr Spectator introduces himself]
Thursday, 1 March 1711

Non fumum ex fulgore, sed ex fumo dare lucem
Cogitat, ut speciosa dehinc miracula promat.   Hor.[1]

I have observed, that a Reader seldom peruses a Book with Pleasure, 'till he knows whether the Writer of it be a black or a fair Man, of a mild or cholerick Disposition, Married or a Batchelor, with other Particulars of the like nature, that conduce very much to the right understanding of an Author. To gratifie this Curiosity, which is so natural to a Reader, I design this Paper, and my next, as Prefatory Discourses to my following Writings, and shall give some Account in them of the several Persons that are engaged in this Work. As the chief Trouble of Compiling, Digesting, and Correcting will fall to my Share, I must do my self the Justice to open the Work with my own History.

I was born to a small Hereditary Estate, which, according to the Tradition of the Village where it lies, was bounded by the same Hedges and Ditches in *William* the Conqueror's Time that it is at present, and has been delivered down from Father to Son whole and entire, without the Loss or Acquisition of a single Field or Meadow, during the Space of six hundred Years. There runs a Story in the Family, that when my Mother was gone with Child of me about three Months, she dreamt that she was brought to Bed of a Judge: Whether this might proceed from a Law-Suit which was then depending in the Family, or my Father's being a Justice of the Peace, I cannot determine; for I am not so vain as to think it presaged any Dignity that I should arrive at in my future Life, though that was the Interpretation which the Neighbourhood put upon it. The Gravity of my Behaviour at my very first Appearance in the World, and all the Time that I sucked, seemed to favour my Mother's Dream: For, as she has often told me, I threw away my Rattle before I was two Months old, and would not make use of my °Coral 'till they had taken away the Bells from it.

As for the rest of my Infancy, there being nothing in it remarkable, I shall pass it over in Silence. I find, that, during my Nonage, I had the Reputation of a very sullen Youth, but was always a Favourite of my School-Master, who used to say, *that my Parts were solid and would wear well.* I had not been long at the University, before I distinguished my self by a most profound Silence: For during the Space of eight Years, excepting in the publick °Exercises of the College, I scarce uttered the Quantity of an hundred Words; and indeed do not remember that I ever spoke three Sentences together in my whole Life. Whilst I was in this Learned Body I applied my self with so much Diligence to my Studies, that there are very few celebrated Books, either in the Learned or the Modern Tongues, which I am not acquainted with.

Upon the Death of my Father I was resolved to travel into Foreign Countries, and therefore left the University, with the Character of an odd unaccountable Fellow, that had a great deal of Learning, if I would but show it. An insatiable Thirst after Knowledge carried me into all the Countries of *Europe*, in which there was any thing new or strange to be seen; nay, to such a Degree was my Curiosity raised, that having read the Controversies of some great Men concerning the Antiquities of *Egypt*, I made a Voyage to *Grand Cairo*, on purpose to take the Measure of a Pyramid; and as soon as I had set my self right in that Particular, returned to my Native Country with great Satisfaction.

I have passed my latter Years in this City, where I am frequently seen in most publick Places, tho' there are not above half a dozen of my select Friends that know me; of whom my next Paper shall give a more particular Account. There is no Place of general Resort, wherein I do not often make my Appearance; sometimes I am seen thrusting my Head into a Round of Politicians at *Will*'s, and listning with great Attention to the Narratives that are made in those little Circular Audiences. Sometimes I smoak a Pipe at

Child's; and whilst I seem attentive to nothing but the °*Post-Man*, over-hear the Conversation of every Table in the Room. I appear on *Sunday* Nights at St. *James*'s Coffee-House, and sometimes join the little Committee of Politicks in the Inner Room, as one who comes there to hear and improve. My Face is likewise very well known at the *Grecian*, the *Cocoa-Tree*, and in the Theatres both of *Drury-Lane* and the *Hay-Market*. I have been taken for a Merchant upon the *Exchange* for above these ten Years, and sometimes pass for a *Jew* in the Assembly of Stock-Jobbers at *Jonathan*'s. In short, where-ever I see a Cluster of People I always mix with them, though I never open my Lips but in my own Club.²

Thus I live in the World, rather as a Spectator of Mankind, than as one of the Species; by which means I have made my self a Speculative Statesman, Soldier, Merchant and Artizan, without ever medling with any Practical Part in Life. I am very well versed in the Theory of an Husband, or a Father, and can discern the Errors in the °Oeconomy, Business and Diversion of others, better than those who are engaged in them; as Standers-by discover °Blots, which are apt to escape those who are in the Game. I never espoused any Party with Violence, and am resolved to observe an exact Neutrality between the Whigs and Tories, unless I shall be forced to declare my self by the Hostilities of either Side. In short, I have acted in all the Parts of my Life as a Looker-on, which is the Character I intend to preserve in this Paper.

I have given the Reader just so much of my History and Character, as to let him see I am not altogether unqualified for the Business I have undertaken. As for other Particulars in my Life and Adventures, I shall insert them in following Papers, as I shall see occasion. In the mean time, when I consider how much I have seen, read and heard, I begin to blame my own Taciturnity; and since I have neither Time nor Inclination to communicate the Fulness of my Heart in Speech, I am resolved to do it in Writing; and to Print my self out, if possible, before I Die. I have been often told by my Friends, that it is Pity so many useful Discoveries which I have made, should be in the Possession of a Silent Man. For this Reason therefore, I shall publish a Sheet-full of Thoughts every Morning, for the Benefit of my Contemporaries; and if I can any way contribute to the Diversion or Improvement of the Country in which I live, I shall leave it, when I am summoned out of it, with the secret Satisfaction of thinking that I have not Lived in vain.

There are three very material Points which I have not spoken to in this Paper, and which, for several important Reasons, I must keep to my self, at least for some Time: I mean, an Account of my Name, my Age, and my Lodgings. I must confess I would gratifie my Reader in any thing that is reasonable; but as for these three Particulars, though I am sensible they might tend very much to the Embellishment of my Paper, I cannot yet come to a Resolution of communicating them to the Publick. They would indeed draw me out of that Obscurity which I have enjoyed for many Years, and expose me in Publick Places to several Salutes and Civilities, which have been always very disagreeable to me; for the greatest Pain I can suffer, is the being talked to, and being stared at. It is for this Reason likewise, that I keep my Complexion and Dress as very great Secrets; tho' it is not impossible but I may make Discoveries of both, in the Progress of the Work I have undertaken.

After having been thus particular upon my self, I shall in to-Morrow's Paper give an Account of those Gentlemen who are concerned with me in this Work. For, as I have before intimated, a Plan of it is laid and concerted (as all other Matters of Importance are) in a Club. However, as my Friends have engaged me to stand in the Front, those who have a mind to correspond with me, may direct their Letters To the SPECTATOR, at Mr. *Buckley's* in *Little Britain*. For I must further acquaint the Reader, that tho' our Club meets only on *Tuesdays* and *Thursdays*, we have appointed a Committee to sit every Night, for the Inspection of all such Papers as may contribute to the Advancement of the Publick Weal.   C

No. 2 [STEELE]

[The Club]

Friday, 2 March 1711

— *Ast Alii sex*
Et plures uno conclamant ore. —   Juv.[1]

The first of our Society is a Gentleman of *Worcestershire*, of antient Descent, a Baronet, his Name Sir ROGER DE COVERLY. His great Grandfather was Inventor of that famous Country-Dance which is called after him.[2] All who know that Shire, are very well acquainted with the Parts and Merits of Sir ROGER. He is a Gentleman that is very singular in his Behaviour, but his Singularities proceed from his good Sense, and are Contradictions to the Manners of the World, only as he thinks the World is in the wrong. However, this Humour creates him no Enemies, for he does nothing with Sourness or Obstinacy; and his being unconfined to Modes and Forms, makes him but the readier and more capable to please and oblige all who know him. When he is in Town he lives in *Soho-Square:* It is said he keeps himself a Batchelor by reason he was crossed in Love, by a perverse beautiful Widow of the next County to him. Before this Disappointment, Sir ROGER was what you call a fine Gentleman, had often supped with my Lord *Rochester* and Sir *George Etherege*, fought a Duel upon his first coming to Town, and kicked Bully *Dawson* in a publick Coffee-house for calling him Youngster.[3] But being ill used by the above-mentioned Widow, he was very serious for a Year and a half; and though, his Temper being naturally jovial, he at last got over it, he grew careless of himself, and never dressed afterwards; he continues to wear a Coat and Doublet of the same Cut that were in Fashion at the Time of his Repulse, which, in his merry Humours, he tells us, has been in and out twelve Times since he first wore it. 'Tis said Sir ROGER grew humble in his Desires after he had forgot this cruel Beauty, insomuch that it is reported he has frequently offended in Point of Chastity with Beggars and Gypsies: But this is looked upon by his Friends rather as Matter of Raillery than Truth. He is now in his Fifty sixth Year, cheerful, gay, and hearty, keeps a good House both in Town and Country; a great Lover of Mankind; but there is such a mirthful Cast in his Behaviour, that he is rather beloved than esteemed: His Tenants grow rich, his Servants look satisfied, all the young Women profess Love to him, and the young Men are glad of his Company: When he comes into a House he calls the Servants by their Names, and talks all the way up Stairs to a Visit. I must not omit that Sir ROGER is a Justice of the °*Quorum*; that he fills the Chair at a Quarter-Session with great Abilities, and three Months ago gained universal Applause by explaining a Passage in the °Game-Act.

The Gentleman next in Esteem and Authority among us, is another Batchelor, who is a Member of the *Inner-Temple*; a Man of great Probity, Wit, and Understanding; but he has chosen his Place of Residence rather to obey the Direction of an old humoursom Father, than in Pursuit of his own Inclinations. He was placed there to study the Laws of the Land, and is the most learned of any of the House in those of the Stage. *Aristotle* and *Longinus* are much better understood by him than *Littleton* or *Cooke*.[4] The Father sends up every Post Questions relating to Marriage-Articles, Leases, and Tenures, in the Neighbourhood; all which Questions he agrees with an Attorney to answer and take care of in the Lump: He is studying the Passions themselves, when he should be inquiring into the Debates among Men which arise from them. He knows the Argument of each of the Orations of *Demosthenes* and *Tully*, but not one Case in the Reports of our own Courts. No one ever took him for a Fool, but none, except his intimate Friends, know he has a great deal of Wit. This Turn makes him at once both disinterested and agreeable: As few of his Thoughts are drawn from Business, they are most of them fit for Conversation. His Taste of Books is a little too just for the Age he lives in; he has read all, but approves of very few. His Familiarity with the Customs, Manners, Actions, and Writings of the Antients, makes him a very delicate Observer of what occurs to him in the present World. He is an excellent Critick, and the Time of the Play is his Hour of Business; exactly at five he passes thro' *New-Inn*, crosses thro' *Russel-Court*, and takes a Turn at *Will*'s 'till the Play begins; he has his Shooes rubbed and his Perriwig powdered at the Barber's as you go into the *Rose*. It is for the Good of the Audience when he is at a Play, for the Actors have an Ambition to please him.[5]

The Person of next Consideration, is Sir ANDREW FREEPORT,

a Merchant of great Eminence in the City of *London*.[6] A Person of indefatigable Industry, strong Reason, and great Experience. His Notions of Trade are noble and generous, and (as every rich Man has usually some sly Way of Jesting, which would make no great Figure were he not a rich Man) he calls the Sea the *British Common*. He is acquainted with Commerce in all its Parts, and will tell you that it is a stupid and barbarous Way to extend Dominion by Arms; for true Power is to be got by Arts and Industry. He will often argue, that if this Part of our Trade were well cultivated, we should gain from one Nation; and if another, from another. I have heard him prove, that Diligence makes more lasting Acquisitions than Valour, and that Sloth has ruined more Nations than the Sword. He abounds in several frugal Maxims, among which the greatest Favourite is, 'A Penny saved is a Penny got.' A General Trader of good Sense, is pleasanter Company than a general Scholar; and Sir ANDREW having a natural unaffected Eloquence, the Perspicuity of his Discourse gives the same Pleasure that Wit would in another Man. He has made his Fortunes himself; and says that *England* may be richer than other Kingdoms, by as plain Methods as he himself is richer than other Men; tho' at the same Time I can say this of him, that there is not a Point in the Compass but blows home a Ship in which he is an Owner.

Next to Sir ANDREW in the Club-room sits Captain SENTRY, a Gentleman of great Courage, good Understanding, but invincible Modesty. He is one of those that deserve very well, but are very awkward at putting their Talents within the Observation of such as should take Notice of them. He was some Years a Captain, and behaved himself with great Gallantry in several Engagements and at several Sieges; but having a small Estate of his own, and being next Heir to Sir ROGER, he has quitted a Way of Life in which no Man can rise suitably to his Merit, who is not something of a Courtier as well as a Soldier. I have heard him often lament, that in a Profession where Merit is placed in so conspicuous a View, Impudence should get the Better of Modesty. When he has talked to this Purpose I never heard him make a sour Expression, but frankly confess that he left the World because he was not fit for it. A strict Honesty and an even regular Behaviour, are in themselves Obstacles to him that must press through Crowds, who endeavour at the same End with himself, the Favour of a Commander. He will however in his way of Talk excuse Generals, for not disposing according to Mens Desert, or enquiring into it: For, says he, that great Man who has a Mind to help me, has as many to break through to come at me, as I have to come at him. Therefore he will conclude, that the Man who would make a Figure, especially in a military Way, must get over all false Modesty, and assist his Patron against the Importunity of other Pretenders, by a proper Assurance in his own Vindication. He says it is a civil Cowardice to be backward in asserting what you ought to expect, as it is a military Fear to be slow in attacking when it is your Duty. With this Candour does the Gentleman speak of himself and others. The same Frankness runs through all his Conversation. The military Part of his Life has furnished him with many Adventures, in the Relation of which he is very agreeable to the Company; for he is never over-bearing, though accustomed to command Men in the utmost Degree below him; nor ever too obsequious, from an Habit of obeying Men highly above him.

But that our Society may not appear a Set of °Humourists unacquainted with the Gallantries and Pleasures of the Age, we have among us the gallant WILL. HONEYCOMB,⁷ a Gentleman who according to his Years should be in the Decline of his Life, but having ever been very careful of his Person, and always had a very easie Fortune, Time has made but very little Impression, either by Wrinkles on his Forehead, or °Traces in his Brain. His Person is well turned, of a good Height. He is very ready at that sort of Discourse with which Men usually entertain Women. He has all his Life dressed very well, and remembers Habits as others do Men. He can smile when one speaks to him, and laughs easily. He knows the History of every Mode, and can inform you from which of the *French* King's Wenches our Wives and Daughters had this Manner of curling their Hair, that Way of placing their Hoods; whose Frailty was covered by such a Sort of Petticoat, and whose Vanity to shew her Foot made that part of the Dress so short in such a Year. In a word, all his Conversation and Knowledge has been in the female World: As other Men of his Age will take notice to you what such a Minister said upon such and such an Occasion, he will tell you when the Duke of *Monmouth* danced at Court such a

Woman was then smitten, another was taken with him at the Head of his Troop in the *Park*. In all these important Relations, he has ever about the same time received a kind Glance or a Blow of a Fan from some celebrated Beauty, Mother of the present Lord such-a-one. If you speak of a young °Commoner that said a lively thing in the House, he starts up, 'He has good Blood in his Veins, *Tom Mirabell* begot him, the Rogue cheated me in that Affair; that young Fellow's Mother used me more like a Dog than any Woman I ever made Advances to.' This way of Talking of his very much enlivens the Conversation among us of a more sedate Turn; and I find there is not one of the Company, but my self, who rarely speak at all, but speaks of him as of that Sort of Man who is usually called a well-bred fine Gentleman. To conclude his Character, where Women are not concerned, he is an honest worthy Man.

I cannot tell whether I am to account him whom I am next to speak of, as one of our Company; for he visits us but seldom, but when he does it adds to every Man else a new Enjoyment of himself. He is a Clergyman, a very philosophick Man, of general Learning, great Sanctity of Life, and the most exact good Breeding. He has the Misfortune to be of a very weak Constitution, and consequently cannot accept of such Cares and Business as Preferments in his Function would oblige him to: He is therefore among Divines what a Chamber-Counsellor is among Lawyers. The Probity of his Mind, and the Integrity of his Life, create him Followers, as being eloquent or loud advances others. He seldom introduces the Subject he speaks upon; but we are so far gone in Years, that he observes, when he is among us, an Earnestness to have him fall on some divine Topick, which he always treats with much Authority, as one who has no Interests in this World, as one who is hastening to the Object of all his Wishes, and conceives Hope from his Decays and Infirmities. These are my ordinary Companions.   R

No. 4 [STEELE]

[Mr Spectator says more of himself]
Monday, 5 March 1711
— *Egregii Mortalem, altique silenti!*   Hor.[1]

An Author, when he first appears in the World, is very apt to believe it has nothing to think of but his Performances. With a good Share of this Vanity in my Heart, I made it my Business these three Days to listen after my own Fame; and as I have sometimes met with Circumstances which did not displease me, I have been encountered by others which gave me as much Mortification. It is incredible to think how empty I have in this Time observed some Part of the Species to be, what mere Blanks they are when they first come abroad in the Morning, how utterly they are at a Stand 'till they are set a going by some Paragraph in a News-Paper: Such Persons are very acceptable to a young Author, for they desire no more in any thing but to be new to be agreeable. If I found Consolation among such, I was as much disquieted by the Incapacity of others. These are Mortals who have a certain Curiosity without Power of Reflection, and perused my Papers like Spectators rather than Readers. But there is so little Pleasure in Enquiries that so nearly concern our selves, (it being the worst Way in the World to Fame, to be too anxious about it) that upon the whole I resolved for the future to go on in my ordinary Way; and without too much Fear or Hope about the Business of Reputation, to be very careful of the Design of my Actions, but very negligent of the Consequences of them.

It is an endless and frivolous Pursuit to act by any other Rule than the Care of satisfying our own Minds in what we do. One would think a silent Man, who concerned himself with no one breathing, should be very little liable to Misinterpretations; and yet I remember I was once °taken up for a Jesuit, for no other Reason but my profound Taciturnity. It is from this Misfortune, that to be out of Harm's Way, I have ever since affected Crowds. He who comes into Assemblies only to gratifie his Curiosity, and not to make a Figure, enjoys the Pleasures of Retirement in a more exquisite Degree, than he possibly could in his Closet; the Lover, the Ambitious, and the Miser, are followed thither by a worse

Crowd than any they can withdraw from. To be exempt from the
Passions with which others are tormented, is the only pleasing
Solitude. I can very justly say with the antient Sage, *I am never less
alone than when alone*.[2] As I am insignificant to the Company in
publick Places, and as it is visible I do not come thither, as most
do, to shew myself; I gratifie the Vanity of all who pretend to make
an Appearance, and have often as kind Looks from well dressed
Gentlemen and Ladies, as a Poet would bestow upon one of his
Audience. There are so many Gratifications attend this publick sort
of Obscurity, that some little Distastes I daily receive have lost
their Anguish; and I did the other Day, without the least
Displeasure, overhear one say of me, *That strange Fellow*; and
another answer, *I have known the Fellow's Face these twelve Years, and
so must you; but I believe you are the first ever asked who he was*. There
are, I must confess, many to whom my Person is as well known as
that of their nearest Relations, who give themselves no further
Trouble about calling me by my Name or Quality, but speak of me
very currently by Mr. *What-d'ye-call-him*.

To make up for these trivial Disadvantages, I have the high
Satisfaction of beholding all Nature with an unprejudiced Eye; and
having nothing to do with Mens Passions or Interests, I can with
the greater Sagacity consider their Talents, Manners, Failings, and
Merits.

It is remarkable, that those who want any one Sense, possess the
others with greater Force and Vivacity. Thus my Want of, or rather
Resignation of Speech, gives me all the Advantages of a dumb
Man. I have, methinks, a more than ordinary Penetration in Seeing;
and flatter my self that I have looked into the Highest and Lowest
of Mankind, and make shrewd Guesses, without being admitted to
their Conversation, at the inmost Thoughts and Reflections of all
whom I behold. It is from hence that good or ill Fortune has no
manner of Force towards affecting my Judgment. I see Men
flourishing in Courts, and languishing in Jayls, without being
prejudiced from their Circumstances to their Favour or Disadvantage; but from their inward Manner of bearing their Condition,
often pity the Prosperous and admire the Unhappy.

Those who converse with the Dumb, know from the Turn of
their Eyes, and the Changes of their Countenance, their Sentiments

of the Objects before them. I have indulged my Silence to such an Extravagance, that the few who are intimate with me, answer my Smiles with concurrent Sentences, and argue to the very Point I shaked my Head at without my speaking. WILL. HONEYCOMB was very entertaining the other Night at a Play to a Gentleman who sat on his right Hand, while I was at his Left. The Gentleman believed WILL. was talking to himself, when upon my looking with great Approbation at a young thing in a Box before us, he said, 'I am quite of another Opinion: She has, I will allow, a very pleasing Aspect, but methinks that Simplicity in her Countenance is rather childish than innocent.' When I observed her a second time, he said, 'I grant her Dress is very becoming, but perhaps the Merit of that Choice is owing to her Mother; for though,' continued he, 'I allow a Beauty to be as much to be commended for the Elegance of her Dress, as a Wit for that of his Language; yet if she has stolen the Colour of her Ribbands from another, or had Advice about her Trimmings, I shall not allow her the Praise of Dress, any more than I would call a Plagiary an Author.' When I threw my Eye towards the next Woman to her, WILL. spoke what I looked, according to his Romantick Imagination, in the following Manner.

'Behold, you who dare, that charming Virgin. Behold the Beauty of her Person chastised by the Innocence of her Thoughts. Chastity, Good-Nature, and Affability, are the Graces that play in her Countenance; she knows she is handsome, but she knows she is good. Conscious Beauty adorned with conscious Virtue! What a Spirit is there in those Eyes! What a Bloom in that Person! How is the whole Woman expressed in her Appearance! Her Air has the Beauty of Motion, and her Look the Force of Language.'

It was Prudence to turn away my Eyes from this Object, and therefore I turned them to the thoughtless Creatures who make up the Lump of that Sex, and move a knowing Eye no more than the Portraitures of insignificant People by ordinary Painters, which are but Pictures of Pictures.

Thus the working of my own Mind, is the general Entertainment of my Life; I never enter into the Commerce of Discourse with any but my particular Friends, and not in Publick even with them. Such an Habit has perhaps raised in me uncommon Reflections; but this Effect I cannot communicate but by my Writings. As my

Pleasures are almost wholly confined to those of the Sight, I take it for a peculiar Happiness that I have always had an easie and familiar Admittance to the fair Sex. If I never praised or flattered, I never belyed or contradicted them. As these compose half the World, and are by the just Complaisance and Gallantry of our Nation the more powerful Part of our People, I shall dedicate a considerable Share of these my Speculations to their Service, and shall lead the Young through all the becoming Duties of Virginity, Marriage, and Widowhood. When it is a Woman's Day, in my Works, I shall endeavour at a Stile and Air suitable to their Understanding. When I say this, I must be understood to mean, that I shall not lower but exalt the Subjects I treat upon. Discourse for their Entertainment, is not to be debased but refined. A man may appear learned, without talking °Sentences; as in his ordinary Gesture he discovers he can Dance, tho' he does not cut Capers. In a Word, I shall take it for the greatest Glory of my Work, if among reasonable Women this Paper may furnish *Tea-Table Talk*. In order to it, I shall treat on Matters which relate to Females, as they are concerned to approach or fly from the other Sex, or as they are tyed to them by Blood, Interest, or Affection. Upon this occasion I think it but reasonable to declare, that whatever Skill I may have in Speculation, I shall never betray what the Eyes of Lovers say to each other in my Presence. At the same Time I shall not think my self obliged, by this Promise, to conceal any false Protestations which I observe made by Glances in publick Assemblies; but endeavour to make both Sexes appear in their Conduct what they are in their Hearts. By this means Love, during the Time of my Speculations, shall be carried on with the same Sincerity as any other Affair of less Consideration. As this is the greatest Concern, Men shall be from henceforth liable to the greatest Reproach for Misbehaviour in it. Falshood in Love shall hereafter bear a blacker Aspect, than Infidelity in Friendship, or Villany in Business. For this great and good End, all Breaches against that noble Passion, the Cement of Society, shall be severely examined. But this, and all other Matters loosely hinted at now, and in my former Papers, shall have their proper Place in my following Discourses: The present Writing is only to admonish the World, that they shall not find me an idle, but a very busie Spectator.   R

No. 10 [ADDISON]

[The reception of *The Spectator*]
Monday, 12 March 1711

Non aliter quam qui adverso vix flumine lembum
Remigiis subigit: si brachia forte remisit,
Atque illum in præceps prono rapit alveus amni.   Virg.[1]

It is with much Satisfaction that I hear this great City inquiring
Day by Day after these my Papers, and receiving my Morning
Lectures with a becoming Seriousness and Attention. My Publisher
tells me, that there are already Three thousand of them distributed
every Day: So that if I allow Twenty Readers to every Paper, which
I look upon as a modest Computation, I may reckon about
Threescore thousand Disciples in *London* and *Westminster*, who I
hope will take care to distinguish themselves from the thoughtless
Herd of their ignorant and unattentive Brethren. Since I have raised
to my self so great an Audience, I shall spare no Pains to make their
Instruction agreeable, and their Diversion useful. For which
Reasons I shall endeavour to enliven Morality with Wit, and to
temper Wit with Morality, that my Readers may, if possible, both
Ways find their °Account in the Speculation of the Day. And to the
End that their Virtue and Discretion may not be short transient
intermitting Starts of Thought, I have resolved to refresh their
Memories from Day to Day, till I have recovered them out of that
desperate State of Vice and Folly into which the Age is fallen. The
Mind that lies fallow but a single Day, sprouts up in Follies that
are only to be killed by a constant and assiduous Culture. It was
said of *Socrates*, that he brought Philosophy down from Heaven, to
inhabit among Men[2]; and I shall be ambitious to have it said of
me, that I have brought Philosophy out of Closets and Libraries,
Schools and Colleges, to dwell in Clubs and Assemblies, at Tea-
Tables and in Coffee-Houses.

I would therefore in a very particular Manner recommend these
my Speculations to all well regulated Families, that set apart an
Hour in every Morning for Tea and Bread and Butter; and would
earnestly advise them for their Good to order this Paper to be
punctually served up, and to be looked upon as a Part of the Tea
Equipage.

Sir *Francis Bacon* observes, that a well-written Book, compared with its Rivals and Antagonists, is like *Moses*'s Serpent, that immediately swallowed up and devoured those of the *Ægyptians*.[3] I shall not be so vain as to think, that where the SPECTATOR appears, the other publick Prints will vanish; but shall leave it to my Reader's Consideration, whether, Is it not much better to be let into the Knowledge of ones self, than to hear what passes in *Muscovy* or *Poland*; and to amuse our selves with such Writings as tend to the wearing out of Ignorance, Passion, and Prejudice, than such as naturally conduce to inflame Hatreds, and make Enmities irreconcilable?

In the next Place, I would recommend this Paper to the daily Perusal of those Gentlemen whom I cannot but consider as my good Brothers and Allies, I mean the Fraternity of Spectators who live in the World without having any thing to do in it; and either by the Affluence of their Fortunes, or Laziness of their Dispositions, have no other Business with the rest of Mankind, but to look upon them. Under this Class of Men are comprehended all contemplative Tradesmen, titular Physicians, Fellows of the Royal Society, °Templers that are not given to be contentious, and Statesmen that are out of Business; in short, every one that considers the World as a Theatre, and desires to form a right Judgment of those who are the Actors on it.

There is another Set of Men that I must likewise lay a Claim to, whom I have lately called the Blanks of Society, as being altogether unfurnished with Ideas, till the Business and Conversation of the Day has supplied them. I have often considered these poor Souls with an Eye of great Commiseration, when I have heard them asking the first Man they have met with, whether there was any News stirring? and by that Means gathering together Materials for thinking. These needy Persons do not know what to talk of, 'till about twelve a Clock in the Morning; for by that Time they are pretty good Judges of the Weather, know which way the Wind sits, and whether the *Dutch* Mail be come in. As they lie at the Mercy of the first Man they meet, and are grave or impertinent all the Day long, according to the Notions which they have imbibed in the Morning, I would earnestly entreat them not to stir out of their Chambers till they have read this Paper, and do promise them that I will daily instil into them such sound and wholesom Sentiments, as shall have a good Effect on their Conversation for the ensuing twelve Hours.

But there are none to whom this Paper will be more useful, than to the Female World. I have often thought there has not been sufficient Pains taken in finding out proper Employments and Diversions for the Fair ones. Their Amusements seem contrived for them rather as they are Women, than as they are reasonable Creatures; and are more adapted to the Sex than to the Species. The °Toilet is their great Scene of Business, and the right adjusting of their Hair the Principal Employment of their Lives. The sorting of a Suit of Ribbons, is reckoned a very good Morning's Work; and if they make an Excursion to a Mercer's or a °Toy-shop, so great a Fatigue makes them unfit for any thing else all the Day after. Their more serious Occupations are Sowing and Embroidery, and their greatest Drudgery the Preparation of Jellies and Sweet-meats. This, I say, is the State of ordinary Women; tho' I know there are Multitudes of those of a more elevated Life and Conversation, that move in an exalted Sphere of Knowledge and Virtue, that join all the Beauties of the Mind to the Ornaments of Dress, and inspire a kind of Awe and Respect, as well as Love, into their Male-Beholders. I hope to encrease the Number of these by Publishing this daily Paper, which I shall always endeavour to make an innocent if not an improving Entertainment, and by that Means at least divert the Minds of my Female Readers from greater Trifles. At the same Time, as I would fain give some finishing Touches to those which are already the most beautiful Pieces in human Nature, I shall endeavour to point out all those Imperfections that are the Blemishes, as well as those Virtues which are the Embellishments, of the Sex. In the mean while I hope these my gentle Readers, who have so much Time on their Hands, will not grudge throwing away a Quarter of an Hour in a Day on this Paper, since they may do it without any Hindrance to Business.

I know several of my Friends and Well-wishers are in great Pain for me, lest I should not be able to keep up the Spirit of a Paper which I oblige my self to furnish every Day: But to make them easie in this Particular, I will promise them faithfully to give it over as soon as I grow dull. This I know will be Matter of great Raillery to the small Wits; who will frequently put me in mind of my Promise, desire me to keep my Word, assure me that it is high Time to give over, with many other little Pleasantries of the like Nature, which Men of a little smart Genius cannot forbear throwing out against their best Friends, when they have such a Handle given them of being witty. But let them remember that I do hereby enter my Caveat against this Piece of Raillery.   C

from No. 555 [STEELE]

[Mr Spectator goes off the stage]
Saturday, 6 December 1712

Respue quod non es —   Pers.[1]

All the Members of the Imaginary Society, which were described in my First Papers, having disappeared one after another, it is high time for the *Spectator* himself to go off the Stage. But, now I am to take my Leave I am under much greater Anxiety than I have known for the Work of any Day since I undertook this Province. It is much more difficult to converse with the World in a real than a personated Character. That might pass for Humour, in the *Spectator*, which would look like Arrogance in a Writer who sets his Name to his Work. The Fictitious Person might contemn those who disapproved him, and extoll his own Performances, without giving Offence. He might assume a Mock-Authority; without being looked upon as vain and conceited. The Praises or Censures of himself fall only upon the Creature of his Imagination, and if any one finds fault with him, the Author may reply with the Philosopher of old, *Thou dost but beat the Case of* Anaxarchus.[2] When I speak in my own private Sentiments, I cannot but address my self to my Readers in a more submissive manner, and with a just Gratitude, for the kind Reception which they have given to these Daily Papers that have been published for almost the space of Two Years last past.

I hope the Apology I have made as to the Licence allowable to a feigned Character, may excuse any thing which has been said in these Discourses of the *Spectator* and his Works; but the Imputation of the grossest Vanity would still dwell upon me, if I did not give some Account by what Means I was enabled to keep up the Spirit of so long and approved a Performance. All the Papers marked with a C, an L, an I, or an O, that is to say, all the Papers which I have distinguished by any Letter in the Name of the Muse *CLIO*, were given me by the Gentleman, of whose Assistance I formerly boasted in the Preface and concluding Leaf of my *Tatlers*.[3] I am indeed much more proud of his long continued Friendship, than I should be of the Fame of being thought the Author of any Writings which he himself is capable of producing. I remember when I finished the *Tender Husband*, I told him there was nothing I so ardently wished, as that we might some time or other publish a Work written by us both, which should bear the Name of *the Monument*, in Memory of our Friendship.[4] I heartily wish what I have done here, were as Honorary to that Sacred Name, as Learning, Wit and Humanity render those Pieces which I have taught the Reader how to distinguish for his. When the Play abovementioned was last Acted, there were so many applauded Stroaks in it which I had from the same Hand, that I thought very meanly of my self that I had never publickly acknowledged them. After I have put other Friends upon importuning him to publish Dramatick, as well as other Writings he has by him, I shall end what I think I am obliged to say on this Head, by giving my Reader this Hint for the better judging of my Productions, that the best Comment upon them would be an Account when the Patron to the *Tender Husband* was in *England*, or Abroad.

The Reader will also find some Papers which are marked with the Letter X, for which he is obliged to the ingenious Gentleman who diverted the Town with the Epilogue to the *Distressed Mother*.[5] I might have owned these several Papers with the free Consent of these Gentlemen, who did not write them with a design of being known for the Authors. But as a candid and sincere Behaviour ought to be preferred to all other Considerations, I would not let my Heart reproach me with a Consciousness of having acquired a Praise which is not my Right.

The other Assistances which I have had have been conveyed by Letter, sometimes by whole Papers, and other times by short Hints from unknown Hands. I have not been able to trace Favours of this kind, with any Certainty, but to the following Names, which I place in the Order wherein I received the Obligation, tho' the first I am going to Name can hardly be mentioned in a List wherein he would not deserve the Precedence. The Persons to whom I am to make these Acknowledgments are Mr. *Henry Martin*, Mr. *Pope*, Mr. *Hughs*, Mr. *Carey* of *New-College* in *Oxford*, Mr. *Tickell* of *Queen*'s in the same University, Mr. *Parnelle*, and Mr. *Eusden* of *Trinity* in *Cambridge*. Thus to speak in the Language of my late Friend Sir ANDREW FREEPORT, I have Ballanced my Accounts with all my Creditors for Wit and Learning. But as these Excellent Performances would not have seen the Light without the means of this Paper, I may still arrogate to my self the Merit of their being communicated to the Publick.

I have nothing more to add, but having swelled this Work to Five hundred and fifty five Papers, they will be disposed into seven Volumes, four of which are already published, and the three others in the Press. It will not be demanded of me why I now leave off, tho' I must own my self obliged to give an Account to the Town of my Time hereafter, since I retire when their Partiality to me is so great, that an Edition of the former Volumes of *Spectators* of above Nine thousand each Book is already sold off,[6] and the Tax on each half Sheet has brought into the Stamp-Office one Week with another above 20 *l.* a Week arising from this single Paper, notwithstanding it at first reduced it to less than half the Number that was usually Printed before this Tax was laid.[7]

I humbly beseech the Continuance of this Inclination to favour what I may hereafter produce, and hope I have in many Occurrences of Life tasted so deeply of Pain and Sorrow, that I am Proof against much more prosperous Circumstances than any Advantages to which my own Industry can possibly exalt me.

 I am,
  My Good-natured Reader,
   Your most Obedient,
    Most Obliged Humble Servant,

            Richard Steele.

    Vos valete & plaudite.   Ter.[8]

POSTSCRIPT.
It had not come to my knowledge, when I left off the *Spectator*, that I owe several excellent sentiments and agreeable Pieces in this Work to Mr. *Ince* of *Grey's-Inn*.

            R. STEELE.

No. 106 [ADDISON]

[Sir Roger's household in the country]
Monday, 2 July 1711
— Hinc tibi Copia
Manabit ad plenum, benigno
Ruris honorum opulenta cornu   Hor.[1]

Having often received an Invitation from my Friend Sir ROGER DE
COVERLY to pass away a Month with him in the Country, I last
Week accompanied him thither, and am settled with him for some
Time at his Country-house, where I intend to form several of my
ensuing Speculations. Sir ROGER, who is very well acquainted
with my Humour, lets me rise and go to Bed when I please, dine
at his own Table or in my Chamber as I think fit, sit still and say
nothing without bidding me be merry. When the Gentlemen of
the Country come to see him, he only shews me at a Distance: As
I have been walking in his Fields I have observed them stealing a
Sight of me over an Hedge, and have heard the Knight desiring
them not to let me see them, for that I hated to be stared at.

I am the more at Ease in Sir ROGER's Family, because it consists
of sober and staid Persons; for as the Knight is the best Master in
the World, he seldom changes his Servants; and as he is beloved by
all about him, his Servants never care for leaving him: By this
Means his Domesticks are all in Years, and grown old with their
Master. You would take his Valet de Chambre for his Brother, his
Butler is grey-headed, his Groom is one of the gravest Men that I
have ever seen, and his Coachman has the Looks of a Privy-
Counsellor. You see the Goodness of the Master even in the old
House-dog, and in a grey Pad that is kept in the Stable with great
Care and Tenderness out of Regard to his past Services, tho' he has
been useless for several Years.

I could not but observe with a great deal of Pleasure the Joy that
appeared in the Countenances of these ancient Domesticks upon
my Friend's Arrival at his Country-Seat. Some of them could not
refrain from Tears at the Sight of their old Master; every one of
them pressed forward to do something for him, and seemed
discouraged if they were not employed. At the same Time the good
old Knight, with a Mixture of the Father and the Master of the

Family, tempered the Enquiries after his own Affairs with several
kind Questions relating to themselves. This Humanity and Good-
nature engages every Body to him, so that when he is pleasant
upon any of them, all his Family are in good Humour, and none
so much as the Person whom he diverts himself with: On the
Contrary, if he coughs, or betrays any Infirmity of old Age, it is
easy for a Stander-by to observe a secret Concern in the Looks of all
his Servants.

My worthy Friend has put me under the particular Care of his
Butler, who is a very prudent Man, and, as well as the rest of his
Fellow-Servants, wonderfully desirous of pleasing me, because they
have often heard their Master talk of me as of his particular Friend.

My chief Companion, when Sir ROGER is diverting himself in
the Woods or the Fields, is a very venerable Man, who is ever with
Sir ROGER, and has lived at his House in the Nature of a Chaplain
above thirty Years. This Gentleman is a Person of good Sense and
some Learning, of a very regular Life and obliging Conversation:
He heartily loves Sir ROGER, and knows that he is very much in
the old Knight's Esteem; so that he lives in the Family rather as a
Relation than a Dependant.

I have observed in several of my Papers, that my Friend Sir
ROGER, amidst all his good Qualities, is something of an
°Humourist; and that his Virtues, as well as Imperfections, are as
it were tinged by a certain Extravagance, which makes them
particularly *his*, and distinguishes them from those of other Men.
This Cast of Mind, as it is generally very innocent in it self, so it
renders his Conversation highly agreeable, and more delightful
than the same Degree of Sense and Virtue would appear in their
common and ordinary Colours. As I was walking with him last
Night, he asked me how I liked the good Man whom I have just
now mentioned? and without staying for my Answer, told me,
That he was afraid of being insulted with Latin and Greek at his
own Table; for which Reason, he desired a particular Friend of his
at the University to find him out a Clergyman rather of plain Sense
than much Learning, of a good Aspect, a clear Voice, a sociable
Temper, and, if possible, a Man that understood a little of Back-
Gammon. My Friend, says Sir ROGER, found me out this
Gentleman, who, besides the Endowments required of him, is,

they tell me, a good Scholar though he does not shew it. I have given him the Parsonage of the Parish; and because I know his Value, have settled upon him a good Annuity for Life. If he out-lives me, he shall find that he was higher in my Esteem than perhaps he thinks he is. He has now been with me thirty Years; and though he does not know I have taken Notice of it, has never in all that Time asked any thing of me for himself, tho' he is every Day solliciting me for something in Behalf of one or other of my Tenants his Parishioners. There has not been a Law-Suit in the Parish since he has lived among them: If any Dispute arises, they apply themselves to him for the Decision; if they do not acquiesce in his Judgment, which I think never happened above once, or twice at most, they appeal to me. At his first settling with me, I made him a Present of all the good Sermons which have been printed in *English*, and only begged of him that every *Sunday* he would pronounce one of them in the Pulpit. Accordingly, he has digested them into such a Series, that they follow one another naturally, and make a continued System of practical Divinity.

As Sir ROGER was going on in his Story, the Gentleman we were talking of came up to us; and upon the Knight's asking him who preached to Morrow (for it was *Saturday* Night) told us, the Bishop of St. *Asaph* in the Morning, and Doctor *South* in the Afternoon. He then shewed us his List of Preachers for the whole Year, where I saw with a great deal of Pleasure Archbishop *Tillotson*, Bishop *Saunderson*, Doctor *Barrow*, Doctor *Calamy*, with several living Authors who have published Discourses of Practical Divinity.[2] I no sooner saw this venerable Man in the Pulpit, but I very much approved of my Friend's insisting upon the Qualifications of a good Aspect and a clear Voice; for I was so charmed with the Gracefulness of his Figure and Delivery, as well as with the Discourses he pronounced, that I think I never passed any Time more to my Satisfaction. A Sermon repeated after this Manner, is like the Composition of a Poet in the Mouth of a graceful Actor.

I could heartily wish that more of our Country-Clergy would follow this Example; and instead of wasting their Spirits in laborious Compositions of their own, would endeavour after a handsome Elocution, and all those other Talents that are proper to enforce what has been penned by greater Masters. This would not

only be more easy to themselves, but more edifying to the
People.   L

No. 108 [ADDISON]

[Will Wimble visits Sir Roger]

Wednesday, 4 July 1711

Gratis anhelans, multa agendo nihil agens.   Phæd.[1]

As I was Yesterday Morning walking with Sir ROGER before his
House, a Country-Fellow brought him a huge Fish, which, he told
him, Mr. *William Wimble* had caught that very Morning; and that
he presented it, with his Service to him, and intended to come and
dine with him. At the same Time he delivered a Letter, which my
Friend read to me as soon as the Messenger left him.

Sir ROGER,

'I desire you to accept of a °Jack, which is the best I have caught
this Season. I intend to come and stay with you a Week, and see
how the Perch bite in the *Black River.* I observed, with some
Concern, the last Time I saw you upon the Bowling Green, that
your Whip wanted a Lash to it: I will bring half a Dozen with me
that I twisted last Week, which I hope will serve you all the Time
you are in the Country. I have not been out of the Saddle for six
Days last past, having been at *Eaton* with Sir *John's* eldest Son. He
takes to his Learning hugely.

         I am,

             SIR,

                Your humble Servant,

                                 Will. Wimble.'

This extraordinary Letter, and Message that accompanied it,
made me very curious to know the Character and Quality of the
Gentleman who sent them; which I found to be as follows; *Will.
Wimble* is younger Brother to a Baronet, and descended of the
ancient Family of the *Wimbles.* He is now between Forty and Fifty;
but being bred to no Business and born to no Estate, he generally
lives with his elder Brother as Superintendant of his Game. He

hunts a Pack of Dogs better than any Man in the Country, and is very famous for finding out a Hare. He is extremely well versed in all the little Handicrafts of an idle Man: He makes a *May*-fly to a Miracle; and furnishes the whole Country with Angle-Rods. As he is a good-natured °officious Fellow, and very much esteemed upon Account of his Family, he is a welcome Guest at every House, and keeps up a good Correspondence among all the Gentlemen about him. He carries a Tulip-Root in his Pocket from one to another, or exchanges a Puppy between a couple of Friends that live perhaps in the opposite Sides of the County. *Will.* is a particular Favourite of all the young Heirs, whom he frequently obliges with a Net that he has weaved, or a Setting-dog that he has °*made* himself: He now and then presents a Pair of Garters of his own knitting to their Mothers or Sisters; and raises a great deal of Mirth among them, by enquiring as often as he meets them *how they wear?* These Gentleman-like Manufactures and obliging little Humours, make *Will.* the Darling of the Country.

Sir ROGER was proceeding in the Character of him, when we saw him make up to us, with two or three Hazle-twigs in his Hand that he had cut in Sir ROGER's Woods, as he came through them, in his Way to the House. I was very much pleased to observe on one Side the hearty and sincere Welcome with which Sir ROGER received him, and on the other the secret Joy which his Guest discovered at Sight of the good old Knight. After the first Salutes were over, *Will.* desired Sir ROGER to lend him one of his Servants to carry a Set of Shuttlecocks he had with him in a little Box to a Lady that lived about a Mile off, to whom it seems he had promised such a Present for above this half Year. Sir ROGER's Back was no sooner turned, but honest *Will.* began to tell me of a large Cock-Pheasant that he had sprung in one of the neighbouring Woods, with two or three other Adventures of the same Nature. Odd and uncommon Characters are the Game that I look for, and most delight in; for which Reason I was as much pleased with the Novelty of the Person that talked to me, as he could be for his Life with the springing of a Pheasant, and therefore listned to him more than ordinary Attention.

In the Midst of his Discourse the Bell rung to Dinner, where the Gentleman I have been speaking of had the Pleasure of seeing the huge Jack, he had caught, served up for the first Dish in a most sumptuous Manner. Upon our sitting down to it he gave us a long Account how he had hooked it, played with it, foiled it, and at length drew it out upon the Bank, with several other Particulars that lasted all the first Course. A Dish of Wild-fowl that came afterwards furnished Conversation for the rest of the Dinner, which concluded with a late Invention of *Will*'s for improving the °Quail Pipe.

Upon withdrawing into my Room after Dinner, I was secretly touched with Compassion towards the honest Gentleman that had dined with us; and could not but consider with a great deal of Concern, how so good an Heart and such busy Hands were wholly employed in Trifles; that so much Humanity should be so little beneficial to others, and so much Industry so little advantageous to himself. The same Temper of Mind and Application to Affairs might have recommended him to the publick Esteem, and have raised his Fortune in another Station of Life. What Good to his Country or himself might not a Trader or Merchant have done with such useful tho' ordinary Qualifications?

Will. Wimble's is the Case of many a younger Brother of a great Family, who had rather see their Children starve like Gentlemen, than thrive in a Trade or Profession that is beneath their Quality. This Humour fills several Parts of *Europe* with Pride and Beggary. It is the Happiness of a trading Nation, like ours, that the younger Sons, tho' uncapable of any liberal Art or Profession, may be placed in such a Way of Life, as may perhaps enable them to vie with the best of their Family: Accordingly we find several Citizens that were launched into the World with narrow Fortunes, rising by an honest Industry to greater Estates than those of their elder Brothers. It is not improbable but *Will.* was formerly tried at Divinity, Law, or Physick; and that finding his Genius did not lie that Way, his Parents gave him up at length to his own Inventions: But certainly, however improper he might have been for Studies of a higher Nature, he was perfectly well °turned for the Occupations of Trade and Commerce. As I think this is a Point which cannot be too much inculcated, I shall desire my Reader to compare what I have here written with what I have said in my Twenty first Speculation.   L

No. 109 [STEELE]

[Sir Roger discourses of his ancestors in his gallery]
Thursday, 5 July 1711

Abnormis sapiens —   Hor.[1]

I was this Morning walking in the Gallery, when Sir ROGER entered at the end opposite to me, and advancing towards me, said, he was glad to meet me among his Relations the DE COVERLEYS and hoped I liked the Conversation of so much good Company, who were as silent as my self. I knew he alluded to the Pictures, and as he is a Gentleman who does not a little value himself upon his ancient Descent, I expected he would give me some Account of them. We were now arrived at the upper End of the Gallery, when the Knight faced towards one of the Pictures, and as we stood before it, he entered into the Matter, after his blunt way of saying things, as they occur to his Imagination, without regular Introduction, or Care to preserve the appearance of Chain of Thought.

'It is, said he, worth while to consider the Force of Dress; and how the Persons of one Age differ from those of another, merely by that only. One may observe also that the General Fashion of one Age has been followed by one particular Set of People in another, and by them preserved from one Generation to another. Thus the vast °Jetting Coat and small Bonnet, which was the Habit in *Harry* the Seventh's time, is kept on in the Yeomen of the Guard; not without a good and Politick View, because they look a Foot taller, and a Foot and an half broader: Besides, that the Cap leaves the Face expanded, and consequently more Terrible, and fitter to stand at the Entrance of Palaces.

'This Predecessor of ours, you see, is dressed after this manner, and his Cheeks would be no larger than mine were he in a Hat as I am. He was the last Man that won a Prize in the Tilt-Yard (which is now a Common Street before *Whitehall*.)[2] You see the broken Lance that lyes there by his right Foot: He shivered that Lance of his Adversary all to pieces; and bearing himself, look you Sir, in this manner, at the same time he came within the Target of the Gentleman who rode again him, and taking him with incredible Force before him on the Pummel of his Saddle, he in that manner

rid the Turnament over, with an Air that shewed he did it rather
to perform the Rule of the Lists, than Expose his Enemy; however,
it appeared he knew how to make use of a Victory, and with a
gentle Trot he marched up to a Gallery where their Mistress sat (for
they were Rivals) and let him down with laudable Courtesy and
pardonable Insolence. I don't know but it might be exactly where
the Coffee-house is now.[3]

'You are to know this my Ancestor was not only of a military
Genius but fit also for the Arts of Peace, for he played on the
Baseviol as well as any Gentleman at Court; you see where his Viol
hangs by his Basket-hilt Sword. The Action at the Tilt-yard you
may be sure won the Fair Lady, who was a Maid of Honour, and
the greatest Beauty of her time; here she stands, the next Picture.
You see, Sir, my Great Great Great Grand-Mother has on the new-
fashioned Petticoat; except that the Modern is gathered at the
Waste; my Grandmother appears as if she stood in a large Drum,
whereas the Ladies now walk as if they were in a °Go-Cart. For all
this Lady was bred at Court, she became an Excellent Country-
Wife, she brought ten Children, and when I shew you the Library,
you shall see in her own hand (allowing for the Difference of the
Language) the best °Receipt now in *England* both for an Hasty-
Pudding and a °Whitepot.

'If you please to fall back a little, because it is necessary to look
at the three next Pictures at one View; these are three Sisters. She
on the right Hand, who is so very beautiful, dyed a Maid; the next
to her, still handsomer, had the same Fate, against her Will; this
homely thing in the middle had both their Portions added to her
own, and was Stolen by a neighbouring Gentleman, a Man of
Stratagem and Resolution, for he poisoned three Mastiffs to come
at her, and knocked down two [Deer]-stealers in carrying her off.
Misfortunes happen in all Families: The Theft of this Romp and so
much Money, was no great matter to our Estate. But the next Heir
that possessed it was this soft Gentleman, whom you see there:
Observe the small Buttons, the little Boots, the Laces, the Slashes
about his Cloaths, and above all the Posture he is drawn in, (which
to be sure was his own chusing;) you see he sits with one Hand on
a Desk writing, and looking as it were another way, like an easie
Writer,[4] or a Sonneteer: He was one of those that had too much

Wit to know how to live in the World; he was a Man of no Justice, but great good Manners; he ruined every body that had any thing to do with him, but never said a rude thing in his Life; the most indolent Person in the World, he would sign a Deed that passed away half his Estate with his Gloves on, but would not put on his Hat before a Lady if it were to save his Country. He is said to be the first that made Love by squeezing the Hand. He left the Estate with ten thousand Pounds Debt upon it, but however by all Hands I have been informed that he was every way the finest Gentleman in the World. That Debt lay heavy on our House for one Generation, but it was retrieved by a Gift from that Honest Man you see there, a Citizen of our Name, but nothing at all a-kin to us. I know Sir ANDREW FREEPORT has said behind my Back, that this Man was descended from one of the ten Children of the Maid of Honour I shewed you above. But it was never made out; we winked at the thing indeed, because Mony was wanting at that time.'

Here I saw my Friend a little embarrassed, and turned my face to the next Portraiture.

Sir ROGER went on with his Account of the Gallery in the following manner. 'This Man (pointing to him I looked at) I take to be the Honour of our House. Sir HUMPHREY DE COVERLEY; he was in his Dealings as punctual as a Tradesman, and as generous as a Gentleman. He would have thought himself as much undone by breaking his Word, as if it were to be followed by Bankruptcy. He served his Country as Knight of this Shire to his dying Day: He found it no easie matter to maintain an Integrity in his Words and Actions, even in things that regarded the Offices which were incumbent upon him, in the care of his own Affairs and Relations of Life, and therefore dreaded (tho' he had great Talents) to go into Employments of State, where he must be exposed to the Snares of Ambition. Innocence of Life and great Ability were the distinguishing Parts of his Character; the latter, he had often observed, had led to the Destruction of the former, and used frequently to lament that Great and Good had not the same Signification. He was an Excellent °Husbandman, but had resolved not to exceed such a degree of Wealth; all above it he bestowed in secret Bounties many Years after the Sum he aimed at for his own use was attained. Yet he did not slacken his Industry, but to a decent old Age spent the

Life and Fortune which was superfluous to himself, in the Service of his Friends and Neighbours.'

Here we were called to Dinner, and Sir ROGER ended the Discourse of this Gentleman, by telling me, as we followed the Servant, that this his Ancestor was a Brave Man, and narrowly escaped being killed in the Civil Wars; 'for,' said he, 'he was sent out of the Field upon a private Message the Day before the Battle of *Worcester*.'⁵ The Whim of narrowly escaping by having been within a Day of Danger; with other Matters above-mentioned, mixed with good Sense, left me at a Loss whether I was more delighted with my Friend's Wisdom or Simplicity.   R

No. 110 [ADDISON]

[Ghosts]
Friday, 6 July 1711

Horror ubique animos, simul ipsa silentia terrent.   Virg.¹

At a little Distance from Sir ROGER's House, among the Ruins of an old Abby, there is a long Walk of aged Elms; which are shot up so very high, that when one passes under them, the Rooks and Crows that rest upon the Tops of them seem to be Cawing in another Region. I am very much delighted with this Sort of Noise, which I consider as a kind of natural Prayer to that Being who supplies the Wants of his whole Creation, and, who in the beautiful Language of the *Psalms*, feedeth the young Ravens that call upon him.² I like this Retirement the better, because of an ill Report it lies under of being *haunted*; for which Reason (as I have been told in the Family) no living Creature ever walks in it besides the Chaplain. My good Friend the Butler desired me with a very grave Face not to venture myself in it after Sun-set, for that one of the Footmen had been almost frighted out of his Wits by a Spirit that appeared to him in the Shape of a black Horse without an Head; to which he added, that about a Month ago one of the Maids coming home late that Way with a Pail of Milk upon her Head, heard such a Rustling among the Bushes that she let it fall.

I was taking a Walk in this Place last Night between the Hours of Nine and Ten, and could not but fancy it one of the most proper

Scenes in the World for a Ghost to appear in. The Ruins of the Abby are scattered up and down on every Side, and half covered with Ivy and Elder-Bushes, the Harbours of several solitary Birds which seldom make their Appearance till the Dusk of the Evening. The Place was formerly a Church-yard, and has still several Marks in it of Graves and Burying-Places. There is such an Eccho among the old Ruins and Vaults, that if you stamp but a little louder than ordinary you hear the Sound repeated. At the same Time the Walk of Elms, with the Croaking of the Ravens which from time to time are heard from the Tops of them, looks exceeding solemn and venerable. These Objects naturally raise Seriousness and Attention; and when Night heightens the Awfulness of the Place, and pours out her supernumerary Horrours upon every thing in it, I do not at all wonder that weak Minds fill it with Spectres and Apparitions.

Mr. *Locke*, in his Chapter of the Association of Ideas, has very curious Remarks to shew how by the Prejudice of Education one Idea often introduces into the Mind a whole Set that bear no Resemblance to one another in the Nature of things.[3] Among several Examples of this Kind, he produces the following Instance. *The Ideas of Goblins and Sprights have really no more to do with Darkness than Light: Yet let but a foolish Maid inculcate these often on the Mind of a Child, and raise them there together, possibly he shall never bee able to separate them again so long as he lives; but Darkness shall ever afterwards bring with it those frightful Ideas, and they shall be so joyned, that he can no more bear the one than the other.*

As I was walking in this Solitude, where the Dusk of the Evening conspired with so many other Occasions of Terrour, I observed a Cow grazing not far from me, which an Imagination that is apt to *startle* might easily have construed into a black Horse without an Head; and I dare say the poor Footman lost his Wits upon some such trivial Occasion.

My friend Sir ROGER has often told me with a great deal of Mirth, that at his first coming to his Estate he found three Parts of his House altogether useless; that the best Room in it had the Reputation of being haunted, and by that Means was locked up; that Noises had been heard in his long Gallery, so that he could not get a Servant to enter it after eight a Clock at Night; that the Door of one of his Chambers was nailed up, because there went a

Story in the Family that a Butler had formerly hanged himself in it; and that his Mother, who lived to a great Age, had shut up half the Rooms in the House, in which either her Husband, a Son, or Daughter had died. The Knight seeing his Habitation reduced to so small a Compass and himself in a Manner shut out of his own House, upon the Death of his Mother ordered all the Apartments to be flung open, and *exorcised* by his Chaplain, who lay in every Room one after another, and by that Means dissipated the Fears which had so long reigned in the Family.

I should not have been thus particular upon these ridiculous Horrours, did not I find them so very much prevail in all Parts of the Country. At the same Time I think a Person who is thus terrifyed with the Imagination of Ghosts and Spectres much more reasonable, than one who contrary to the Reports of all Historians sacred and prophane, ancient and modern, and to the Traditions of all Nations, thinks the Appearance of Spirits fabulous and groundless: Could not I give my self up to this general Testimony of Mankind, I should to the Relations of particular Persons who are now living, and whom I cannot distrust in other Matters of Fact. I might here add, that not only the Historians, to whom we may joyn the Poets, but likewise the Philosophers of Antiquity have favoured this Opinion. *Lucretius* himself, though by the Course of his Philosophy he was obliged to maintain that the Soul did not exist separate from the Body, makes no Doubt of the Reality of Apparitions, and that Men have often appeared after their Death. This I think very remarkable; he was so pressed with the Matter of Fact which he could not have the Confidence to deny, that he was forced to account for it by one of the most absurd unphilosophical Notions that was ever started. He tells us, That the Surfaces of all Bodies are perpetually flying off from their respective Bodies, one after another; and that these Surfaces or thin Cases that included each other whilst they were joined in the Body like the Coats of an Onion, are sometimes seen entire when they are separated from it; by which Means we often behold the Shapes and Shadows of Persons who are either dead or absent.[4]

I shall dismiss this Paper with a Story out of *Josephus*, not so much for the Sake of the Story it self, as for the moral Reflections with which the Author concludes it, and which I shall here set down in his own Words.[5] 'Glaphyra the Daughter of King Archilaus, after the Death of her two first Husbands (being married to a third, who was Brother to her first Husband, and so passionately in Love with her that he turned off his former Wife to make Room for this Marriage) had a very odd kind of Dream. She fancied that she saw her first Husband coming towards her, and that she embraced him with great Tenderness; when in the Midst of the Pleasure which she expressed at the Sight of him, he reproached her after the following Manner: Glaphyra, says he, thou hast made good the old Saying, That Women are not to be trusted. Was not I the Husband of thy Virginity? have I not Children by thee? How couldst thou forget our Loves so far as to enter into a second Marriage, and after that into a third, nay to take for thy Husband a Man who has so shamele[s]sly crept into the Bed of his Brother? However, for the Sake of our passed Loves, I shall free thee from thy present Reproach, and make thee mine for ever. Glaphyra told this Dream to several Women of her Acquaintance, and died soon after. I thought this Story might not be impertinent in this Place, wherein I speak of those Things: Besides that, the Example deserves to be taken Notice of, as it contains a most certain Proof of the Immortality of the Soul, and of Divine Providence. If any Man thinks these Facts incredible, let him enjoy his Opinion to himself; but let him not endeavour to disturb the Belief of others, who by Instances of this Nature are excited to the Study of Virtue.'   L

No. 112 [ADDISON]

[Sir Roger at church]
Monday, 9 July 1711

Ἀθανάτους μὲν πρῶτα Θεοὺς, νόμῳ ὡς διάκειται, τιμα. Pyth.[1]

I am always very well pleased with a Country Sunday; and think, if keeping holy the Seventh Day were only a human Institution, it would be the best Method that could have been thought of for the polishing and civilizing of Mankind. It is certain the Country-People would soon degenerate into a kind of Savages and Barbarians, were there not such frequent Returns of a stated Time, in which the whole Village meet together with their best Faces, and in their cleanliest Habits, to converse with one another upon indifferent Subjects, hear their Duties explained to them, and join together in Adoration of the supreme Being. *Sunday* clears away the Rust of the whole Week, not only as it refreshes in their Minds the Notions of Religion, but as it puts both the Sexes upon appearing in their most agreeable Forms, and exerting all such Qualities as are apt to give them a Figure in the Eye of the Village. A Country-Fellow distinguishes himself as much in the *Church-yard*, as a Citizen does upon the *Change*; the whole Parish-Politicks being generally discussed in that Place either after Sermon or before the Bell rings.

My friend Sir ROGER being a good Churchman, has beautified the Inside of his Church with several Texts of his own chusing: He has likewise given a handsome Pulpit-Cloth, and railed in the Communion-Table at his own Expence. He has often told me, that at his coming to his Estate he found his Parishioners very irregular; and that in order to make them kneel and join in the Responses, he gave every one of them a Hassock and a Common-prayer Book; and at the same Time employed an itinerant Singing-Master, who goes about the Country for that Purpose, to instruct them rightly in the Tunes of the Psalms; upon which they now very much value themselves, and indeed out-do most of the Country Churches that I have ever heard.

As Sir ROGER is Landlord to the whole Congregation, he keeps them in very good Order, and will suffer no Body to sleep in it besides himself; for if by Chance he has been surprized into a short Nap at Sermon, upon recovering out of it he stands up and looks about him, and if he sees any Body else nodding, either wakes them himself, or sends his Servant to them. Several other of the old Knight's Particularities break out upon these Occasions: Sometimes he will be lengthening out a Verse in the Singing-Psalms, half a Minute after the rest of the Congregation have done with it; sometimes, when he is pleased with the Matter of his Devotion, he pronounces *Amen* three or four times to the same Prayer; and sometimes stands up when every Body else is upon their Knees, to count the Congregation, or see if any of his Tenants are missing.

I was Yesterday very much surprized to hear my old Friend, in the Midst of the Service, calling out to one *John Matthews* to mind what he was about, and not disturb the Congregation. This *John*

Matthews it seems is remarkable for being an idle Fellow, and at that Time was kicking his Heels for his Diversion. This Authority of the Knight, though exerted in that odd Manner which accompanies him in all Circumstances of Life, has a very good Effect upon the Parish, who are not polite enough to see any thing ridiculous in his Behaviour; besides that, the general good Sense and Worthiness of his Character, make his Friends observe these little Singularities as Foils that rather set off than blemish his good Qualities.

As soon as the Sermon is finished, no Body presumes to stir till Sir ROGER is gone out of the Church. The Knight walks down from his Seat in the Chancel between a double Row of his Tenants, that stand bowing to him on each Side; and every now and then enquires how such an one's Wife, or Mother, or Son, or Father do whom he does not see at Church; which is understood as a secret Reprimand to the Person that is absent.

The Chaplain has often told me, that upon a Catechizing-day, when Sir ROGER has been pleased with a Boy that answers well, he has ordered a Bible to be given him next Day for his Encouragement; and sometimes accompanies it with a Flitch of Bacon to his Mother. Sir ROGER has likewise added five Pounds a Year to the Clerk's Place; and that he may encourage the young Fellows to make themselves perfect in the Church Service, has promised upon the Death of the present Incumbent, who is very old, to bestow it according to Merit.

The fair Understanding between Sir ROGER and his Chaplain, and their mutual Concurrence in doing Good, is the more remarkable, because the very next Village is famous for the Differences and Contentions that rise between the Parson and the 'Squire, who live in a perpetual State of War. The Parson is always preaching at the 'Squire, and the 'Squire to be revenged on the Parson never comes to Church. The 'Squire has made all his Tenants Atheists and Tithe-Stealers; while the Parson instructs them every *Sunday* in the Dignity of his Order, and insinuates to them in almost every Sermon, that he is a better Man than his Patron. In short, Matters are come to such an Extremity, that the 'Squire has not said his Prayers either in publick or private this half

Year; and that the Parson threatens him, if he does not mend his Manners, to pray for him in the Face of the whole Congregation.

Feuds of this Nature, though too frequent in the Country, are very fatal to the ordinary People; who are so used to be dazled with Riches, that they pay as much Deference to the Understanding of a Man of an Estate, as of a Man of Learning; and are very hardly brought to regard any Truth, how important soever it may be, that is preached to them, when they know there are several Men of five hundred a Year who do not believe it.   L

No. 113 [STEELE]

[Sir Roger's disappointment in love]
Tuesday, 10 July 1711

— Hærent infixi Pectore vultus.   Virg.[1]

In my first Description of the Company in which I pass most of my Time, it may be remembered that I mentioned a great Affliction which my Friend Sir ROGER had met with in his Youth, which was no less than a Disappointment in Love. It happened this Evening, that we fell into a very pleasing Walk at a Distance from his House: As soon as we came into it, 'It is, quoth the good old Man, looking round him with a Smile, very hard, that any Part of my Land should be settled upon one who has used me so ill as the perverse Widow did; and yet I am sure I could not see a Sprig of any Bough of this whole Walk of Trees, but I should reflect upon her and her Severity. She has certainly the finest Hand of any Woman in the World. You are to know this was the Place wherein I used to muse upon her; and by that Custom I can never come into it, but the same tender Sentiments revive in my Mind, as if I had actually walked with that beautiful Creature under these Shades. I have been Fool enough to carve her Name on the Bark of several of these Trees; so unhappy is the Condition of Men in Love, to attempt the removing of their Passion by the Methods which serve only to imprint it deeper. She has certainly the finest Hand of any Woman in the World.'

Here followed a profound Silence; and I was not displeased to observe my Friend falling so naturally into a Discourse, which I had ever before taken Notice he industriously avoided. After a very long Pause, he entered upon an Account of this great Circumstance in his Life, with an Air which I thought raised my *Idea* of him above what I had ever had before; and gave me the Picture of that chearful Mind of his, before it received that Stroke which has ever since affected his Words and Actions. But he went on as follows.

'I came to my Estate in my Twenty second Year, and resolved to follow the Steps of the most worthy of my Ancestors, who have inhabited this Spot of Earth before me, in all the Methods of Hospitality and good Neighbourhood, for the Sake of my Fame; and in Country Sports and Recreations, for the Sake of my Health. In my Twenty third Year I was obliged to serve as Sheriff of the County; and in my Servants, Officers, and whole Equipage, indulged the Pleasure of a young Man (who did not think ill of his own Person) in taking that publick Occasion of shewing my Figure and Behaviour to Advantage. You may easily imagine to yourself what Appearance I made, who am pretty tall, rid well, and was very well dressed, at the Head of a whole County, with Musick before me, a Feather in my Hat, and my Horse well bitted. I can assure you I was not a little pleased with the kind Looks and Glances I had from all the Balconies and Windows, as I rode to the Hall where the Assizes were held. But when I came there, a beautiful Creature in a Widow's Habit sat in Court, to hear the Event of a Cause concerning her Dower. This commanding Creature (who was born for Destruction of all who behold her) put on such a Resignation in her Countenance, and bore the Whispers of all around the Court with such a pretty Uneasiness, I warrant you, and then recovered her self from one Eye to another, till she was perfectly confused by meeting something so wistful in all she encountered, that at last, with a °Murrain to her, she casts her bewitching Eye upon me. I no sooner met it, but I bowed like a great surprized Booby; and knowing her Cause to be the first which came on, I cried, like a captivated Calf as I was, Make Way for the Defendant's Witness. This sudden Partiality made all the County immediately see the Sheriff also was become a Slave to the fine Widow. During the Time her Cause was upon Trial, she behaved her self, I warrant you, with such a deep Attention to her Business, took Opportunities to have little Billets handed to her Counsel, then would be in such a pretty Confusion, occasioned, you must know, by acting before so much Company, that not only I but the whole Court was prejudiced in her Favour; and all that the next Heir to her Husband had to urge, was thought so groundless and frivolous, that when it came to her Counsel to reply, there was not half so much said as every one besides in the Court thought he could have urged to her Advantage. You must understand, Sir, this perverse Woman is one of those unaccountable Creatures that secretly rejoyce in the Admiration of Men, but indulge themselves in no further Consequences. Hence it is that she has ever had a Train of Admirers, and she removes from her Slaves in Town to those in the Country, according to the Seasons of the Year. She is a reading Lady, and far gone in the Pleasures of Friendship: She is always accompanied by a Confident, who is Witness to her daily Protestations against our Sex, and consequently a Bar to her first Steps towards Love, upon the Strength of her own Maxims and Declarations.

'However, I must needs say this accomplished Mistress of mine has distinguished me above the rest, and has been known to declare Sir ROGER DE COVERLEY was the tamest and most human of all the Brutes in the Country. I was told she said so by one who thought he rallied me; but upon the Strength of this slender Encouragement of being thought least detestable, I made new Liveries, new paired my Coach-Horses, sent them all to Town to be bitted, and taught to throw their Legs well, and move [all together], before I °pretended to cross the Country and wait upon her. As soon as I thought my Retinue suitable to the Character of my Fortune and Youth, I set out from hence to make my Addresses. The particular Skill of this Lady has ever been to inflame your Wishes, and yet command Respect. To make her Mistress of this Art, she has a greater Share of Knowledge, Wit, and good Sense, than is usual even among Men of Merit. Then she is beautiful beyond the Race of Women. If you won't let her go on with a certain Artifice with her Eyes, and the Skill of Beauty, she will arm her self with her real Charms, and strike you with Admiration instead of Desire. It is certain that if you were to behold the whole Woman, there is that Dignity in her Aspect, that Composure in her Motion, that Complacency in her Manner, that if her Form makes you hope, her Merit makes you fear. But then again, she is such a desperate Scholar, that no Country-Gentleman can approach her without being a Jest. As I was going to tell you, when I came to her House I was admitted to her Presence with great Civility; at the same Time she placed her self to be first seen by me in such an Attitude, as I think you call the Posture of a Picture, that she discovered new Charms, and I at last came towards her with such an Awe as made me speechless. This she no sooner observed but she made her Advantage of it, and began a Discourse to me concerning Love and Honour, as they both are followed by °Pretenders, and the real Votaries to them. When she discussed these Points in a Discourse, which I verily believe was as learned as the best Philosopher in *Europe* could possibly make, she asked me whether she was so happy as to fall in with my Sentiments on these important Particulars. Her Confident sat by her, and upon my being in the last Confusion and Silence, this malicious Aide of hers turning to her says, I am very glad to observe Sir ROGER pauses upon this Subject, and seems resolved to deliver all his Sentiments upon the Matter when he pleases to speak. They both kept their Countenances, and after I had sat half an Hour meditating how to behave before such profound Casuists, I rose up and took my Leave. Chance has since that Time thrown me very often in her Way, and she as often has directed a Discourse to me which I do not understand. This Barbarity has kept me ever at a Distance from the most beautiful Object my Eyes ever beheld. It is thus also she deals with all Mankind, and you must make Love to her, as you would conquer the Sphinx, by posing her. But were she like other Women, and that there were any talking to her, how constant must the Pleasure of that Man be, who could converse with a Creature – But, after all, you may be sure her Heart is fixed on some one or other; and yet I have been credibly informed; but who can believe half that is said! After she had done speaking to me, she put her Hand to her Bosom and adjusted her °Tucker. Then she cast her Eyes a little down, upon my beholding her too earnestly. They say she sings excellently: Her Voice in her ordinary Speech has something in it inexpressibly sweet. You must know I dined with her at a publick Table the Day after I first saw her, and she helped me to some °Tansy in the Eye of all the Gentlemen in the Country: She has certainly the finest Hand of any Woman in the World. I can assure you, Sir, were you to behold her, you would be in the same Condition; for as her Speech is Musick, her Form is Angelick. But I find I grow irregular while I am talking of her; but indeed it would be Stupidity to be unconcerned at such Perfection. Oh the excellent Creature, she is as inimitable to all Women, as she is inaccessible to all Men!'

I found my Friend begin to rave, and insensibly led him towards the House, that we might be joined by some other Company; and am convinced that the Widow is the secret Cause of all that Inconsistency which appears in some Parts of my Friend's Discourse; tho' he has so much Command of himself as not directly to mention her, yet according to that of *Martial*, which one knows not how to render in English, *Dum tacet hanc loquitur*.[2] I shall end this Paper with that whole Epigram, which represents with much Humour my honest Friend's Condition.

> *Quicquid agit, Rufus, nihil est, nisi Nævia Rufo,*
>   *Si gaudet, si flet, si tacet, hanc loquitur:*
> *Cænat, propinat, poscit, negat, annuit, una est*
>   *Nævia: Si non sit Nævia, mutus erit.*
> *Scriberet hesterna Patri cum Luce Salutem.*
>   *Nævia lux, inquit, Nævia numen, ave.*

> Let Rufus *weep, rejoice, stand, sit, or walk,*
> *Still he can nothing but of* Nævia *talk:*
> *Let him eat, drink, ask Questions, or dispute,*
> *Still he must speak of* Nævia, *or be mute.*
> *He writ to his Father, ending with this Line,*
> *I am, my lovely* Nævia, *ever thine.*   R

No. 117 [ADDISON]

[Witchcraft: Sir Roger and Moll White][1]
Saturday, 14 July 1711

— Ipsi sibi somnia fingunt.   Virg.[2]

There are some Opinions in which a Man should stand Neuter, without engaging his Assent to one side or the other. Such a hovering Faith as this, which refuses to settle upon any Determination, is absolutely necessary in a Mind that is careful to avoid Errors and Prepossessions. When the Arguments press equally on both sides in Matters that are indifferent to us, the safest Method is to give up our selves to neither.

It is with this Temper of Mind that I consider the Subject of Witchcraft. When I hear the Relations that are made from all Parts of the World, not only from *Norway* and *Lapland*, from the *East* and *West Indies*, but from every particular Nation in *Europe*, I cannot forbear thinking that there is such an Intercourse and Commerce with Evil Spirits, as that which we express by the Name of Witchcraft. But when I consider that the ignorant and credulous Parts of the World abound most in these Relations, and that the Persons among us who are supposed to engage in such an Infernal Commerce are People of a weak Understanding and crazed Imagination, and at the same time reflect upon the many Impostures and Delusions of this Nature that have been detected in all Ages, I endeavour to suspend my Belief till I hear more certain Accounts than any which have yet come to my Knowledge. In short, when I consider the Question, Whether there are such Persons in the World as those we call Witches? my Mind is divided between the two opposite Opinions; or rather (to speak my Thoughts freely) I believe in general that there is, and has been such a thing as Witchcraft; but at the same time can give no Credit to any Particular Instance of it.

I am engaged in this Speculation, by some Occurrences that I met with Yesterday, which I shall give my Reader an Account of at large. As I was walking with my Friend Sir ROGER by the side of one of his Woods, an old Woman applied her self to me for my Charity. Her Dress and Figure put me in mind of the following Description in *Otway*.

In a close Lane as I pursued my Journey, [. . .]
I spyed a wrinkled Hag, *with Age grown double,*
Picking dry Sticks, and mumbling to her self.
Her Eyes with scalding Rheum were galled and red;
Cold Palsy shook her Head; her Hands seemed withered;
And on her crooked Shoulders had she wrapped
The tatter'd Remnants of an old striped Hanging,
Which served to keep her Carcass from the Cold:
So there was nothing of a-piece about her.
Her lower Weeds were all o'er coarsly patched
With diff'rent-coloured Rags, black, red, white, yellow,
And seemed to speak Variety of Wretchedness.[3]

As I was musing on this Description, and comparing it with the
Object before me, the Knight told me, that this very old Woman
had the Reputation of a Witch all over the Country, that her Lips
were observed to be always in Motion, and that there was not a
Switch about her House which her Neighbours did not believe had
carried her several hundreds of Miles. If she chanced to stumble,
they always found Sticks or Straws that lay in the Figure of a Cross
before her. If she made any Mistake at Church, and cryed *Amen* in
a wrong Place, they never failed to conclude that she was saying her
Prayers backwards. There was not a Maid in the Parish that would
take a Pin of her, though she should offer a Bag of Money with it.
She goes by the Name of *Moll White*, and has made the Country
ring with several imaginary Exploits which are palmed upon her.
If the Dairy Maid does not make her Butter come so soon as she
would have it, *Moll White* is at the bottom of the Churn. If a Horse
sweats in the Stable, *Moll White* has been upon his Back. If a Hare
makes an unexpected Escape from the Hounds, the Huntsman
curses *Moll White*. Nay, (says Sir ROGER) I have known the Master
of the Pack, upon such an Occasion, send one of his Servants to see
if *Moll White* had been out that Morning.

This Account raised my Curiosity so far, that I begged my Friend
Sir ROGER to go with me into her Hovel, which stood in a solitary
Corner under the side of the Wood. Upon our first entring Sir
ROGER winked to me, and pointed at something that stood behind
the Door, which upon looking that way I found to be an old

Broomstaff. At the same time he whispered me in the Ear to take notice of a Tabby Cat that sat in the Chimney-Corner, which, as the Knight told me, lay under as bad a Report as *Moll White* her self; for besides that *Moll* is said often to accompany her in the same Shape, the Cat is reported to have spoken twice or thrice in her Life, and to have played several Pranks above the Capacity of an ordinary Cat.

I was secretly concerned to see Human Nature in so much Wretchedness and Disgrace, but at the same time could not forbear smiling to hear Sir ROGER, who is a little puzzled about the old Woman, advising her as a Justice of Peace to avoid all Communication with the Devil, and never to hurt any of her Neighbours Cattle. We concluded our Visit with a Bounty, which was very acceptable.

In our Return home Sir ROGER told me, that old *Moll* had been often brought before him for making Children spit Pins, and giving Maids the Night-Mare; and that the Country People would be tossing her into a Pond and trying Experiments with her every Day, if it was not for him and his Chaplain.

I have since found, upon Enquiry, that Sir ROGER was several times °staggered with the Reports that had been brought him concerning this old Woman, and would frequently have bound her over to the County Sessions, had not his Chaplain with much ado perswaded him to the contrary.

I have been the more particular in this Account, because I hear there is scarce a Village in *England* that has not a *Moll White* in it. When an old Woman begins to doat, and grow chargeable to a Parish, she is generally turned into a Witch, and fills the whole Country with extravagant Fancies, imaginary Distempers, and terrifying Dreams. In the mean time, the poor Wretch that is the innocent Occasion of so many Evils begins to be frighted at her self, and sometimes confesses secret Commerces and Familiarities that her Imagination forms in a delirious old Age. This frequently cuts off Charity from the greatest Objects of Compassion, and inspires People with a Malevolence towards those poor decrepid Parts of our Species, in whom Human Nature is defaced by Infirmity and Dotage.   L

No. 122 [ADDISON]

[Sir Roger at the County-Assizes]

Friday, 20 July 1711

Comes jucundus in via pro vehiculo est.   Publ. Syr. Frag.[1]

A man's first Care should be to avoid the Reproaches of his own Heart; his next, to escape the Censures of the World: If the last interferes with the former, it ought to be entirely neglected; but otherwise, there cannot be a greater Satisfaction to an honest Mind, than to see those Approbations which it gives itself seconded by the Applauses of the Publick: A Man is more sure of his Conduct, when the Verdict which he passes upon his own Behaviour is thus warranted, and confirmed by the Opinion of all that know him.

My worthy Friend Sir ROGER is one of those who is not only at Peace within himself, but beloved and esteemed by all about him. He receives a suitable Tribute for his universal Benevolence to Mankind, in the Returns of Affection and Good-will, which are paid him by every one that lives within his Neighbourhood. I lately met with two or three odd Instances of that general Respect which is shewn to the good old Knight. He would needs carry *Will. Wimble* and my self with him to the County-Assizes: As we were upon the Road *Will. Wimble* joyned a couple of plain Men who rid before us, and conversed with them for some Time; during which my Friend Sir ROGER acquainted me with their Characters.

The first of them, says he, that has a Spaniel by his Side, is a Yeoman of about an hundred Pounds a Year, an honest Man: He is just within the °Game-Act, and qualified to kill an Hare or a Pheasant: He knocks down a Dinner with his Gun twice or thrice a Week; and by that Means lives much cheaper than those who have not so good an Estate as himself. He would be a good Neighbour if he did not destroy so many Partridges: In short, he is a very sensible Man; °shoots flying; and has been several Times Foreman of the Petty-Jury.

The other that rides along with him is *Tom Touchy*, a Fellow famous for *taking the Law* of every Body. There is not one in the Town where he lives that he has not sued at a Quarter-Sessions. The Rogue had once the Impudence to go to Law with the *Widow*. His Head is full of Costs, Damages, and Ejectments: He plagued a couple of honest Gentlemen so long for a Trespass in breaking one of his Hedges, till he was forced to sell the Ground it enclosed to defray the Charges of the Prosecution: His Father left him fourscore Pounds a Year; but he has °*cast* and been cast so often, that he is not now worth thirty. I suppose he is going upon the old Business of the Willow-Tree.

As Sir ROGER was giving me this Account of *Tom Touchy*, *Will. Wimble* and his two Companions stopped short till we came up to them. After having paid their Respects to Sir ROGER, *Will.* told him that• Mr. *Touchy* and he must appeal to him upon a Dispute that arose between them. *Will.* it seems had been giving his Fellow Travellers an Account of his angling one Day in such a Hole; when *Tom Touchy*, instead of hearing out his Story, told him, that Mr. such an One, if he pleased, might *take the Law of him* for fishing in that Part of the River. My Friend Sir ROGER heared them both, upon a round Trot; and after having paused some Time told them, with the Air of a Man who would not give his Judgment rashly, that *much might be said on both Sides.* They were neither of them dissatisfied with the Knight's Determination, because neither of them found himself in the Wrong by it: Upon which we made the best of our Way to the Assizes.

The Court was sat before Sir ROGER came, but notwithstanding all the Justices had taken their Places upon the Bench, they made room for the old Knight at the Head of them; who for his Reputation in the Country took Occasion to whisper in the Judge's Ear, That *he was glad his Lordship had met with so much good Weather in his Circuit*. I was listening to the Proceedings of the Court with much Attention, and infinitely pleased with that great Appearance and Solemnity which so properly accompanies such a publick Administration of our Laws; when, after about an Hour's Sitting, I observed to my great Surprize, in the Midst of a Trial, that my Friend Sir ROGER was getting up to speak. I was in some Pain for him, till I found he had acquitted himself of two or three Sentences, with a Look of much Business and great Intrepidity.

Upon his first Rising the Court was hushed, and a general W[h]isper ran among the Country-People that Sir ROGER *was up*. The Speech he made was so little to the Purpose, that I shall not trouble my Readers with an Account of it; and I believe was not so much designed by the Knight himself to inform the Court, as to give him a Figure in my Eye, and keep up his Credit in the Country.

I was highly delighted, when the Court rose, to see the Gentlemen of the Country gathering about my old Friend, and striving who should compliment him most; at the same Time that the ordinary People gazed upon him at a Distance, not a little admiring his Courage, that was not afraid to speak to the Judge.

In our Return home we met with a very odd Accident; which I cannot forbear relating, because it shews how desirous all who know Sir ROGER are of giving him Marks of their Esteem. When we were arrived upon the Verge of his Estate, we stopped at a little Inn to rest our selves and our Horses. The Man of the House had it seems been formerly a Servant in the Knight's Family; and to do Honour to his old Master, had some Time since, unknown to Sir ROGER, put him up in a Sign-post before the Door; so that *the Knight's Head* had hung out upon the Road about a Week before he himself knew any thing of the Matter. As soon as Sir ROGER was acquainted with it, finding that his Servant's Indiscretion proceeded wholly from Affection and Good-will, he only told him that he had made him too high a Compliment; and when the Fellow seemed to think that could hardly be, added with a more decisive Look, That it was too great an Honour for any Man under a Duke; but told him at the same time that it might be altered with a very few Touches, and that he himself would be at the Charge of it. Accordingly they got a Painter by the Knight's Directions to add a Pair of Whiskers to the Face, and by a little Aggravation of the Features to change it into the *Saracen's Head*. I should not have known this Story, had not the Inn-keeper upon Sir ROGER's alighting told him in my Hearing, That his Honour's Head was brought back last Night with the Alterations that he had ordered to be made in it. Upon this my Friend with his usual Chearfulness related the Particulars above-mentioned, and ordered the Head to be brought into the Room. I could not forbear discovering greater Expressions of Mirth than ordinary upon the Appearance of this monstrous Face, under which, notwithstanding it was made to frown and stare in a most extraordinary Manner, I could still discover a distant Resemblance of my old Friend. Sir ROGER, upon seeing me laugh, desired me to tell him truly if I thought it possible for People to know him in that Disguise. I at first kept my usual Silence; but upon the Knight's conjuring me to tell him whether it was not still more like himself than a *Saracen*, I composed my Countenance in the best Manner I could, and replied, *That much might be said on both Sides*.

These several Adventures, with the Knight's Behaviour in them, gave me as pleasant a Day as ever I met with in any of my Travels.   L

No. 131 [ADDISON]

[Mr Spectator resolves to return to Town]
Tuesday, 31 July 1711

— *Ipsæ rursum concedite Sylvæ.*   Virg.[1]

It is usual for a Man who loves Country Sports to preserve the Game in his own Grounds, and divert himself upon those that belong to his Neighbour. My Friend Sir ROGER generally goes two or three Miles from his House, and gets into the Frontiers of his Estate, before he beats about in search of an Hare or Partridge, on purpose to spare his own Fields, where he is always sure of finding Diversion when the worst comes to the worst. By this means the Breed about his House has time to encrease and multiply, besides that the Sport is the more agreeable where the Game is the harder to come at, and [where it] does not lie so thick as to produce any Perplexity or Confusion in the Pursuit. For these Reasons the Country Gentleman, like the Fox, seldom preys near his own Home.

In the same manner I have made a Month's Excursion out of the Town, which is the great Field of Game for Sportsmen of my Species, to try my Fortune in the Country, where I have started several Subjects, and hunted them down, with some Pleasure to my self, and I hope to others. I am here forced to use a great deal of Diligence before I can spring any thing to my Mind, whereas in Town, whilst I am following one Character, it is ten to one but I am crossed in my Way by another, and put up such a Variety of odd Creatures in both Sexes, that they foil the Scent of one another, and puzzle the Chace. My greatest

Difficulty in the Country is to find Sport, and in Town to chuse it. In the mean time, as I have given a whole Month's Rest to the Cities of *London* and *Westminster*, I promise my self abundance of new Game upon my return thither.

It is indeed high time for me to leave the Country, since I find the whole Neighbourhood begin to grow very inquisitive after my Name and Character. My Love of Solitude, Taciturnity, and particular way of Life, having raised a great Curiosity in all these Parts.

The Notions which have been framed of me are various; some look upon me as very proud, [some as very modest], and some as very melancholy. *Will. Wimble*, as my Friend the Butler tells me, observing me very much alone, and extreamly silent when I am in Company, is afraid I have killed a Man. The Country People seem to suspect me for a °Conjurer; and some of them hearing of the Visit that I made to *Moll. White*, will needs have it that Sir ROGER has brought down a °Cunning Man with him, to cure the old Woman, and free the Country from her Charms. So that the Character which I go under in part of the Neighbourhood, is what they here call a °*White Witch*.

A Justice of Peace, who lives about five Miles off, and is not of Sir ROGER's Party, has it seems said twice or thrice at his Table, that he wishes Sir ROGER does not harbour a Jesuit in his House, and that he thinks the Gentlemen of the Country would do very well to make me give some Account of my self.

On the other side, some of Sir ROGER's Friends are afraid the old Knight is imposed upon by a designing Fellow; and as they have heard that he converses very promiscuously when he is in Town, do not know but he has brought down with him some discarded Whig, that is sullen, and says nothing, because he is out of Place.

Such is the Variety of Opinions that are here entertained of me, so that I pass among some for a disaffected Person, and among others for a Popish Priest; among some for a Wizard, and among others for a Murderer; and all this for no other Reason, that I can imagine, but because I do not hoot and hollow and make a Noise. It is true my Friend Sir ROGER, tells them *that it is my way*, and that I am only a Philosopher, but [this] will not satisfy them. They think there is more in me than he discovers, and that I do not hold my Tongue for nothing.

For these and other Reasons I shall set out for *London* to Morrow, having found by Experience that the Country is not a Place for a Person of my Temper, who does not love Jollity, and what they call Good-Neighbourhood. A Man that is out of Humour when an unexpected Guest breaks in upon him, and does not care for sacrificing an Afternoon to every Chance-comer; that will be the Master of his own Time, and the Pursuer of his own Inclinations, makes but a very unsociable Figure in this kind of Life. I shall therefore retire into the Town, if I may make use of that Phrase, and get into the Crowd again as fast as I can, in order to be alone. I can there raise what Speculations I please upon others without being observed my self, and at the same time enjoy all the Advantages of Company with all the Privileges of Solitude. In the mean while, to finish the Month, and conclude these my Rural Speculations, I shall here insert a Letter from my Friend WILL. HONEYCOMB, who has not lived a Month for these forty Years out of the Smoke of *London*, and rallies me after his way upon my Country Life.

   Dear SPEC.

'I suppose this Letter will find thee picking of Daisies, or smelling to a Lock of Hay, or passing away thy time in some innocent Country Diversion of the like nature. I have however Orders from the Club to summon thee up to Town, being all of us cursedly afraid thou wilt not be able to relish our Company, after thy Conversations with *Moll. White* and *Will. Wimble*. Prithee don't send us up any more Stories of a Cock and a Bull, nor frighten the Town with Spirits and Witches. Thy Speculations begin to smell confoundedly of Woods and Meadows. If thou dost not come up quickly, we shall conclude thou art in Love with one of Sir ROGER's Dairy Maids. Service to the Knight. Sir ANDREW is grown the Cock of the Club since he left us, and if he does not return quickly will make every Mother's Son of us Common-wealths Men.

                    Dear SPEC,
                    Thine Eternally,
C   WILL. HONEYCOMB.'

No. 383 [ADDISON]

[A visit to Spring-Garden with Sir Roger]
Tuesday, 20 May 1712

Criminibus debent Hortos —   [Juvenal][1]

As I was sitting in my Chamber, and thinking on a Subject for my next *Spectator*, I heard two or three irregular Bounces at my Landlady's Door, and upon the opening of it, a loud chearful Voice enquiring whether the Philosopher was at Home. The Child who went to the Door answered very Innocently, that he did not lodge there. I immediately recollected that it was my good Friend Sir ROGER's Voice: and that I had promised to go with him on the Water to *Spring-Garden*,[2] in case it proved a good Evening. The Knight put me in mind of my Promise from the Bottom of the Stair-Case, but told me that if I was Speculating he would stay below till I had done. Upon my coming down I found all the Children of the Family got about my old Friend, and my Landlady herself, who is a notable prating Gossip, engaged in a Conference with him, being mightily pleased with his stroaking her little Boy upon the Head, and bidding him be a good Child, and mind his Book.

We were no sooner come to the *Temple* Stairs, but we were surrounded with a Crowd of Water-men, offering us their respective Services. Sir ROGER, after having looked about him very attentively, spied one with a Wooden-Leg, and immediately gave him Orders to get his Boat ready. As we were walking towards it, *You must know*, says Sir ROGER, *I never make use of any Body to row me that has not either lost a Leg or an Arm. I would rather bate him a few Strokes of his Oar, than not employ an honest Man that has been wounded in the Queen's Service. If I was a Lord or a Bishop, and kept a Barge, I would not put a Fellow in my Livery that had not a Wooden Leg.*

My old Friend, after having seated himself, and trimmed the Boat with his Coachman, who, being a very sober Man, always serves for Ballast on these Occasions, we made the best of our way for °*Fox-hall*. Sir ROGER obliged the Waterman to give us the History of his Right Leg, and hearing that he had left it at °*La Hogue*, with many Particulars which passed in that glorious Action, the Knight in the Triumph of his Heart made several Reflections on the Greatness of the *British* Nation; as, that one *Englishman* could beat three *Frenchmen*; that we cou'd never be in Danger of Popery so long as we took care of our Fleet; that the *Thames* was the noblest River in *Europe*; that *London-Bridge* was a greater Piece of Work than any of the Seven Wonders of the World; with many other honest Prejudices which naturally cleave to the Heart of a true *Englishman*.

After some short Pause, the old Knight turning about his Head twice or thrice, to take a Survey of this great Metropolis, bid me observe how thick the City was set with Churches, and that there was scarce a single Steeple on this side *Temple-bar. A most Heathenish Sight!* says Sir ROGER: *There is no Religion at this End of the Town. The Fifty new Churches will very much mend the Prospect; but Church-work is slow, Church-work is slow!*[3]

I do not remember I have any where mentioned, in Sir ROGER's Character, his Custom of saluting every Body that passes by him with a Good-morrow or a Good-night. This the old Man does out of the Overflowings of his Humanity, though at the same time it renders him so popular among all his Country Neighbours, that it is thought to have gone a good way in making him once or twice °Knight of the Shire. He cannot forbear this Exercise of Benevolence even in Town, when he meets with any one in his Morning or Evening Walk. It broke from him to several Boats that passed by us upon the Water; but, to the Knight's great Surprize, as he gave the Good-night to two or three young Fellows a little before our Landing, one of them, instead of returning the Civility, asked us what queer old Putt we had in the Boat; and whether he was not ashamed to go a Wenching at his Years? with a great deal of the like *Thames*-Ribaldry. Sir ROGER seemed a little shocked at first, but at length assuming a Face of Magistracy, told us, *That if he were a* Middlesex *Justice, he would make such Vagrants know that her Majesty's Subjects were no more to be abused by Water than by Land.*

We were now arrived at *Spring-Garden*, which is exquisitely pleasant at this Time of Year. When I considered the Fragrancy of the Walks and Bowers, with the Choirs of Birds that sung upon the Trees, and the loose Tribe of People that walked under their Shades, I could not but look upon the Place as a kind of *Mahometan* Paradise. Sir ROGER told me it put him in mind of a little Coppice

by his House in the Country, which his Chaplain used to call an
Aviary of Nightingales. *You must understand*, says the Knight, *there
is nothing in the World that pleases a Man in Love so much as your
Nightingale. Ah Mr.* SPECTATOR! *The many Moon-light Nights that
I have walked by my self and thought on the Widow by the Musick of the
Nightingale!* He here fetched a deep Sigh, and was falling into a Fit
of musing, when a Mask, who came behind him, gave him a gentle
Tap upon the Shoulder, and asked him if he would drink a Bottle
of Mead with her? But the Knight being startled at so unexpected
a Familiarity, and displeased to be interrupted in his Thoughts of
the Widow, told her, *She was a wanton Baggage*, and bid her go
about her Business.

We concluded our Walk with a Glass of °*Burton*-Ale, and a Slice
of °Hung-Beef. When we had done eating our selves, the Knight
called a Waiter to him, and bid him carry the Remainder to a
Waterman that had but one Leg. I perceived the Fellow stared
upon him at the Oddness of the Message, and was going to be
saucy; upon which I ratified the Knight's Commands with a
peremptory Look.

As we were going out of the Garden, my old Friend thinking
himself obliged, as a member of the °*Quorum*, to animadvert upon
the Morals of the Place, told the Mistress of the House, who sat at
the Bar, That he should be a better Customer to her Garden, if
there were more Nightingales, and fewer Strumpets.   I

No. 517 [ADDISON]

[The death of Sir Roger][1]
Thursday, **2**3 *October* 1712

Heu pietas! heu prisca fides! —   Virg.[2]

We last Night received a Piece of ill News at our Club, which very
sensibly afflicted every one of us. I question not but my Readers
themselves will be troubled at the hearing of it. To keep them no
longer in Suspence Sir ROGER DE COVERLY *is dead*. He departed
this Life at his House in the Country, after a few Weeks Sickness. Sir
ANDREW FREEPORT has a Letter from one of his Correspondents in
those Parts, that informs him the old Man caught a Cold at the

County Sessions, as he was very warmly promoting an Address of his own penning, in which he succeeded according to his Wishes. But this Particular comes from a Whig Justice of Peace, who was always Sir ROGER's Enemy and Antagonist. I have Letters both from the Chaplain and Captain *Sentry* which mention Nothing of it, but are filled with many Particulars to the Honour of the good old Man. I have likewise a Letter from the Butler, who took so much Care of me last Summer when I was at the Knight's House. As my Friend the Butler mentions, in the Simplicity of his Heart, several Circumstances the others have passed over in Silence, I shall give my Reader a Copy of his Letter, without any Alteration or Diminution.

Honoured Sir,
'Knowing that you was my old Master's good Friend, I could not forbear sending you the melancholy News of his Death, which has afflicted the whole Country, as well as his poor Servants, who loved him, I may say, better than we did our Lives. I am afraid he caught his Death the last County Sessions, where he would go to see Justice done to a poor Widow Woman, and her Fatherless Children that had been wronged by a Neighbouring Gentleman; for you know, Sir, my good Master was always the poor Man's Friend. Upon his coming home, the first Complaint he made was, that he had lost his Roast-Beef Stomach, not being able to touch a Sirloin, which was served up according to Custom; and you know he used to take great Delight in it. From that Time forward he grew worse and worse, but still kept a good Heart to the last. Indeed we were once in great Hope of his Recovery, upon a kind Message that was sent him from the Widow Lady whom he had made Love to the forty last Years of his Life; but this only proved a Light'ning before Death. He has bequeathed to this Lady, as a Token of his Love, a great Pearl Necklace, and a Couple of Silver Bracelets set with Jewels, which belonged to my good old Lady his Mother: He has bequeathed the fine white Guelding, that he used to ride a hunting upon, to his Chaplain, because he thought he would be kind to him, and has left you all his Books. He has, moreover, bequeathed to the Chaplain a very pretty Tenement with good Lands about it. It being a very cold Day when he made his Will, he left for Mourning, to every Man in the Parish a great °Frize Coat, and to

every Woman a black Riding-hood. It was a most moving Sight to
see him take Leave of his poor Servants, commending us all for our
Fidelity, whilst we were not able to speak a Word for weeping. As
we most of us are grown gray-headed in our Dear Master's Service,
he has left us Pensions and Legacies, which we may live very
comfortably upon, the remaining Part of our Days. He has
bequeathed a great Deal more in Charity, which is not yet come to
my Knowledge, and it is peremptorily said in the Parish, that he
has left Money to build a Steeple to the Church; for he was heard
to say some Time ago, that if he lived two Years longer *Coverly*
Church should have a Steeple to it. The Chaplain tells every Body
that he made a very good End, and never speaks of him without
Tears. He was buried, according to his own Directions, among the
Family of the *Coverly's*, on the left Hand of his Father, Sir *Arthur*.
The Coffin was carried by Six of his Tenants, and the Pall held up
by Six of the °*Quorum*: The whole Parish followed the Corps with
heavy Hearts, and in their Mourning-Suits, the Men in Frize, and
the Women in Riding-hoods. Captain *Sentry*, my Master's Nephew,
has taken Possession of the Hall-House, and the whole Estate.
When my old Master saw him a little before his Death, he shook
him by the Hand, and wished him Joy of the Estate which was
falling to him, desiring him only to make a good Use of it, and to
pay the several Lagacies, and the Gifts of Charity which he told
him he had left as Quit-rents upon the Estate. The Captain truly
seems a courteous Man, though he says but little. He makes much
of those whom my Master loved, and shews great Kindness to the
old House-dog, that you know my poor Master was so fond of. It
wou'd have gone to your Heart to have heard the Moans the dumb
Creature made on the Day of my Master's Death. He has ne'er joyed
himself since; no more has any of us. 'Twas the melancholiest Day
for the poor People that ever happened in *Worcestershire*. This being
all from,

> Honoured Sir,
>> Your most sorrowful Servant,

Edward Biscuit.'

P.S. 'My Master desired, some Weeks before he died, that a Book
which comes up to you by the Carrier should be given to Sir *Andrew
Freeport* in his Name.'

This Letter, notwithstanding the poor Butler's Manner of Writing it, gave us such an Idea of our good old Friend, that upon the Reading of it there was not a dry Eye in the Club. Sir *Andrew* opening the Book found it to be a Collection of Acts of Parliament. There was in Particular the °Act of Uniformity, with some Passages in it marked by Sir *Roger*'s own Hand. Sir *Andrew* found that they related to two or three Points, which he had disputed with Sir *Roger* the last Time he appeared at the Club. Sir *Andrew*, who would have been merry at such an Incident on another Occasion, at the Sight of the old Man's Hand-writing burst into Tears, and put the Book into his Pocket. Captain *Sentry* informs me, that the Knight has left °Rings and Mourning for every one in the Club.   O

II *Men, Women, Manners*

[Male and female roles]
Saturday, 5 May 1711

Quem præstare potest mulier galeata pudorem,
Quæ fugit à Sexu? —   Juv.[1]

When the Wife of *Hector*, in *Homer's Iliads*, discourses with her
Husband about the Battel in which he was going to engage, the
Hero, desiring her to leave that Matter to his Care, bids her go to her
Maids and mind her Spinning:[2] By which the Poet intimates, that
Men and Women ought to busie themselves in their proper Spheres,
and on such Matters only as are suitable to their respective Sex.

I am at this time acquainted with a young Gentleman, who has
passed a great Part of his Life in the Nursery, and, upon Occasion,
can make a °Caudle or a °Sack Posset better than any Man in
England. He is likewise a wonderful Critick in Cambrick and
Muslins, and will talk an Hour together upon a Sweetmeat. He
entertains his Mother every Night with Observations that he makes
both in Town and Court: As what Lady shows the nicest Fancy in
her Dress; what Man of Quality wears the fairest [Wig]; who has
the finest Linnen, who the prettiest Snuff-box, with many other the
like curious Remarks that may be made in good Company.

On the other hand I have very frequently the Opportunity of
seeing a Rural *Andromache*, who came up to Town last Winter,[3]
and is one of the greatest Fox Hunters in the Country. She talks of
Hounds and Horses, and makes nothing of leaping over a Six-bar
Gate. If a Man tells her a waggish Story, she gives him a Push with
her Hand in jest, and calls him an impudent Dog; and if her
Servant neglects his Business, threatens to kick him out of the
House. I have heard her, in her Wrath, call a Substantial Tradesman a Lousie Cur; and remember one Day, when she could not

think of the Name of a Person, she described him, in a large Company of Men and Ladies, by the Fellow with the Broad Shoulders.

If those Speeches and Actions, which in their own Nature are indifferent, appear ridiculous when they proceed from a wrong Sex, the Faults and Imperfections of one Sex transplanted into another, appear black and monstrous. As for the Men, I shall not in this Paper any further concern my self about them; but as I would fain contribute to make Woman-kind, which is the most beautiful Part of the Creation, entirely amiable, and wear out all those little Spots and Blemishes that are apt to rise among the Charms which Nature has poured out upon them, I shall dedicate this Paper to their Service. The Spot which I would here endeavour to clear them of, is that Party-Rage which of late Years is very much crept into their Conversation. This is, in its nature, a Male Vice, and made up of many angry and cruel Passions that are altogether repugnant to the Softness, the Modesty, and those other endearing Qualities which are natural to the Fair Sex. Women were formed to temper Mankind, and sooth them into Tenderness and Compassion; not to set an Edge upon their Minds, and blow up in them those Passions which are too apt to rise of their own Accord. When I have seen a pretty Mouth uttering Calumnies and Invectives, what would I not have given to have stopt it? How have I been troubled to see some of the finest Features in the World grow pale, and tremble with Party-Rage? *Camilla* is one of the greatest Beauties in the *British* Nation, and yet values herself more upon being the *Virago* of one Party, than upon being the Toast of both. The Dear Creature, about a Week ago, encountred the fierce and beautiful *Penthesilea*[4] across a Tea-Table; but in the height of her Anger, as her Hand chanced to shake with the Earnestness of the Dispute, she scalded her Fingers, and spilt a Dish of Tea upon her Petticoat. Had not this Accident broke off the Debate, no Body knows where it would have ended.

There is one Consideration which I would earnestly recommend to all my Female Readers, and which, I hope, will have some weight with them. In short it is this, that there is nothing so bad for the Face as Party-Zeal. It gives an ill-natured Cast to the Eye, and a disagreeable Sourness to the Look; besides, that it makes the Lines too strong, and flushes them worse than Brandy. I have seen a Woman's Face break out in Heats, as she has been talking against a great Lord, whom she had never seen in her Life; and indeed never knew a Party-Woman that kept her Beauty for a Twelve-month. I would therefore advise all my Female Readers, as they value their Complexions, to let alone all Disputes of this Nature; though, at the same time, I would give free Liberty to all superannuated motherly Partizans to be as violent as they please, since there will be no danger either of their spoiling their Faces, or of their gaining Converts.

For my own part, I think a Man makes an odious and despicable Figure, that is violent in a Party; but a Woman is too sincere to mitigate the Fury of her Principles with Temper and Discretion, and to act with that Caution and Reservedness which are requisite in our Sex. When this unnatural Zeal gets into them, it throws them into ten thousand Heats and Extravagances; their generous Souls set no Bounds to their Love, or to their Hatred; and whether a Whig or Tory, a Lap-Dog or a Gallant, an Opera or a Puppet-Show, be the Object of it, the Passion, while it reigns, engrosses the whole Woman.

I remember when Dr. *Titus Oates* was in all his Glory,[5] I accompanied my friend WILL. HONEYCOMB in a Visit to a Lady of his Acquaintance: We were no sooner sate down, but upon casting my Eyes about the Room, I found in almost every Corner of it a Print that represented the Doctor in all Magnitudes and Dimensions. A little after, as the Lady was discoursing my Friend, and held her Snuff-Box in her Hand, who should I see in the Lid of it but the Doctor. It was not long after this, when she had occasion for her Handkerchief, which upon the first opening discovered among the Plaites of it the Figure of the Doctor. Upon this my Friend WILL. who loves Raillery, told her, That if he was in Mr. *Truelove*'s Place (for that was the Name of her Husband) he should be made as uneasie by a Handkerchief as ever *Othello* was. *I am afraid*, said she, *Mr.* HONEYCOMB, *you are a Tory; tell me truly, are you a Friend to the Doctor or not?* WILL. instead of making her a Reply, smiled in her Face (for indeed she was very pretty) and told her that one of her Patches was dropping off. She immediately adjusted it, and looking a little seriously, *Well*, says she, *I'll be hanged if you and your silent Friend there are not against the Doctor in your Hearts, I suspected as much by his saying nothing.* Upon this she took her Fan into her Hand, and upon the opening of it again displayed to us the Figure of the Doctor, who was placed with great Gravity among the Sticks of it. In a word, I found that the Doctor had taken Possession of her Thoughts, her Discourse, and most of her °Furniture; but finding my self pressed too close by her Question, I winked upon my Friend to take his Leave, which he did accordingly.   C

No. 66 [STEELE]

[The education of girls]
Wednesday, 16 May 1711

Motus Doceri gaudet Jonicos
Matura Virgo, & fingitur Artubus
Jam nunc, & incestos amores
De Tenero meditatur Ungui.   Hor.[1]

The two following Letters are upon a Subject of very great Importance, tho' expressed without any Air of Gravity.[2]

To the SPECTATOR.

SIR,

'I take the Freedom of asking your Advice in Behalf of a young Country Kinswoman of mine who is lately come to Town, and under my Care for her Education. She is very pretty, but you can't imagine how unformed a Creature it is. She comes to my Hands just as Nature left her, half finished, and without any acquired Improvements. When I look on her I often think of the *Belle Sauvage* mentioned in one of your Papers.[3] Dear Mr. SPECTATOR, help me to make her comprehend the visible Graces of Speech, and the dumb Eloquence of Motion; for she is at present a perfect Stranger to both. She knows no Way to express her self but by her Tongue, and that always to signifie her Meaning. Her Eyes serve her yet only to see with, and she is utterly a Foreigner to the Language of Looks and Glances. In this I fancy you could help her better than any Body. I have bestowed two Months in teaching her to Sigh when she is not concerned, and to Smile when she is not pleased; and am ashamed to own she makes little or no Improvement. Then she is no more able now to walk, than she was to go at a Year old. By Walking you will easily know I mean that regular but easie Motion, which gives our Persons so irresistible a Grace as if we moved to Musick, and is a kind of disengaged Figure, or, if I may so speak, recitative Dancing. But the want of this I cannot blame in her, for I find she has no Ear, and means nothing by Walking but to change her Place. I could pardon too her Blushing, if she knew how to carry her self in it, and if it did not manifestly injure her Complexion.

'They tell me you are a Person who have seen the World, and are a Judge of fine Breeding; which makes me ambitious of some Instructions from you for her Improvement: Which when you have favoured me with, I shall further advise with you about the Disposal of this fair °Forrester in Marriage; for I will make it no Secret to you, that her Person and Education are to be her Fortune.'

   I am, SIR,
      Your very Humble Servant,
            CELIMENE.'

  SIR,
'Being employed by *Celimene* to make up and send to you her Letter, I make bold to recommend the Case therein mentioned to your Consideration, because she and I happen to differ a little in our Notions. I, who am a rough Man, am afraid the young Girl is in a fair Way to be spoiled; Therefore pray, Mr. SPECTATOR, let us have your Opinion of this fine thing called *Fine Breeding*; for I am afraid it differs too much from that plain thing called *Good Breeding*.
            Your most humble Servant.'

The general Mistake among us in the Educating our Children, is, That in our Daughters we take Care of their Persons and neglect their Minds; in our Sons, we are so intent upon adorning their Minds, that we wholly neglect their Bodies. It is from this that you shall see a young Lady celebrated and admired in all the Assemblies about Town; when her elder Brother is afraid to come into a Room. From this ill Management it arises, That we frequently observe a Man's Life is half spent before he is taken Notice of; and a Woman in the Prime of her Years is out of Fashion and neglected. The Boy I shall consider upon some other Occasion, and at present stick to the Girl: And I am the more inclined to this, because I have several Letters which complain to me that my Female Readers have not understood me for some Days last past, and take themselves to be unconcerned in the present Turn of my Writings. When a Girl is safely brought from her Nurse, before she is capable of forming one simple Notion of any thing in Life, she is delivered to the Hands of her Dancing-Master; and with a °Collar round her Neck, the pretty wild Thing is taught a fantastical Gravity of Behaviour, and forced to a particular Way of holding her Head, heaving her Breast, and moving with her whole Body; and all this under Pain of never having an Husband, if she steps, looks, or moves awry. This gives the young Lady wonderful Workings of imagination, what is to pass between her and this Husband, that she is every Moment told of, and for whom she seems to be educated. Thus her Fancy is engaged to turn all her Endeavours to the Ornament of her Person, as what must determine her Good and Ill in this Life; and she naturally thinks, if she is tall enough, she is wise enough for any thing for which her Education makes her think she is designed. To make her an agreeable Person is the main Purpose of her Parents; to that is all their Cost, to that all their Care directed; and from this general Folly of Parents we owe our present numerous Race of Coquets. These Reflections puzzle me, when I think of giving my Advice on the Subject of managing the wild Thing mentioned in the Letter of my Correspondent. But sure there is a middle Way to be followed; the Management of a young Lady's Person is not to be overlooked, but the °Erudition of her Mind is much more to be regarded. According as this is managed, you will see the Mind follow the Appetites of the Body, or the Body express the Virtues of the Mind.

Cleomira dances with all the Elegance of Motion imaginable; but her Eyes are so chastised with the Simplicity and Innocence of her Thoughts, that she raises in her Beholders Admiration and good

Will, but no loose Hope or wild Imagination. The true Art in this Case is, To make the Mind and Body improve together; and if possible, to make Gesture follow Thought, and not let Thought be employed upon Gesture.   R

No. 189 [ADDISON]

[Fathers and sons]

Saturday, 6 October 1711

—Patriæ pietatis imago.   Virg.[1]

The following Letter being written to my Bookseller, upon a Subject of which I treated some time since, I shall publish it in this Paper, together with the Letter that was inclosed in it.

    Mr. *Buckley*,

'Mr. SPECTATOR having of late descanted upon the Cruelty of Parents to their Children, I have been induced (at the Request of several of Mr. SPECTATOR's Admirers) to enclose this Letter, which I assure you is the Original from a Father to his own Son, notwithstanding the latter gave but little or no Provocation. It would be wonderfully obliging to the World, if Mr. SPECTATOR would give his Opinion of it, in some of his Speculations, and particularly to

         (Mr. *Buckley*)
         Your humble Servant.'

    SIRRAH,

'You are a sawcy audacious Rascal, and both Fool and Mad, and I care not a Farthing whether you comply or no; that does not raze out my Impressions of your Insolence, going about Railing at me, and the next Day to sollicit my Favour: These are Inconsistencies, such as discover thy Reason depraved. To be brief, I never desire to see your Face; and, Sirrah, if you go to the Work-house, it's no Disgrace to me for you to be supported there; and if you Starve in the Streets, I'll never give any thing underhand in your behalf. If I have any more of your scribling Nonsense, I'll break your Head, the first time I set Sight on you: You are a stubborn Beast; is this your Gratitude for my giving you Mony? You Rogue I'll better your Judgment, and give you a greater Sense of your Duty to (I regret to say) your Father, &c.

'*P.S.* It's Prudence for you to keep out of my Sight; for to reproach me, that Might overcomes Right, on the outside of your Letter, I shall give you a great Knock on the Skull for it.'

Was there ever such an Image of Paternal Tenderness! It was usual among some of the *Greeks* to make their Slaves drink to excess, and then expose them to their Children, who by that means conceived an early Aversion to a Vice which makes Men appear so monstrous and irrational.[2] I have exposed this Picture of an unnatural Father with the same Intention, that its Deformity may deter others from its Resemblance. If the Reader has a mind to see a Father of the same Stamp represented in the most exquisite Stroaks of Humour, he may meet with it in one of the finest Comedies that ever appeared upon the *English* Stage: I mean the part of Sir *Sampson* in *Love for Love*.[3]

I must not however engage my self blindly on the Side of the Son, to whom the fond Letter above-written was directed. His Father calls him a *sawcy and audacious Rascal* in the first Line, and I am afraid upon Examination he will prove but an ungracious Youth. *To go about Railing* at his Father, and to find no other place but *the outside of his Letter* to tell him *that Might overcomes Right*, if it does not discover *his Reason to be depraved*, and *that he is either Fool or Mad*, as the Cholerick old Gentleman tells him, we may at least allow that the Father will do very well in endeavouring to *better his Judgment, and give him a greater Sense of his Duty*. But whether this may be brought about *by breaking his Head*, or *giving him a great Knock on the Skull*, ought I think to be well considered. Upon the whole, I wish the Father has not met with his Match, and that he may not be as equally paired with a Son, as the Mother in *Virgil*.

> — *Crudelis tu quoque mater:*
> *Crudelis mater magis an puer improbus ille?*
> *Improbus ille puer, crudelis tu quoque mater.*[4]

Or like the Crow and her Egg in the *Greek* Proverb.

> Κακοῦ κόρακος κακὸν ᾠόν.[5]

I must here take Notice of a Letter which I have received from an unknown Correspondent, upon the Subject of my Paper, upon which the foregoing Letter is likewise founded. The Writer of it seems very much concerned least that Paper should seem to give Encouragement to the Disobedience of Children towards their Parents; but if the Writer of it will take the Pains to read it over again attentively, I dare say his Apprehensions will vanish. Pardon and Reconciliation are all the Penitent Daughter requests, and all that I contend for in her behalf; and in this Case I may use the Saying of an eminent Wit, who upon some great Mens pressing him to forgive his Daughter who had married against his Consent, told them he could refuse nothing to their Instances, but that he would have them remember there was Difference between *Giving* and *Forgiving*.

I must confess, in all Controversies between Parents and their Children, I am naturally prejudiced in favour of the former. The Obligations on that side can never be acquitted, and I think it is one of the greatest Reflections upon Humane Nature that Paternal Instinct should be a stronger Motive to Love than Filial Gratitude; that the receiving of Favours should be a less Inducement to Goodwill, Tenderness and Commiseration, than the conferring of them; and that the taking Care of any Person should endear the Child or Dependant more to the Parent or Benefactor, than the Parent or Benefactor to the Child or Dependant; yet so it happens, that for one cruel Parent we meet with a thousand undutiful Children. This is indeed wonderfully contrived (as I have formerly observed)[6] for the Support of every living Species; but at the same time that it shews the Wisdom of the Creator, it discovers the Imperfection and Degeneracy of the Creature.

The Obedience of Children to their Parents is the Basis of all Government, and set forth as the measure of that Obedience which we owe to those whom Providence hath placed over us.

It is Father *le Conte*, if I am not mistaken, who tells us how want of Duty in this Particular is punished among the *Chinese*, insomuch that if a Son should be known to kill or so much as to strike his Father, not only the Criminal but his whole Family would be rooted out, nay the Inhabitants of the Place where he lived would be put to the Sword, nay the Place it self would be razed to the Ground, and its Foundations sown with Salt: For, say they, there must have been an utter Depravation of Manners in that Clan or Society of People, who could have bred up among them so horrible an Offender.[7] To this I shall add a Passage out of the first Book of *Herodotus*. That Historian in his Account of the *Persian* Customs and Religion tells us, it is their Opinion that no Man ever killed his Father, or that it is possible such a Crime should be in Nature; but that if anything like it should ever happen, they conclude that the reputed Son must have been illegitimate, Suppostitious, or begotten in Adultery. Their Opinion in this Particular shews sufficiently what a Notion they must have had of Undutifulness in general. L

No. 261 [ADDISON]

[Courtship]

Saturday, 29 December 1711

Γάμος γὰρ ἀνθρώποισιν εὐκταῖον κακόν   Frag. vet. Po.[1]

My Father, whom I mentioned in my first Speculation, and whom I must always Name with Honour and Gratitude, has very frequently talked to me upon the Subject of Marriage. I was in my younger Years engaged, partly by his Advice, and partly by my own Inclinations, in the Courtship of a Person who had a great Deal of Beauty, and did not at my first Approaches seem to have any Aversion to me; but as my natural Taciturnity hindered me from shewing my self to the best Advantage, she by Degrees began to look upon me as a very silly Fellow, and being resolved to regard Merit more than any Thing else in the Persons who made their Applications to her, she married a Captain of Dragoons who happened to be beating up for Recruits in those Parts.

This unlucky Accident has given me an Aversion to pretty Fellows ever since, and discouraged me from trying my Fortune with the fair Sex. The Observations which I made in this Conjuncture, and the repeated Advices which I received at that Time from the good old Man above-mentioned, have produced the following Essay upon Love and Marriage.

The pleasantest Part of a Man's Life is generally that which passes in Courtship, provided his Passion be sincere, and the Party beloved kind with Discretion. Love, Desire, Hope, all the pleasing Motions of the Soul rise in the Pursuit.

It is easier for an artful Man, who is not in Love, to persuade his Mistress he has a Passion for her, and to succeed in his Pursuits, than for one who loves with the greatest Violence. True Love hath ten thousand Griefs, Impatiencies and Resentments, that render a Man unamiable in the Eyes of the Person whose Affection he sollicits; besides that, it sinks his Figure, gives him Fears, Apprehensions, and Poorness of Spirit, and often makes him appear ridiculous where he has a Mind to recommend himself.

Those Marriages generally abound most with Love and Constancy, that are preceded by a long Courtship. The Passion should strike Root, and gather Strength before Marriage be grafted on it. A long Course of Hopes and Expectations fixes the Idea in our Minds, and habituates us to a Fondness of the Person beloved.

There is Nothing of so great Importance to us, as the good Qualities of one to whom we join our selves for Life; they do not only make our present State agreeable, but often determine our Happiness to all Eternity. Where the Choice is left to Friends, the chief Point under Consideration is an Estate: Where the Parties chuse for themselves, their Thoughts turn most upon the Person. They have both their Reasons. The first would procure many Conveniencies and Pleasures of Life to the Party whose Interests they espouse; and at the same Time may hope that the Wealth of their Friend will turn to their own Credit and Advantage. The others are preparing for themselves a perpetual Feast. A good Person does not only raise, but continue Love, and breeds a secret Pleasure and Complacency in the Beholder, when the first Heats of Desire are extinguished. It puts the Wife or Husband in Countenance both among Friends and Strangers, and generally fills the Family with a healthy and beautiful Race of Children.

I should prefer a Woman that is agreeable in my own Eye, and not deformed in that of the World, to a celebrated Beauty. If you marry one remarkably beautiful, you must have a violent Passion for her, or you have not the proper Taste of her Charms; and if you have such a Passion for her, it is odds but it will be imbittered with Fears and Jealousies.

Good Nature, and Evenness of Temper, will give you an easie Companion for Life; Vertue and good Sense, an agreeable Friend; Love and Constancy, a good Wife or Husband. Where we meet one Person with all these Accomplishments, we find an Hundred without any one of them. The World notwithstanding, is more intent on Trains and Equipages, and all the showy Parts of Life; we love rather to dazzle the Multitude, than consult our proper Interest; and, as I have elsewhere observed,[2] it is one of the most unaccountable Passions of humane Nature, that we are at greater Pains to appear easie and happy to others, than really to make our selves so. Of all Disparities, that in Humour makes the most unhappy Marriages, yet scarce enters into our Thoughts at the contracting of them. Several that are in this Respect unequally yoaked, and uneasie for Life, with a Person of a particular Character, might have been pleased and happy with a Person of a contrary one, notwithstanding they are both perhaps equally vertuous and laudable in their Kind.

Before Marriage we cannot be too inquisitive and discerning in the Faults of the Person beloved, nor after it too dim sighted and superficial. However perfect and accomplished the Person appears to you at a Distance, you will find many Blemishes and Imperfections in her Humour, upon a more intimate Acquaintance, which you never discovered or perhaps suspected. Here therefore Discretion and good Nature are to shew their Strength; the first will hinder your Thoughts from dwelling on what is disagreeable, the other will raise in you all the Tenderness of Compassion and Humanity, and by Degrees soften those very Imperfections into Beauties.

Marriage enlarges the Scene of our Happiness and Miseries. A Marriage of Love is pleasant; a Marriage of Interest easie; and a Marriage, where both meet, happy. A happy Marriage has in it all the Pleasures of Friendship, all the Enjoyments of Sense and Reason, and, indeed, all the Sweets of Life. Nothing is a greater Mark of a degenerate and vitious Age, than the common Ridicule which passes on this State of Life. It is, indeed, only happy in those who can look down with Scorn or Neglect on the Impieties of the Times, and tread the Paths of Life together in a constant uniform Course of Virtue.   [C]

No. 182 [STEELE]

[Seduction]

Friday, 28 September 1711

Plus aloes quam mellis habet —   Juv.[1]

As all Parts of humane Life come under my Observation, my
Reader must not make uncharitable Inferences from my speaking
knowingly of that sort of Crime which is at present treated of. He
will, I hope, suppose I know it only from the Letters of
Correspondents, two of which you shall have as follow.

Mr. SPECTATOR,

'It is wonderful to me, that among the many Enormities which you
have treated of you have not mentioned that of Wenching, and
particularly the insnaring Part; I mean, that it is a thing very fit for
your Pen to expose the Villany of the Practice of deluding Women.
You are to know, Sir, that I my self am a Woman who have been
one of the Unhappy that have fallen into this Misfortune, and that
by the Insinuation of a very worthless Fellow who served others in
the same Manner both before my Ruin and since that Time. I had,
as soon as the Rascal left me, so much Indignation and Resolution,
as not to °go upon the Town, as the Phrase is, but took to work for
my Living in an obscure Place, out of the Knowledge of all with
whom I was before acquainted.

'It is the ordinary Practice and Business of Life with a Sett of idle
Fellows about this Town, to write Letters, send Messages, and form
Appointments with little raw unthinking Girls, and leave them
after Possession of them without any Mercy to Shame, Infamy,
Poverty, and Disease. Were you to read the nauseous Impertinencies
which are written on these Occasions, and to see the silly Creatures
sighing over them, it could not but be Matter of Mirth as well as
Pity. A little Prentice Girl of mine has been for some time applied
to by an *Irish* Fellow, who dresses very fine, and struts in a laced
Coat, and is the Admiration of Semstresses who are under Age in
Town. Ever since I have had some Knowledge of the Matter, I have
debarred my Prentice from Pen, Ink, and Paper. But the other Day
he bespoke some Cravats of me: I went out of the Shop, and left his
Mistress to put them up into a °Band-Box in order to be sent to

him when his Man called. When I came into the Shop again I took Occasion to send her away, and found in the Bottom of the Box written these Words, *Why would you ruin a harmless Creature that loves you?* then in the Lid, *There is no resisting* Strephon: I searched a little further, and found in the Rim of the Box, *At eleven of Clock at Night come in an Hackney-Coach at the End of our Street*. This was enough to alarm me; I sent away the things, and took my Measures accordingly. An Hour or two before the appointed Time I examined my young Lady and found her Trunk stuffed with impertinent Letters, and an old Scrole of Parchment in Latin, which her Lover had sent her as a Settlement of fifty Pounds a Year; among other things there was also the best Lace I had in my Shop to make him a Present for Cravats. I was very glad of this last Circumstance, because I could very conscienciously swear against him that he had enticed my Servant away, and was her Accomplice in robbing me. I procured a Warrant against him accordingly. Every thing was now prepared, and the tender Hour of Love approaching, I who had acted for my self in my Youth the same senseless Part, knew how to manage accordingly. Therefore after having locked up my Maid, and not being so much unlike her in Height and Shape, as in a huddled way not to pass for her, I delivered the Bundle designed to be carried off to her Lover's Man, who came with the Signal to receive them. Thus I followed after to the Coach, where when I saw his Master take them in, I cryed out Thieves! Thieves! and the Constable with his Attendants seized my expecting Lover. I kept my self unobserved 'till I saw the Crowd sufficiently encreased, and then appeared to declare the Goods to be mine; and had the Satisfaction to see my Man of Mode[2] put into the °Round-house with the stolen Wares by him, to be produced in Evidence against the next Morning. This Matter is notoriously known to be Fact, and I have been contented to save my Prentice, and take a Year's Rent of this mortified Lover not to appear further in the Matter. This was some Penance; but, Sir, is this enough for a Villany of much more pernicious Consequence than the Trifles for which he was to have been indicted? Should not you, and all Men of any Parts or Honour, put things upon so right a Foot, as that such a Rascal should not laugh at the Imputation of what he was really guilty, and dread being accused of that for which he was arrested?

'In a Word, Sir, it is in the Power of you, and such as I hope you are, to make it as infamous to rob a poor Creature of her Honour as her Cloaths. I leave this to your Consideration, only take Leave (which I cannot do without sighing) to remark to you, that if this had been the Sense of Mankind thirty Years ago, I should have avoided a Life spent in Poverty and Shame.

            I am, SIR,

                         Your most humble Servant,
                         Alice Threadneedle.'

Mr. SPECTATOR   °*Round-house, Sept.* 9.

'I am a Man of Pleasure about Town, but by the Stupidity of a dull Rogue of a Justice of Peace and an insolent Constable, upon the Oath of an old Harridan, am imprisoned here for Theft when I designed only Fornication. The °Midnight Magistrate as he conveyed me along had you in his Mouth, and said this would make a °pure Story for the SPECTATOR. I hope, Sir, you won't pretend to Wit, and take the Part of dull Rogues of Business. The World is so altered of late Years, that there was not a Man who would knock down a Watchman in my Behalf, but I was carried off with as much Triumph as if I had been a Pick-pocket. At this Rate there is an End to all the Wit and Humour in the World. The Time was when all the honest Whore-masters in the Neighbour-hood, would have rose against the Cuckolds to my Rescue. If Fornication is to be scandalous, half the fine Things that have been writ by most of the Wits of the last Age may be burnt by the common Hangman. Harkee, SPEC. do not be queer; after having done some things pretty well, don't begin to write at that Rate that no Gentleman can read thee. Be true to Love, and burn your *Seneca.* You do not expect me to write my Name from hence, but I am

                         Your unknown humble, &c.'

                                          T

No. 266 [STEELE]

[Poor and publick whores]
Friday, 4 January 1712

Id vero est, quod ego mihi puto palmarium,
Me reperisse, quomodo adolescentulus
Meretricum ingenia & mores possit noscere:
Mature ut cum cognorit perpetuo oderit.   Ter.[1]

No Vice or Wickedness, which People fall into from Indulgence to Desires which are natural to all, ought to place them below the Compassion of the virtuous Part of the World; which indeed often makes me a little apt to suspect the Sincerity of their Virtue, who are too warmly provoked at other Peoples personal Sins. The unlawful Commerce of the Sexes is of all other the hardest to avoid; and yet there is no one which you shall hear the rigider Part of Womankind speak of with so little Mercy. It is very certain that a modest Woman cannot abhor the Breach of Chastity too much; but pray let her hate it for herself, and only pity it in others. WILL. HONEYCOMB calls these over-offended Ladies, the outragiously virtuous.

I do not design to fall upon Failures in general, with Relation to the Gift of Chastity, but at present enter upon that large Field, and begin with the Consideration of poor and publick Whores. The other Evening passing along near *Covent-Garden*, I was jogged on the Elbow as I turned into the Piazza, on the right Hand coming out of *James-Street*, by a slim young Girl of about Seventeen, who with a pert Air asked me if I was for a Pint of Wine. I do not know but I should have indulged my Curiosity in having some Chat with her, but that I am informed the Man of the *Bumper* knows me;[2] and it would have made a Story for him not very agreeable to some Part of my Writings, though I have in others so frequently said that I am wholly unconcerned in any Scene I am in, but merely as a Spectator. This Impediment being in my Way, we stood under one of the Arches by Twilight; and there I could observe as exact Features as I had ever seen, the most agreeable Shape, the finest Neck and Bosom, in a Word, the whole Person of a Woman exquisitely beautiful. She affected to allure me with a forced Wantonness in her Look and Air; but I saw it checked

with Hunger and Cold; Her Eyes were wan and eager, her Dress
thin and tawdry, her [Mien] genteel and childish. This strange
Figure gave me much Anguish of Heart, and to avoid being seen
with her I went away, but could not forbear giving her a °Crown.
The poor Thing sighed, curtsied, and with a Blessing, expressed
with the utmost Vehemence, turned from me. This Creature is
what they call °*newly come upon the Town*, but who, I suppose, falling
into cruel Hands, was left in the first Month from her Dishonour,
and exposed to pass through the Hands and Discipline of one of
those Hags of Hell whom we call Bawds. But least I should grow
too suddenly grave on this Subject, and be my self outragiously
good, I shall turn to a Scene in one of *Fletcher*'s Plays, where this
Character is drawn, and the Oeconomy of Whoredom most
admirably described. The Passage I would point to is in the third
Scene of the second Act of the *Humorous Lieutenant*.[3] *Leucippe*, who
is Agent for the King's Lust, and bawds at the same Time for the
whole Court, is very pleasantly introduced, reading her Minutes as
a Person of Business, with two Maids, her Under-Secretaries, taking
Instructions at a Table before her. Her Women, both those under
her present Tutelage, and those which she is laying Wait for, are
alphabetically set down in her Book; and she is looking over the
Letter *C*, in a muttering Voice, as if between Soliloquy and
speaking out, she says,

> *Her Maiden-head will yield me; let me see now;*
> *She is not Fifteen they say: For her Complexion —*
> Cloe, Cloe, Cloe, *here I have her,*
> Cloe, *the Daughter of a Country Gentleman;*
> *Her Age upon Fifteen. Now her Complexion,*
> *A lovely brown; here 'tis; Eyes black and rowling,*
> *The Body neatly built; she strikes a Lute well,*
> *Sings most enticingly: These Helps consider'd,*
> *Her Maiden-head will amount to some three hundred,*
> *Or three hundred and fifty Crowns, 'twill bear it handsomly.*
> *Her Father's poor, some little Share deducted,*
> *To buy him a Hunting-Nag . . .*

These Creatures are very well instructed in the Circumstances
and Manners of all who are any Way related to the fair one whom

they have a Design upon. As *Cloe* is to be purchased with 350 Crowns, and the Father taken off with a Pad; the Merchant's Wife next to her, who abounds in Plenty, is not to have downright Money, but the mercenary Part of her Mind is engaged with a Present of Plate and a little Ambition: She is made to understand that it is a Man of Quality who dies for her. The Examination of a young Girl for Business, and the crying down her Value for being a slight Thing, together with every other Circumstance in the Scene, are inimitably excellent, and have the true Spirit of Comedy; tho' it were to be wished the Author had added a Circumstance which should make *Leucippe*'s Baseness more odious.

It must not be Thought a Digression from my intended Speculation, to talk of Bawds in a Discourse upon Wenches; for a Woman of the Town is not thoroughly and properly such, without having gone through the Education of one of these Houses: But the compassionate Case of very many is, that they are taken into such Hands without any the least Suspicion, previous Temptation, or Admonition to what Place they are going. The last Week I went to an Inn in the City, to enquire for some Provisions which were sent by a Waggon out of the Country; and as I waited in one of the °Boxes till the Chamberlain had looked over his Parcels, I heard an old and a young Voice repeating the Questions and Responces of the Church-Catechism. I thought it no Breach of good Manners to peep at a Crevise, and look in at People so well employed; but who should I see there but the most artful Procuress in the Town, examining a most beautiful Country-Girl, who had come up in the same Waggon with my Things,[4] *Whether she was well educated, could forbear playing the Wanton with Servants, and idle Fellows, of which this Town*, says she, *is too full:* At the same Time, *Whether she knew enough of Breeding; as that if a Squire or a Gentleman, or one that was her Betters, should give her a civil Salute, she could curtsie and be humble nevertheless. Her innocent forsooths, yes's, and't please you's, and she would do her Endeavour*, moved the good old Lady to take her out of the Hands of a Country Bumkin her Brother, and hire her for her own Maid. I stayed till I saw them all marched out to take Coach; the Brother loaded with a great Cheese, he prevailed upon her to take for her Civilities to Sister. This poor Creature's Fate is not far off that of her's whom I spoke of above; and it is not to be doubted, but after she has been long enough a Prey to Lust she will be delivered over to Famine; the Ironical Commendation of the Industry and Charity of these antiquated Ladies, these Directors of Sin, after they can no longer commit it, makes up the Beauty of the inimitable Dedication to the *Plain Dealer*, and is a Master-piece of Railery on this Vice: But to understand all the °Purlues of this Game the better, and to illustrate this Subject in future Discourses, I must venture my self, with my Friend WILL, into the Haunts of Beauty and Gallantry; from pampered Vice in the Habitations of the Wealthy, to distressed indigent Wickedness expelled the Harbours of the Brothel.   T

No. 276 [STEELE]

[Responses to S 266]
Wednesday, 16 January 1712

Errori nomen virtus posuisset honestum.   Hor.[1]

Mr. SPECTATOR,

'I hope you have Philosophy enough to be capable of bearing the Mention of your Faults. Your Papers which regard the fallen Part of the fair Sex, are, I think, written with an Indelicacy which makes them unworthy to be inserted in the Writings of a Moralist who knows the World. I cannot allow that you are at Liberty to observe upon the Actions of Mankind with the Freedom which you seem to resolve upon; at least if you do so, you should take along with you the Distinction of Manners of the World, according to the Quality and Way of Life of the Persons concerned. A Man of Breeding speaks of even Misfortune among Ladies, without giving it the most terrible Aspect it can bear; and this Tenderness towards them, is much more to be preserved when you speak of Vices. All Mankind are so far related, that Care is to be taken, in things to which all are liable, you do not mention what concerns one in Terms which shall disgust another. Thus to tell a rich Man of the Indigence of a Kinsman of his, or abruptly inform a virtuous Woman of the Lapse of one who till then was in the same Degree of Esteem with her self, is in a kind involving each of them in some Participation of those Disadvantages. It is therefore expected from every Writer, to treat his Argument in such a Manner, as is most proper to entertain the sort of Readers to whom his Discourse is directed. It is not necessary, when you write to the Tea-Table, that you should draw Vices which carry all the Horrour of Shame and Contempt: If you paint an impertinent Self-love, an artful Glance, an assumed Complection, you say all which you ought to suppose they can possibly be guilty of. When you talk with this Limitation, you behave your self so as that you may expect others in Conversation may second your Raillery; but when you do it in a Stile which every Body else forbears in Respect to their Quality, they have an easy Remedy in forbearing to read you, and hearing no more of their Faults. A Man that is now and then guilty of an Intemperance, is not to be called a Drunkard; but the Rule of polite Raillery, is to speak of a Man's Faults as if you loved him. Of this Nature is what was said by *Cæsar*: When one was railing with an uncourtly Vehemence, and broke out, What must we call him who was taken in an Intrigue with another Man's Wife? *Cæsar* answered very gravely, *A careless Fellow*. This was at once a Reprimand for speaking of a Crime which in those Days had not the Abhorrence attending it as it ought, as well as an Intimation that all intemperate Behaviour before Superiours loses its Aim, by accusing in a Method unfit for the Audience. A Word to the Wise. All I mean here to say to you is, That the most free Person of Quality can go no further than being an unkind Woman; and you should never say of a Man of Figure worse, than that he knows the World.

> *I am*,
>
> > *SIR*,
> >
> > > *Your most humble Servant*,
> > >
> > > > Francis Courtly.'

Mr. SPECTATOR,

'I am a Woman of an unspotted Reputation, and know Nothing I have ever done which should encourage such Insolence; but here was one the other Day, and he was dressed like a Gentleman too, who took Liberty to Name the Words lusty Fellow in my Presence. I doubt not but you will resent it in Behalf of,

> > *SIR*,
> >
> > > *Your humble Servant*,
> > >
> > > > Celia.'

Mr. SPECTATOR,

'You lately put out a dreadful Paper, wherein you promise a full
Account of the State of criminal Love; and call all the Fair who have
transgressed in that Kind by one very rude Name which I do not
care to repeat: But I Desire to know of you whether I am or I am
not one of those? My Case is as follows. I am kept by an old
Batchelour, who took me so young that I knew not how he came
by me: He is a Bencher of one of the Inns of Court, a very gay
healthy old Man; which is a very lucky Thing for him, who has
been, he tells me, a °Scowrer, a °Scamperer, a Breaker of Windows,
and Invader of Constables, in the Days of Yore, when all Dominion
ended with the Day, and Males and Females met helter-skelter,
and the Scowrers drove before them all who pretended to keep up
Order or Rule to the Interruption of Love and Honour. This is his
Way of Talk, for he is very gay when he visits me; but as his former
Knowledge of the Town has alarmed him into an invincible
Jealousy, he keeps me in a Pair of Slippers, neat Boddice, warm
Petticoats, and my own Hair woven in Ringletts, after a Manner,
he says, he remembers. I am not Mistress of one Farthing of
Money, but have all Necessaries provided for me, under the Guard
of one who procured for him while he had any Desires to gratify.
I know Nothing of a Wench's Life, but the Reputation of it: I have
a natural Voice, and a pretty untaught Step in Dancing. His
Manner is to bring an old Fellow who has been his Servant from his
Youth, and is grey-headed: This Man makes on the Violin a certain
Jiggish Noise, to which I dance, and when that is over I sing to
him some loose Air that has more Wantonness than Musick in it.
You must have seen a strange windowed House near *Hide-Park;*
which is so built that no one can look out of any of the Apartments;
my Rooms are after that Manner, and I never see Man, Woman or
Child but in Company with the two Persons abovementioned. He
sends me in all the Books, Pamphlets, Plays, Operas and Songs
that come out; and his utmost Delight in me, as a Woman, is to
talk over all his old Amours in my Presence, to play with my Neck,
say *the Time was*, give me a Kiss, and bid me be sure to follow the
Directions of my Guardian, (the abovementioned Lady) and I shall
never want. The Truth of my Case is, I suppose, that I was educated
for a Purpose he did not know he should be unfit for when I came

to Years. Now, Sir, what I ask of you, as a Casuist, is to tell me how far in these Circumstances I am innocent, though submissive; he guilty, though impotent?

> *I am,*
>
> SIR,
>
> *Your constant Reader,*

PUCELLA.'

To the Man called the SPECTATOR.

Friend,

'Forasmuch as at the Birth of thy Labour, thou didst promise upon thy Word, that letting alone the Vanities that do abound, thou wouldest only endeavour to strengthen the crooked Morals of this our *Babylon*, I gave Credit to thy fair Speeches, and admitted one of thy Papers, every Day, save *Sunday*, into my House; for the Edification of my Daughter *Tabitha*, and to the End that *Susanna* the Wife of my Bosom might profit thereby. But alas! my Friend, I find that thou art a Liar, and that the Truth is not in thee; else why didst thou in a Paper which thou didst lately put forth, make Mention of those vain Coverings for the Heads of our Females, which thou lovest to liken unto Tulips,[2] and which are lately sprung up among us? Nay, why didst thou make Mention of them in such a Seeming, as if thou didst approve the Invention, insomuch that my Daughter *Tabitha* beginneth to wax wanton, and to lust after these foolish Vanities? Surely thou dost see with the Eyes of the Flesh. Verily therefore, unless thou dost speedily amend and leave off following thine own Imaginations, I will leave off thee.

Thy Friend as hereafter thou dost demean thy self,

T   Hezekiah Broadbrim.'

No. 203 [ADDISON]

[Illegitimate children]
Tuesday, 23 October 1711

— *Phœbe pater, si das hujus mihi nominis usum,*
Nec falsâ Clymene culpam sub imagine celat;
Pignora da, Genitor —   Ov. Met.[1]

There is a loose Tribe of Men whom I have not yet taken Notice of, that ramble into all the Corners of this great City, in order to seduce such unfortunate Females as fall into their Walks. These abandoned Profligates raise up Issue in every Quarter of the Town, and very often for a valuable Consideration father it upon the Church-warden. By this means there are several Married Men who have a little Family in most of the Parishes of *London* and *Westminster*, and several Batchelors who are undone by a Charge of Children.

When a Man once gives himself this Liberty of preying at large, and living upon the Common, he finds so much Game in a populous City, that it is surprising to consider the Numbers which he sometimes Propagates. We see many a young Fellow, who is scarce of Age, that could lay his Claim to the *Jus trium Liberorum*, or the Privileges which were granted by the *Roman* Laws to all such as were Fathers of three Children: Nay, I have heard a Rake who was not quite Five and Twenty declare himself the Father of a Seventh Son,[2] and very prudently determine to breed him up a Physician. In short, the Town is full of these young Patriarchs, not to mention several battered Beaus, who, like heedless Spend-thrifts that squander away their Estates before they [are] Masters of them, have raised up their whole stock of Children before Marriage.

I must not here omit the particular Whim of an Impudent Libertine that had a little smattering of Heraldry, and observing how the Genealogies of great Families were often drawn up in the shape of Trees, had taken a Fancy to dispose of his own Illegitimate Issue in a Figure of the same kind.

— *Nec longum tempus et ingens,*
Exiit ad cœlum ramis felicibus arbos,
Miraturque novas frondes, et non sua poma.   Virg.[3]

The Trunk of the Tree was marked with his own Name, *Will. Maple*. Out of the Side of it grew a large Barren Branch, Inscribed *Mary Maple*, the Name of his unhappy Wife. The Head was adorned with five huge Boughs. On the bottom of the first was Written in Capital Characters *Kate Cole*, who branched out into three Sprigs, *viz. William, Richard* and *Rebecca. Sal Twiford* gave birth to another Bough that shot up into *Sarah, Tom. Will.* and *Frank*. The third Arm of the Tree had only a single Infant in it, with a space left for a second, the Parent from whom it sprung being near her time, when the Author took this Ingenious Device into his Head. The two other great Boughs were very plentifully loaden with Fruit of the same kind; besides which there were many Ornamental Branches that did not bear. In short, a more flourishing Tree never came out of the Herald's Office.

What makes this Generation of Vermin so very Prolifick, is the indefatigable Diligence with which they apply themselves to their Business. A Man does not undergo more watchings and fatigues in a Campaign, than in the Course of a vicious Amour. As it is said of some Men, that they make their Business their Pleasure, these Sons of Darkness may be said to make their Pleasure their Business. They might conquer their corrupt Inclinations with half the Pains they are at in gratifying them.

Nor is the Invention of these Men less to be admired than their Industry and Vigilance. There is a Fragment of *Apollodorus* the Comick Poet (who was Contemporary with *Menander*) which is full of Humour, as follows. *Thou may'st shut up thy Doors*, says he, *with Bars and Bolts: It will be impossible for the Blacksmith to make them so fast, but a Cat and a Whore-master will find a way through them.*[4] In a Word, there is no Head so full of Stratagems as that of a Libidinous Man.

Were I to propose a Punishment for this infamous Race of Propagators, it should be to send them, after the second or third Offence, into our *American* Colonies, in order to People those Parts of her Majesty's Dominions where there is a want of Inhabitants, and in the Phrase of *Diogenes*[,] to *Plant Men*.[5] Some Countries punish this Crime with Death; but I think such a Banishment would be sufficient, and might turn this generative Faculty to the Advantage of the Publick.

In the mean time, till these Gentlemen may be thus disposed of, I would earnestly exhort them to take Care of those unfortunate Creatures whom they have brought into the World by these indirect Methods, and to give their spurious Children such an Education as may render them more virtuous than their Parents. This is the best Attonement they can make for their own Crimes, and indeed the only Method that is left them to repair their past Miscarriages.

I would likewise desire them to consider, whether they are not bound in common Humanity, as well as by all the Obligations of Religion and Nature, to make some Provision for those whom they have not only given Life to, but entailed upon them, though very unreasonably, a degree of Shame and Disgrace. And here I cannot but take notice of those depraved Notions which prevail among us, and which must have taken Rise from our natural Inclination to favour a Vice to which we are so very prone, namely, that *Bastardy* and *Cuckoldom* should be looked upon as Reproaches, and that the Ignominy which is only due to Lewdness and Falshood, should fall in so unreasonable a manner upon the Persons who are Innocent.

I have been insensibly drawn into this Discourse by the following Letter, which is drawn up with such a Spirit of Sincerity, that I question not but the Writer of it has represented his Case in a true and genuine Light.

   SIR,

'I am one of those People who by the general Opinion of the World are counted both Infamous and Unhappy.

'My Father is a very eminent Man in this Kingdom, and one who bears considerable Offices in it. I am his Son, but my Misfortune is, that I dare not call him Father, nor he without shame own me as his Issue, I being Illegitimate, and therefore deprived of that endearing Tenderness and unparalleled Satisfaction which a good Man finds in the Love and Conversation of a Parent; Neither have I the Opportunities to render him the Duties of a Son, he having always carried himself at so vast a Distance, and with such Superiority towards me, that by long use I have contracted a Timorousness when before him, which hinders me from declaring my own Necessities, and giving him to understand the Inconveniences I undergo.

'It is my Misfortune to have been neither bred a Scholar, a Soldier, nor to any kind of Business, which renders me entirely uncapable of making Provision for my self without his Assistance; and this creates a continual Uneasiness in my Mind, fearing I shall in time want Bread; my Father, if I may so call him, giving me but very faint Assurances of doing any thing for me.

'I have hitherto lived somewhat like a Gentleman, and it would be very hard for me to labour for my Living. I am in continual Anxiety for my future Fortune, and under a great Unhappiness in losing the sweet Conversation and Friendly Advice of my Parents; so that I cannot look upon my self otherwise than as a Monster strangely sprung up in Nature, which every one is ashamed to own.

'I am thought to be a Man of some natural Parts, and by the continual reading what you have offered the World, become an Admirer thereof, which has drawn me to make this Confession; at the same time hoping, if any thing herein shall touch you with a Sense of Pity, you would then allow me the favour of your Opinion thereupon, as also what part, I, being unlawfully born, may claim of the Man's Affection who begot me, and how far in your Opinion I am to be thought his Son, or he acknowledged as my Father. Your Sentiments and Advice herein will be a great Consolation and Satisfaction to,

> SIR,
>> Your Admirer and
>> Humble Servant,

C

>> W. B.'

No. 119 [ADDISON]

[Manners in Town and in the country]
Tuesday, 17 July 1711

Urbem quam dicunt Romam, Meliboee, putavi
Stultus ego huic nostræ similem—   Virg.[1]

The first and most obvious Reflections which arise in a man who changes the City for the Country, are upon the different Manners of the People whom he meets with in those two different Scenes of

Life. By Manners I do not mean Morals, but Behaviour and Good Breeding, as they shew themselves in the Town and in the Country.

And here, in the first place, I must observe a very great Revolution that has happened in this Article of Good Breeding. Several obliging Deferencies, Condescensions and Submissions, with many outward Forms and Ceremonies that accompany them, were first of all brought up among the politer Part of Mankind who lived in Courts and Cities, and distinguished themselves from the Rustick part of the Species (who on all Occasions acted bluntly and naturally) by such a mutual Complaisance and Intercourse of Civilities. These Forms of Conversation by degrees multiplied and grew troublesome; the Modish World found too great a Constraint in them, and have therefore thrown most of them aside. Conversation, like the *Romish* Religion, was so encumbered with Show and Ceremony, that it stood in need of a Reformation to retrench its Superfluities, and restore it to its natural good Sense and Beauty. At present therefore an unconstrained Carriage, and a certain Openness of Behaviour, are the height of Good Breeding. The Fashionable World is grown free and easie; our Manners sit more loose upon us: Nothing is so modish as an agreeable Negligence. In a word, Good Breeding shows it self most, where to an ordinary Eye it appears the least.

If after this we look on the People of Mode in the Country, we find in them the Manners of the last Age. They have no sooner fetched themselves up to the fashion of the Polite World, but the Town has dropped them, and are nearer to the first State of Nature than to those Refinements which formerly reigned in the Court, and still prevail in the Country. One may now know a Man that never conversed in the World by his Excess of Good Breeding. A Polite Country Squire shall make you as many Bows in half an Hour, as would serve a Courtier for a Week. There is infinitely more to do about Place and Precedency in a Meeting of Justices Wives, than in an Assembly of Dutchesses.

This Rural Politeness is very troublesome to a Man of my Temper, who generally take the Chair that is next me, and walk first or last, in the Front or in the Rear, as Chance directs. I have known my Friend Sir ROGER's Dinner almost cold before the Company could adjust the Ceremonial, and be prevailed upon to sit down; and have heartily pitied my old Friend, when I have seen him forced to pick and cull his Guests, as they sat at the several Parts of his Table, that he might drink their Healths according to their respective Ranks and Qualities. Honest *Will. Wimble*, who I should have thought had been altogether uninfected with Ceremony, gives me abundance of Trouble in this Particular. Though he has been fishing all the Morning, he will not help himself at Dinner 'till I am served. When we are going out of the Hall, he runs behind me; and last Night, as we were walking in the Fields, stopped short at a Stile till I came up to it, and upon my making Signs to him to get over, told me, with a serious Smile, that sure I believed they had no Manners in the Country.

There has happened another Revolution in the Point of Good Breeding, which relates to the Conversation among Men of Mode, and which I cannot but look upon as very extraordinary. It was certainly one of the first Distinctions of a well-bred Man, to express every thing that had the most remote Appearance of being obscene, in modest Terms and distant Phrases; whilst the Clown, who had no such Delicacy of Conception and Expression, cloathed his *Ideas* in those plain homely Terms that are the most obvious and natural. This kind of Good Manners was perhaps carried to an Excess, so as to make Conversation too stiff, formal and precise; for which Reason (as Hypocrisy in one Age is generally succeeded by Atheism in another) Conversation is in a great measure relapsed into the first Extream; So that at present several of our Men of the Town, and particularly those who have been polished in *France*, make use of the most coarse uncivilized Words in our Language, and utter themselves often in such a manner as a Clown would blush to hear.

This infamous Piece of Good Breeding, which reigns among the Coxcombs of the Town, has not yet made its way into the Country; and as it is impossible for such an irrational way of Conversation to last long among a People that make any Profession of Religion, or Show of Modesty, if the Country Gentlemen get into it they will certainly be left in the Lurch. Their Good Breeding will come too late to them, and they will be thought a parcel of lewd Clowns, while they fancy themselves talking together like Men of Wit and Pleasure.

As the two Points of Good Breeding, which I have hitherto

insisted upon, regard Behaviour and Conversation, there is a third
which turns upon Dress. In this too the Country are very much
behind hand. The Rural Beaus are not yet got out of the Fashion
that took place at the time of the Revolution, but ride about the
Country in red Coats and laced Hats, while the Women in many
Parts are still trying to out-vie one another in the Height of their
Head-Dresses.

But a Friend of mine, who is now upon the Western Circuit, having
promised to give me an Account of the several Modes and Fashions
that prevail in the different Parts of the Nation through which he
passes, I shall defer the enlarging upon this last Topick till I have
received a Letter from him, which I expect every Post.[2]   L

No. 132 [STEELE]

[Company in a stage-coach]
Wednesday, 1 August 1711

*— Qui, aut Tempus quid postulet non videt, aut plura loquitur, aut se ostentat, aut
eorum quibuscum est rationem non habet, is ineptus esse dicitur.*   Tull.[1]

Having notified to my good Friend Sir ROGER that I should set out
for *London* the next Day, his Horses were ready at the appointed
Hour in the Evening; and, attended by one of his Grooms, I arrived
at the Country Town at Twilight, in order to be ready for the Stage-
Coach the Day following. As soon as we arrived at the Inn, the
Servant who waited upon me, enquired of the Chamberlain in my
Hearing what Company he had for the Coach? The Fellow
answered, Mrs. *Betty Arable*, the great Fortune, and the Widow her
Mother, a recruiting Officer (who took a Place because they were
to go,) young Squire *Quickset* her Cousin (that her Mother wished
her to be married to,) *Ephraim* the Quaker her Guardian, and a
Gentleman that had studied himself dumb from Sir ROGER DE
COVERLEY's. I observed by what he said of my self, that according
to his Office he dealt much in Intelligence; and doubted not but
there was some Foundation for his Reports of the rest of the
Company, as well as for the whimsical Account he gave of me. The
next Morning at Day-break we were all called; and I, who know
my own natural Shyness, and endeavour to be as little liable to be

disputed with as possible, dressed immediately, that I might make
no one wait. The first Preparation for our Setting out was, that the
Captain's °Half-Pike was placed near the Coach-man, and a Drum
behind the Coach. In the mean Time the Drummer, the Captain's
°Equipage, was very loud, that none of the Captain's things should
be placed so as to be spoiled; upon which his Cloak-bag was fixed
in the Seat of the Coach: And the Captain himself, according to a
frequent, tho' invidious Behaviour of military Men, ordered his
Man to look sharp, that none but one of the Ladies should have the
Place he had taken fronting to the Coach-box.

We were in some little Time fixed in our Seats, and sat with that
Dislike which People not too good-natured, usually conceive of
each other at first Sight. The Coach jumbled us insensibly into
some sort of Familiarity; and we had not moved above two Miles,
when the Widow asked the Captain what Success he had in his
Recruiting? The Officer, with a Frankness he believed very graceful,
told her, 'That indeed he had but very little Luck, and had suffered
much by Desertion, therefore should be glad to end his Warfare in
the Service of her or her fair Daughter. In a Word, continued he,
I am a Soldier, and to be plain is my Character: You see me,
Madam, young, sound, and impudent; take me your self, Widow,
or give me to her, I will be wholly at your Disposal. I am a Soldier
of Fortune, ha!' This was followed by a vain Laugh of his own, and
a deep Silence of all the rest of the Company. I had nothing left for
it but to fall fast asleep, which I did with all Speed. 'Come, said
he, resolve upon it, we will make a Wedding at the next Town: We
will wake this pleasant Companion who is fallen asleep, to be the
Brideman, and (giving the Quaker a Clap on the Knee) he
concluded, 'This sly Saint, who, I'll warrant understands what's
what as well as you or I, Widow, shall give the Bride as Father.'
The Quaker, who happened to be a Man of Smartness, answered,
'Friend, I take it in good Part that thou hast given me the Authority
of a Father over this comely and virtuous Child; and I must assure
thee, that if I have the giving her, I shall not bestow her on thee.
Thy Mirth, Friend, savoureth of Folly: Thou art a Person of a light
Mind; thy Drum is a Type of thee, it soundeth because it is empty.
Verily, it is not from thy Fullness, but thy Emptiness, that thou
hast spoken this Day. Friend, Friend, we have hired this Coach in

Partnership with thee, to carry us to the great City; we cannot go
any other Way. This worthy Mother must hear thee if thou wilt
needs utter thy Follies; we cannot help it Friend, I say; if thou wilt,
we must hear thee: But if thou wert a Man of Understanding, thou
wouldst not take Advantage of thy couragious Countenance to
abash us Children of Peace. Thou art, thou sayest, a Soldier; give
Quarter to us, who cannot resist thee. Why didst thou fleer at our
Friend, who feigned himself asleep? he said nothing; but how dost
thou know what he containeth? If thou speakest improper things
in the Hearing of this virtuous young Virgin, consider it is an
Outrage against a distressed Person that cannot get from thee: To
speak indiscreetly what we are obliged to hear, by being °hasped
up with thee in this publick Vehicle, is in some Degree assaulting
on the high Road.'

Here *Ephraim* paused, and the Captain with an happy and
uncommon Impudence (which can be convicted and support itself
at the same time) crys, 'Faith Friend, I thank thee; I should have
been a little impertinent if thou hadst not reprimanded me. Come,
thou art, I see, a °smoaky old Fellow, and I'll be very orderly the
ensuing Part of the Journey. I was a going to give my self Airs, but
Ladies I beg Pardon.'

The Captain was so little out of Humour, and our Company was
so far from being sowered by this little Ruffle, that *Ephraim* and he
took a particular Delight in being agreeable to each other for the
future; and assumed their different Provinces in the Conduct of the
Company. Our Reckonings, Apartments, and Accommodation,
fell under *Ephraim*; and the Captain looked to all Disputes on the
Road, as the good Behaviour of our Coachman, and the Right we
had of taking Place as going to *London* of all Vehicles coming from
thence. The Occurrences we met with were ordinary, and very
little happened which could entertain by the Relation of them: But
when I considered the Company we were in, I took it for no small
good Fortune that the whole Journey was not spent in Impertin-
ences, which to one Part of us might be an Entertainment, to the
other a Suffering. What therefore *Ephraim* said when we were
almost arrived at *London*, had to me an Air not only of good
Understanding, but good Breeding. Upon the young Lady's
expressing her Satisfaction in the Journey, and declaring how

delightful it had been to her, *Ephraim* delivered himself as follows; 'There is no ordinary Part of humane Life which expresseth so much a good Mind, and a right inward Man, as his Behaviour upon Meeting with Strangers, especially such as may seem the most unsuitable Companions to him: Such a Man when he falleth in the Way with Persons of Simplicity and Innocence, however knowing he may be in the Ways of Men, will not vaunt himself thereof; but will the rather hide his Superiority to them, that he may not be painful unto them. My good Friend, continued he, turning to the Officer, thee and I are to part by and by, and peradventure we may never meet again: But be advised by a plain Man; Modes and Apparels are but trifles to the real man, therefore do not think such a Man as thy self terrible for thy Garb, nor such a one as me contemptible for mine. When two such as thee and I meet, with Affections as we ought to have towards each other, thou shouldst rejoyce to see my peaceable Demeanour, and I should be glad to see thy Strength and Ability to protect me in it.'   T

III   *The Town and Daily Life*

No. 28 [ADDISON]

[Street signs][1]
Monday, 2 April 1711

— *Neque semper arcum*
Tendit Apollo   Hor.[2]

I shall here present my Reader with a Letter from a °Projector, concerning a new Office which he thinks may very much contribute to the Embellishment of the City, and to the driving Barbarity out of our Streets. I consider it as a Satyr upon Projectors in general, and a lively Picture of the whole Art of Modern Criticism.

SIR,
'Observing that you have Thoughts of creating certain Officers under you, for the Inspection of several petty Enormities which you your self cannot attend to; and finding a daily Absurdities hung out upon the Sign-Posts of this City, to the great Scandal of Foreigners, as well as those of our own Country, who are curious Spectators of the same: I do humbly propose, that you would be pleased to make me your Superintendant of all such Figures and Devices as are or shall be made use of on this Occasion; with full Powers to rectifie or expunge whatever I shall find irregular or defective. For want of such an Officer, there is nothing like sound Literature and good Sense to be met with in those Objects, that are every where thrusting themselves out to the Eye, and endeavouring to become visible. Our Streets are filled with blue Boars, black Swans, and red Lions; not to mention flying Pigs, and Hogs in Armour, with many other Creatures more extraordinary than any in the Desarts of *Africk*. Strange! that one who has all the Birds and Beasts in Nature to chuse out of, should live at the Sign of an °*Ens Rationis!*

'My first Task therefore should be, like that of *Hercules*, to clear the City from Monsters. In the second Place I would forbid, that Creatures of jarring and incongruous Natures should be joined together in the same Sign; such as the Bell and the Neats-Tongue, the Dog and Gridiron. The Fox and Goose may be supposed to have met; but what has the Fox and the Seven Stars to do together? And when did the Lamb and Dolphin ever meet, except upon a Sign-Post? As for the Cat and Fiddle, there is a Conceit in it; and therefore I do not intend that any thing I have here said should affect it.³ I must however observe to you upon this Subject, that it is usual for a young Tradesman, at his first setting up, to add to his own Sign that of the Master whom he served; as the Husband after Marriage, gives a Place to his Mistress's Arms in his own Coat. This I take to have given Rise to many of those Absurdities which are committed over our Heads; and, as I am informed, first occasioned the three Nuns and a Hare, which we see so frequently joined together. I would therefore establish certain Rules, for the determining how far one Tradesman may *give* the Sign of another, and in what Cases he may be allowed to quarter it with his own.

'In the third Place, I would enjoin every Shop to make use of a Sign which bears some Affinity to the Wares in which it deals. What can be more inconsistent, than to see a Bawd at the Sign of the Angel, or a Taylor at the Lion? A Cook should not live at the Boot, nor a Shooemaker at the roasted Pig; and yet, for want of this Regulation, I have seen a Goat set up before the Door of a Perfumer, and the *French* King's Head at a Sword-Cutler's.

'An ingenious Foreigner observes, that several of those Gentlemen who value themselves upon their Families, and overlook such as are bred to Trade, bear the Tools of their Forefathers in their Coats of Arms.⁴ I will not examine how true this is in Fact: But though it may not be necessary for Posterity thus to set up the Sign of their Forefathers; I think it highly proper for those who actually profess the Trade, to show some such Marks of it before their Doors.

'When the Name gives an Occasion for an ingenious Sign-Post, I would likewise advise the Owner to take that Opportunity of letting the World know who he is. It would have been ridiculous for the Ingenious Mrs. *Salmon* to have lived at the Sign of the Trout;[5] for which Reason she has erected before her House the Figure of the Fish that is her Name-sake. Mr. *Bell* has likewise distinguished himself by a Device of the same Nature: And here, Sir, I must beg Leave to observe to you, that this particular Figure of a Bell has given Occasion to several Pieces of Wit in this kind. A Man of your Reading, must know that *Abel Drugger* gained great Applause by it in the Time of *Ben. Johnson*.[6] Our Apocryphal Heathen God is also represented by this Figure;[7] which, in Conjunction with the Dragon, makes a very handsome Picture in several of our Streets. As for the Bell-Savage,[8] which is the Sign of a Savage Man standing by a Bell, I was formerly very much puzzled upon the Conceit of it, till I accidentally fell into the reading of an old Romance translated out of the *French*; which gives an Account of a very beautiful Woman who was found in a Wilderness, and is called in the *French la belle Sauvage*; and is every where translated by our Country-man the Bell-Savage. This Piece of Philology will, I hope, convince you that I have made Sign-Posts my Study, and consequently qualified my self for the Employment which I sollicit at your Hands. But before I conclude my Letter, I must communicate to you another Remark which I have made upon the Subject with which I am now entertaining you, namely, that I can give a shrewd Guess at the Humour of the Inhabitant by the Sign that hangs before his Door. A surly cholerick Fellow, generally makes Choice of a Bear; as Men of milder Dispositions frequently live at the Lamb. Seeing a Punch-Bowl painted upon a Sign near *Charing-Cross*, and very curiously garnished, with a couple of Angels hovering over it and squeezing a Lemmon into it, I had the Curiosity to ask after the Master of the House, and found upon Enquiry, as I had guessed by the little *Agréemens* upon his Sign, that he was a *Frenchman.* I know, Sir, it is not requisite for me to enlarge upon these Hints to a Gentleman of your great Abilities; so humbly recommending my self to your Favour and Patronage,

I remain, &c.'

I shall add to the foregoing Letter, another which came to me by the same Penny-Post.

From my own Apartment near Charing-Cross.

Honoured Sir,

'Having heard that this Nation is a great Encourager of Ingenuity, I have brought with me a °Rope-Dancer that was caught in one of the Woods belonging to the Great *Mogul*. He is by Birth a Monkey; but swings upon a Rope, takes a Pipe of Tobacco, and drinks a Glass of Ale, like any reasonable Creature. He gives great Satisfaction to the Quality; and if they will make a Subscription for him, I will send for a Brother of his out of *Holland* that is a very good Tumbler; and also for another of the same Family whom I design for my °*Merry-Andrew*, as being an excellent Mimick, and the greatest Drole in the Country where he now is. I hope to have this Entertainment in a Readiness for the next Winter; and doubt not but it will please more than the Opera or Puppet-Show. I will not say that a Monkey is a better Man than some of the Opera Heroes; but certainly he is a better Representative of a Man, than the most artificial Composition of Wood and Wire. If you will be pleased to give me a good Word in your Paper, you shall be every Night a Spectator at my Show for nothing.

C   *I am*, &c.'

No. 49 [STEELE]

[The coffee-house]
Thursday, 26 April 1711

—Hominem pagina nostra sapit.   Mart.[1]

It is very natural for a Man, who is not turned for Mirthful Meetings of Men, or Assemblies of the fair Sex, to delight in that sort of Conversation which we find in Coffee-houses. Here a Man, of my Temper, is in his Element; for, if he cannot talk, he can still be more agreeable to his Company, as well as pleased in himself, in being only an Hearer. It is a Secret known but to few, yet of no small use in the Conduct of Life, that when you fall into a Man's Conversation, the first thing you should consider is, whether he has a greater Inclination to hear you, or that you should hear him. The latter is the more general Desire, and I know very able Flatterers that never speak a word in Praise of the Persons from whom they

i

obtain daily Favours, but still practise a skilful Attention to whatever is uttered by those with whom they converse. We are very Curious to observe the Behaviour of Great Men and their Clients; but the same Passions and Interests move Men in lower Spheres; and I (that have nothing else to do, but make Observations) see in every Parish, Street, Lane, and Alley of this Populous City, a little Potentate that has his Court, and his Flatterers who lay Snares for his Affection and Favour, by the same Arts that are practised upon Men in higher Stations.

In the Place I most usually frequent, Men differ rather in the Time of Day in which they make a Figure, than in any real Greatness above one another. I, who am at the Coffee-house at Six in a Morning, know that my Friend *Beaver* the Haberdasher has a Levy of more undissembled Friends and Admirers, than most of the Courtiers or Generals of *Great Britain*. Every Man about him has, perhaps, a News-Paper in his Hands; but none can pretend to guess what Step will be taken in any one Court of *Europe*, 'till Mr. *Beaver* has thrown down his Pipe, and declares what Measures the Allies must enter into upon this new Posture of Affairs. Our Coffee-house is near one of the Inns of Court, and *Beaver* has the Audience and Admiration of his Neighbours from Six 'till within a Quarter of Eight, at which time he is interrupted by the Students of the House; some of whom are ready dressed for *Westminster*, at Eight in a Morning, with Faces as busie as if they were retained in every Cause there; and others come in their °Night-Gowns to saunter away their Time, as if they never designed to go thither. I do not know that I meet, in any of my Walks, Objects which move both my Spleen and Laughter so effectually, as those Young Fellows at the *Grecian, Squire*'s, *Searle*'s; and all other Coffee-houses adjacent to the Law,² who rise early for no other Purpose but to publish their Laziness. One would think these young °*Virtuoso's* take a gay Cap and Slippers, with a Scarf and Party-coloured Gown, to be Ensigns of Dignity; for the vain Things approach each other with an Air, which shews they regard one another for their Vestments. I have observed, that the Superiority among these proceeds from an Opinion of Gallantry and Fashion: The Gentleman in the Strawberry Sash, who presides so much over the rest, has, it seems, subscribed to every Opera this last Winter, and is supposed to receive Favours from one of the Actresses.

When the Day grows too busie for these Gentlemen to enjoy any longer the Pleasures of their *Deshabilé*, with any manner of Confidence, they give Place to Men who have Business or good Sense in their Faces, and come to the Coffee-house either to transact Affairs, or enjoy Conversation. The Persons to whose Behaviour and Discourse I have most regard, are such as are between these two sorts of Men: Such as have not Spirits too Active to be happy and well pleased in a private Condition, nor Complexions too warm to make them neglect the Duties and Relations of Life. Of these sort of Men consist the worthier Part of Mankind; of these are all good Fathers, generous Brothers, sincere Friends, and faithful Subjects. Their Entertainments are derived rather from Reason than Imagination: Which is the Cause that there is no Impatience or Instability in their Speech or Action. You see in their Countenances they are at home, and in quiet Possession of the present Instant, as it passes, without desiring to quicken it by gratifying any Passion, or prosecuting any new Design. These are the Men formed for Society, and those little Communities which we express by the Word *Neighbourhoods*.

The Coffee-house is the Place of Rendezvous to all that live near it, who are thus turned to relish calm and ordinary Life. *Eubulus* presides over the middle Hours of the Day, when this Assembly of Men meet together. He enjoys a great Fortune handsomely, without launching into Expence; and exerts many noble and useful Qualities, without appearing in any publick Employment. His Wisdom and Knowledge are serviceable to all that think fit to make use of them; and he does the Office of a Council, a Judge, an Executor, and a Friend to all his Acquaintance, not only without the Profits which attend such Offices, but also without the Deference and Homage which are usually paid to them. The giving of Thanks is displeasing to him. The greatest Gratitude you can shew him, is to let him see you are the better Man for his Services; and that you are as ready to oblige others, as he is to oblige you.

In the private Exigencies of his Friends he lends, at legal Value, considerable Sums, which he might highly increase by °rolling in the Publick Stocks. He does not consider in whose Hands his Mony will improve most, but where it will do most Good.

Eubulus has so great an Authority in his little Diurnal Audience, that when he shakes his Head at any Piece of publick News, they all of them appear dejected; and, on the contrary, go home to their Dinners with a good Stomach and chearful Aspect, when *Eubulus* seems to intimate that Things go well. Nay, their Veneration towards him is so great, that when they are in other Company they speak and act after him; are Wise in his °Sentences, and are no sooner sate down at their own Tables, but they hope or fear, rejoice or despond as they saw him do at the Coffee-house. In a word, every Man is *Eubulus* as soon as his Back is turned.

Having here given an Account of the several Reigns that succeed each other from Day-break 'till Dinner-time,[3] I shall mention the Monarchs of the Afternoon on another occasion, and shut up the whole Series of them with the History of *Tom* the Tyrant;[4] who, as first Minister of the Coffee-house, takes the Government upon him between the Hours of Eleven and Twelve at Night, and gives his Orders in the most Arbitrary manner to the Servants below him, as to the Disposition of Liquors, Coal and Cinders.   R

No. 155 [STEELE]

[The coffee-house again]

Tuesday, 28 August 1711

— Hæ nugæ seria ducunt
In mala —   Hor.[1]

I have more than once taken Notice of an indecent License taken in Discourse, wherein the Conversation on one Part is involuntary, and the Effect of some necessary Circumstance. This happens in travelling together in the same hired Coach, sitting near each other in any publick Assembly, or the like. I have upon making Observations of this sort received innumerable Messages, from that Part of the fair Sex whose Lot in Life it is to be of any Trade or publick Way of Life. They are all to a Woman urgent with me to lay before the World the unhappy Circumstances they are under, from the unreasonable Liberty which is taken in their Presence, to talk on what Subject it is thought fit by every Coxcomb who wants Understanding or Breeding. One or two of these Complaints I shall set down.

   Mr. SPECTATOR,
'I keep a Coffee-house, and am one of those whom you have thought fit to mention as an Idol some Time ago.[2] I suffered a good deal of Raillery upon that Occasion; but shall heartily forgive you, who were the Cause of it, if you will do me Justice in another Point. What I ask of you, is, to acquaint my Customers (who are otherwise very good ones) that I am unavoidably °hasped in my Bar, and cannot help hearing the improper Discourses they are pleased to entertain me with. They strive who shall say the most immodest things in my Hearing: At the same Time half a Dozen of them loll at the Bar staring just in my Face, ready to interpret my Looks and Gestures according to their own Imaginations. In this passive Condition I know not where to cast my Eyes, place my Hands, or what to employ my self in: But this Confusion is to be a Jest, and I hear them say in the End, with an insipid Air of Mirth and Subtlety, Let her alone, she knows as well as we for all she looks so. Good Mr. SPECTATOR, perswade Gentlemen that it is out of all Decency: Say it is possible a Woman may be modest, and yet keep a publick House. Be pleased to argue that in Truth the Affront is the more unpardonable because I am obliged to suffer it, and cannot fly from it. I do assure you, Sir, the Chearfulness of Life which would arise from the honest Gain I have, is utterly lost to me from the endless, flat, impertinent Pleasantries which I hear from Morning to Night. In a Word, it is too much for me to bear; and I desire you to acquaint them, that I will keep Pen and Ink at the Bar, and write down all they say to me, and send it to you for the Press. It is possible when they see how empty what they speak, without the Advantage of an impudent Countenance and Gesture, will appear, they may come to some Sense of themselves, and the Insults they are guilty of towards me. I am,
     SIR,
      Your most humble Servant,
           The Idol.'

This Representation is so just, that it is hard to speak of it without an Indignation which perhaps would appear too elevated to such as can be guilty of this inhuman Treatment, where they see they affront a modest, plain, and ingenuous Behaviour. This Correspondent is not the only Sufferer in this Kind, for I have long Letters both from the *Royal* and *New Exchange*[3] on the same Subject. They tell me that a young Fop cannot buy a Pair of Gloves, but he is at the same Time straining for some ingenious Ribaldry to say to the young Woman who helps them on. It is no small Addition to the Calamity, that the Rogues °buy as hard as the plainest and modestest Customers they have; besides which they loll upon their Counters half an Hour longer than they need, to drive away other Customers, who are to share their Impertinencies with the Milliner, or go to another Shop. Letters from °*Change-Alley* are full of the same Evil, and the Girls tell me except I can chace some eminent Merchants from their Shops they shall in a short Time fail. It is very unaccountable, that Men can have so little Deference to all Mankind who pass by them, as to bear being seen toying by two's and three's at a Time, with no other Purpose but to appear gay enough to keep up a light Conversation of common-place Jests, to the Injury of her whose Credit is certainly hurt by it, tho' their own may be strong enough to bear it. When we come to have exact Accounts of these Conversations, it is not to be doubted but that their Discourses will raise the usual Stile of buying and selling: Instead of the plain down-right lying, and asking and bidding so unequally to what they will really give and take, we may hope to have from these fine Folks an Exchange of Complements. There must certainly be a great deal of pleasant Difference between the Commerce of Lovers, and that of all other Dealers, who are, in a Kind, Adversaries. A sealed Bond or a Bank Note, would be a pretty Gallantry to convey unseen into the Hands of one whom a Director is charmed with; otherwise the City Loiterers are still more unreasonable than those at the other End of the Town: At the *New Exchange* they are eloquent for want of Cash, but in the City they ought with Cash to supply their want of Eloquence.

If one might be serious on this prevailing Folly, one might observe, that it is a melancholy thing, when the World is mercenary even to the buying and selling our very Persons, that young Women, tho' they have never so great Attractions from Nature, are never the nearer being happily disposed of in Marriage; I say, it is very hard under this Necessity, it shall not be possible for them to go into a Way of Trade for their Maintenance, but their very Excellencies and personal Perfections shall be a Disadvantage to them, and subject them to be treated as if they stood there to sell their Persons to Prostitution. There cannot be a more melancholy Circumstance to one who has made any Observation in the World, than one of these erring Creatures exposed to Bankruptcy. When that happens, none of these toying Fools will do any more than any other Man they meet to preserve her from Infamy, Insult, and °Distemper. A Woman is naturally more helpless than the other Sex; and a Man of Honour and Sense should have this in his View in all Manner of Commerce with her. Were this well weighed, Inconsideration, Ribaldry, and Nonsense, would not be more natural to entertain Women with than Men; and it would be as much Impertinence to go into a Shop of one of these young Women without buying, as into that of any other Trader. I shall end this Speculation with a Letter I have received from a pretty Milliner in the City.

Mr. SPECTATOR,
'I have read your Account of Beauties,[4] and was not a little surprized to find no Character of my self in it. I do assure you I have little else to do but to give Audience as I am such. Here are Merchants of no small Consideration, who call in as certainly as they go to *'Change* to say something of my roguish Eye: And here is one who makes me once or twice a Week tumble over all my Goods, and then owns it was only a Gallantry to see me act with these pretty Hands; then lays out three Pence in a little Ribbon for his Wrist-bands, and thinks he is a Man of great Vivacity. There is an ugly thing not far off me, whose Shop is frequented only by People of Business, that is all Day long as busy as possible. Must I that am a Beauty be treated with for nothing but my Beauty? Be pleased to assign Rates to my kind Glances, or make all pay who come to see me, or I shall be undone by my Admirers for want of Customers. *Albacinda*, *Eudosia*, and all the rest would be used just as we are, if they were

in our Condition; therefore pray consider the Distress of us the lower Order of Beauties, and I shall be

T   *Your oblig'd humble Servant.'*

No. 88 [STEELE]

[Servants]

Monday, 11 June 1711

Quid Domini facient, audent cum talia Fures?   Virg.[1]

Mr. SPECTATOR,   *May 30. 1711.*

'I have no small Value for your Endeavours to lay before the World what may escape their Observation, and yet highly conduces to their Service. You have, I think, succeeded very well on many Subjects; and seem to have been conversant in very different Scenes of Life. But in the Considerations of Mankind, as a SPECTATOR, you should not omit Circumstances which relate to the inferiour Part of the World, any more than those which concern the greater. There is one thing in particular which I wonder you have not touched upon, and that is, the general Corruption of Manners in the Servants of *Great Britain*. I am a Man that have travelled and seen many Nations, but have for seven Years last past resided constantly in *London* or within twenty Miles of it: In this Time I have contracted a numerous Acquaintance among the best Sort of People, and have hardly found one of them happy in their Servants. This is Matter of great Astonishment to Foreigners, and all such as have visited foreign Countries; especially since we cannot but observe, That there is no Part of the World where Servants have those Privileges and Advantages as in *England*: They have no where else such plentiful Diet, large Wages, or indulgent Liberty: There is no Place wherein they labour less, and yet where they are so little respectful, more wasteful, more negligent, or where they so frequently change their Masters. To this I attribute, in a great Measure, the frequent Robberies and Losses which we suffer on the high Road and in our own Houses. That indeed which gives me the present Thought of this Kind, is, that a careless Groom of mine has spoiled me the prettiest Pad in the World, with only riding him ten Miles; and I assure you, if I were to make a Register of all the

Horses I have known thus abused by Negligence of Servants, the
Number would mount a Regiment. I wish you would give us your
Observations, that we may know how to treat these Rogues, or that
we Masters may enter into Measures to reform them. Pray give us
a Speculation in general about Servants, and you make me

Yours,

Philo-Britannicus.'

'Pray do not omit the Mention of Grooms in particular.'

This honest Gentleman, who is so desirous that I should write
a Satyr upon Grooms, has a great deal of Reason for his Resentment;
and I know no Evil which touches all Mankind so much, as this of
the Misbehaviour of Servants.

The Complaint of this Letter runs wholly upon Men-Servants; and
I can attribute the Licentiousness which as at present prevailed among
them, to nothing but what an hundred before me have ascribed it to,
The Custom of giving °Board-Wages: This one Instance of false
°Oeconomy, is sufficient to debauch the whole Nation of Servants,
and makes them as it were but for some Part of their Time in that
Quality. They are either attending in Places where they meet and run
into Clubs, or else, if they wait at Taverns, they eat after their
Masters, and reserve their Wages for other Occasions. From hence it
arises, That they are but in a lower Degree what their Masters
themselves are; and usually affect an Imitation of their Manners: And
you have in Liveries Beaux, Fops, and Coxcombs, in as high Perfection, as among People that keep °Equipages. It is a common Humour
among the Retinue of People of Quality, when they are in their
Revels, that is when they are out of their Masters Sight, to assume in
an humourous Way the Names and Titles of those whose Liveries they
wear. By which Means Characters and Distinctions become so familiar to them, that it is to this, among other Causes, one may impute
a certain Insolence among our Servants, that they take no Notice of
any Gentleman though they know him ever so well, except he is an
Acquaintance of their Masters.

My Obscurity and Taciturnity leave me at Liberty, without
Scandal, to dine, if I think fit, at a common °Ordinary, in the
meanest as well as the most sumptuous House of Entertainment.
Falling in the other Day at a Victualling-house near the House of

Peers, I heard the Maid come down and tell the Landlady at the Bar, That my Lord Bishop swore he would throw her out at Window if she did not bring up more Mild-beer, and that my Lord Duke would have a double Mug of °Purle. My Surprise was encreased, in hearing loud and rustick Voices speak and answer to each other upon the publick Affairs, by the Names of the most Illustrious of our Nobility; till of a sudden one came running in, and cryed the House was rising. Down came all the Company together, and away: The Ale-house was immediately filled with Clamour, and scoring one Mug to the Marquis of such a Place, Oyl and Vinegar to such an Earl, three Quarts to my new Lord for wetting his Title, and so forth. It is a thing too notorious to mention the Crowds of Servants, and their Insolence, near the Courts of Justice, and the Stairs towards the supreme Assembly; where there is an universal Mockery of all Order, such riotous Clamour and licentious Confusion, that one would think the whole Nation lived in Jest, and there were no such thing as Rule and Distinction among us.

The next Place of Resort, wherein the servile World are let loose, is at the Entrance of *Hide-Park*, while the Gentry are at the °Ring. Hither People bring their Lacqueys out of State, and here it is that all they say at their Tables and act in their Houses is communicated to the whole Town. There are Men of Wit in all Conditions of Life; and mixing with these People at their Diversions, I have heard Coquets and Prudes as well rallied, and Insolence and Pride exposed, (allowing for their want of Education,) with as much Humour and good Sense, as in the politest Companies. It is a general Observation, That all Dependants run in some Measure into the Manners and Behaviour of those whom they serve: You shall frequently meet with Lovers and Men of Intrigue among the Lacqueys, as well as at *White*'s[2] or in the °Side-Boxes. I remember some Years ago an Instance of this Kind. A Footman to a Captain of the Guard used frequently, when his Master was out of the Way, to carry on Amours and make Assignations in his Master's Cloaths. The Fellow had a very good Person, and there are very many Women that think no further than the Outside of a Gentleman; besides which, he was almost as learned a Man as the Collonel himself. I say, thus qualified, the Fellow could scrawl *Billets doux* so well, and furnish a Conversation on the common Topicks, that he had, as they call it, a great deal of good Business on his Hands. It happened one Day, that coming down a Tavern-stairs in his Master's fine Guard-Coat, with a well-dressed Woman masked, he met the Collonel coming up with other Company; but with a ready Assurance he quitted his Lady, came up to him, and said, *Sir, I know you have too much Respect for your self to cane me in this honourable Habit: But you see there is a Lady in the Case, and I hope on that Score also you will put off your Anger till I have told you all another Time.* After a little Pause the Collonel cleared up his Countenance, and with an Air of Familiarity whispered his Man apart, *Sirrah, bring the Lady with you to ask Pardon for you*; then aloud, *Look to it* Will. *I'll never forgive you else.* The Fellow went back to his Mistress, and telling her with a loud Voice and an Oath, That was the honestest Fellow in the World, conveyed her to an Hackney-Coach.

But the many Irregularities committed by Servants in the Places above-mentioned, as well as in the Theatres, of which Masters are generally the Occasions, are too various not to need being resumed on another Occasion.   R

No. 137 [STEELE]

[Complaints of servants]
Tuesday, 7 August 1711

At hæc etiam Servis semper libera fuerunt, timerent, gauderent, dolerent suo potius quam alterius arbitrio.   Tull. Epist.[1]

It is no small Concern to me, that I find so many Complaints from that Part of Mankind whose Portion it is to live in Servitude, that those whom they depend upon will not allow them to be even as happy as their Condition will admit of. There are, as these unhappy Correspondents inform me, Masters who are offended at a chearful Countenance, and think a Servant has broke loose from them, if he does not preserve the utmost Awe in their Presence. There is one who says, if he looks satisfied his Master asks him what makes him so pert this Morning; if a little sower, Hark ye, Sirrah, are not you paid your Wages? The poor Creatures live in the most extreme Misery together: The Master knows not how to preserve Respect, nor the Servant how to give it. If seems this Person is of so sullen a Nature, that he knows but little Satisfaction in the Midst of a plentiful Fortune, and secretly frets to see any Appearance of Content in one that lives upon the hundredth Part of his Income, who is unhappy in the Possession of the Whole. Uneasy Persons, who cannot possess their own Minds, vent their Spleen upon all who depend upon them; which, I think, is expressed in a lively Manner in the following Letters.

SIR,   *August* 2, 1711.
'I have read your *Spectator* of the 3d of the last Month, and wish I had the Happiness of being preferred to serve so good a Master as Sir ROGER. The Character of my Master is the very Reverse of that good and gentle Knight's. All his Directions are given, and his Mind revealed by Way of Contraries: As when any thing is to be remembered, with a peculiar Cast of Face he cries, *Be sure to forget now*. If I am to make Haste back, *Don't come these two Hours; be sure to call by the Way upon some of your Companions*. Then another excellent Way of his is, if he sets me any thing to do, which he knows must necessarily take up Half a Day, he calls ten times in a Quarter of an Hour to know whether I have done yet. This is his Manner, and the same Perverseness runs through all his Actions, according as the Circumstances vary. Besides all this, he is so suspicious, that he submits himself to the Drudgery of a Spy. He is as unhappy himself as he makes his Servants: He is constantly watching us, and we differ no more in Pleasure and Liberty than as a Gaoler and a Prisoner. He lays Traps for Faults, and no sooner makes a Discovery, but falls into such Language, as I am more ashamed of for coming from him, than for being directed to me. This, Sir, is a short Sketch of a Master I have served upwards of nine Years; and tho' I have never wronged him, I confess my Despair of pleasing him has very much abated my Endeavour to do it. If you will give me Leave to steal a Sentence out of my Master's *Clarendon*, I shall tell you my Case in a Word, *Being used worse than I deserved, I cared less to deserve well than I had done.* [2]

              I am,
         SIR,
              Your humble Servant,
                             RALPH VALET.'

Dear Mr. SPECTER,

'I am the next thing to a Lady's Woman, and am under both my Lady and her Woman. I am so used by them both, that I should be very glad to see them in the SPECTER. My Lady herself is of no Mind in the World, and for that Reason her Woman is of twenty Minds in a Moment. My Lady is one that never knows what to do with her self; she pulls on and puts off every thing she wears twenty times before she resolves upon it for that Day. I stand at one End of the Room, and reach things to her Woman. When my Lady asks for a thing, I hear and have half brought it, when the Woman meets me in the Middle of the Room to receive it, and at that Instant she says No she will not have it. Then I go back, and her Woman comes up to her, and by this Time she will have that, and two or three things more in an Instant: The Woman and I run to each other; I am loaded and delivering the things to her when my Lady says she wants none of these things, and we are the dullest Creatures in the World, and she the unhappiest Woman living, for she shan't be dressed in any time. Thus we stand not knowing what to do, when our good Lady with all the Patience in the World tells us as plain as she can speak, that she will have °Temper because we have no manner of Understanding, and begins again to dress, and see if we can find out of our selves what we are to do. When she is Dressed she goes to Dinner, and after she has disliked every thing there, she calls for the Coach, then commands it in again, and then she will not go out at all, and then will go too, and orders the °Chariot. Now good Mr. SPECTER, I desire you would, in the Behalf of all who serve froward Ladies, give out in your Paper, that nothing can be done without allowing Time for it, and that one cannot be back again with what one was sent for if one is called back before one can go a Step for that they want. And if you please let them know that all Mistresses are as like as all Servants.

I am

Your loving Friend
PATIENCE GIDDY.'

These are great Calamities; but I met the other Day in the five Fields towards *Chelsea*,[3] a pleasanter Tyrant than either of the above represented. A fat Fellow was puffing on in his open Wastcoat; a

Boy of fourteen in a Livery carrying after him his Cloak, upper Coat, Hat, Wig, and Sword. The poor Lad was ready to sink with the Weight, and could not keep up with his Master, who turned back every half Furlong, and wondered what made the lazy young Dog lag behind.

There is something very unaccountable, that People cannot put themselves in the Condition of the Persons below them when they consider the Commands they give. But there is nothing more common, than to see a Fellow (who, if he were reduced to it, would not be hired by any Man living) lament that he is troubled with the most worthless Dogs in Nature.

It would, perhaps, be running too far out of common Life to urge, that he who is not Master of himself and his own Passions, cannot be a proper Master of another. Æquanimity in a Man's own Words and Actions, will easily diffuse it self through his whole Family. *Pamphilio* has the happiest Houshold of any Man I know, and that proceeds from the human Regard he has to them in their private Persons, as well as in respect that they are his Servants. If there be any Occasion, wherein they may in themselves be supposed to be unfit to attend their Master's Concerns, by reason of an Attention to their own, he is so good as to place himself in their Condition. I thought it very becoming in him, when at Dinner the other Day he made an Apology for want of more Attendants. He said, *One of my Footmen is gone to the Wedding of his Sister; and the other I don't expect to Wait, because his Father died but two Days ago.*   T

No. 251 [ADDISON]

[The cries of London][1]
Tuesday, 18 December 1711

— Linguæ centum sunt, oraque centum,
Ferrea vox —   Virg.[2]

There is nothing which more astonishes a Foreigner, and frights a Country Squire, than the *Cries of London*. My good Friend Sir ROGER often declares, that he cannot get them out of his Head, or go to sleep for them the first Week that he is in Town. On the contrary, WILL. HONEYCOMB calls them the °*Ramage de la Ville*,, and prefers them to the Sounds of Larks and Nightingales, with all the Musick of the Fields and Woods. I have lately received a Letter from some very odd Fellow upon this Subject, which I shall leave with my Reader, without saying any thing further of it.

SIR,
'I am a Man out of all Business, and would willingly turn my Head to any thing for an honest Livelihood. I have invented several Projects for raising many Millions of Money without burthening the Subject, but I cannot get the Parliament to listen to me, who look upon me, forsooth, as a [°Crack and a] °Projector; so that despairing to enrich either myself or my Country by this Publick-spiritedness, I would make some Proposals to you relating to a Design which I have very much at Heart, and which may procure me an handsome Subsistance, if you will be pleased to recommend it to the Cities of *London* and *Westminster*.

'The Post I would aim at is to be Comptroller general of the *London* Cries, which are at present under no manner of Rules or Discipline. I think I am pretty well qualified for this Place, as being a Man of very strong Lungs, of great Insight into all the Branches of our *British* Trades and Manufactures, and of a competent Skill in Musick.

'The Cries of *London* may be divided into Vocal and Instrumental. As for the latter, they are at present under a very great Disorder. A Freeman of *London* has the Privilege of disturbing a whole Street for an Hour together, with the Twancking of a brass Kettle or a Frying-pan. The Watch-man's Thump at Midnight startles us in our Beds, as much as the breaking in of a Thief. The Sow-gelder's Horn has indeed something musical in it, but this is seldom heard within the Liberties. I would therefore propose, that no Instrument of this Nature should be made use of, which I have not tuned and licensed, after having carefully examined in what manner it may affect the Ears of her Majesty's liege Subjects.

'Vocal Cries are of much larger Extent, and indeed so full of Incongruities and Barbarisms, that we appear a distracted City to Foreigners, who do not comprehend the Meaning of such °enormous Outcries. Milk is generally sold in a Note above °*Elah*, and in Sounds so exceeding shrill, that it often sets our Teeth an edge.

The Chimney-sweeper is confined to no certain Pitch; he sometimes utters himself in the deepest Base, and sometimes in the sharpest Treble; sometimes in the highest, and sometimes in the lowest Note of the Gamut. The same Observation might be made on the Retailers of Small-coal, not to mention broken Glasses or Brick-dust.[3] In these, therefore, and the like Cases, it should be my Care to sweeten and mellow the Voices of these itinerant Tradesmen, before they make their Appearance in our Streets; as also to accommodate their Cries to their respective Wares; and to take Care in particular that those may not make the most Noise, who have the least to sell, which is very observable in the Venders of Card-matches to whom I cannot but apply that old Proverb of *Much Cry but little Wool.*

'Some of these last-mentioned Musicians are so very loud in the Sale of these trifling Manufactures, that an honest splenetick Gentleman of my Acquaintance bargained with one of them never to come into the Street where he lived: But what was the Effect of this Contract? why, the whole Tribe of Cardmatch-makers which frequent that Quarter, passed by his Door the very next Day, in hopes of being bought off after the same manner.

'It is another great Imperfection in our *London* Cries, that there is no just Time nor Measure observed in them. Our News should indeed be published in a very quick Time, because it is a Commodity that will not keep cold. It should not however be cried with the same Precipitation as *Fire*: Yet this is generally the Case: A bloody Battel alarms the Town from one End to another in an Instant. Every Motion of the *French* is published in so great an Hurry, that one would think the Enemy were at our Gates. This likewise I would take upon me to regulate in such a manner, that there should be some Distinction made between the spreading of a Victory, a March, or an Incampment, a *Dutch*, a *Portugal*, or a *Spanish* Mail. Nor must I omit under this Head, those excessive Alarms with which several boisterous Rusticks infest our Streets in Turnip Season; and which are more inexcusable, because these are Wares which are in no Danger of Cooling upon their Hands.

'There are others who affect a very slow Time, and are in my Opinion much more tuneable than the former; the Cooper in particular swells his last Note in an hollow Voice, that is not without its Harmony; nor can I forbear being inspired with a most agreeable Melancholy, when I hear that sad and solemn Air with which the Publick is very often asked, if they have any Chairs to mend. Your own Memory may suggest to you many other lamentable Ditties of the same Nature, in which the Musick is wonderfully languishing and melodious.

'I am always pleased with that particular Time of the Year which is proper for the pickling of Dill and Cucumbers; but alas this Cry, like the Song of the Nightingales, is not heard above two Months. It would therefore be worth while to consider whether the same Air might not in some Cases be adapted to other Words.

'It might likewise deserve our most serious Consideration, how far, in a well-regulated city, those Humourists are to be tolerated, who not contented with the traditional Cries of their Fore-fathers, have invented particular Songs and Tunes of their own: Such as was, not many Years since, the Pastry-man, commonly known by the Name of the Colly-Molly-Puff;[4] and such as is at this Day the Vender of Powder and °Washballs, who, if I am rightly informed, goes under the Name of *Powder-Watt*.

'I must not here omit one particular Absurdity which runs thro' this whole vociferous Generation, and which renders their Cries very often not only incommodious, but altogether useless to the Publick. I mean that idle Accomplishment which they all of them aim at, of Crying so not to be understood. Whether or no they have learned this from several of our affected Singers, I will not take upon me to say; but most certain it is, that People know the Wares they deal in rather by their Tunes than by their Words; insomuch that I have sometimes seen a Country Boy run out to buy Apples of a Bellows-mender, and Gingerbread from a Grinder of Knives and Scissars. Nay, so strangely infatuated are some very eminent Artists of this particular Grace in a Cry, that none but their Acquaintance are able to guess at their Profession; for who else can know, that *Work if I had it*, should be the Signification of a Corn-Cutter.

'Forasmuch therefore as Persons of this Rank are seldom Men of Genius or Capacity, I think it would be very proper that some Man of good Sense and sound Judgment should preside over these publick Cries, who should permit none to lift up their Voices in our Streets, that have not tuneable Throats, and are not only able to overcome the Noise of the Croud, and the rattling of Coaches, but also to vend their respective Merchandizes in apt Phrases, and in the most distinct and agreeable Sounds. I do therefore humbly recommend my self as a Person rightly qualified for this Post, and if I meet with fitting Encouragements, shall communicate some other Projects which I have by me, that may no less conduce to the Emolument of the Publick.

                    I am,

                              SIR, &c.
C   Ralph Crotchett.'

No. 324 [STEELE]

[Mohawks]¹

Wednesday, 12 March 1712

O curvæ in terris animæ, & cœlestium inanes.   Pers.²

Mr. SPECTATOR,

'The Materials you have collected together towards a general History of Clubs,³ makes so bright a Part of your Speculations, that I think it is but a Justice we all owe the learned World to furnish you with such Assistances as may promote that useful Work. For this Reason I could not forbear communicating to you some imperfect Informations of a Set of Men (if you will allow them a Place in that Species of Being) who have lately erected themselves into a Nocturnal Fraternity, under the Title of *The Mohock Club*, a Name borrowed it seems from a Sort of *Cannibals* in *India*, who subsist by Plundering and Devouring all the Nations about them. The President is stiled *Emperor of the Mohocks*; and his Arms are a *Turkish* Crescent, which his Imperial Majesty bears at present in a very extraordinary Manner engraven upon his Forehead. Agreeable to their Name, the avowed Design of their Institution is Mischief; and upon this Foundation all their Rules and Orders are framed. An outragious Ambition of doing all possible Hurt to their Fellow-Creatures, is the great Cement of their Assembly, and the only Qualification required in the Members. In order to exert this Principle in its full Strength and Perfection, they take Care to drink themselves to a Pitch, that is, beyond the Possibility of attending to any Motions of Reason or Humanity; then make a general Sally, and attack all that are so unfortunate as to walk the Streets through which they patroll. Some are knocked down, others stabbed, others cut and °carbonadoed. To put the Watch to a total Rout, and mortify some of those inoffensive Militia, is reckoned a *Coup d'eclat*. The particular Talents by which these *Misanthropes* are distinguished from one another, consist in the various Kinds of Barbarities which they execute upon their Prisoners. Some are celebrated for a happy Dexterity in Tipping the Lion upon them; which is performed by squeezing the Nose flat to the Face, and boring out the Eyes with their Fingers: Others are called the Dancing-Masters, and teach their Scholars to cut Capers by running Swords thro' their Legs; a new Invention, whether originally *French* I cannot tell: A third Sort are the Tumblers, whose Office it is to set Women upon their Heads and commit certain Indecencies, or rather Barbarities, on the Limbs which they expose. But these I forbear to mention, because they can't but be very shocking to the Reader, as well as the SPECTATOR. In this Manner they carry on a War against Mankind; and by the standing Maxims of their Policy, are to enter into no Alliances but one, and that is Offensive and Defensive with all Bawdy-Houses in general, of which they have declared themselves Protectors and Guarantees.

'I must own, Sir, these are only broken incoherent Memoirs of this wonderful Society, but they are the best I have been yet able to procure; for being but of late Establishment, it is not ripe for a just History: And to be serious, the chief Design of this Trouble is to hinder it from ever being so. You have been pleased, out of a Concern for the Good of your Countrymen, to act under the Character of SPECTATOR not only the Part of a Looker-on, but an Overseer of their Actions; and whenever such Enormities as this infest the Town, we immediately fly to you for Redress. I have Reason to believe, that some thoughtless Youngsters, out of a false Notion of Bravery, and an immoderate Fondness to be distinguished for Fellows of Fire, are insensibly hurried into this senseless scandalous Project: Such will probably stand corrected by your Reproofs, especially if you inform them, that it is not Courage for half a Score Fellows, mad with Wine and Lust, to set upon two or three soberer than themselves; and that the Manners of *Indian* Savages are no becoming Accomplishments to an *English* fine Gentleman. Such of them as have been Bullies and °Scowrers of a long Standing, and are grown Veterans in this Kind of Service, are I fear too hardned to receive any Impressions from your Admonitions. But I beg you would recommend to their Perusal your ninth Speculation: They may there be taught to take Warning from the Club of Duellists; and be put in Mind, that the common Fate of those Men of Honour was to be hanged.

I am,

SIR,

March the 10th,   *Your most humble Servant,*
1711–12.   Philanthropos.'

The following Letter is of a quite contrary Nature; but I add it here that the Reader may observe at the same View, how amiable Ignorance may be when it is shewn in its Simplicities, and how detestable in Barbarities. It is written by an honest Countryman to his Mistress, and came to the Hands of a Lady of good Sense wrapped about a Thread-Paper, who has long kept it by her as an Image of artless Love.

To her I very much Respect, Mrs. Margaret Clark.

'Lovely, and oh that I could write loving Mrs. *Margaret Clark*, I pray you let Affection excuse Presumption. Having been so happy as to enjoy the Sight of your sweet Countenance and comely Body, sometimes when I had Occasion to buy Treacle or Liquorish Powder at the Apothecary's Shop, I am so enamoured with you, that I can no more keep close my flaming Desire to become your Servant. And I am the more bold now to write to your sweet self, because I am now my own Man, and may match where I please; for my Father is taken away, and now I am come to my Living, which is Ten Yard Land, and a House; and there is never a Yard of Land in our Field but it is as well worth ten Pound a Year as a Thief is worth a Halter; and all my Brothers and Sisters are provided for: Besides I have good Houshold stuff, though I say it, both Brass and Pewter, Linnens and Woollens; and though my House be thatched, yet, if you and I match, it shall go hard but I will have one Half of

it slated. If you think well of this Motion, I will wait upon you as
soon as my new Cloaths is made and Hay-Harvest is in. I could,
though I say it, have good . . .' The rest is torn off;[4] and Posterity
must be contented to know that Mrs. *Margaret Clark* was very
pretty, but are left in the Dark as to the Name of her Lover.   T

No. 454 [STEELE]

[Twenty-four hours in London][1]
Monday, 11 August 1712

Sine me, Vacivom tempus ne quod duim mihi Laboris.   Ter. Heau.[2]

It is an inexpressible Pleasure to know a little of the World, and
be of no Character or Significancy in it. To be ever unconcerned,
and ever looking on new Objects with an endless Curiosity, is a
Delight known only to those who are turned for Speculation: Nay,
they who enjoy it, must value things only as they are the Objects
of Speculation, without drawing any worldly Advantage to themselves from them, but just as they are what contribute to their
Amusement, or the Improvement of the Mind. I lay one Night
last Week at *Richmond*; and being restless, not out of Dissatisfaction, but a certain busie Inclination one sometimes has, I arose at
Four in the Morning, and took Boat for *London*, with a Resolution
to rove by Boat and Coach for the next Four and twenty Hours,
till the many different Objects I must needs meet with should tire
my Imagination, and give me an Inclination to a Repose more
profound than I was at that Time capable of. I beg People's Pardon
for an odd Humour I am guilty of, and was often that Day,
which is saluting any Person whom I like, whether I know him
or not. This is a Particularity would be tolerated in me, if they
considered that the greatest Pleasure I know I receive at my Eyes,
and that I am obliged to an agreeable Person for coming abroad
into my View, as another is for a Visit of Conversation at their
own Houses.

The Hours of the Day and Night are taken up in the Cities of
London and *Westminster* by Peoples as different from each other as
those who are Born in different Centuries. Men of Six-a-Clock give
way to those of Nine, they of Nine to the Generation of Twelve,

and they of Twelve disappear, and make Room for the fashionable World, who have made Two-a-Clock the Noon of the Day.

When we first put off from Shoar, we soon fell in with a Fleet of Gardiners bound for the several Market-Ports of *London*; and it was the most pleasing Scene imaginable to see the Chearfulness with which those industrious People ply'd their Way to a certain Sale of their Goods. The Banks on each Side are as well Peopled, and beautified with as agreeable Plantations, as any Spot on the Earth; but the *Thames* it self, loaded with the Product of each Shoar, added very much to the Landskip. It was very easie to observe by their Sailing, and the Countenances of the ruddy Virgins who were Supercargos, the Parts of the Town to which they were bound. There was an Air in the Purveyors for *Covent-Garden*, who frequently converse with Morning Rakes, very unlike the seemly Sobriety of those bound for *Stocks-Market*.

Nothing remarkable happened in our Voyage; but I landed with Ten Sail of Apricock Boats at *Strand-Bridge*, after having put in at *Nine-Elmes*, and taken in Melons, consigned by Mr. *Cuffe* of that Place, to *Sarah Sewell* and Company, at their Stall in *Covent-Garden*. We arrived at *Strand-Bridge* at Six of the Clock, and were unloading; when the Hackney-Coachmen of the foregoing Night took their Leave of each other at the *Dark-House*, to go to Bed before the Day was too far spent. Chimney-Sweepers passed by us as we made up to the Market, and some Raillery happened between one of the Fruit-Wenches and those black Men, about the Devil and *Eve*, with Allusion to their several Professions. I could not believe any Place more entertaining than *Covent-Garden*; where I strolled from one Fruit-Shop to another, with Crowds of agreeable young Women around me, who were purchasing Fruit for their respective Families. It was almost Eight of the Clock before I could leave that Variety of Objects. I took Coach and followed a young Lady, who tripped into another just before me, attended by her Maid. I saw immediately she was of the Family of the *Vainloves*. There are a Sett of these, who of all things affect the Play of *Blindman's-Buff*, and leading Men into Love for they know not whom, who are fled they know not where. This sort of Woman is usually a janty Slattern; she hangs on her Cloaths, plays her Head, varies her Posture, and changes Place incessantly; and all with an Appearance of striving at the same time to hide her self, and yet give you to understand she is in Humour to laugh at you. You must have often seen the Coachmen make Signs with their Fingers as they drive by each other, to intimate how much they have got that Day. They can carry on that Language to give Intelligence where they are driving. In an instant my Coachman took the Wink to pursue, and the Lady's Driver gave the Hint that he was going through *Long-Acre* towards St. *James's*: While he whipped up *James-Street*, we drove for *King-Street*, to save the Pass at St. *Martins Lane*. The Coachmen took Care to meet, justle, and threaten each other for Way, and be intangled at the End of *Newport-Street*, and *Long-Acre*. The Fright, you must believe, brought down the Lady's Coach Door, and obliged her, with her Mask off, to enquire into the Bustle, when she sees the Man she would avoid. The Tackle of the Coach-Window is so bad she cannot draw it up again, and she drives on sometimes wholly discovered, and sometimes half escaped, according to the Accident of Carriages in her Way. One of these Ladies keeps her Seat in an Hackney-Coach as well as the best Rider does on a managed Horse. The laced Shooe on her Left Foot, with a careless Gesture, just appearing on the opposite Cushion, held her both firm, and in a proper Attitude to receive the next Jolt.

As she was an excellent Coach-Woman, many were the Glances at each other which we had for an Hour and an Half in all Parts of the Town by the Skill of our Drivers; till at last my Lady was conveniently lost with Notice from her Coachman to ours to make off, and he should hear where she went. This Chase was now at an End, and the Fellow who drove her came to us, and discovered that he was ordered to come again in an Hour, for that she was a Silk-Worm. I was surprized with this Phrase, but found it was a Cant among the Hackney Fraternity for their best Customers, Women who ramble twice or thrice a Week from Shop to Shop, to turn over all the Goods in Town without buying any thing. The Silk-Worms are, it seems, indulged by the Tradesmen; for tho' they never buy, they are ever talking of new Silks, Laces and Ribbands, and serve the Owners in getting them Customers, as their common Dunners do in making them pay.

The Day of People of Fashion began now to break, and Carts and Hacks were mingled with Equipages of Show and Vanity; when

I resolved to walk it out of Cheapness; but my unhappy Curiosity is such, that I find it always my Interest to take Coach, for some odd Adventure among Beggars, Ballad Singers, or the like, detains and throws me into Expence. It happened so immediately; for at the Corner of *Warwick-Street*, as I was listning to a new Ballad, a ragged Rascal, a Beggar who knew me, came up to me, and began to turn the Eyes of the good Company upon me, by telling me he was extream Poor, and should die in the Streets for want of Drink, except I immediately would have the Charity to give him Six-pence to go into the next Ale-House and save his Life. He urged, with a melancholy Face, that all his Family had died of Thirst. All the Mob have Humour, and two or three began to take the Jest; by which Mr. *Sturdy* carried his Point, and let me sneak off to a Coach. As I drove along, it was a pleasing Reflection to see the World so prettily chequered since I left *Richmond*, and the Scene still filling with Children of a new Hour. This Satisfaction encreased as I moved towards the City; and gay Signs, well disposed Streets, magnificent publick Structures, and wealthy Shops, adorned with contented Faces, made the Joy still rising till we came into the Centre of the City, and Centre of the World of Trade, the *Exchange* of *London*.[3] As other Men in the Crowds about me were pleased with their Hopes and Bargains, I found my °Account in observing them, in Attention to their several Interests. I, indeed, looked upon my self as the richest Man that walked the *Exchange* that Day; for my Benevolence made me share the Gains of every Bargain that was made. It was not the least of the Satisfactions in my Survey, to go up Stairs, and pass the Shops of agreeable Females; to observe so many pretty Hands busie in the Foldings of Ribbands, and the utmost Eagerness of agreeable Faces in the Sale of Patches, Pins, and Wires, on each Side the Counters, was an Amusement, in which I should longer have indulged my self, had not the dear Creatures called to me to ask what I wanted, when I could not answer, only *To look at you.* I went to one of the Windows which opened to the Area below, where all the several Voices lost their Distinction, and rose up in a confused Humming; which created in me a Reflection that could not come into the Mind of any but of one a little too studious; for I said to my self, with a kind of Punn in Thought, *What Nonsense is all the Hurry of this World to those who are above it?* In these, or not much wiser Thoughts, I had like to have lost my Place at the Chop-House; where every Man, according to the natural Bashfulness or Sullenness of our Nation, eats in a publick Room a Mess of Broth, or Chop of Meat, in dumb Silence, as if they had no Pretence to speak to each other on the Foot of being Men, except they were of each other's Acquaintance.

I went afterwards to *Robin's*,[4] and saw People who had dined with me at the Five-penny °Ordinary just before, give Bills for the Value of large Estates; and could not but behold with great Pleasure, Property lodged in, and transferred in a Moment from such as would never be Masters of half as much as is seemingly in them, and given from them every Day they live. But before Five in the Afternoon I left the City, came to my common Scene of *Covent-Garden*, and passed the Evening at *Will's* in attending the Discourses of several Sets of People, who relieved each other within my Hearing on the Subjects of Cards, Dice, Love, Learning and Politicks. The last Subject kept me till I heard the Streets in the Possession of the °Bell-man, who had now the World to himself, and cryed, *Past Two of Clock*. This roused me from my Seat, and I went to my Lodging, led by a °Light, whom I put into the Discourse of his private Oeconomy, and made him give me an Account of the Charge, Hazard, Profit and Loss of a Family that depended upon a Link, with a Design to end my trivial Day with the Generosity of Six-pence, instead of a third Part of that Sum. When I came to my Chamber I writ down these Minutes; but was at a Loss what Instruction I should propose to my Reader from the Enumeration of so many insignificant Matters and Occurrences; and I thought it of great Use, if they could learn with me to keep their Minds open to Gratification, and ready to receive it from any thing it meets with. This one Circumstance will make every Face you see give you the Satisfaction you now take in beholding that of a Friend; will make every Object a pleasing one; will make all the Good which arrives to any Man, an Encrease of Happiness to your self.   T

No. 552 [STEELE]

[The industrious part of mankind]
Wednesday, 3 December 1712

—Qui prægravat artes
Infra se positas extinctus amabitur idem.   Hor.[1]

As I was tumbling about the Town the other Day in an Hackney-Coach, and delighting my self with busie Scenes in the Shops of each Side of me, it came into my Head, with no small Remorse, that I had not been frequent enough in the Mention and Recommendation of the industrious Part of Mankind. It very naturally, upon this Occasion, touched my Conscience in particular, that I had not acquitted my self to my Friend Mr. *Peter Motteux*. That industrious Man of Trade, and formerly Brother of the Quill, has dedicated to me a Poem upon Tea.[2] It would injure him, as a Man of Business, if I did not let the World know that the Author of so good Verses writ them before he was concerned in Traffick. In order to expiate my Negligence towards him, I immediately resolved to make him a Visit. I found his spacious Warehouses filled and adorned with Tea, China, and Indian Ware. I could observe a beautiful °Ordonnance of the Whole, and such different and considerable Branches of Trade carried on in the same House, I exulted in seeing disposed by a Poetical Head. In one Place were exposed to view Silks of various Shades and Colours, rich Brocades, and the wealthiest Products of foreign Looms. Here you might see the finest Laces held up by the fairest Hands; and there examined by the beauteous Eyes of the Buyers the most delicate Cambricks, Muslins, and Linnens. I could not but congratulate my Friend on the humble, but, I hoped, beneficial use he had made of his Talents, and wished I could be a Patron to his Trade, as he had [been] pleased to make me of his Poetry. The honest Man has, I know, that modest Desire of Gain which is peculiar to those who understand better Things than Riches; and I dare say he would be contented with much less than what is called Wealth in that Quarter of the Town which he inhabits, and will oblige all his Customers with Demands agreeable to the Moderation of his Desires.

Among other Omissions of which I have been also guilty with

Relation to Men of Industry of a superior Order, I must acknowledge my Silence towards a Proposal frequently enclosed to me by Mr. *Renatus Harris, Organ-Builder*. The Ambition of this Artificer[3] is to erect an Organ in St. *Paul*'s Cathedral over the West Door at the Entrance into the Body of the Church, which in Art and Magnificence shall transcend any Work of that Kind ever before invented. The Proposal in perspicuous Language sets forth the Honour and Advantage such a Performance would be to the *British* Name, as well as that it would apply the Power of Sounds in a Manner more amazingly forcible than, perhaps, has yet been known, and I am sure to an End much more worthy. Had the vast Sums which have been laid out upon Opera's without Skill or Conduct, and to no other Purpose but to suspend or vitiate our Understandings, been disposed this Way, we should now, perhaps, have had an Engine so formed as to strike the Minds of half a People at once in a Place of Worship with a Forgetfulness of present Care and Calamity, and an Hope of endless Rapture, Joy and Hallelujah hereafter.

When I am doing this Justice, I am not to forget the best Mechanick of my Acquaintance, that useful Servant to Science and Knowledge, Mr. *John Rowley*; but think I lay a great Obligation on the Publick, by acquainting them with his Proposals for a °Pair of new Globes.[4] After his Preamble, he promises in the said Proposals that,

In the Celestial Globe,

'Care shall be taken that the Fixed Stars be placed according to their true Longitude and Latitude, from the many and correct Observations of *Hevelius, Cassini,* Mr. *Flamsteed*, Reg. Astronomer, Dr. *Halley, Savilian* Professor of Geometry in *Oxon*;[5] and from whatever else can be procured to render the Globe more exact, instructive, and useful.

'That all the Constellations be drawn in a curious, new, and particular Manner; each Star in so just, distinct, and conspicuous a Proportion, that its true Magnitude may be readily known by bare Inspection, according to the different *Light* and *Sizes* of the Stars. That the Tract or Way of such Comets as have been well observed, but not hitherto expressed in any Globe, be carefully delineated in this.'

In the Terrestrial Globe,

'That by reason the Descriptions formerly made, both in the *English* or *Dutch* great Globes, are Erroneous, *Asia, Africa,* and *America* be drawn in a Manner wholly new; by which Means it is to be noted that the °Undertakers will be obliged to alter the Latitude of some Places in 10 Degrees, the Longitude of others in 20 Degrees: Besides which great and necessary Alterations, there be many remarkable Countries, Cities, Towns, Rivers, and Lakes, omitted in other Globes, inserted here according to the best Discoveries made by our late Navigators. Lastly, That the Course of the Trade-Winds, the *Monsoons* and other Winds periodically shifting between the Tropicks, be visibly expressed.

'Now in Regard that this Undertaking is of so universal Use, as the Advancement of the most necessary Parts of the Mathematicks, as well as tending to the Honour of the *British* Nation, and that the Charge of carrying it on is very expensive, it is desired that all Gentlemen who are willing to promote so great a Work, will be pleased to subscribe the following Conditions.

'I. The Undertakers engage to furnish each Subscriber with a Celestial and Terrestrial Globe, each of 30 Inches Diameter in all Respects curiously adorned, the Stars gilded, the Capital Cities plainly distinguished, the Frames, Meridians, Horizons, Hour-Circles and Indexes so exactly finished up and accurately divided, that a Pair of these Globes will really appear, in the Judgment of any disinterested and intelligent Person, worth Fifteen Pounds more than will be demanded for them by the Undertakers.

'II. Whosoever will be pleased to Subscribe, and pay Twenty Five Pounds in the manner following for a Pair of these Globes, either for their own Use, or to present them to any College in the Universities, or any publick Library or School, shall have his Coat of Arms, Name, Title, Seat, or Place of Residence, &c. inserted in some convenient Place of the Globe.

'III. That every Subscriber do at first pay down the Sum of Ten Pounds, and Fifteen Pounds more upon the Delivery of each Pair of Globes perfectly fitted up: And that the said Globes be delivered within Twelve Months after the Number of Thirty Subscribers be compleated; and that the Subscribers be served with Globes in the Order in which they subscribed.

'IV. That a Pair of these Globes shall not hereafter be sold to any Person but the Subscribers under Thirty Pounds.

'V. That if there be not thirty Subscribers within four Months after the first of *December*, 1712, the Money paid shall be returned on Demand by Mr. *John Warner*, Goldsmith, near *Temple-Bar*, who shall receive and pay the same according to the above-mentioned Articles.'   T

IV *Essays in Criticism*

No. 18 [ADDISON]

[The Italian opera]¹
Wednesday, 21 March 1711

— Equitis quoque jam migravit ab aure voluptas
Omnis ad incertos oculos & gaudia vana.   Hor.²

It is my Design in this Paper to deliver down to Posterity a faithful Account of the *Italian* Opera, and of the gradual Progress which it has made upon the *English* Stage: For there is no question but our great Grand-children will be very curious to know the Reason why their Forefathers used to sit together like an Audience of Foreigners in their own Country, and to hear whole Plays acted before them in a Tongue which they did not understand.

Arsinoe was the first Opera that gave us a Taste of *Italian* Musick.³ The great Success this Opera met with, produced some Attempts of forming Pieces upon *Italian* Plans, which should give a more natural and reasonable Entertainment than what can be met with in the elaborate Trifles of that Nation. This alarmed the Poetasters and Fidlers of the Town, who were used to deal in a more ordinary kind of Ware; and therefore laid down an established Rule, which is received as such to this Day, *That nothing is capable of being well set to Musick, that is not Nonsense.*

This Maxim was no sooner received, but we immediately fell to translating the *Italian* Operas; and as there was no great Danger of hurting the Sense of those extraordinary Pieces, our Authors would often make Words of their own which were entirely foreign to the Meaning of the Passages they pretended to translate; their chief Care being to make the Numbers of the *English* Verse answer to those of the *Italian*, that both of them might go to the same Tune. Thus the famous Song in *Camilla*,

Barbara si t' intendo, &c.
Barbarous Woman, yes, I know your Meaning.

which expresses the Resentments of an angry Lover, was translated
into that *English* Lamentation,

Frail are a Lover's Hopes, &c.[4]

And it was pleasant enough to see the most refined Persons of the
British Nation dying away and languishing to Notes that were
filled with a Spirit of Rage and Indignation. It happened also very
frequently, where the Sense was rightly translated, the necessary
Transportation of Words which were drawn out of the Phrase of one
Tongue into that of another, made the Musick appear very absurd
in one Tongue that was very natural in the other. I remember an
Italian Verse that ran thus Word for Word,

And turn'd my Rage into Pity;

which the *English* for Rhime sake translated,

And into Pity turn'd my Rage.

By this means the soft Notes that were adapted to *Pity* in the
Italian, fell upon the Word *Rage* in the *English*; and the angry
Sounds that were tuned to *Rage* in the Original, were made to
express *Pity* in the Translation. It oftentimes happened likewise,
that the finest Notes in the Air fell upon the most insignificant
Words in the Sentence. I have known the Word *And* pursued
through the whole °Gamut, have been entertained with many a
melodious *The*, and have heard the most beautiful Graces Quavers
and °Divisions bestowed upon *Then, For*, and *From*; to the eternal
Honour of our *English* Particles.

The next Step to our Refinement, was the introducing of *Italian*
Actors into our Opera; who sung their Parts in their own Language,
at the same time that our Countrymen performed theirs in our native
Tongue. The King or Hero of the Play generally spoke in *Italian*,
and his Slaves answered him in *English*: The Lover frequently made
his Court, and gained the Heart of his Princess, in a Language
which she did not understand. One would have thought it very
difficult to have carried on Dialogues after this manner, without an
Interpreter between the Persons that conversed together; but this

was the State of the *English* Stage for about three Years.

At length the Audience grew tired of understanding Half the Opera, and therefore to ease themselves intirely of the Fatigue of Thinking, have so ordered it at present that the whole Opera is performed in an unknown Tongue. We no longer understand the Language of our own Stage; insomuch that I have often been afraid, when I have seen our *Italian* Performers chattering in the Vehemence of Action, that they have been calling us Names, and abusing us among themselves; but I hope, since we do put such an entire Confidence in them, they will not talk against us before our Faces, though they may do it with the same Safety as if it were behind our Backs. In the mean time, I cannot forbear thinking how naturally an Historian who writes two or three hundred Years hence, and does not know the Taste of his wise Forefathers, will make the following Reflection, *In the Beginning of the Eighteenth Century the* Italian *Tongue was so well understood in* England, *that Operas were acted on the publick Stage in that Language.*

One scarce knows how to be serious in the Confutation of an Absurdity that shews it self at the first Sight. It does not want any great measure of Sense to see the Ridicule of this monstrous Practice; but what makes it the more astonishing, it is not the Taste of the Rabble, but of Persons of the greatest Politeness, which has established it.

If the *Italians* have a Genius for Musick above the *English*, the *English* have a Genius for other Performances of a much higher Nature, and capable of giving the Mind a much nobler Entertainment. Would one think it was possible (at a Time when an Author lived that was able to write the *Phædra and Hippolitus*)[5] for a People to be so stupidly fond of the *Italian* Opera, as scarce to give a third Day's Hearing to that admirable Tragedy? Musick is certainly a very agreeable Entertainment, but if it would take the entire Possession of our Ears, if it would make us incapable of hearing Sense, if it would exclude Arts that have a much greater Tendency to the Refinement of human Nature; I must confess I would allow it no better Quarter than *Plato* has done, who banishes it out of his Common-wealth.

At present, our Notions of Musick are so very uncertain, that we do not know what it is we like; only, in general, we are transported with any thing that is not *English*: So it be of a foreign Growth, let it be *Italian*, *French*, or *High-Dutch*, it is the same thing. In short, our *English* Musick is quite rooted out, and nothing yet planted in its stead.

When a Royal Palace is burnt to the Ground, every Man is at Liberty to present his Plan for a new one; and though it be but indifferently put together, it may furnish several Hints that may be of Use to a good Architect. I shall take the same Liberty in a following Paper, of giving my Opinion upon the Subject of Musick; which I shall lay down only in a °problematical Manner, to be considered by those who are Masters in the Art.   C

[ENGLISH TRAGEDY]

No. 39 [ADDISON]

[English tragedy: Style, language and verse]
Saturday, 14 April 1711

Multa fero, ut placem genus irritabile vatum,
Cum scribo —   Hor.[1]

As a perfect Tragedy is the noblest Production of human Nature, so it is capable of giving the Mind one of the most delightful and most improving Entertainments.[2] A virtuous Man (says *Seneca*)[3] strugling with Misfortunes, is such a Spectacle as Gods might look upon with Pleasure: And such a Pleasure it is which one meets with in the Representation of a well-written Tragedy. Diversions of this kind wear out of our Thoughts every thing that is mean and little. They cherish and cultivate that Humanity which is the Ornament of our Nature. They soften Insolence, sooth Affliction, and subdue the Mind to the Dispensations of Providence.

It is no Wonder therefore that in all the Polite Nations of the World, this Part of the *Drama* has met with Publick Encouragement.

The Modern Tragedy excels that of *Greece* and *Rome*, in the Intricacy and Disposition of the Fable: but, what a Christian Writer would be ashamed to own, falls infinitely short of it in the Moral Part of the Performance.

This I may shew more at large hereafter; and in the mean time, that I may contribute something towards the Improvement of the *English* Tragedy, I shall take notice, in this and in other following Papers, of some particular Parts in it that seem liable to Exception.

Aristotle observes, that the *Iambick* Verse in the *Greek* Tongue was the most proper for Tragedy; Because at the same time that it lifted up the Discourse from Prose, it was that which approached nearer to it than any other kind of Verse. For, says he, we may observe that Men in ordinary Discourse very often speak *Iambicks*, without taking Notice of it.[4] We may take the same Observation of our *English* Blank Verse, which often enters into our common Discourse, though we do not attend to it, and is such a due Medium between Rhyme and Prose, that it seems wonderfully adapted to Tragedy.[5] I am therefore very much offended when I see a Play in Rhyme; which is as absurd in *English*, as a Tragedy of *Hexameters* would have been in *Greek* or *Latin*. The Solæcism is, I think, still greater, in those Plays that have some Scenes in Rhyme and some in Blank Verse, which are to be looked upon as two several Languages; or where we see some particular Similies dignified with Rhyme, at the same time that every thing about them lyes in Blank Verse. I would not however debar the Poet from concluding his Tragedy, or, if he pleases, every Act of it, with two or three Couplets, which may have the same Effect as an Air in the *Italian* Opera after a long *Recitativo*, and give the Actor a graceful *Exit*. Besides, that we see a Diversity of Numbers in some Parts of the Old Tragedy, in order to hinder the Ear from being tired with the same continued Modulation of Voice. For the same Reason I do not dislike the Speeches in our *English* Tragedy that close with an *Hemistick*, or half Verse, notwithstanding the Person who speaks after it begins a new Verse, without filling up the preceding one; nor with abrupt Pauses and Breakings-off in the middle of a Verse, when they humour any Passion that is expressed by it.

Since I am upon this Subject, I must observe that our *English* Poets have succeeded much better in the Stile, than in the Sentiments of their Tragedies. Their Language is very often noble and sonorous, but the Sense either very trifling or very common. On the contrary, in the ancient Tragedies, and indeed in those of

Corneille and *Racine*, tho' the Expressions are very great, it is the
Thought that bears them up and swells them. For my own part, I
prefer a noble Sentiment that is depressed with homely Language,
infinitely before a vulgar one that is blown up with all the Sound
and Energy of Expression. Whether this Defect in our Tragedies
may arise from Want of Genius, Knowledge, or Experience in the
Writers, or from their Compliance with the vicious Taste of their
Readers, who are better Judges of the Language than of the
Sentiments, and consequently relish the one more than the other,
I cannot determine. But I believe it might rectifie the Conduct
both of the one and of the other, if the Writer laid down the whole
Contexture of his Dialogue in plain *English*, before he turned it
into Blank Verse; and if the Reader, after the Perusal of a Scene,
would consider the naked Thought of every Speech in it, when
divested of all its Tragick Ornaments: By this means, without
being imposed upon by Words, we may judge impartially of the
Thought, and consider whether it be natural or great enough for
the Person that utters it, whether it deserves to shine in such a
Blaze of Eloquence, or shew it self in such a variety of Lights as are
generally made use of by the Writers of our *English* Tragedy.

I must in the next place observe, that when our Thoughts are
great and just, they are often obscured by the sounding Phrases,
hard Metaphors, and forced Expressions in which they are cloathed.
Shakespear is often very faulty in this Particular. There is a fine
Observation in *Aristotle* to this purpose, which I have never seen
quoted.[6] The Expression, says he, ought to be very much laboured
in the unactive Parts of the Fable, as in Descriptions, Similitudes,
Narrations, and the like; in which the Opinions, Manners, and
Passions of Men are not represented; for these (namely the Opinions,
Manners, and Passions) are apt to be obscured by pompous Phrases
and elaborate Expressions. *Horace*, who copied most of his Criti-
cisms after *Aristotle*, seems to have had his Eye on the foregoing
Rule, in the following Verses:

> *Tragædian too lay by their State, to grieve.*
> Peleus *and* Telephus, *exil'd and poor,*
> *Forget their swelling and gigantick Words.*
>   Ld. ROSCOMMON.[7]

Among our Modern *English* Poets, there is none who was better
°turned for Tragedy than *Lee*; if instead of favouring the Impetuosity
of his Genius, he had restrained it, and kept it within its proper
Bounds. His Thoughts are wonderfully suited to Tragedy, but
frequently lost in such a Cloud of Words, that it is hard to see the
Beauty of them: There is an infinite Fire in his Works, but so
involved in Smoak, that it does not appear in half its Lustre. He
frequently succeeds in the passionate Parts of the Tragedy, but
more particularly where he slackens his Efforts, and eases the Stile
of those Epithets and Metaphors, in which he so much abounds.
What can be more natural, more soft, or more passionate, than
that Line in *Statira*'s Speech, where she describes the Charms of
Alexander's Conversation?

> *Then he would talk: Good Gods! how he would talk!*[8]

That unexpected Break in the Line, and turning the Description
of his manner of Talking into an Admiration of it, is inexpressibly
beautiful, and wonderfully suited to the fond Character of the
Person that speaks it. There is a Simplicity in the Words, that
outshines the utmost Pride of Expression.

Otway[9] has followed Nature in the Language of his Tragedy, and
therefore shines in the Passionate Parts, more than any of our
English Poets. As there is something Familiar and Domestick in
the Fable of his Tragedy, more than in those of any other Poet, he
has little Pomp, but great Force in his Expressions. For which
Reason, tho' he has admirably succeeded in the tender and melting
Part of his Tragedies, he sometimes falls into too great a Familiarity
of Phrase in those Parts, which, by *Aristotle*'s Rule, ought to have
been raised and supported by the Dignity of Expression.

It has been observed by others, that this Poet has founded his
Tragedy of *Venice Preserved* on so wrong a Plot, that the greatest
Characters in it are those of Rebels and Traitors. Had the Hero of
his Play discovered the same good Qualities in the Defence of his

Country, that he shewed for its Ruin and Subversion, the Audience could not enough pity and admire him: But as he is now represented, we can only say of him, what the *Roman* Historian says of *Catiline*, that his Fall would have been glorious (*si pro Patriâ sic concidisset*) had he so fallen in the Service of his Country.[10]   C

No. 40 [ADDISON]

[English tragedy: Poetic justice, tragi-comedy, double plots, rant][1]
Monday, 16 April 1711

> *Ac ne forte putes me, quæ facere ipse recusem,*
> *Cum recte tractant alii, laudare, maligne;*
> *Ille per extentum funem mihi posse videtur*
> *Ire Poeta, meum qui pectus inaniter angit,*
> *Irritat, mulcet, falsis terroribus implet,*
> *Ut magus; & modo me Thebis, modo ponit Athenis.*   Hor.[2]

The *English* Writers of Tragedy are possessed with a Notion, that when they represent a virtuous or innocent Person in Distress, they ought not to leave him till they have delivered him out of his Troubles, or made him triumph over his Enemies. This Error they have been led into by a ridiculous Doctrine in Modern Criticism, that they are obliged to an equal Distribution of Rewards and Punishments, and an impartial Execution of Poetical Justice. Who were the first that established this Rule I know not; but I am sure it has no Foundation in Nature, in Reason, or in the Practice of the Ancients. We find that Good and Evil happen alike to all Men on this Side the Grave; and as the principal Design of Tragedy is to raise Commiseration and Terror in the Minds of the Audience, we shall defeat this great End, if we always make Virtue and Innocence happy and successful. Whatever Crosses and Disappointments a good Man suffers in the Body of the Tragedy, they will make but small Impression on our Minds, when we know that in the last Act he is to arrive at the End of his Wishes and Desires. When we see him engaged in the Depth of his Afflictions, we are apt to comfort our selves, because we are sure he will find his Way out of them; and that his Grief, how great soever it may be at present, will soon terminate in Gladness. For this Reason the ancient Writers of Tragedy treated Men in their Plays, as they are dealt with in the World, by making Virtue sometimes happy and sometimes miserable, as they found it in the Fable which they made choice of, or as it might affect their Audience in the most agreeable Manner. *Aristotle* considers the Tragedies that were written in either of these Kinds, and observes, That those which ended unhappily, had always pleased the People, and carried away the Prize in the publick Disputes of the Stage, from those that ended happily. Terror and Commiseration leave a pleasing Anguish in the Mind; and fix the Audience in such a serious Composure of Thought, as is much more lasting and delightful than any little transient Starts of Joy and Satisfaction.[3] Accordingly we find, that more of our *English* Tragedies have succeeded, in which the Favourites of the Audience sink under their Calamities, than those in which they recover themselves out of them. The best Plays of this Kind are the *Orphan, Venice preserved, Alexander the Great, Theodosius, All for Love, Oedipus, Oroonoko, Othello, &c.*[4] *King Lear* is an admirable Tragedy of the same Kind, as *Shakespear* wrote it; but as it is reformed according to the chymerical Notion of Poetical Justice, in my humble Opinion it has lost half its Beauty.[5] At the same time I must allow, that there are very noble Tragedies which have been framed upon the other Plan, and have ended happily; as indeed most of the good Tragedies, which have been written since the starting of the above-mentioned Criticism, have taken this Turn: As the *Mourning Bride, Tamerlane, Ulysses, Phædra and Hyppolitus*, with most of Mr. *Dryden*'s. I must also allow, that many of *Shakespear*'s, and several of the celebrated Tragedies of Antiquity, are cast in the same Form.[6] I do not therefore dispute against this way of writing Tragedies, but against the Criticism that would establish this as the only Method; and by that Means would very much cramp the *English* Tragedy, and perhaps give a wrong Bent to the Genius of our Writers.

The Tragi-Comedy, which is the Product of the *English* Theatre, is one of the most monstrous Inventions that ever entered into a Poet's Thoughts. An Author might as well think of weaving the Adventures of *Æneas* and *Hudibras* into one Poem, as of writing such a motly Piece of Mirth and Sorrow. But the Absurdity of these Performances is so very visible, that I shall not insist upon it.

The same Objections which are made to Tragi-Comedy, may in some Measure be applied to all Tragedies that have a double Plot in them; which are likewise more frequent upon the *English* Stage, than upon any other: For though the Grief of the Audience, in such Performances, be not changed into another Passion, as in Tragi-Comedies; it is diverted upon another Object, which weakens their Concern for the principal Action, and breaks the Tide of Sorrow, by throwing it into different Channels. This Inconvenience, however, may in a great Measure be cured, if not wholly removed, by the skilful Choice of an Under-Plot, which may bear such a near Relation to the principal Design, as to contribute towards the Completion of it, and be concluded by the same Catastrophe.

There is also another Particular, which may be reckoned among the Blemishes, or rather the false Beauties, of our *English* Tragedy: I mean those particular Speeches which are commonly known by the Name of *Rants*. The warm and passionate Parts of a Tragedy, are always the most taking with the Audience; for which Reason we often see the Players pronouncing, in all the Violence of Action, several Parts of the Tragedy which the Author writ with great °Temper, and designed that they should have been so acted. I have seen *Powell* very often raise himself a loud Clap by this Artifice. The Poets that were acquainted with this Secret, have given frequent Occasion for such Emotions in the Actor, by adding Vehemence to Words where there was no Passion, or inflaming a real Passion into Fustian. This hath filled the Mouths of our Heroes with Bombast; and given them such Sentiments, as proceed rather from a Swelling than a Greatness of Mind. Unnatural Exclamations, Curses, Vows, Blasphemies, a Defiance of Mankind, and an Outraging of the Gods, frequently pass upon the Audience for towering Thoughts, and have accordingly met with infinite Applause.

I shall here add a Remark, which I am afraid our Tragick Writers may make an ill use of. As our Heroes are generally Lovers, their Swelling and Blustring upon the Stage very much recommends them to the fair Part of their Audience. The Ladies are wonderfully pleased to see a Man insulting Kings, or affronting the Gods, in one Scene, and throwing himself at the Feet of his Mistress in another. Let him behave himself insolently towards the Men, and abjectly towards the Fair One, and it is ten to one but he proves a Favourite of the Boxes. *Dryden* and *Lee*, in several of their Tragedies, have practised this Secret with good Success.

But to shew how a *Rant* pleases beyond the most just and natural Thought that is not pronounced with Vehemence, I would desire the Reader, when he sees the Tragedy of *Oedipus*, to observe how quietly the Hero is dismissed at the End of the third Act, after having pronounced the following Lines, in which the Thought is very natural, and apt to move Compassion.

> *To you, good Gods, I make my last Appeal,*
> *Or clear my Virtues, or my Crimes reveal.*
> *If in the Maze of Fate I blindly run,*
> *And backward trod those Paths I fought to shun;*
> *Impute my Errors to your own Decree:*
> *My Hands are guilty, but my Heart is free.*

Let us then observe with what Thunder-claps of Applause he leaves the Stage, after the Impieties and Execrations at the End of the fourth Act; and you will wonder to see an Audience so cursed and so pleased at the same Time.

> *O that as oft I have at* Athens *seen,*
> [Where, by the way, there was no Stage
>   till many Years after *Oedipus.*]
> *The Stage arise, and the big Clouds descend;*
> *So now, in very deed, I might behold*
> *This pond'rous Globe, and all yon marble Roof,*
> *Meet, like the Hands of* Jove, *and crush Mankind.*
> *For all the Elements,* &c.

ADVERTISEMENT.

Having spoken of Mr. Powell, *as sometimes raising himself Applause from the ill Taste of an Audience; I must do him the Justice to own, that he is excellently formed for a Tragœdian, and, when he pleases, deserves the Admiration of the best Judges; as I doubt not but he will in the Conquest of* Mexico, *which is acted for his own Benefit To-morrow Night.*[7]   C

No. 42 [ADDISON]

[English tragedy: Staging]

Wednesday, 18 April 1711

Garganum mugire putes nemus aut mare Thuscum,
Tanto cum strepitu ludi spectantur, & artes,
Divitiæque peregrinæ; quibus oblitus actor
Cum stetit in Scena, concurrit dextera lævæ.
Dixit adhuc aliquid? Nil sane. Quid placet ergo?
Lana Tarentino violas imitata veneno.   Hor.[1]

Aristotle has observed, that ordinary Writers in Tragedy endeavour to raise Terror and Pity in their Audience, not by proper Sentiments and Expressions, but by the Dresses and Decorations of the Stage.[2] There is something of this kind very ridiculous in the *English* Theatre. When the Author has a mind to terrifie us, it thunders; when he would make us melancholy, the Stage is darkened. But among all our Tragick Artifices, I am the most offended at those which are made use of to inspire us with magnificent Ideas of the Persons that speak. The ordinary Method of making an Hero, is to clap a huge Plume of Feathers upon his Head, which rises so very high, that there is often a greater Length from his Chin to the Top of his Head, than to the Sole of his Foot. One would believe, that we thought a great Man and a tall Man the same thing. This very much embarrasses the Actor, who is forced to hold his Neck extreamly stiff and steady all the while he speaks; and notwithstanding any Anxieties which he pretends for his Mistress, his Country, or his Friends, one may see by his Action, that his greatest Care and Concern is to keep the Plume of Feathers from falling off his Head. For my own part, when I see a Man uttering his Complaints under such a Mountain of Feathers, I am apt to look upon him rather as an unfortunate Lunatick, than a distressed Hero. As these superfluous Ornaments upon the Head make a great Man, a Princess generally receives her Grandeur from those additional Incumbrances that fall into her Tail: I mean the broad sweeping Train that follows her in all her Motions, and finds constant Employment for a Boy who stands behind her to open and spread it to Advantage. I do not know how others are affected at this Sight, but, I must confess, my Eyes are wholly taken up with the

Page's Part; and as for the Queen, I am not so attentive to any thing she speaks, as to the right adjusting of her Train, lest it should chance to trip up her Heels, or incommode her, as she walks to and fro upon the Stage. It is, in my Opinion, a very odd Spectacle, to see a Queen venting her Passion in a disordered Motion, and a little Boy taking Care all the while that they do not ruffle the Tail of her Gown. The Parts that the two Persons act on the Stage at the same Time, are very different: The Princess is afraid lest she should incur the Displeasure of the King her Father, or lose the Hero her Lover, whilst her Attendant is only concerned lest she should entangle her Feet in her Petticoat.

We are told, that an ancient Tragick Poet, to move the Pity of his Audience for his exiled Kings and distressed Heroes, used to make the Actors represent them in Dresses and Cloaths that were thread-bare and decayed.[3] This Artifice for moving Pity, seems as ill contrived, as that we have been speaking of to inspire us with a great Idea of the Persons introduced upon the Stage. In short, I would have our Conceptions raised by the Dignity of Thought and Sublimity of Expression, rather than by a Train of Robes or a Plume of Feathers.

Another Mechanical Method of making great Men, and adding Dignity to Kings and Queens, is to accompany them with Halberts and Battel-axes. Two or three Shifters of Scenes, with the two Candle-Snuffers, make up a compleat Body of Guards upon the *English* Stage; and by the Addition of a few Porters dressed in red Coats, can represent above a dozen Legions. I have sometimes seen a Couple of Armies drawn up together upon the Stage, when the Poet has been disposed to do Honour to his Generals. It is impossible for the Reader's Imagination to multiply twenty Men into such prodigious Multitudes, or to fancy that two or three hundred thousand Soldiers are fighting in a Room of forty or fifty Yards in Compass. Incidents of such nature should be told, not represented.

> *— Non tamen intus*
> *Digna geri promes in scenam: multaque tolles*
> *Ex oculis, quæ mox narret facundia præsens.*

Hor.[4]

> *Yet there are things improper for a Scene,*
> *Which Men of Judgment only will relate.*
>
> Ld. ROSCOMMON.

I should therefore, in this Particular, recommend to my Countrymen the Example of the *French* Stage, where the Kings and Queens always appear unattended, and leave their Guards behind the Scenes. I should likewise be glad if we imitated the *French* in banishing from our Stage the Noise of Drums, Trumpets, and Huzzas; which is sometimes so very great, that when there is a Battel in the *Hay-Market* Theatre, one may hear it as far as *Charing-Cross*.

I have here only touched upon those Particulars which are made use of to raise and aggrandize the Persons of a Tragedy; and shall shew in another Paper the several Expedients which are practised by Authors of a vulgar Genius to move Terror, Pity, or Admiration, in their Hearers.

The Taylor and the Painter often contribute to the Success of a Tragedy more than the Poet. Scenes affect ordinary Minds as much as Speeches; and our Actors are very sensible, that a well-dressed Play has sometimes brought them as full Audiences, as a well-written one. The *Italians* have a very good Phrase to express this Art of imposing upon the Spectators by Appearances: They call it the *Fourberia della Scena, The Knavery or trickish Part of the Drama.* But however the Show and Outside of the Tragedy may work upon the Vulgar, the more understanding Part of the Audience immediately see through it, and despise it.

A good Poet will give the Reader a more lively idea of an Army or a Battel in a Description, than if he actually saw them drawn up in Squadrons and Battalions, or engaged in the Confusion of a Fight. Our Minds should be opened to great Conceptions, and inflamed with glorious Sentiments, by what the Actor speaks, more than by what he appears. Can all the Trappings or Equipage of a King or Hero, give *Brutus* half that Pomp and Majesty which he receives from a few Lines in *Shakespear*?   C

No. 44 [ADDISON]

[English tragedy: Strictures on English methods of moving
pity and terror]
Friday, 20 April 1711

Tu quid ego & populus mecum desideret audi.   Hor.[1]

Among the several Artifices which are put in Practice by the Poets
to fill the Minds of an Audience with Terror, the first Place is due
to Thunder and Lightning, which are often made use of at the
Descending of a God, or the Rising of a Ghost, at the Vanishing
of a Devil, or at the Death of a Tyrant. I have known a Bell
introduced into several Tragedies with good Effect; and have seen
the whole Assembly in a very great Alarm all the while it has been
ringing. But there is nothing which delights and terrifies our
English Theatre so much as a Ghost, especially when he appears in
a bloody Shirt. A Spectre has very often saved a Play, though he
has done nothing but stalked across the Stage, or rose through a
Cleft of it, and sunk again without speaking one Word. There may
be a proper Season for these several Terrors; and when they only
come in as Aids and Assistances to the Poet, they are not only to
be excused, but to be applauded. Thus the sounding of the Clock
in *Venice preserved*,[2] makes the Hearts of the whole Audience quake;
and conveys a stronger Terror to the Mind, than it is possible for
Words to do. The Appearance of the Ghost in *Hamlet* is a Master-
piece in its kind, and wrought up with all the Circumstances that
can create either Attention or Horror. The Mind of the Reader is
wonderfully prepared for his Reception, by the Discourses that
precede it: His dumb Behaviour at his first Entrance, strikes the
Imagination very strongly; but every time he enters, he is still
more terrifying. Who can read the Speech with which young
Hamlet accosts him, without trembling?

> Hor. *Look, my Lord, it comes!*
> Ham. *Angels and Ministers of Grace defend us!*
> *Be thou a Spirit of Health, or Goblin damn'd;*
> *Bring with thee Airs from Heav'n, or Blasts from Hell;*
> *Be thy Events wicked or charitable;*
> *Thou com'st in such a questionable Shape*

That I will speak to thee. I'll call thee Hamlet,
King, Father, Royal Dane: Oh! Oh! Answer me,
Let me not burst in Ignorance; but tell
Why thy canoniz'd Bones, hearsed in Death,
Have burst their Cearments? Why the Sepulchre,
Wherein we saw thee quietly inurn'd,
Hath op'd his ponderous and marble Jaws
To cast thee up again? What may this mean?
That thou dead Coarse again in compleat Steel
Revisit'st thus the Glimpses of the Moon,
Making Night hideous?[3]

I do not therefore find Fault with the Artifices abovementioned, when they are introduced with Skill, and accompanied by proportionable Sentiments and Expressions in the Writing.

For the moving of Pity, our principal Machine is the Handkerchief; and indeed in our common Tragedies, we should not know very often that the Persons are in Distress by any thing they say, if they did not from time to time apply their Handkerchiefs to their Eyes. Far be it from me to think of banishing this Instrument of Sorrow from the Stage; I know a Tragedy could not subsist without it: All that I would contend for, is, to keep it from being misapplied. In a Word, I would have the Actor's Tongue sympathize with his Eyes.

A disconsolate Mother, with a Child in her Hand, has frequently drawn Compassion from the Audience, and has therefore gained a Place in several Tragedies. A Modern Writer, that observed how this had took in other Plays, being resolved to double the Distress, and melt his Audience twice as much as those before him had done, brought a Princess upon the Stage with a little Boy in one Hand and a Girl in the other. This too had a very good Effect. A third Poet, being resolved to out-write all his Predecessors, a few Years ago introduced three Children, with great Success: And, as I am informed, a young Gentleman, who is fully determined to break the most obdurate Hearts, has a Tragedy by him, where the first Person that appears upon the Stage is an afflicted Widow in her Mourning-Weeds, with half a Dozen fatherless Children attending her, like those that usually hang about the Figure of Charity. Thus several Incidents that are beautiful in a good Writer, become ridiculous by falling into the Hands of a bad one.

But among all our Methods of moving Pity or Terror, there is none so absurd and barbarous, and what more exposes us to the Contempt and Ridicule of our Neighbours, than that dreadful butchering of one another, which is so very frequent upon the *English* Stage. To delight in seeing Men stabbed, poisoned, racked, or impaled, is certainly the Sign of a cruel Temper: And as this is often practised before the *British* Audience, several *French* Criticks, who think these are grateful Spectacles to us, take Occasion from them to represent us as a People that delight in Blood.[4] It is indeed very odd, to see our Stage strowed with Carcasses in the last Scene of a Tragedy; and to observe in the Ward-robe of the Play-house several Daggers, Poniards, °Wheels, Bowls for Poison, and many other Instruments of Death. Murders and Executions are always transacted behind the Scenes in the *French* Theatre; which in general is very agreeable to the Manners of a polite and civilized People: But as there are no Exceptions to this Rule on the *French* Stage, it leads them into Absurdities almost as ridiculous as that which falls under our present Censure. I remember in the famous Play of *Corneille*, written upon the Subject of the *Horatii* and *Curiatii*;[5] the fierce young Hero who had overcome the *Curiatii* one after another (instead of being congratulated by his Sister for his Victory, being upbraided by her for having slain her Lover) in the height of his Passion and Resentment kills her. If any thing could extenuate so brutal an Action, it would be the doing of it on a sudden, before the Sentiments of Nature, Reason, or Manhood could take Place in him. However, to avoid *publick Blood-shed*, as soon as his Passion is wrought to its Height, he follows his Sister the whole length of the Stage, and forbears killing her till they are both with drawn behind the Scenes. I must confess, had he murdered her before the Audience, the Indecency might have been greater; but as it is, it appears very unnatural, and looks like killing in cold Blood. To give my Opinion upon this Case; the Fact ought not to have been represented, but to have been told, if there was any Occasion for it.

It may not be unacceptable to the Reader, to see how *Sophocles* has conducted a Tragedy under the like delicate Circumstances.[6]

Orestes was in the same Condition with *Hamlet* in *Shakespear*, his Mother having murdered his Father, and taken Possession of his Kingdom in Conspiracy with her Adulterer. That young Prince therefore, being determined to revenge his Father's Death upon those who filled his Throne, conveys himself by a beautiful Stratagem into his Mother's Apartment, with a Resolution to kill her. But because such a Spectacle would have been too shocking to the Audience, this dreadful Resolution is executed behind the Scenes: The Mother is heard calling out to her Son for Mercy; and the Son answering her, that she shewed no Mercy to his Father: After which she shrieks out that she is wounded, and by what follows we find that she is slain. I do not remember that in any of our Plays there are Speeches made behind the Scenes, though there are other Instances of this Nature to be met with in those of the Ancients: And I believe my Reader will agree with me, that there is something infinitely more affecting in this dreadful Dialogue between the Mother and her Son behind the Scenes, than could have been in any thing transacted before the Audience. *Orestes* immediately after meets the Usurper at the Entrance of his Palace; and by a very happy Thought of the Poet avoids killing him before the Audience, by telling him that he should live some Time in his present Bitterness of Soul before he would dispatch him, and by ordering him to retire into that part of the Palace where he had slain his Father, whose Murther he would revenge in the very same Place where it was committed. By this Means the Poet observes that Decency, which *Horace* afterwards established by a Rule, of forbearing to commit Parricides or unnatural Murthers before the Audience.

> *Nec coram populo natos* Medea *trucidet.*

> Let *not* Medea *draw her murth'ring Knife,*
> *And spill her Childrens Blood upon the Stage.* [7]

The *French* have therefore refined too much upon *Horace*'s Rule, who never designed to banish all Kinds of Death from the Stage; but only such as had too much Horror in them, and which would have a better Effect upon the Audience when transacted behind the Scenes. I would therefore recommend to my Countrymen the

Practice of the ancient Poets, who were very sparing of their
publick Executions, and rather chose to perform them behind the
Scenes, if it could be done with as great an Effect upon the
Audience. At the same Time I must observe, that though the
devoted Persons of the Tragedy were seldom slain before the
Audience, which has generally something ridiculous in it, their
Bodies were often produced after their Death, which has always in
it something melancholy or terrifying; so that the killing on the
Stage does not seem to have been avoided only as an Indecency, but
also as an Improbability.

> *Nec pueros coram populo* Medea *trucidet;*
> *Aut humana palam coquat exta nefarius* Atreus;
> *Aut in Avem* Progne *vertatur,* Cadmus *in anguem,*
> *Quodcunq; ostendis mihi sic, incredulus odi.*   Hor.

> Medea *must not draw her murth'ring Knife,*
> Nor Atreus *there his horrid Feast prepare.*
> Cadmus *and* Progne's *Metamorphosis,*
> *(She to a Swallow turn'd, he to a Snake)*
> *And whatsoever contradicts my Sense,*
> *I hate to see, and never can believe.*
>   Ld. ROSCOMMON.[8]

I have now gone through the several dramatick Inventions which
are made use of by the ignorant Poets to supply the Place of
Tragedy, and by the skilful to improve it; some of which I could
wish entirely rejected, and the rest to be used with Caution. It
would be an endless Task to consider Comedy in the same Light,
and to mention the innumerable Shifts that small Wits put in
practice to raise a Laugh. *Bullock* in a short Coat, and *Norris* in a
long one, seldom fail of this Effect. In ordinary Comedies, a broad
and a narrow brim'd Hat are different Characters. Sometimes the
Wit of the Scene lies in a Shoulder-Belt, and sometimes in a Pair
of Whiskers. A Lover running about the Stage, with his Head
peeping out of a Barrel,[9] was thought a very good Jest in King
Charles the Second's time; and invented by one of the first Wits of
that Age. But because Ridicule is not so delicate as Compassion,
and because the Objects that make us laugh are infinitely more

numerous than those that make us weep, there is a much greater
Latitude for comick than tragick Artifices, and by consequence a
much greater Indulgence to be allowed them.   C

[HUMOUR]

No. 35 [ADDISON]

[False and true humour]
Tuesday, 10 April 1711

Risu inepto res ineptior nulla est.   [Catullus][1]

Among all kinds of Writing, there is none in which Authors are
more apt to miscarry than in Works of Humour, as there is none in
which they are more ambitious to excel. It is not an Imagination
that teems with Monsters, an Head that is filled with extravagant
Conceptions, which is capable of furnishing the World with
Diversions of this nature; and yet if we look into the Productions
of several Writers, who set up for Men of Humour, what wild
irregular Fancies, what unnatural Distortions of Thought, do we
meet with? If they speak Nonsense, they believe they are talking
Humour; and when they have drawn together a Scheme of absurd
inconsistent Ideas, they are not able to read it over to themselves
without laughing. These poor Gentlemen endeavour to gain
themselves the Reputation of Wits and Humourists, by such
monstrous Conceits as almost qualifie them for *Bedlam*;[2] not
considering that Humour should always lye under the Check of
Reason, and that it requires the Direction of the nicest Judgment,
by so much the more as it indulges it self in the most boundless
Freedoms. There is a kind of Nature that is to be observed in this
sort of Compositions, as well as in all other; and a certain Regularity
of Thought which must discover the Writer to be a Man of Sense,
at the same time that he appears altogether given up to Caprice:
For my part, when I read the delirious Mirth of an unskilful
Author, I cannot be so barbarous as to divert my self with it, but
am rather apt to pity the Man, than to laugh at any thing he
writes.

The Deceased Mr. *Shadwell*, who had himself a great deal of the Talent which I am treating of, represents an empty Rake, in one of his Plays, as very much surprized to hear one say that breaking of Windows was not Humour;[3] and I question not but several *English* Readers will be as much startled to hear me affirm, that many of those raving incoherent Pieces, which are often spread among us, under odd Chymerical Titles, are rather the Offsprings of a distempered Brain, than Works of Humour.

It is indeed much easier to describe what is not Humour, than what is; and very difficult to define it otherwise than as *Cowley* has done Wit, by Negatives.[4] Were I to give my own Notions of it, I would deliver them after *Plato*'s manner, in a kind of Allegory, and by supposing Humour to be a Person, deduce to him all his Qualifications, according to the following Genealogy.[5] TRUTH was the Founder of the Family, and the Father of GOOD SENSE. GOOD SENSE was the Father of WIT, who married a Lady of Collateral Line called MIRTH, by whom he had Issue HUMOUR. HUMOUR therefore being the youngest of this Illustrious Family, and descended from Parents of such different Dispositions, is very various and unequal in his Temper; sometimes you see him putting on grave Looks and a solemn Habit, sometimes airy in his Behaviour and fantastick in his Dress: Insomuch that at different times he appears as serious as a Judge, and as jocular as a °*Merry-Andrew*. But as he has a great deal of the °Mother in his Constitution, whatever Mood he is in, he never fails to make his Company laugh.

But since there is an Impostor abroad, who takes upon him the Name of this young Gentleman, and would willingly pass for him in the World; to the end that well-meaning Persons may not be imposed upon by Cheats, I would desire my Readers, when they meet with this °Pretender, to look into his Parentage, and to examine him strictly, whether or no he be remotely allied to TRUTH, and lineally descended from GOOD SENSE? if not, they may conclude him a Counterfeit. They may likewise distinguish him by a loud and excessive Laughter, in which he seldom gets his Company to join with him. For as TRUE HUMOUR generally looks serious, whilst every Body laughs about him; FALSE HUMOUR is always laughing, whilst every Body about him looks serious. I shall only add, if he has not in him a Mixture of both Parents, that is, if he would pass for the Offspring of WIT without MIRTH, or MIRTH without WIT, you may conclude him to be altogether Spurious, and a Cheat.

The Impostor of whom I am speaking, descends Originally from FALSEHOOD, who was the Mother of NONSENSE, who was brought to Bed of a Son called FRENZY, who Married one of the Daughters of FOLLY, commonly known by the Name of LAUGH-TER, on whom he begot that Monstrous Infant of which I have been here speaking. I shall set down at length the Genealogical Table of FALSE HUMOUR, and, at the same time, place under it the Genealogy of TRUE HUMOUR, that the Reader may at one View behold their different Pedigrees and Relations.

FALSEHOOD.

NONSENSE.

FRENZY. — LAUGHTER.

FALSE HUMOUR.

TRUTH.

GOOD SENSE.

WIT. — MIRTH.

HUMOUR.

I might extend the Allegory, by mentioning several of the Children of FALSE HUMOUR, who are more in Number than the Sands of the Sea, and might in particular enumerate the many Sons and Daughters which he has begot in this Island. But as this would be a very invidious Task, I shall only observe in general, that FALSE HUMOUR differs from the TRUE, as a Monkey does from a Man.

First of all, He is exceedingly given to little Apish Tricks and Buffooneries.

Secondly, He so much delights in Mimickry, that it is all one to him whether he exposes by it Vice and Folly, Luxury and Avarice; or, on the contrary, Virtue and Wisdom, Pain and Poverty.

Thirdly, He is wonderfully unlucky, insomuch that he will bite the Hand that feeds him, and endeavour to ridicule both Friends and Foes indifferently. For having but small Talents, he must be merry where he *can*, not where he *should*.

Fourthly, Being entirely void of Reason, he pursues no Point either of Morality or Instruction, but is Ludicrous only for the sake of being so.

Fifthly, Being incapable of any thing but Mock-Representations; his Ridicule is always Personal, and aimed at the Vicious Man, or the Writer; not at the Vice, or at the Writing.

I have here only pointed at the whole Species of False Humourists, but as one of my principal Designs in this Paper is to beat down that malignant Spirit, which discovers it self in the Writings of the present Age, I shall not scruple, for the future, to single out any of the small Wits, that infest the World with such Compositions as are ill-natured, immoral and absurd. This is the only Exception which I shall make to the General Rule I have prescribed my self, of *attacking Multitudes*: Since every honest Man ought to look upon himself as in a Natural State of War with the Libeller and Lampooner, and to annoy them wherever they fall in this way. This is but retaliating upon them, and treating them as they treat others.

C

No. 47 [ADDISON]

[Laughter]

Tuesday, 24 April 1711

Ride si sapis —   Mart.[1]

Mr. *Hobbs*, in his Discourse of Human Nature,[2] which, in my humble Opinion, is much the best of all his Works, after some very curious Observations upon Laughter, concludes thus: 'The Passion of Laughter is nothing else but sudden Glory arising from some sudden Conception of some Eminency in our selves, by Comparison with the Infirmity of others, or with our own formerly: For Men laugh at the Follies of themselves past, when they come suddenly to Remembrance, except they bring with them any present Dishonour.'

According to this Author therefore, when we hear a Man laugh excessively, instead of saying he is very Merry, we ought to tell him he is very Proud. And indeed, if we look into the bottom of this Matter, we shall meet with many Observations to confirm us in his Opinion. Every one laughs at somebody that is in an inferior

State of Folly to himself. It was formerly the Custom for every great House in *England* to keep a tame Fool dressed in Petticoats, that the Heir of the Family might have an Opportunity of joking upon him, and divert himself with his Absurdities. For the same Reason Ideots are still in request in most of the Courts of *Germany*, where there is not a Prince of any great Magnificence who has not two or three dressed, distinguished, undisputed Fools in his Retinue, whom the rest of the Courtiers are always breaking their Jests upon.

The *Dutch*, who are more famous for their Industry and Application, than for Wit and Humour, hang up in several of their Streets what they call the Sign of the *Gaper*, that is, the Head of an Ideot dressed in a Cap and Bells, and gaping in a most immoderate manner; This is a standing Jest at *Amsterdam*.

Thus every one diverts himself with some Person or other that is below him in Point of Understanding, and triumphs in the Superiority of his Genius, whilst he has such Objects of Derision before his Eyes. Mr. *Dennis* has very well expressed this in a Couple of humorous Lines, which are part of a Translation of a Satyr in Monsieur *Boileau*.

> *Thus one Fool lolls his Tongue out at another,*
> *And shakes his empty Noddle at his Brother.*[3]

Mr. *Hobbs*'s Reflection gives us the Reason why the insignificant People above-mentioned are Stirrers up of Laughter among Men of a gross Taste: But as the more understanding Part of Mankind do not find their Risibility affected by such ordinary Objects, it may be worth the while to examine into the several Provocatives of Laughter in Men of superior Sense and Knowledge.

In the first Place I must observe, that there is a Sett of merry Drolls, whom the common People of all Countries admire, and seem to love so well, *that they could eat them*, according to the old Proverb: I mean those °circumforaneous Wits whom every Nation calls by the Name of that Dish of Meat which it loves best. In *Holland* they are termed *Pickled Herrings*; in *France, Jean Pottages*; in *Italy, Maccaronies*; and in *Great Britain, Jack Puddings*. These merry Wags, from whatsoever Food they receive their Titles, that they may make their Audiences laugh, always appear in a Fool's Coat, and commit such Blunders and Mistakes in every Step they take, and every Word they utter, as those who listen to them would be ashamed of.

But this little Triumph of the Understanding, under the Disguise of Laughter, is no where more visible than in that Custom which prevails every where among us on the First Day of the present Month, when every Body takes it in his Head to make as many Fools as he can.[4] In proportion as there are more Follies discovered, so there is more Laughter raised on this Day, than on any other in the whole Year. A Neighbour of mine, who is a Haberdasher by Trade, and a very shallow conceited Fellow, makes his Boasts that for these ten Years successively he has not made less than an hundred *April* Fools. My Landlady had a falling out with him about a Fortnight ago, for sending every one of her Children upon some *Sleeveless Errand*, as she terms it. Her eldest Son went to buy an Half-penny worth of °Inkle at a Shoe-maker's; the eldest Daughter was dispatched half a Mile to see a Monster; and in short, the whole Family of innocent Children made *April* Fools. Nay, my Landlady her self did not escape him. This empty Fellow has laughed upon these Conceits ever since.

This Art of Wit is well enough, when confined to one Day in a Twelve-month; but there is an ingenious Tribe of Men sprung up of late Years, who are for making *April* Fools every Day in the Year. These Gentlemen are commonly distinguished by the Name of °*Biters*;[5] a Race of Men that are perpetually employed in laughing at those Mistakes which are of their own Production.

Thus we see, in proportion as one Man is more refined than another, he chuses his Fool out of a lower or higher Class of Mankind; or, to speak in a more Philosophical Language, That secret Elation and Pride of Heart which is generally called Laughter, arises in him from his comparing himself with an Object below him, whether it so happens that it be a Natural or an Artificial Fool. It is indeed very possible, that the Persons we laugh at may in the main of their Characters be much wiser Men than our selves; but if they would have us laugh at them, they must fall short of us in those Respects which stir up this Passion.

I am afraid I shall appear too °Abstracted in my Speculations, if I shew that when a Man of Wit makes us laugh, it is by betraying some Oddness or Infirmity in his own Character, or in the

Representation which he makes of others; and that when we laugh at a Brute or even at an inanimate thing, it is at some Action or Incident that bears a remote Analogy to any Blunder or Absurdity in reasonable Creatures.

But to come into common Life: I shall pass by the Consideration of those Stage Coxcombs that are able to shake a whole Audience, and take Notice of a particular sort of Men who are such Provokers of Mirth in Conversation, that it is impossible for a Club or Merry-meeting to subsist without them; I mean, those honest Gentlemen that are always exposed to the Wit and Raillery of their Well-wishers and Companions; that are pelted by Men, Women, and Children, Friends, and Foes, and, in a word, stand as *Butts* in Conversation, for every one to shoot at that pleases. I know several of these *Butts* who are Men of Wit and Sense, though by some odd Turn of Humour, some unlucky Cast in their Person or Behaviour, they have always the Misfortune to make the Company merry. The Truth of it is, a Man is not qualified for a *Butt*, who has not a good deal of Wit and Vivacity, even in the ridiculous Side of his Character. A stupid *Butt* is only fit for the Conversation of ordinary People: Men of Wit require one that will give them Play, and bestir himself in the absurd Part of his Behaviour. A *Butt* with these Accomplishments frequently gets the Laugh of his Side, and turns the Ridicule upon him that attacks him. Sir *John Falstaff* was an Hero of this Species, and gives a good Description of himself in his Capacity of a *Butt*, after the following manner; *Men of all sorts* (says that merry Knight) *take a Pride to gird at me. The Brain of Man is not able to invent any thing that tends to Laughter more than I invent, or is invented on me. I am not only Witty in my self, but the Cause that Wit is in other Men.*

C

[WIT]

No. 61 [ADDISON]

[False wit: punning]
Thursday, 10 May 1711

Non equidem studeo, bullatis ut mihi nugis
Pagina turgescat, dare pondus idonea fumo.   *Pers.*[1]

There is no kind of false Wit which has been so recommended by the Practice of all Ages, as that which consists in a Jingle of Words, and is comprehended under the general Name of *Punning*. It is indeed impossible to kill a Weed, which the Soil has a natural Disposition to produce. The Seeds of Punning are in the Minds of all Men, and tho' they may be subdued by Reason, Reflection, and good Sense, they will be very apt to shoot up in the greatest Genius, that is not broken and cultivated by the Rules of Art. Imitation is natural to us, and when it does not raise the Mind to Poetry, Painting, Musick, or other more noble Arts, it often breaks out in Punns and Quibbles.

Aristotle, in the Eleventh Chapter of his Book of Rhetorick, describes two or three kinds of Punns, which he calls Paragrams, among the Beauties of good Writing, and produces Instances of them out of some of the greatest Authors in the *Greek* Tongue.[2] *Cicero* has sprinkled several of his Works with Punns, and in his Book where he lays down the Rules of Oratory, quotes abundance of Sayings as Pieces of Wit, which also upon Examination prove arrant Punns.[3] But the Age in which *the Punn* chiefly flourished, was the Reign of King *James* the First. That learned Monarch was himself a tolerable Punnster, and made very few Bishops or Privy-Counsellors that had not some time or other signalized themselves by a °Clinch, or a °*Conundrum*. It was therefore in this Age that the Punn appeared with Pomp and Dignity. It had before been admitted into merry Speeches and ludicrous Compositions, but was now delivered with great Gravity from the Pulpit, or pronounced in the most solemn manner at the Council-Table. The greatest Authors, in their most serious Works, made frequent use of Punns. The Sermons of Bishop *Andrews*,[4] and the Tragedies of

Shakespear, are full of them. The Sinner was punned into Repentance by the former, as in the latter nothing is more usual than to see a Hero weeping and quibbling for a dozen Lines together.

I must add to these great Authorities, which seem to have given a kind of Sanction to this Piece of false Wit, that all the Writers of Rhetorick have treated of Punning with very great Respect, and divided the several kinds of it into hard Names, that are reckoned among the Figures of Speech, and recommended as Ornaments in Discourse. I remember a Country School-master of my Acquaintance told me once, that he had been in Company with a Gentleman whom he looked upon to be the greatest *Paragrammatist* among the Moderns. Upon Enquiry, I found my learned Friend had dined that Day with Mr. *Swan*, the famous Punnster;[5] and desiring him to give me some Account of Mr. *Swan*'s Conversation, he told me that he generally talked in the °*Paranomasia*, that he sometimes gave into the °*Plocè*, but that in his humble Opinion he shined most in the °*Antanaclasis*.

I must not here omit, that a famous University of this Land was formerly very much infested with Punns;[6] but whether or no this might not arise from the Fens and Marshes in which it was situated, and which are now drained, I must leave to the Determination of more skilful Naturalists.

After this short History of Punning, one would wonder how it should be so entirely banished out of the Learned World, as it is at present, especially since it had found a Place in the Writings of the most ancient Polite Authors. To account for this, we must consider, that the first Race of Authors, who were the great Heroes in Writing, were destitute of all Rules and Arts of Criticism; and for that Reason, though they excel later Writers in Greatness of Genius, they fall short of them in Accuracy and Correctness. The Moderns cannot reach their Beauties, but can avoid their Imperfections. When the World was furnished with these Authors of the first Eminence, there grew up another Set of Writers, who gained themselves a Reputation by the Remarks which they made on the Works of those who preceded them. It was one of the Employments of these Secondary Authors, to distinguish the several kinds of Wit by Terms of Art, and to consider them as more or less perfect, according as they were founded in Truth. It is no wonder therefore, that even such Authors as *Isocrates, Plato*, and *Cicero*, should have such little Blemishes as are not to be met with in Authors of a much inferior Character, who have written since those several Blemishes were discovered. I do not find that there was a proper Separation made between Punns and true Wit by any of the ancient Authors, except *Quintilian* and *Longinus*. But when this Distinction was once settled, it was very natural for all Men of Sense to agree in it. As for the Revival of this false Wit, it happened about the time of the °Revival of Letters; but as soon as it was once detected, it immediately vanished and disappeared. At the same time there is no question, but as it has sunk in one Age and rose in another, it will again recover it self in some distant Period of Time, as Pedantry and Ignorance shall prevail upon Wit and Sense. And, to speak the Truth, I do very much apprehend, by some of the last Winter's Productions, which had their Sets of Admirers, that our Posterity will in a few Years degenerate into a Race of Punnsters: At least, a Man may be very excusable for any Apprehensions of this kind, that has seen *Acrosticks* handed about the Town with great Secresie and Applause; to which I must also add a little *Epigram* called the *Witches Prayer*, that fell into Verse when it was read either backward or forward, excepting only that it Cursed one way and Blessed the other. When one sees there are actually such Pains-takers among our *British* Wits, who can tell what it may end in? If we must Lash one another, let it be with the manly Strokes of Wit and Satyr; for I am of the old Philosopher's Opinion, That if I must suffer from one or the other, I would rather it should be from the Paw of a Lion, than the Hoof of an Ass.[7] I do not speak this out of any Spirit of Party. There is a most crying Dulness on both Sides. I have seen Tory *Acrosticks* and Whig *Anagrams*, and do not quarrel with either of them, because they are *Whigs* or *Tories*, but because they are *Anagrams* and *Acrosticks*.

But to return to Punning. Having pursued the History of a Punn, from its Original to its Downfal, I shall here define it to be a Conceit arising from the use of two Words that agree in the Sound, but differ in the Sense. The only way therefore to try a Piece of Wit, is to translate it into a different Language: If it bears the Test you may pronounce it true; but if it vanishes in the Experiment you may conclude it to have been a Punn. In short, one may say of a Punn as the Country-man described his Nightingale, that it is *vox & præterea nihil*,[8] a Sound, and nothing but a Sound. On the contrary, one may represent true Wit by the Description which *Aristinetus* makes of a fine Woman, When she is *dressed* she is Beautiful, when she is *undressed* she is Beautiful: Or, as *Mercerus* has translated it more Emphatically, *Induitur, formosa est: Exuitur, ipsa forma est.*[9]   C

No. 62 [ADDISON]

[True, false and mixed wit]
Friday, 11 May 1711

Scribendi recte Sapere est & principium & fons.   Hor.[1]

Mr. *Lock* has an admirable Reflection upon the Difference of Wit and Judgment, whereby he endeavours to shew the Reason why they are not always the Talents of the same Person.[2] His Words are as follow: *And hence, perhaps, may be given some Reason of that common Observation, That Men who have a great deal of Wit and prompt Memories, have not always the clearest Judgment, or deepest Reason. For Wit lying most in the Assemblage of Ideas, and putting those together with Quickness and Variety, wherein can be found any Resemblance or Congruity, thereby to make up pleasant Pictures and agreeable Visions in the Fancy; Judgment, on the contrary, lies quite on the other Side, In separating carefully one from another, Ideas wherein can be found the least Difference, thereby to avoid being mis-led by Similitude, and by Affinity to take one thing for another. This is a Way of proceeding quite contrary to Metaphor and Allusion; wherein, for the most Part, lies that Entertainment and Pleasantry of Wit which strikes so lively on the Fancy, and is therefore so acceptable to all People.*

This is, I think, the best and most philosophical Account that I have ever met with of Wit, which generally, though not always, consists in such a Resemblance and Congruity of Ideas as this Author mentions. I shall only add to it, by way of Explanation, That every Resemblance of Ideas is not that which we call Wit, unless it be such an one that gives *Delight* and *Surprize* to the Reader: These two Properties seem essential to Wit, more particularly the last of them. In order therefore that the Resemblance in the Ideas be Wit, it is necessary that the Ideas should not lie too near one another in the Nature of things; for where the Likeness is obvious, it gives no Surprize. To compare one Man's Singing to that of another, or to represent the Whiteness of any Object by that of Milk and Snow, or the Variety of its Colours by those of the Rainbow, cannot be called Wit, unless, besides this obvious Resemblance, there be some further Congruity discovered in the two Ideas that is capable of giving the Reader some Surprize. Thus when a Poet tells us, the Bosom of his Mistress is as white as Snow, there is no Wit in the Comparison; but when he adds, with a Sigh, that it is as cold too, it then grows into Wit. Every Reader's Memory may supply him with innumerable Instances of the same Nature. For this Reason, the Similitudes in Heroick Poets, who endeavour rather to fill the Mind with great Conceptions, than to divert it with such as are new, and surprizing, have seldom any thing in them that can be called Wit. Mr. *Lock*'s Account of Wit, with this short Explanation, comprehends most of the Species of Wit, as Metaphors, Similitudes, Allegories, Ænigmas, Mottos, Parables, Fables, Dreams, Visions, dramatick Writings, Burlesque, and all the Methods of Allusion: As there are many other Pieces of Wit (how remote soever they may appear at first Sight from the foregoing Description) which upon Examination will be found to agree with it.

As *true Wit* generally consists in this Resemblance and Congruity of Ideas, *false Wit* chiefly consists in the Resemblance and Congruity sometimes of single Letters, as in Anagrams, °Chronograms, °Lipograms, and Acrosticks: Sometimes of Syllables, as in Ecchos and Doggerel Rhymes: Sometimes of Words, as in Punns and Quibbles; and sometimes of whole Sentences or Poems, cast into the Figures of *Eggs, Axes* or *Altars:* Nay, some carry the Notion of Wit so far, as to ascribe it even to external Mimickry; and to look upon a Man as an ingenious Person, that can resemble the Tone, Posture, or Face of another.

As *true Wit* consists in the Resemblance of Ideas, and *false Wit* in the Resemblance of Words, according to the foregoing Instances; there is another kind of Wit which consists partly in the Resemblance of Ideas, and partly in the Resemblance of Words; which for Distinction Sake I shall call *mixt Wit*. This Kind of Wit is that which abounds in *Cowley*, more than in any Author that ever wrote. Mr. *Waller* has likewise a great deal of it.[3] Mr. *Dryden* is very sparing in it. *Milton* had a Genius much above it. *Spencer* is in the same Class with *Milton*. The *Italians*, even in their Epic Poetry, are full of it. Monsieur *Boileau*, who formed himself upon the Ancient Poets, has every where rejected it with Scorn. If we look after mixt Wit among the *Greek* Writers, we shall find it no where but in the Epigrammatists. There are indeed some Strokes of it in the little Poem ascribed to *Musæus*, which by that, as well as many other Marks, betrays it self to be a Modern Composition.[4] If we look into the *Latin* Writers, we find none of this mixt Wit in *Virgil, Lucretius*, or *Catullus*; very little in *Horace*, but a great deal of it in *Ovid*, and scarce any thing else in *Martial*.

Out of the innumerable Branches of *mixt Wit*, I shall chuse one Instance which may be met with in all the Writers of this Class. The Passion of Love in its Nature has been thought to resemble Fire; for which Reason the Words Fire and Flame are made use of to signifie Love. The witty Poets therefore have taken an Advantage from the doubtful Meaning of the Word Fire, to make an infinite Number of Witticisms. *Cowley* observing the cold Regard of his Mistress's Eyes, and at the same Time their Power of producing Love in him, considers them as Burning-Glasses made of Ice; and finding himself able to live in the greatest Extremities of Love, concludes the Torrid Zone to be habitable. When his Mistress has read his Letter written in Juice of Lemmon by holding it to the Fire, he desires her to read it over a second time by Love's Flames. When she weeps, he wishes it were inward Heat that distilled those Drops from the °Limbeck. When she is absent he is beyond eighty, that is, thirty Degrees nearer the Pole than when she is with him. His ambitious Love is a Fire that naturally mounts upwards; his happy Love is the Beams of Heaven, and his unhappy Love Flames of Hell. When it does not let him sleep, it is a Flame that sends up no Smoak; when it is opposed by Counsel and Advice, it is a Fire that rages the more by the Wind's blowing upon it. Upon the dying of a Tree in which he had cut his Loves, he observes that his written Flames had burnt up and withered the Tree. When he resolves to give over his Passion, he tells us that one burnt like him for ever dreads the Fire. His Heart is an *Ætna*, that instead of

Vulcan's Shop encloses *Cupid*'s Forge in it. His endeavouring to drown his Love in Wine, is throwing Oil upon the Fire. He would insinuate to his Mistress, that the Fire of Love, like that of the Sun (which produces so many living Creatures) should not only warm but beget. Love in another Place cooks Pleasure at his Fire. Sometimes the Poet's Heart is frozen in every Breast, and sometimes scorched in every Eye. Sometimes he is drowned in Tears, and burnt in Love, like a Ship set on fire in the Middle of the Sea.

The Reader may observe in every one of these Instances, that the Poet mixes the Qualities of Fire with those of Love; and in the same Sentence speaking of it both as a Passion, and as real Fire, surprizes the Reader with those seeming Resemblances or Contradictions that make up all the Wit in this kind of Writing. Mixt Wit therefore is a Composition of Punn and true Wit, and is more or less perfect as the Resemblance lies in the Ideas or in the Words: Its Foundations are laid partly in Falsehood and partly in Truth: Reason puts in her Claim for one Half of it, and Extravagance for the other. The only Province therefore for this kind of Wit, is Epigram, or those little occasional Poems that in their own Nature are nothing else but a Tissue of Epigrams. I cannot conclude this Head of *mixt Wit*, without owning that the admirable Poet out of whom I have taken the Examples of it, had as much true Wit as any Author that ever writ; and indeed all other Talents of an extraordinary Genius.

It may be expected, since I am upon this Subject, that I should take Notice of Mr. *Dryden*'s Definition of Wit[5]; which, with all the Deference that is due to the Judgment of so great a Man, is not so properly a Definition of Wit, as of good Writing in general. Wit, as he defines it, is 'a Propriety of Words and Thoughts adapted to the Subject.' If this be a true Definition of Wit, I am apt to think that *Euclid* was the greatest Wit that ever set Pen to Paper: It is certain there never was a greater Propriety of Words and Thoughts adapted to the Subject, than what that Author has made use of in his Elements. I shall only appeal to my Reader, if this Definition agrees with any Notion he has of Wit: If it be a true one, I am sure Mr. *Dryden* was not only a better Poet, but a great Wit than Mr. *Cowley*; and *Virgil* a much more facetious Man than either *Ovid* or *Martial*.

Bouhours, whom I look upon to be the most penetrating of all the *French* Criticks, has taken Pains to shew, That it is impossible for any Thought to be beautiful which is not just, and has not its Foundation in the Nature of things: That the Basis of all Wit is Truth; and that no Thought can be valuable, of which good Sense is not the Ground-work. *Boileau* has endeavoured to inculcate the same Notion[6] in several Parts of his Writings, both in Prose and Verse. This is that natural Way of Writing, that beautiful Simplicity, which we so much admire in the Compositions of the Ancients; and which no Body deviates from, but those who want Strength of Genius to make a Thought shine in its own natural Beauties. Poets who want this Strength of Genius to give that Majestick Simplicity to Nature, which we so much admire in the Works of the Ancients, are forced to hunt after foreign Ornaments, and not to let any Piece of Wit of what Kind soever escape them. I look upon these Writers as *Goths* in Poetry, who, like those in Architecture, not being able to come up to the beautiful Simplicity of the old *Greeks* and *Romans*, have endeavoured to supply its Place with all the Extravagances of an irregular Fancy. Mr. *Dryden* makes a very handsome Observation on *Ovid*'s Writing a Letter from *Dido* to *Æneas*, in the following Words:[7] '*Ovid* (says he, speaking of *Virgil*'s Fiction of *Dido* and *Æneas*) takes it up after him, even in the same Age, and makes an Ancient Heroine of *Virgil*'s new-created *Dido*; dictates a Letter for her just before her Death to the ungrateful Fugitive; and, very unluckily for himself, is for measuring a Sword with a Man so much superior in Force to him, on the same Subject. I think I may be Judge of this, because I have translated both. The famous Author of the Art of Love has nothing of his own; he borrows all from a greater Master in his own Profession, and, which is worse, improves nothing which he finds: Nature fails him, and being forced to his old Shift, he has Recourse to Witticism. This passes indeed with his soft Admirers, and gives him the Preference to *Virgil* in their Esteem.'

Were not I supported by so great an Authority as that of Mr. *Dryden*, I should not venture to observe, That the Taste of most of our *English* Poets, as well as Readers, is extremely *Gothick*. He quotes Monsieur *Segrais* for a threefold Distinction of the Readers of Poetry:[8] In the first of which he comprehends the Rabble of

Readers, whom he does not treat as such with regard to their Quality, but to their Numbers and the Coarseness of their Taste. His Words are as follow: 'Segrais has distinguished the Readers of Poetry, according to their Capacity of judging, into three Classes. (He might have said the same of Writers too, if he had pleased.) In the lowest Form he places those whom he calls *Les Petits Esprits*, such things as are our Upper-Gallery Audience in a Play-house; who like nothing but the Husk and Rind of Wit, prefer a Quibble, a Conceit, an Epigram, before solid Sense and elegant Expression: These are Mob-Readers. If *Virgil* and *Martial* stood for Parliament-Men, we know already who would carry it. But though they make the greatest Appearance in the Field, and cry the loudest, the best on't is they are but a Sort of *French* Huguenots, or *Dutch* Boors, brought over in Herds, but not Naturalized; who have not Lands of two Pounds *per Annum* in *Parnassus*, and therefore are not privileged to Poll. Their Authors are of the same Level, fit to represent them on a Mountebank's Stage, or to be Masters of the Ceremonies in a Bear-Garden: Yet these are they who have the most Admirers. But it often happens, to their Mortification, that as their Readers improve their Stock of Sense, (as they may by reading better Books, and by Conversation with Men of Judgment) they soon forsake them.'

I must not dismiss this Subject without observing, that as Mr. *Lock* in the Passage above-mentioned has discovered the most fruitful Source of Wit, so there is another of a quite contrary Nature to it which does likewise branch it self out into several Kinds. For not only the *Resemblance* but the *Opposition* of Ideas does very often produce Wit; as I could shew in several little Points, Turns, and Antitheses, that I may possibly enlarge upon in some future Speculation.

                                                      C

[BALLADS]

No. 70 [ADDISON]

['Chevy-Chase']¹
Monday, 21 May 1711

Interdum vulgus rectum videt.   Hor.²

When I travelled, I took a particular Delight in hearing the Songs and Fables that are come from Father to Son, and are most in vogue among the common People of the Countries through which I passed, for it is impossible that any thing should be universally tasted and approved by a Multitude, tho' they are only the Rabble of a Nation, which hath not in it some peculiar Aptness to please and gratifie the Mind of Man. Human Nature is the same in all reasonable Creatures; and whatever falls in with it, will meet with Admirers amongst Readers of all Qualities and Conditions. *Moliere*, as we are told by Monsieur *Boileau*,³ used to read all his Comedies to an old Woman who was his House-keeper, as she sat with him at her Work by the Chimney-Corner; and could foretel the Success of his Play in the Theatre, from the Reception it met at his Fire-Side: For he tells us the Audience always followed the old Woman, and never failed to laugh in the same Place.

I know nothing which more shews the essential and inherent Perfection of Simplicity of Thought, above that which I call the Gothick Manner in Writing, than this, that the first pleases all Kinds of Palates, and the latter only such as have formed to themselves a wrong artificial Taste upon little fanciful Authors and Writers of Epigram. *Homer*, *Virgil*, or *Milton*, so far as the Language of their Poems is understood, will please a Reader of plain common Sense, who would neither relish nor comprehend an Epigram of *Martial*, or a Poem of *Cowley*: So, on the contrary, an ordinary Song or Ballad that is the Delight of the common People, cannot fail to please all such Readers as are not unqualified for the Entertainment by their Affectation or Ignorance; and the Reason is plain, because the same Paintings of Nature which recommend it to the most ordinary Reader, will appear beautiful to the most refined.

The old Song of *Chevy-Chase* is the favourite Ballad of the common

People of *England*; and *Ben. Johnson* used to say he had rather have been the Author of it than of all his Works.[4] Sir *Philip Sidney* in his Discourse of Poetry speaks of it in the following Words;[5] *I never heard the old Song of* Piercy *and* Douglas, *that I found not my Heart more moved than with a Trumpet; and yet is [it] sung [but] by some blind Crowder with no rougher Voice than rude Stile; which being so evil apparelled in the Dust and [Cobwebs] of that uncivil Age, what would it work trimmed in the gorgeous Eloquence of* Pindar? For my own Part, I am so professed an Admirer of this antiquated Song, that I shall give my Reader a °Critick upon it, without any further Apology for so doing.

The greatest Modern Cricticks have laid it down as a Rule, That an Heroick Poem should be founded upon some important Precept of Morality, adapted to the Constitution of the Country in which the Poet writes.[6] *Homer* and *Virgil* have formed their Plans in this View. As *Greece* was a Collection of many Governments, who suffered very much among themselves, and gave the *Persian* Emperor, who was their common Enemy, many Advantages over them by their mutual Jealousies and Animosities, *Homer*, in order to establish among them an Union, which was so necessary for their Safety, grounds his Poem upon the Discords of the several *Grecian* Princes who were engaged in a Confederacy against an *Asiatick* Prince, and the several Advantages which the Enemy gained by such their Discords. At the Time the Poem we are now treating of was written, the Dissentions of the Barons, who were then so many petty Princes, ran very high, whether they quarrelled among themselves, or with their Neighbours, and produced unspeakable Calamities to the Country: The Poet, to deter Men from such unnatural Contentions, describes a bloody Battel and dreadful Scene of Death, occasioned by the mutual Feuds which reigned in the Families of an *English* and *Scotch* Nobleman. That he designed this for the Instruction of his Poem, we may learn from his four last Lines, in which, after the Example of the Modern Tragedians, he draws from it a Precept for the Benefit of his Readers.

> *God save the King, and bless the Land*
> *In Plenty, Joy, and Peace;*
> *And grant henceforth that foul Debate*
> *'Twixt Noblemen may cease.*

The next Point observed by the greatest Heroic Poets, hath been to celebrate Persons and Actions which do Honour to their Country: Thus *Virgil*'s Hero was the Founder of *Rome*, *Homer*'s a Prince of *Greece*; and for this Reason *Valerius Flaccus* and *Statius*, who were both *Romans*, might be justly derided for having chosen the Expedition of the *Golden Fleece* and *the Wars of Thebes*, for the Subjects of their Epic Writings.[7]

The Poet before us, has not only found out an Hero in his own Country, but raises the Reputation of it by several beautiful Incidents. The *English* are the first who take the Field, and the last who quit it. The *English* bring only Fifteen hundred to the Battel, the *Scotch* Two thousand. The *English* keep the Field with Fifty three: The *Scotch* retire with Fifty five: All the rest on each Side being slain in Battel. But the most remarkable Circumstance of this Kind, is the different Manner in which the *Scotch* and *English* Kings receive the News of this Fight, and of the great Mens Deaths who commanded in it.

> *This News was brought to* Edinburgh,
>   *Where* Scotland's *King did reign,*
> *That brave Earl* Douglas *suddenly*
>   *Was with an Arrow slain.*
>
> *O heavy News, King* James *did say,*
>   Scotland *can Witness be,*
> *I have not any Captain more*
>   *Of such Account as he.*
>
> *Like Tydings to King* Henry *came*
>   *Within as short a Space,*
> *That* Piercy *of* Northumberland
>   *Was slain in* Chevy-Chace.
>
> *Now God be with him, said our King,*
>   *Sith 'twill no better be,*
> *I trust I have within my Realm*
>   *Five hundred as good as he.*
>
> *Yet shall not* Scot *nor* Scotland *say*
>   *But I will Vengeance take,*

> *And be revenged on them all*
> *For brave Lord* Piercy's *Sake.*
>
> *This Vow full well the King perform'd*
> *After on* °Humble-down,
> *In one Day Fifty Knights were slain*
> *With Lords of great Renown.*
>
> *And of the rest of small Account*
> *Did many Thousands dye,* &c.

At the same Time that our Poet shews a laudable Partiality to his Country-men, he represents the *Scots* after a Manner not unbecoming so bold and brave a People.

> Earl *Douglas on a milk-white Steed,*
> *Most like a Baron bold,*
> *Rode foremost of the Company*
> *Whose Armour shone like Gold.*

His Sentiments and Actions are every Way suitable to an Hero. One of us two, says he, must dye: I am an Earl as well as your self, so that you can have no Pretence for refusing the Combat: However, says he, 'tis Pity, and indeed would be a Sin, that so many innocent Men should perish for our Sakes; rather let you and I end our Quarrel in single Fight.

> *E'er thus I will out-braved be,*
> *One of us two shall dye;*
> *I know thee well, an Earl thou art,*
> *Lord* Piercy, *so am I.*
>
> *But trust me,* Piercy, *Pity it were,*
> *And great Offence, to kill*
> *Any of these our harmless Men,*
> *For they have done no Ill.*
>
> *Let thou and I the Battel try,*
> *And set our Men aside;*
> *Accurst be he, Lord* Piercy *said,*
> *By whom this is deny'd.*

When these brave Men had distinguished themselves in the Battel and in single Combat with each other, in the Midst of a generous Parly, full of heroic Sentiments, the *Scotch* Earl falls; and with his Dying Words encourages his Men to revenge his Death, representing to them, as the most bitter Circumstance of it, that his Rival saw him fall.

> *With that there came an Arrow keen*
> *Out of an* English *Bow,*
> *Which struck Earl* Douglas *to the Heart*
> *A deep and deadly Blow.*

> *Who never spoke more Words than these,*
> *Fight on my merry Men all;*
> *For why, my Life is at an End,*
> Lord *Piercy sees my Fall.*

Merry Men, in the Language of those Times, is no more than a chearful Word for Companions and Fellow-Soldiers. A Passage in the Eleventh Book of *Virgil's Æneids* is very much to be admired, where *Camilla* in her last Agonies, instead of weeping over the Wound she had received, as one might have expected from a Warrior of her Sex, considers only (like the Hero of whom we are now speaking) how the Battel should be continued after her Death.

> *Tum sic exspirans,* &c.[8]

> *A gathering Mist o'erclouds her chearful Eyes;*
> *And from her Cheeks the rosie Colour flies.*
> *Then, turns to her, whom, of her Female Train,*
> *She trusted most, and thus she speaks with Pain.*
> *Acca, 'tis past! He swims before my Sight,*
> *Inexorable Death; and claims his Right.*
> *Bear my last Words to* Turnus, *fly with Speed,*
> *And bid him timely to my Charge succeed:*
> *Repel the* Trojans, *and the Town relieve:*
> *Farewell. —*

Turnus did not die in so heroic a Manner; tho' our Poet seems to have had his Eye upon *Turnus's* Speech in the last Verse,

> *Lord* Piercy *sees my Fall.*

> *— Vicisti, & victum tendere palmas*
> *Ausonii videre —*[9]

Earl *Piercy*'s Lamentation over his Enemy is generous, beautiful, and passionate; I must only caution the Reader not to let the Simplicity of the Stile, which one may well pardon in so old a Poet, prejudice him against the Greatness of the Thought.

> *Then leaving Life Earl* Piercy *took*
> *The dead Man by the Hand,*
> *And said, Earl* Douglas *for thy Life*
> *Would I had lost my Land.*

> *O Christ! My very Heart doth bleed*
> *With Sorrow for thy Sake;*
> *For sure a more renowned Knight*
> *Mischance did never take.*

That beautiful Line *Taking the dead Man by the Hand*, will put the Reader in Mind of *Æneas*'s Behaviour towards *Lausus*, whom he himself had Slain as he came to the Rescue of his aged Father.

> *At vero ut vultum vidit morientis, & ora,*
> *Ora modis Anchisiades, pallentia miris:*
> *Ingemuit, miserans graviter, dextramque tetendit, &c.*[10]

> *The pious Prince beheld young* Lausus *dead;*
> *He griev'd, he wept; then grasp'd his Hand, and said,*
> *Poor hapless Youth! What Praises can be paid*
> *To Worth so great —!*

I shall take another Opportunity to consider the other Parts of this old Song.

No. 74 [ADDISON]

['Chevy-Chase' continued]
Friday, 25 May 1711
— Pendent opera interrupta —   Virg.[1]

In my last *Monday*'s Paper I gave some general Instances of those beautiful Strokes which please the Reader in the old Song of *Chevy-Chase*; I shall here, according to my Promise, be more particular, and shew that the Sentiments in that Ballad are extreamly Natural and Poetical, and full of the majestick Simplicity which we admire in the greatest of the ancient Poets: For which Reason I shall quote several Passages of it, in which the Thought is altogether the same with what we meet in several Passages of the *Æneid*; not that I would infer from thence, that the Poet (whoever he was) proposed to himself any Imitation of those Passages, but that he was directed to them in general, by the same kind of Poetical Genius, and by the same Copyings after Nature.

Had this old Song been filled with Epigrammatical Turns and Points of Wit, it might perhaps have pleased the wrong Taste of some Readers; but it would never have become the Delight of the common People, nor have warmed the Heart of Sir *Philip Sidney* like the Sound of a Trumpet; it is only Nature that can have this Effect, and please those Tastes which are the most unprejudiced or the most refined. I must however beg leave to dissent from so great an Authority as that of Sir *Philip Sidney*, in the Judgment which he has passed as to the rude Stile and evil Apparel of this antiquated Song; for there are several Parts in it where not only the Thought but the Language is majestick, and the Numbers sonorous; at least, the *Apparel* is much more *gorgeous* than many of the Poets made use of in Queen *Elizabeth*'s Time, as the Reader will see in several of the following Quotations.

What can be greater than either the Thought or the Expression in that Stanza,

> *To drive the Deer with Hound and Horn*
>   *Earl* Piercy *took his Way;*
> *The Child may rue that was unborn*
>   *The Hunting of that Day?*

This Way of considering the Misfortunes which this Battel would
bring upon Posterity, not only on those who were born immediately
after the Battel and lost their Fathers in it, but on those also who
perished in future Battels which took their rise from this Quarrel
of the two Earls, is wonderfully beautiful, and conformable to the
Way of Thinking among the ancient Poets.

> *Audiet pugnas vitio parentum*
> *Rara juventus.*   Hor.[2]

What can be more sounding and poetical, or resemble more the
majestick Simplicity of the Ancients, than the following Stanzas?

> *The stout Earl of* Northumberland
>   *A Vow to God did make,*
> *His Pleasure in the* Scottish *Woods*
>   *Three Summer's Days to take.*
>
> *With fifteen hundred Bowmen bold,*
>   *All chosen Men of Might,*
> *Who knew full well, in Time of Need,*
>   *Tho aim their Shafts aright.*
>
> *The Hounds ran swiftly thro' the Woods*
>   *The nimble Deer to take,*
> *And with their Cries the Hills and Dales*
>   *An Echo shrill did make.*

– Vocat ingenti Clamore Cithæron
Taygetique canes, domitrixque Epidaurus equorum:
Et vox assensu nemorum ingeminata remugit.[3]

> *Lo, yonder doth Earl* Dowglas *come,*
>   *His Men in Armour bright;*
> *Full twenty hundred* Scottish *Spears,*
>   *All marching in our Sight.*
>
> *All Men of pleasant* °Tividale,
>   *Fast by the River* Tweed, &c.

The Country of the *Scotch* Warriors, described in these two last
Verses, has a fine romantick Situation, and affords a Couple of

smooth Words for Verse. If the Reader compares the foregoing six Lines of the Song with the following *Latin* Verses, he will see how much they are written in the Spirit of *Virgil*.

> *Adversi campo apparent, hastasque reductis*
> *Protendunt longe dextris; & spicula vibrant:* [. . .]
> *Quique altum Preneste viri, quique arva Gabinæ*
> *Junonis, gelidumque Anienem, & roscida rivis*
> *Hernica saxa colunt:* [. . .] *qui rosea rura Velini,*
> *Qui Tetricæ horrentes rupes, montemque Severum,*
> *Casperiamque colunt, Forulosque & flumen Himellæ:*
> *Qui Tiberim Fabarimque bibunt.* [. . .]⁴

But to proceed.

> *Earl* Dowglas *on a milk-white Steed,*
>   *Most like a Baron bold,*
> *Rode foremost of the Company*
>   *Whose Armour shone like Gold.*

Turnus ut antevolans tardum precesserat agmen, &c.
Vidisti, quo Turnus equo, quibus ibat in armis
Aureus. —⁵

> *Our* English *Archers bent their Bows,*
>   *Their Hearts were good and true;*
> *At the first Flight of Arrows sent,*
>   *Full threescore Scots they slew.*

> *They clos'd full fast on ev'ry Side,*
>   *No Slackness there was found;*
> *And many a gallant Gentleman*
>   *Lay gasping on the Ground.*

> *With that there came an Arrow keen*
>   *Out of an* English *Bow,*
> *Which struck Earl* Dowglas *to the Heart*
>   *A deep and deeply Blow.*

Æneas was wounded after the same Manner by an unknown Hand in the midst of a Parly.

Has inter voces, media inter talia verba,
Ecce viro stridens alis allapsa sagitta est,
Incertum quâ pulsa manu —[6]

But of all the descriptive Parts of this Song, there are none more beautiful than the four following Stanzas, which have a great Force and Spirit in them, and are filled with very natural Circumstances. The Thought in the third Stanza was never touched by any other Poet, and is such an one as would have shined in *Homer* or in *Virgil*.

> *So thus did both these Nobles die,*
> *Whose Courage none could stain;*
> *An* English *Archer then perceiv'd*
> *The noble Earl was slain.*

> *He had a Bow bent in his Hand,*
> *Made of a trusty Tree,*
> *An Arrow of a Cloth-yard long*
> *Unto the Head drew he.*

> *Against Sir* Hugh Montgomery
> *So right his Shaft he set,*
> *The grey-goose Wing that was thereon —*
> *In his Heart-blood was wet.*

> *This Fight did last from Break of Day*
> *Till setting of the Sun;*
> *For when they rung the Evening Bell*
> *The Battel scarce was done.*

One may observe likewise, that in the Catalogue of the Slain the Author has followed the Example of the greatest ancient Poets, not only in giving a long List of the Dead, but by diversifying it with little Characters of particular Persons.

> *And with Earl* Douglas *there was slain*
> *Sir* Hugh Montgomery,
> *Sir* Charles Carrel, *that from the Field*
> *One Foot would never fly:*

> *Sir* Charles Murrel *of Ratcliff too,*
> *His Sister's Son was he,*

> *Sir* David Lamb, *so well esteem'd,*
> *Yet saved could not be.*

The familiar Sound in these Names destroys the Majesty of the Description; for this Reason I do not mention this Part of the Poem but to shew the natural Cast of Thought which appears in it, as the two last Verses look almost like a Translation of *Virgil*.

> — *Cadit & Ripheus justissimus unus*
> *Qui fuit in Teucris & servantissimus æqui,*
> *Diis aliter visum est —*[7]

In the Catalogue of the *English* who fell, *Witherington*'s Behaviour is in the same Manner particularized very artfully, as the Reader is prepared for it by that Account which is given of him in the Beginning of the Battel; though I am satisfied your little Buffoon Readers (who have seen that Passage ridiculed in *Hudibras*) will not be able to take the Beauty of it: For which Reason I dare not so much as quote it.

> *Then stept a gallant Squire forth,*
>   Witherington *was his Name,*
> *Who said, I would not have it told*
>   *To* Henry *our King for Shame,*

> *That e'er my Captain fought on Foot,*
>   *And I stood looking on.*[8]

We meet with the same Heroic Sentiment in *Virgil*.

> *Non pudet, O Rutuli, cunctis pro talibus unam*
> *Objectare animam? numerone an viribus æqui*
> *Non sumus —?*[9]

What can be more natural or more moving, than the Circumstances in which he describes the Behaviour of those Women who had lost their Husbands on this fatal Day?

> *Next Day did many Widows come*
>   *Their Husbands to bewail,*

They wash'd their Wounds in brinish Tears,
But all would not prevail.

Their Bodies bath'd in purple Blood
They bore with them away;
They kiss'd them dead a thousand times,
When they were clad in Clay.

Thus we see how the Thoughts of this Poem, which naturally arise from the Subject, are always simple, and sometimes exquisitely noble; that the Language is often very sounding, and that the whole is written with a true Poetical Spirit.

If this Song had been written in the *Gothic* Manner, which is the Delight of all our little Wits, whether Writers or Readers, it would not have hit the Taste of so many Ages, and have pleased the Readers of all Ranks and Conditions. I shall only beg Pardon for such a Profusion of *Latin* Quotations; which I should not have made use of, but that I feared my own Judgment would have looked too singular on such a Subject, had not I supported it by the Practice and Authority of *Virgil*.   C

No. 85 [ADDISON]

[Broadsides and 'The Two Children in the Wood']¹
Thursday, 7 June 1711

Interdum speciosa locis, morataque recte
Fabula nullius Veneris, sine pondere & Arte,
Valdius oblectat populum, meliusque moratur,
Quam versus inopes rerum, nugæq; canoræ.   Hor.²

It is the Custom of the *Mahometans*, if they see any printed or written Paper upon the Ground, to take it up and lay it aside carefully, as not knowing but it may contain some Piece of their *Alcoran*.³ I must confess I have so much of the *Mussulman* in me, that I cannot forbear looking into every Printed Paper which comes in my way under whatsoever despicable Circumstances it may appear: For as no Mortal Author, in the ordinary Fate and Vicissitude of Things, knows to what use his Works may, some time or other, be applied; a Man may often meet with very celebrated Names in a Paper of Tobacco. I have lighted my Pipe more than once with the Writings of a Prelate; and know a Friend of mine who, for these several Years, has converted the Essays of a Man of Quality into a kind of Fringe for his Candlesticks. I remember, in particular, after having read over a Poem of an Eminent Author on a Victory,[4] I met with several Fragments of it upon the next Rejoycing-day, which had been employed in Squibs and Crackers, and by that means celebrated its Subject in a double Capacity. I once met with a Page of Mr. *Baxter* under a *Christmas* Pye.[5] Whether or no the Pastry-Cook had made use of it through Chance, or Waggery, for the defence of that Superstitious *Viande*, I know not; but, upon the Perusal of it, I conceived so good an Idea of the Author's Piety, that I bought the whole Book. I have often profited by these accidental Readings, and have sometimes found very Curious Pieces, that are either out of Print, or not to be met with in the Shops of our *London* Booksellers. For this Reason, when my Friends take a Survey of my Library, they are very much surprised to find, upon the Shelf of Folios, two long °Band-boxes standing upright among my Books; till I let them see that they are both of them lined with deep Erudition and abstruse Literature. I might likewise mention a Paper Kite, from which I have received great Improvement; and a Hat-Case, which I would not exchange for all the Beavers in *Great Britain*. This my inquisitive Temper, or rather impertinent Humour of prying into all sorts of Writing, with my natural Aversion to Loquacity, give me a good deal of Employment when I enter any House in the Country; for I can't, for my Heart, leave a Room before I have thoroughly studied the Walls of it, and examined the several printed Papers which are usually pasted upon them. The last Piece that I met with upon this Occasion, gave me a most exquisite Pleasure. My Reader will think I am not serious, when I acquaint him that the Piece I am going to speak of was the old Ballad of the *Two Children in the Wood*, which is one of the Darling Songs of the Common People, and has been the Delight of most *Englishmen* in some Part of their Age.

This Song is a plain simple Copy of Nature, destitute of all the Helps and Ornaments of Art. The Tale of it is a pretty Tragical Story; and pleases for no other Reason, but because it is a Copy of Nature. There is even a despicable Simplicity in the Verse; and yet, because the Sentiments appear genuine and unaffected, they are able to move the Mind of the most polite Reader with inward Meltings of Humanity and Compassion. The Incidents grow out of the Subject, and are such as are the most proper to excite Pity. For which Reason the whole Narration has something in it very moving; notwithstanding the Author of it (whoever he was) has delivered it in such an abject Phrase, and poorness of Expression, that the quoting any part of it would look like a Design of turning it into Ridicule. But though the Language is mean, the Thoughts, as I have before said, from one end to the other are natural; and therefore cannot fail to please those who are not Judges of Language, or those who notwithstanding they are Judges of Language, have a true and unprejudiced Taste of Nature. The Condition, Speech, and Behaviour of the dying Parents, with the Age, Innocence, and Distress of the Children, are set forth in such tender Circumstances, that it is impossible for a Reader of common Humanity not to be affected with them. As for the Circumstance of the *Robin-red-breast*, it is indeed a little Poetical Ornament; and to shew the Genius of the Author amidst all his Simplicity, it is just the same kind of Fiction which one of the greatest of the *Latin* Poets has made use of upon a Parallel Occasion; I mean that Passage in *Horace*, where he describes himself when he was a Child, fallen asleep in a Desart Wood, and covered with Leaves by the Turtles that took pity on him.

> *Me fabulosæ Vulture in Appulo,*
> *Altricis extra limen Apuliæ,*
>   *Ludo fatigatumque somno*
>   *Fronde novâ puerum palumbes*
>   *Texere —*[6]

I have heard that the late Lord DORSET,[7] who had the greatest Wit tempered with the greatest Candour, and was one of the finest Criticks as well as the best Poets of his Age, had a numerous Collection of old *English* Ballads, and took a particular Pleasure in the Reading of them. I can affirm the same of Mr. DRYDEN; and know several of the most refined Writers of our present Age, who are of the same Humour.

I might likewise refer my Reader to MOLIERE's Thoughts on

this Subject, as he has expressed them in the Character of the *Misanthrope*;[8] but those only who are endowed with a true Greatness of Soul and Genius, can divest themselves of the little Images of Ridicule, and admire Nature in her Simplicity and Nakedness. As for the little conceited Wits of the Age, who can only shew their Judgment by finding Fault; they cannot be supposed to admire these Productions which have nothing to recommend them but the Beauties of Nature, when they do not know how to relish even those Compositions that, with all the Beauties of Nature, have also the additional Advantages of Art.   L

[THE PLEASURES OF THE IMAGINATION]*

No. 409 [ADDISON]

[1. Introduction: the fine taste in writing]
Thursday, 19 June 1712

— *Musæo contingere cuncta lepore.*   Lucr.[1]

Gratian very often recommends *the fine Taste*, as the utmost Perfection of an accomplished Man.[2] As this Word arises very often in Conversation, I shall endeavour to give some Account of it, and to lay down Rules how we may know whether we are possessed of it, and how we may acquire that fine Taste of Writing, which is so much talked of among the Polite World.

Most Languages make use of this Metaphor, to express that Faculty of the Mind, which distinguishes all the most concealed Faults and nicest Perfections in Writing. We may be sure this Metaphor would not have been so general in all Tongues, had there not been a very great Conformity between that Mental Taste, which is the Subject of this Paper, and that Sensitive Taste which gives us a Relish of every different Flavour that affects the Pálate. Accordingly we find, there are as many Degrees of Refinement in the intellectual Faculty, as in the Sense, which is marked out by this common Denomination.

I knew a Person who possessed the one in so great a Perfection, that after having tasted ten different Kinds of Tea, he would distinguish, without seeing the Colour of it, the particular Sort which was offered him; and not only so, but any two Sorts of them that were mixt together in an equal Proportion; nay, he has carried the Experiment so far, as upon tasting the Composition of three different Sorts, to name the Parcels from whence the three several Ingredients were taken. A Man of a fine Taste in Writing will discern after the same manner, not only the general Beauties and Imperfections of an Author, but discover the several Ways of thinking and expressing himself, which diversify him from all other Authors, with the several Foreign Infusions of Thought and Language, and the particular Authors from whom they were borrowed.

After having thus far explained what is generally meant by a fine Taste in Writing, and shewn the Propriety of the Metaphor which is used on this Occasion, I think I may define it to be *that Faculty of the Soul, which discerns the Beauties of an Author with Pleasure, and the Imperfections with Dislike.* If a Man would know whether he is possessed of this Faculty, I would have him read over the celebrated Works of Antiquity, which have stood the Test of so many different Ages and Countries; or those Works among the Moderns, which have the Sanction of the Politer Part of our Contemporaries. If upon the Perusal of such Writings he does not find himself delighted in an extraordinary Manner, or if, upon reading the admired Passages in such Authors, he finds a Coldness and Indifference in his Thoughts, he ought to conclude, not (as is too usual among tasteless Readers) that the Author wants those Perfections which have been admired in him, but that he himself wants the Faculty of discovering them.

He should, in the second Place, be very careful to observe, whether he tastes the distinguishing Perfections, or, if I may be allowed to call them so, the Specifick Qualities of the Author whom he peruses; whether he is particularly pleased with *Livy* for his Manner of telling a Story, [with] *Sallust* for his entring into those internal Principles of Action which arise from the Characters and Manners of the Persons he describes, or with *Tacitus* for his displaying those outward Motives of Safety and Interest, which give birth to the whole Series of Transactions which he relates.

He may likewise consider, how differently he is affected by the same Thought, which presents it self in a great Writer, from what he is when he finds it delivered by a Person of an ordinary Genius. For there is as much difference in apprehending a Thought cloathed in *Cicero*'s Language, and that of a common Author, as in seeing an Object by the Light of a Taper, or by the Light of the Sun.

It is very difficult to lay down Rules for the Acquirement of such a Taste as that I am here speaking of. The Faculty must in some degree be born with us, and it very often happens, that those who have other Qualities in Perfection are wholly void of this. One of the most eminent Mathematicians of the Age has assured me, that the greatest Pleasure he took in reading *Virgil*, was in examining *Æneas* his Voyage by the Map; as I question not but many a Modern Compiler of History would be delighted with little more in that Divine Author, than in the bare Matters of Fact.

But notwithstanding this Faculty must in some measure be born with us, there are several Methods for Cultivating and Improving it, and without which it will be very uncertain, and of little use to the Person that possesses it. The most natural Method for this Purpose is to be conversant among the Writings of the most Polite Authors. A Man who has any Relish for fine Writing, either discovers new Beauties, or receives stronger Impressions from the Masterly Stroaks of a great Author every time he peruses him: Besides that he naturally wears himself into the same manner of Speaking and Thinking.

Conversation with Men of a Polite Genius is another Method for improving our Natural Taste. It is impossible for a Man of the greatest Parts to consider any thing in its whole Extent, and in all its variety of Lights. Every Man, besides those general Observations which are to be made upon an Author, forms several Reflections that are peculiar to his own manner of Thinking; so that Conversation will naturally furnish us with Hints which we did not attend to, and make us enjoy other Mens Parts and Reflections as well as our own. This is the best reason I can give for the Observation which several have made, that Men of great Genius in the same way of Writing seldom rise up singly, but at certain Periods of Time appear together, and in a Body; as they did at *Rome* in the Reign of *Augustus*, and in *Greece* about the Age of *Socrates*. I cannot think that *Corneille, Racine, Moliere, Boileau, la*

Fontaine, Bruyere, Bossu, or the *Daciers,* would have written so well as they have done, had they not been Friends and Contemporaries.[3]

It is likewise necessary for a Man who would form to himself a finished Taste of good Writing, to be well versed in the Works of the best *Criticks* both Ancient and Modern. I must confess that I could wish there were Authors of this kind, who, beside the Mechanical Rules which a Man of very little Taste may discourse upon, would enter into the very Spirit and Soul of fine Writing, and shew us the several Sources of that Pleasure which rises in the Mind upon the Perusal of a noble Work. Thus altho' in Poetry it be absolutely necessary that the Unities of Time, Place and Action, with other Points of the same Nature, should be thoroughly explained and understood; there is still something more essential to the Art, something that elevates and astonishes the Fancy, and gives a Greatness of Mind to the Reader, which few of the Criticks besides *Longinus* have considered.[4]

Our general Taste in *England* is for Epigram, turns of Wit, and forced Conceits, which have no manner of Influence, either for the bettering or enlarging the Mind of him who reads them, and have been carefully avoided by the greatest Writers, both among the Ancients and Moderns. I have endeavoured in several of my Speculations to banish this *Gothic* Taste, which has taken Possession among us. I entertained the Town for a Week together with an Essay upon Wit,[5] in which I endeavoured to detect several of those false Kinds which have been admired in the different Ages of the World; and at the same time to shew wherein the Nature of true Wit consists. I afterwards gave an Instance of the great Force which lyes in a natural Simplicity of Thought to affect the Mind of the Reader, from such vulgar Pieces as have little else besides this single Qualification to recommend them.[6] I have likewise examined the Works of the greatest Poet which our Nation or perhaps any other has produced, and particularized most of those rational and manly Beauties which give a Value to that Divine Work.[7] I shall next *Saturday* enter upon an Essay *on the Pleasures of the Imagination,* which, though it shall consider that Subject at large, will perhaps suggest to the Reader what it is that gives a Beauty to many Passages of the finest Writers both in Prose and Verse. As an Undertaking of this Nature is entirely new, I question not but it will be received with Candour.   O

No. 411 [ADDISON]

[2. The topic stated]

Saturday, 21 June 1712

Avia Pieridum peragro loca, nullius ante
Trita solo; juvat integros accedere fonteis;
Atque haurire: —   Lucr.[1]

Our Sight is the most perfect and most delightful of all our Senses. It fills the Mind with the largest Variety of Ideas, converses with its Objects at the greatest Distance, and continues the longest in Action without being tired or satiated with its proper Enjoyments. The Sense of Feeling can indeed give us a Notion of Extention, Shape, and all other Ideas that enter at the Eye, except Colours; but at the same time it is very much streightned and confined in its Operations, to the Number, Bulk, and Distance of its particular Objects. Our Sight seems designed to supply all these Defects, and may be considered as a more delicate and diffusive Kind of Touch, that spreads its self over an infinite Multitude of Bodies, comprehends the largest Figures, and brings into our reach some of the most remote Parts of the Universe.

It is this Sense which furnishes the Imagination with its Ideas; so that by the Pleasures of the Imagination or Fancy (which I shall use promiscuously) I here mean such as arise from visible Objects, either when we have them actually in our View, or when we call up their Ideas into our Minds by Paintings, Statues, Descriptions, or any the like Occasion. We cannot indeed have a single Image in the Fancy that did not make its first Entrance through the Sight; but we have the Power of retaining, altering and compounding those Images, which we have once received, into all the Varieties of Picture and Vision that are most agreeable to the Imagination; for by this Faculty a Man in a Dungeon is capable of entertaining himself with Scenes and Landskips more beautiful than any that can be found in the whole Compass of Nature.

There are few Words in the *English* Language which are employed in a more loose and uncircumscribed Sense than those of the *Fancy* and the *Imagination*. I therefore thought it necessary to fix and determine the Notion of these two Words,[2] as I intend to make use of them in the Thread of my following Speculations, that the

Reader may conceive rightly what is the Subject which I proceed upon. I must therefore desire him to remember, that by the Pleasures of the Imagination, I mean only such Pleasures as arise originally from Sight, and that I divide these Pleasures in two Kinds: My Design being first of all to discourse of those Primary Pleasures of the Imagination, which entirely proceed from such Objects as are before our Eyes; and in the next place to speak of those Secondary Pleasures of the Imagination which flow from the Ideas of visible Objects, when the Objects are not actually before the Eye, but are called up into our Memories, or formed into agreeable Visions of Things that are either Absent or Fictitious.

The Pleasures of the Imagination, taken in their full Extent, are not so gross as those of Sense, nor so refined as those of the Understanding. The last are, indeed, more preferable, because they are founded on some new Knowledge or Improvement in the Mind of Man; yet it must be confest, that those of the Imagination are as great and as transporting as the other. A beautiful Prospect delights the Soul, as much as a Demonstration; and a Description in *Homer* has charmed more Readers than a Chapter in *Aristotle*. Besides, the Pleasures of the Imagination have this Advantage, above those of the Understanding, that they are more obvious, and more easie to be acquired. It is but opening the Eye, and the Scene enters. The Colours paint themselves on the Fancy, with very little Attention of Thought or Application of Mind in the Beholder. We are struck, we know not how, with the Symmetry of any thing we see, and immediately assent to the Beauty of an Object, without enquiring into the particular Causes and Occasions of it.

A man of a Polite Imagination is let into a great many Pleasures, that the Vulgar are not capable of receiving. He can converse with a Picture, and find an agreeable Companion in a Statue. He meets with a secret Refreshment in a Description, and often feels a greater Satisfaction in the Prospect of Fields and Meadows, than another does in the Possession. It gives him, indeed, a kind of Property in every thing he sees, and makes the most rude uncultivated Parts of Nature administer to his Pleasures: So that he looks upon the World, as it were, in another Light, and discovers in it a Multitude of Charms, that conceal themselves from the generality of Mankind.

There are indeed, but very few who know how to be idle and

innocent, or have a Relish of any Pleasures that are not Criminal; every Diversion they take is at the Expence of some one Virtue or another, and their very first Step out of Business is into Vice or Folly. A Man should endeavour, therefore, to make the Sphere of his innocent Pleasures as wide as possible, that he may retire into them with Safety, and find in them such a Satisfaction as a wise Man would not blush to take. Of this Nature are those of the Imagination, which do not require such a Bent of Thought as is necessary to our more serious Employments, nor at the same Time, suffer the Mind to sink into that Negligence and Remissness, which are apt to accompany our more sensual Delights, but, like a gentle Exercise to the Faculties, awaken them from Sloth and Idleness, without putting them upon any Labour or Difficulty.

We might here add, that the Pleasures of the Fancy are more conducive to Health than those of the Understanding, which are worked out by Dint of Thinking, and attended with too violent a Labour of the Brain. Delightful Scenes, whether in Nature, Painting, or Poetry, have a kindly Influence on the Body, as well as the Mind, and not only serve to clear and brighten the Imagination, but are able to disperse Grief and Melancholy, and to set the Animal Spirits in pleasing and agreeable Motions. For this Reason Sir *Francis Bacon*, in his Essay upon Health, has not thought it improper to prescribe to his Reader a Poem or a Prospect, where he particularly dissuades him from knotty and subtle Disquisitions, and advises him to pursue Studies, that fill the Mind with splendid and illustrious Objects, as Histories, Fables, and Contemplations of Nature.[3]

I have in this Paper, by way of Introduction, settled the Notion of those Pleasures of the Imagination which are the Subject of my present Undertaking, and endeavoured, by several Considerations, to recommend to my Reader the Pursuit of those Pleasures. I shall, in my next Paper, examine the several Sources from whence these Pleasures are derived.   O

No. 412 [ADDISON]

[3. How the imagination is affected by the survey of outward
objects: the primary pleasures]

Monday, 23 June 1712

Divisum sic breve fiet Opus.   Mart.[1]

I shall first consider those Pleasures of the Imagination, which arise
from the actual View and Survey of outward Objects: And these,
I think, all proceed from the Sight of what is *Great, Uncommon* or
Beautiful. There may, indeed, be something so terrible or offensive,
that the Horrour or Loathsomeness of an Object may over-bear the
Pleasure which results from its *Greatness, Novelty* or *Beauty*; but
still there will be such a Mixture of Delight in the very Disgust it
gives us, as any of these three Qualifications are most conspicuous
and prevailing.

By *Greatness*, I do not only mean the Bulk of any single Object,
but the Largeness of a whole View, considered as one entire Piece.
Such are the Prospects of an open Champian Country, a vast
uncultivated Desart, of huge Heaps of Mountains, high Rocks and
Precipicies, or a wide Expanse of Waters, where we are not struck
with the Novelty or Beauty of the Sight, but with that rude kind
of Magnificence which appears in many of these stupendous Works
of Nature. Our Imagination loves to be filled with an Object, or to
grasp at any thing that is too big for its Capacity. We are flung into
a pleasing Astonishment at such unbounded Views, and feel a
delightful Stillness and Amazement in the Soul at the Apprehension
of them. The Mind of Man naturally hates every thing that looks
like a Restraint upon it, and is apt to fancy it self under a sort of
Confinement, when the Sight is pent up in a narrow Compass, and
shortned on every side by the Neighbourhood of Walls or Mountains. On the contrary, a spacious Horison is an Image of Liberty,
where the Eye has Room to range abroad, to expatiate at large on
the Immensity of its Views, and to lose it self amidst the Variety
of Objects that offer themselves to its Observation. Such wide and
undetermined Prospects are as pleasing to the Fancy, as the
Speculations of Eternity or Infinitude are to the Understanding.
But if there be a Beauty or Uncommonness joined with this
Grandeur, as in a troubled Ocean, a Heaven adorned with Stars

and Meteors, or a spacious Landskip cut out into Rivers, Woods, Rocks, and Meadows, the Pleasure still grows upon us, as it arises from more than a single Principle.

Every thing that is *new* or *uncommon* raises a Pleasure in the Imagination, because it fills the Soul with an agreeable Surprise, gratifies its Curiosity, and gives it an Idea of which it was not before possest. We are indeed so often conversant with one Sett of Objects, and tired out with so many repeated Shows of the same Things, that whatever is *new* or *uncommon* contributes a little to vary human Life, and to divert our Minds, for a while, with the Strangeness of its Appearance: It serves us for a Kind of Refreshment, and takes off from that Satiety we are apt to complain of in our usual and ordinary Entertainments. It is this that bestows Charms on a Monster, and makes even the Imperfections of Nature please us. It is this that recommends Variety, where the Mind is every Instant called off to something new, and the Attention not suffered to dwell too long, and waste it self on any particular Object. It is this, likewise, that improves what is great or beautiful, and makes it afford the Mind a double Entertainment. Groves, Fields, and Meadows, are at any Season of the Year pleasant to look upon, but never so much as in the opening of the Spring, when they are all new and fresh, with their first Gloss upon them, and not yet too much accustomed and familiar to the Eye. For this Reason there is nothing that more enlivens a Prospect than Rivers, °Jetteaus, or Falls of Water, where the Scene is perpetually shifting, and entertaining the Sight every Moment with something that is new. We are quickly tired with looking upon Hills and Vallies, where every thing continues fixt and settled in the same Place and Posture, but find our Thoughts a little agitated and relieved at the Sight of such Objects as are ever in Motion, and sliding away from beneath the Eye of the Beholder.

But there is nothing that makes its way more directly to the Soul than *Beauty*, which immediately diffuses a secret Satisfaction and Complacency through the Imagination, and gives a Finishing to any thing that is Great or Uncommon. The very first Discovery of it strikes the Mind with an inward Joy, and spreads a Chearfulness and Delight through all its Faculties. There is not perhaps any real Beauty or Deformity more in one piece of Matter than another, because we might have been so made, that whatsoever now appears loathsom to us, might have shewn it self agreeable; but we find by Experience, that there are several Modifications of Matter which the Mind, without any previous Consideration, pronounces at first sight Beautiful or Deformed. Thus we see that every different Species of sensible Creatures has its different Notions of Beauty, and that each of them is most affected with the Beauties of its own Kind. This is no where more remarkable than in Birds of the same Shape and Proportion, where we often see the Male determined in his Courtship by the single Grain or Tincture of a Feather, and never discovering any Charms but in the Colour of its Species.

> Scit thalamo servare fidem, sanctasque veretur
> Connubii leges, non illum in pectore candor
> Sollicitat niveus; neque pravum accendit amorem
> Splendida Lanugo, vel honesta in vertice crista,
> Purpureusve nitor pennarum; ast agmina latè
> Fœminea explorat cautus, maculasque requirit
> Cognatas, paribusque interlita corpora guttis:
> Ni faceret, pictis sylvam circum undique monstris
> Confusam aspiceres vulgò, partusque biformes,
> Et genus ambiguum, & Veneris monumenta nefandæ.
> Hinc merula in nigro se oblectat nigra marito,
> Hinc socium lasciva petit Philomela canorum,
> Agnoscitque pares sonitus, hinc Noctua tetram
> Caniteiem alarum, & glaucos miratur ocellos.
> Nempe sibi semper constat, crescitque quotannis
> Lucida progenies, castos confessa parentes;
> Dum virides inter saltus locosque sonoros
> Vere novo exultat, plumasque decora Juventus
> Explicat ad solem, patriisque coloribus ardet.[2]

[The feather'd Husband, to his Partner true,
Preserves connubial Rites inviolate.
With cold Indifference every Charm he sees,
The milky Whiteness of the stately Neck,
The shining Down, proud Crest, and purple Wings:
But cautious with a searching Eye explores
The female Tribes, his proper Mate to find,

With kindred Colours mark'd: Did he not so,
The Grove with painted Monsters wou'd abound,
Th' ambiguous Product of unnatural Love.
The Black-bird hence selects her sooty Spouse;
The Nightingale her musical Compeer,
Lur'd by the well-known Voice: the Bird of Night,
Smit with his dusky Wings, and greenish Eyes,
Wo[o]s his dun Paramour. The beauteous Race
Speak the chaste Loves of their Progenitors;
When, by the Spring invited, they exult
In Woods and Fields, and to the Sun unfold
Their Plumes, that with paternal Colours glow.]

There is a second Kind of *Beauty* that we find in the several Products of Art and Nature, which does not work in the Imagination with that Warmth and Violence as the Beauty that appears in our proper Species, but is apt however to raise in us a secret Delight, and a kind of Fondness for the Places or Objects in which we discover it. This consists either in the Gaiety or Variety of Colours, in the Symmetry and Proportion of Parts, in the Arrangement and Disposition of Bodies, or in a just Mixture and Concurrence of all together. Among these several Kinds of Beauty the Eye takes most Delight in Colours. We no where meet with a more glorious or pleasing Show in Nature, than what appears in the Heavens at the rising and setting of the Sun, which is wholly made up of those different Stains of Light that shew themselves in Clouds of a different Situation. For this Reason we find the Poets, who are always addressing themselves to the Imagination, borrowing more of their Epithets from Colours than from any other Topic.

As the Fancy delights in every thing that is Great, Strange, or Beautiful, and is still more pleased the more it finds of these Perfections in the same Object, so is it capable of receiving a new Satisfaction by the Assistance of another Sense. Thus any continued Sound, as the Musick of Birds, or a Fall of Water, awakens every moment the Mind of the Beholder, and makes him more attentive to the several Beauties of the Place that lye before him. Thus if there arises a Fragrancy of Smells or Perfumes, they heighten the Pleasures of the Imagination, and make even the Colours and Verdure of the Landskip appear more agreeable; for the Ideas of both Senses recommend each other, and are pleasanter together than when they enter the Mind separately: As the different Colours of a Picture, when they are well disposed, set off one another, and receive an additional Beauty from the Advantage of their Situation.   O

No. 413 [ADDISON]

[4. Primary pleasures: effects on the imagination from nature]
Tuesday, 24 June 1712

— *Causa latet, vis est notissima* —   Ovid.[1]

Though in Yesterday's Paper we considered how every thing that is *Great*, *New*, or *Beautiful*, is apt to affect the Imagination with Pleasure, we must own that it is impossible for us to assign the °necessary Cause of this Pleasure, because we know neither the Nature of an Idea, nor the Substance of a Human Soul, which might help us to discover the Conformity or Disagreeableness of the one to the other; and therefore, for want of such a Light, all that we can do in Speculations of this kind, is to reflect on those Operations of the Soul that are most agreeable, and to range, under their proper Heads, what is pleasing or displeasing to the Mind, without being able to trace out the several necessary and °efficient Causes from whence the Pleasure or Displeasure arises.

°*Final Causes* lye more bare and open to our Observation, as there are often a great Variety that belong to the same Effect; and these, tho' they are not altogether so satisfactory, are generally more useful than the other, as they give us greater Occasion of admiring the Goodness and Wisdom of the first Contriver.

One of the Final Causes of our Delight, in any thing that is *great*, may be this. The Supreme Author of our Being has so formed the Soul of Man, that nothing but himself can be its last, adequate, and proper Happiness. Because, therefore, a great Part of our Happiness must arise from the Contemplation of his Being, that he might give our Souls a just Relish of such a Contemplation, he has made them naturally delight in the Apprehension of what is Great or Unlimited. Our Admiration, which is a very pleasing Motion of the Mind, immediately rises at the Consideration of any Object that takes up a great deal of room in the Fancy, and, by consequence, will improve into the highest pitch of Astonishment and Devotion when we contemplate his Nature, that is neither circumscribed by Time nor Place, nor to be comprehended by the largest Capacity of a Created Being.

He has annexed a secret Pleasure to the Idea of any thing that is *new* or *uncommon*, that he might encourage us in the Pursuit after Knowledge, and engage us to search into the Wonders of his Creation; for every new Idea brings such a Pleasure along with it, as rewards any Pains we have taken in its Acquisition, and consequently serves as a Motive to put us upon fresh Discoveries.

He has made every thing that is *beautiful in our own Species* pleasant, that all Creatures might be tempted to multiply their Kind, and fill the World with Inhabitants; for 'tis very remarkable that where-ever Nature is crost in the Production of a Monster (the Result of any unnatural Mixture) the Breed is incapable of propagating its Likeness, and of founding a new Order of Creatures, so that unless all Animals were allured by the Beauty of their own Species, Generation would be at an end, and the Earth unpeopled.

In the last place, he has made every thing that is beautiful in all other Objects pleasant, or rather has made so many Objects appear beautiful, that he might render the whole Creation more gay and delightful. He has given almost every thing about us the Power of raising an agreeable Idea in the Imagination: So that it is impossible for us to behold his Works with Coldness or Indifference, and to survey so many Beauties without a secret Satisfaction and Complacency. Things would make but a poor Appearance to the Eye,[2] if we saw them only in their proper Figures and Motions: And what Reason can we assign for their exciting in us many of those Ideas which are different from any thing that exists in the Objects themselves, (for such are Light and Colours) were it not to add Supernumary Ornaments to the Universe, and make it more agreeable to the Imagination? We are every where entertained with pleasing Shows and Apparitions, we discover imaginary Glories in the Heavens, and in the Earth, and see some of this Visionary Beauty poured out upon the whole Creation; but what a rough unsightly Sketch of Nature should we be entertained with, did all her Colouring disappear, and the several Distinctions of Light and Shade vanish? In short, our Souls are at present delightfully lost and bewildered in a pleasing Delusion, and we walk about like the

Enchanted Hero of a Romance, who sees beautiful Castles, Woods and Meadows; and at the same time hears the warbling of Birds, and the purling of Streams; but upon the finishing of some secret Spell, the fantastick Scene breaks up, and the disconsolate Knight finds himself on a barren Heath, or in a solitary Desart. It is not improbable that something like this may be the State of the Soul after its first Separation, in respect of the Images it will receive from Matter; tho' indeed the Ideas of Colours are so pleasing and beautiful in the Imagination, that it is possible the Soul will not be deprived of them, but perhaps find them excited by some other °Occasional Cause, as they are at present by the different Impressions of the subtle Matter on the Organ of Sight.

I have here supposed that my Reader is acquainted with that great Modern Discovery, which is at present universally acknowledged by all the Enquirers into Natural Philosophy: Namely, that Light and Colours, as apprehended by the Imagination, are only Ideas in the Mind, and not Qualities that have any Existence in Matter. As this is a Truth which has been proved incontestably by many Modern Philosophers, and is indeed one of the finest Speculations in that Science, if the *English* Reader would see the Notion explained at large, he may find it in the Eighth Chapter of the Second Book of Mr. *Lock*'s Essay on Human Understanding. O

No. 414 [ADDISON]

[5. Primary pleasures: the effects of nature and art compared and contrasted]

Wednesday, 25 June 1712

— *Alterius sic*

Altera poscit opem res & conjurat amicè.   Hor.[1]

If we consider the Works of *Nature* and *Art*, as they are qualified to entertain the Imagination, we shall find the last very defective, in Comparison of the former; for though they may sometimes appear as Beautiful or Strange, they can have nothing in them of that Vastness and Immensity, which afford so great an Entertainment to the Mind of the Beholder. The one may be as Polite and Delicate as the other, but can never shew her self so August and

Magnificent in the Design. There is something more bold and
masterly in the rough careless Strokes of Nature, than in the nice
Touches and Embellishments of Art. The Beauties of the most
stately Garden or Palace lie in a narrow Compass, the Imagination
immediately runs them over, and requires something else to gratifie
her; but, in the wide Fields of Nature, the Sight wanders up and
down without Confinement, and is fed with an infinite variety of
Images, without any certain Stint or Number. For this Reason we
always find the Poet in Love with a Country-Life, where Nature
appears in the greatest Perfection, and furnishes out all those Scenes
that are most apt to delight the Imagination.

> Scriptorum chorus omnis amat nemus & fugit Urbes.   Hor.[2]

> Hìc Secura quies, & nescia fallere vita,
> Dives opum variarum; hìc latis otia fundis,
> Speluncæ, vivique lacus, hìc frigida Tempe,
> Mugitusque boum, mollesque sub arbore somni.   Vir.[3]

But tho' there are several of these wild Scenes, that are more
delightful than any artificial Shows; yet we find the Works of
Nature still more pleasant, the more they resemble those of Art:
For in this case our Pleasure rises from a double Principle; from the
Agreeableness of the Objects to the Eye, and from their Similitude
to other Objects: We are pleased as well with comparing their
Beauties, as with surveying them, and can represent them to our
Minds, either as Copies or Originals. Hence it is that we take
Delight in a Prospect which is well laid out, and diversified with
Fields and Meadows; Woods and Rivers; in those accidental
Landskips of Trees, Clouds and Cities, that are sometimes found in
the Veins of Marble; in the curious Fret-work of Rocks, and
Grottos; and, in a Word, in any thing that hath such a Variety or
Regularity as may seem the Effect of Design, in what we call the
Works of Chance.

If the Products of Nature rise in Value, according as they more
or less resemble those of Art, we may be sure that artificial Works
receive a greater Advantage from their Resemblance of such as are
natural; because here the Similitude is not only pleasant, but the
Pattern more perfect. The prettiest Landskip I ever saw,[4] was one-

drawn on the Walls of a dark Room, which stood opposite on one side to a navigable River, and on the other to a Park. The Experiment is very common in Opticks. Here you might discover the Waves and Fluctuations of the Water in strong and proper Colours, with the Picture of a Ship entering at one end, and sailing by Degrees through the whole Piece. On another there appeared the Green Shadows of Trees, waving to and fro with the Wind, and Herds of Deer among them in Miniature, leaping about upon the Wall. I must confess, the Novelty of such a Sight may be one occasion of its Pleasantness to the Imagination, but certainly the chief Reason is its near Resemblance to Nature, as it does not only, like other Pictures, give the Colour and Figure, but the Motion of the Things it represents.

We have before observed, that there is generally in Nature something more Grand and August, than what we meet with in the Curiosities of Art. When, therefore, we see this imitated in any measure, it gives us a nobler and more exalted kind of Pleasure than what we receive from the nicer and more accurate Productions of Art. On this Account our *English* Gardens are not so entertaining to the Fancy as those in *France* and *Italy*, where we see a large Extent of Ground covered over with an agreeable mixture of Garden and Forest, which represent every where an artificial Rudeness, much more charming than that Neatness and Elegancy which we meet with in those of our own Country.[5] It might, indeed, be of ill Consequence to the Publick, as well as unprofitable to private Persons, to alienate so much Ground from Pasturage, and the Plow, in many Parts of a Country that is so well peopled, and cultivated to a far greater Advantage. But why may not a whole Estate be thrown into a kind of Garden by frequent Plantations, that may turn as much to the Profit, as the Pleasure of the Owner? A Marsh overgrown with Willows, or a Mountain shaded with Oaks, are not only more beautiful, but more beneficial, than when they lie bare and unadorned. Fields of Corn make a pleasant Prospect, and if the Walks were a little taken care of that lie between them, if the natural Embroidery of the Meadows were helpt and improved by some small Additions of Art, and the several Rows of Hedges set off by Trees and Flowers, that the Soil was capable of receiving, a Man might make a pretty Landskip of his own Possessions.

Writers, who have given us an Account of *China*, tell us, the Inhabitants of that Country laugh at the Plantations of our *Europeans*, which are are laid by the Rule and Line; because, they say, any one may place Trees in equal Rows and uniform Figures. They chuse rather to shew a Genius in Works of this Nature, and therefore always conceal the Art by which they direct themselves. They have a Word it seems in their Language, by which they express the particular Beauty of a Plantation that thus strikes the Imagination at first Sight, without discovering what it is that has so agreeable an Effect.[6] Our *British* Gardeners, on the contrary, instead of humouring Nature, love to deviate from it as much as possible. Our Trees rise in Cones, Globes, and Pyramids. We see the Marks of the Scissars upon every Plant and Bush. I do not know whether I am singular in my Opinion, but, for my own part, I would rather look upon a Tree in all its Luxuriancy and Diffusion of Boughs and Branches, than when it is thus cut and trimmed into a Mathematical Figure; and cannot but fancy that an Orchard in Flower looks infinitely more delightful than all the little Labyrinths of the most finished Parterre. But as our great Modellers of Gardens have their Magazines of Plants to dispose of, it is very natural for them to tear up all the Beautiful Plantations of Fruit Trees, and contrive a Plan that may most turn to their own Profit, in taking off their Evergreens, and the like Moveable Plants, with which their Shops are plentifully stocked.[7]   O

No. 415 [ADDISON]

[6. Primary pleasures: architecture, the art most immediately producing such imaginative pleasure]

Thursday, 26 June 1712

Adde tot egregias urbes, operumque laborem: Virg.[1]

Having already shewn how the Fancy is affected by the Works of Nature, and afterwards considered in general, both the Works of Nature and of Art, how they mutually assist and compleat each other, in forming such Scenes and Prospects as are most apt to

delight the Mind of the Beholder, I shall in this Paper throw
together some Reflections on that Particular Art, which has a more
immediate Tendency, than any other, to produce those primary
Pleasures of the Imagination, which have hitherto been the Subject
of this Discourse. The Art I mean is that of Architecture, which I
shall consider only with regard to the Light in wich the foregoing
Speculations have placed it, without entring into those Rules and
Maxims which the great Masters of Architecture have laid down,
and explained at large in numberless Treatises upon that Subject.

Greatness, in the Works of Architecture, may be considered as
relating to the Bulk and Body of the Structure, or to the *Manner*
in which it is built. As for the first, we find the Antients, especially
among the Eastern Nations of the World, infinitely superior to the
Moderns. [2]

Not to mention the Tower of *Babel*, of which an old Author says,
there were the Foundations to be seen in his time, which looked
like a Spacious Mountain; what could be more noble than the Walls
of *Babylon*, its hanging Gardens, and its Temple to *Jupiter Belus*,
that rose a Mile high by Eight several Stories, each Story a Furlong
in Height, and on the Top of which was the *Babylonian* Observatory?
I might here, likewise, take Notice of the huge Rock that was cut
into the Figure of *Semiramis*, with the smaller Rocks that lay by it
in the Shape of Tributary Kings; the prodigious Basin, or artificial
Lake, which took in the whole *Euphrates*, 'till such time as a new
Canal was formed for its Reception, with the several Trenches
through which that River was conveyed. I know there are Persons
who look upon some of these Wonders of Art as fabulous, but I
cannot find any Grounds for such a Suspicion, unless it be that we
have no such Works among us at present. There were indeed many
greater Advantages for Building in those Times, and in that Part
of the World, than have been met with ever since. The Earth was
extreamly fruitful, Men lived generally on Pasturage, which
requires a much smaller number of Hands than Agriculture: There
were few Trades to employ the busie Part of Mankind, and fewer
Arts and Sciences to give Work to Men of Speculative Tempers;
and what is more than all the rest, the Prince was absolute; so that
when he went to War, he put himself at the Head of a whole
People: As we find *Semiramis* leading her three Millions to the

Field, and yet overpowered by the Number of her Enemies. 'Tis no wonder, therefore, when she was at Peace, and turned her Thoughts on Building, that she could accomplish so great Works, with such a prodigious Multitude of Labourers: Besides that, in her Climate, there was small Interruption of Frosts and Winters, which make the Northern Workmen lye half the Year Idle. I might mention too, among the Benefits of the Climate, what Historians say of the Earth, that it sweated out a Bitumen or natural kind of Mortar, which is doubtless the same with that mentioned in Holy Writ, as contributing to the Structure of *Babel. Slime they used instead of Mortar*.[3]

In *Egypt* we still see their Pyramids, which answer to the Descriptions that have been made of them; and I question not but a Traveller might find out some Remains of the Labyrinth that covered a whole Province, and had a hundred Temples disposed among its several Quarters and Divisions.

The Wall of *China* is one of these Eastern Pieces of Magnificence, which makes a Figure even in the Map of the World, altho' an Account of it would have been thought Fabulous, were not the Wall it self still extant.

We are obliged to Devotion for the noblest Buildings that have adorned the several Countries of the World. It is this which has set Men at work on Temples and Publick Places of Worship, not only that they might, by the Magnificence of the Building, invite the Deity to reside within it, but that such stupendous Works might, at the same time, open the Mind to vast Conceptions, and fit it to converse with the Divinity of the Place. For every thing that is Majestick, imprints an Awfulness and Reverence on the Mind of the Beholder, and strikes in with the Natural Greatness of the Soul.

In the second place we are to consider *Greatness of Manner* in Architecture, which has such force upon the Imagination, that a small Building, where *it* appears, shall give the Mind nobler Ideas than one of twenty times the Bulk, where the Manner is ordinary or little. Thus, perhaps, a Man would have been more astonished with the Majestick Air that appeared in one of *Lysippus*'s Statues of *Alexander*, tho' no bigger than the Life, than he might have been with Mount *Athos*, had it been cut into the Figure of the Heroe, according to the Proposal of *Phidias*, with a River in one Hand, and a City in the other.[4]

Let any one reflect on the Disposition of Mind he finds in himself, at his first Entrance into the *Pantheon* at *Rome*, and how his Imagination is filled with something Great and Amazing; and, at the same time, consider how little, in proportion, he is affected with the Inside of a *Gothick* Cathedral, tho' it be five times larger than the other; which can arise from nothing else, but the Greatness of the Manner in the one, and the Meanness in the other.

I have seen an Observation upon this Subject in a *French* Auther, which very much pleased me. It is in Monsieur *Freart*'s Parallel of the Ancient and Modern Architecture.[5] I shall give it the Reader with the same terms of Art which he has made use of. *I am observing* (says he) *a thing, which in my Opinion, is very curious, whence it proceeds, that in the same quantity of Superficies, the one* Manner *seems great and magnificent, and the other poor and trifling; the Reason is fine and uncommon. I say then, that to introduce into Architecture this Grandeur of Manner, we ought so to proceed, that the Division of the Principal Members of the Order may consist but of few Parts, that they be all great and of a bold and ample °Relievo, and Swelling; and that the Eye, beholding nothing little and mean, the Imagination may be more vigorously touched and affected with the Work that stands before it. For Example; In a Cornice, if the °Gola or Cynatium of the Corona, the Coping, the Modillions or °Dentelli, make a noble Show by their graceful Projections, if we see none of that ordinary Confusion which is the Result of those little Cavities, Quarter Rounds of the °Astragal, and I know not how many other intermingled Particulars, which produce no effect in great and massy Works, and which very unprofitably take up Place to the prejudice of the Principal Member, it is most certain that this Manner will appear Solemn and Great; as on the contrary, that will have but a poor and mean Effect, where there is a Redundancy of those smaller Ornaments, which divide and scatter the [Angles] of the Sight into such a Multitude of Rays, so pressed together that the whole will appear but a Confusion.*

Among all the Figures in Architecture, there are none that have a greater Air than the Concave and the Convex; and we find in all the Ancient and Modern Architecture, as well in the remote Parts of *China*, as in Countries nearer home, that round Pillars and Vaulted Roofs make a great part of those Buildings which are designed for Pomp and Magnificence. The Reason I take to be, because in these Figures we generally see more of the Body, than in those of other Kinds. There are, indeed, Figures of Bodies, where the Eye may take in two Thirds of the Surface; but as in such Bodies the Sight must split upon several Angles, it does not take in one uniform Idea, but several Ideas of the same kind. Look upon the Outside of a Dome, your Eye half surrounds it; look up into the Inside, and at one Glance you have all the Prospect of it; the entire Concavity falls into your Eye at once, the Sight being as the Center that collects and gathers into it the Lines of the whole Circumference: In a Square Pillar, the Sight often takes in but a fourth Part of the Surface, and, in a Square Concave, must move up and down to the different Sides, before it is Master of all the inward Surface. For this Reason, the Fancy is infinitely more struck with the view of the open Air, and Skies, that passes through an Arch, than what comes through a Square, or any other Figure. The Figure of the Rainbow does not contribute less to its Magnificence, than the Colours to its Beauty, as it is very Poetically described by the Son of *Sirach: Look upon the Rainbow, and praise him that made it; very beautiful it is in its Brightness; it encompasses the Heavens with a glorious Circle, and the Hands of the most High have bended it.*[6]

Having thus spoken of that Greatness which affects the Mind in Architecture, I might next shew the Pleasure that rises in the Imagination from what appears new and beautiful in this Art; but as every Beholder has naturally a greater Taste of these two Perfections in every Building which offers it self to his View, than of that which I have hitherto considered, I shall not trouble my Reader with any Reflections upon it. It is sufficient for my present Purpose, to observe, that there is nothing in this whole Art which pleases the Imagination, but as it is Great, Uncommon, or Beautiful.   O

No. 416 [ADDISON]

[7. Secondary pleasures of the imagination: consideration limited to literature]

Friday, 27 June 1712

Quatenûs hoc simile est oculis, quod mente videmus.   Lucr.[1]

I at first divided the Pleasures of the Imagination, into such as arise from Objects that are actually before our Eyes, or that once entered in at our Eyes, and are afterwards called up into the Mind, either barely by its own Operations, or on occasion of something without us, as Statues or Descriptions. We have already considered the first Division, and shall therefore enter on the other, which, for Distinction sake, I have called the Secondary Pleasures of the Imagination. When I say the Ideas we receive from Statues, Descriptions, or such like Occasions, are the same that were once actually in our View, it must not be understood that we had once seen the very Place, Action, or Person which are carved or described. It is sufficient, that we have seen Places, Persons, or Actions, in general, which bear a Resemblance or at least some remote Analogy with what we find represented. Since it is in the Power of the Imagination, when it is once Stocked with particular Ideas, to enlarge, compound, and vary them at her own Pleasure.

Among the different Kinds of Representation, *Statuary* is the most natural, and shews us something *likest* the Object that is represented. To make use of a common Instance, let one who is born Blind take an Image in his Hands, and trace out with his Fingers the different Furrows and Impressions of the Chissel, and he will easily conceive how the Shape of a Man, or Beast, may be represented by it; but should he draw his Hand over a *Picture*, where all is smooth and uniform, he would never be able to imagine how the several Prominencies and Depressions of a human Body could be shewn on a plain Piece of Canvas, that has in it no Unevenness or Irregularity. *Description* runs yet further from the things it represents than Painting; for a Picture bears a real Resemblance to its Original, which Letters and Syllables are wholly void of. Colours speak all Languages, but Words are understood only by such a People or Nation. For this reason, tho'

Mens Necessities quickly put them on finding out Speech, Writing is probably of a later Invention than Painting; particularly we are told, that in *America* when the *Spaniards* first arrived there, Expresses were sent to the Emperor of *Mexico* in Paint, and the News of his Country delineated by the Strokes of a Pencil, which was a more natural Way than that of Writing, tho' at the same time much more imperfect, because it is impossible to draw the little Connexions of Speech, or to give the Picture of a Conjunction or an Adverb. It would be yet more strange, to represent visible Objects by Sounds that have no Ideas annexed to them, and to make something like Description in *Musick.* Yet it is certain, there may be confused, imperfect Notions of this Nature raised in the Imagination by an Artificial Composition of Notes; and we find that great Masters in the Art are able, sometimes, to set their Hearers in the heat and hurry of a Battel, to overcast their Minds with melancholy Scenes and Apprehensions of Deaths and Funerals, or to lull them into pleasing Dreams of Groves and Elisiums.

In all these Instances, this Secondary Pleasure of the Imagination proceeds from that Action of the Mind, which compares the Ideas arising from the Original Objects, with the Ideas we receive from the Statue, Picture, Description, or Sound that represents them. It is impossible for us to give the necessary Reason, why this Operation of the Mind is attended with so much Pleasure, as I have before observed on the same Occasion;[2] but we find a great variety of Entertainments derived from this single Principle: For it is this that not only gives us a relish of Statuary, Painting and Description, but makes us delight in all the Actions and Arts of Mimickry. It is this that makes the several kinds of Wit pleasant, which consists, as I have formerly shewn, in the Affinity of Ideas. And we may add, it is this also that raises the little Satisfaction we sometimes find in the different Sorts of false Wit; whether it consist in the Affinity of Letters, as in Anagram, Acrostick; or of Syllables, as in Doggerel Rhimes, Ecchos; or of Words, as in Puns, Quibbles; or of a whole Sentence or Poem, to Wings, and Altars. The °*final Cause*, probably, of annexing Pleasure to this Operation of the Mind, was to quicken and encourage us in our Searches after Truth, since the distinguishing one thing from another, and the right discerning betwixt our Ideas, depends wholly upon our comparing them together, and observing the Congruity or Disagreement that appears among the several Works of Nature.

But I shall here confine my self to those Pleasures of the Imagination, which proceed from Ideas raised by *Words*, because most of the Observations that agree with Descriptions, are equally Applicable to Painting and Statuary.

Words, when well chosen, have so great a Force in them, that a Description often gives us more lively Ideas than the Sight of Things themselves. The Reader finds a Scene drawn in stronger Colours, and painted more to the Life in his Imagination, by the help of Words, than by an actual Survey of the Scene which they describe. In this Case the Poet seems to get the better of Nature; he takes, indeed, the Landskip after her, but gives it more vigorous Touches, heightens its Beauty, and so enlivens the whole Piece, that the Images which flow from the Objects themselves appear weak and faint, in Comparison of those that come from the Expressions. The Reason, probably, may be, because in the Survey of any Object we have only so much of it painted on the Imagination, as comes in at the Eye; but in its Description, the Poet gives us as free a View of it as he pleases, and discovers to us several Parts, that either we did not attend to, or that lay out of our Sight when we first beheld it. As we look on any Object, our Idea of it is, perhaps, made up of two or three simple Ideas; but when the Poet represents it, he may either give us a more complex Idea of it, or only raise in us such Ideas as are most apt to affect the Imagination.

It may be here worth our while to examine, how it comes to pass that several Readers, who are all acquainted with the same Language, and know the Meaning of the Words they read, should nevertheless have a different Relish of the same Descriptions. We find one transported with a Passage, which another runs over with Coldness and Indifference, or finding the Representation extreamly natural, where another can perceive nothing of Likeness and Conformity. This different Taste must proceed, either from the *Perfection of Imagination* in one more than in another, or from the *different Ideas* that several Readers affix to the same Words. For, to have a true Relish, and form a right Judgment of a Description, a Man should be born with a good Imagination, and must have well weighed the Force and Energy that lye in the several Words of a Language, so as to be able to distinguish which are most significant and expressive of their proper Ideas, and what additional Strength and Beauty they are capable of receiving from Conjunction with others. The Fancy must be warm, to retain the Print of those Images it hath received from outward Objects; and the Judgment discerning, to know what Expressions are most proper to cloath and adorn them to the best Advantage. A Man who is deficient in either of these Respects, tho' he may receive the general Notion of a Description, can never seen distinctly all its particular Beauties: As a Person, with a weak Sight, may have the confused Prospect of a Place that lyes before him, without entering into its several Parts, or discerning the variety of its Colours in their full Glory and Perfection.   O

No. 417 [ADDISON]

[8. Secondary pleasures: the expansive effect of images in poetry: Homer, Virgil, Ovid, Milton]

Saturday, 2 June 1712

Quem tu Melpomene semel
Nascentem placido lumine videris,
    Non illum labor Istmius
Clarabit pugilem, non equus impiger, &c.
Sed quæ Tibur aquæ fertile perfluunt,
    Et Spissæ nemorum comæ
Fingent Æolio carmine nobilem.   Hor.[1]

We may observe, that any single Circumstance of what we have formerly seen often raises up a whole Scene of Imagery, and awakens numberless Ideas that before slept in the Imagination; such a particular Smell or Colour is able to fill the Mind, on a sudden, with the Picture of the Fields or Gardens where we first met with it, and to bring up into View all the Variety of Images that once attended it. Our Imagination takes the Hint, and leads us unexpectedly into Cities or Theatres, Plains or Meadows. We may further observe, when the Fancy thus reflects on the Scenes that have past in it formerly, those, which were at first pleasant to behold, appear more so upon Reflection, and that the Memory heightens the Delightfulness of the Original. A *Cartesian* would account for both these Instances in the following Manner.[2]

The Sett of Ideas, which we received from such a Prospect or Garden, having entered the Mind at the same time, have a Sett of °Traces belonging to them in the Brain, bordering very near upon one another; when, therefore, any one of these Ideas arises in the Imagination, and consequently dispatches a flow of Animal Spirits to its proper Trace, these Spirits, in the Violence of their Motion, run not only into the Trace, to which they were more particularly directed, but into several of those that lye about it: By this means they awaken other Ideas of the same Sett, which immediately determine a new Dispatch of Spirits, that in the same manner open other Neighbouring Traces, till at last the whole Sett of them is blown up, and the whole Prospect or Garden flourishes in the Imagination. But because the Pleasure we received from these Places far surmounted and overcame the little Disagreeableness we found in them, for this Reason there was at first a wider Passage worn in the Pleasure Traces, and, on the contrary, so narrow a one in those which belonged to the disagreeable Ideas, that they were quickly stopt up, and rendered incapable of receiving any Animal Spirits, and consequently of exciting any unpleasant Ideas in the Memory.

It would be in vain to enquire, whether the Power of imagining Things strongly proceeds from any greater Perfection in the Soul, or from any nicer Texture in the Brain of one Man than of another. But this is certain, that a noble Writer should be born with this Faculty in its full Strength and Vigour, so as to be able to receive lively Ideas from outward Objects, to retain them long, and to range them together, upon occasion, in such Figures and Representations as are most likely to hit the Fancy of the Reader. A Poet should take as much Pains in forming his Imagination, as a Philosopher in cultivating this Understanding. He must gain a due Relish of the Works of Nature, and be throughly conversant in the various Scenary of a Country Life.

When he is stored with Country Images, if he would go beyond

Pastoral, and the lower kinds of Poetry, he ought to acquaint himself with the Pomp and Magnificence of Courts. He should be very well versed in every thing that is noble and stately in the Productions of Art, whether it appear in Painting or Statuary, in the great Works of Architecture which are in their present Glory, or in the Ruins of those which flourished in former Ages.

Such Advantages as these help to open a Man's Thoughts, and to enlarge his Imagination, and will therefore have their Influence on all kinds of Writing, if the Author knows how to make right use of them. And among those of the learned Languages who excel in this Talent, the most perfect in their several kinds, are perhaps *Homer*, *Virgil*, and *Ovid*. The first strikes the imagination wonderfully with what is Great, the second with what is Beautiful, and the last with what is Strange. Reading the *Iliad* is like travelling through a Country uninhabited, where the Fancy is entertained with a thousand Savage Prospects of vast Desarts, wide uncultivated Marshes, huge Forests, mis-shapen Rocks and Precipices. On the contrary, the *Æneid* is like a well ordered Garden, where it is impossible to find out any Part unadorned, or to cast our Eyes upon a single Spot, that does not produce some beautiful Plant or Flower. But when we are in the *Metamorphosis*, we are walking on enchanted Ground, and see nothing but Scenes of Magick lying round us.

Homer is in his Province, when he is describing a Battel or a Multitude, a Heroe or a God. *Virgil* is never better pleased, than when he is in his *Elysium*, or copying out an entertaining Picture. *Homer*'s Epithets generally mark out what is Great, *Virgil*'s what is Agreeable. Nothing can be more Magnificent than the Figure *Jupiter* makes in the first *Iliad*, nor more Charming than that of *Venus* in the first *Æneid*,

> Ἦ, καὶ κυανέησιν ἐπ' ὀφρύσι νεῦσε Κρονίων·
> Ἀμβρόσιαι δ' ἄρα χαῖται ἐπερρώσαντο ἄνακτος,
> Κρατὸς ἄπ' Ἀθανάτοιο μέγαν δ' ἐλέλιξεν Ὄλυμπον.[3]

> *Dixit, & avertens roseâ cervice refulsit:*
> *Ambrosiæque comæ divinum vertice odorem*
> *Spiravere: Pedes vestis defluxit ad imos:*
> *Et vera incessu patuit Dea* —[4]

Homer's Persons are most of them God-like and Terrible: *Virgil* has scarce admitted any into his Poem, who are not beautiful, and has taken particular Care to make his Heroe so.

— lumenque juventæ
Purpureum, & lætos oculis afflavit honores. [5]

In a Word, *Homer* fills his Readers with Sublime *Ideas*, and, I believe, has raised the Imagination of all the good Poets that have come after him. I shall only instance *Horace*, who immediately takes Fire at the first Hint of any Passage in the *Iliad* or *Odyssey*, and always rises above himself, when he has *Homer* in his View. *Virgil* has drawn together, into his *Æneid*, all the pleasing Scenes his Subject is capable of admitting, and in his *Georgics* has given us a Collection of the most delightful Landskips that can be made out of Fields and Woods, Herds of Cattle, and Swarms of Bees.

Ovid, in his *Metamorphoses*, has shewn us how the Imagination may be affected by what is Strange. He describes a Miracle in every Story, and always gives us the Sight of some new Creature at the end of it. His Art consists chiefly in well-timing his Description, before the first Shape is quite worn off, and the new one perfectly finished; so that he every where entertains us with something we never saw before, and shews Monster after Monster, to the end of the *Metamorphoses*.

If I were to name a Poet that is a perfect Master in all these Arts of working on the Imagination, I think *Milton* may pass for one: And if his *Paradise Lost* falls short of the *Æneid* or *Iliad* in this respect, it proceeds rather from the Fault of the Language in which it is written, than from any Defect of Genius in the Author. So Divine a Poem in *English*, is like a stately Palace built of Brick, where one may see Architecture in as great a Perfection as in one of Marble, tho' the Materials are of a coarser Nature. But to consider it only as it regards our present Subject: What can be conceived greater than the Battel of Angels, the Majesty of Messiah, the Stature and Behaviour of Satan and his Peers? What more beautiful than *Pandæmonium*, Paradise, Heaven, Angels, *Adam* and *Eve*? What more strange, than the Creation of the World, the several Metamorphoses of the fallen Angels, and the surprising Adventures their Leader meets with in his Search after Paradise? No other

Subject could have furnished a Poet with Scenes so proper to strike the Imagination, as no other Poet could have painted those Scenes in more strong and lively Colours.   O

No. 418 [ADDISON]

[9. Secondary pleasures related to words wider than those joined to sight: pleasure from mental comparison]

Monday, 30 June 1712

—ferat & rubus asper amomum.   Virg.[1]

The Pleasures of these Secondary Views of the Imagination, are of a wider and more universal Nature than those it has when joined with Sight; for not only what is Great, Strange or Beautiful, but any Thing that is Disagreeable when looked upon, pleases us in an apt Description. Here, therefore, we must enquire after a new Principle of Pleasure, which is nothing else but the Action of the Mind, which *compares* the Ideas that arise from Words, with the Ideas that arise from the Objects themselves; and why this Operation of the Mind is attended with so much Pleasure, we have before considered. For this Reason therefore, the Description of a Dunghill is pleasing to the Imagination, if the Image be represented to our Minds by suitable Expressions; tho', perhaps, this may be more properly called the Pleasure of the Understanding than of the Fancy, because we are not so much delighted with the Image that is contained in the Description, as with the Aptness of the Description to excite the Image.

But if the Description of what is Little, Common or Deformed, be acceptable to the Imagination, the Description of what is Great, Surprising or Beautiful, is much more so; because here we are not only delighted with *comparing* the Representation with the Original, but are highly pleased with the Original it self. Most Readers, I believe, are more charmed with *Milton*'s Description of Paradise, than of Hell; they are both, perhaps, equally perfect in their Kind, but in the one the Brimstone and Sulphur are not so refreshing to the Imagination, as the Beds of Flowers and the Wilderness of Sweets in the other.

There is yet another Circumstance which recommends a Description more than all the rest, and that is, if it represents to us such Objects as are apt to raise a secret Ferment in the Mind of the Reader, and to work, with Violence, upon his Passions. For, in this Case, we are at once warmed and enlightened, so that the Pleasure becomes more Universal, and is several ways qualified to entertain us. Thus, in Painting, it is pleasant to look on the Picture of any Face, where the Resemblance is hit, but the Pleasure encreases, if it be the Picture of a Face that is beautiful, and is still greater, if the Beauty be softned with an Air of Melancholly or Sorrow. The two leading Passions which the more serious Parts of Poetry endeavour to stir up in us, are Terror and Pity. And here, by the way, one would wonder how it comes to pass, that such Passions as are very unpleasant at all other times, are very agreeable when excited by proper Descriptions. It is not strange, that we should take Delight in such Passages as are apt to produce Hope, Joy, Admiration, Love, or the like Emotions in us, because they never rise in the Mind without an inward Pleasure which attends them. But how comes it to pass, that we should take delight in being terrified or dejected by a Description, when we find so much Uneasiness in the Fear or Grief which we receive from any other Occasion?

If we consider, therefore, the Nature of this Pleasure, we shall find that it does not arise so properly from the Description of what is Terrible, as from the Reflection we make on our selves at the time of reading it. When we look on such hideous Objects, we are not a little pleased to think we are in no Danger of them. We consider them at the same time, as Dreadful and Harmless; so that the more frightful Appearance they make, the greater is the Pleasure we receive from the Sense of our own Safety. In short, we look upon the Terrors of a Description, with the same Curiosity and Satisfaction that we survey a dead Monster.

> — *Informe cadaver*
> *Protrahitur, nequeunt expleri corda tuendo*
> *Terribiles oculos: vultum, villosaque setis*
> *Pectora semiferi, atque extinctos faucibus ignes.* Virg.[2]

It is for the same Reason that we are delighted with the reflecting upon Dangers that are past, or in looking on a Precipice at a distance, which would fill us with a different kind of Horrour, if we saw it hanging over our Heads.

In the like manner, when we read of Torments, Wounds, Deaths, and the like dismal Accidents, our Pleasure does not flow so properly from the Grief which such melancholly Descriptions give us, as from the secret Comparison which we make between our selves and the Person who suffers. Such Representations teach us to set a just Value upon our own Condition, and make us prize our good Fortune which exempts us from the like Calamities. This is, however, such a kind of Pleasure as we are not capable of receiving, when we see a Person actually lying under the Tortures that we meet with in a Description; because, in this Case, the Object presses too close upon our Senses, and bears so hard upon us, that it does not give us Time or Leisure to reflect on our selves. Our Thoughts are so intent upon the Miseries of the Sufferer, that we cannot turn them upon our own Happiness. Whereas, on the contrary, we consider the Misfortunes we read in History or Poetry, either as past, or as fictitious, so that the Reflection upon our selves rises in us insensibly, and over-bears the Sorrow we conceive for the Sufferings of the Afflicted.

But because the Mind of Man requires something more perfect in Matter, than what it finds there, and can never meet with any Sight in Nature which sufficiently answers its highest Ideas of Pleasantness; or, in other Words, because the Imagination can fancy to it self Things more Great, Strange, or Beautiful, than the Eye ever saw, and is still sensible of some Defect in what it has seen; on this account it is the part of a Poet to humour the Imagination in its own Notions, by mending and perfecting Nature where he describes a Reality, and by adding greater Beauties than are put together in Nature, where he describes a Fiction.

He is not obliged to attend her in the slow Advances which she makes from one Season to another, or to observe her Conduct, in the successive Production of Plants and Flowers. He may draw into his Description all the Beauties of the Spring and Autumn, and make the whole Year contribute something to render it the more agreeable. His Rose-trees, Wood-bines, and Jessamines, may flower together, and his Beds be covered at the same time with Lillies, Violets, and Amaranths. His Soil is not restrained to any particular

Sett of Plants, but is proper either for Oaks or Mirtles, and adapts it self to the Products of every Climate. Oranges may grow wild in it; Myrrh may be met with in every Hedge, and if he thinks it proper to have a Grove of Spices, he can quickly command Sun enough to raise it. If all this will not furnish out an agreeable Scene, he can make several new Species of Flowers, with richer Scents and higher Colours, than any that grow in the Gardens of Nature. His Consorts of Birds may be as full and harmonious, and his Woods as thick and gloomy as he pleases. He is at no more Expence in a long Vista, than a short one, and can as easily throw his Cascades from a Precipice of half a Mile high, as from one of twenty Yards. He has his Choice of the Winds, and can turn the Course of his Rivers in all the variety of *Meanders*, that are most delightful to the Reader's Imagination. In a Word, he has the modelling of Nature in his own Hands, and may give her what Charms he pleases, provided he does not reform her too much, and run into Absurdities, by endeavouring to excel.   O

No. 419 [ADDISON]

[10. Fantasy: writing wholly out of the poet's own invention]
Tuesday, 1 July 1712

—mentis gratissimus Error.   Hor.[1]

There is a kind of Writing, wherein the Poet quite loses sight of Nature, and entertains his Reader's Imagination with the Characters and Actions of such Persons as have many of them no Existence, but what he bestows on them. Such are Fairies, Witches, Magicians, Demons, and departed Spirits. This Mr. *Dryden* calls *the Fairy way of Writing*,[2] which is, indeed, more difficult than any other that depends on the Poet's Fancy, because he has no Pattern to follow in it, and must work altogether out of his own Invention.

There is a very odd turn of Thought required for this sort of Writing, and it is impossible for a Poet to succeed in it, who has not a particular Cast of Fancy, and an Imagination naturally fruitful and superstitious. Besides this, he ought to be very well versed in Legends and Fables, antiquated Romances, and the Traditions of Nurses and old Women, that he may fall in with our natural

Prejudices, and humour those Notions which we have imbibed in our Infancy. For, otherwise, he will be apt to make his Fairies talk like People of his own Species, and not like other Setts of Beings, who converse with different Objects, and think in a different manner from that of Mankind;

> *Sylvis deducti caveant, me Judice, Fauni*
> *Ne velut innati triviis ac pæne forenses*
> *Aut nimium teneris juvenentur versibus* — Hor.[3]

I do not say with Mr. *Bays* in the *Rehearsal*, that Spirits must not be confined to speak Sense,[4] but it is certain their Sense ought to be a little discoloured, that it may seem particular, and proper to the Person and the Condition of the Speaker.

These Descriptions raise a pleasing kind of Horrour in the Mind of the Reader, and °amuse his Imagination with the Strangeness and Novelty of the Persons who are represented in them. They bring up into our Memory the Stories we have heard in our Childhood, and favour those secret Terrours and Apprehensions to which the Mind of Man is naturally subject. We are pleased with surveying the different Habits and Behaviours of Foreign Countries, how much more must we be delighted and surprised when we are led, as it were, into a new Creation, and see the Persons and Manners of another Species? Men of cold Fancies, and Philosophical Dispositions, object to this kind of Poetry, that it has not Probability enough to affect the Imagination. But to this it may be answered, that we are sure, in general, there are many intellectual Beings in the World besides our selves, and several Species of Spirits, who are subject to different Laws and °Oeconomies from those of Mankind; when we see, therefore, any of these represented naturally, we cannot look upon the Representation as altogether impossible; nay, many are prepossest with such false Opinions, as dispose them to believe these particular Delusions; at least, we have all heard so many pleasing Relations in favour of them, that we do not care for seeing through the Falshood, and willingly give our selves up to so agreeable an Imposture.

The Ancients have not much of this Poetry among them, for, indeed, almost the whole Substance of it owes its Original to the Darkness and Superstition of later Ages, when pious Frauds were made use of to amuse mankind, and frighten them into a Sense of their Duty. Our Forefathers looked upon Nature with more Reverence and Horrour, before the World was enlightened by Learning and Philosophy, and loved to astonish themselves with the Apprehensions of Witchcraft, Prodigies, Charms and Enchantments. There was not a Village in *England* that had not a Ghost in it, the Church-yards were all haunted, every large Common had a Circle of Fairies belonging to it, and there was scarce a Shepherd to be met with who had not seen a Spirit.

Among all the Poets of this Kind our *English* are much the best, by what I have yet seen, whether it be that we abound with more Stories of this Nature, or that the Genius of our Country is fitter for this sort of Poetry. For the *English* are naturally Fanciful, and very often disposed by that Gloominess and Melancholly of Temper, which is so frequent in our Nation, to many wild Notions and Visions, to which others are not so liable.

Among the *English*, Shakespear has incomparably excelled all others. That noble Extravagance of Fancy, which he had in so great Perfection, throughly qualified him to touch this weak superstitious Part of his Reader's Imagination; and made him capable of succeeding, where he had nothing to support him besides the Strength of his own Genius. There is something so wild and yet so solemn in the Speeches of his Ghosts, Fairies, Witches, and the like Imaginary Persons, that we cannot forbear thinking them natural, tho' we have no Rule by which to judge of them, and must confess, if there are such Beings in the World, it looks highly probable they should talk and act as he has represented them.

There is another sort of Imaginary Beings, that we sometimes meet with among the Poets, when the Author represents any Passion, Appetite, Virtue or Vice, under a visible Shape, and makes it a Person or an Actor in his Poem. Of this Nature are the Descriptions of Hunger and Envy in *Ovid*, of Fame in *Virgil*, and of Sin and Death in *Milton*.[5] We find a whole Creation of the like shadowy Persons in *Spencer*, who had an admirable Talent in Representations of this kind. I have discoursed of these Emblematical Persons in former Papers, and shall therefore only mention them in this Place. Thus we see how many ways Poetry addresses it self to the Imagination, as it has not only the whole Circle of

Nature for its Province, but makes new Worlds of its own, shews us Persons who are not to be found in Being, and represents even the Faculties of the Soul, with her several Virtues and Vices, in a sensible Shape and Character.

I shall, in my two following Papers, consider in general, how other kinds of Writing are qualified to please the Imagination, with which I intend to conclude this Essay.   O

No. 420 [ADDISON]

[11. Imagination contrasted with understanding: imaginative importance of history, natural philosophy, etc.: bounds and defects of imagination]

Wednesday, 2 July 1712

—Quocunque volunt mentem Auditoris agunto.   Hor.[1]

As the Writers in Poetry and Fiction borrow their several Materials from outward Objects, and join them together at their own Pleasure, there are others who are obliged to follow Nature more closely, and to take entire Scenes out of her. Such are Historians, natural Philosophers, Travellers, Geographers, and, in a Word, all who describe visible Objects of a real Existence.

It is the most agreeable Talent of an Historian, to be able to draw up his Armies and fight his Battels in proper Expressions, to set before our Eyes the Divisions, Cabals, and Jealousies of Great Men, and to lead us Step by Step into the several Actions and Events of his History. We love to see the Subject unfolding it self by just Degrees, and breaking upon us insensibly, that so we may be kept in a pleasing Suspence, and have Time given us to raise our Expectations, and to side with one of the Parties concerned in the Relation. I confess this shews more the Art than the Veracity of the Historian, but I am only to speak of him as he is qualified to please the Imagination. And in this respect *Livy* has, perhaps, excelled all who went before him, or have written since his Time. He describes every thing in so lively a manner, that his whole History is an admirable Picture, and touches on such proper Circumstances in every Story, that [his] Reader becomes a kind of Spectator, and feels in himself all the variety of Passions, which are correspondent to the several Parts of the Relation.

But among this Sett of Writers, there are none who more gratifie and enlarge the Imagination, than the Authors of the °new Philosophy, whether we consider their Theories of the Earth or Heavens, the Discoveries they have made by °Glasses, or any other of their Contemplations on Nature. We are not a little pleased to find every green Leaf swarm with Millions of Animals, that at their largest Growth are not visible to the naked Eye. There is something very engaging to the Fancy, as well as to our Reason, in the Treatises of Metals, Minerals, Plants and Meteors. But when we survey the whole Earth at once, and the several Planets that lye within its Neighbourhood, we are filled with a pleasing Astonishment, to see so many Worlds hanging one above another, and sliding round their Axles in such an amazing Pomp and Solemnity. If, after this, we contemplate those wide Fields of *Ether*, that reach in height as far as from *Saturn* to the fixt Stars, and run abroad almost to an infinitude, our Imagination finds its Capacity filled with so immense a Prospect, and puts its self upon the Stretch to comprehend it. But if we yet rise higher, and consider the fixt Stars as so many vast Oceans of Flame, that are each of them attended with a different Sett of Planets, and still discover new Firmaments and new Lights, that are sunk farther in those unfathomable Depths of *Ether*, so as not to be seen by the strongest of our Telescopes, we are lost in such a Labarynth of Suns and Worlds, and confounded with the Immensity and Magnificence of Nature.

Nothing is more pleasant to the Fancy, than to enlarge it self, by Degrees, in its Contemplation of the various Proportions which its several Objects bear to each other, when it compares the Body of Man to the Bulk of the whole Earth, the Earth to the Circle it describes round the Sun, that Circle to the Sphere of the fixt Stars, the Sphere of the fixt Stars to the Circuit of the whole Creation, the whole Creation it self to the infinite Space that is every where diffused about it; or when the Imagination works downward, and considers the Bulk of a Human Body, in respect of an Animal a hundred times less than a Mite, the particular Limbs of such an Animal, the different Springs which actuate the Limbs, the Spirits which set these Springs a going, and the proportionable Minuteness of these several Parts, before they have arrived at their full Growth and Perfection. But if, after all this, we take the least Particle of these Animal Spirits, and consider its Capacity of being wrought into a World, that shall contain within those narrow Dimensions a Heaven and Earth, Stars and Planets, and every different Species of living Creatures, in the same Analogy and Proportion they bear to each other in our own Universe; such a Speculation, by reason of its Nicety, appears ridiculous to those who have not turned their Thoughts that way, tho', at the same time, it is founded on no less than the Evidence of a Demonstration. Nay, we might yet carry it farther, and discover in the smallest Particle of this little World, a new inexhausted Fund of Matter, capable of being spun out into another Universe.

I have dwelt the longer on this Subject, because I think it may shew us the proper Limits, as well as the Defectiveness, of our Imagination; how it is confined to a very small Quantity of Space, and immediately stopt in its Operations, when it endeavours to take in any thing that is very great, or very little. Let a Man try to conceive the different Bulk of an Animal, which is twenty, from another which is a hundred times less than a Mite, or to compare, in his Thoughts, a length of a thousand Diameters of the Earth, with that of a Million, and he will quickly find that he has no different Measures in his Mind, adjusted to such extraordinary Degrees of Grandeur or Minuteness. The Understanding, indeed, opens an infinite Space on every side of us, but the Imagination, after a few faint Efforts, is immediately at a stand, and finds her self swallowed up in the Immensity of the Void that surrounds it: Our Reason can pursue a Particle of Matter through an infinite variety of Divisions, but the Fancy soon loses sight of it, and feels in it self a kind of Chasm, that wants to be filled with Matter of a more sensible Bulk.[2] We can neither widen nor contract the Faculty to the Dimensions of either Extream: The Object is too big for our Capacity, when we would comprehend the Circumference of a World, and dwindles into nothing, when we endeavour after the Idea of an Atome.

It is possible this Defect of Imagination may not be in the Soul it self, but as it acts in Conjunction with the Body. Perhaps there may not be room in the Brain for such a variety of Impressions, or the Animal Spirits may be incapable of figuring them in such a manner, as is necessary to excite so very large or very minute Ideas.

However it be, we may well suppose that Beings of a higher Nature very much excel us in this respect, as it is probable the Soul of Man will be infinitely more perfect hereafter in this Faculty, as well as in all the rest; insomuch that, perhaps, the Imagination will be able to keep Pace with the Understanding, and to form in it self distinct Ideas of all the different Modes and Quantities of Space.   O

No. 421 [ADDISON]

[12. Appeal to the imagination in writing on abstract subjects by allusion to the natural world: imagination liable to cause pain as well as pleasure]

Thursday, 3 July 1712

Ignotis errare locis, ignotis videre
Flumina gaudebat; studio minuente laborem.   Ovid.[1]

The Pleasures of the Imagination are not wholly confined to such particular Authors as are conversant in material Objects, but are often to be met with among the Polite Masters of Morality, Criticism, and other Speculations abstracted from Matter, who, tho' they do not directly treat of the visible Parts of Nature, often draw from them their Similitudes, Metaphors, and Allegories. By these Allusions a Truth in the Understanding is as it were reflected by the Imagination; we are able to see something like Colour and Shape in a Notion, and to discover a Scheme of Thoughts traced out upon Matter. And here the Mind receives a great deal of Satisfaction, and has two of its Faculties gratified at the same time, while the Fancy is busie in copying after the Understanding, and transcribing Ideas out of the Intellectual World into the Material.

The Great Art of a Writer shews it self in the Choice of pleasing Allusions, which are generally to be taken from the *great* or *beautiful* Works of Art or Nature; for though whatever is New or Uncommon is apt to delight the Imagination, the chief Design of an Allusion being to illustrate and explain the Passages of an Author, it should be always borrowed from what is more known and common, than the Passages which are to be explained.

Allegories, when well chosen, are like so many Tracks of Light in a Discourse, that make every thing about them clear and beautiful. A noble Metaphor, when it is placed to an Advantage, casts a kind of Glory round it, and darts a Lustre through a whole Sentence: These different Kinds of Allusion are but so many different Manners of Similitude, and, that they may please the Imagination, the Likeness ought to be very exact, or very agreeable, as we love to see a Picture where the Resemblance is just, or the Posture and Air graceful. But we often find eminent Writers very faulty in this respect; great Scholars are apt to fetch their Comparisons and Allusions from the Sciences in which they are most conversant, so that a Man may see the Compass of their Learning in a Treatise on the most indifferent Subject. I have read a Discourse upon Love, which none but a profound Chymist could understand, and have heard many a Sermon that should only have been preached before a Congregation of °*Cartesians*. On the contrary, your Men of Business usually have recourse to such Instances as are too mean and familiar. They are for drawing the Reader into a Game of Chess or Tennis, or for leading him from Shop to Shop, in the Cant of particular Trades and Employments. It is certain, there may be found an infinite Variety of very agreeable Allusions in both these kinds, but, for the generality, the most entertaining ones lie in the Works of Nature, which are obvious to all Capacities, and more delightful than what is to be found in Arts and Sciences.

It is this Talent of affecting the Imagination, that gives an Embellishment to good Sense, and makes one Man's Compositions more agreeable than another's. It setts off all Writings in general, but is the very Life and highest Perfection of Poetry. Where it shines in an Eminent Degree, it has preserved several Poems for many Ages, that have nothing else to recommend them; and where all the other Beauties are present, the Work appears dry and insipid, if this single one be wanting. It has something in it like Creation; It bestows a kind of Existence, and draws up to the Reader's View several Objects which are not to be found in Being. It makes Additions to Nature, and gives a greater Variety to God's Works. In a word, it is able to beautifie and adorn the most illustrious Scenes in the Universe, or to fill the Mind with more glorious Shows and Apparitions, than can be found in any Part of it.

We have now discovered the several Originals of those Pleasures that gratifie the Fancy; and here, perhaps, it would not be very difficult to cast under their proper Heads those contrary Objects, which are apt to fill it with Distaste and Terrour; for the Imagination is as liable to Pain as Pleasure. When the Brain is hurt by any Accident, or the Mind disordered by Dreams or Sickness, the Fancy is over-run with wild dismal Ideas, and terrified with a thousand hideous Monsters of its own framing.

> *Eumenidum veluti demens videt Agmina Pantheus,*
> *Et solem geminum, & duplices se ostendere Thebas.*
> *Aut Agamemnonius scenis agitatus Orestes,*
> *Armatam facibus matrem & serpentibus atris*
> *Cum videt, ultricesque sedent in limine Diræ.*   Virg.[2]

There is not a Sight in Nature so mortifying as that of a Distracted Person, when his Imagination is troubled, and his whole Soul disordered and confused. *Babylon* in Ruins is not so melancholy a Spectacle. But to quit so disagreeable a Subject, I shall only consider, by way of Conclusion, what an infinite Advantage this Faculty gives an Almighty Being over the Soul of Man, and how great a measure of Happiness or Misery we are capable of Receiving from the Imagination only.

We have already seen the Influence that one Man has over the Fancy of another, and with what Ease he conveys into it a Variety of Imagery; how great a Power then may we suppose lodged in him, who knows all the ways of affecting the Imagination, who can infuse what Ideas he pleases, and fill those Ideas [with] Terrour and Delight to what Degree he thinks fit? He can excite Images in the Mind, without the help of Words, and make Scenes rise up before us and seem present to the Eye, without the Assistance of Bodies or Exterior Objects. He can transport the Imagination with such beautiful and glorious Visions as cannot possibly enter into our present Conceptions, or haunt it with such ghastly Spectres and Apparitions as would make us hope for Annihilation, and think Existence no better than a Curse. In short, he can so exquisitely ravish or torture the Soul through this single Faculty, as might suffice to make up the whole Heaven or Hell of any finite Being.

This Essay on the Pleasures of the Imagination having been published in separate Papers, I shall conclude it with a Table of the principal Contents in each Paper.

The CONTENTS

PAPER V.

Of Architecture *as it affects the Imagination.* Greatness *in Architecture relates either to the* Bulk *or to the* Manner. *Greatness of Bulk in the* Ancient Oriental Buildings. *The ancient Accounts of these Buildings confirmed,* 1. *From the Advantages, for raising such Works, in the first Ages of the World and in the Eastern Climates:* 2. *From several of them which are still Extant. Instances how* Greatness of Manner *affects the Imagination. A* French *Author's Observation on this Subject. Why* Concave *and* Convex Figures *give a Greatness of Manner to Works of Architecture. Every thing that pleases the Imagination in Architecture is either,* Great, Beautiful, *or* New.

PAPER VI.

The Secondary *Pleasures of the Imagination. The several Sources of these Pleasures* (Statuary, Painting, Description and Musick) *compared together. The* Final Cause *of our receiving Pleasure from these several Sources. Of* Descriptions *in Particular. The Power of* Words *over the Imagination. Why one Reader* more pleased *with Descriptions than another*,

PAPER VII.

How a whole Set of Ideas Hang together, &c. *A Natural Cause assigned for it. How to* perfect *the Imagination of a Writer. Who among the* Ancient Poets *had this Faculty in its greatest Perfection.* Homer *excelled in Imagining what is* Great; Virgil *in Imagining what is* Beautiful; Ovid *in Imagining what is* New. *Our own Country-Man* Milton, *very perfect in all three respects.*

PAPER VIII.

Why any thing that is unpleasant *to behold, pleases the Imagination when well Described. Why the Imagination receives a more Exquisite Pleasure from the Description of what is* Great, New, *or* Beautiful. *The Pleasure still heightned, if what is described raises* Passion *in the Mind.* Disagreeable *Passions pleasing when raised by apt Descriptions. Why* Terrour *and* Grief *are pleasing to the Mind, when excited by Descriptions. A particular Advantage the Writers in Poetry and Fiction have to please the Imagination. What Liberties are allowed them.*

PAPER IX.

Of that kind of Poetry *which* Mr. Dryden *calls the* Fairy-way of Writing. *How a Poet should be* Qualified *for it. The* Pleasures *of the* Imagination *that arise from it. In this respect, why the* Moderns *excell the* Ancients. *Why the* English *excell the Moderns. Who the Best among the* English. *Of* Emblematical *Persons.*

PAPER X.

What Authors please the Imagination who have nothing to do with Fiction. *How* History *pleases the Imagination. How the* Authors of the New Philosophy *please the Imagination. The* Bounds *and* Defects *of the Imagination. Whether these Defects are* Essential *to the Imagination.*

PAPER XI.

How those please the Imagination who treat of Subjects abstracted from Matter, *by Allusions taken from it. What* Allusions *most pleasing to the Imagination. Great Writers how* Faulty *in this respect. Of the Art of* Imagining *in General. The Imagination capable of* Pain *as well as* Pleasure. In what Degree *the Imagination is capable either of Pain or* Pleasure. O

[PRACTICAL CRITICISM]

No. 65 [STEELE]

[Etherege's *The Man of Mode: or Sir Fopling Flutter*][1]
Tuesday, 15 May 1711

— Demetri teque Tigelli
Discipularum inter Jubeo plorare cathedras. Hor.[2]

After having at large explained what Wit is, and described the false Appearances of it, all that Labour seems but an useless Enquiry, without some Time be spent in considering the Application of it. The Seat of Wit, when one speaks as a Man of the Town and the World, is the Playhouse; I shall therefore fill this Paper with Reflections upon the Use of it in that Place. The Application of Wit in the Theatre has as strong an Effect upon the Manners of our Gentlemen, as the Taste of it has upon the Writings of our Authors.

It may, perhaps, look like a very presumptuous Work, though not Foreign from the Duty of a SPECTATOR, to tax the Writings of such as have long had the general Applause of a Nation: But I shall always make Reason, Truth, and Nature the Measures of Praise and Disapraise; if those are for me, the Generality of Opinion is of no Consequence against me; if they are against me, the general Opinion cannot long support me.

Without further Preface, I am going to look into some of our most applauded Plays, and see whether they deserve the Figure they at present bear in the Imaginations of Men, or not.

In reflecting upon these Works, I shall chiefly dwell upon that for which each respective Play is most celebrated. The present Paper shall be employed upon Sir *Foplin Flutter*. The received Character of this Play is, That it is the Pattern of °Gentile Comedy. *Dorimant* and *Harriot* are the Characters of greatest Consequence, and if these are Low and Mean, the Reputation of the Play is very Unjust.

I will take for granted, that a fine Gentleman should be honest in his Actions, and refined in his Language. Instead of this, our Hero, in this Piece, is a direct Knave in his Designs, and a Clown in his Language. *Bellair* is his Admirer and Friend; in return for which, because he is forsooth a greater Wit than his said Friend, he thinks it reasonable to perswade him to Marry a young Lady, whose Virtue, he thinks, will last no longer than till she is a Wife, and then she cannot but fall to his Share, as he is an irresistible fine Gentleman. The Falshood to Mrs. *Loveit*, and the Barbarity of Triumphing over her Anguish for losing him, is another Instance of his Honesty, as well as his good Nature. As to his fine Language; he calls the Orange Woman, who, it seems, is inclined to grow Fat, *An Over-grown Jade, with a Flasket of Guts before her*; and salutes her with a pretty Phrase of, *How now, Double Tripe?*[3] Upon the Mention of a Country Gentlewoman, whom he knows nothing of, (no one can imagine why) he *will lay his Life she is some awkard, ill-fashioned Country Toad, who not having above four Dozen of Hairs on her Head, has adorned her Baldness with a large white °Fruz, that she may look Sparkishly in the Fore-front of the King's Box at an old Play*.[3] Unnatural Mixture of senseless Common Place!

As to the Generosity of his Temper, he tells his poor Footman, *If he did not wait better* — he would turn him away, in the insolent Phrase of, *I'll Uncase you*.[3]

Now for Mrs. *Harriot*: She laughs at Obedience to an absent Mother, whose Tenderness *Busie* describes to be very exquisite, for *that she is so pleased with finding* Harriot *again, that she cannot chide her for being out of the Way*.[4] This Witty Daughter, and Fine Lady, has so little Respect for this good Woman, that she Ridicules her Air in taking Leave, and cries, *In what Struggle is my poor Mother yonder? See, see, her Head tottering, her Eyes staring, and her under Lip trembling*.[5] But all this is atoned for, because *she has more Wit than is usual in her Sex, and as much Malice, though she is as wild as you would wish her, and has a Demureness in her Looks that makes it so surprising!*[6] Then to recommend her as a fit Spouse for his Hero, the Poet makes her speak her Sense of Marriage very ingeniously. *I think*, says she, *I might be brought to endure him, and that is all a reasonable Woman should expect in an Husband*.[7] It is, methinks, unnatural that we are not made to understand how she that was bred under a silly pious old Mother, that would never trust her out of her Sight, came to be so Polite.

It cannot be denied, but that the Negligence of every thing, which engages the Attention of the sober and valuable Part of Mankind, appears very well drawn in this Piece: But it is denied, that it is necessary to the Character of a Fine Gentleman, that he should in that manner Trample upon all Order and Decency. As for the Character of *Dorimant*, it is more of a Coxcomb than that of *Foplin*. He says of one of his Companions,[8] that a good Correspondence between them is their mutual Interest. Speaking of that Friend, he declares, their being much together *makes the Women think the better of his Understanding, and judge more favourably of my Reputation. It makes him pass upon some for a Man of very good Sense, and me upon others for a very civil Person*.[3]

This whole celebrated Piece is a perfect Contradiction to good Manners, good Sense, and common Honesty; and as there is nothing in it but what is built upon the Ruin of Virtue and Innocence, according to the Notion of Merit in this Comedy, I take the Shooe-maker to be, in reality, the Fine Gentleman of the Play: For it seems he is an Atheist, if we may depend upon his Character as given by the Orange Woman, who is her self far from being the lowest in the Play. She says of a Fine Man, who is *Dorimant's* Companion, There *is not such another Heathen in the Town*, *except the Shooe-maker*.[3] His Pretention to be the hero of the *Drama* appears still more in his own Description of his way of Living with his Lady. *There is*, says he, *never a Man in Town lives more like a Gentleman with his Wife than I do; I never mind her Motions; she never enquires into mine. We speak to one another civilly, hate one another heartily; and because it is Vulgar to Lye and Soak together, we have each of us our several Settle-Bed*.[3] That of *Soaking together* is as good as if *Dorimant* had spoken it himself; and, I think, since he puts human Nature in as ugly a Form as the Circumstance will bear, and is a staunch Unbeliever, he is very much Wronged in having no part of the good Fortune bestowed in the last Act.

To speak plainly of this whole Work, I think nothing but being lost to a Sense of Innocence and Virtue can make any one see this Comedy, without observing more frequent Occasion to move Sorrow and Indignation, than Mirth and Laughter. At the same time I allow it to be Nature, but it is Nature in its utmost Corruption and Degeneracy.   R

No. 290 [STEELE]

[Ambrose Philips's *The Distress'd Mother*][1]
Friday, 1 February 1712
Projicit ampullas & sesquipedalia verba.   Hor.[2]

The Players, who know I am very much their Friend, take all Opportunities to express a Gratitude to me for being so. They could not have a better Occasion of obliging me, than one which they lately took Hold of. They desired my Friend WILL HONEY-COMB to bring me to the Reading of a new Tragedy, it is called *The distressed Mother*. I must confess, tho' some Days are passed since I enjoyed that Entertainment, the Passions of the several Characters dwell strongly upon my Imagination; and I congratulate to the Age, that they are at last to see Truth and humane Life represented in the Incidents which concern Heroes and Heroines. The Stile of the Play is such as becomes those of the first Education, and the Sentiments worthy those of the highest Figure. It was a most exquisite Pleasure to me, to observe real Tears drop from the Eyes of those who had long made it their Profession to dissemble

Affliction; and the Player who read, frequently throw down the Book, till he had given Vent to the Humanity which rose in him at some irresistible Touches of the imagined Sorrow. We have seldom had any Female Distress on the Stage, which did not, upon cool Imagination, appear to flow from the Weakness rather than the Misfortune of the Person represented: But in this Tragedy you are not entertained with the ungoverned Passions of such as are enamoured of each other meerly as they are Men and Women, but their Regards are founded upon high Conceptions of each other's Virtue and Merit; and the Character which gives Name to the Play, is one who has behaved her self with heroick Virtue in the most important Circumstances of a female Life, those of a Wife, a Widow, and a Mother. If there be those whose Minds have been too attentive upon the Affairs of Life, to have any Notion of the Passion of Love in such Extremes as are known only to particular Tempers, yet in the abovmentioned Considerations, the Sorrow of the Heroine will move even the Generality of Mankind. Domestick Virtues concern all the World, and there is no one living who is not interested that *Andromache* should be an imitable Character. The generous Affection to the Memory of her deceased Husband, that tender Care for her Son, which is ever heightned with the Consideration of his Father, and these Regards preserved in spite of being tempted with the Possession of the highest Greatness, are what cannot but be venerable even to such an Audience as at present frequents the *English* Theatre. My Friend WILL HONEYCOMB commended several tender Things that were said, and told me they were very genteel; but whispered me, that he feared the Piece was not busy enough for the present Taste. To supply this, he recommended to the Players to be very careful in their Scenes, and above all Things, that every Part should be perfectly new dressed. I was very glad to find that they did not neglect my Friend's Admonition, because there are a great many in his Class of Criticism who may be gained by it; but indeed the Truth is, that as to the Work itself, it is every where Nature. The Persons are of the highest Quality in Life, even that of Princes; but their Quality is not represented by the Poet with Direction that Guards and °Waiters should follow them in every Scene, but their Grandure appears in greatness of Sentiments, flowing from Minds worthy their Condition. To make a Character truly Great, this Author understands that it should have its Foundation in superior Thoughts and Maxims of Conduct. It is very certain, that many an honest Woman would make no Difficulty, tho' she had been the Wife of *Hector*, for the Sake of a Kingdom, to marry the Enemy of her Husband's Family and Country; and indeed who can deny but she might be still an honest Woman, but no Heroine? That may be defensible, nay laudable in one Character, which would be in the highest Degree exceptionable in another. When *Cato Uticensis* killed himself, *Cottius*, a *Roman* of ordinary Quality and Character, did the same Thing; upon which one said, smiling, '*Cottius* might have lived tho' *Caesar* has seized the *Roman* Liberty.' *Cottius*'s Condition might have been the same, let Things at the Upper-End of the World pass as they would. What is further very extraordinary in this Work, is, that the Persons are all of them laudable, and their Misfortunes arise rather from unguarded Virtue than Propensity to Vice. The Town has an Opportunity of doing it self Justice in supporting the Representations of Passion, Sorrow, Indignation, even Despair it self, within the Rules of Decency, Honour, and good Breeding; and since there is no one can flatter himself his Life will be always fortunate, they may here see Sorrow as they would wish to bear it whenever it arrives.

Mr. SPECTATOR,

'I am appointed to act a Part in the new Tragedy, called *The distressed Mother*: It is the celebrated Grief of *Orestes* which I am to personate; but I shall not act as I ought, for I shall feel it too intimately to be able to utter it. I was last night repeating a Paragraph to my self, which I took to be an Expression of Rage, and in the Middle of the Sentence there was a Stroke of Self-pity which quite unmanned me.[3] Be pleased, Sir, to print this Letter, that when I am oppressed in this Manner at such an Interval, a certain Part of the Audience may not think I am out; and I hope with this Allowance to do it to Satisfaction.

I am,

SIR,

Your most humble Servant,

George Powell.'

Mr. SPECTATOR,

'As I was walking t'other Day in the *Park*, I saw a Gentleman with
a very short Face; I desire to know whether it was you. Pray inform
me assoon as you can, lest I become the most heroick *Hecatissa's*
Rival.

Your humble Servant to Command,
Sophia.'

Dear *Madam*,

'It is not me you are in love with, for I was very ill, and kept my
Chamber all that Day.

Your most humble Servant,
The SPECTATOR,'
T

[FROM THE SERIES OF PAPERS ON *PARADISE LOST*]*

No. 267 [ADDISON]

[*Paradise Lost* examined by the rules of epic poetry:
the fable and action][1]
Saturday, 5 January 1712

Cedite Romani Scriptores, cedite Graii.   Propert.[2]

There is Nothing in Nature so irksome as general Discourses,
especially when they turn chiefly upon Words. For this Reason I
shall wave the Discussion of that Point which was started some
Years since, Whether *Milton's Paradise Lost* may be called an *Heroick
Poem?* Those who will not give it that Title, may call it (if they
please) a *Divine Poem.*[3] It will be sufficient to its Perfection, if it has
in it all the Beauties of the highest Kind of Poetry; and as for those
who alledge it is not an Heroick Poem, they advance no more to
the Diminution of it, than if they should say *Adam* is not *Æneas*,
nor *Eve Helen.*

I shall therefore examine it by the Rules of Epic Poetry, and see
whether it falls short of the *Iliad* or *Æneid*, in the Beauties which
are essential to that Kind of Writing. The first Thing to be

considered in an Epic Poem, is the Fable, which is perfect or imperfect, according as the Action which it relates is more or less so. This Action should have three Qualifications in it. First, It should be but one Action. Secondly, It should be an entire Action; and Thirdly, it should be a great Action. To consider the Action of the *Iliad*, *Æneid*, and *Paradise Lost*, in these three several Lights. *Homer* to preserve the Unity of his Action hastens into the Midst of Things, as *Horace* has observed[4]: Had he gone up to °*Leda's* Egg, or begun much later, even at the Rape of *Helen*, or the Investing of *Troy*, it is manifest that the Story of the Poem would have been a Series of several Actions. He therefore opens his Poem with the Discord of his Princes, and [artfully] interweaves in the several succeeding Parts of it, an Account of every Thing material which relates to them, and had passed before that fatal Dissension. After the same Manner *Æneas* makes his first Appearance in the *Tyrrhene* Seas, and within Sight of *Italy*, because the Action proposed to be celebrated was that of his settling himself in *Latium*. But because it was necessary for the Reader to know what had happened to him in the taking of *Troy*, and in the preceding Parts of his Voyage, *Virgil* makes his Heroe relate it by Way of Episode in the second and third Books of the *Æneid*. The Contents of both which Books come before those of the first Book in the Thread of the Story, tho' for preserving of this Unity of Action, they follow [it] in the Disposition of the Poem. *Milton*, in Imitation of these two great Poets, opens his *Paradise Lost*, with an infernal Council plotting the Fall of Man, which is the Action he proposed to celebrate; and as for those great Actions which preceded, in Point of Time, the Battle of the Angels, and the Creation of the World, (which would have entirely destroyed the Unity of his principal Action, had he related them in the same Order that they happened) he cast them into the fifth, sixth and seventh Books, by way of Episode to this noble Poem.

Aristotle himself allows, that *Homer* has nothing to boast of as to the Unity of his Fable, tho' at the same Time that great Critick and Philosopher endeavours to palliate this Imperfection in the *Greek* Poet, by imputing it in some Measure to the very Nature of an Epic Poem.[5] Some have been of Opinion, that the *Æneid* °labours also in this Particular, and has Episodes which may be looked upon as Excrescencies rather than as Parts of the Action. On the contrary, the Poem which we have now under our Consideration, hath no other Episodes than such as naturally arise from the Subject, and yet is filled with such a Multitude of astonishing Incidents, that it gives us at the same Time a Pleasure of the greatest Variety, and of the greatest Simplicity.

I must observe also, that as *Virgil* in the Poem which was designed to celebrate the Original of the *Roman* Empire, has described the Birth of its great Rival, the *Carthaginian* Commonwealth: *Milton* with the like Art in his Poem on the Fall of Man, has related the Fall of those Angels who are his professed Enemies. Besides the many other Beauties in such an Episode, it's running parallel with the great Action of the Poem, hinders it from breaking the Unity so much as another Episode would have done, that had not so great an Affinity with the principal Subject. In short, this is the same Kind of Beauty which the Criticks admire in the *Spanish Fryar*, or the *Double Discovery*, where the two different Plots look like Counterparts and Copies of one another.

The second Qualification required in the Action of an Epic Poem is, that it should be an *entire* Action: An Action is entire when it is compleat in all its Parts; or as *Aristotle* describes it, when it consists of a Beginning, a Middle, and an End.[6] Nothing should go before it, be intermixed with it, or follow after it, that is not related to it. As on the contrary, no single Step should be omitted in that just and regular [Progress] which it must be supposed to take from its Original to its Consummation. Thus we see the Anger of *Achilles* in its Birth, its Continuance and Effects, and *Æneas*'s Settlement in *Italy*, carried on through all the Oppositions in his Way to it both by Sea and Land. The Action in *Milton* excels (I think) both the former in this Particular; we see it contrived in Hell, executed upon Earth, and punished by Heaven. The Parts of it are told in the most distinct Manner, and grow out of one another in the most natural Method.

The third Qualification of an Epic Poem is its *Greatness*. The Anger of *Achilles* was of such Consequence, that it embroiled the Kings of *Greece*, destroyed the Heroes of *Troy*, and engaged all the Gods in Factions. *Æneas*'s Settlement in *Italy* produced the *Cæsars*, and gave Birth to the *Roman* Empire. *Milton*'s Subject was still

greater than either of the former; it does not determine the Fate of
single Persons or Nations, but of a whole Species. The united
Powers of Hell are joined together for the Destruction of Mankind,
which they effected in Part, and would have completed, had not
Omnipotence it self interposed. The principal Actors are Man in
his greatest Perfection, and Woman in her highest Beauty. Their
Enemies are the fallen Angels: The Messiah their Friend, and the
Almighty their Protector. In short, every Thing that is great in the
whole Circle of Being, whether within the Verge of Nature, or out
of it, has a proper Part assigned it in this noble Poem.

In Poetry, as in Architecture, not only the Whole, but the
principal Members, and every Part of them, should be Great. I will
not presume to say, that the Book of Games in the *Æneid*, or that
in the *Iliad*, are not of this Nature, nor to reprehend *Virgil's* Simile
of a Top,[7] and many other of the same Nature in the *Iliad*, as liable
to any Censure in this Particular; but I think we may say, without
derogating from those wonderful Performances, that there is an
unquestionable Magnificence in every Part of *Paradise Lost*, and
indeed a much greater than could have been formed upon any Pagan
System.

But *Aristotle*, by the Greatness of the Action, does not only
mean that it should be great in its Nature, but also in its Duration,
or in other Words, that it should have a due Length in it, as well
as what we properly call Greatness. The just Measure of this Kind
of Magnitude, he explains by the following Similitude. An Animal,
no bigger than a Mite, cannot appear perfect to the Eye, because
the Sight takes it in at once, and has only a confused Idea of the
Whole, and not a distinct Idea of all its Parts; If on the contrary
you should suppose an Animal of ten thousand Furlongs in Length,
the Eye would be so filled with a single Part of it, that it could not
give the Mind an Idea of the Whole.[8] What these Animals are to
the Eye, a very short or a very long Action would be to the memory.
The first would be, as it were, lost and swallowed up by it, and the
other difficult to be contained in it. *Homer* and *Virgil* have shewn
their principal Art in this Particular; the Action of the *Iliad*, and
that of the *Æneid*, were in themselves exceeding short, but are so
beautifully extended and diversified by the Invention of *Episodes*,
and the Machinery of Gods, with the like poetical Ornaments,[9]

that they make up an agreeable Story sufficient to employ the Memory without over-charging it. *Milton*'s Action is enriched with such a Variety of Circumstances, that I have taken as much Pleasure in reading the Contents of his Books, as in the best invented Story I ever met with. It is possible, that the Traditions on which the *Iliad* and *Æneid* were built, had more Circumstances in them than the History of *the Fall of Man*, as it is related in Scripture. Besides it was easier for *Homer* and *Virgil* to dash the Truth with Fiction, as they were in no danger of offending the Religion of their Country by it. But as for *Milton*, he had not only a very few Circumstances upon which to raise his Poem, but was also obliged to proceed with the greatest Caution in every Thing that he added out of his own Invention. And, indeed, notwithstanding all the Restraints he was under, he has filled his Story with so many surprising Incidents, which bear so close an Analogy with what is delivered in Holy Writ, that it is capable of pleasing the most delicate Reader, without giving Offence to the most scrupulous.

The modern Criticks have collected from several Hints in the *Iliad* and *Æneid* the Space of Time, which is taken up by the Action of each of those Poems;[10] but as a great Part of *Milton*'s Story was transacted in Regions that lie out of the reach of the Sun and the Sphere of Day, it is impossible to gratifie the Reader with such a Calculation, which indeed would be more curious than instructive; None of the Criticks, either Antient or Modern, having laid down Rules to circumscribe the Action of an Epic Poem with any determined Number of Years, Days or Hours.

This Piece of Criticism on Milton's Paradise Lost *shall be carried on in the following* Saturdays *Papers.*   L

No. 273 [ADDISON]

[Continued: the characters or actors]
Saturday, 12 January 1712

— *Notandi sunt tibi* Mores.   Hor.[1]

Having examined the Action of *Paradise Lost*, let us in the next Place consider the Actors. This is *Aristotle*'s Method of considering; first the Fable, and secondly the Manners, or as we generally call them in *English*, the Fable and the Characters.

Homer has excelled all the heroic Poets that ever wrote, in the Multitude and Variety of his Characters. Every God that is admitted into his Poem, acts a Part which would have been suitable to no other Deity. His Princes are as much distinguished by their Manners as by their Dominions; and even those among them, whose Characters seem wholly made up of Courage, differ from one another as to the particular Kinds of Courage in which they excel. In short, there is scarce a Speech or Action in the *Iliad*, which the Reader may not ascribe to the Person that speaks or acts, without seeing his Name at the Head of it.

Homer does not only out-shine all other Poets in the Variety, but also in the Novelty of his Characters. He has introduced among his *Grecian* Princes a Person, who had lived thrice the Age of Man,[2] and conversed with *Theseus*, *Hercules*, *Polyphemus*, and the first Race of Heroes. His principal Actor is the Son of a Goddess, not to mention the Off-spring of other Deities, who have likewise a Place in his Poem, and the venerable *Trojan* Prince who was the Father of so many Kings and Heroes. There is in these several Characters of *Homer*, a certain Dignity as well as Novelty, which adapts them in a more peculiar manner to the Nature of an heroic Poem. Tho', at the same Time, to give them the greater Variety, he has described a *Vulcan*, that is, a Buffoon among his Gods, and a *Thersites* among his Mortals.

Virgil falls infinitely short of *Homer* in the Characters of his Poem, both as to their Variety and Novelty. *Æneas* is indeed a perfect Character, but as for *Achates*, tho' he is stiled the Hero's Friend, he does nothing in the whole Poem which may deserve that Title. *Gyas*, *Mnesteus*, *Sergestus* and *Cloanthus*, are all of them Men of the same Stamp and Character,

> *Fortemque Gyan, fortemque Cloanthum*:   Virg.[3]

There are indeed several very natural Incidents in the Part of *Ascanius*; as that of *Dido* cannot be sufficiently admired. I do not see any Thing new or particular in *Turnus*. *Pallas* and *Evander* are remote Copies of *Hector* and *Priam*, as *Lausus* and *Mezentius* are almost Parallels to *Pallas* and *Evander*. The Characters of *Nisus* and *Eurialus* are beautiful, but common. We must not forget the Parts of *Sinon*, *Camilla*, and some few others, which are beautiful Improvements on the Greek Poet. In short, there is neither that Variety nor Novelty in the Persons of the *Æneid*, which we meet with in those of the *Iliad*.

If we look into the Characters of *Milton*, we shall find that he has introduced all the Variety his {Fable} was capable of receiving. The whole Species of Mankind was in two Persons at the Time to which the Subject of his Poem is confined. We have, however, four distinct Characters in these two Persons. We see Man and Woman in the highest Innocence and Perfection, and in the most abject State of Guilt and Infirmity. The two last Characters are, indeed, very common and obvious, but the two first are not only more magnificent, but more new than any Characters either in *Virgil* or *Homer*, or indeed in the whole Circle of Nature.

Milton was so sensible of this Defect in the Subject of his Poem, and of the few Characters it would afford him, that he has brought into it two Actors of a shadowy and fictitious Nature, in the Persons of Sin and Death, by which Means he has interwoven in the Body of his Fable a very beautiful and well invented Allegory.[4] But notwithstanding the Fineness of this Allegory may atone for it in some Measure; I cannot think that Persons of such a chymerical Existence are proper Actors in an Epic Poem; because there is not that Measure of Probability annexed to them, which is requisite in Writings of this Kind, as I shall shew more at large hereafter.

Virgil has, indeed, admitted Fame as an Actress in the *Æneid*, but the Part she acts is very short, and none of the most admired Circumstances in that Divine Work.[5] We find in Mock-Heroic Poems, particularly in the *Dispensary* and the *Lutrin*,[6] several allegorical Persons of this Nature, which are very beautiful in those Compositions, and may, perhaps, be used as an Argument, that

the Authors of them were of Opinion, such Characters might have
a Place in an Epic Work. For my own Part, I should be glad the
Reader would think so, for the sake of the Poem I am now
examining, and must further add, that if such empty unsubstantial
Beings may be ever made Use of on this Occasion, there were never
any more nicely imagined, and employed in more proper Actions,
than those of which I am now speaking.

Another principal Actor in this Poem is the great Enemy of
Mankind. The Part of *Ulysses* in *Homer's Odyssey* is very much
admired by *Aristotle*,[7] as perplexing that Fable with very agreeable
Plots and Intricacies, not only by the many Adventures in his
Voyage, and the Subtilty of his Behaviour, but by the various
Concealments and Discoveries of his Person in several Parts of that
Poem. But the crafty Being I have now mentioned, makes a much
longer Voyage than *Ulysses*, puts in Practice many more Wiles and
Stratagems, and hides himself under a greater Variety of Shapes
and Appearances, all of which are severally detected, to the great
Delight and Surprise of the Reader.

We may likewise observe with how much Art the Poet has varied
several Characters of the Persons that speak in his infernal
Assembly. On the contrary, how has he represented the whole
Godhead exerting it self towards Man in its full Benevolence under
the Three-fold Distinction of a Creator, a Redeemer and a
Comforter!

Nor must we omit the Person of *Raphael*, who amidst his
Tenderness and Friendship for Man, shews such a Dignity and
Condescention in all his Speech and Behaviour, as are suitable to a
Superior Nature. The Angels are indeed as much diversified in
Milton, and distinguished by their proper Parts, as the Gods are in
Homer or *Virgil*. The reader will find nothing ascribed to *Uriel*,
Gabriel, *Michael* or *Raphael*, which is not in a particular manner
suitable to their respective Characters.

There is another Circumstance in the principal Actors of the
Iliad and *Æneid*, which gives a peculiar Beauty to those two Poems,
and was therefore contrived with very great Judgment. I mean the
Authors having chosen for their Heroes Persons who were so nearly
related to the People for whom they wrote. *Achilles* was a *Greek*,
and *Æneas* the remote Founder of *Rome*. By this means their

Countrymen (whom they principally proposed to themselves for their Readers) were particularly attentive to all the Parts of their Story, and sympathized with their Heroes in all their Adventures. A *Roman* could not but rejoice in the Escapes, Successes and Victories of *Æneas*, and be grieved at any Defeats, Misfortunes or Disappointments that befel him; as a *Greek* must have had the same regard for *Achilles*. And it is plain, that each of those Poems have lost this great Advantage, among those Readers to whom their Heroes are as Strangers, or indifferent Persons.

Milton's Poem is admirable in this respect, since it is impossible for any of its Readers, whatever Nation, Country or People he may belong to, not to be related to the Persons who are the principal Actors in it; but what is still infinitely more to its Advantage, the principal Actors in this Poem are not only our Progenitors, but our Representatives. We have an actual Interest in every Thing they do, and no less than our utmost Happiness is concerned, and lies at Stake in all their Behaviour.

I shall subjoyn as a Corollary to the foregoing Remark, an admirable Observation out of *Aristotle*, which hath been very much misrepresented in the Quotations of some Modern Criticks.[8] 'If a Man of perfect and consummate Virtue falls into a Misfortune, it raises our Pity, but not our Terror, because we do not fear that it may be our own Case, who do not resemble the Suffering Person.' But as that great Philosopher adds, 'If we see a Man of Virtues mixt with Infirmities, fall into any Misfortune, it does not only raise our Pity but our Terror; because we are afraid that the like Misfortunes may happen to our selves, who resemble the Character of the suffering Person.'

I shall take another Opportunity to observe, that a Person of an absolute and consummate Virtue should never be introduced in Tragedy, and shall only remark in this Place, that the foregoing Observation of *Aristotle*, tho' it may be true in other Occasions, does not hold in this; because in the present Case, though the Persons who fall into Misfortune are of the most perfect and consummate Virtue, it is not to be considered as what may possibly be, but what actually is our own Case; since we are embarked with them on the same Bottom, and must be Partakers of their Happiness or Misery.

In this, and some other very few Instances, *Aristotle*'s Rules for Epic Poetry (which he had drawn from his Reflections upon *Homer*) cannot be supposed to [square] exactly with the heroic Poems which have been made since his Time; as it is plain his Rules would have been still more perfect, could he have perused the *Æneid* which was made some hundred Years after his Death.

In my next I shall go through other Parts of *Milton*'s Poem; and hope that what I shall there advance, as well as what I have already written, will not only serve as a Comment upon *Milton*, but upon *Aristotle*.   L

No. 291 [ADDISON]

[Qualities necessary for a just critic of *Paradise Lost*]
Saturday, 2 February 1712

> — *Ubi plura nitent in carmine, non ego paucis*
> *Offendor maculis, quas aut Incuria fudit,*
> *Aut Humana parum cavit Natura* —   Hor.[1]

I have now considered *Milton*'s *Paradise Lost* under those four great Heads of the Fable, the Characters, the Sentiments, and the Language; and have shewn that he excels, in general, under each of these Heads. I hope that I have made several Discoveries which may appear new, even to those who are versed in Critical Learning. Were I indeed to chuse my Readers, by whose Judgment I would stand or fall, they should not be such as are acquainted only with the *French* and *Italian* Criticks, but also with the Antient and Modern who have written in either of the learned Languages. Above all, I would have them well versed in the *Greek* and *Latin* Poets, without which a Man very often fancies that he understands a Critick, when in reality he does not comprehend his Meaning.

It is in Criticism, as in all other Sciences and Speculations; one who brings with him any implicit Notions and Observations which he has made in his reading of the Poets, will find his own Reflections methodized and explained, and perhaps several little Hints that had passed in his Mind, perfected and improved in the Works of a good Critick; whereas one who has not these previous

Lights, is very often an utter Stranger to what he reads, and apt to put a wrong Interpretation upon it.

Nor is it sufficient, that a Man who sets up for a Judge in Criticism, should have perused the Authors above-mentioned, unless he has also a clear and logical Head. Without this Talent he is perpetually puzzled and perplexed amidst his own Blunders, mistakes the Sense of those he would confute, or if he chances to think right, does not know how to convey his Thoughts to another with Clearness and Perspicuity. *Aristotle*, who was the best Critick, was also one of the best Logicians that ever appeared in the World.

Mr. *Lock*'s Essay on Human Understanding would be thought a very odd Book for a Man to make himself Master of, who would get a Reputation by Critical Writings; though at the same Time it is very certain, that an Author who has not learned the Art of distinguishing between Words and Things, and of ranging his Thoughts, and setting them in proper Lights, whatever Notions he may have, will lose himself in Confusion and Obscurity. I might further observe, that there is not a *Greek* or *Latin* Critick who has not shewn, even in the Stile of his Criticisms, that he was a Master of all the Elegance and Delicacy of his Native Tongue.

The Truth of it is, there is nothing more absurd, than for a Man to set up for a Critick, without a good Insight into all the Parts of Learning; whereas many of those who have endeavoured to signalize themselves by Works of this Nature among our *English* Writers, are not only defective in the above-mentioned Particulars, but plainly discover by the Phrases which they make use of, and by their confused way of thinking, that they are not acquainted with the most common and ordinary Systems of Arts and Sciences. A few general Rules extracted out of the *French* Authors,[2] with a certain Cant of Words, has sometimes set up an illiterate heavy Writer for a most judicious and formidable Critick.

One great Mark, by which you may discover a Critick who has neither Taste nor Learning, is this, that he seldom ventures to praise any Passage in an Author which has not been before received and applauded by the Publick, and that his Criticism turns wholly upon little Faults and Errors. This Part of a Critick is so very easy to succeed in, that we find every ordinary Reader, upon the publishing of a new Poem, has Wit and Ill-nature enough to turn several Passages of it into Ridicule, and very often in the right Place. This Mr. *Dryden* has very agreeably remarked in those two celebrated Lines,

> *Errors, like Straws, upon the Surface flow;*
> *He who would search for Pearls must dive below.*[3]

A true Critick ought to dwell rather upon Excellencies than Imperfections, to discover the concealed Beauties of a Writer, and communicate to the World such Things as are worth their Observation. The most exquisite Words and finest Strokes of an Author are those which very often appear the most doubtful and exceptionable, to a man who wants a Relish for polite Learning; and they are these, which a soure undistinguishing Critick generally attacks with the greatest Violence. *Tully* observes, that it is very easy to brand or fix a Mark upon what he calls *Verbum ardens*, or, as it may be rendered into *English*, *a glowing bold Expression*, and to turn it into Ridicule by a cold ill-natured Criticism.[4] A little Wit is equally capable of exposing a Beauty, and of aggravating a Fault; and though such a Treatment of an Author naturally produces Indignation in the Mind of an understanding Reader, it has however its Effect among the Generality of those whose Hands it falls into, the Rabble of Mankind being very apt to think that every Thing which is laughed at with any Mixture of Wit, is ridiculous in it self.

Such a Mirth as this, is always unseasonable in a Critick, as it rather prejudices the Reader than convinces him, and is capable of making a Beauty, as well as a Blemish, the Subject of Derision. A Man, who cannot write with Wit on a proper Subject, is dull and stupid, but one who shews it in an improper Place, is as impertinent and absurd. Besides, a Man who has the Gift of Ridicule is apt to find Fault with any Thing that gives him an Opportunity of exerting his beloved Talent, and very often censures a Passage, not because there is any Fault in it, but because he can be merry upon it. Such Kinds of Pleasantry are very unfair and disingenuous in Works of Criticism, in which the greatest Masters, both antient and modern, have always appeared with a serious and instructive Air.

As I intend in my next Paper to shew the Defects in *Milton's Paradise Lost*, I thought fit to premise these few Particulars, to the

End that the Reader may know I enter upon it, as on a very ungrateful Work, and that I shall just point at the Imperfections, without endeavouring to enflame them with Ridicule. I must also observe with *Longinus*,[5] that the Productions of a great Genius, with many Lapses and Inadvertencies, are infinitely preferable to the Works of an inferior Kind of Author, which are scrupulously exact and conformable to all the Rules of correct Writing.

I shall conclude my Paper with a Story out of *Boccalini*,[6] which sufficiently shews us the Opinion that judicious Author entertained of the Sort of Criticks I have been here mentioning. A famous Critick, says he, having gathered together all the Faults of an eminent Poet, made a Present of them to *Apollo*, who received them very graciously, and resolved to make the Author a suitable Return for the Trouble he had been at in collecting them. In order to this, he set before him a Sack of Wheat, as it had been just threshed out of the Sheaf. He then bid him pick out the Chaff from among the Corn, and lay it aside by it self. The Critick applied himself to the Task with great Industry and Pleasure, and after having made the due Separation, was presented by *Apollo* with the Chaff for his Pains. L

No. 297 [ADDISON]

[Defects in the fable, characters, sentiments and
language of *Paradise Lost*]
Saturday, 9 February 1712

—velut si
Egregio inspersos reprendas corpore nævos. Hor.[1]

After what I have said in my last *Saturday*'s Paper, I shall enter on the Subject of this without farther Preface, and remark the several Defects which appear in the Fable, the Characters, the Sentiments, and the Language of *Milton*'s *Paradise Lost*; not doubting but the Reader will pardon me, if I alledge at the same Time whatever may be said for the Extenuation of such Defects. The first Imperfection which I shall observe in the Fable is, that the Event of it is unhappy.

The Fable of every Poem is according to *Aristotle*'s Division either

Simple or *Implex*.[2] It is called Simple when there is no Change of
Fortune in it, Implex when the Fortune of the chief Actor changes
from Bad to Good, or from Good to Bad. The Implex Fable is
thought the most perfect; I suppose, because it is more proper to
stir up the Passions of the Reader, and to surprize him with a
greater Variety of Accidents.

The Implex Fable is therefore of two Kinds: In the first the chief
Actor makes his way through a long Series of Dangers and
Difficulties, 'till he arrives at Honour and Prosperity, as we see in
the Story of *Ulysses*. In the second, the chief Actor in the Poem falls
from some eminent Pitch of Honour and Prosperity, into Misery
and Disgrace. Thus we see *Adam* and *Eve* sinking from a State of
Innocence and Happiness, into the most abject Condition of Sin
and Sorrow.

The most taking Tragedies among the Antients were built on
this last Sort of Implex Fable, particularly the Tragedy of *Œdipus*,
which proceeds upon a Story, if we may believe *Aristotle*, the most
proper for Tragedy that could be invented by the Wit of Man. I
have taken some pains in a former Paper to shew, that this Kind
of Implex Fable, wherein the Event is unhappy, is more apt to
affect an Audience than that of the first Kind;[3] notwithstanding
many excellent Pieces among the Antients, as well as most of those
which have been written of late Years in our own Country, are
raised upon contrary Plans. I must however own, that I think this
Kind of Fable, which is the most perfect in Tragedy, is not so
proper for an Heroick Poem.

Milton seems to have been sensible of this Imperfection in his
Fable, and has therefore endeavoured to cure it by several Expedients; particularly by the Mortification which the great Adversary of
Mankind meets with upon his Return to the Assembly of Infernal
Spirits, as it is described in a beautiful Passage of the tenth Book;[4]
and likewise by the Vision, wherein *Adam* at the Close of the Poem
sees his Off-spring triumphing over his great Enemy, and himself
restored to a happier *Paradise* than that from which he fell.[5]

There is another Objection against *Milton*'s Fable, which is
indeed almost the same with the former, tho' placed in a different
Light, namely, That the Hero in the *Paradise Lost* is unsuccessful,
and by no means a match for his Enemies. This gave Occasion to

Mr. *Dryden's* Reflection, that the Devil was in reality *Milton's* Hero.[6] I think I have obviated this Objection in my first Paper. The *Paradise Lost* is an Epic, or a Narrative Poem, he that looks for an Hero in it, searches for that which *Milton* never intended; but if he will needs fix the Name of an Hero upon any Person in it, 'tis certainly the *Messiah* who is the Hero, both in the Principal Action, and in the chief Episodes. Paganism could not furnish out a real Action for a Fable greater than that of the *Iliad* or *Æneid*, and therefore an Heathen could not form a higher Notion of a Poem than one of that Kind, which they call an Heroick. Whether *Milton's* is not of a sublimer Nature I will not presume to determine: It is sufficient that I shew there is in the *Paradise Lost* all the Greatness of Plan, Regularity of Design, and masterly Beauties which we discover in *Homer* and *Virgil*.

I must in the next Place observe, that *Milton* has interwoven in the Texture of his Fable some Particulars which do not seem to have Probability enough for an Epic Poem, particularly in the Actions which he ascribes to *Sin* and *Death*, and the Picture which he draws of the *Lymbo of Vanity*, with other Passages in the second Book.[7] Such Allegories rather favour of the Spirit of *Spencer* and *Ariosto*, than of *Homer* and *Virgil*.

In the Structure of his Poem he has likewise admitted of too many Digressions. It is finely observed by *Aristotle*, that the Author of an Heroick Poem should seldom speak himself, but throw as much of his Work as he can into the Mouths of those who are his principal Actors.[8] *Aristotle* has given no Reason for this Precept; but I presume it is because the Mind of the Reader is more awed and elevated when he hears *Æneas* or *Achilles* speak, than when *Virgil* or *Homer* talk in their own Persons. Besides that assuming the Character of an eminent Man is apt to fire the Imagination, and raise the Ideas of the Author. *Tully* tells us, mentioning his Dialogue of Old Age, in which *Cato* is the chief Speaker, that upon a Review of it he was agreeably imposed upon, and fancied that it was *Cato*, and not he himself, who uttered his Thoughts on that Subject.[9]

If the Reader would be at the pains to see how the Story of the *Iliad* and the *Æneid* is delivered by those Persons who act in it, he will be surprized to find how little in either of these Poems proceeds from the Authors. *Milton* has, in the general Disposition of his Fable, very finely observed this great Rule; insomuch, that there is scarce a third Part of it which comes from the Poet; the rest is spoken either by *Adam* and *Eve*, or by some Good or Evil Spirit who is engaged either in their Destruction or Defence.

From what has been here observed it appears, that Digressions are by no means to be allowed of in an Epic Poem. If the Poet, even in the ordinary Course of his Narration, should speak as little as possible, he should certainly never let his Narration sleep for the sake of any Reflections of his own. I have often observed, with a secret Admiration, that the longest Reflection in the *Æneid* is in that Passage of the Tenth Book, where *Turnus* is represented as dressing himself in the Spoils of *Pallas*, whom he had slain. *Virgil* here lets his Fable stand still for the sake of the following Remark. *How is the Mind of Man ignorant of Futurity, and unable to bear prosperous Fortune with Moderation? The Time will come when* Turnus *shall wish that he had left the Body of* Pallas *untouched, and curse the Day on which he dressed himself in these Spoils.*[10] As the great Event of the *Æneid*, and the Death of *Turnus*, whom *Æneas* slew because he saw him adorned with the Spoils of *Pallas*, turns upon this Incident, *Virgil* went out of his way to make this Reflection upon it, without which so small a Circumstance might possibly have slipped out of his Reader's Memory. *Lucan*, who was an Injudicious Poet, lets drop his Story very frequently for the sake of his unnecessary Digressions, or his *Diverticula*, as *Scaliger* calls them.[11] If he gives us an Account of the Prodigies which preceded the Civil War, he declaims upon the Occasion, and shews how much happier it would be for Man, if he did not feel his Evil Fortune before it comes to pass, and suffer not only by its real Weight, but by the Apprehension of it. *Milton*'s Complaint of his Blindness, his Panegyrick on Marriage, his Reflections on *Adam* and *Eve*'s going naked, of the Angels eating, and several other Passages in his Poem, are liable to the same Exception, tho' I must confess there is so great a Beauty in these very Digressions, that I would not wish them out of his Poem.[12]

I have, in a former Paper, spoken of the *Characters* of *Milton*'s *Paradise Lost*, and declared my Opinion, as to the Allegorical Persons who are introduced in it.

If we look into the *Sentiments*, I think they are sometimes defective under the following Heads; First, as there are several of them too much pointed, and some that degenerate even into Punns. Of this last Kind I am afraid is that in the First Book, where, speaking of the Pigmies, he calls them.

> . . . *The small* Infantry
> *Warr'd on by Cranes* . . . [13]

Another Blemish that appears in some of his Thoughts, is his frequent Allusion to Heathen Fables, which are not certainly of a Piece with the Divine Subject, of which he treats. I do not find fault with these Allusions, where the Poet himself represents them as fabulous, as he does in some Places, but where he mentions them as Truths and Matters of Fact. The Limits of my Paper will not give me leave to be particular in Instances of this Kind: The Reader will easily remark them in his Perusal of the Poem.

A third Fault in his Sentiments, is an unnecessary Ostentation of Learning, which likewise occurs very frequently. It is certain that both *Homer* and *Virgil* were Masters of all the Learning of their Times, but it shews it self in their Works after an indirect and concealed Manner. *Milton* seems ambitious of letting us know, by his Excursions on Free-Will and Predestination, and his many Glances upon History, Astronomy, Geography and the like, as well as by the Terms and Phrases he sometimes makes use of, that he was acquainted with the whole Circle of Arts and Sciences.

If, in the last Place, we consider the *Language* of this great Poet, we must allow what I have hinted in a former Paper, that it is often too much laboured, and sometimes obscured by old [Words], Transpositions, and Foreign Idioms. *Seneca's* Objection to the Stile of a great Author, *Riget ejus oratio, nihil in ea placidum nihil lene*, is what many Criticks make to *Milton*:[14] As I cannot wholly refute it, so I have already apologized for it in another Paper; to which I may further add, that *Milton's* Sentiments and Ideas were so wonderfully sublime, that it would have been impossible for him to have represented them in their full Strength and Beauty, without having Recourse to these Foreign Assistances. Our Language sunk under him, and was unequal to that Greatness of Soul, which furnished him with such glorious Conceptions.

A second Fault in his Language is, that he often affects a Kind of Jingle in his Words,[15] as in the following Passages,[16] and many others:

> And brought into the World a World of woe.

> . . . Begirt th' Almighty throne
> Beseeching or besieging . . .

> This tempted our Attempt . . .

> At one slight Bound high overleapt all Bound.

I know there are Figures for this Kind of Speech, that some of the greatest Antients have been guilty of it, and that *Aristotle* himself has given it a Place in his Rhetorick among the Beauties of that Art.[17] But as it is in itself poor and trifling, it is I think at present universally exploded by all the Masters of polite Writing.

The last Fault which I shall take notice of in *Milton*'s Stile, is the frequent Use of what the Learned call *Technical Words*, or Terms of Art. It is one of the great Beauties of Poetry, to make hard Things intelligible, and to deliver what is abstruse of it self in such easy Language as may be understood by ordinary Readers: Besides that the Knowledge of a Poet should rather seem born with him, or inspired, than drawn from Books and Systems. I have often wondered how Mr. *Dryden* could translate a Passage of *Virgil* after the following manner

> Tack to the Larboard, and stand off to Sea.
> Veer Star-board Sea and Land . . .

Milton makes use of *Larboard* in the same manner.[18] When he is upon Building he mentions *Doric Pillars*, *Pilasters*, *Cornice*, *Freeze*, *Architrave*. When he talks of Heavenly Bodies, you meet with °*Ecliptic*, and *Eccentric*, the °*Trepidation*, *Stars dropping from the Zenith*, *Rays culminating from the Equator*. To which might be added many Instances of the like Kind in several other Arts and Sciences.

I shall in my next Papers give an Account of the many particular Beauties in *Milton*, which would have been too long to insert under those general Heads I have already treated of, and with which I intend to conclude this Piece of Criticism.   L

V Politics and Public Affairs

No. 3 [ADDISON]

[The Bank of England: a vision][1]
Saturday, 3 March 1711

Quoi quisque ferè studio devinctus adhæret:
Aut quibus in rebus multùm sumus antè morati:
Atque in quà ratione fuit contenta magis mens;
In somnis eadem plerumque videmur obire.   Lucr. L. 4.[2]

In one of my late Rambles, or rather Speculations, I looked into
the great Hall where the Bank is kept, and was not a little pleased
to see the Directors, Secretaries, and Clerks, with all the other
Members of that wealthy Corporation, ranged in their several
Stations, according to the Parts they act in that just and regular
°Oeconomy. This revived in my Memory the many Discourses
which I had both read and heard concerning the Decay of Publick
Credit, with the Methods of restoring it, and which, in my
Opinion, have always been defective, because they have always
been made with an Eye to separate Interests, and Party Principles.

The Thoughts of the Day gave my Mind Employment for the
whole Night, so that I fell insensibly into a kind of Methodical
Dream, which disposed all my Contemplations into a Vision or
Allegory, or what else the Reader shall please to call it.

Methoughts I returned to the Great Hall, where I had been the
Morning before, but, to my Surprize, instead of the Company
that I left there, I saw towards the upper end of the Hall, a
beautiful Virgin, seated on a Throne of Gold. Her Name (as they
told me) was *Publick Credit*. The Walls, instead of being adorned
with Pictures and Maps, were hung with many Acts of Parliament
written in Golden Letters. At the Upper end of the Hall was the
Magna Charta, with the °Act of Uniformity on the right Hand,

and the °Act of Toleration on the left. At the Lower end of the
Hall was the °Act of Settlement, which was placed full in the Eye
of the Virgin that sat upon the Throne. Both the Sides of the
Hall were covered with such Acts of Parliament as had been made
for the Establishment of Publick Funds. The Lady seemed to set
an unspeakable Value upon these several Pieces of Furniture,
insomuch that she often refreshed her Eye with them, and often
smiled with a Secret Pleasure, as she looked upon them; but, at
the same time, showed a very particular Uneasiness, if she saw
any thing approaching that might hurt them. She appeared indeed
infinitely timorous in all her Behaviour: And, whether it was from
the Delicacy of her Constitution, or that she was troubled with
°Vapours, as I was afterwards told by one who I found was none of
her Well-wishers, she changed Colour, and startled at every thing
she heard. She was likewise (as I afterwards found) a greater
Valetudinarian than any I had ever met with, even in her own Sex,
and subject to such Momentary Consumptions, that in the
twinkling of an Eye, she would fall away from the most florid
Complexion, and the most healthful State of Body, and wither into
a Skeleton. Her Recoveries were often as sudden as her Decays,
insomuch that she would revive in a Moment out of a wasting
Distemper, into a Habit of the highest Health and Vigour.

I had very soon an Opportunity of observing these quick Turns
and Changes in her Constitution. There sat at her Feet a Couple
of Secretaries, who received every Hour Letters from all Parts of
the World, which the one or the other of them was perpetually
reading to her; and, according to the News she heard, to which
she was exceedingly attentive, she changed Colour, and discovered
many Symptoms of Health or Sickness.

Behind the Throne was a prodigious Heap of Bags of Mony,
which were piled upon one another so high that they touched the
Ceiling. The Floor, on her right Hand and on her left, was
covered with vast Sums of Gold that rose up in Pyramids on either
side of her: But this I did not so much wonder at, when I heard,
upon Enquiry, that she had the same Virtue in her Touch, which
the Poets tell us a °*Lydian* King was formerly possessed of; and

that she could convert whatever she pleased into that precious Metal.

After a little Dizziness, and confused Hurry of Thought, which a Man often meets with in a Dream, methoughts the Hall was alarmed, the Doors flew open, and there entered half a dozen of the most hideous Phantoms that I had ever seen (even in a Dream) before that Time. They came in two by two, though matched in the most dissociable Manner, and mingled together in a kind of Dance. It would be tedious to describe their Habits and Persons, for which Reason I shall only inform my Reader that the first Couple were Tyranny and Anarchy, the second were Bigotry and Atheism, the third the Genius of a Common-Wealth and a young Man of about twenty two Years of Age, whose Name I could not learn.[3] He had a Sword in his right Hand, which in the Dance he often brandished at the Act of Settlement; and a Citizen, who stood by me, whispered in my Ear, that he saw a Spunge in his left Hand.[3] The Dance of so many jarring Natures, put me in Mind of the Sun Moon and Earth, in the *Rehearsal*, that danced together for no other end but to eclipse one another.[4]

The Reader will easily suppose, by what has been before said, that the Lady on the Throne would have been almost frighted to Distraction, had she seen but any one of these Spectres; what then must have been her Condition when she saw them all in a Body? She fainted and dyed away at the Sight.

> *Et neq; jam color est misto candore rubori;*
> *Nec Vigor, & Vires, & quæ modo visa placebant;*
> *Nec Corpus remanet* – Ov. Met. Lib. 3.[5]

There was as great a Change in the Hill of Mony Bags, and the Heaps of Mony, the former shrinking, and falling into so many empty Bags, that I now found not above a tenth part of them had been filled with Mony. The rest that took up the same Space, and made the same Figure as the Bags that were really filled with Mony, had been blown up with Air, and called into my Memory the Bags full of Wind, which *Homer* tells us his Hero received as a Present from *Æolus*.[6] The great Heaps of Gold, on either side the Throne, now appeared to be only Heaps of Paper, or little Piles of notched Sticks,[7] bound up together in Bundles, like *Bath*-Faggots.

Whilst I was lamenting this sudden Desolation that had been made before me, the whole Scene vanished: In the Room of the frightful Spectres, there now entered a second Dance of Apparitions very agreeably matched together, and made up of very amiable Phantoms. The first Pair was Liberty with Monarchy at her right Hand: The second was Moderation leading in Religion; and the third a Person whom I had never seen,[8] with the Genius of *Great Britain*. At their first Entrance the Lady revived, the Bags swelled to their former Bulk, the Piles of Faggots and Heaps of Paper changed into Pyramids of Guineas: And for my own part I was so transported with Joy, that I awaked, tho', I must confess, I would fain have fallen asleep again to have closed my Vision, if I could have done it.   C

No. 50   [SWIFT and ADDISON]

[The Indian kings in London][1]
Friday, 27 April 1711
Nunquam aliud Natura, aliud Sapientia dixit.   Juv.[2]

When the four *Indian* Kings were in this Country about a Twelve-month ago, I often mixed with the Rabble, and followed them a whole Day together, being wonderfully struck with the Sight of every thing that is new or uncommon. I have, since their Departure, employed a Friend to make many Enquiries of their Landlord the Upholsterer, relating to their Manners and Conversation, as also concerning the Remarks which they made in this Country: For, next to the forming a right Notion of such Strangers, I should be desirous of learning what Ideas they have conceived of us.

The Upholsterer finding my Friend very inquisitive about these his Lodgers, brought him some time since a little Bundle of Papers, which he assured him were written by King *Sa Ga Yean Qua Rash Tow*, and, as he supposes, left behind by some mistake. These Papers are now translated, and contain abundance of very odd Observations, which I find this little Fraternity of Kings made during their Stay in the Isle of *Great Britain*. I shall present my Reader with a short Specimen of them in this Paper, and may, perhaps, communicate more to him hereafter. In the Article of *London* are the following Words, which without doubt are meant of the Church of St. *Paul*.

'On the most rising Part of the Town there stands a huge House, big enough to contain the whole Nation of which I am King. Our good Brother *E Tow O Koam*, King of the *Rivers*, is of Opinion it was made by the Hands of that great God to whom it is consecrated. The Kings of *Granajah* and of the *Six Nations* believe that it was created with the Earth, and produced on the same Day with the Sun and Moon. But for my own Part, by the best Information that I could get of this Matter, I am apt to think that this prodigious Pile was fashioned into the Shape it now bears by several Tools and Instruments, of which they have a wonderful Variety in this Country. It was probably at first an huge mis-shapen Rock that grew upon the Top of the Hill, which the Natives of the Country (after having cut it into a kind of regular Figure) bored and hollowed with incredible Pains and Industry, till they had wrought in it all those beautiful Vaults and Caverns into which it is divided at this Day. As soon as this Rock was thus curiously scooped to their Liking, a prodigious Number of Hands must have been employed in chipping the Outside of it, which is now as smooth as the Surface of a Pebble; and is in several Places hewn out into Pillars that stand like the Trunks of so many Trees bound about the Top with Garlands of Leaves. It is probable that when this great Work was begun, which must have been many Hundred Years ago, there was some Religion among this People; for they give it the Name of a Temple, and have a Tradition that it was designed for Men to pay their Devotions in. And indeed, there are several Reasons which make us think, that the Natives of this Country had formerly among them some sort of Worship; for they set apart every seventh Day as sacred: But upon my going into one of these holy Houses on that Day, I could not observe any Circumstance of Devotion in their Behaviour: There was indeed a Man in Black who was mounted above the rest, and seemed to utter something with a great deal of Vehemence; but as for those underneath him, instead of paying their Worship to the Deity of the Place, they were most

of them bowing and curtsying to one another, and a considerable
Number of them fast asleep.

'The Queen of the Country appointed two Men to Attend us,
that had enough of our Language to make themselves understood
in some few Particulars. But we soon perceived these two were
great Enemies to one another, and did not always agree in the
same Story. We could make a Shift to gather out of one of them,
that this Island was very much infested with a monstrous Kind of
Animals, in the Shape of Men, called *Whigs*; and he often told
us, that he hoped we should meet with none of them in our Way,
for that if we did, they would be apt to knock us down for being
Kings.

'Our other Interpreter used to talk very much of a kind of
Animal called a *Tory*, that was as great a Monster as the *Whig*,
and would treat us as ill for being Foreigners. These two Creatures,
it seems, are born with a secret Antipathy to one another, and
engage when they meet as naturally as the Elephant and the
Rhinoceros. But as we saw none of either of these Species, we are
apt to think that our Guides deceived us with Misrepresentations
and Fictions, and amused us with an Account of such Monsters
as are not really in their Country.

'These Particulars we made a Shift to pick out from the
Discourse of our Interpreters; which we put together as well as we
could, being able to understand but here and there a Word of
what they said, and afterwards making up the Meaning of it
among our selves. The Men of the Country are very cunning and
ingenious in handicraft Works; but withal so very idle, that we
often saw young lusty raw-boned Fellows carried up and down the
Streets in little covered Rooms by a Couple of Porters, who are
hired for that Service. Their Dress is likewise very barbarous, for
they almost strangle themselves about the Neck, and bind their
Bodies with many Ligatures, that we are apt to think are the
Occasion of several Distempers among them which our Country
is entirely free from. Instead of those beautiful Feathers with
which we adorn our Heads, they often buy up a monstrous Bush
of Hair, which covers their Heads, and falls down in a large Fleece
below the Middle of their Backs; with which they walk up and

down the Streets, and are as proud of it as if it was of their own
Growth.

'We were invited to one of their publick Diversions, where we
hoped to have seen the great Men of their Country running down
a Stag or pitching a Bar, that we might have discovered who were
the Persons of the greatest Abilities among them; but instead of
that, they conveyed us into an huge Room lighted up with
abundance of Candles, where this lazy People sate still above three
Hours to see several Feats of Ingenuity performed by others, who
it seems were paid for it.

'As for the Women of the Country, not being able to talk with
them, we could only make our Remarks upon them at a Distance.
They let the Hair of their Heads grow to a great Length; but as
the Men make a great Show with Heads of Hair that are none of
their own, the Women, who they say have very fine Heads of
Hair, tie it up in a Knot, and cover it from being seen. The
Women look like Angels, and would be more beautiful than the
Sun, were it not for little black Spots that are apt to break out in
their Faces, and sometimes rise in very odd Figures.[3] I have
observed that those little Blemishes wear off very soon; but when
they disappear in one Part of the Face, they are very apt to break
out in another, insomuch that I have seen a Spot upon the
Forehead in the Afternoon, which was upon the Chin in the
Morning.'

The Author then proceeds to shew the Absurdity of Breeches
and Petticoats, with many other curious Observations, which I
shall reserve for another Occasion. I cannot however conclude this
Paper without taking Notice, That amidst these wild Remarks
there now and then appears something very reasonable. I cannot
likewise forbear observing, That we are all guilty in some Measure
of the same narrow way of Thinking, which we meet with in this
Abstract of the *Indian* Journal; when we fancy the Customs,
Dresses, and Manners of other Countries are ridiculous and
extravagant, if they do not resemble those of our own.   C

No. 69 [ADDISON]

[The Royal Exchange][1]

Saturday, 19 May 1711

Hic segetes, illic veniunt felicius uvæ:
Arborei fætus alibi, atque injussa virescunt
Gramina. Nonne vides, croceos ut Tmolus odores,
India mittit ebur, molles sua thura Sabæi?
At Chalybes nudi ferrum, virosaque Pontus
Castorea, Eliadum palmas Epirus equarum?
Continuo has leges æternaque fœdera certis
Imposuit Natura locis —   Vir.[2]

There is no Place in the Town which I so much love to frequent as the *Royal Exchange*. It gives me a secret Satisfaction, and, in some measure, gratifies my Vanity, as I am an *Englishman*, to see so rich an Assembly of Country-men and Foreigners consulting together upon the private Business of Mankind, and making this Metropolis a kind of *Emporium* for the whole Earth. I must confess I look upon °High-Change to be a great Council, in which all considerable Nations have their Representatives. °Factors in the Trading World are what Ambassadors are in the Politick World; they negotiate Affairs, conclude Treaties, and maintain a good Correspondence between those wealthy Societies of Men that are divided from one another by Seas and Oceans, or live on the different Extremities of a Continent. I have often been pleased to hear Disputes adjusted between an Inhabitant of *Japan* and an Alderman of *London*, or to see a Subject of the *Great Mogul* entering into a League with one of the *Czar* of *Muscovy*. I am infinitely delighted in mixing with these several Ministers of Commerce, as they are distinguished by their different Walks and different Languages: Sometimes I am justled among a Body of *Armenians*: Sometimes I am lost in a Crowd of *Jews*; and sometimes make one in a Groupe of *Dutch-men*. I am a *Dane*, *Swede*, or *French-man* at different times, or rather fancy my self like the old Philosopher, who upon being asked what Country-man he was, replied, That he was a Citizen of the World.[3]

Though I very frequently visit this busie Multitude of People, I am known to no Body there but my Friend Sir ANDREW, who often smiles upon me as he sees me bustling in the Croud, but at the same time connives at my Presence without taking any further Notice of me. There is indeed a Merchant of *Egypt*, who just knows me by sight, having formerly remitted me some Mony to *Grand Cairo*;[4] but as I am not versed in the Modern *Coptick*, our Conferences go no further than a Bow and a °Grimace.

This grand Scene of Business gives me an infinite Variety of solid and substantial Entertainments. As I am a great Lover of Mankind, my Heart naturally overflows with Pleasure at the sight of a prosperous and happy Multitude, insomuch that at many publick Solemnities I cannot forbear expressing my Joy with Tears that have stoln down my Cheeks. For this reason I am wonderfully delighted to see such a Body of Men thriving in their own private Fortunes, and at the same time promoting the Publick Stock; or in other Words, raising Estates for their own Families, by bringing into their Country whatever is wanting, and carrying out of it whatever is superfluous.

Nature seems to have taken a particular Care to disseminate her Blessings among the different Regions of the World, with an Eye to this mutual Intercourse and Traffick among Mankind, that the Natives of the several Parts of the Globe might have a kind of Dependance upon one another, and be united together by their common Interest. Almost every *Degree* produces something peculiar to it. The Food often grows in one Country, and the Sauce in another. The Fruits of *Portugal* are corrected by the Products of *Barbadoes*: The Infusion of a *China* Plant sweetned with the Pith of an *Indian* Cane: The °*Philippick* Islands give a Flavour to our *European* Bowls. The single Dress of a Woman of Quality is often the Product of an hundred Climates. The Muff and the Fan come together from the different Ends of the Earth. The Scarf is sent from the Torrid Zone, and the Tippet from beneath the Pole. The Brocade Petticoat rises out of the Mines of *Peru*, and the Diamond Necklace out of the Bowels of *Indostan*.

If we consider our own Country in its natural Prospect, without any of the Benefits and Advantages of Commerce, what a barren uncomfortable Spot of Earth falls to our Share! Natural Historians tell us, that no Fruit grows originally among us, besides Hips and Haws, Acorns and Pig-Nutts, with other Delicacies of the like Nature; That our Climate of itself, and without the Assistances of

Art, can make no further Advances towards a Plumb than to a Sloe, and carries an Apple to no greater a Perfection than a Crab: That our Melons, our Peaches, our Figs, our Apricots, and Cherries, are Strangers among us, imported in different Ages, and naturalized in our *English* Gardens; and that they would all degenerate and fall away into the Trash of our own Country, if they were wholly neglected by the Planter, and left to the Mercy of our Sun and Soil. Nor has Traffick more enriched our Vegetable World, than it has improved the whole Face of Nature among us. Our Ships are laden with the Harvest of every Climate: Our Tables are stored with Spices, and Oils, and Wines: Our Rooms are filled with Pyramids of *China*, and adorned with the Workmanship of *Japan*: Our Morning's-Draught comes to us from the remotest Corners of the Earth: We repair our Bodies by the Drugs of *America*, and repose our selves under *Indian* Canopies. My friend Sir ANDREW calls the Vineyards of *France* our Gardens; the Spice-Islands our Hot-Beds; the *Persians* our Silk-Weavers, and the *Chinese* our Potters. Nature indeed furnishes us with the bare Necessaries of Life, but Traffick gives us a great Variety of what is Useful, and at the same time supplies us with every thing that is Convenient and Ornamental. Nor is it the least Part of this our Happiness, that whilst we enjoy the remotest Products of the North and South, we are free from those Extremities of Weather which give them Birth; That our Eyes are refreshed with the green Fields of *Britain*, at the same time that our Palates are feasted with Fruits that rise between the Tropicks.

For these Reasons there are not more useful Members in a Commonwealth than Merchants. They knit Mankind together in a mutual Intercourse of good Offices, distribute the Gifts of Nature, find Work for the Poor, add Wealth to the Rich, and Magnificence to the Great. Our *English* Merchant converts the Tin of his own Country into Gold, and exchanges his Wooll for Rubies. The *Mahometans* are cloathed in our *British* Manufacture, and the Inhabitants of the Frozen Zone warmed with the Fleeces of our Sheep.

When I have been upon the *'Change*, I have often fancied one of our old Kings standing in Person, where he is represented in Effigy, and looking down upon the wealthy Concourse of People with which that Place is every Day filled. In this Case, how would he be surprized to hear all the Languages of *Europe* spoken in this little Spot of his former Dominions, and to see so many private Men, who in his Time would have been the Vassals of some powerful Baron, Negotiating like Princes for greater Sums of Mony than were formerly to be met with in the Royal Treasury! Trade, without enlarging the *British* Territories, has given us a kind of additional Empire: It has multiplied the Number of the Rich, made our Landed Estates infinitely more Valuable than they were formerly, and added to them an Accession of other Estates as Valuable as the Lands themselves.   C

No. 81 [ADDISON]

[Party among women]
Saturday, 2 June 1711

Qualis ubi audito venantum murmure Tigris
Horruit in maculas —   Statius.[1]

About the middle of last Winter I went to see an *Opera* at the Theatre in the *Hay-Market*, where I could not but take notice of two Parties of very Fine Women, that had placed themselves in the opposite °Side-Boxes,[2] and seemed drawn up in a kind of Battle-Array one against another. After a short Survey of them, I found they were *Patched* differently; the Faces, on one Hand, being Spotted on the Right Side of the Forehead, and those upon the other on the Left. I quickly perceived that they cast Hostile Glances upon one another; and that their Patches were placed in those different Situations, as Party-Signals to distinguish Friends from Foes.[3] In the Middle-Boxes, between these two opposite Bodies, were several Ladies who Patched indifferently on both sides of their Faces, and seemed to sit there with no other Intention but to see the *Opera*. Upon Enquiry I found, that the Body of *Amazons* on my Right Hand, were Whigs; and those on my Left, Tories; and that those who had placed themselves in the Middle-Boxes were a Neutral Party, whose Faces had not yet declared themselves. These last, however, as I afterwards found, diminished daily, and took their Party with one Side or the other; insomuch that I observed in several of them, the Patches which were before dispersed equally, are now all gone over to the Whig or Tory Side of the Face. The Censorious say, That the Men whose Hearts are aimed at are very often the Occasions that one part of the Face is thus Dishonoured, and lyes under a kind of Disgrace, while the other is so much Set off and Adorned by the Owner; and that the Patches turn to the Right or to the Left, according to the Principles of the Man who is most in Favour. But whatever may be the Motives of a few Fantastical Coquets, who do not Patch for the Publick Good, so much as for their own Private Advantage; it is certain, that there are several Women of Honour who Patch out of Principle, and with an Eye to the Interest of their Country. Nay, I am informed, that some of them adhere so stedfastly to their Party, and are so far from Sacrificing their Zeal for the Publick to their Passion for any particular Person, that in a late Draught of Marriage-Articles a Lady has stipulated with her Husband, That, whatever his Opinions are, she shall be at Liberty to Patch on which side she pleases.

I must here take notice, that *Rosalinda*, a Famous Whig Partizan, has most unfortunately a very beautiful Mole on the Tory part of her Forehead; which, being very conspicuous, has occasioned many Mistakes, and given an Handle to her Enemies to misrepresent her Face, as though it had Revolted from the Whig Interest. But whatever this natural Patch may seem to intimate, it is well known that her Notions of Government are still the same. This unlucky Mole however has mis-led several Coxcombs; and, like the hanging out of false Colours, made some of them converse with *Rosalinda* in what they thought the Spirit of her Party, when on a sudden she has given them an unexpected Fire, that has sunk them all at once. If *Rosalinda* is unfortunate in her Mole, *Nigranilla* is as unhappy in a Pimple, which forces her, against her Inclinations, to Patch on the Whig side.

I am told that many Virtuous Matrons, who formerly have been taught to believe that this Artificial Spotting of the Face was unlawful, are now reconciled by a Zeal for their Cause, to what they could not be prompted by a Concern for their Beauty. This way of declaring War upon one another, puts me in mind of what is reported of the Tigress, that several Spots rise in her Skin when she is angry; or as Mr. *Cowley* has imitated the Verses that stand as the Motto of this Paper,

> *— She Swells with angry Pride,*
> *And calls forth all her Spots on ev'ry side.* [4]

When I was in the Theatre the time above-mentioned, I had the Curiosity to count the Patches on both Sides, and found the Tory Patches to be about twenty Stronger than the Whig; but to make amends for this small Inequality, I the next Morning found the whole Puppet-show filled with Faces spotted after the Whiggish manner. Whether or no the Ladies had retreated hither in order to rally their Forces I cannot tell; but the next Night they came in so great a Body to the Opera, that they outnumbered the Enemy.

This Account of Party-Patches will, I am afraid, appear improbable to those who live at a distance from the fashionable World; but as it is a Distinction of a very singular Nature, and what perhaps may never meet with a Parallel, I think I should not have discharged the Office of a faithful Spectator had I not recorded it.

I have, in former Papers, endeavoured to expose this Party-Rage in Women, as it only serves to aggravate the Hatreds and Animosities that reign among Men, and in a great measure deprives the Fair Sex of those peculiar Charms with which Nature has endowed them.

When the *Romans* and *Sabines* were at War, and just upon the point of giving Battle, the Women, who were allied to both of them, interposed with so many Tears and Intreaties, that they prevented the mutual Slaughter which threatned both Parties, and united them together in a firm and lasting Peace.

I would recommend this noble Example to our *British* Ladies, at a time when their Country is torn with so many unnatural Divisions, that if they continue, it will be a Misfortune to be born in it. The *Greeks* thought it so improper for Women to interest themselves in Competitions and Contentions, that for this Reason, among others, they forbad them, under Pain of Death, to be present at the *Olympick* Games, notwithstanding these were the Publick Diversions of all *Greece*.

As our *English* Women excel those of all Nations in Beauty, they should endeavour to outshine them in all other Accomplishments proper to the Sex, and to distinguish themselves as tender Mothers and faithful Wives, rather than as furious Partizans. Female Virtues are of a Domestick turn. The Family is the proper Province for Private Women to Shine in. If they must be showing their Zeal for the Publick, let it not be against those who are perhaps of the same Family, or at least of the same Religion or Nation, but against those who are the open, professed, undoubted Enemies of their Faith, Liberty, and Country. When the *Romans* were pressed with a Foreign Enemy, the Ladies voluntarily contributed all their Rings and Jewels to assist the Government under a publick Exigence; which appeared so laudable an Action in the Eyes of their Countrymen, that from thenceforth it was permitted by a Law to pronounce publick Orations at the Funeral of a Woman in Praise of the deceased Person, which till that time was peculiar to Men. Would our *English* Ladies, instead of sticking on a patch against those of their own Country, shew themselves so truly Publick-spirited as to Sacrifice every one her Necklace against the Common Enemy, what Decrees ought not to be made in favour of them?

Since I am recollecting upon this Subject such Passages as occur to my Memory out of ancient Authors, I cannot omit a Sentence in the Celebrated Funeral Oration of *Pericles*,[5] which he made in Honour of those Brave *Athenians* that were Slain in a Fight with the *Lacedemonians*. After having addressed himself to the several Ranks and Orders of his Countrymen, and shewn them how they should behave themselves in the Publick Cause, he turns to the Female part of his Audience; 'And as for you (says he) I shall advise you in very few Words: Aspire only to those Virtues that are peculiar to your Sex; follow your natural Modesty, and think it your greatest Commendation not to be talked of one way or other.'   C

No. 125 [ADDISON]

[The rage of party]
Tuesday, 24 July 1711

Ne pueri, ne tanta animis assuescite bella:
Neu patriæ validas in viscera vertite vires.   Vir.[1]

My worthy Friend Sir ROGER, when we are talking of the Malice of Parties, very frequently tells us an Accident that happened to him when he was a School-Boy, which was at the Time when the

Feuds ran high between the Round-heads and Cavaliers. This worthy Knight being then but a Strippling, had Occasion to enquire which was the Way to St. *Anne's* Lane,[2] upon which the Person whom he spoke to, instead of answering his Question, called him a young Popish Cur, and asked him who had made *Anne* a Saint? The Boy being in some Confusion, enquired of the next he met, which was the Way to *Anne's* Lane; but was called a Prick-eared Cur for his Pains, and instead of being shewn the Way, was told, that she had been a Saint before he was born, and would be one after he was hanged. Upon this, says Sir ROGER, I did not think fit to repeat the former Question, but going into every Lane of the Neighbourhood, asked what they called the Name of that Lane. By which ingenious Artifice he found out the Place he enquired after, without giving Offence to any Party. Sir ROGER, generally closes this Narrative with Reflections on the Mischief that Parties do in the Country; how they spoil good Neighbourhood, and make honest Gentlemen hate one another; besides that they manifestly tend to the Prejudice of the Land-Tax, and the Destruction of the Game.

There cannot a greater Judgment befall a Country than such a dreadful Spirit of Division as rends a Government into two distinct People, and makes them greater Strangers and more averse to one another, than if they were actually two different Nations. The Effects of such a Division are pernicious to the last degree, not only with Regard to those Advantages which they give the Common Enemy, but to those private Evils which they produce in the Heart of almost every particular Person. This Influence is very fatal both to Mens Morals and their Understandings; It sinks the Virtue of a Nation, and not only so, but destroys even Common Sense.

A furious Party-Spirit, when it rages in its full Violence, exerts it self in Civil War and Bloodshed; and when it is under its greatest Restraints naturally breaks out in Falshood, Detraction, Calumny, and a partial Administration of Justice. In a Word, It fills a Nation with Spleen and Rancour, and extinguishes all the Seeds of Good-Nature, Compassion and Humanity.

Plutarch says very finely,[3] That a Man should not allow himself to hate even his Enemies, because, says he, if you indulge this Passion in some Occasions, it will rise of it self in others; if you hate your Enemies, you will contract such a vicious Habit of Mind, as by Degrees will break out upon those who are your Friends, or those who are indifferent to you. I might here observe how admirably this Precept of Morality (which derives the Malignity of Hatred from the Passion it self, and not from its Object) answers to that great Rule which was dictated to the World about an Hundred Years before this Philosopher wrote;[4] but instead of that, I shall only take notice, with a real Grief of Heart, that the Minds of many good Men among us appear sowered with Party-Principles, and alienated from one another in such a manner, as seems to me altogether inconsistent with the Dictates either of Reason or Religion. Zeal for a Publick Cause is apt to breed Passions in the Hearts of virtuous Persons, to which the Regard of their own private Interest would never have betrayed them.

If this Party-Spirit has so ill an Effect on our Morals, it has likewise a very great one upon our Judgments. We often hear a poor insipid Paper or Pamphlet cryed up, and sometimes a noble Piece depreciated, by those who are of a different Principle from the Author. One who is actuated by this Spirit is almost under an Incapacity of discerning either real Blemishes or Beauties. A Man of Merit in a different Principle, is like an Object seen in two different Mediums, that appears crooked or broken, however streight and entire it may be in it self. For this Reason there is scarce a Person of any Figure in *England* who does not go by two contrary Characters, as opposite to one another as Light and Darkness. Knowledge and Learning suffer in a particular manner from this strange Prejudice, which at present prevails amongst all Ranks and Degrees in the *British* Nation. As Men formerly became eminent in learned Societies by their Parts and Acquisitions, they now distinguish themselves by the Warmth and Violence with which they espouse their respective Parties. Books are valued upon the like Considerations: An Abusive Scurrilous Style passes for Satyr, and a dull Scheme of Party-Notions is called fine Writing.

There is one Piece of Sophistry practised by both Sides, and that is the taking any scandalous Story that has been ever whispered or invented of a private Man, for a known undoubted Truth, and raising suitable Speculations upon it. Calumnies that have been never proved, or have been often refuted, are the ordinary

Postulatums of these infamous Scribblers, upon which they proceed as upon first Principles granted by all Men, though in their Hearts they know they are false, or at best very doubtful. When they have laid these Foundations of Scurrility, it is no wonder that their Superstructure is every way answerable to them. If this shameless Practice of the present Age endures much longer, Praise and Reproach will cease to be Motives of Action in good Men.

There are certain Periods of Time in all Governments when this inhuman Spirit prevails. *Italy* was long torn in pieces by the °*Guelfes* and *Gibellines*, and *France* by those who were for and against the °League: But it is very unhappy for a Man to be born in such a stormy and tempestuous Season. It is the restless Ambition of Artful Men that thus breaks a People into Factions, and draws several well-meaning Persons to their Interest by a Specious Concern for their Country. How many honest Minds are filled with uncharitable and barbarous Notions, out of their Zeal for the Publick Good? What Cruelties and Outrages would they not commit against Men of an adverse Party, whom they would honour and esteem, if instead of considering them as they are represented, they knew them as they are? Thus are Persons of the greatest Probity seduced into shameful Errors and Prejudices, and made bad Men even by that noblest of Principles, the Love of their Country. I cannot here forbear mentioning the Famous *Spanish* Proverb, *If there were neither Fools, nor Knaves in the World, all People would be of one Mind.*

For my own part, I could heartily wish that all Honest Men would enter into an Association, for the Support of one another against the Endeavours of those whom they ought to look upon as their Common Enemies, whatsoever side they may belong to. Were there such an honest Body of Neutral Forces, we should never see the worst of Men in great Figures of Life, because they are useful to a Party; nor the best unregarded, because they are above practising those Methods which would be grateful to their Faction. We should then single every Criminal out of the Herd, and hunt him down, however formidable and overgrown he might appear: On the contrary, we should shelter distressed Innocence, and defend Virtue, however beset with Contempt or Ridicule, Envy or Defamation. In short, we should not any longer regard our Fellow-

Subjects as Whigs or Tories, but should make the Man of Merit our Friend, and the Villain our Enemy.   C

No. 174 [STEELE]

[Sir Andrew Freeport defends commerce]

Wednesday, 19 September 1711

Hæc memini & victum frustra contendere Thyrsin.   Virg.[1]

There is scarce any thing more common than Animosities between Parties that cannot subsist but by their Agreement: This was well represented in the Sedition of the Members of the human Body in the old *Roman* Fable.[2] It is often the Case of lesser confederate States against a superior Power, which are hardly held together though their Unanimity is necessary for their common Safety: And this is always the Case of the landed and trading Interest of *Great Britain*; the Trader is fed by the Product of the Land, and the landed Man cannot be cloathed but by the Skill of the Trader; and yet those Interests are ever jarring.

We had last Winter an Instance of this at our Club, in Sir ROGER DE COVERLY and Sir ANDREW FREEPORT, between whom there is generally a constant, though friendly, Opposition of Opinions. It happened that one of the Company, in an historical Discourse, was observing, that *Carthaginian* Faith was a proverbial Phrase to intimate Breach of Leagues.[3] Sir ROGER said it could hardly be otherwise: That the *Carthaginians* were the greatest Traders in the World; and as Gain is the chief End of such a People, they never pursue any other: The Means to it are never regarded; they will, if it comes easily, get Money honestly; but if not, they will not scruple to attain it by Fraud or Cosenage: And indeed what is the whole Business of the Trader's Accompt, but to over-reach him who trusts to his Memory? But were that not so, what can there great and noble be expected from him whose Attention is for ever fixed upon ballancing his Books, and watching over his Expences? And at best, let Frugality and Parsimony be the Virtues of the Merchant, how much is his punctual Dealing below a Gentleman's Charity to the Poor, or Hospitality among his Neighbours?

Captain SENTRY observed Sir ANDREW very diligent in hearing Sir ROGER, and had a Mind to turn the Discourse, by taking Notice in general from the highest to the lowest Parts of humane Society, there was a secret, tho' unjust Way among Men, of indulging the Seeds of Ill-nature and Envy, by comparing their own State of Life to that of another, and grudging the Approach of their Neighbour to their own Happiness; and on the other Side, he who is the less at his Ease repines at the other who, he thinks, has unjustly the Advantage over him. Thus the civil and military List look upon each other with much Ill-nature; the Soldier repines at the Courtier's Power, and the Courtier rallies the Soldier's Honour; or to come to lower Instances, the private Men in the Horse and Foot of an Army, the °Carmen and Coachmen in the City-streets, mutually look upon each other with Ill-will, when they are in Competition for Quarters or the Way in their respective Motions.

It is very well, good Captain, interrupted Sir ANDREW: You may attempt to turn the Discourse, if you think fit, but I must however have a Word or two with Sir ROGER; who, I see, thinks he has paid me off, and been very severe upon the Merchant. I shall not, continued he, at this Time remind Sir ROGER of the great and noble Monuments of Charity and publick Spirit which have been erected by Merchants since the Reformation, but at present content my self with what he allows us, Parsimony and Frugality. If it were consistent with the Quality of so antient a Baronet as Sir ROGER, to keep an Accompt or measure things by the most infallible Way, that of Numbers, he would prefer our Parsimony to his Hospitality. If to drink so many Hogsheads is to be hospitable, we do not contend for the Fame of that Virtue; but it would be worth while to consider, whether so many Artificers at work ten Days together by my Appointment, or so many Peasants made merry on Sir ROGER's Charge, are the Men more obliged: I believe the Families of the Artificers will thank me, more than the Housholds of the Peasants shall Sir ROGER. Sir ROGER gives to his Men, but I place mine above the Necessity or Obligation of my Bounty. I am in very little Pain for the *Roman* Proverb upon the *Carthaginian* Traders; the *Romans* were their professed Enemies: I am only sorry no *Carthaginian* Histories have come to our Hands; we might have been taught perhaps by them some Proverbs against the *Roman*

Generosity, in fighting for and bestowing other People's Goods. But since Sir ROGER has taken Occasion from an old Proverb to be out of Humour with Merchants, it should be no Offence to offer one not quite so old in their Defence. When a Man happens to °break in *Holland*, they say of him that *he has not kept true Accompts*. This Phrase, perhaps, among us would appear a soft or humorous way of speaking, but with that exact Nation it bears the highest Reproach; for a Man to be mistaken in the Calculation of his Expence, in his Ability to answer future Demands, or to be impertinently sanguine in putting his Credit to too great Adventure, are all Instances of as much Infamy, as with gayer Nations to be failing in Courage or common Honesty.

Numbers are so much the Measure of every thing that is valuable, that it is not possible to demonstrate the Success of any Action, or the Prudence of any Undertaking, without them. I say this in Answer to what Sir ROGER is pleased to say, That little that is truly noble can be expected from one who is ever poring on his Cash-book or ballancing his Accompts. When I have my Returns from Abroad, I can tell to a Shilling by the Help of Numbers the Profit or Loss by my Adventure; but I ought also to be able to shew that I had Reason for making it, either from my own Experience or that of other People, or from a reasonable Presumption that my Returns will be sufficient to answer my Expence and Hazard; and this is never to be done without the Skill of Numbers. For Instance, if I am to trade to *Turkey*, I ought beforehand to know the Demand of our Manufactures there as well as of their Silks in *England*, and the customary Prices that are given for both in each Country. I ought to have a clear Knowledge of these Matters before-hand, that I may presume upon sufficient Returns to answer the Charge of the Cargo I have fitted out, the Freight and Assurance out and home, the Customs to the Queen, and the Interest of my own Money, and besides all these Expences a reasonable Profit to my self. Now what is there of Scandal in this Skill? What has the Merchant done that he should be so little in the good Graces of Sir ROGER? he throws down no Man's Enclosures, and tramples upon no Man's Corn; he takes nothing from the industrious Labourer; he pays the poor Man for his Work; he communicates his Profit with Mankind; by the Preparation of his Cargo and the Manufacture of his Returns, he furnishes Employment and Subsistence to greater Numbers than the richest Nobleman; and even the Nobleman is obliged to him for finding out foreign Markets for the Produce of his Estate, and for making a great Addition to his Rents; and yet 'tis certain that none of all these Things could be done by him without the Exercise of his Skill in Numbers.

This is the °Oeconomy of the Merchant, and the Conduct of the Gentleman must be the same, unless by scorning to be the Steward, he resolves the Steward shall be the Gentleman. The Gentleman no more than the Merchant is able without the Help of Numbers to account for the Success of any Action, or the Prudence of any Adventure. If, for Instance, the Chace is his whole Adventure, his only Returns must be the Stag's Horns in the great Hall, and the Fox's Nose upon the Stable Door. Without Doubt Sir ROGER knows the full Value of these Returns; and if before-hand he had computed the Charges of the Chace, a Gentleman of his Discretion would certainly have hanged up all his Dogs, he would never have brought back so many fine Horses to the Kennel, he would never have gone so often like a Blast over Fields of Corn. If such too had been the Conduct of all his Ancestors, he might truly have boasted at this Day that the Antiquity of his Family had never been sullied by a Trade; a Merchant had never been permitted with his whole Estate to purchase a Room for his Picture in the Gallery of the COVERLYS, or to claim his Descent from the Maid of Honour.[4] But 'tis very happy for Sir ROGER that the Merchant paid so dear for his Ambition. 'Tis the Misfortune of many other Gentlemen to turn out of the Seats of their Ancestors, to make Way for such new Masters as have been more exact in their Accompts than themselves; and certainly he deserves the Estate a great deal better who has got it by his Industry, than he who has lost it by his Negligence.   T

No. 232 [?]¹

[The economics of charity]
Monday, 26 November 1711
Nihil largiundo gloriam adeptus est.   Sallust.²

My wise and good Friend Sir ANDREW FREEPORT divides himself almost equally between the Town and the Country: His Time in Town is given up to the Publick and the Management of his private Fortune; and after every three or four Days spent in this Manner, he retires for as many to his Seat within a few Miles of the Town, to the Enjoyment of himself, his Family, and his Friend. Thus Business and Pleasure, or rather, in Sir ANDREW, Labour and Rest, recommend each other: They take their Turns with so quick a Vicissitude, that neither becomes a Habit, or takes Possession of the whole Man; nor is it possible he should be surfeited with either. I often see him at our Club in good Humour, and yet sometimes too with an Air of Care in his Looks: But in his Country Retreat he is always unbent, and such a Companion as I could desire; and therefore I seldom fail to make one with him when he is pleased to invite me.

The other Day, as soon as we were got into his °Chariot, two or three Beggars on each side hung upon the Doors, and sollicited our Charity with the usual Rhetoric of a sick Wife or Husband at Home, three or four helpless little Children all starving with Cold and Hunger. We were forced to part with some Money to get rid of their Importunity; and then we proceeded on our Journey with the Blessings and Acclamations of these People.

'Well then, says Sir ANDREW, we go off with the Prayers and good Wishes of the Beggars, and perhaps too our Healths will be [drunk] at the next Ale-House: So all we shall be able to value our selves upon, is, that we have promoted the Trade of the Victualler, and the Excises of the Government. But how few Ounces of Wooll do we see upon the Backs of those poor Creatures? And when they shall next fall in our Way, they will hardly be better drest; they must always live in Rags to look like Objects of Compassion. If their Families too are such as they are represented, 'tis certain they cannot be better cloathed, and must be a great deal worse fed: One would think Potatoes should be all their Bread, and their Drink the pure Element; and then what goodly Customers are the Farmers like to have for their Wooll, Corn and Cattel? Such Customers and such a Consumption cannot chuse but advance the landed interest, and hold up the Rents of the Gentlemen.

'But of all Men living, we Merchants, who live by Buying and Selling, ought never to encourage Beggars. The Goods which we export are indeed the Product of the Lands, but much the greatest Part of their Value is the Labour of the People: But how much of these Peoples Labour shall we export, whilst we hire them to sit still? The very Alms they receive from us, are the Wages of Idleness. I have often thought that no Man should be permitted to take Relief from the Parish, or to ask it in the Street, till he has first purchased as much as possible of his own Livelihood by the Labour of his own Hands; and then the Publick ought only to be taxed to make good the Deficiency. If this Rule was strictly observed, we should see every where such a Multitude of new Labourers, as would in all Probability reduce the Prices of all our Manufactures. It is the very Life of Merchandise to buy cheap and sell dear. The Merchant ought to make his °Out-set as cheap as possible, that he may find the greater Profit upon his Returns; and nothing will enable him to do this like the reduction of the Price of Labour upon all our Manufactures. This too would be the ready Way to increase the Number of our foreign Markets: The Abatement of the Price of the Manufacture would pay for the Carriage of it to more distant Countries; and this Consequence would be equally beneficial both to the landed and trading Interests. As so great an Addition of labouring Hands would produce this happy Consequence both to the Merchant and the Gentleman; our Liberality to common Beggars, and every other Obstruction to the Increase of Labourers, must be equally pernicious to both.'

Sir ANDREW then went on to affirm, That the Reduction of the Prices of our Manufactures by the Addition of so many new Hands, would be no Inconvenience to any Man: But observing I was something startled at the Assertion, he made a short Pause, and then resumed the Discourse. 'It may seem, says he, a Paradox, that the Price of Labour should be reduced without an Abatement of Wages, or that Wages can be abated without any Inconvenience to the Labourer; and yet nothing is more certain than that both those things may happen. The Wages of the Labourers make the greatest Part of the Price of every thing that is useful; and if in Proportion with the wages the Prices of all other things shall be abated, every Labourer with less Wages would be still able to purchase as many Necessaries of Life, where then would be the Inconvenience? But the Price of Labour may be reduced by the Addition of more Hands to a Manufacture, and yet the Wages of Persons remain as high as ever. The admirable Sir *William Petty* has given Examples of this in some of his Writings: One of them, as I remember, is that of a Watch, which I shall endeavour to explain so as shall suit my present Purpose.[3] It is certain that a single Watch could not be made so cheap in Proportion by one only Man, as a hundred Watches by a hundred; for as there is vast Variety in the Work, no one Person could equally suit himself to all the Parts of it; the Manufacture would be tedious, and at last but clumsily performed: But if an hundred Watches were to be made by a hundred Men, the Cases may be assigned to one, the Dials to another, the Wheels to another, the Springs to another, and every other Part to a proper °Artist; as there would be no need of perplexing any one Person with too much Variety, every one would be able to perform his single Part with greater Skill and Expedition; and the hundred Watches would be finished in one fourth Part of the Time of the first one, and every one of them at one-fourth Part of the Cost, though the wages of every Man were equal. The Reduction of the Price of the Manufacture would increase the Demand of it, all the same Hands would be still employed and as well paid. The same Rule will hold in the Cloathing, the Shipping, and all the other Trades whatsoever. And thus an Addition of Hands to our Manufactures will only reduce the Price of them; the Labourer will still have as much Wages, and will consequently be enabled to purchase more Conveniences of Life; so that every Interest in the Nation would receive a Benefit from an Increase of our working People.

'Besides, I see no Occasion for this Charity to common Beggars, since every Beggar is an Inhabitant of a Parish, and every Parish is taxed to the Maintenance of their own Poor.[4] For my own Part, I cannot be mightily pleased with the Laws which have done this, which have provided better to feed than employ the Poor. We have a Tradition from our Forefathers, that after the first of those Laws was made, they were insulted with that famous Song,

> *Hang Sorrow, and cast away Care,*
> *The Parish is bound to find us*, &c.

And if we will be so good-natured as to maintain them without Work, they can do no less in Return than sing us *The merry Beggars*.[5]

'What then? am I against all Acts of Charity? God forbid! I know of no Virtue in the Gospel that is in more pathetical Expressions recommended to our Practice. *I was hungry and* [ye] *gave me no Meat, thirsty and* [ye] *gave me no Drink; naked and* [ye] *cloathed me not, a Stranger and* [ye] *took me not in; sick and in Prison, and* [ye] *visited me not*.[6] Our Blessed Saviour treats the Exercise or Neglect of Charity towards a poor Man, as the Performance or Breach of this Duty towards himself. I shall endeavour to obey the Will of my Lord and Master. And therefore if an industrious Man shall submit to the hardest Labour and coarsest Fare, rather than endure the Shame of taking Relief from the Parish or asking it in the Street, this is the Hungry, the Thirsty, the Naked; and I ought to believe if any Man is come hither for Shelter against Persecution or Oppression, this is the Stranger, and I ought to take him in. If any Countryman of our own is fallen into the Hands of Infidels, and lives in a State of miserable Captivity, this is the Man in Prison, and I should contribute to his Ransom. I ought to give to an Hospital of Invalids, to recover as many useful Subjects as I can; but I shall bestow none of my Bounties upon an Alms-house of idle People; and for the same Reason I should not think it a Reproach to me if I had with-held my Charity from those common Beggars. But we prescribe better Rules than we are able to practise; we are ashamed not to give into the mistaken Customs of our Country: But at the same Time I cannot but think it a Reproach worse than that of common Swearing, that the Idle and the Abandoned are suffered in the Name of Heaven and all that is sacred, to extort from christian and tender Minds a Supply to a profligate Way of Life, that is always to be supported but never relieved.   Z

No. 384 [STEELE and FLEETWOOD]

[A bold stroke in the party war][1]
Wednesday, 21 May 1712

Hague, May 24. °N. S. The same Republican Hands, who have so often since the Chevalier de St. George's Recovery, killed him in our publick Prints, have now reduced the young Dauphin of France to that desperate Condition of Weakness, and Death it self, that it is hard to conjecture what Method they will take to bring him to Life again. Mean time we are assured by a very good Hand from Paris, That on the 20th Instant this young Prince was as well as ever he was known to be since the Day of his Birth. As for the other, they are now sending his Ghost, we suppose, (for they never had the Modesty to contradict their Assertions of his Death) to Commerci in Lorrain, attended only by four Gentlemen, and a few Domesticks of little Consideration. [. . .] The Baron *de Bothmar* having delivered in his Credentials, to qualify him as an Ambassador to this State, (an *Office* to which his greatest Enemies will acknowledge him to be *equal*) is gone to *Utrecht*, whence he will proceed to *Hanover*, but not stay long at that Court, for fear the Peace should be made during his *lamented* Absence.   °*Post-Boy*, May 20.[2]

I should be thought not able to read, should I overlook some excellent Pieces lately come out. My Lord Bishop of St. Asaph has just now published some Sermons, the Preface to which seems to me to determine a great Point. He has, like a good Man and a good Christian, in Opposition to all the Flattery and base Submission of false Friends to Princes, asserted, That Christianity left us where it found us as to our Civil Rights. The present Entertainment shall consist only of a Sentence out of the °Post-Boy, and the said Preface of the Lord of St. Asaph. I should think it a little odd if the Author of the Post-Boy should with Impunity call Men Republicans for a Gladness on Report of the Death of the Pretender; and treat Baron Bothmar, the Minister of Hanover, in such a manner as you see in my Motto. I must own, I think every Man in England concerned to support the Succession of that Family.

'The publishing a few Sermons whilst I live, the latest of which was preached about eight Years since, and the first above seventeen, will make it very natural for People to enquire into the occasion of doing so: And to such I do very willingly assign these following Reasons.

'First, from the Observations I have been able to make, for these many Years last past, upon our publick Affairs; and from the natural Tendency of several Principles and Practices, that have, of late been studiously revived; and from what has followed thereupon, I could not help both fearing and presaging, that these Nations would some time or other, if ever we should have an Enterprizing Prince upon the Throne, of more Ambition than Virtue, Justice and true Honour, fall into the Way of all other Nations, and lose their *Liberty*.

'Nor could I help foreseeing to whose Charge a great deal of this dreadful Mischief, whenever it should happen, would be laid, whether justly or unjustly was not my Business to determine; but I resolved, for my own particular Part, to deliver my self, as well as I could, from the Reproaches and the Curses of Posterity, by publickly declaring to all the World, that although in the constant Course of my Ministry, I have never failed, on proper Occasions, to recommend, urge, and insist upon the loving, honouring, and the reverencing the Prince's Person, and holding it, according to the Laws, inviolable and sacred, and paying all Obedience and Submission to the Laws, tho' never so hard and inconvenient to private People: Yet did I never think my self at Liberty, or authorized to tell the People, that either *Christ*, St. *Peter*, or St. *Paul*, or any other Holy Writer, had, by any Doctrine delivered by them, subverted the *Laws* and *Constitutions* of the Country in which they lived, or put them in a worse Condition, with respect to their Civil Liberties, than they would have been had they not been Christians. I ever thought it a most impious Blasphemy against that Holy Religion, to father any thing upon it that might encourage Tyranny, Oppression, or Injustice in a Prince, or that easily tended to make a free and happy People *Slaves* and *miserable*. No: People may make themselves as wretched as they will, but let not God be called into that wicked Party. When Force, and Violence, and hard Necessity have brought the Yoak of Servitude upon a People's Neck, Religion will supply them with a patient and submissive Spirit under it till they can innocently shake it off; but certainly Religion never puts it on. This always was, and this at present is, my Judgment of these Matters: And I would be transmitted to Posterity (for the little Share of Time such Names as mine can live) under the Character of one who loved his Country, and would be thought a *good Englishman* as well as a *good Clergyman*.

'This Character I thought would be transmitted by the following Sermons, which were made for, and preached in a private Audience, when I could think of nothing else but doing my Duty on the Occasions that were then offered by God's Providence, without any manner of Design of making them publick: And for that Reason I give them now as they were then delivered; by which I hope to satisfie those People who have objected a Change of Principles to me, as if I were not now the same Man I formerly was. I never had but one Opinion of these Matters; and that I think is so reasonable and well-grounded, that I believe I never can have any other.

'Another Reason of my publishing these Sermons at this Time, is, that I have a mind to do my self some Honour, by doing what Honour I could to the Memory of two most excellent Princes,[3] and who have very highly deserved at the Hands of all the People of these Dominions, who have any true Value for the *Protestant Religion*, and the *Constitution* of the *English Government*, of which they were the great *Deliverers* and *Defenders*. I have lived to see their illustrious Names very rudely handled, and the great Benefits they did this Nation treated slightly and contemptuously. I have lived to see our Deliverance from *Arbitrary Power* and *Popery*, traduced and villified by some who formerly thought it was their greatest Merit, and made it part of their Boast and Glory to have had a little Hand and Share in bringing it about; and others who, without it, must have lived in Exile, Poverty, and Misery, meanly disclaiming it, and using ill the *glorious Instruments* thereof. Who could expect such a Requital of such Merit? I have, I own it, an Ambition of exempting my self from the Number of *unthankful* People: And as I loved and honoured those great Princes living, and lamented over them when dead, so I would gladly raise them up a Monument of Praise as lasting as any thing of mine can be; and I choose to do it at this Time, when it is so unfashionable a Thing to speak honourably of them.

'The Sermon that was preached upon the Duke of *Gloucester*'s Death[4] was printed quickly after, and is now, because the Subject was so suitable, joined to the others. The Loss of that most promising and hopeful Prince was, at that Time, I saw, unspeakably great; and many Accidents since have convinced us, that it could not have been over-valued. That precious Life, had it pleased God to have prolonged it the usual Space, had saved us many Fears, and Jealousies, and dark Distrusts, and prevented many Alarms, that have long kept us, and will keep us still, waking and uneasy. Nothing remained to comfort and support us under this heavy Stroke, but the Necessity it brought the King and Nation under, of settling the *Succession* in the House of HANOVER, and giving it an *Hereditary Right*, by *Act of Parliament*, as long as it continues *Protestant*.[5] So much Good did God, in his merciful Providence, produce from a Misfortune, which we could never otherwise have sufficiently deplored.

'The fourth Sermon was preached upon the Queen's *Accession* to the Throne,[6] and the first Year in which that Day was solemnly observed, (for, by some Accident or other, it had been over-looked the Year before;) and every one will see, without the Date of it, that it was preached very early in this Reign, since I was able only to *promise* and *presage* its future Glories and Successes, from the good Appearances of Things, and the happy Turn our Affairs began to take; and could not then count up the Victories and Triumphs that, for seven Years after, made it in the Prophet's Language, *a Name and a Praise among all the People of the Earth*.[7] Never did seven such Years together pass over the Head of any *English Monarch*, nor cover it with so much Honour: The Crown and Sceptre seemed to be the *Queen's* least Ornaments; those other Princes wore in common with Her, and her great personal Virtues were the same before and since; but such was the Fame of Her Administration of Affairs at home, such was the Reputation of Her Wisdom and Felicity in choosing Ministers, and such was then esteemed their Faithfulness and Zeal, their Diligence and great Abilities in executing Her Commands; to such a Height of military Glory did Her Great *General* and Her *Armies* carry the *British* Name abroad; such was the Harmony and Concord betwixt Her and Her *Allies*, and such was the Blessing of God upon all Her Counsels and Undertakings, that I am as sure as History can make me, no Prince of ours was ever yet so Prosperous and Successful, so loved, esteemed, and

honoured by their Subjects and their Friends, nor near so formidable
to their Enemies. We were, as all the World imagined then just
entring on the Ways that promised to lead to such a Peace, as
would have answered all the Prayers of our Religious Queen, the
Care and Vigilance of a most able Ministry, the Payments of a
willing and obedient People, as well as all the glorious Toils and
Hazards of the Soldiery; when God, for our Sins, permitted *the
Spirit of Discord* to go forth, and, by troubling sore the Camp, the
City, and the Country, (as oh that it had altogether spared the
Places sacred to his Worship!) to spoil for a Time, this beautiful
and pleasing Prospect, and give us in its Stead, I know not what
– Our Enemies will tell the rest with Pleasure. It will become me
better to pray to God to restore us to the Power of obtaining such
a Peace, as will be to his Glory, the Safety, Honour, and the
Welfare of the Queen and Her Dominions, and the general
Satisfaction of all Her High and Mighty Allies.'
May 2, 1712.   T

No. 445 [ADDISON]

[The Stamp Act][1]
Thursday, 31 July 1712

Tanti non es ais. Sapis, Luperce.   Mart.[2]

This is the Day on which many eminent Authors will probably
Publish their Last Words. I am afraid that few of our Weekly
Historians, who are Men that above all others delight in War, will
be able to subsist under the Weight of a Stamp, and an approaching
Peace. A Sheet of Blank Paper that must have this new Imprimatur
clapt upon it, before it is qualified to Communicate any thing to
the Publick, will make its way in the World but very heavily. In
short, the Necessity of carrying a Stamp, and the Improbability of
notifying a Bloody Battel, will, I am afraid, both concur to the
sinking of those thin Folios, which have every other Day retailed
to us the History of *Europe* for several Years last past. A Facetious
Friend of mine, who loves a Punn, calls this present Mortality
among Authors, *The Fall of the Leaf.*

I remember, upon Mr. *Baxter*'s Death,[3] there was Published a

Sheet of very good Sayings, inscribed, *The last Words of Mr.* Baxter. The Title sold so great a Number of these Papers, that about a Week after, there came out a second Sheet, inscribed, *More last Words of Mr.* Baxter. In the same Manner, I have Reason to think, that several Ingenious Writers, who have taken their Leave of the Publick, in farewell Papers, will not give over so, but intend to appear again, tho' perhaps under another Form, and with a different Title. Be that as it will, it is my Business, in this place, to give an Account of my own Intentions, and to acquaint my Reader with the Motives by which I Act, in this great Crisis of the Republick of Letters.

I have been long debating in my own Heart, whether I should throw up my Pen, as an Author that is cashiered by the Act of Parliament, which is to Operate within these Four and Twenty Hours, or whether I should still persist in laying my Speculations, from Day to Day, before the Publick. The Argument which prevails with me most on the first side of the Question is, that I am informed by my Bookseller he must raise the Price of every single Paper to Two-pence, or that he shall not be able to pay the Duty of it. Now as I am very desirous my Readers should have their Learning as cheap as possible, it is with great Difficulty that I comply with him in this Particular.

However, upon laying my Reasons together in the Balance, I find that those which plead for the Continuance of this Work have much the greater Weight. For, in the first Place, in Recompence for the Expence to which this will put my Readers, it is to be hoped they may receive from every Paper so much Instruction, as will be a very good Equivalent. And, in order to this, I would not advise any one to take it in, who, after the Perusal of it, does not find himself Twopence the wiser, or the better Man for it; or who, upon Examination, does not believe that he has had Two penny-worth of Mirth or Instruction for his Mony.

But I must confess there is another Motive which prevails with me more than the former. I consider that the Tax on Paper was given for the Support of the Government; and as I have Enemies, who are apt to pervert every thing I do or say, I fear they would ascribe the laying down my Paper, on such an occasion, to a Spirit of Malecontentedness, which I am resolved none shall ever justly upbraid me with. No, I shall glory in contributing my utmost to the Weal Publick; and if my Country receives Five or Six Pounds a-Day by my Labours,[4] I shall be very well pleased to find my self so useful a Member. It is a received Maxim, that no honest Man should enrich himself by Methods that are prejudicial to the Community in which he lives, and by the same Rule I think we may pronounce the Person to deserve very well of his Country-men, whose Labours bring more into the Publick Coffers, than into his own Pocket.

Since I have mentioned the Word Enemies, I must explain my self so far as to acquaint my Reader, that I mean only the insignificant Party Zealots on both sides; Men of such poor narrow Souls, that they are not capable of thinking on any thing but with an Eye to Whig or Tory. During the Course of this Paper, I have been accused by these despicable Wretches of Trimming, Time-serving, Personal Reflection, secret Satire, and the like. Now, tho' in these my Compositions, it is visible to any Reader of Common Sense, that I consider nothing but my Subject, which is always of an Indifferent Nature; how is it possible for me to write so clear of Party, as not to lie open to the Censures of those who will be applying every Sentence, and finding out Persons and Things in it which it has no regard to?

Several Paltry Scribblers and Declaimers have done me the Honour to be dull upon me in Reflections of this Nature; but notwithstanding my Name has been sometimes traduced by this contemptible Tribe of Men, I have hitherto avoided all Animad-versions upon 'em. The truth of it is, I am afraid of making them appear considerable by taking notice of them, for they are like those Imperceptible Insects which are discovered by the Microscope, and cannot be made the Subject of Observation without being magnified.

Having mentioned those few who have shewn themselves the Enemies of this Paper, I should be very ungrateful to the Publick, did not I at the same time testifie my Gratitude to those who are its Friends, in which number I may reckon many of the most distinguished Persons of all Conditions, Parties, and Professions in the Isle of *Great Britain*. I am not so vain as to think this Approbation is so much due to the Performance as to the Design.

There is, and ever will be, Justice enough in the World, to afford Patronage and Protection for those who endeavour to advance Truth and Virtue, without regard to the Passions and Prejudices of any particular Cause or Faction. If I have any other Merit in me, it is that I have new-pointed all the Batteries of Ridicule. They have been generally planted against Persons who have appeared Serious rather than Absurd; or at best, have aimed rather at what is Unfashionable than what is Vicious. For my own part, I have endeavoured to make nothing Ridiculous that is not in some measure Criminal. I have set up the Immoral Man as the Object of Derision: In short, if I have not formed a new Weapon against Vice and Irreligion, I have at least shewn how that Weapon may be put to a right use, which has so often fought the Battels of Impiety and Prophaneness.   C

VI *Religion and the Conduct of Life*

No. 11 [STEELE]

[Male hypocrisy: the story of Inkle and Yarico]
Tuesday, 13 March 1711

Dat veniam corvis, vexat censura columbas. Juv.[1]

Arietta is visited by all Persons of both Sexes, who have any Pretence to Wit and Gallantry. She is in that time of Life which is neither affected with the Follies of Youth, or Infirmities of Age; and her Conversation is so mixed with Gaiety and Prudence, that she is agreeable both to the Young and the Old. Her Behaviour is very frank, without being in the least blameable; and as she is out of the Tract of any amorous or ambitious Pursuits of her own, her Visitants entertain her with Accounts of themselves very freely, whether they concern their Passions or their Interests. I made her a Visit this Afternoon, having been formerly introduced to the Honour of her Acquaintance, by my Friend WILL. HONEYCOMB, who has prevailed upon her to admit me sometimes into her Assembly, as a civil inoffensive Man. I found her accompanied with one Person only, a Common-Place Talker, who, upon my Entrance, rose, and after a very slight Civility sat down again; then turning to *Arietta*, pursued his Discourse, which I found was upon the old Topick, of Constancy in Love. He went on with great Facility in repeating what he talks every Day of his Life; and, with the Ornaments of insignificant Laughs and Gestures, enforced his Arguments by Quotations out of Plays and Songs, which allude to the Perjuries of the Fair, and the general Levity of Women. Methought he strove to shine more than ordinarily in his Talkative Way, that he might insult my Silence, and distinguish himself before a Woman of *Arietta*'s Taste and Understanding. She had often an Inclination to interrupt him, but could find no Opportunity, till the Larum ceased of it self; which it did not 'till he had repeated and murdered the celebrated Story of the *Ephesian* Matron.[2]

Arietta seemed to regard this Piece of Raillery as an Outrage done to her Sex; as indeed I have always observed that Women, whether out of a nicer Regard to their Honour, or what other Reason I cannot tell, are more sensibly touched with those general Aspersions which are cast upon their Sex, than Men are by what is said of theirs.

When she had a little recovered her self from the serious Anger she was in, she replied in the following manner.

Sir, When I consider how perfectly new all you have said on this Subject is, and that the Story you have given us is not quite Two thousand Years old, I cannot but think it a Piece of Presumption to dispute with you: But your Quotations put me in Mind of the Fable of the Lion and the Man.[3] The Man walking with that noble Animal, shewed him, in the Ostentation of Human Superiority, a Sign of a Man killing a Lion. Upon which the Lion said very justly, *We Lions are none of us Painters, else we could shew a hundred Men killed by Lions, for one Lion killed by a Man.* You Men are Writers, and can represent us Women as Unbecoming as you please in your Works, while we are unable to return the Injury. You have twice or thrice observed in your Discourse, that Hypocrisie is the very Foundation of our Education; and that an Ability to dissemble our Affections, is a professed Part of our Breeding. These, and such other Reflections, are sprinkled up and down the Writings of all Ages, by Authors, who leave behind them Memorials of their Resentment against the Scorn of particular Women, in Invectives against the whole Sex. Such a Writer, I doubt not, was the celebrated *Petronius*, who invented the pleasant Aggravations of the Frailty of the *Ephesian* Lady; but when we consider this Question between the Sexes, which has been either a Point of Dispute or Raillery ever since there were Men and Women, let us take Facts from plain People, and from such as have not either Ambition or Capacity to embellish their Narrations with any Beauties of Imagination. I was the other Day amusing my self with *Ligon*'s Account of *Barbadoes*;[4] and, in Answer to your well-wrought Tale, I will give you (as it dwells upon my Memory) out of that honest Traveller, in his fifty fifth Page, the History of *Inkle* and *Yarico*.

Mr. *Thomas Inkle*, of *London*, aged twenty Years, embarked in the *Downs* on the good Ship called the *Achilles*, bound for the *West-Indies*, on the 16th of *June*, 1647, in order to improve his Fortune by Trade and Merchandize. Our Adventurer was the third Son of an eminent Citizen, who had taken particular Care to instill into his Mind an early Love of Gain, by making him a perfect Master of Numbers, and consequently giving him a °quick View of Loss and Advantage, and preventing the natural Impulses of his Passions, by Prepossession towards his Interests. With a Mind thus turned, young *Inkle* had a Person every way agreeable, a ruddy Vigour in his Countenance, Strength in his Limbs, with Ringlets of fair Hair loosely flowing on his Shoulders. It happened, in the Course of the Voyage, that the *Achilles*, in some Distress, put into a Creek on the Main of *America*, in Search of Provisions: The Youth, who is the Hero of my Story, among others, went ashore on this Occasion. From their first Landing they were observed by a Party of *Indians*, who hid themselves in the Woods for that Purpose. The *English* unadvisedly marched a great distance from the Shore into the Country, and were intercepted by the Natives, who slew the greatest Number of them. Our Adventurer escaped among others, by flying into a Forest. Upon his coming into a remote and pathless Part of the Wood, he threw himself, tired and breathless, on a little Hillock, when an *Indian* Maid rushed from a Thicket behind him: After the first Surprize, they appeared mutually agreeable to each other. If the *European* was highly Charmed with the Limbs, Features, and wild Graces of the Naked *American*; the *American* was no less taken with the Dress, Complexion, and Shape of an *European*, covered from Head to Foot. The *Indian* grew immediately enamoured of him, and consequently sollicitous for his Preservation: She therefore conveyed him to a Cave, where she gave him a delicious Repast of Fruits, and led him to a Stream to slake his Thirst. In the midst of these good Offices, she would sometimes play with his Hair, and delight in the Opposition of its Colour to that of her Fingers: Then open his Bosom, then laugh at him for covering it. She was, it seems, a Person of Distinction, for she every Day came to him in a different Dress, of the most beautiful Shells, °Bugles, and Bredes. She likewise brought him a great many Spoils, which her other Lovers had presented to her; so that his Cave was richly adorned with all the spotted Skins of Beasts, and most Party-coloured Feathers of Fowls, which that World afforded. To make his Confinement more tolerable, she would carry him in the Dusk of the Evening, or by the favour of Moon-light, to unfrequented Groves and Solitudes, and shew him where to lye down in Safety, and sleep amidst the Falls of Waters, and Melody of Nightingales. Her Part was to watch and hold him awake in her Arms, for fear of her Country-men, and wake him on Occasions to consult his Safety. In this manner did the Lovers pass away their Time, till they had learned a Language of their own, in which the Voyager communicated to his Mistress, how happy he should be to have her in his Country, where she should be Cloathed in such Silks as his Wastecoat was made of, and be carried in Houses drawn by Horses, without being exposed to Wind or Weather. All this he promised her the Enjoyment of, without such Fears and Alarms as they were there tormented with. In this tender Correspondence these Lovers lived for several Months, when *Yarico*, instructed by her Lover, discovered a Vessel on the Coast, to which she made Signals; and in the Night, with the utmost Joy and Satisfaction, accompanied him to a Ship's-Crew of his Countrymen, bound for *Barbadoes*. When a Vessel from the Main arrives in that Island, it seems the Planters come down to the Shoar, where there is an immediate Market of the *Indians* and other Slaves, as with us of Horses and Oxen.

To be short, Mr. *Thomas Inkle*, now coming into *English* Territories, began seriously to reflect upon his loss of Time, and to weigh with himself how many Days Interest of his Mony he had lost during his Stay with *Yarico*. This Thought made the young Man very pensive, and careful what Account he should be able to give his Friends of his Voyage. Upon which Considerations, the prudent and frugal young Man sold *Yarico* to a *Barbadian* Merchant; notwithstanding that the poor Girl, to incline him to commiserate her Condition, told him that she was with Child by him: But he only made use of that Information, to rise in his Demands upon the Purchaser.

I was so touched with this Story, (which I think should be always a Counterpart to the *Ephesian* Matron) that I left the Room with Tears in my Eyes; which a Woman of *Arietta*'s good Sense, did, I am sure, take for greater Applause, than any Compliments I could make her.   R

No. 159 [ADDISON]

[Human life and eternity: the vision of Mirzah][1]
Saturday, 1 September 1711

—*Omnem quæ nunc obducta tuenti*
Mortales hebetat visus tibi, & humida circum
Caligat, nubem eripiam—   Virg.[2]

When I was at *Grand Cairo* I picked up several Oriental Manuscripts, which I have still by me. Among others I met with one entituled, *The Visions of Mirzah*, which I have read over with great Pleasure. I intend to give it to the Publick when I have no other Entertainment for them; and shall begin with the first Vision, which I have translated Word for Word as follows.

'On the fifth Day of the Moon, which according to the Custom of my Forefathers I always keep holy, after having washed my self and offered up my Morning Devotions, I ascended the high Hills of *Bagdat*, in order to pass the rest of the Day in Meditation and Prayer. As I was here airing my self on the Tops of the Mountains, I fell into a profound Contemplation on the Vanity of humane Life; and passing from one Thought to another, Surely, said I, Man is but a Shadow and Life a Dream. Whilst I was thus musing, I cast my Eyes towards the Summit of a Rock that was not far from me, where I discovered one in the Habit of a Shepherd, with a little Musical Instrument in his Hand. As I looked upon him he applied it to his Lips, and began to play upon it. The Sound of it was exceeding sweet, and wrought into a Variety of Tunes that were inexpressibly melodious, and altogether different from any thing I had ever heard. They put me in mind of those heavenly Airs that are played to the departed Souls of good Men upon their first Arrival in Paradise, to wear out the Impressions of their last

Agonies, and qualify them for the Pleasures of that happy Place. My Heart melted away in secret Raptures.

'I had been often told that the Rock before me was the Haunt of a Genius; and that several had been entertained with Musick who had passed by it, but never heard that the Musician had before made himself visible. When he had raised my Thoughts, by those transporting Airs which he played, to taste the Pleasures of his Conversation, as I looked upon him like one astonished, he beckoned to me, and by the waving of his Hand directed me to approach the Place where he sat. I drew near with that Reverence which is due to a superior Nature; and as my Heart was entirely subdued by the captivating Strains I had heard, I fell down at his Feet and wept. The Genius smiled upon me with a Look of Compassion and Affability that familiarized him to my Imagination, and at once dispelled all the Fears and Apprehensions with which I approached him. He lifted me from the Ground, and taking me by the Hand, *Mirzah*, said he, I have heard thee in thy Soliloquies, follow me.

'He then led me to the highest Pinnacle of the Rock, and placing me on the Top of it, Cast thy Eyes Eastward, said he, and tell me what thou seest. I see, said I, a huge Valley and a prodigious Tide of Water rolling through it. The Valley that thou seest, said he, is the Vale of Misery, and the Tide of Water that thou seest is Part of the Great Tide of Eternity. What is the Reason, said I, that the Tide I see rises out of a thick Mist at one End, and again loses it self in a thick Mist at the other? What thou seest, said he, is that Portion of Eternity which is called Time, measured out by the Sun, and reaching from the Beginning of the World to its Consummation. Examine now, said he, this Sea that is thus bounded with Darkness at both Ends, and tell me what thou discoverest in it. I see a Bridge, said I, standing in the Midst of the Tide. The Bridge thou seest, said he, is humane Life; consider it attentively. Upon a more leisurely Survey of it, I found that it consisted of threescore and ten entire Arches, with several broken Arches, which added to those that were entire made up the Number about an hundred. As I was counting the Arches, the Genius told me that this Bridge consisted at first of a thousand Arches; but that a great Flood swept away the rest, and left the Bridge in the ruinous Condition I now beheld it. But tell me further, said he, what thou discoverest on it. I see Multitudes of People passing over it, said I, and a black Cloud hanging on each End of it. As I looked more attentively, I saw several of the Passengers dropping thro' the Bridge, into the great Tide that flowed underneath it; and upon further Examination, perceived there were innumerable Trap-doors that lay concealed in the Bridge, which the Passengers no sooner trod upon, but they fell through them into the Tide and immediately disappeared. These hidden Pit-falls were set very thick at the Entrance of the Bridge, so that Throngs of People no sooner broke through the Cloud, but many of them fell into them. They grew thinner towards the Middle, but multiplied and lay closer together towards the End of the Arches that were entire.

'There were indeed some Persons, but their Number was very small, that continued a kind of hobbling March on the broken Arches, but fell through one after another, being quite tired and spent with so long a Walk.

'I passed some Time in the Contemplation of this wonderful Structure, and the great Variety of Objects which it presented. My Heart was filled with a deep Melancholy to see several dropping unexpectedly in the Midst of Mirth and Jollity, and catching at every thing that stood by them to save themselves. Some were looking up towards the Heavens in a thoughtful Posture, and in the Midst of a Speculation stumbled and fell out of Sight. Multitudes were very busy in the Pursuit of Bubbles that glittered in their Eyes and danced before them, but often when they thought themselves within the Reach of them their Footing failed and down they sunk. In this Confusion of Objects, I observed some with Scymetars in their Hands, and others with °Urinals, who ran to and fro upon the Bridge, thrusting several Persons on Trap-doors which did not seem to lie in their Way, and which they might have escaped had they not been thus forced upon them.

'The Genius seeing me indulge my self in this melancholy Prospect, told me I had dwelt long enough upon it: Take thine Eyes off the Bridge, said he, and tell me if thou yet seest any thing thou dost not comprehend. Upon looking up, What mean said I, those great Flights of Birds that are perpetually hovering about the Bridge, and settling upon it from Time to Time? I see Vultures,

Harpyes, Ravens, Cormorants; and among many other feathered
Creatures several little winged Boys, that perch in great Numbers
upon the middle Arches. These said the Genius, are Envy, Avarice,
Superstition, Despair, Love, with the like Cares and Passions that
infest humane Life.

'I here fetched a deep Sigh, Alass, said I, Man was made in vain!
How is he given away to Misery and Mortality! tortured in Life,
and swallowed up in Death! The Genius being moved with
Compassion towards me, bid me quit so uncomfortable a Prospect:
Look no more, said he, on Man in the first Stage of his Existence,
in his setting out for Eternity; but cast thine Eye on that thick Mist
into which the Tide bears the several Generations of Mortals that
fall into it. I directed my Sight as I was ordered, and (whether or
no the good Genius strengthened it with any supernatural Force,
or dissipated Part of the Mist that was before too thick for the Eye
to penetrate) I saw the Valley opening at the further End, and
spreading forth into an immense Ocean, that had a huge Rock of
Adamant running through the Midst of it, and dividing it into two
equal Parts. The Clouds still rested on one Half of it, insomuch
that I could discover nothing in it; but the other appeared to me
a vast Ocean planted with innumerable Islands, that were covered
with Fruits and Flowers, and interwoven with a thousand little
shining Seas that ran among them. I could see Persons dressed in
glorious Habits, with Garlands upon their Heads, passing among
the Trees, lying down by the Sides of Fountains, or resting on Beds
of Flowers; and could hear a confused Harmony of singing Birds,
falling Waters, humane Voices, and musical Instruments. Gladness
grew in me upon the Discovery of so delightful a Scene. I wished
for the Wings of an Eagle, that I might fly away to those happy
Seats; but the Genius told me there was no Passage to them, except
through the Gates of Death that I saw opening every Moment upon
the Bridge. The Islands, said he, that lie so fresh and green before
thee, and with which the whole Face of the Ocean appears spotted
as far as thou canst see, are more in Number than the Sands on the
Sea-shore; there are Myriads of Islands behind those which thou
here discoverest, reaching further than thine Eye or even thine
Imagination can extend it self. These are the Mansions of good
Men after Death, who according to the Degree and Kinds of Virtue

in which they excelled, are distributed among these several Islands, which abound with Pleasures of different Kinds and Degrees, suitable to the Relishes and Perfections of those who are settled in them; every Island is a Paradise accommodated to its respective Inhabitants. Are not these, O *Mirzah*, Habitations worth contending for? Does Life appear miserable, that gives thee Opportunities of earning such a Reward? Is Death to be feared, that will convey thee to so happy an Existence? Think not Man was made in vain, who has such an Eternity reserved for him. I gazed with inexpressible Pleasure on these happy Islands. At length said I, shew me now, I beseech thee, the Secrets that lie hid under those dark Clouds which cover the Ocean on the other Side of the Rock of Adamant. The Genius making me no Answer, I turned about to address my self to him a second time, but I found that he had left me; I then turned again to the Vision which I had been so long contemplating, but instead of the rolling Tide, the arched Bridge, and the happy Islands, I saw nothing but the long hollow Valley of *Bagdat*, with Oxen, Sheep, and Camels, grazing upon the Sides of it.'

The End of the first Vision of Mirzah. C

No. 264 [STEELE]

[Choice of life]
Wednesday, 2 January 1711

— Secretum iter & fallentis Semita vitæ. Hor.[1]

It has been from Age to Age an Affectation to love the Pleasure of Solitude, among those who cannot possibly be supposed qualified for passing Life in that Manner. This People have taken up from reading the many agreeable Things which have been writ on that Subject, for which we are beholden to excellent Persons who delighted in being retired and abstracted from the Pleasures that enchant the Generality of the World. This Way of Life is recommended indeed with great Beauty, and in such a Manner as disposes the Reader for the Time to a pleasing Forgetfulness, or Negligence of the particular Hurry of Life in which he is engaged, together with a longing for that State which he is charmed with in

Description. But when we consider the World it self, and how few there are capable of a religious, learned, or philosophick Solitude, we shall be apt to change a Regard to that Sort of Solitude, for being a little singular in enjoying Time after the Way a Man himself likes best in the World, without going so far as wholly to withdraw from it. I have often observed, there is not a Man breathing who does not differ from all other Men, as much in the Sentiments of his Mind, as the Features of his Face. The Felicity is, when any one is so happy as to find out and follow what is the proper Bent of his Genius, and turn all his Endeavours to exert himself according as that prompts him. Instead of this, which is an innocent Method of enjoying a Man's self, and turning out of the general °Tracts wherein you have Crouds of Rivals, there are those who pursue their own Way out of a Sourness and Spirit of Contradiction: These Men do every Thing which they are able to support, as if Guilt and Impunity could not go together. They chuse a Thing only because another dislikes it; and affect forsooth an inviolable Constancy in Matters of no manner of Moment. Thus sometimes an old Fellow shall wear this or that Sort of Cut in his Cloaths with great Integrity, while all the rest of the World are degenerated into Buttons, Pockets and Loops unknown to their Ancestors. As insignificant as even this is, if it were searched to the Bottom, you perhaps would find it not sincere, but that he is in the Fashion in his Heart, and holds out from mere Obstinacy. But I am running from my intended Purpose, which was to celebrate a certain particular Manner of passing away Life, and is a Contradiction to no Man, but a Resolution to contract none of the exorbitant Desires by which others are enslaved. The best Way of separating a Man's self from the World, is to give up the Desire of being known to it. After a Man has preserved his Innocence, and performed all Duties incumbent upon him, his Time spent his own Way is what makes his Life differ from that of a Slave. If they who affect Show and Pomp knew how many of their Spectators derided their trivial Taste, they would be very much less elated, and have an Inclination to examine the Merit of all they have to do with: They would soon find out that there are many who make a Figure below what their Fortune or Merit entitles them to, out of mere Choice, and an elegant Desire of Ease and Disincumbrance. It would look like Romance to tell you in this Age of an old Man who is contented to pass for an °Humourist, and one who does not understand the Figure he ought to make in the World, while he lives in a Lodging of ten Shillings a Week with only one Servant. While he dresses himself according to the Season in °Cloath or in °Stuff, and has no one necessary Attention to any Thing but the Bell which calls to Prayers twice a Day. I say it would look like a Fable to report that this Gentleman gives away all which is the Overplus of a great Fortune, by secret Methods, to other Men. If he has not the Pomp of a numerous Train, and of Professors of Service to him, he has every Day he lives the °Conscience that the Widow, the Fatherless, the Mourner, and the Stranger bless his unseen Hand in their Prayers. This °Humourist gives up all the Compliments which People of his own Condition could make to him, for the Pleasures of helping the afflicted, supplying the needy, and befriending the neglected. This Humourist keeps to himself much more than he wants, and gives a vast Refuse of his Superfluities to purchase Heaven, and by freeing others from the Temptations of worldly Want, to carry a Retinue with him thither.

Of all Men who affect living in a particular Way, next to this admirable Character, I am the most enamoured of *Irus*,[2] whose Condition will not admit of such Largesses, and perhaps would not be capable of making them, if it were. *Irus*, tho' he is now turned of fifty, has not appeared in the World, in his real Character, since five and twenty, at which Age he ran out a small Patrimony, and spent some Time after with Rakes who had lived upon him: A Course of ten Years Time passed in all the little Alleys, By Paths, and sometimes open Taverns and Streets of this Town, gave *Irus* a perfect Skill in judging of the Inclinations of Mankind, and acting accordingly. He seriously considered he was poor, and the general Horrour which most Men have of all who are in that Condition. *Irus* judged very rightly, that while he could keep his Poverty a Secret, he should not feel the Weight of it; he improved this Thought into an Affectation of Closeness and Covetousness. Upon this one Principle he resolved to govern his future Life; and in the thirty sixth Year of his Age he repaired to °*Long-lane*, and looked upon several Dresses which hung there deserted by their first Masters, and exposed to the Purchase of the best Bidder. At this

Place he exchanged his gay Shabbyness of Cloaths fit for a much younger Man, to warm ones that would be decent for a much older one. Irus came out thoroughly equipped from Head to Foot, with a little oaken Cane in the Form of a substantial Man that did not mind his Dress, turned of fifty. He had at this Time fifty Pounds in ready Money; and in this Habit, with this Fortune, he took his present Lodging in °St. John-street, at the °Mansion-House of a Taylor's Widow, who washes and can clear-starch his °Bands. From that Time to this, he has kept the main Stock, without Alteration under or over, to the Value of five Pounds. He left off all his old Acquaintance to a Man, and all his Arts of Life, except the Play of Back-gammon, upon which he has more than bore his Charges. Irus has, ever since he came into this Neighbourhood, given all the Intimations, he skilfully could, of being a °close Hunks worth Money: No body comes to visit him, he receives no Letters, and tells his Money Morning and Evening. He has from the publick Papers, a Knowledge of what generally passes, shuns all Discourses of Money, but shrugs his Shoulder when you talk of Securities; he denies his being rich with the Air, which all do who are vain of being so: He is the Oracle of a neighbouring Justice of Peace who meets him at the Coffee-House; the Hopes that what he has must come to Somebody, and that he has no Heirs, have that Effect where-ever he is known, that he every Day has three or four Invitations to dine at different Places, which he generally takes Care to chuse in such a manner, as not to seem inclined to the richer Man. All the young Men respect him, and say he is just the same Man he was when they were Boys. He uses no Artifice in the World, but makes Use of Men's Designs upon him to get a Maintenance out of them. This he carries on by a certain Peevishness, (which he acts very well) that no one would believe could possibly enter into the Head of a poor Fellow. His [Mien], his Dress, his Carriage, and his Language are such, that you would be at a Loss to guess, whether in the active Part of his Life he had been a sensible Citizen, or Scholar that knew the World. These are the great Circumstances in the Life of Irus, and thus does he pass away his Days a Stranger to Mankind; and at his Death, the worst that will be said of him will be, that he got by every Man, who had Expectations from him, more than he had to leave him.

I have an Inclination to print the following Letters; for that I have heard the Author of them has some where or other seen me, and by an excellent Faculty in Mimickry my Correspondents tell me he can assume my Air, and give my Taciturnity a Slyness which diverts more than any Thing I could say if I were present. Thus I am glad my Silence is atoned for to the good Company in Town. He has carryed his Skill in Imitation so far, as to have forged a Letter from my Friend Sir ROGER in such a manner, that any one but I who am thoroughly acquainted with him, would have taken it for genuine.

Mr. SPECTATOR,
'Having observed in *Lily*'s Grammar how sweetly *Bacchus* and *Apollo* run in a Verse³: I have (to preserve the Amity between them) called in *Bacchus* to the Aid of my Profession of the *Theatre*. So that while some People of Quality are bespeaking Plays of me to be acted upon such a Day, and others, Hogsheads for their Houses, against such a Time; I am wholly employed in the agreeable Service of Wit and Wine: Sir, I have sent you Sir *Roger de Coverly*'s Letter to me, which pray comply with in Favour of the *Bumper* Tavern. Be kind, for you know a Player's utmost Pride is the Approbation of the SPECTATOR.

> *I am your Admirer, tho' unknown,*
> Richard Estcourt.'⁴

To Mr. *Estcourt* at his House in *Covent-Garden.*
Coverly, December the 18th, 1711.

Old Comical [*One*],
'The Hogsheads of °Neat Port came safe, and have gotten [thee] good Reputation in these Parts; and I am glad to hear, that a Fellow who has been laying out his Money, ever since he was born, for the meer Pleasure of Wine, has bethought himself of joining Profit and Pleasure together. Our Sexton (poor Man) having received Strength from thy Wine, since his Fit of the Gout is hugely taken with it: He says it is given by Nature for the Use of Families, that no Steward's Table can be without it, that it strengthens Digestion, excludes Surfeits, Fevers and Physick;

which Green Wines of any Kind can't do. Pray get a °pure snug Room, and I hope next Term to help fill your [Bumper] with our People of the Club; but you must have no Bells stirring when the *Spectator* comes; I forbore ringing to Dinner while he was down with me in the Country. Thank you for the little Hams and *Portugal* Onions; pray keep some always by you. You know my Supper is only good *Cheshire* Cheese, best Mustard, a Golden Pippin, attended with a Pipe of °*John Sly*'s Best. Sir *Harry* has stoln all your Songs, and tells the Story of the 5th of *November* to Perfection.

Yours to serve you,
Roger de Coverly.

'We've lost old *John* since you were here.'   T

No. 543 [ADDISON]

[Anatomy argues for Providence]
Saturday, 22 November 1712

—facies non omnibus una
Nec diversa tamen —   Ov.[1]

Those who were skillful in Anatomy among the Ancients, concluded from the outward and inward Make of an Human Body, that it was the Work of a Being transcendently Wise and Powerful. As the World grew more enlightened in this Art, their Discoveries gave them fresh Opportunities of admiring the Conduct of Providence in the Formation of an Human Body. *Galen* was converted by his Dissections, and could not but own a Supreme Being upon a Survey of this his Handywork.[2] There were, indeed, many Parts of which the old Anatomists did not know the certain Use, but as they saw that most of those which they examined were adapted with admirable Art to their several Functions, they did not question but those, whose Uses they could not determine, were contrived with the same Wisdom for respective Ends and Purposes. Since the Circulation of the Blood has been found out, and many other great Discoveries have been made by our Modern Anatomists, we see new Wonders in the Human Frame, and discern several important Uses for those Parts, which Uses the Ancients knew nothing of. In short, the Body of Man is such a Subject as stands the utmost Test of Examination. Tho' it appears formed with the nicest Wisdom upon the most superficial Survey of it, it still mends upon the Search, and produces our Surprise and Amazement in Proportion as we pry into it. What I have here said of an Human Body, may be applied to the Body of every Animal which has been the Subject of Anatomical Observations.

The Body of an Animal is an Object adequate to our Senses. It is a particular System of Providence, that lies in a narrow Compass. The Eye is able to command it, and by successive Enquiries can search into all its Parts. Could the Body of the whole Earth, or indeed the whole Universe, be thus submitted to the Examination of our Senses, were it not too big and disproportioned for our Enquiries, too unwieldy for the Management of the Eye and Hand, there is no Question but it would appear to us as curious and well-contrived a Frame as that of an human Body. We should see the same Concatenation and Subserviency, the same Necessity and Usefulness, the same Beauty and Harmony in all and every of its Parts, as what we discover in the Body of every single Animal.

The more extended our Reason is, and the more able to grapple with immense Objects, the greater still are those Discoveries which it makes of Wisdom and Providence in the Work of the Creation. A Sir *Isaac Newton*, who stands up as the Miracle of the present Age, can look through a whole Planetary System; consider it in its Weight, Number, and Measure; and draw from it as many Demonstrations of infinite Power and Wisdom, as a more confined Understanding is able to deduce from the System of an Human Body.

But to return to our Speculations on Anatomy, I shall here consider the Fabrick and Texture of the Bodies of Animals in one particular View, which, in my Opinion, shews the Hand of a thinking and all-wise Being in their Formation, with the Evidence of a thousand Demonstrations. I think we may lay this down as an incontested Principle, that Chance never acts in a perpetual Uniformity and Consistence with it self. If one should always fling the same Number with ten thousand Dice, or see every Throw just five times less, or five times more in Number, than the Throw which immediately preceded it, who would not imagine there is some invisible Power which directs the Cast? This is the Proceeding which we find in the Operations of Nature. Every kind of Animal is diversifyed by different Magnitudes, each of which gives Rise to a different Species. Let a Man trace the Dog or Lion Kind, and he will observe how many of the Works of Nature are published, if I may use the Expression, in a variety of Editions. If we look into the Reptile World, or into those different Kinds of Animals that fill the Element of Water, we meet with the same Repetitions among several Species, that differ very little from one another, but in Size and Bulk. You find the same Creature, that is drawn at large, copied out in several Proportions, and ending in Miniature. It would be tedious to produce Instances of this regular Conduct in Providence, as it would be superfluous to those who are versed in the Natural History of Animals. The Magnificent Harmony of the Universe is such, that we may observe innumerable °*Divisions* running upon the same *Ground*. I might also extend this Speculation to the dead Parts of Nature, in which we may find Matter disposed into many *similar* Systems, as well in our Survey of Stars and Planets, as of Stones, Vegetables, and other sublunary Parts of the Creation. In a Word, Providence has shewn the Richness of its Goodness and Wisdom, not only in the Production of many Original Species, but in the Multiplicity of Descants, which it has made on every Original Species in particular.

But to pursue this Thought still farther: Every living Creature, considered in it self, has many very complicated Parts that are exact Copies of some other Parts which it possesses, and which are complicated in the same manner. One *Eye* would have been sufficient for the Subsistence and Preservation of an Animal; but, in order to better his Condition, we see another placed with a Mathematical Exactness in the same most advantageous Situation, and in every Particular of the same Size and Texture. Is it possible for Chance to be thus delicate and uniform in her Operations? Should a Million of Dice turn up twice together the same Number, the Wonder would be nothing in Comparison with this. But when we see this Similitude and Resemblance in the Arm, the Hand, the Fingers; when we see one half of the Body entirely correspond with the other in all those minute Strokes, without which a Man might have very well subsisted; nay, when we often see a single Part repeated an hundred times in the same Body, notwithstanding it consists of the most intricate weaving of numberless Fibres, and these Parts differing still in Magnitude, as the Convenience of their particular Situation requires; sure a Man must have a strange Cast of Understanding, who does not discover the Finger of God in so wonderful a Work. These Duplicates in those Parts of the Body, without which a Man might have very well subsisted, tho' not so well as with them, are a plain Demonstration of an all-wise Contriver; as those more numerous Copyings, which are found among the Vessels of the same Body, are evident Demonstrations that they could not be the Work of Chance. This Argument receives additional Strength, if we apply it to every Animal and Insect, within our Knowledge, as well as to those numberless living Creatures that are Objects too minute for an Human Eye; and if we consider how the several Species in this whole World of Life resemble one another in very many Particulars, so far as is convenient for their respective States of Existence. It is much more probable that an hundred Million of Dice should be casually thrown an hundred Million of Times in the same Number, than that the Body of any single Animal should be produced by the fortuitous Concourse of Matter. And that the like Chance should arise in innumerable Instances, requires a Degree of Credulity that is not under the direction of Common-Sense. We may carry this Consideration yet further, if we reflect on the two Sexes in every living Species, with their Resemblances to each other, and those particular Distinctions that were necessary for the keeping up of this great World of Life.

There are many more Demonstrations of a Supreme Being, and of his transcendent Wisdom, Power and Goodness in the Formation of the Body of a living Creature, for which I refer my Reader to other Writings, particularly to the Sixth Book of the Poem Entitled *Creation*, where the Anatomy of the human Body is described with Great Perspicuity and Elegance.[3] I have been particular on the Thought which runs through this Speculation, because I have not seen it enlarged upon by others.   O

No. 385 [BUDGELL]

[Friendship]

Thursday, 22 May 1712

— *Theseâ pectora juncta fide.* Ovid.[1]

I intend the Paper for this Day as a loose Essay upon *Friendship*, in which I shall throw my Observations together without any set Form, that I may avoid repeating what has been often said on this Subject.

Friendship is *a strong and habitual Inclination in two Persons to Promote the Good and Happiness of one another.* Tho' the Pleasures and Advantages of Friendship have been largely celebrated by the best moral Writers, and are considered by all as great Ingredients of human Happiness, we very rarely meet with the Practice of this Virtue in the World.

Every Man is ready to give in a long Catalogue of those Virtues and good Qualities he expects to find in the Person of a Friend, but very few of us are careful to cultivate them in our selves.

Love and Esteem are the first Principles of Friendship, which always is imperfect where either of these two is wanting.

As, on the one Hand, we are soon ashamed of loving a Man whom we cannot esteem; so, on the other, tho' we are truly sensible of a Man's Abilities, we can never raise our selves to the Warmths of Friendship, without an affectionate Good-Will towards his Person.

Friendship immediately banishes Envy under all its Disguises. A Man who can once doubt whether he should rejoice in his Friend's being happier than himself, may depend upon it that he is an utter Stranger to this Virtue.

There is something in Friendship so very great and noble, that in those fictitious Stories which are invented to the Honour of any particular Person, the Authors have thought it as necessary to make their Hero a Friend as a Lover. *Achilles* has his *Patroclus*, and *Æneas* his *Achates*.[2] In the first of these Instances we may observe, for the Reputation of the Subject I am treating of, that *Greece* was almost ruined by the Heroe's Love, but was preserved by his Friendship.

The Character of *Achates* suggests to us an Observation we may often make on the Intimacies of great Men, who frequently chuse their Companions rather for the Qualities of the Heart than those of the Head, and prefer Fidelity in an easy inoffensive complying Temper to those Endowments which make a much great Figure among Mankind. I do not remember that *Achates*, who is represented as the first Favourite, either gives his Advice, or strikes a Blow, thro' the whole *Æneid*.

A Friendship which makes the least Noise is very often most useful, for which Reason I should prefer a prudent Friend to a zealous one.

[3]*Atticus*, one of the best Men of ancient *Rome*, was a very remarkable instance of what I am here speaking [of]. This extraordinary Person, amidst the Civil Wars of his Country, when he saw the Designs of all Parties equally tended to the Subversion of Liberty, by constantly preserving the Esteem and Affection of both the Competitors, found Means to serve his Friends on either Side; and while he sent Money to young *Marius*, whose Father was declared an Enemy of the Common-wealth, he was himself one of *Sylla*'s chief Favourites, and always near that General.

During the War between *Cæsar* and *Pompey*, he still maintained the same Conduct. After the Death of *Cæsar* he sent Money to *Brutus* in his troubles, and did a Thousand good Offices to *Anthony*'s Wife and Friends when that Party seemed ruined. Lastly, even in that bloody War between *Anthony* and *Augustus*, *Atticus* still kept his Place in both their Friendships, insomuch that the first, says *Cornelius Nepos*, whenever he was absent from *Rome* in any Part of the Empire, writ punctually to him what he was doing, what he read, and whither he intended to go; and the latter gave him constantly an exact Account of all his Affairs.

A Likeness of Inclinations in every Particular is so far from being requisite to form a Benevolence in two Minds towards each other, as it is generally imagined, that I believe we shall find some of the firmest Friendships to have been contracted between Persons of different Humours; the Mind being often pleased with those Perfections which are new to it, and which it does not find among its own Accomplishments. Besides that a Man in some Measure supplies his own Defects, and fancies himself at second hand possessed of those good Qualities and Endowments which are in the Possession of him who in the Eye of the World is looked on as his *other self*.

The most difficult Province in Friendship is the letting a Man see his Faults and Errors; which should, if possible, be so contrived, that he may perceive our Advice is given him not so much to please our selves as for his own Advantage. The Reproaches therefore of a Friend should always be strictly just, and not too frequent.

The violent Desire of pleasing in the Person reproved, may otherwise change into a Despair of doing it, while he finds himself censured for Faults he is not conscious of. A mind that is softened and humanised by Friendship, cannot bear frequent Reproaches; either it must quite sink under the Oppression, or abate considerably of the Value and Esteem it had for him who bestows them.

The proper Business of Friendship is to inspire Life and Courage; and a Soul thus supported outdoes it self; whereas if it be unexpectedly deprived of these Succours, it droops and languishes.

We are in some Measure more inexcusable if we violate our Duties to a Friend, than to a Relation; since the former arise from a voluntary Choice, the latter from a Necessity to which we could not give our own Consent.

As it has been said on one Side, that a Man ought not to break with a faulty Friend, that he may not expose the Weakness of his Choice; it will doubtless hold much stronger with respect to a worthy one, that he may never be upbraided for having lost so valuable a Treasure which was once in his Possession.   X

APPENDIX
Papers Related to The Tatler
and The Spectator

A. *Steele's Preface to the Collected* Tatlers
(*first printed in the fourth volume of the first collected edition*)

In the last *Tatler* I promised some Explanation of Passages and Persons mentioned in this Work, as well as some Account of the Assistances I have had in the Performance. I shall do this in very few Words; for when a Man has no Design but to speak plain Truth, he may say a great deal in a very narrow Compass. I have in the Dedication of the First Volume made my Acknowledgments to Dr. *Swift*, whose pleasant Writings, in the Name of *Bickerstaff*, created an Inclination in the Town towards any Thing that could appear in the same Disguise. I must acknowledge also, that at my first entring upon this Work, a certain uncommon Way of Thinking, and a Turn in Conversation peculiar to that agreeable Gentleman, rendered his Company very advantageous to one whose Imagination was to be continually employed upon obvious and common Subjects, though at the same Time obliged to treat of them in a new and unbeaten Method. His Verses on the *Shower in Town*, and the *Description of the Morning*, are Instances of the Happiness of that Genius, which could raise such pleasing Ideas upon Occasions so barren to an ordinary Invention.[1]

When I am upon the House of *Bickerstaff*, I must not forget that Genealogy of the Family sent to me by the Post, and written, as I since understand, by Mr. *Twisden*, who died at the Battle of *Mons*, and has a Monument in *Westminster-Abbey* suitable to the Respect which is due to his Wit and his Valour.[2] There are through the Course of the Work very many Incidents which were written by unknown Correspondents. Of this Kind is the Tale in the Second *Tatler*, and the Epistle from Mr. *Downes* the Prompter, with others which were very well received by the Publick.[3] But I have only one Gentleman, who will be nameless, to thank for any frequent Assistance to me, which indeed it would have been barbarous in him to have denied to one with whom he has lived in an Intimacy from Childhood, considering the great Ease with which he is able to dispatch the most entertaining Pieces of this Nature. This good Office he performed with such Force of Genius, Humour, Wit, and Learning, that I fared like a distressed Prince who calls in a powerful Neighbour to his Aid; I was undone by my Auxiliary; when I had once called him in, I could not subsist without Dependance on him.[4]

The same Hand writ the distinguishing Characters of Men and Women under the Names of *Musical Instruments*, *the Distress of the News-Writers*, *the Inventory of the Play-house*, and the *Description of the Thermometer*, which I cannot but look upon as the greatest Embellishments of this Work.[5]

Thus far I thought necessary to say relating to the great Hands which have been concerned in these Volumes, with Relation to the Spirit and Genius of the Work; and am far from °pretending to Modesty in making this Acknowledgment. What a Man obtains from the good Opinion and Friendship of worthy Men, is a much greater Honour than he can possibly reap from any Accomplishments of his own. But all the Credit of Wit which was given me by the Gentlemen above-mentioned (with whom I have now accounted) has not been able to attone for the Exceptions made against me for some Raillery in Behalf of that learned Advocate for the Episcopacy of the Church, and the Liberty of the People, Mr. *Hoadley*.[6] I mention this only to defend my self against the Imputation of being moved rather by Party than Opinion; and I think it is apparent I have with the utmost Frankness allowed Merit wherever I found it, though joined in Interests different from those for which I have declared my self. When my *Favonius* is acknowledged to be Dr. *Smalridge*, and the amiable Character of the Dean in the Sixty fifth *Tatler* drawn for Dr. *Atterbury*, I hope I need say no more as to my Impartiality.[7]

I really have acted in these Cases with Honesty, and am concerned it should be thought otherwise: For Wit, if a Man had it, unless it be directed to some useful End, is but a wanton frivolous Quality; all that one should value himself upon in this Kind is, that he had some honourable Intention in it.

As for this Point, never Hero in Romance was carry'd away with a more furious Ambition to conquer Giants and Tyrants, than I have been in extirpating Gamesters and Duellists. And indeed, like one of those Knights too, tho' I was calm before, I am apt to fly out again, when the Thing that first disturbed me is presented to my Imagination. I shall therefore leave off when I am well, and fight with Windmills no more: Only shall be so Arrogant as to say of my self, that in Spite of all the Force of Fashion and Prejudice, in the Face of all the World, I alone bewailed the Condition of an *English* Gentleman, whose Fortune and Life are at this Day precarious; while His Estate is liable to the Demands of Gamesters, through a false Sense of Justice; and to the Demands of Duellists, through a false Sense of Honour. As to the First of these Orders of Men, I have not one Word more to say of them: As to the latter, I shall conclude all I have more to offer against them (with Respect to their being prompted by the Fear of Shame) by applying to the Duellist what I think Dr. *South* says somewhere of the Lyar, *He is a Coward to Man, and a Brave to God*.[8]

B. *The Subscription Lists of the Collected* Tatlers *and* Spectators

The octavo edition of the collected *Tatlers* was published as a subscription venture, one set on ordinary paper at ten shillings a volume, another on 'fine Royal' paper at a pound. This is apparently the first publication in England of a collected periodical by such a method. The octavo collected *Spectators* were likewise published by subscription. As was the custom, lists of the subscribers' names were printed in the sets, to throw reflected glory on the books, the authors and the publishers, not to mention the subscribers themselves. A letter survives from Steele to Lord Halifax, dated 26 January 1710, in which he says that he encloses 'Mr. Bickerstaffe's proposal for a Subscription' and asks 'your Lordship's favour in promoting it . . .' (R. Blanchard, ed., *The Correspondence of Richard Steele*, Oxford, 1941, 35–6.) The *Tatler* list, it seems reasonable to conclude, was indeed vigorously promoted; more so than that of the *Spectator*, since it contains 737 names to the latter's 402. 122 persons subscribed to both publications. There are more peers in the *Tatler* list, and altogether it reads more like a careful effort to promote and exploit the publication. An analysis of the two lists cannot be too solemn, though, because there may be a few hidden overlaps. *Spectator* subscriber 'Mr. Smith' might be the same as one of the *Tatler* Smiths; elements of haphazard nomenclature are not surprisingly to be found in what might have been a complicated printing chore; the whole Ashurst family seem to have been given *Spectator* subscriptions by their generous *paterfamilias*, Sir William, 'Knight and Alderman', and the Bull family's subscriptions to the same periodical account for four of the subscriptions by women. 'Mrs. Ann Admirer' was no doubt a real lady who did not wish her identity to be made public even among *Spectator* readers, but was 'Mr. Pheasant Crisp *Merchant*' in the same position among the *Tatler* group? These are minor reservations, however, in reading a fascinating intellectual and social document.

Although the *Tatler* list is more elaborate, there does not seem to be any major difference in the composition of the two lists, except that thirty-nine *Tatler* names are entered for multiple subscriptions, a detail not at least recorded in the *Spectator* list: Whitgift Aylmer, for example, put

himself down for six books, Halifax himself for five, and 'Francis Popham
Esq.', the biggest spender, for seven. Both lists emphasize the political
connections of Steele and Addison: many of the Whig grandees appear,
to whom were dedicated volumes of the collected essays, Lord Chancellor
◊ Cowper, the Earl of ◊ Orford, Lord ◊ Somers and the Earl of ◊ Wharton.
Marlborough and Godolphin are also there, and Harley (Oxford) and St
John (Bolingbroke), the leaders of the succeeding Tory administration, are
absent. While among the writers ◊ Maynwaring, ◊ Martyn (Martin) and
◊ Budgell subscribed, the names of Arbuthnot, ◊ Swift (a compulsive
non-subscriber though) and ◊ Pope are missing. It is of course hazardous
to argue from the subscription lists about the composition of the
readership, since there are many reasons for subscribing which may not
involve reading, pressure by salesmen (quite apparent here), ostentation,
good intentions, or simply business obligation (which might account for
the name of '*Mr*. Richard Bull, *Druggist*'). Nevertheless, the make-up of
the total of 1,139 names gathered together does suggest more interesting
lines of thought. Ninety-three women subscribed (*Tatler*, fifty-nine;
Spectator, thirty-four); some half of these are wives or widows of peers,
some are the dependants of male subscribers. None the less, as befits
periodicals which devoted much space to the welfare of women, many
seem to be independent subscribers. There is quite a large group of names
with distinguishing marks of military or naval service (fifty-three: *Tatler*,
thirty-three; *Spectator*, twenty), quite apart from peers who also held field
rank (e.g. Argyle, Marlborough), or men who are not given their official
rank (e.g. Adam Cardon[n]el, Marlborough's military secretary). Similarly, a large group of civil office-holders is noticeable. These range from
◊ Godolphin, the Lord Treasurer, through aristocratic courtiers whose
places have political significance (e.g. the '*Duke of* Somerset, *Master of the
Horse*') to minor place-men such as '*Mr*. Edwards *of the* Exchequer'. Several
administrative mandarins are enrolled, like 'Josiah Burchet[t] *Esq*.',
Pepys's successor at the Admiralty, and 'William Lowndes *Esq. Secretary
of the Treasury*'. Similar figures are not clearly indicated, such as 'Edward
Southwell *Esq*.', M.P., one of the Clerks of the Privy Council and as the
holder of a little-known office, Secretary of State for Ireland, the
government's London-based Irish administrator. Of this group denoted by
offices held, there are thirty-eight (*Tatler*, twenty-eight; *Spectator*, ten).
The subscription lists also offer further important evidence of the middle-
class, monied audience to whom the periodicals were addressed. There is
a large group of London, mercantile, financial and commercial subscribers.
Fourteen of these are described as *merchant*; the Governor (Sir Gilbert

Heathcote) and the Deputy Governor ('Nathaniel Gould *Esq.*') of the Bank of England are specifically so identified, as well as twelve *aldermen* of the London corporation (*Tatler*, five; *Spectator*, seven); a druggist, two apothecaries, Thomas Tompion the famous watchmaker, two goldsmiths and a dyer give their business interests. Many other mercantile names, foreign and British, may easily be traced (e.g. 'Moses de Medina *Esq.*' and '*Sir* Solomon de Medina', two of the great army contractors; Matthew Decker, the rich philanthropist). Finally, generally distinguished men of the age to be met with number Sir Isaac Newton, James Thornhill, the painter, Vanbrugh, playwright and architect, Sir Godfrey Kneller, General Wade and George Berkeley, the philosopher.

The two lists have been conflated here, and each name is followed by T or S, indicating a subscription to the *Tatler* or *Spectator* sets. A number in brackets following T represents the multiple subscription indicated. Words within brackets indicate differences between entries for the same subscriber in the two lists. The original arrangement of peers, peeresses and commoners under each alphabetical letter is preserved. Alphabetization has occasionally been adjusted and punctuation simplified.

A

Earl of Abercorn   T
Earl of Abingdon   T
Duke of St. Albans   T
Duke of Argyle   T
Earl of Arran   T
Lord Bishop of St. Asaph   T
Lord Ashburnham   T, S

Lady Abergavenny   T
Right Hon. Lady Arran   T

Sir — Abercrom[*b*]ly *Bart.*   T
Sir Thomas Abney *Knight and Alderman*   T, S
— Acquiccavy   T
Mr. Benjamin Adams   S
Jo. Addison *Esq.*   T
Mrs. Ann Admirer   S
John Aislabie *Esq.*   T
Richard Aleworth *Esq.*   S
Charles Selby Amherst *Esq.*   S
Edward Ash *Esq.*   S
Sir James Ash   T

James Ashburn(e)   T, S
J. Ashburnham *Esq.*   T
Mr. Mor. Ashley   T
Sir William Ashurst *Knight and Alderman*   S
Lady Ashurst   S
William Ashurst *Esq.*   T, S
Mr. Benjamin Ashurst   S
Mr. Samuel Ashurst   S
Mrs. Elizabeth Ashurst   S
Sir Thomas Aston *of Aston* in Cheshire *Bart.*   T
Mr. Robert Attwood *Merchant*   T
Admiral Aylmer   T
Whitgift Aylmer *Esq.*   T(6)
Philip Ayscough, *A.M.*   T

B

Earl of Barrymore   T
Earl of Bath   T
Lord Bathurst   S
Duke of Beaufort   T, S
Duke of Bedford   T(3)

Lord Blessington   T
Duke of Bolton   T(2)
Earl of Bridgewater   T(2)
Duke of Buckinghamshire   T
Earl of Burlington   T, S
Lord Byron   T

Lady Bridgewater   T
Lady Buckingham   T
Lady Buckworth   T
Lady Burlington   T(2)

Montague Bacon *Esq.*   S
Mr. Thomas Bacon   S
Water Bagnal *Esq.*   S
Mr. Baignean   S
Henry Baker *Esq.*   T, S
Thomas Baker *Esq.*   S
Mr. Barnes   T
Da[c]re Barrett *Esq.*   T
Mr. Moses Barrow   T
Mr. Henry Bartelett   S
Mr. Barton   T
Charles le Bas *Esq.*   S
John Basket *Esq.*   S
Mr. Giles Batcheler   S
Mr. Bateman   S
Sir James Bateman   T
Thomas Bateman *Esq.*   S
Mr. Bathurst   T
Arthur Bayley *Esq.*   T
(*Mr.*) Alexander Bayne (*Esq.*)   T, S
Thomas Bacon *Esq.*   S
Justus Beck *Esq.*   T, S
William Bellamy *Esq.*   T
Mr. Richard Bellasyse, of Lincoln's
   Inn   T
Mr. Bellitha   T
Sir J. Bennet   T
John Benson *Esq.*   T, S
Mr. Benson   T
Mr. J. Bentinck   T
Mr. Moses Beranger   T, S
Thomas Bere *Esq.*   S
George Berkley, *A.M. Fellow of Trin.
   Coll.* Dublin   T

The Hon. Peregrine Bertie *Esq.*   T, S
Dr. Beson   S
Hugh Bethell *Esq.*   T
Sir George Bing   T
John Bird *Esq.*   S
Francis Bithel *Esq.*   T
Abraham Blackmore *Esq.*   S
Sir Richard Blackmore   S
Sir Lambert Blackwell   T, S
(*Mr.*) Jonathan Blackwell (*Esq.*)   T, S
Colonel Bladen   T
Captain Blakely   S
Charles Blunt *Esq.*   S
Mr. John Blunt *Esq.*   S
The Hon. Veere Boothe *Esq.*   T
Hugh Boscawen *Esq.*   S
Mr. Boucher   S
Mr. Peter Bowen   T
Brigadier Phineas Bowles   S
Lady Bowyer   T
Right Hon. H. Boyle *Esq. Principal
   Secretary of State*   T(3)
Mr. James Brain *Junior*   T
Mr. Tho. Brand   T
Charles Bressey *Esq.*   T
Col. Breton   T
John Brewer *Esq.*   T
Brooke Brides *Esq.*   S
John Bridges *Esq.*   S
William Bridges *Esq.*   S
(*The Honourable*) William Bridges *Esq.
   Surveyor General of the Ordnance*   T,
   S
Mrs. Katherine Bridgman   T
(*Mr.*) Robert Bristow (*Esq.*)   T, S
Mr. William Brockman   T
Mr. Tho. Brodrick   T
Mr. Edmund Brome *Fellow of* St.
   John's *College*, Cambridge   T
Dr. Brookes   S
Mr. Thomas Brookes *Merchant*   S
William Brown *Esq.*   S
Mr. Philip Browne   T
James Bruce *Esq.*   T
Mr. Walter Brudenell   T

Mr. William Bryan   T
Francis Brydges Esq.   T
Mr. John ô Bryen   T
John Buckmaster Esq.   S
Sir John Buckworth Bart.   S
(Mr.) Eustace Budgell (Esq.)   T, S
Capt. Peter Buer   T
Mr. Richard Bull (Druggist)   T, S
Mrs. Elizabeth Bull   S
Mrs. Mary Bull   S
Mrs. Jane Bull   S
Mrs. Sarah Bull   S
Mr. Richard Bull Junior   S
Josias Burchett Esq. (Secretary of the
   Admiralty) T, S
Mr. Tho. Burgh   T
John Buridg Esq.   T
William Burt Esq.   T
Mr. Lancelot Burton   T, S
Mr. Baron Bury   T
J. Buxton Esq.   T
John Byde Esq.   S
Mr. John Bythel   S

C

His Grace the Lord Archbishop of
   Canterbury   S
Earl of Carlisle   S
Lord Carteret   T, S
Lord Viscount Castlecomer   T
Lord Bishop of Chester   T
Earl of Cholmondely   T(5),S
Lord Colrain   T
Lord Coningsby   T
Lord Conway   T
Lord Cornwallis   T, S
(Lord) (William) Cowper (Lord
   Wingham, Lord High Chancellor of
   Great Britain)   T, S
Lord Craven   T
Earl of Crawford   T

Lady Cairnes   S
Countess of Carlisle   T, S

The Right Honourable the Lady
   Crew   T, S

Mrs. Bridget Cadogan   T
Mr. John Cadwell Merchant   T
Mrs. Cadworth   T
Mr. Tho. Caesar   T
Sir Alexander Cairns Baronet   T
Mr. George Camocke   T
David Campbell Esq.   S
Charles Carcass Esq. Secretary to the
   Customs House   S
Andrew Card Esq.   S
A(dam) Cardon[n]el Esq.   T, S
Sir Nich. Carew Baronet   T
Mr. John Carruthers   T
Capt. Henry Cartwright at
   Antwerp   T
The Hon. Mrs. Cartwright of Agno in
   Northamptonshire   T
Mrs. Mary Cary   T
Mr. Nat Castletoy   T(2)
Mr. George Caswall (Goldsmith)   T, S
Mr. John Catesby   S
Tho. Caverley (Cavalry) Esq.   T, S
Mr. John Chadwick   T
Hugh Chamberlen M.D.   T
Thomas Chambers Esq.   S
John Champante Esq.   S
Mr. Jo. Charlton   T
Mr. Robert Chester   T
— Chetwynd Esq.   T
Stephen Child Esq.   T
Charles Cholmondely of Chester
   Esq.   T
Hugh Chomley Esq.   T
Col. George Churchill   S
Mr. John Churchill   S
Mr. Edmund Clark   T
George Clark Esq.   S
John Clark of Hackney Esq.   S
Sir John Clark   S
Mr. Samuel Clark   S
Sir Samuel Clark   S
Mr. James Clarke   T

Mr. Sam. Clarke T

Stephen Clay *of the* Inner-Temple
  Esq. T

William Clayton *Esq.* T, S

Mr. Clerk S

Mr. Cobington T

Mr. John Cock *Merchant* T(2),S

Thomas Coleby *Esq.* S

Mrs. Collins T

The Honble Spencer Compton
  Esq. T, S

(*Mr.*) Gerrard Conyers (*Esq.*
  Alderman) T, S

Mr. Cook *Vice-Chamberlain* T

Mr. Thomas Cootes *Merchant* T

Sir John Cope T, S

Mr. John Corbet T

Thomas Corbet *Esq.* T

(*Mr.*) (William Henry) Cornelison
  (*Esq.*) T, S

Henry Cornish *Esq.* T

William Cotesworth *Esq.* T

Sir Clement Cotterel S

(*Mr.*) (William) Coventry (*Esq.*) T,
  S

Sir Charles Cox T

John Cox *Esq.* S

Mr. Thomas Cox T

(*Mr.*) (James) Craggs (*Esq.*) T(5), S

Mrs. Crake T

The Reverend Mr. Crank S

John Crew *Esq.* T

Mr. Pheasant Crisp *Merchant* T

Col. Crofts T

Sir John Cropley (*Bar.*) T, S

Mr. Robert Cross T

Mr. Crouch S

D

Lord Delawar T

Earl of Delorain T

Earl of Derby T

Duke of Devonshire T(3),S

Marquis of Dorchester T(3),S

Earl of Dorset T, S

The Lady Dacres T

Dutchess of Devonshire T

Mr. Robert Dalgardno T

Sir David Dalrymple T

Sir Abstrupus Danby *of* Swinton *in*
  Yorkshire T

Mr. Thomas D'Ath T

Major-General Davenport T

Ralph Davison *Gent.* T

Mr. William Dawson T

Matthew Decker *Esq.* S

Mr. Francis Delaferelle T(2)

Captain Delaval S

Mr. Delavall T

William Delaune *D.D.* T

Mr. Peter Delme(e) T, S

Alexander Denton *Esq.* T

Mr. John Devink T

Mr. Robert Dickins T

Mr. Samuel Diggle S

Col. Henry Disney S

Josiah Diston *Esq.* T, S

Mr. Thomas Dodd T

George Doddington *Esq. one of the*
  Lords Commissioners of the
  Admiralty T, S

Sir Gilbert Dolben *Bar.* T

Mrs. Dolben T

Mr. James Dolliffe T

John Dormer *Esq.* T, S

(*Col.* Richard) (*Brigadier*) Dormer T,
  S

Capt. Dorrell T

Mr. Henry Dottin T

Mr. Douglas S

Mr. Peter Downer T

Mr. William Dowson T

John Drummond, *Esq.* S

Mr. Charles Dubois *Merchant* T

Sir Matthew Dudley (*Bar.*) T, S

Mr. Matthew Dukes T

Thomas Dummer, *Esq.* S

Edward Dunce *Esq.* S

Mr. Dunch T

Henry Durley *Esq.* S
Mrs. Dutton T
Richard Dyett, *Esq.* T

E

Lord Bishop of Ely T, S
Earl of Essex T, S

Countess of Essex T

William East *Esq.* T
Mr. Eaton S
Mr. James Eckersall T
Lieutenant-General Ecklin T
Kenrick Edesbury, *Esq.* T
R. Edgecomb, *Esq.* T, S
Francis Edwards *Esq.* T
Capt. John Edwards T
Samuel Edwards *Esq.* S
Mr. Edwards *of the* Exchequer T
Samuel Edwin *Esq.* S
Sir G. Elliott T
Mr. William Elliott T
Mr. John Emilie T
Lieutenant-General Erle T
Mr. Erle T
Henry Erthman *Esq.* T(2)
William Etherick *Esq.* T(2)
John Evelyn *Esq.* S
John Ewer *Esq.* T
Francis Eyles, *Esq.* (*Alderman*) T, S
Lady Eyre T
Sir Robert Eyres (*Knight*) *one of the*
  Justices of (*the Court of*) *the Queen's*
  Bench T, S

F

Lord Ferrers T
Lord Viscount Fitzharding T
Lord Foley S

Hon. Lady Mildmay Fane T
Hon. John Fane T
Edward Farmer *Esq.* T
Mr. Farr S
Lieutenant-General Farrington T

Mr. Edward Faulkner T
Mr. Nath. Fran. Fauquier T
Mr. John Francis Fauquier S
Mrs. Fawkner S
Capt. Thos. Fazakerley T
Mr. James Fell T
John Fellowes, *Esq.* S
Henry Fern *Esq. Receiver of Her*
  Majesty's Customs S
Mr. James Fern T
Mr. Isaac Fernandez-Nunes T
Thomas Ferrers, *Esq.* T
The Rev. Mr. James Field T
Mr. Robert Findley S
Mr. Fisher S
Mrs. Frances Fitzherbert T
Mr. Robert Floyd *A.M.* T
Sir William Forrester T
Mr. Forrester T
Hugh Fortesque *Esq.* T, S
Major Patrick Fox T
Sir Thomas Frankland T
Thomas Frankland *Esq.* T, S
Will. Frankland *Esq.* T
Mr. Richard Franks T
Mr. Freeman S
Ash. Frowde *Esq.* T
Alderman Fryer T
Sir Henry Furness (*Kt. and Bar.*)
  (*Alderman*) T, S
(*Mr.*) Ro(bert) Furness (*Esq.*) T, S
Sir Comport Fytche T

G

Earl of Gainsborough S
Lord Gerard T
Earl of Godolphin *Lord High Treasurer*
  of Great Britain T(3)
Duke of Grafton T, S
Earl of Grantham T

Dutchess of Grafton T
Lady Guise T

Robert Gardner *Esq.* S
Mr. Nathaniel Garland T

Dr. Garth   T(3), S
Mr. Robert Gay *Surgeon*   S
Major Thomas Gay   S
Robert Gayer *Esq.*   T
Mr. Barnabas Geary   T
Mr. Edward Gee   T
Mr. Joshua Gee   T
Mr. Charles Gere   T
Mr. Charles Gervas   T
Edward Gibbon   S
The Reverend Dr. Gibson   S
William Glanvill *Esq.*   S
Colonel Gledhill   T
(Colonel) (Brigadier) Godfrey   T, S
Mr. Francis Godfrey   T
John Godfrey *Esq.*   T
Mr. De Gols   S
Mr. Goodal   S
George Goodday *Esq.*   T
Mr. Richard Goodlad   T
John Gore *Esq.*   S
William Gore *Esq.*   T
Mr. Harry Goring   T
William Gosselin *Esq.*   T, S
Mr. Christian Gottlieb-Pauli   T
Richard Gough *Esq.*   T
Mr. Gough   S
Nathaniel Gould *Esq. (Deputy Governor of the Bank of England)*   T, S
Mr. John Gould   T
Richard Graham *Esq.*   T
Colonel Grant   T
Mr. Kend. Grantham   T
Charles Grayden *Esq.*   T
Mr. Nathaniel Green   T
Mr. Thomas Green   T
Mr. William Greenwood   T
Mr. Isaac Guiger   T
Philip Gybbon *Esq.*   T
Mr. D. Gybbon   T
Mr. R. Gypps   T

H

Earl of Haddington   T
Lord Halifax   T(5), S

Duke of Hamilton   T
(Sir) Simon *(Lord)* Harcourt *(Baron of Stanton Harcourt, Lord Keeper of the Great Seal of* Great Britain) *(Knt.)*   T, S
(Earl) (Marquis) of Har(r)old *son to the Duke of Kent*   T, S
Lord William Hay   T
Lord Herbert   T
Lord Hertford   T
Lord Hervey   T
Earl of Holderness   T

Dutchess of Hamilton   S
Rt. Hon. Lady Eliz. Harris   T
Rt. Hon. Lady Eliz. Hastings   T

Mr. William Hales   T
Edmund Halsey *Esq.*   S
Hugh Ham(m)ersley *Esq. of the* Inner-Temple   T, S
Sir David Hamilton   S
Lady Hamilton   S
Mr. Thomas Hamilton   S
Mr. Hanbel   T
Mrs. Hanbury   T
Mr. John Hanger   S
Mrs. Catherine Harbon   T
(Mr.) Edward Harley *(Esq.)*   T, S
Mr. Went. Harman   T
Mr. George Harrison *of* Lyons-Inn   T
Moses Hart *Esq.*   S
Lieutenant-General Harvey   T
Mr. Henry Harwood   S
Mr. Nath. Hathed   T
Francis Hawes (Hawse) *Esq.*   T, S
Captain Heath   T
Sir Gilbert Heathcote *(Knight and Alderman) (Governor of the Bank of* England)   T, S
John Hedges *Esq.*   T
Mr. William Hedges   T
Mr. John Hellier *Merchant*   S
Charles Hendage *Esq.*   S
John Henley *Esq.*   S

Nathaniel Hern *Esq.* T
John Hiccocks *Esq.* S
William Hide *Esq.* T
Mr. Humphrey Hill S
Mr. Richard Hoar S
Mrs. Susan Hobbs T
Mrs. Hobbs S
Sir William Hodges *Bart* T, S
Charles Hodges *Esq.* T
John Holbatch *Esq.* T
Mr. Abraham Holditch T
Sir J. Holland *Bar. Comptroller of
the Household* T
Sir Charles Holt T
Robert Holt *Esq.* T
Mr. Holt S
John Holworthy *Esq.* S
Mrs. Elizabeth Hoole S
Mrs. Mary Hoole S
Nicholas Hooper *Esq. Serjeant at
Law* T
Colonel Hope T, S
Sir Thomas Hope S
Tho. Hopkins *Esq.* T
Mrs. Parnel Horton S
Sir Charles Hotham T
Sir John Houblon T
Mr. Howell S
Mrs. Huffam S
Mr. John Hughes T
Sir John Humble S
Sir Andrew Hume S
Sir William Humphreis *Knight and
Alderman* T
His Excellency Colonel Hunter *Governor
of New York* T
Mrs. Hussey T, S
Peter Hussy *Esq.* S
Mr. Hutchison of Newcastle T
William Hyde *Esq.* S

I

Earl of Ilay T
Lord Irwin T, S

Lord Johnson T

(The Reverend Mr.) (Benjamin) Ibbot
(*A.M.*) T, S
Mr. H. Ireton T
John Irwin *Esq.* T
Mr. Isaac S
Mr. Nath. Jackson T
Mr. Philip Jackson S
Mr. Stephen Jackson T
Mr. Jacobson S
Mr. Theodore Jacobson S
(*Mr.*) (*Sir*) Theodore Janssen T, S
Mr. Jarvis S
Edward Jefferies *Esq.* S
John Jefferies *Esq.* S
Edward Jeffrey *Esq.* T
John Jeffreys *Esq.* T
Sir Jos. Jekyll T
Lady Jekyll T
Sir John Jenings T
Lady Jermin S
Mr. Ch. Jervas T
Thomas Jett *Esq.* S
Sir Henry St. John *Bar.* T
John Johnson *Esq.* S
William Johnson *Esq.* S
Mr. Edward Jones T
Mr. Roger Jones T
Charles Joy *Esq.* T
Mr. James Joy T

K

Duke of Kent T, S
Earl of Kingston T(2)
Lord Kennedy T

Dutchess of Kent S

Mr. Kecke T
Mr. Robert Kelway *Surgeon* S
Nicholas Kemeys *Esq.* T
Mr. William Kerr T
Mr. Robert Keylway T
Captain Keyser *Merchant* T
Mr. Henry King T

Mr. J. King T
Sir Peter King *Recorder of*
    Lond[on] T
Sir Godfrey Kneller S

L

Lord Lansdowne S
Lord Lempster T
Lord Leven T
Lord Lexington T
(*Rt. Hon.*) *Earl of* Lincoln T, S
Lord *Bishop of* Lincoln T
Earl of Loudon T, S
Lord Lumley T

Mrs. Lacey T
Mr. L. Laconde T
William Lamb *Esq.* T
Sir John Lambert S
Mr. Ra. Lambert T
John Landsel *Esq.* S
Mr. Lattieu S
Mr. Richard Laurence (Lawrence) T,
    S
Sir J. Leake *one of the Commissioners of*
    the Admiralty T
William Le(t)chmere *Esq.* T, S
Mr. Bernard Levis T
Mr. Lewin T
Mr. Lewis S
Mr. Stephen Lilly S
Mr. William Lingren T
Mr. Linton T
Mr. Edward Lloyd T
Mr. Thomas Lloyd *Merchant* T
W. Lloyd *D.D.* T
William Lloyd *A.M. Chancellor of*
    Worcester T
Mr. Lockert T
Colonel Long S
Mr. John Long S
Mrs. Jane Lowman T
William Lowndes *Esq. Secretary of the*
    Treasury T, S
Mr. Robert Lowther T

Mrs. Margaret Lowther T
Otto Luis *Esq.* S
Lieutenant-General Lumley T

M

Lord Mackwell T
Earl of Manchester T(2), S
Lord Mark [K]err T
Duke of Marlborough T(3)
Earl of Marr T(2)
Lord Mohun T, S
Earl of Montrath T
Duke of Montross T
Duke of Mountague T, S
Lord Mountjoy T

Dutchess of Marlborough T
Dutchess of Monmouth S
Dutchess of Mountague T

Randle McDonnell *of the* Middle-
    Temple *Esq.* T
Mr. Kenneth Mackenzie S
Mr. Charles Maddocks T
Mr. Robert Maddocks T
Mr. Thomas Maddocks T
John Manley *Esq.* S
Sir John Manly T
Sir George Markham T
Mrs. Isabella Marro T
Sir Robert Marsham S
Henry Martin *Esq.* S
Richard Martyn *Esq.* T
Mr. Will Martyn T
Colonel Samuel Masham T
Mr. Robert Masham T
Sir Strensham Masters S
Mr. Harcourt Masters S
Reverend Mr. Masters T
Mr. Masters T
Thomas Maule *Esq.* T, S
(*Mr.*) (*Arthur*) Maynwaring
    (*Esq.*) T, S
Mrs. Mayowe S
Mr. John Mead T, S
Mr. James Meade T

G. Medcalf *Esq.* S
Moses de Medina *Esq.* T, S
Sir Solomon de Medina S
(*Mr.*) Charles Mein (Esq.) T, S
Mr. David Mercatur T
Lieutenant-General Meredith T
Richard Meriweather *Esq.* T
Mr. Alexander Merreal T
John Methuen *Esq.* S
P. Methuen *Esq.* T
D'Oyley Michel *Esq.* T
Robert Michell *Esq.* T
Thomas Mickelthwaite *Esq.* S
Mr. Benjamin Middleton T
Mr. Thomas Middleton T
The Hon. Benj. Mildmay *Esq.* T
Carew Mildmay *Esq.* T
Mr. John Mille T
Edmund Miller *Esq.* S
The Reverend Mr. Mills *Master,*
   Croyden *School* S
Mr. John Mitchell S
Colonel Molesworth *of the Guards* T
John Molesworth *Esq.* T
Col. Moncall T
Mr. Moncton T
John Montague *Esq.* T
John Montgomery *Esq.* S
Mr. Moor T
Mr. Thomas Moore T
William Morgan *Esq.* S
Mr. Henry Morison T
Brigadier Henry Morrison S
Mr. John Morrys T
Mr. John Morton S
Mr. Charles Morton *Junior* S
Captain Moses T
Mr. Mottley T
Christopher Mountague *Esq.* T
Edward Wortley Mountague *Esq.* T
Sir James Mountague *Attorney
   General* T
John Mountague *Esq.* S
Samuel Wortley Mountague *Esq.* T

William Mowbray *of the* Inner-Temple
   Gent. T
Joseph Moyle *Esq.* S
Brigadier Munden S

N

Duke of Newcastle T(3)
Lord Henry Newport T
Lord North and Grey T
Earl of Northesk T
Lord Bishop of Norwich T

Rt. Hon. Lady Northampton T
Dutchess of Northumberland T

Sir David Nairne T
Mr. (George) (G.) Naylor T, S
Mr. Negus S
Mrs. Ann Nelthorp T
Mr. James Nelthrop S
Gray Neville *Esq.* T
The Hon. Thomas Newport *Esq.* T
The Hon. Mrs. Newport S
Henry Newton *L.L.D.* S
Sir Isaac Newton T, S
Denton Nicholas *M.D.* T
Colonel Francis Nicholson T
Cloberry Noel *Esq.* T
Sir John Norris T
Mr. Robert Norris *Merchant* T
Sir Edward Northey (*Knight, Her
   Majesty's Attorney General*) T, S

O

Earl of Orford T
Earl of Orkney T(2)
Earl of Orrery T
Lord Ossulston T
Lord Bishop of Oxford T

Mr. William Ogbourne S
Lady Oglethorpe S
Sir Richard Onslow *Speaker of the
   House of Commons* T
Thomas Onslow *Esq.* S
Mr. John Osgood T

John Owen *of the* Inner-Temple
   Esq. T
Mr. Michael Owen   T
Newdigate Owsley *Esq.*   T
Sir Henry Oxenden   T, S

P

Lord Pagete   T
Lord Chief Justice Parker/*Sir* Thomas
   Parker, *Knight, Lord Chief Justice of*
   the Court of Queen's Bench   T, S
Lord Pelham   T, S
Lord Pembroke   T
Earl of Plymouth   T
Lord Pollworth   T
Earl of Portland   T(4), S
Earl Poulett   T

Lady M. Pierrepoint   T
Lady Portland   T

Mr. Page   T
Mr. Thomas Paget   T
Mr. John Pain   T
Lieutenant General Palmes   S
Sir P. Parker   S
William Parker *Esq.*   S
Mr. Henry Parsons   T
The Hon. Mrs. Ann Paston   T
Mr. William Pate   T
Edward Paunceforth *Esq.*   S
Mr. Pearce   S
Mr. James Pearse   T
Sir Charles Peers *Knight and*
   Alderman   T, S
Henry Pelham *Esq. of* Lewes *in*
   Sussex   S
Thomas Pelham *Esq.*   T
Colonel John Pendlebury   S
Mr. Matt. Pennyfeather   T
Mr. H. Penrice   T
Mr. J. C(hristopher) Pepusch   T, S
Mr. John Percivale   T
Micaiah Perry *Esq.*   T
Peter Pershouse *Esq.*   T

Mr. John Pettit   T
Mr. Gravett Phillips   T
Constantine Phipps *Esq.*   T
Brigadier Pierce   T
Mrs. Anne Pitfield   T
Mrs. Andrew Pitt   T, S
Fitz-William Plumptre *Esq.*   T
Henry Plumptre *Esq.*   T
John Plumptree *Esq.*   T
David Polhill *Esq.*   T
Robert Pooley *Esq.*   T, S
Francis Popham *Esq.*   T(7)
John Popham *of the City of*
   Westminster *Esq.*   T
J. Poulteney *Esq.*   T
Mrs. Elizabeth Poultney   S
Mr. Jeremiah Powell   S
Richard Powis *Esq.*   S
Sir Thomas Powis   T
Mrs. Jane Powlett   S
Mr. Baron Price   T
Mr. John Prince   T
Mr. H. Pyne   T

Q

Duke of Queensberry *and* Dover
   Principal Secretary of State   T

Mr. Jeremiah Quare *Merchant*   T
Mr. Daniel Quare   T
Sir William St. Quintin   T

R

Right Hon. Earl of Radnor   T
Duke of Richmond   T
Earl Rivers   T
Lord Rockingham   T(2)
Earl of Rolles   T
Earl of Rosebery   T
Lord Rosse   T
Earl of Rothes   T
Lord Edward Russell   T
Duke of Rutland   T
Lord Ryalton   T, S

Mr. Rene Rane   T
Mr. Thomas Raper   T
Mr. Matthew Raper   T
(*Sir*) Robert Raymond (*Esq.*) (*Her Majesty's*) *Solicitor-General*   T, S
Mr. James Raymond   T
Sir Thomas Read   T
Sir William Read *Her Majesty's Oculist*   T
Sir Robert Rich   S
Edward Richards *of* Exeter-College (*Oxon.*) *L.L.B.*   T, S
Mr. John Richardson   T
Mr. Barnham Rider   T
John Ridge *Esq.*   T
The Hon. Russell Robartes   T
Mr. Christopher Robinson   S
Sir William Robinson   T
Mrs. Elinor Rogers   S
Mr. Rolfe *of* Lincolns-Inn   T
Sir Edward Rolt   S
Edward Rolt *Esq.*   S
Stephen Ronjat *Serjeant-Surgeon to* King William III   T
Mr. Ch. Rosse   T
Joseph Rous *Esq.*   T
Mr. Nathaniel Rous   T
Guy Roussignac *of* Bromley *in Kent M.D.*   T
John Rudge *Esq.*   S
Colonel Russel   T
Philip Ryley *Esq.*   S
Mr. John Rymer   T(2)

S

Earl of Salisbury   T
Lord Bishop of Sarum   T
Earl of Scarborough   T
Earl of Scarsdale   T
Duke of Schonberg   T
Earl of Seafield   T
Lord Percy Seymour   T
Lord Shannon   T, S
Lord Shelburne   T
Lord Sherrard   T

Duke of Shrewsbury *Lord Chamberlain*   T
Duke of Somerset *Master of the Horse*   T
Lord Som(m)ers (*President of Her Majesty's Council*)   T(2), S
Earl of Sunderland   T

Rt. Hon. Lady Caroline Schonburg   T
Lady Scudamore   S
Dutchess of Somerset   S
Countess of Sunderland   T

Mr. Jacob Salemo   T
Sir Richard Sandford   S
Mr. William Sankey   T
Mr. Andrew Sansom   T
Mr. Nicholas Santini   T
Major Saule   T, S
John Savage *D.D.*   T
Sir George Savill *Bar.*   T(2)
Jacob Sawbridge *Esq.*   S
Mr. G. Sayer   T
Mr. Tho. Scawen   T
Thomas Scawen *Esq.*   T, S
Sir William Scawen   T
Thomas Scot *Esq.*   S
Sir John Scott   T
Mr. Gervase Scroop   S
Mr. Baron Scroop   S
Mrs. Elizabeth Scurlock   T
Sir Thomas Se(a)bright (*Bar.*)   T, S
— Sedgwick *of the* Middle-Temple *Esq.*   T
Mrs. Henry Segar   S
James Selby *Serjeant at Law*   T
Mr. J. Selwyn   T
Mr. William Semserf   T
Lieutenant-General (William) Seymour   T, S
Dr. Shadwell   T, S
Mark Shaftoe *Esq.*   T
Mr. Charles Shales   S
Mr. Samuel Sheafe   T
Mr. Henry Sheibell *Apothecary*   T
Samuel Shepherd *Esq.*   S

Mr. Robey Sherwin S

Mr. George Ship(p)man T, S

John Shute *Esq. Commissioner of the Customs* T

Mr. Peter Siris T

Mr. Abel Slany T

Hans Sloane *M.D.* T

Mr. Sloper S

William Sloper *Esq.* S

The Reverend Dr. Smallbrooke S

George Smalridge *D.D.* T

Mr. John Smart *of the Town-Clerk's Office* T

John Smith *Esq. Chancellor of the Exchequer* T

John Smith *Esq. of Beaufort-Buildings* T

Tho. Smith *Esq.* T(2)

Mr. T. Smith T

Mr. Smith S

Mr. John Smyth *B.B.* T

Mr. Christopher Soan *Senior* T

Mr. T. Southerne T(2)

Edward Southwell *Esq.* T, S

Mr. Spragg T

Thomas Spratt *Archdeacon of* Rochester T

Lieutenant General Stanhope T, S

Charles Stanhope *of the* Inner-Temple *Esq.* T

Mr. Philip Stanhope S

Sir Samuel Stanier *Knight and Alderman* T

Sir John Stanley *Bar.* T

Mr. Henry Stannyford S

Mrs. Mary Steele T

Walter Stephens *of* Dublin *Esq.* T

Mrs. Dorothy Stepney S

Alexander Stevenson *Esq.* S

General William Stewart S

Jo. Stillingfleet *A.M.* T

Mr. Robert Stockdale T, S

Mr. John Stone T

Mr. Henry Stratford T

Sir William Strickland T

Mr. Strickland T

(*Mr.*) George Stubbs (A.M. Fellow of Exeter *College*, Oxon) T, S

Mr. John Styleman S

Mr. Abr. Swift T(2)

Arthur Swift *Esq.* S

T

Lord Tamworth S

Earl of Thanet T

Earl of Thomond S

Lord Toumult T

Lord Tyrawly T

John Tayleur *Esq.* T

James Taylor *Esq.* S

John Taylor *Esq.* S

John Taylor *of the War Office Esq.* T

Jos. Taylor *of the* Inner Temple *Esq.* T

Mr. Jonah Taylor T

Mr. Taylor T

Mr. J. Taylour T

Sir Richard Temple *Bart.* T, S

Fisher Tench *Esq.* T

Mr. Tennison S

Mr. Nicholas Terrell T

Belbey Thompson *Esq.* T

William Thompson *Esq.* T

Mr. James Thornhill *Painter* T

Robert Thornhill *Esq.* S

Mr. Thomas Thynne T

Lieutenant General Tidcombe T

Mr. Titus T

Mr. Thomas Tompion *Watchmaker* T

Mr. Tounton T

John Tournay *Gent.* T

Christoph. Tower *of the County of* Bucks. *Esq.* T

George Townsend *Esq.* S

Samuel Travers *Esq.* S

Mr. Travers T(2)

George Treby *Esq.* T

Major General Trelawney S

Mr. Henry Trelawney T(3)

John Morley Trevor *Esq.*   T
John Trimmer *Esq.*   S
Mr. Rowland Tryon *Merchant*   T
Benjamin Tudman *Esq.*   S
Samuel Tuffnel *Esq.*   S
Sir C. Turner   T
Richard Tye *Esq.*   S
Christopher Tylson *Esq.*   S
Mr. J. Tyrrell   T
Sir John Tyrwhit   S

V

Lady Ann Vaughan   T, S

(*Mr.*) J(ohn) Vanbrugh (*Esq.*)   T, S
Hon. William Vane *Esq.*   T
Mr. Robert Vansittart   T(2)
James Vernon *Esq.*   T
Thomas Vernon *Esq.*   T
Dr. Vernon   S
William Vesey *Esq.*   T
Mrs. Villiers   T
Marinier de Vryberge *Envoy from the States-General*   T

W

Earl of Warwick *and* Holland   T, S
Earl of Weems   T, S
Earl of Westmoreland   T
Lord Viscount Weymouth   T
Earl of Wharton   T, S
Earl of Winchelsea   T
Lord P. Winchendon   T
Lord Bishop of Winchester   S
Marquis of Winchester   T

Countess of Warwick   T
Lady Viscountess Weymouth   T, S
Countess of Winchelsea   T

Lieutenant General Wade   S
Sir Charles Wager   T
Mr. Humphr(e)y Walcot(t)   T, S
Thomas Walker *Esq.*   S
William Walker *Esq.*   T
Mr. Ben. Wall *Merchant*   T

Richard Waller *Esq. F.R.S.*   T
Mr. Wallis   S
Mr. Samuel Wallis   S
Mr. G. Walpole   T
Mr. H. Walpole *Junior*   T
Horatio Walpole *Esq.*   T
R(obert) Walpole *Esq.* (*Treasurer of the Navy*)   T, S
John Ward *Esq.*   S
William Wardour *Esq.*   T
Mr. (John) Warner *Goldsmith*   T, S
Mr. Warren   S
Mrs. Warter   T
Mr. Waterhouse   T
Hon. E. Watson   T
Jonathan Watson *Esq.*   S
Mr. John Webster   T
Sir Tho. Webster *Bar.*   T
Abraham Weekes *of* Rookely in *Hants Esq.*   T
Mr. Weld   T
Jos. Wells *Esq. Serjeant at Law*   T
Sir John Wentworth   T
Mr. Charles West *Apothecary*   T
Mr. John West   T
Mr. T. Wharton   T
Brigadier-General Whetham   T
Mr. William Whidden   T
Mr. Joseph Whiston Dyer   T
Sir Paul Whitchcote *Bar.*   T
Mr. George Whitehead   T(2)
Mr. Samuel Whitshed   T
Charles Whitworth *Esq.*   S
Mr. Richard Whitworth   T(2)
John Wilkes *Esq.*   S
Mr. Wilkinson   S
Mr. Robert Wilks   T
Lady Williams   S
Mr. John Williams   S
Robert Williamson *Esq.*   S
Dr. Wilmot   S
Mr. Windar   S
Sir William Windham   S
Lieutenant-Colonel Windham   T
Mr. Windham   T

Mr. Henry Wise   S
Lieutenant-General Wood   T
Charles Woodroffe *of the City of*
   Winchester *D.D.*   T
Sir Jo. Woolf *Knight and Alderman*   T
John Coden Woolf   T
Mr. George Woolley   T
Mr. H. Worsley   T(2)
Christopher Wren *Esq*.   S

Mr. Joseph Wright   T(2)
Mr. Thomas Wylde   T
Richard Wynne *Esq*.   T

Y

Mr. Yale   S

Z

Mr. Zachary   S

Notes,
Biographical Index,
Maps and
Glossary

Notes

1. *motto*] Juvenal, *Satires*, 85 . . . 86: 'Whatever men do [will make up] the hotch-potch of my book.' This stood at the head of each of the first forty numbers in the folio half-sheets.

2. *Tuesday, Thursday,* and *Saturday*] The days the post left London for provincial towns.

3. *All Accounts . . .*] Steele is joking with the newspaper practice of date-heading news paragraphs from various European and English towns. Visitors to London often commented on the large numbers of coffee-houses which were frequented for conversation, newspapers and periodicals, a fire, coffee and in the different houses different interest-groups for business or pleasure. See also *S*1, *S*49, *S*155.

White's Chocolate-house] Founded by Francis White in 1693, by this time it was a fashionable haunt of gamblers on the west side of St James's Street near the bottom, close to the palace; it is the ancestor of White's Club.

Will's Coffee-house] Called after its proprietor, stood on the north side of Russell Street, Covent Garden, at the corner of Bow Street; its hey-day was at the turn of the century when Dryden and his circle met in the first-floor 'wits' room'.

Græcian] Dating from 1652, it was probably the oldest coffee-house in London; standing in Devereux Court in the Strand next to the °Temple, it was a meeting-place for lawyers, as well as scholars and members of the Royal Society.

St James's Coffee-house] A rendezvous for Whig politicians, at the end of St James's Street, looking down Pall-Mall; it was kept by Mrs Elliot.

4. *Tho' the other Papers . . . our Superiors*] The four paragraphs of this plan, printed across both columns, were repeated in nos. 2 and 3 of the original folio half-sheets.

5. *Mr. Betterton's benefit night*] On 7 April 1709, the veteran actor Thomas ◊ Betterton, at the age of well over seventy, appeared in his benefit at Drury Lane as Valentine in William Congreve's *Love for Love*; he had created this youthful part in April 1695 in the play's extremely

successful première given by his breakaway actors' company at Lisle's
Tennis Court in Lincoln's Inn Fields. The benefit performance was said to
have brought him £500. Mrs Elizabeth ◊ Barry, who had long adhered to
Betterton's company, had retired from the stage through ill-health in
1707, but returned in the part of Mrs Frail and spoke an Epilogue written
for the occasion by Nicholas Rowe. Mrs Anne ◊ Bracegirdle had also
retired two years previously, but acted Angelica. Thomas ◊ Doggett had
created the part of Ben Sampson. Steele's little piece is characteristic of his
interest, as a dramatist and a man of the theatre, in the reform of the
stage, under serious attack at this time (see S65, p. 406).

6. *Mithridates . . . Theodosius*] Nathaniel Lee's 'pathetic' tragedy, *Mithridates, King of Pontus*, was first acted in 1678; his heroic tragedy,
Theodosius, or The Force of Love, first acted in 1680, was most famous for
the part of Pulcheria, created by Mrs Betterton.

7. *a Comedy now in Rehearsal*] Thomas ◊ D'Urfey's *The Modern Prophets,
or New Wit for a Husband*, acted in May 1709, exploited the newsworthy
activities of refugee millenarians, the so-called *French Prophets*, and their
English followers.

8. *News*] On 11 July 1708, at Oudenarde, Marlborough had defeated
but not destroyed the French army under ◊ Vendôme. The French had
fought well, though hampered by inefficient command, and their morale
was severely damaged. In early 1709, following this defeat, the fall of
Lille and a severe winter, the French had initiated peace negotiations at
The Hague, but the Allies' terms were pushed unrealistically high, and
a campaign was inevitable in summer 1709. On account of the abortive
peace negotiations, Marlborough did not take the field at Ghent until the
end of June, at the head of the largest allied army yet mustered, consisting
of 110,000 men. By a supreme effort, despite their strained economy, the
French fielded 100,000 men under Marshal ◊ Villars, so far undefeated.

9. *The death of Mr Partridge*] John ◊ Partridge, the astrologer; see
p. 26.

T3

1. *The Country Wife*] William ◊ Wycherley's comedy was first acted at
Drury Lane in January 1675. Steele's critique of the play shows quite
clearly his reformist sentimental, moralizing conception of comedy, but
also how actively he tries to defend the stage against current polemics
such as Jeremy Collier's hostile *A Short View of the Immorality and Profaneness
of the English Stage* (1698).

2. *Instructions to Vanderbank*] Sir Richard Blackmore's *Advice to the Poets:
A Poem occasion'd by the wonderful Success of Her Majesty's Arms in Flanders*

appeared in 1706 (two editions); the sequel *Advice to Vander Bank* in 1709 ran to three editions. A Whig, Blackmore was physician-in-ordinary to William III and Queen Anne; his lengthy *Creation: A Philosophical Poem* (1712) earned the praise of Addison for its religious tone, but 'Blackmore's endless line' was scorned by Pope in his *Dunciad*. Steele apologized for this 'Raillery upon his Work', in *Tatler* 14. Hangings such as those described by Blackmore were a feature at this time in great houses: see Alan Wace, *The Marlborough Tapestries at Blenheim Palace and Their Relation to Other Military Tapestries of the War of the Spanish Succession* (1968).

3. *Waller and Denham*] Edmund Waller, *Instructions to a Painter for the Drawing of the Posture and Progress of His Majesties Forces at Sea* (1666); Sir John Denham, *The Second and Third Advice to a Painter* (1667, etc.). Such works became a minor genre.

4. *the Pretender and the Duke of Burgundy*] After the dangerous but abortive descent on the Firth of Forth by a French fleet in spring 1708, Louis XIV allowed the disappointed Pretender to serve on the staff of his young grandson, the Duke of Burgundy, nominal commander-in-chief of the French army in Flanders. Burgundy's fumbling cost Vendôme the battle of Oudenarde.

5. *his Royal Highness*] Prince ◊ Eugène of Savoy, Marlborough's colleague and friend.

6. *the Stratagem*] George Farquhar's sparkling comedy, *The Beaux' Stratagem*, was first acted at the Queen's Theatre, Haymarket, on 8 March 1707.

7. *only on the Stage*] George ◊ Powell acted the title role in Nathaniel Lee's most popular heroic tragedy, *The Rival Queens, or The Death of Alexander the Great*, in Greenwich on 5 and 6 July 1710.

from T4

1. *Show-business*] Steele was much interested and engaged in the politics of the theatre. The opposition to the fashionable Italian opera voiced in this piece was made on social grounds, that it had become a craze of the ignorant rich (see *Spectator* 212), and probably that it split the small wealthy audience for the legitimate theatre. Addison's opposition to the Italian opera was on grounds of (literary) taste (e.g. *Spectator* 5). In 1708—9, in a precarious truce imposed on the theatrical factions by the Lord Chamberlain, the Queen's Theatre, Haymarket, the acoustics of which were relatively unkind to spoken drama, was allocated to the opera under the management of Owen ◊ Swiney; Drury Lane presented drama given by the united companies of ◊ Betterton and Christopher ◊ Rich.

2. *Opera of Pyrrhus and Demetrius*] An adaptation by N. F. Haym, first

performed 14 December 1708, of Alessandro Scarlatti's *Pirro e Demetrio*, English translation by Owen Swiney, though Nicolo Grimaldi sang the male title role in Italian; it was published 20 January 1709 (*Daily Courant*).

3. *a great Critick*] John ◊ Dennis's *An Essay on the Operas after the Italian Manner: with some reflections on the damage which they may bring to the publick* had been published in 1706.

4. *Discourse of Mrs. Manly . . . concerning Samplers*] The humourist Dr William King quite elaborately satirized the *Philosophical Transactions* of the Royal Society in a periodical with the title *Useful Transactions in Philosophy, and other Sorts of Learning*, announcing that it was 'to be continu'd Monthly, as they Sell'; they didn't, and only three numbers appeared. The first, for the months of January and February 1709, contained 'An Essay on the Invention of Samplers, communicated by Mrs Judith Bagford: with an Account of her Collections for the Same. By Mrs Arabella Manly, School Mistress at Hackney'. This piece, equipped with marginal references, travestied the essay by John Bagford on the invention of printing in the 1707 volume of *Philosophical Transactions*, communicated by Humfry Wanley, F.R.S.

5. *Mr. Pinkethman . . . Greenwich*] William ◊ Pinkethman (or Penkethman).

from T5

1. *A Project*] Jonathan ◊ Swift's anonymous pamphlet *A Project for the Advancement of Religion, and the Reformation of Manners. By a Person of Quality* was published on 9 April 1709 ('This Day', *Daily Courant*) by Benjamin ◊ Tooke. A second printing followed by the pirate Henry Hills, suggesting it aroused some interest.

T9

1. *The Old Batchelor*] William Congreve's earliest comedy, first acted at Drury Lane, 9 March 1693.

2. *an ingenious Kinsman of mine*] Jonathan ◊ Swift.

3. *Dr. Anderson . . . Sir William Read . . . Monsieur Roselli*] Three names commonly associated with advertisements for proprietary medical treatments; for Anderson, see *T224, n5*.

4. *Mr. Scoggin, the famous Droll*] John Scogan or Scoggin, said to have been a fool at the court of Edward IV; various printings of Scoggins' *Jests* are found, the earliest dating from 1626.

5. *our famous Noy*] William Noye or Noy (1577–1634), Attorney-

General for Charles I from 1631; his famous will left the bulk of his estate to his eldest son, with the rough jest mentioned by Steele.

from T 12

1. *little King Oberon*] Thomas ◊ Betterton, who had 'ruled' over his colleagues in the actors' company.

2. *Divito . . . the most skilful of all Politicians*] Christopher ◊ Rich.

3. *an Architect . . . Song and Dance*] Sir John ◊ Vanbrugh's huge echoing new Queen's Theatre, Haymarket, opened 9 April 1705 with an unsuccessful production of Giacomo Greber's Italian pastoral opera *The Loves of Ergasto*, succeeded by more failures. The second season started on 30 October 1706 with Vanbrugh's own comedy *The Confederacy* followed on 27 December with Betterton in his *The Mistake*, but with legitimate theatre he could make no headway against the competition of Drury Lane and he turned again to operas. He continued to lose money as an impresario, and finally sold all interest in the opera company to Owen ◊ Swiney at the beginning of 1708; thereafter, ironically, with plays only at Drury Lane, the Italian opera at the Haymarket prospered.

4. *a Surgeon*] Owen ◊ Swiney (see *T* 4, *n* 1).

from T 18

1. *The Approach of a Peace*] The conclusion of this paper is by Addison; see Preface to *The Tatler*, p. 486.

2. *the Duke of Alva, or Prince Waldeck*] Ferdinand Álvarez de Toledo, Duke of Alva, or Alba (1507–82), Captain-General in the Spanish Netherlands, 1567, until he asked to be recalled in 1573; his military campaign against protestant separatism was ruthless, but was eventually counter-productive. Prince George Frederic of Waldeck (1620–92), Field-Marshal and Prince of the Empire, commander-in-chief of the Dutch and allied forces fighting against the French, 1689.

3. *There is not a Yard of Linnen . . . Shirts on every Hedge.*] Shakespeare, *I Henry IV*, IV, ii, 40–46: '*Falstaff* . . . There's not a shirt and a half in all my company, and the half-shirt is two napkins tacked together and thrown over the shoulders like a herald's coat without sleeves; and the shirt, to say the truth, stol'n from my host at Saint Albans, or the red-nosed innkeeper of Daventry. But that's all one; they'll find linen enough on every hedge.'

4. *Post-Men or Post-Boys*] Jean de Fonvive's paper *The Post-Man* was Whig; Abel Roper's *The Post-Boy* Tory.

5. *Marius of Ancient Rome*] Gaius Marius (157–86 B.C.), uncle by marriage of Julius Caesar. He captured Jugurtha and ended the invasion

of Italy by Germanic tribes, 102—101 B.C. Overthrown by Sulla, he returned to Rome and after being elected consul for the seventh time, savagely massacred his opponents.

from T 25

1. *If you neglect to do all this . . .*] ◇ Swift, *A Tale of A Tub*, Section IV; the reference is to the burlesque papal bull addressed 'To all Mayors, Sheriffs, Jaylors, Constables, Bayliffs, Hangmen, &c . . .', concluding 'And if you fail hereof, G— d—mn you and yours to all Eternity. And so we bid you heartily Farewell./Your most Humble/Man's Man,/Emperor Peter.'

from T 29

1. *Novell and Oldfox in the Plain-Dealer*] William ◇ Wycherley's comedy was first acted in January 1676; in 'The Persons' of the printed play, *Novell* is described as 'A pert railing Coxcomb, and an Admirer of Novelties' and *Oldfox* as 'An old impertinent Fop, given to Scribling'.

from T 30

1. *The Suspension of the Playhouse*] The Lord Chamberlain closed Drury Lane Theatre on 6 June 1709 to settle a dispute between the players and the over-bearing Christopher ◇ Rich, who was to lose his patent.

2. *the Battle of Almanza*] on 14 April 1707, the Earl of ◇ Galway, allied commander-in-chief in Spain, was decisively beaten by a larger force under the Duke of Berwick, Marshal of France. Thereafter there was no chance that military victory could be gained in Spain to replace the French Philip V as King with the allied candidate Charles VI. There was a long and acrimonious post-mortem in Parliament on Galway's defeat.

from T 31

1. *Landbadernawz in Cardiganshire*] ? Llanbadarn Fawr, near Aberystwith.

2. *Fitzherbert's Grand Abridgment*] Sir Anthony Fitzherbert (1470—1538), one of the Justices of the Common Pleas, produced *The Grand Abridgement of the Common Law* (1516), the earliest digest of English law, a much-used reference work several times revised and extended.

3. *the ancient Bear-Garden . . . Gorman*] A bear-garden was a pit for the 'sport' of bear-baiting, setting dogs against a chained bear; it was also used for bull-baiting, sword-play, cudgell-play, wrestling and other rough pastimes. Steele in *Spectator* 436 gives a description of a 'Tryal of Skill' between James Miller and Timothy Buck, 'two Masters of the Noble

Science of Defence [swordsmen]' at the 'Bear Garden at °Hockley in the Hole', with all its ceremonies, using the same mock-heroic overtones as he employs here, comparing the activities in the bear-garden with the events in classical myths.

4. *Oyster-Woman*] Thetis, one of the Nereids.

5. *Dares, and Entellus*] Virgil, *Aeneid*, V, 362ff. At the boxing match in the games which Aeneas holds to celebrate the death of his father, a 'Sword and Casque' are given to the defeated Dares; to Entellus 'the Palm and Sword remain' (Dryden).

6. *400 Senators entered the List*] and 600 Knights, many of them rich and respectable, do battle in the arena, at one of Nero's gladiatorial shows (Suetonius, *The Twelve Caesars*, trans. Robert Graves (1957), 'Nero, section 12').

7. *A mortifying letter from the country*] This is plausibly nominated as Swift's writing, on the grounds of its subject matter, its satire of both sides of a question, its parallel with his satire *A Complete Collection of Genteel and Ingenious Conversation, according to the most Polite Mode and Method now used at Court, and in the Best Companies of England. In Three Dialogues,* which, though not finally published until 1738, was certainly under way at this time.

T37

1. *Banister and King*] John Banister (1630–79), violinist, composer and leader of Charles II's band.

2. *Valentine or Orson*] There were many broadside versions of this story, drawn from French Romance, of the twin sons of Bellisaunt, sister of King Pepin and wife of Alexander, emperor of Constantinople. Orson was brought up by a bear, terrorized France as a wild man, but was rehabilitated by the courtly Valentine.

T55

1. *A blind young man gains his sight*] Steele presents as a genuine case, and a suitable vehicle for his moral, aesthetic and scientific interests, an incident that provoked much controversy in 1709, and was therefore good for a summer essay and short story. Roger ◊ Grant claimed the cure of William James on 19 June, but on 10 September Timothy Childe published an 'exposure' of Grant in *A Full and True Account of a Miraculous Cure, of a Young Man in Newington, that was born blind, and was in five minutes brought to perfect sight*. Childe claims that the twenty-year-old James was not born blind, and that his imperfect sight is worse after the 'cure'; that in July, James and his mother sought a certificate of the cure from the

parish priest of St Mary's, Newington, presumably to forestall refutation, pleading that otherwise Grant would charge for the operation. Childe further alleges that Dr William ◊ Taswell, D.D., refused to give such a certificate and thereafter his signature was forged, the 'affidavit' being published in advertisements in *The Daily Courant* for 29 July, and other papers. The attack on Grant further says he had been a cobbler or a tinker and was an anabaptist preacher, in other words an illiterate impostor of mad religious opinions. The practice of cutting cataracts demanded ingenuity, nerve and extreme physical control, which Grant may well have possessed, and which orthodox medical men might well lack. A correspondent in *Spectator* 472 claims to have been himself cured by 'that skilful Artist' of a 'weakness in my Eyes next to Blindness', and mentions 'several Hundreds' who had benefited from Grant's ability.

2. *motto*] Virgil, *Eclogues* IV, 1: 'Let us attempt a nobler theme.'
3. *Mr Caswell*] Dr William ◊ Taswell.
4. *Charles XII of Sweden defeated at Poltava*] 'Hide, blushing Glory, hide Pultowa's day:/The vanquish'd hero leaves his broken bands,/And shews his miseries in distant lands . . .' (Samuel Johnson, *The Vanity of Human Wishes*, 1749, 210—12). ◊ Charles, wounded in the foot, fled from Poltava in the Ukraine to Bender (Bendery) in Turkish territory, now Moldavia.

from T56

1. ραϲκαλ] 'rascal' in Greek letters.
2. *Myrmidons*] The followers of Achilles; Steele continues with a mock-heroic comment on Homer's *Iliad*.
3. *Job Gadbury . . . Mr. Partridge*] John Gadbury (1627—1724) and John ◊ Partridge, two astrologers and almanac writers.

from T62

1. *Mr. Dryden's Definition of Wit*] 'A propriety of thoughts and words; or, in other terms, thoughts and words elegantly adapted to the subject' ('The Author's *Apology* for Heroick Poetry' preceding *The State of Innocence and Fall of Man: An Opera. Written in Heroique Verse*, published 1677, never performed); see *S62*, p. 344.

from T77

1. *A burlesque letter*] Marshal ◊ Boufflers is supposed to be writing about the small but crucial action that took place at Wynendael on 28 September 1708. Major-General John Webb with a smaller force beat off a powerful French attack under La Motte on the supply convoy from

Ostend to Marlborough's siege of Lille. One of the smaller tapestry panels at Blenheim Palace is entitled 'Wynendael' and shows part of the convoy, the woods, and the flight of the French attackers (see Wace, *Marlborough Tapestries*, 1968, pp. 78ff. and plate).

2. *Mr. Powel*] Steele used the name of Martin ◊ Powell, the puppeteer, in a series of running-gags satirizing Dr Offspring Blackall, Bishop of Exeter, a haughty proponent of the Tory doctrine of passive obedience to the crown.

T81

1. *The Tables of Fame: a vision*] Swift allowed a statement to stand in *Collected Works* of 1735 that one of the hints he furnished for *The Tatler* was for the Tables of Fame (see *T*249, *n*1), but this piece as written is clearly not from his pen. The idea of a Palace of Fame, with three tables for 12, 20 and 100 of the most famous men in descending degrees of renown, together with a side table for persons of great fame but dubious existence, like Hercules or Aeneas, had been sketched out in *Tatler* 67. Readers were asked to send their lists of suggestions for the first table only to Mr Bickerstaff at Mr ◊ Morphew's. Clearly the idea was meant to be a running activity, and there was also a hint of a vault for great villains. The build-up to the appearance of *T*81 was carried on by mention of the scheme in *Tatler*s 68 and 73, another plea for help from readers in *Tatler* 74 and a burlesque letter in *Tatler* 78. But either because it excited little reader participation, or because Steele lost interest in it, the present paper by Steele and Addison – the format of the vision is perhaps the latter's – is the only embodiment of the idea. It obviously telescopes into a single paper what was meant to furnish at least three. In *Tatler* 84, a letter asks why there were no women at the tables, mentioning Lucretia, a very pertinent query considering *The Tatler*'s discussion of women.

2. *motto*] Virgil, *Aeneid*, VI, 660, 662–4: 'Here is the band of those who suffered wounds fighting for their native land . . . and the worthy poets whose words were worthy of Phoebus Apollo, and the men who improved life by their skill and ingenuity, and those who earned remembrance by their other deeds.'

3. *Quintus Curtius . . . Arrian . . . Plutarch*] Quintus Curtius Rufus wrote a good narrative history in Latin of Alexander the Great, readable if uncritical, some time in the first century A.D. Arrian (Flavius Arrianus, *c*.95–175), a Greek from Nicomedia in Bithynia who served the Roman state as an army officer and administrator, wrote in Greek the best ancient account of Alexander's campaigns, in the form of a parallel to Xenophon's *Anabasis*. Plutarch (*c*.46–*c*.120), the Greek moralist and biographer,

included Alexander and Julius Caesar as one of the pairs of Greek and Roman biographies in his *Lives*. The spirit of Plutarch's lively, ethical, anecdotal interest in character-drawing, long familiar to English readers in North's translation, is echoed in Steele's own essays.

4. *Julius Cæsar . . . would have no Conductor but himself*] Caesar's surviving writings are two historical works, both self-justifications, the first subtly and brilliantly in the 'Commentary' on the Gallic War, the second more tendentiously political in the unfinished 'Commentary' on the Civil War.

5. *Lucceius . . . Sallust*] L. Lucceius was a wealthy senator, praetor in 67, a friend of Pompey but also friendly with Cicero, who sought a eulogy of his actions to be included in Lucceius's historical writings, not now extant. Gaius Sallustius Crispus (86–*c*.35 B.C.) was a wealthy pro-consul, who devoted his retirement to writing. One of his two surviving historical monographs, both vivid and dramatic pieces, *The Conspiracy of Catiline*, presents a much less favourable account of Cicero's public life than that offered by the orator himself.

6. *Polybius*] A Greek historian, diplomat, traveller, *c*.202–120 B.C. His perceptive *History*, which survives only in part, traces the rise of Rome to Mediterranean supremacy, from the beginning of the first war against Carthage; he was present with Scipio, his friend and patron, at the siege and destruction of that city in 147–146 B.C.

7. *Lucan the Poet*] Marcus Annaeus Lucanus (39–65); his only surviving work is a Latin epic, the unfinished *Pharsalia (De Bello Civile)*, in ten books, dealing with the war between Caesar and Pompey, strongly sympathetic with the latter. Lucan's epigrammatic poem was much admired in the Middle Ages; he is awarded a very prominent place in Chaucer's *Hous of Fame*; it fell out of fashion and by Steele's day was considered a repertory of 'false wit'.

8. *Diogenes the Laertian*] Diogenes Laertius (*c*.200–*c*.250), author of a set of *Lives and Opinions of* [82] *Eminent Philosophers* in Greek.

9. *Pythagoras . . . a very great Harlot in your Time*] Pythagoras believed in transmigration of souls.

10. *Phalaris and Musæus*] Phalaris, reputed tyrant of Acragas in Sicily in the first half of the sixth century B.C., who employed the punishment of roasting in a brazen bull, and to whom a set of *Epistles* were attributed, just at this time proved by Richard Bentley to be later forgeries. Musaeus, a legendary Thracian poet, pupil of Orpheus and fore-runner of Homer.

11. *the taking of Mons*] captured 21 October N.S. (10 October O.S.) 1709, the only result of Marlborough's campaign that year, after the bloody battle of Malplaquet.

from T86

1. *Dick's Coffee-house*] Dick's (or Richard's) Coffee-house in Fleet Street was opened in 1680 by Richard Turner.

T87

1. *the Cold-stream Regiment of Foot-guards*] Steele's own regiment; see p. 28.

2. *Bouhours and Rapin*] Dominique Bouhours (see S62, *n*6) and Nicholas Rapin (?1535–?1609), two French theorists of literary criticism. English readers had Rapin's *Whole Critical Works* in two volumes in 1706.

3. *the Action*] Malplaquet, fought on Wednesday, 11 September N.S. (31 August O.S.), described by Marlborough as 'a very bloody battle'. The French army under Villars and Boufflers withdrew in good order; the Allies, though masters of the field, suffered higher casualties.

4. *the Siege*] Of Mons; see T81, *n*11.

5. *the Battle of Coldstream in Scotland*] Following the death of Cromwell, General George Monck with an army of 6,000 men crossed the Tweed into England at Coldstream on 1 January 1659, the start of the military initiative that restored Charles II to the crown.

6. *Blenheim or Blaregnies*] In the battle called after the village of Blenheim on the Danube in Bavaria, 13 August N.S. 1704, Marlborough with Prince Eugène defeated the French Marshal Tallard, the first and most famous of his great victories. The battle of Malplaquet was offered by the French in an unsuccessful attempt to deny Marlborough the opportunity of besieging Mons. Blaregnies lies between Mons and Malplaquet.

T89

1. *motto*] Virgil, *Georgics*, II, 485–6: 'Let my delight be the country and the running streams through the dells; may I love the waters and woods though fame be lost.'

2. *Tom's, Will's, White's or St James's*] Coffee-houses. There were several called Tom's; this is probably the establishment opposite Button's in Russell Street, Covent Garden, called after its proprietor Captain Thomas West, and an after-theatre rendezvous. For the others, see T1, *n*3.

3. *Dick's Coffee-house, the Trumpet in Sheer-Lane*] For Dick's see T86, *n*1; the Trumpet was a tavern half-way up Sheer or Shire Lane running from the north side of the Strand to Carey Street, on the site of the present Law Courts. Isaac Bickerstaff's club met there: see T132.

from T101

1. *A Set of Wretches we Authors call Pirates*] Steele had clearly got wind

of a pirated collection of the first hundred *Tatlers* being printed by the
notorious pirate Henry Hills, Jr, and advertised this very week in Abel
Boyer's *Post-Boy*, 1-3 December 1709: 'This Day is published one
Hundred *Tatlers*, by Isaac Bickerstaff, Esq., on a fine Paper in a neat
Pocket Volume. Price, bound, 4s., which is less than half the Price of a
Set in Folio. Sold by H. Hills, in Blackfriars, near the Water-Side.' In
addition to this piece, *Tatler* 102 replied with an 'Advertisement' for an
authorized collected edition: 'Whereas I am informed, that there is a
spurious and very incorrect Edition of these Papers printed in a small
Volume; these are to give Notice, that there is in the Press, and will
speedily be Published, a very neat Edition, fitted for the Pocket, on
extraordinary good Paper, a new Brevier Letter, like the *Elizevir* Editions,
and adorned with several Cuts by the best Artists. To which is added a
Preface, Index, and many Notes, for the better Explanation of these
Lucubrations, by the Author, who has revised, amended and made many
Additions to the whole. N.B. — Notice shall be given in this Paper, when
I conclude my first Volume.' This 12mo edition did not appear until July
1710, at 2s 6d a volume, with the £1 and 10s volumes of the 8vo editions.
The notes and cuts advertised did not materialize (see p. 191). For further
information on Hills and the piracy, see R. P. Bond, 'The Pirates and the
Tatler', *The Library*, 5th series, 18 (1963), 257-74.

2. *motto*] Juvenal, *Satires*, VII, 86-7: 'The audience sits dumbfounded
at his poetry, but [Statius] starves unless he sells a fresh libretto to Paris
[the director of the Opera].'

3. *An ingenious Drole . . . Poor Tom!*] Thomas (Tom) Brown
(1663-1704), a voluminous satirical, miscellaneous and popular writer.
His *Amusements, Serious and Comical, calculated for the Meridian of London*
(based on Dufresny's *Amusemens sérieux et comiques*, 1699) first appeared in
1700.

4. *A liberal Education is the only one which a polite Nation makes
unprofitable*] The first legislation giving an author copyright in his work
was 'An Act for the Encouragement of Learning, by vesting the Copies of
printed Books in the Authors, or Purchasers, of such Copies during the
Times therein mentioned' (fourteen years plus a further fourteen years if
the author was still alive). 8 Anne *c*.19 was given the Royal Assent on 5
April 1710. The petition to draw up the Bill was presented in the
Commons on 12 December 1709, the week after this paper, which was
perhaps partly designed to influence the debates.

5. *the late Archbishop of Canterbury*] John Tillotson (1630-96); from the
1717 edition onwards, the *Works* of this very influential Anglican preacher
contained 254 sermons.

6. *the Memoirs of Sir William Temple . . . Tom Thumb*] Three separate, uniform, unauthorized titles of Sir William Temple's works, 'Printed and Sold by the Booksellers of London and Westminster', were issued in 1709: viz. *Memoirs: 1672–79*; *Memoirs, Part III*; *Miscellenea: the First part*, 'the 5th edition'. These are pamphlet-sized publications in a very small letter.

7. *Browner Paper*] The folio *Tatlers* were printed on notoriously cheap, brown paper: 'The Tobacco-paper on which your own Writings are usually Printed' (*Tatler*, 160).

from T 105

1. *Cheapside or Cornhill*] Part of the City (of London), the district of wealthy merchants.

2. *the admirable Poem called the Dispensary*] This popular burlesque poem supporting the physicians in their quarrel with the apothecaries first appeared in 1699. It was written by a physician, (Sir) Samuel Garth (*c*.1660–1719), a friend of Addison's and one of Steele's fellow-members of the Whig Kit-Cat Club of writers and political magnates.

T 112

1. *motto*] Cicero (Tully), *Laelius, sive De Amicitia* (*Laelius: On Friendship*), xviii, 66: 'Next, there should be a certain pleasantness of conversation and manners; such things add a certain relish to friendship: but shun sadness and harshness in every thing. There should be some seriousness in it, indeed, but a relationship ought to be more relaxed, freer and more agreeable, inclining more to good temper and affability.'

2. *Scipio and Lelius*] In the work from which Steele takes his motto, Cicero casts his essay in the form of a discussion in which Gaius Laelius Sapiens (b. 186 B.C), consul, orator and military hero, speaks of his friendship with Scipio (Aemilianus) Africanus, the younger, (*c*.185–129 B.C.), consul and destroyer of Carthage. The anecdote about the sea-shore, however, comes from Cicero's *De Oratore* (*The Orator*), II, vi, 22.

3. *Agesilaus . . . the Ambassadors of Sparta*] Agesilaus (*c*.444–361 B.C) was the lame king of Sparta; in the story the ambassadors are from Persia.

from T 130

1. *motto*] Horace, II, *Satires*, i, 75–7: 'Even Envy must confess in spite of herself, that I have lived with the great.'

2. *Pliny . . . Claritas & Nitor Saeculi*] Pliny the Younger (*c*.62–*c*.113) served in important offices under Trajan: the bright lustre of the age.

3. *a General . . . Posts suitable to their Characters*] These three paragraphs offer fulsome and open support for the administration threatened by a

crisis at court. The men praised are: the Duke of ◊ Marlborough; Lord Treasurer ◊ Godolphin; Lord ◊ Somers; Lord Chancellor ◊ Cowper; Edward ◊ Russell, Earl of Orford; the Earl of ◊ Wharton, Lord Lieutenant of Ireland and Addison's chief; and perhaps the two Secretaries of State, the Earl of ◊ Sunderland and Henry ◊ Boyle, M.P.

T132

1. *motto*] Cicero (Tully), *De Senectute* (*On Old Age*), 46: 'I am really grateful to old age which has increased my eagerness for conversation but destroyed my greed for drinking and eating.'

2. *the Trumpet*] See T89, *n*3.

3. *the Fight of Marston-Moor . . . the Rising of the London Apprentices*] A royalist army under Prince Rupert was routed by parliamentary forces under Fairfax, Cromwell and others, with a Scottish army, at Marston Moor near York, on 2 July 1644. A serious confrontation with Parliament took place in London on 28 July 1647 during which a petition on behalf of Charles I, who had been kidnapped by agents of the army, was carried by force into the Commons chamber by a crowd of pro-presbyterian London apprentices.

4. *Jack Ogle*] 'Mad' Ogle (?1647–?1685). His 'Humours' entered chap-book literature. His sister was one of the Duke of York's mistresses, and the Duke made Ogle a gentleman trooper in the body of guards commanded by the Duke of Monmouth, the King's bastard son (D.N.B.). The story referred to by Steele has Ogle pawning his rich trooper's cloak and borrowing his landlady's daughter's red petticoat to roll up on his saddle for parade. Monmouth, noticing this, gives the order, 'Cloak all!'

5. *the Battle of Naseby*] Between Coventry and Bedford, on 21 May 1645, the New Model Army under Fairfax and Cromwell completely defeated Charles I's army, and destroyed his infantry.

6. *a Stick rhimes with Ecclesiastick*] Samuel Butler's anti-Puritan anti-romance, *Hudibras*, Part I (1663), canto i, 11–12: 'And Pulpit, Drum Ecclesiastick,/ Was beat with fist instead of a stick.'

7. *Edge-hill Fight*] The indecisive first battle of the Civil War, fought on 23 October 1642 on the border of Warwickshire and Oxfordshire, in which the parliamentary forces under Essex showed that the King and Prince Rupert could not seize the military initiative.

8. *Discourse like that of Nestor, which Homer compares . . . His Tongue drop[pe]d Manna*] Homer, *Iliad*, I, 249: 'Nestor . . . the clear voiced orator . . . whose speech ran sweeter than honey off his tongue.' Milton, *Paradise Lost*, II, 112–14: 'But all was false and hollow; though his

Tongue/Dropd Manna, and could make the worse appear/The better reason . . .'

T 149

1. Sir *Francis Bacon . . . Maxim*} Francis Bacon, *The Essays or Counsels, Civill and Moral* (1625), no. 8, 'Of Marriage and Single Life': 'It is one of the best Bonds, both of Chastity and Obedience, in the *Wife*, if she thinks her *Husband* Wise, which she must never doe, if She finde him *Jealous.*'

2. *Three Letters of Pliny*} Pliny the Younger, *Letters*, vi, 4 ('To Calpurnia'), 7, and viii, 5.

3. *a beautiful Passage out of Milton*} *Paradise Lost*, VIII, 39–59, three lines omitted.

T 155

1. *motto*} Horace, II, *Satires*, iii, 19–20: 'He looks after affairs foreign to him and neglects his own business.'

2. *Accounts . . . from Bender . . . this great Monarch*} See *T* 55, *n* 4.

T 172

1. *The unhappy end of Mr Eustace*} After his essay on the effect of ungoverned passions, Steele introduces a short story based on a real murder which had taken place in Ireland on 26 March. Francis Eustace, Jr, stabbed his pregnant wife, daughter of Mr Bartholomew Wybrants, and escaped. On Sunday, 16 April, Eustace was apprehended by a Dublin constable, whom he fatally shot in the stomach and by whom he was in turn shot in the head and killed. The events were reported in the Dublin papers, and the London press printed reports of them. Relevant press extracts are given by R. P. Bond in *The Tatler: The Making of a Literary Journal* (Harvard U.P., Cambridge, Mass., 1971), pp. 224–6, Appendix C, 'The Murder of Mrs Eustace'. From these it is clear that the Eustace murder is a great deal more socially complex than the 'psychological' story that Steele chooses to dramatize. Francis Eustace was heir to a good estate; his name indicates he was a member of a catholic 'Old English' family, but he himself was a convert to protestantism of two years standing; he is described as 'formerly of *Castlemore* in the County of *Catherlough*, now of the City of *Dublin*'. Under the penal laws, a son who became a protestant could claim the estate of a catholic father. The murder took place, not as Steele's story suggests in Eustace's own country house, but in the Church of Ireland Bishop of Raphoe's house in Smithfield, Dublin. Pursuit of Eustace was undertaken and reward offered by the Wybrants family and the Bishop of Raphoe. The Bishop's 'gentleman' was concerned in Eustace's

apprehension, five or six miles out of the city, as he fled in disguise, ten days after the murder. He had during that time been sheltered and helped by people in the egg-market. A surgeon was imprisoned for treating the lacerations Eustace sustained as he escaped from the scene of the crime. The differences between the Irish murder recorded in the press, and clearly familiar to Steele, and the story in *The Tatler* point very clearly to the strong emphasis in Steele's fiction on sentiment, domesticity and personal relationships.

2. *motto*] Horace, II *Odes*, xiii, 13–14: 'Man does not pay enough attention from hour to hour to what he should avoid.'

T181

1. *motto*] Virgil, *Aeneid*, V, 49–50: 'This is the day, unless I am mistaken, which (such was your will, O Gods) I shall ever observe with grief and hold in honour.'

2. *a Hamper of Wine . . . at Garraway's Coffee-house*] 'Notice is hereby given, that 46 hogsheads and one half of extraordinary French claret will be put up for sale at £20 per hogshead, in Garraway's Coffee-house in Exchange-Alley on Thursday the 8th instant at three in the afternoon, and to be tasted in a vault under Messrs. Lane and Harrison's in Sweethings Lane, Lombard Street, from this day until the time of sale': advertisement in *Tatler* 181 (folio). Garraway's, founded by Thomas Garraway, is reputed to have been the first house to sell tea; it was a merchants' rendezvous.

from T195

1. *the Staggering Party*] The administration's affairs were going from crisis to crisis at court, as Harley's plans to take Godolphin's place went ahead with the Queen's approval. In June, Marlborough's son-in-law the Whig Earl of ♭ Sunderland had been replaced as Secretary of State by the Earl of Dartmouth.

T214

1. *Political change*] On 2 August, the Queen had dismissed Lord Treasurer Godolphin, replacing him four days later with a Treasury Commission in which Robert Harley was Chancellor of the Exchequer, the final move before the total collapse of the Whig administration.

2. *motto*] Virgil, *Georgics*, I, 393–4: 'Then, after showers, 'tis easy to descry/Returning suns, and a serener Sky' (Dryden).

3. *Mr. D'Urfey . . . writ a Dedication . . . upon a Misinformation*] Thomas D'Urfey dedicated the second comedy in a trilogy, *The Comical History of Don Quixote: part the second* (first acted at the Duke's Theatre,

Dorset Garden, in June 1694), to Charles, Earl of Dorset, 'To whom the world united give this Due,/Best Judge of Men, and best of Poets too.'

4. *Cardan . . . Machiavel*] Girolamo Cardano (Pavia, 1501–Rome, 1576), mathematician, physician and astrologer. Niccolò Machiavelli (Florence, 1469–Florence, 1527), political theorist, diplomat and historian.

5. *Non ulla Laborum . . . mecum ante peregi*] Virgil, *Aeneid*, VI, 103–5: 'No kind of struggle, maiden, breaks on me unexpectedly or unprovided for; all these things I have foreseen and inwardly pondered.'

T224

1. *motto*] Ovid, *Metamorphoses*, II, 5: 'The workmanship excelled the material.'

2. *John Bartlett of Goodman's Fields*] at the Golden Ball, by the Ship Tavern in Prescott Street, advertised trusses and 'Divers Instruments to help the Weak and Crooked'.

3. *The Inventors of Strops for Razors*] 'Jacob's Famous Strops' were available 'only at Jacob's Coffee-house, in Threadneedle Street'; Reynold's strops were to be had at Sam's Coffee-house in Ludgate Street; the 'Famous Original Venetian Strops' were sold only at 'Mr Allcraft's, a °Toy-shop', at the Blue-Coat-Boy, next to the Royal Exchange in Cornhill etc.

4. *the Case of the Morning Gowns*] There were regularly running, rival advertisements for 'bankrupt stock' silk, stuff and calico morning gowns for men and women; one lot at the Golden Sugar Loaf, next to the Horse, at Charing Cross (e.g. in *Tatler* 222); the other at the Black Lion, next to Foster Lane, Cheapside (e.g. *Examiner*, 7–14 December 1710).

5. *the several Proprietors of Dr. Anderson's Pills*] The 'famous Scots Pills' of Dr Patrick Anderson (see *T9, n3*) were sold by at least three rivals: John Gray's product, available at the Golden Head, between the little Turnstile and the Bull Inn on High Holborn (e.g. *Post-Boy*, 3 January 1699), did not have 'that griping Quality that is in the Pill of a perpetual Vain-boaster'; J. Inglish 'faithfully prepared' pills sealed in specially marked boxes, and sold them at the Golden Unicorn, next to the Maypole, in the Strand (e.g. *Post-Boy*, 23 October 1700); Mrs Man at Old Man's Coffee-house, Charing Cross, offered 'the right Scotch Pills, used by the Heirs of Dr Anderson in Scotland' (e.g. *Post-Man*, 23 October 1703).

6. *Dr. Clark . . . Sir William ◊ Read*] Clark's 'Ophthalmic Secret' was available at his house in Old Southampton Buildings, Holborn (e.g. *Post-Man*, 24–26 August 1710).

7. *Michael Parrot . . . a certain Worm*] 'Affidavits' by Michael Parot (or Parrot) appeared regularly certifying that he had 'brought away' a worm

sixteen feet long 'by taking the Medicines of J. Moore, Apothecary' (*Post-Boy*, 11 April 1710 etc.).

8. *The true Spanish Blacking for Shoes, &c.*] The advertisements referred to in the concluding section of this paper are:

Spanish Blacking] Advertised in *Spectator* 108 etc.: makes the shoes 'always look like New, never Daubs the Hands in putting on, or Soils the Stockings in wearing; neither has it the ordinary Gloss of German Balls, or the intolerable Stink of Syze . . . 1s 6d the Pot . . . from Mr John Hannam's °Toyshop at the 3 Angels near Fetterlane in Cheapside.'

The Beautifying Cream for the Face] 'An incomparable Beautifying Cream for the Face, Neck, and Hands; takes away all Freckles, Spots, Pimples, Wrinkles, Roughness, Scurf, Yellowness, Sun-burns . . . Sold only at Mr Lawrence's Toy Shop at the Griffin, the corner of the Poultry near Cheapside, at 2s 6d a Gallipot, with Directions' (*Tatler* 140). Also available were 'The Chrystal Cosmetick approved by the worthy Dr Paul Chamberlain' and 'The Britannick Beautifier: or the greatest Cleanser of the Skin in Nature'.

Nectar and Ambrosia] 'The highest Cordial in the World . . . the Cordial Dram the Czar of Muscovy so highly approved. Sold in 1s and 2s Bottles . . .'

Annotations upon the Tatler] Published by Bernard ◊ Lintot, August 1707; a satirical disparagement of *The Tatler* in the form of passages from the essays with comments, 'Written in French by Monsieur Bournelle: and Translated into English by Walter Wagstaffe, Esq.'; perhaps by William Oldisworth, a Tory journalist.

B.L. Bookseller] Perhaps a knock at Lintot, in retaliation for the *Annotations*.

T230

1. *The continual corruption of our English tongue*] The letter to Isaac Bickerstaff is by Swift, as the entries in his *Journal to Stella* show: 'To-day I dined with Mr Stratford at Mr Addison's retirement near Chelsea; then came to town; got home early, and begun a letter to the *Tatler* about the corruptions of style and writing &c.' (18 September 1710); 'I have sent a long letter to Bickerstaff: let the Bishop of Clogher smoak it [detect it] if he can' (23 September); 'Have you smoakt the *Tatler* that I writ? It is much liked here, and I think it a °pure one' (1 October). T230 is included by Faulkner in Swift's *Works* (1735), presumably by Swift's authority.

2. *Hooker*] Richard Hooker (*c.*1554–1600), author of tracts and sermons, and of a massive argument in defence of the Church of England,

Of the Laws of Ecclesiastical Polity, in eight books (printed 1593–1661). The latter is a monument of English prose.

3. *Parsons*] Robert Parsons, S.J. (1546–1610), controversialist and educationalist; his chief work is *A Christian Directorie* (1581, 1585 etc.), which also appeared in several editions in a protestant version, a book of devotional instruction.

4. *Sir H. Wootton, Sir Rob. Naunton, Osborn, Daniel the Historian*] Sir Henry Wootton (1586–1639), poet, diplomat and provost of Eton, whose writings appeared in a posthumous collection, *Reliquiae Wottonianae* (1651). Sir Robert Naunton (1563–1635), Secretary of State, 1617–18, whose *Fragmenta Regalia: Observations on the late Queen Elizabeth, her times and favourites* were several times reprinted from 1641 to 1663 and in later collections. Francis Osbourne (1593–1659), sceptical controversialist and historian, best known for his witty *Advice to a Son* (Oxford, 1656–8; many editions). Samuel Daniel (1563–1619), poet laureate after Spenser, dramatist and historian; his historical writing is partly in verse – *The Civil Warr between the Houses of Lancaster and York* (1595–1609) – and partly in prose – *The Collection of the Historie of England to the death of Edward III* (1612–18; several later editions with continuations).

T238

1. *The Description of a City Shower*] The poem, one of his best, is by Swift, who detailed its writing in his *Journal to Stella*: 'And now I am going in charity to send Steele a *Tatler*, who is very low of late' (7 October 1710); 'My *Shower* with you; why, the bishop of Clougher says, he has seen something of mine of the same sort, better than the *Shower*. I suppose he means *The Morning*; but it is not half so good. I want your judgement of things, and not your country's . . .' (30 November).

2. *motto*] Juvenal, *Satires*, XII, 23–4: 'The poetic storm rose.'

3. *Aches*] Pronounced *aitches*.

T242

1. *motto*] Juvenal, *Satires*, I, 30–31: 'Who could endure this lewd town, however hard-hearted, and restrain his anger?'

2. *Virgil said*] *Eclogues*, III, 90: 'Qui Bavium non odit, amet tua carmina Maevi . . .': 'The man who doesn't like Bavius, let him appreciate your songs, Maevius . . .'

3. *The best good Man, with the worst-natured Muse*] Written by John Wilmot, Earl of Rochester, in his verses *To Lord Buckhurst* (later Earl of Dorset).

T249

1. *The life and adventures of a shilling*] Swift claimed, or allowed it to be claimed on his behalf in *Works* (1735), '*it is well known that the Author writ several* Tatlers, *and some* Spectators: *and furnished Hints for many more. Particularly*, The Tables of Fame, The Life and Adventures of a Shilling, The Account of England by an Indian King [*S*50] *and some others. But, as we are informed, he would never tell his best Friends the particular Papers.*' Though well-written, *T*249 as it stands is not from his pen.

2. *motto*] Virgil, *Aeneid*, I, 204–5: 'Through various hazards, and events, we move' (Dryden).

3. *a monstrous Pair of Breeches*] The coins of 'The Commonwealth of England' bore on the verso, the date, the motto 'God with Us' and two joined triangular shields with the cross of St George and the Irish harp, respectively, which roughly resemble a pair of breeches.

4. *this Change of Sex*] Re-minted with the head of William III in the re-coinage of 1696, which was largely forced by the practice of clipping described above.

5. *The Splendid Shilling*] A mock-heroic poem in Miltonic blank verse by John Philips (1676–1709), published in 1705.

T271

1. *The Hand that has assisted me*] Addison.

2. *which of the whole have been written by me, and which by others*] See Preface, p. 485.

3. *all my Imperfections on my Head*] Hamlet, I, v, 79.

S1

1. *motto*] Horace, *Ars Poetica*, 143–4: 'He is not intending to produce smoke after flame, but after smoke, fire, so that he may offer striking marvels.'

2. *Will's . . . Child's . . . St. James's . . . Grecian . . . Cocoa-Tree . . . Jonathan's*] For Will's, St James's and the Grecian coffee-houses, see *T*1, *n*3; the Cocoa-Tree was a chocolate-house at the corner of St James's and Pall-Mall, the rendezvous of Tories and Jacobites, just as the St James's was a Whig house; Jonathan's in °Change-Alley was frequented by stock-jobbers.

S2

1. *motto*] Juvenal, *Satires*, VII, 167–8: 'Half-a-dozen or more shout with one voice.'

2. *Sir Roger de Coverly . . . that famous Country-Dance*] Sir Roger's name

is given as *Coverly* on its first appearance in the folio half-sheet paper and this spelling was kept in the first reprint. In later numbers, however, the spelling *Coverley* becomes established and remains the form by which the greatest character created by the *Spectator* essays is known to all readers of English literature. 'Roger of Coverly', the name of a country-dance and the tune to go with it, seems to date from the 1680s; the popularity of *The Spectator* imposed the new form of the name on the dance and tune too. *Roger of Coverly* had been used earlier as a name for a fictional character, with overtones of honest rusticity, in Tutchin's *Observator* for 25 March 1704. Dr Johnson remarks in his 'Life of Addison' that the 'personages introduced' are 'not merely ideal', basing his comment on a paragraph, perhaps revised by Addison himself, in ◊Budgell's 'Introduction' to his translation of the *Moral Characters of Theophrastus*, 1714. In line with this suggestion editors have spent a good deal of time attempting identifications of the characters in the *Tatler* and *Spectator* papers. It will be noted that Sir Roger is first introduced by Steele, though he was developed as a character by Addison, who assumed a kind of proprietorial care of him. There are thus two Sir Rogers to be distinguished in the essays.

3. *Lord Rochester . . . Etherege . . . Bully Dawson*] the juxtaposition of these names allows Steele, while acknowledging genius and talent, neatly and humourously to give a denigrating knock to the past age and besmirch in the friendliest way the early life of Sir Roger. John Wilmot (1647–80), Earl of Rochester, was a considerable poet (often quoted by Steele), a courtier and a rake; Sir George Etherege (?1635–91) wrote three of the most famous Restoration comedies, *The Comical Revenge: or, Love in a Tub* (1664), *She Would if She Could* (1668) and *The Man of Mode* (1676; given a critique by Steele in *S*65, p. 406). Steele admired Etherege's skill, but himself represents a new, softer comedy of feeling. Several tales and jests are preserved of Bully Dawson, a seedy swaggerer, sharper and man-about-town of Restoration London.

4. *Aristotle . . . Longinus . . . Littleton . . . Cooke*] The *Poetics* of Aristotle and the treatise *On the Sublime* of Longinus (*c*. A.D. 50) represent the interest in the theatre and literature followed by the young law students instead of studying Sir Edward Coke's *First Part of the Laws of England, or Commentaries upon Littleton* (1628 etc.), a basic law text book. Longinus's Greek work was available in translation, and just beginning the great vogue it enjoyed during the following decades.

5. *the Time of the Play . . . New-Inn . . . the Rose*] At this time the play usually began about 6 p.m. New-Inn, one of the nine Inns of Chancery, was a building housing attorneys dependent on the Middle Temple; it lay

in Wych Street, now obliterated by Aldwych. The Rose was a tavern frequented by actors at the Drury Lane end of Russell Street, which ran from Drury Lane to Covent Garden.

6. *Sir Andrew Freeport*] Sir Andrew is the Whig, mercantile, monied foil to the Tory country gentleman, Sir Roger; he is a knight raised by his own efforts juxtaposed with a baronet inheriting his title and position.

7. *the gallant Will. Honeycomb*] This proto-typical member of the Drones' Club is somewhat rehabilitated as the dedicatee of the 'Eighth and Last' volume of the collected *Spectators*, when we learn that he escaped from the past age's ideal of the fine gentleman, satirized here; he at last confessed his age, and 'very ingenuously step'd into your Grand Climaterick'; married and retired to his own estate.

S4

1. *motto*] Horace, II *Satires*, vi, 58: 'A man out of the ordinary for his silence and reserve.'

2. *the antient Sage . . .*] Cicero, *De Officiis* (On Duties, a letter to his son Marcus) '. . . nec minus solum, quam quum solus esset.' One of the fourteen *Spectator* mottoes taken from this one work of Cicero alone. The works of Cicero with the blend they offer of familiar discourse, moral and ethical reflection, and the mingling of public activity and private life represent one of the most important classical parallels with the essays of *The Tatler* and *The Spectator*.

S10

1. *motto*] Virgil, *Georgics*, I, 201–5: 'Just as when a man whose sculls can scarcely force his skiff against the stream should by chance let his arms go slack, then headlong the current sweeps him off down the river.'

2. *It was said of Socrates . . .*] Cicero, *Tusculan Disputations*, V, iv, 10: 'Socrates, however, took the initiative in summoning philosophy down from the heavens. He transferred it to the actual cities inhabited by mankind, and moved it right into people's own houses; and he compelled it to ask questions about how one ought to live and behave . . .' (trans. Michael Grant).

3. *Sir Francis Bacon observes*] *Advancement of Learning*, II, Introduction, 14.

from S555

1. *motto*] Persius, *Satires*, iv, 51: 'Put aside your assumed character.'

2. *the Philosopher of old . . . Anaxarchus*] Anaxarchus, a philosopher of Abdera, a follower of Democritus and a friend of Alexander the Great,

offended Mecreon, tyrant of Cyprus, who had him pounded to death with iron pestles. The tale is often referred to by ancient authors: e.g. Diogenes Laertius, *Lives of the Philosophers*, ix, 59; Cicero, *Tusculan Disputations*, II, 22.

3. *the Gentleman, of whose Assistance I formerly boasted*] Addison; see the Preface to the collected *Tatlers*, p. 485.

4. *the Tender Husband*] Steele's comedy of sentiment was acted at Drury Lane, 23 April 1705; Addison wrote the Prologue and is believed to have had some hand in the play itself; the printed copy is headed by a Dedicatory Letter to him.

5. *the ingenious Gentleman . . . Distressed Mother*] Eustace ◊ Budgell, but the lines were sometimes attributed to Addison, e.g. by Dr Johnson, 'Life of Addison'. Ambrose Philips's tragedy, based on Racine's *Andromaque*, was first acted at Drury Lane, 17 March 1712 (published 28 March). Steele wrote the Prologue.

6. *an Edition of the former Volumes of Spectators*] i.e. vols. I and II, published in January 1712; Steele does not say whether he means the 12mo or the 8vo, or both sets.

7. *the Tax on each half Sheet . . . above 20l. a Week . . .*] This statement strictly interpreted means that after the imposition of the tax of ½d per half-sheet on 1 August 1712, *The Spectator* had a printing of about 1,600–1,700 weekly, therefore about 3,200–3,400 before the tax. (Say £21 weekly = £3.50 daily = 1,680 half-pennies.)

8. *vos valete & plaudite.*] The last words of Terence's comedies, *The Self-Tormentor*, *The Eunuch* and *Phormio*: 'Farewell and applaud.'

S 106

1. *motto*] Horace, I *Odes*, xvii, 14–16: 'In this place, a glorious abundance of the countryside's riches shall all for you form a cornucopia.'

2. *Bishop of St. Asaph . . . Doctor South . . . Tillotson . . . Saunderson . . . Barrow . . . Calamy*] William ◊ Fleetwood; Robert ◊ South; John Tillotson (1610–94), Archbishop of Canterbury (see *T* 101, *n* 5); Robert Sa[u]nderson (1587–1662), Bishop of Lincoln, chaplain to Charles I and a friend of Archbishop Laud, whose popular Tory sermons on topics like passive obedience and non-resistance were available in several printings; Isaac Barrow (1630–77), D.D., who was succeeded by his pupil Isaac Newton as Lucasian professor of mathematics at Cambridge, and whose influential sermons were edited by Tillotson; Benjamin Calamy (1642–86), D.D., prebendary of St Paul's, whose Tory sermons in support of the church establishment were published in 1690 (several later editions).

S 108

1. *motto*] Phaedrus, *Fables*, II, v, 3: 'Out of breath to no purpose and busy about nothing at all.'

S 109

1. *motto*] Horace, II *Satires*, ii, 3: 'A philosopher of no particular school of thought.'

2. *the Tilt-Yard . . . now a Common Street before Whitehall*] The Tilt-Yard for jousting, constructed by Henry VIII at Whitehall Palace, lay in front of what is now the Banqueting House, and stretched over to the present Horse Guards Parade.

3. *where the Coffee-house is now*] Jenny Mann's Tilt-Yard Coffee-house, a haunt of the military, stood on the site of the Paymaster-General's office in Whitehall, between the Horse Guards and the Old Admiralty.

4. *an easie Writer*] See T9.

5. *the Battle of Worcester*] On 3 September 1651, Cromwell defeated Charles II and his Scottish army, forcing him to flee abroad.

S 110

1. *motto*] Virgil, *Aeneid*, II, 755: 'Terror everywhere attacks my spirits, and the very silence terrifies me.'

2. *feedeth the young Ravens*] Psalms, cxlvii, 9.

3. *Mr. Lock in his Chapter of the Association of Ideas*] Locke, *An Essay Concerning Human Understanding* (1690, etc.), II, xxxiii, 10.

4. *Lucretius himself . . . tells us . . . Persons who are either dead or absent*]. *De Rerum Natura*, IV, 26ff.

5. *a Story out of Josephus*] *Antiquities of the Jews*, xiii, 4; related also in Bayle's *Dictionary*, under 'Glaphyra', remark C.

S 112

1. *motto*] Pythagoras, *Carmina Aurea*, 1–2: 'First, devote to the immortal gods the appointed service.'

S 113

1. *motto*] Virgil, *Aeneid*, IV, 4: 'Her looks were deep imprinted in his heart.'

2. *Dum tacet hanc loquitur*] Martial, *Epigrams*, I, lxviii, 1–6.

S 117

1. *Witchcraft: Sir Roger and Moll White*] Addison's cool, satirical essay on witchcraft is typical of his mind and of the temper of his periodical.

It is not absolutely sceptical, but, advocating a 'hovering Faith', would have been quite powerful and persuasive to readers of his age. In England, under statutes of Elizabeth (1563) and James I (1603), prosecutions for witchcraft and executions, mainly by hanging, were at different times and places not infrequent, and became numerous in the early years of the Commonwealth. The last person in England to be condemned to death for witchcraft was Jane Wenham, at Hertford on 4 March 1712, less than a year after this piece was written; though the jury found her guilty, the judge first obtained a reprieve for her and finally a pardon. In Scotland, in the sixteenth and seventeenth centuries, prosecutions and condemnations were numerous, following trials in which judicial torture was permitted; the last judicial burning for the 'crime' was at Loth in Sutherland in 1722; five years earlier, at Dornoch in the same county, a mother and daughter were found guilty, and the former lynched and burned. In 1736, the English and Scottish capital statutes were repealed. The ill-treatment in local communities of old folk like Moll White remained, and remains, another matter.

2. *motto*] Virgil, *Eclogues*, VIII, 108: 'They create their own dreams.'

3. *the following description in Otway*] Thomas Otway's popular tragedy, which held the stage until the beginning of the nineteenth century, *The Orphan: or, The Unhappy Marriage* (first acted and printed, 1680), II, 244–56 (omitting 245).

S122

1. *motto*] Publilius Syrus, *Sententiae*, 113: 'On a journey, a pleasant companion is as good as a carriage.'

S131

1. *motto*] Virgil, *Eclogues*, X, 63: 'Even you, O woods, away with you!'

S383

1. *motto*] Juvenal, *Satires*, I, 75: 'Their pleasure grounds are the fruit of crimes.'

2. *Spring-Garden*] These pleasure gardens at Foxhall or Vauxhall (from 'Fulke's Hall'), across the river from what is now the Tate Gallery, were first laid out in 1661, and from then until the early nineteenth century were one of the chief leisure resorts of fashionable London; they closed in 1859. On Saturday, 19 July 1710, Z. C. von Uffenbach 'drove [from Lambeth Wells] further along this side of the Thames to Foxhall, where there is a large garden of matchless elegance called the Spring Garden because it is most agreeable in spring, when vast quantities of birds nest

and sing there. It consists entirely of avenues and covered walks where people stroll up and down, and green huts, in which one can get a glass of wine, snuff and other things, although everything is very dear and bad. Generally; vast crowds are to be seen here, especially females of doubtful morals, who are dressed as finely as ladies of quality, most of them having a gold watch hanging from their neck' (trans. and ed. W. H. Quarrell and M. Mare, *London in 1710*, 1934, p. 131).

3. *The Fifty new Churches*] The Act of 1711, promoted by the Tory-dominated Commons, was an asseveration of Church of England power. It placed a tax on coal entering the capital, the revenue to be employed 'for building fifty new churches in or near the cities of London and Westminster and their suburbs' and for certain other ecclesiastical building purposes. The growth of London had made the old churches inappropriately concentrated in the medieval city, and left large numbers of citizens without parochial or church provision. The money raised could never have financed the grandiose programme legislated for, if it were seriously intended. After twenty years of haggling, twelve splendid new churches had been built, including St Mary-le-Strand (designed by Gibbs), St George, Bloomsbury (Hawksmoor), and St John's, Smith Square (Archer). Several steeples were also added to existing churches. The tax was collected until the mid nineteenth century, paying for suburban churches, church repairs and other (unintended) purposes.

S517

1. *The death of Sir Roger*] By killing off Sir Roger, Addison clearly signals an early end to the *Spectator* papers. Eustace ◊ Budgell, in his periodical *The Bee, or The Universal Weekly Pamphlet*, no. 1 (3 February 1733), relates that 'Mr. *Addison* was so fond of this character, that a little before he laid down the *Spectator* (foreseeing that some nimble Gentleman would catch up his Pen the Moment he quitted it) he said to an intimate Friend, with a certain *Warmth* in his Expression, which he was not often guilty of, By G—d, *I'll* KILL *Sir* Roger, *that no Body else may* MURDER *him*. Accordingly, the whole *Spectator*, No. 517 consists of nothing else but an Account of the *Old Knight's Death*, and some *moving circumstances* which attended it.' The clergyman's serious illness had been reported in *Spectator* 513, and Will Honeycomb's marriage is announced in *Spectator* 530. *Spectator* 541 is the 'Farewell Essay' of the Templar, who is said to have 'determined to lay aside his Poetical Studies, in order to a closer Pursuit of the Law'.

2. *motto*] Virgil, *Aeneid*, VI, 878: 'I mourn his goodness and his old-fashioned honour.'

S 57

1. *motto*] Juvenal, *Satires*, VI, 252–3: 'What sense of shame can you expect in a steel-helmeted woman, a renegade from her sex?'

2. *The Wife of Hector in Homer's Iliads*] *Iliad*, VI, 490–93.

3. *a Rural Andromache*] Cf. 'the Yorkshire Huntress', Mrs Alice Copswood, in *T* 37.

4. *Camilla . . . Penthesilea*] Camilla, the maiden warrior in *Aeneid* XI; Penthesilea, Queen of the Amazons, slain by Achilles.

5. *when Dr. Titus Oates was in all his Glory*] Titus Oates (1649–1705), the chief instigator of the Popish Plot (1679–80), but also by implication Dr Henry Sacheverell (*c.* 1674–1744), high-church preacher; on 5 November 1709, in an inflammatory sermon preached in St Paul's before the Lord Mayor, on 'The Perils of False Brethren', Sacheverell attacked Lord Treasurer Godolphin and the Whigs as enemies to the church. The administration was stung into impeaching him, probably because a prosecution in the courts would certainly have failed by reason of the strong, popular Tory feeling. Lord Chancellor ◊ Cowper presided at his month-long trial before the House of Lords; on 23 March 1710, by a majority of seventeen he was found guilty, but punished only by a suspension from preaching for three years. This was a severe blow to the prestige and confidence of the government and hastened their slide from influence and power. The trial caused tremendous popular, party excitement in London. *Tatler* 142 mentions the partisanship of the Tory ladies for Sacheverell.

S 66

1. *motto*] Horace, III *Odes*, vi, 21–4: 'The maiden at an early age relishes learning Greek dancing, and even then is trained in wanton wiles, and passionately gives herself up to future lawless love-affairs.'

2. *The two following Letters*] By John ◊ Hughes.

3. *the Belle Sauvage mentioned in one of your Papers*] *S* 28, p. 285.

S 189

1. *motto*] Virgil, *Aeneid*, X, 824: 'The picture of filial affection.'

2. *It was usual among some of the Greeks*] As Plutarch relates the Spartans treated the Helots ('Life of Lycurgus').

3. *Sir Sampson in Love for Love*] Sir Sampson Legend, father of Valentine and Ben in Congreve's popular comedy, first acted in 1695.

4. *the mother in Virgil*] *Eclogues*, VIII, 48–52: 'You are a cruel mother, but were you worse than the ruthless boy? The boy was heartless; you were a cruel mother.'

5. *the Greek Proverb*] 'Evil crow, evil egg.'

6. *as I have formerly observed*] S182, p. 263.

7. *It is Father le Conte . . . who tells us*] Louis le Conte, *Memories and Observations . . . made in a late Journey through the Empire of China* (first published in French, Paris, 1696, 1697, 1701; translated, 1697): Part II, letter i, to the Cardinal d'Estrée, p. 28.

S261

1. *motto*] Menander, *Monostichoi*, 159 (Winterton, p. 505; *see* S203, *n* 4): 'Wedlock's an ill men eagerly embrace.'

2. *I have elsewhere observed*] Spectators 188, 255, 256, 257.

S182

1. *motto*] Juvenal, *Satires*, VI, 182: 'There is more of aloes than honey in it.'

2. *Man of Mode*] Perhaps a glance at Etherege's comedy: see S65, p. 407.

S266

1. *motto*] Terence, *The Eunuch*, 930–33: 'I look on this as my claim to fame that I have been able to show this young man how to detect the tricks of whores and by knowing these early detest them ever afterwards.'

2. *the Man of the Bumper knows me*] For the Bumper tavern, see S264, *n* 4, p. 564.

3. *the second Act of the Humorous Lieutenant*] John Fletcher's *The Humorous Lieutenant, or Generous Enemies: a Comedy*, II, iii, 15–26; the play was first acted in 1619 and first printed 1697, 'as it is now acted by his Majesties servants at the Theatre-Royal in Drury Lane'. It was acted there on 11 April 1709, and revived on 11 and 12 February 1712.

4. *a most beautiful Country-Girl, who had come up in the same Waggon with my Things*] Cf. William Hogarth's *Harlot's Progress* (1732), plate I.

S276

1. *motto*] Horace, I *Satires*, iii, 42: 'I wish the virtuous man could give the man who makes a mistake some credit for meaning well.'

2. *a Paper which thou didst lately put forth*] Spectator 265.

S203

1. *motto*] Ovid, *Metamorphoses*, II, 36–8: 'Illustrious parent! Since you don't despise,/The parent's name, some certain token give,/That I may Clymene's proud boast believe,/Nor longer under false reproaches grieve'

(Addison). His translations of two fables from *Metamorphoses* II and nine from III appeared in *Poetical Miscellanies*, ed. John Dryden and Nicholas Rowe, fifth part (1704).

2. *the Father of a Seventh Son*] A seventh son was popularly supposed to possess 'powers', especially in healing, and quacks so advertised themselves. In the Scottish Highlands, the seventh son of a seventh son has the 'second sight', the faculty of foreseeing death.

3. *nec longum tempus et ingens*] Virgil, *Georgics*, II, 80—82: 'And a short time [after the graft] a huge tree thrusts up to the sky with flourishing boughs and wonders at its strange foliage and fruits not its own.'

4. *a Fragment of Apollodorus*] The fragment and the information about Apollodorus comes from *Poetae Minores Graeci*, ed. Winterton (Cambridge, 1677), a book which Addison possessed and several times makes use of in producing *Spectator* papers.

5. *the phrase of Diogenes[,] to Plant Men*] 'The phrase probably comes through Bayle [*Dictionary*], article Hipparchia, remark D. Bayle there cites it from Cardinal Du Perron and adds "No Antient that I know of, tells the Story . . ." ' (D. F. Bond).

S 119

1. *motto*] Virgil, *Eclogues*, I, 19—20: 'Fool that I was, Meliboeus; I used to think the city they call Rome was like our Mantua.'

2. *an Account of the several Modes and Fashions*] *Spectator* 129.

S 132

1. *motto*] Cicero, *De Oratore*, II, iv, 7 (adapted): 'He might indeed be called impertinent, who pays no attention to the demands of time, or hogs the conversation, or makes himself the topic of discourse.'

S 28

1. *Street signs*] The numbering of entries from streets was practically unknown in London at this time. Hatton's *New View of London* (1708) notes as remarkable that 'in Prescott Street, Goodman's Fields, instead of Signs, the Houses there are distinguished by Numbers, as the Stair Cases in the *Inns of Court* and *Chancery*'. Signs were used for every kind of building and oddities of signs and mis-match of signs and occupants was a frequent source of jokes (e.g. *Tatler* 18); see B. Lillywhite, *London Signs* (1972).

2. *motto*] Horace, II *Odes*, x, 19—20: 'Nor does Apollo always bend his bow.'

3. *the Cat and Fiddle . . . a Conceit . . .*] Popularly supposed to be a version of '*le chat fidèle*'.

4. *An ingenious Foreigner observes . . . Coats of Arms*] One of the numerous hints Addison draws from a useful anthology based on the writings of the learned Gilles Ménage (d. 1692): *Menagiana, ou Bons mots, rencontres agréeables, pensées judicieuses et observations curieuses de M. Ménage* (Amsterdam, 1693; several later editions).

5. *the ingenious Mrs. Salmon*] Mrs Salmon's popular waxworks were advertised in *Tatler* 251, 30 November 1710; she had recently moved to new premises in Fleet Street, at the sign of the Golden Salmon.

6. *Abel Drugger*] Ben Jonson, *The Alchemist*, II, i, where Subtle gives Abel Drugger, 'the Tobacco Man', a rebus or punning logo for a sign, *a bell* with (Dr) *Dee* (the astrologer and scientist) in a *rug* gown, 'anenst him a dog snarling *er*'.

7. *Our Apocryphal Heathen God*] The apocryphal addition to the book of David, 'The History of the Destruction of Bel and the Dragon'. The Bell and Dragon was a sign popular with chemists and druggists, perhaps because a resinous preparation called 'dragon's blood' was used in pharmacy.

8. *As for the Bell-Savage*] Addison's is only one of the explanations offered for this sign.

S 49

1. *motto*] Martial, *Epigrams*, X, iv, 10: 'My page smacks of man.'

2. *the Grecian, Squire's, Searle's; and all other Coffee-houses adjacent to the Law*] For the Grecian, near the Temple, see *T* 1, *n* 3; Squire's was in Fuller's Rents, which ran north from Holborn opposite the top of Chancery Lane to Gray's Inn; Searle's was near Lincoln's Inn, at the corner of Searle or Serle Street and Portugal Street.

3. *Dinner-time*] Probably about 3 p.m.; the gradual advance of the dinner hour from noon, in some early, healthy time, to later and later hours was long a moralist's commonplace as a sign of decadence.

4. *Tom the Tyrant*] The waiter at White's Chocolate-house.

S 155

1. *motto*] Horace, *Ars Poetica*, 451 (adapted): 'These trifles will lead to serious trouble.'

2. *whom you have thought fit to mention as an Idol*] *Spectators* 75 and 87. '. . . the vain Part of the Sex . . . her Business and Employment to gain Admirers.'

3. *the Royal and New Exchange*] For the Royal Exchange, see *S* 69, p. 437. The New Exchange was a fashionable lounging place in the Strand,

beside what is now Bedford Street, with boutiques and gift shops; it was a favourite place of assignation, often mentioned in Restoration comedies.

4. *your Account of Beauties*] *Spectator* 144.

S88

1. *motto*] Virgil, *Eclogues*, III, 16: 'What can the master do when servants are as bold as this?'

2. *White's*] See *T*1, *n*3.

S137

1. *motto*] Cicero, *Epistula ad Familiares*, XI, xxviii, 3: 'Even slaves always at liberty to fear, rejoice and grieve at their own rather than another's pleasure.'

2. *Clarendon . . . Being used worse than I deserved . . . I had done*] Clarendon, *The History of the Great Rebellion*, Book I, para. 9, discussing the divisions and jealousies he saw among the councillors of Charles I, attributes these words to Richard Weston, Lord Treasurer 1628–33; Earl of Portland 1633.

3. *the five Fields towards Chelsea*] A pleasant country walk, though robbers lurked there; the King's Road now runs through this area, which covered Belgravia and Pimlico.

S251

1. *The cries of London*] Street cries are a form of folk music formerly found in all large towns and cities. Most of the cries mentioned in this essay are represented in Marcellus Laroon, *The Cryes of London Drawn after the Life*, engraved by René Tempest (1709; re-issued in 1711 by Henry Overton, which may have prompted Addison's essay); von Uffenbach bought a set of the original engravings with the words they cry in 'seventy-four sheets for half a guinea' on 27 October 1710; he adds that they were also available 'with notes, for the curious tones that they call or sing can be freakishly imitated on the violin' (*London in 1710*, pp. 164–5).

2. *motto*] Virgil, *Aeneid*, VI, 625–6 (adapted): 'Had I a hundred tongues, a hundred mouths and a voice of iron.'

3. *Retailers of . . . broken Glasses or Brick-dust*] Abrasive materials for making cleansers; '*Brick Dust* Moll *had Scream'd through half a Street*' in Swift's 'Description of the Morning', *T*9.

4. *Colly-Molly-Puff*] Laroon (see *n* 1), no. 19; he carries a basket on his head, and his name came from his jingle.

S 324

1. *Mohawks*] On the night of 11 March there was an outbreak of hooliganism in the streets of central London; a number of people were arrested, including Lord Hinchingbroke, Sir Mark Cole and other well-to-do bullies. Swift wrote in his *Journal to Stella* the next day, 'Here is the D— and all to do with these Mohocks. Grubstreet Papers about them fly like Lightening; and a List of near 80 put in [se]vrll Prisons, and all a lye.' There was certainly a situation in which rumours were rife; the Tories suggested the Mohawks were 'young, lew'd, debauchd Sparks, all of the Whiggish Gang' (Hearne, *Diary*, 30 March). On 15 April, Gay published his 'tragi-comical farce', *The Mohocks*. See L. C. Jones, *The Clubs of Georgian London* (New York, 1942), chapter 2, 'The Tradition of the Mohawks'.

2. *motto*] Persius, *Satires*, II, 61: 'O souls, bent down to the earth, and empty of the heavenly spark.'

3. *a general History of Clubs*] Accounts of clubs (the Ugly Club, Punning Club, Amorous Club etc.) formed a running theme in the *Spectator* papers; see especially *Spectator* 9.

4. *the rest is torn off*] A continuation of the letter appeared in the folio half-sheet, *Spectator* 328; another piece was substituted in the collected sets. Bishop Percy told a story that the letter was real, and really was transmitted in the manner described.

S 454

1. *Twenty-four hours in London*] Starting at Richmond, Mr Spectator roves by boat and coach; the topography may be outlined as follows: he sails down the Thames with the flotilla of boats loaded with fruit and vegetables either for Covent Garden, or for the Stocks Market, on the site of the present Mansion House at the end of Cornhill; a stop is made *en route* at Nine Elms on the south bank between the present Chelsea and Vauxhall bridges; he lands at Strand Bridge, a landing stage at the bottom of Strand Lane running up from the river on the east side of Somerset House and originally under the Strand; after strolling round the fruit stalls in Covent Garden, he takes a coach and follows a young lady in another; she goes west on Long Acre; he travels parallel and to the south on King Street; this allows him to reach St Martin's Lane before she does and his coachman turns north on this street to tangle with hers at the end of Newport Street. Thereafter they both travel about the town for an hour and a half. Mr Spectator takes to his feet, and listens to a ballad singer at the corner of Warwick Street, either to the west of Charing Cross, south of and parallel with Pall Mall, or more likely the street running parallel

with the west side of Golden Square, half-way between Piccadilly and Oxford Street. Thence he takes coach again eastward into the City. He spends some time lounging in the Royal Exchange, between Cornhill and Threadneedle Street, managing to dine before the rush starts in the chophouse. He visits a coffee-house in °Exchange Alley, then leaves the City before 5 p.m. and travels west again to the fashionable area of Covent Garden, and passes the evening at Will's Coffee-house in Russell Street, at the corner of Bow Street, near the present Opera House.

2. *motto*] Terence, *Heauton-timorumenos* (The Self-Tormentor), 90: 'Don't prevent me from giving myself a holiday from work.'

3. *the Exchange of London*] The Royal Exchange; see S69, p. 437.

4. *Robin's*] A coffee-house in °Exchange Alley, a rendezvous for merchants and brokers.

S552

1. *motto*] Horace, II *Epistles*, i, 13–14: 'Whoever eclipses the rest [by his brilliant performance], when his light goes out, then he will be loved.'

2. *Peter Motteux . . . a Poem upon Tea*] The writer, a Huguenot, playwright, journalist and translator of Rabelais, had published his poem on 26 July, dedicated to Mr Spectator.

3. *Renatus Harris, Organ-Builder. The Ambition of this Artificer*] d. 1724; one of a family of famous organ-builders. There was an organ in the choir of St Paul's built by his rival Father Bernard Smith. Harris published a *Proposal for the Erecting of an Organ in St. Paul's Cathedral, over the West Door* . : . (c. 1712). This was intended as a concert instrument, with several novel features, but nothing came of his suggestion.

4. *John Rowley . . . his Proposals for a Pair of new Globes*] d. 1728; maker of orreries, though not the inventor of them, and Master of Mechanics to George I.

5. *Hevelius, Cassini . . . Flamsteed . . . Halley*] These astronomers were: Johannes Hevelius (1611–87) of Danzig, publisher of a star catalogue; Giovanni Domenico Cassini (1625–1712), director of the Paris Observatory, discoverer of four of Saturn's satellites; the Rev. John Flamsteed (1646–1719), the first Astronomer Royal, whose star catalogue, *Historia Coelestis*, had just been imperfectly hurried into print against the old man's will; Edmund Halley (1656–1742), predictor of the return of (Halley's) comet of 1682, Savilian professor of geometry at Oxford, who succeeded Flamsteed as Astronomer Royal; he published a *General Chart of the Variations of the Compass* (1701) and compiled lunar observations and a star-map of the southern hemisphere.

S 18

1. *The Italian opera*] The Restoration stage developed a native English opera, musical dramas of very various kinds; only two baroque masterpieces of this output are still performed, Purcell and Tate's *Dido and Aeneas* (1689) and Dryden and Purcell's *King Arthur* (1691). This vigorous tradition continued during part of the first decade of the eighteenth century. There was concomitantly an increasing interest in music itself, vocal and instrumental, as is indicated by the development of public concerts as well as the popularity of music in the theatres. No clear artistic or professional policy existed for music in the theatre, however, nor was there any powerful innovating genius, and when the international, prestigious Italian opera with its star system was after a period of tentative experiment finally established in London, the English opera was driven from the stage amid a flurry of pamphlets and periodical writing. Addison, with the feeble composer Thomas Clayton, devised an opera in English, on an English historical theme, but following the Italian model; *Rosamund*, produced 4 March 1707 at Drury Lane, was a failure. Addison's essay on Italian opera is interesting in its date, in the information it contains and also as exemplifying a particularly English attitude to musical drama. As a devotee of the legitimate theatre, Addison argues for the primacy of the text, for the event as a play, and for the play as a conscious didactic act willed by the author of the text. He rejects the musical intensity of the Italian opera. His kind of taste, seeking to make all culture literary, is still powerful. For some idea of the complexity of the theatrical scene at the time, see A. H. Scouten, 'Dramatic Opera', in J. Loftis et al., *The Revels History of Drama in English*, V: 1660–1750, pp. 288–95.

2. *motto*] Horace, II *Epistles*, i, 187–8: 'As far as all the audience are concerned, including the quality, Delight has migrated from the understanding of words, to the uncertainties of spectacle and tawdry decoration.'

3. *Arsinoe*] *Arsinoë, Queen of Egypt*, libretto by Peter Motteux based on an Italian piece, had music composed and arranged by Thomas Clayton and others.

4. *the famous Song in Camilla*] *Il Trionfo di Camilla, Regina de' Volsci*, based on an episode in the *Aeneid*, was the most successful opera of Antonio Maria, brother of Giovanni ◊ Bononcini. The piece was first given in Naples in 1696; for the London production, the music was adapted and the libretto translated by Owen ◊ Swiney and others for a performance at Drury Lane in March 1706; thereafter, reverting more or less to an Italian text, it was the most successful opera in London.

5. *the Phædra and Hippolitus*] Written by Addison's late friend, Edmund

Smith (1667–1710), it was unsuccessfully acted on 21 April 1707 at the
Haymarket, with a Prologue by Addison and an Epilogue by Prior.

S 39

1. *motto*] Horace, II *Epistles*, ii, 102–3: 'Much do I suffer, much, to
keep in peace/This jealous, waspish, wrong-headed, rhyming race' (Pope).

2. *a perfect Tragedy is the noblest Production*] Addison follows Aristotle's
Poetics, xxvi, against Dryden, 'Dedication of the *Aeneis*', and French neo-
classic critics of the previous century, who all placed the epic first.

3. *A virtuous Man (says Seneca)*] *De Providentia*, ii, 8–9.

4. *Aristotle observes . . . without taking Notice of it*] *Poetics*, iv, and
Rhetoric, III, 1.

5. *our English Blank Verse*] A point discussed by Dryden in his *Essay of
Dramatic Poesy* (1668), where also is to be found discussion of plays in
rhyme, the Hemistich and Pauses.

6. *a fine Observation in Aristotle*] *Poetics*, xxiv (end).

7. *Horace . . . in the following Verses*] *Ars Poetica*, 95–8; Roscommon
notes that Telephus and Peleus are the subjects respectively of tragedies
(neither extant) by Euripides and Sophocles; exiled from their dominions,
they solicited assistance throughout Greece, dressed as beggars.

8. *none who was better turned for Tragedy than Lee . . . that Line in
Statira's Speech*] Nathaniel Lee (?1649–92), whose 'pathetic' tragedies
were much admired and often acted. His rhyming, rhetorical, heroic plays
were mostly based on classical themes or French versions of them. Statira's
speech referred to, not quite correctly, is from Lee's most successful piece,
The Rival Queens, or The Death of Alexander the Great (1677), I, i.

9. *Otway*] Thomas Otway (1652–85). Though he also wrote rhyming
heroic tragedies like Lee, his two best pieces are in blank verse, and are
also powerful, 'domestic' tragedies: *The Orphan* (*S* 117, *n*3, p. 529) and
Venice Preserv'd, or A Plot Discover'd (1682), both with excellent, pathetic,
acting parts, which kept them in the repertory until the nineteenth
century.

10. *what the Roman Historian says of Catiline*] Florus, *Epitome*, IV, i, 12.

S 40

1. *English tragedy . . . poetic justice*] Poetic justice, meaning the distribution of rewards to the good and (particularly) punishments to the vicious
at the end of a poem or drama, seems to be used first as a phrase by
Thomas Rymer, *Tragedies of the Last Age* (1678), in ed. Zimansky, *Rymer's
Critical Works*, pp. 22 and 26. Any theorists like Rymer or John Dennis,
with a strong interest in the social place of literature, in other words who

move their discussions away from formal description to the relationship between works of art and the audience, tend to write rather categorically on poetic justice, though in practice they might be less simplistic. Dryden defended his own practice (e.g. *Essay on Dramatic Poesy*, in ed. G. Watson, pp. 150–52) by appealing to the practice of the ancients. Addison and Steele took a moderate stance on the question.

2. *motto*] Horace, II *Epistles*, i, 208–13:

> But please don't think that I am unwilling to praise
> Well-written plays, even though I don't write them myself.
> The dramatist walks on a tight-rope, it seems to me,
> Making me catch my breath and clutch at my heart
> With his words, mere words, making me glad or sad,
> Filling me full of false fears, whisking me off
> To Thebes or Athens at will: the illusion is magic.
>
> (S. P. Bovie)

3. *Aristotle considers the Tragedies that were written in either of these Kinds*] *Poetics*, xiii.

4. *the best Plays of this kind*] For *The Orphan* and *Venice Preserv'd*, see *S*39, *n* 9, p. 539. *The Rival Queens* and *Theodosius, or the Force of Love* are by Lee (see *S*39, *n* 8); *All for Love* (1678) by Dryden, *Oedipus* (1679) by Dryden and Lee; *Oroonoko* by Thomas Southerne. All the plays mentioned, except *Theodosius*, were in the repertory at Drury Lane.

5. *King Lear . . . as it is reformed*] Nahum Tate's adaptation replaced Shakespeare's original from 1681. Tate not only altered the ending but re-wrote the play to give a Cordelia–Edgar love relationship that motivates Lear's rage, produces a large actable part for a star actress, and re-organizes the story into a heroic tragedy of private love *versus* public duty.

6. *very noble Tragedies which have been framed upon the other Plan*] Congreve's *The Mourning Bride*, the most popular of his plays at this time, was first acted in 1697; *Tamerlane* (1701) and *Ulysses* (1705) are both by Nicholas Rowe (1674–1715); for *Phaedra and Hippolitus*, see *S*18, p. 317.

7. *the Conquest of Mexico . . . To-morrow Night*] This benefit performance for Powell as Cortez in Dryden's play, better known as *The Indian Emperor*, is advertised in *Spectator* 41.

*S*42

1. *motto*] Horace, II *Epistles*, i, 202–7:

> Loud as the Wolves on Orcas' stormy steep,
> Howl to the roarings of the Northern deep.
> Such is the shout, the long-applauding note,

At Quin's high plume, or Oldfield's petticoat,
Or when from Court a birth-day suit bestow'd
Sinks the lost Actor in the tawdry load.
Booth enters — hark! the Universal Peal!
'But has he spoken?' Not a syllable.
'What shook the stage, and made the people stare?'
Cato's long Wig, flowr'd gown, and laquer'd chair.
                    (Pope, *The First Epistle* . . . *Imitated*, 1737)

2. *Aristotle has observed . . . by the : . . Decorations of the Stage*] *Poetics*, xiv.

3. *an ancient Tragick Poet, to move the Pity of his Audience*] Aristophanes, *Frogs* (trans. J. H. Frere), 1375 ff.: 'Aeschylus . . . A practice which nature and reason allow,/But which you disannul'd and rejected./Euripides: As how?/Aes.: When you brought forth your kings in a villainous fashion,/In patches and rags, as a claim for compassion.' See *S* 39, *n* 7, p. 539.

4. *Non tamen intus . . .*] Horace, *Ars Poetica*, 182–4.

S 44

1. *motto*] Horace, *Ars Poetica*, 153: 'Hear what I, and the general public, expect in a play.'

2. *the sounding of the Clock in Venice preserved*] In Act 1 of Otway's play, Jaffeir and Pierre meet as arranged on the Rialto at midnight; Pierre enters saying 'The Clock has struck'. There is talk of clocks a little later in the scene, which suggests, although there is no stage direction, that an important place has been given to the admonitory sound of the bell.

3. *Hor. Look, my Lord, it comes*] *Hamlet*, I, i, 38–54.

4. *several French Criticks . . . take Occasion . . . to represent us as a People that delight in Blood*] e.g. René Rapin, s.j. (1621–87), in his systematic treatise, *Réflexions sur la Poétique* (1674), translated by Thomas Rymer under the misleading title *Reflections on Aristotle's Treatise of Poesie* (1674), part ii, chapters xx and xxiii: '[the English] our Neighbours love Blood in their Sports by the Quality of their Temperament . . . We are more humane' and 'The *English* have more of the *Genius* for *Tragedy* than Any People, as well by the Spirit of their Nation which delights in Cruelty, as also by the Character of their Language which is proper for great Expressions.'

5. *the famous Play of Corneille*] *Horace* (1640), IV, v; a tragedy drawing on an incident in Livy. Corneille himself complained that many thought the death of Camille spoiled the play, because the actors played the killing on the stage, against his directions (*Examen*, 1660).

6. *Sophocles has conducted a Tragedy*] *Electra*; but in the play it is Electra,

shouting from outside the closed doors, not Orestes inside, who upbraids
Clytemnestra.

7. *Nec coram populo . . .*] Horace, *Ars Poetica*, 185.

8. *Nec pueros coram . . . Ld. Roscommon*] Horace, *Ars Poetica*, 185–8.
Medea kills her children in Euripides' tragedy of that name; Atreus
murdered the children of his brother Thyestes, and caused them to be
served in a feast to their father; the story is treated in Seneca's tragedy
Thyestes. Cadmus and Procne are changed in Ovid, *Metamorphoses*, IV,
576, and VI, 668.

9. *A Lover . . . Barrel*] Dufoy, 'a saucy, impertinent Frenchman', in
Etherege's first play, *The Comic Revenge, or Love in a Tub*, produced 1664;
IV, vi and vii; V, i.

S 35

1. *motto*] Catullus, *Carmina*, xxxix, 16: 'Nothing is more foolish than
a laugh out of place.'

2. *Bedlam*] Henry VIII gave the priory of Bethlehem in St Botolph
Without, Bishopsgate, to the Corporation of London who organized it as
a hospital for the mad; in 1675 it moved to a new building, housing 150
sufferers, in Moorfields near London Wall. The hospital, which cost
£17,000, was open to the public to raise money.

3. *The Deceased Mr. Shadwell*] Thomas Shadwell (?1642–92), a
successful dramatist, often introduced °scowrers and window-breaking by
young hooligans in comedies such as *The Woman Captain* (1679) and *The
Squire of Alsatia* (1685).

4. *difficult to define it otherwise than as Cowley has done Wit*] In his poem
'Of Wit'.

5. *the following Genealogy*] A not uncommon journalistic device at this
time; cf. Swift's 'Poetical Genealogy and Description of Merit' in *The
Examiner* no. 30 for 1 March 1710.

S 47

1. *motto*] Martial, *Epigrams*, II, xli, 1: 'Laugh if you are wise.'

2. *Mr. Hobbs in his Discourse of Human Nature*] ix, 13; published 1650.
The Discourse consisted of the first thirteen chapters of the first part of
Elements of Law, Natural and Politick (circulating in manuscript in 1640);
the concluding six chapters of the first part and the whole of the second
part formed a separate treatise, *De Corpore Politico* (1650). The whole
manuscript was a fore-runner of *Leviathan* (1651).

3. *Mr. Dennis . . . in a Couple of humorous Lines*] Nicholas Boileau,
Satire IV; ◊ Dennis took exception to this satiric quotation of lines he said

he wrote as a boy (*Critical Works*, ed. Hooker, ii, 24); this is the only reference to him by name in the *Spectator*.

4. *that Custom . . . on the First Day of the present Month*} The custom of celebrating April Fool's Day by practical jokes seems to have become firmly established in the late seventeenth century, perhaps by the transference of periods of permitted disorder to this date. Swift held to the observance strongly, and the invention of Isaac Bickerstaff with his attendant papers was his greatest contribution to it. In the same way, legitimated mis-rule is an important thread in the *Tatler* and *Spectator* papers.

5. *Biters*} See *T* 12.

S61

1. *motto*} Persius, *Satires*, V, 19–20: 'It is not at all my aim to plump out my page with pretentious trifles, fit only to give substance to smoke.'

2. *Aristotle, in . . . his Book of Rhetorick*} III, xi.

3. *Cicero . . . in his . . . Rules of Oratory*} De Oratore, II, 61–3.

4. *The Sermons of Bishop Andrews*} Launcelot Andrewes (1555–1626), chaplain to Queen Elizabeth and made by James VI and I successively Bishop of Chichester, Ely and Winchester; sermons of his were printed during his lifetime: *XCVI Sermons* (1629). He has a learned, witty, condensed style meant for theological connoisseurs.

5. *Mr. Swan, the famous Punnster*} Richard Swan; mentioned by Dryden in *Discourse concerning Satire*, in ed. G. Watson, *Essays* (1962), ii, 139

6. *a famous University*} Cambridge.

7. *the old Philosopher's Opinion*} Aesop's *Fables*.

8. *vox & praeterea nihil*} Plutarch, 'Sayings of Spartans', *Moralia*, 233 A: '[You are] a voice and nothing else.'

9. *Aristinetus . . . Mercerus*} The saying of the Greek Aristinetus (*Epistles*, I, i) translated by Mercerus (Mercier) is taken from *Menagiana* (see *S* 28, *n* 4, p. 534).

S62

1. *motto*} Horace, *Ars Poetica*, 309: 'The foundation and fount of good writing is good understanding.'

2. *Mr. Lock has an admirable Reflection*} John Locke, *Essay concerning Humane Understanding* (1690), II, xi, 2.

3. *This Kind of Wit . . . in Cowley . . . Mr. Waller*} Abraham Cowley (1618–67) in his own age had a tremendous reputation, but the change in taste was moderating his fame, though his work was esteemed. Edmund Waller (1606–87) was still considered a great poet, but coming to be

judged more a fore-runner of poets greater than himself, such as Dryden (and later, Pope).

4. *the little Poem ascribed to Musaeus . . . a Modern Composition*] 'Hero and Leander', printed in a collection used by Addison, *Poetas Minores Graecae*, ed. Winterton, (Cambridge, 1635), pp. 330–47: *Menagiana* contains a brief discussion of its modernity.

5. *Mr. Dryden's Definition of Wit*] In the *Apology* prefixed to *The Age of Innocence*, 1677; *Essays*, ed. G. Watson, (1962), i, 207: 'The definition of wit (which has been so often attempted, and ever unsuccessfully, by many poets) is only this; that it is a propriety of thoughts and words; or, in other terms, thoughts and words elegantly adapted to the subject.' See T62. It will be noted that Addison omits Dryden's 'elegantly', allowing himself more freedom to push the old definition aside, though deferentially.

6. *Bouhours . . . the most penetrating of all the French Criticks . . . Boileau . . . the same Notion*] Dominique Bouhours (1628–1702), S.J., a philologist and critic; his most influential work, characterized by a commonsense and flexible handling of French neo-classic doctrines, was *Manière de bien penser dans les ouvrages d'esprit* (1687; rev. 1692; translated into English, 1705). Addison is using the discussion of 'ingenious thoughts' to be found in the first of the four dialogues.

7. *Mr. Dryden makes a very handsome Observation*] 'Dedication' to Lord Normanby of his translated *Aeneis*, 1697, about half-way through.

8. *Mr. Dryden . . . quotes Monsieur Segrais for a threefold Distinction of the Readers of Poetry*] Jean Regnauld de Segrais (1624–1701), member of the circle at the Hôtel de Rambouillet and miscellaneous writer; published a verse translation of the *Aeneid* prefaced by a dissertation on Virgil, to which Dryden makes several laudatory references in his 'Dedication'.

S70

1. *Chevy-Chase*] The set of verses quoted and commented on by Addison represents a popular broadside version, dating from the sixteenth century, of the border ballad known as 'The Hunting of the Cheviot'. This explains the alternative title, *Chevy* (= Cheviot) *Chase*. Addison returns to broadsides in *S*85, p. 361 see *n* 1, p. 546. Texts of both the old ballad and the broadside version, the latter often characterized by ballad scholars as impaired, impoverished, degenerate doggerel, are printed in *The English and Scottish Popular Ballads* (1882–98), ed. F. J. Child, III, 303 ff. (Child 162). The traditional ballad seems to have been already an old and popular song in the sixteenth century, and it is related to an even older ballad, 'The Ballad of Otterburn' (Child 161) commemorating, though long after the event, a border affray fought between Percy and

Douglas on 19 August 1388. It is not clear from Sir Philip Sidney's comment, quoted by Addison, which ballad or version(s) the former had heard. A blind harper could have had a traditional ballad, not a written-over piece. Addison of course is either ignorant of the complexities of the situation or does not distinguish different versions he knows (if any). The ballad of *Chevy Chase*, in any version, was a commonplace of rustic life, like the songs of *Robin Hood*, and also in broadside versions in popular circulation throughout the country. This is the point of Addison's selecting it for his literary discussion. See James Reed, *The Border Ballads* (1975), pp. 124 ff. English and Scottish versions of these ballads with divergent nationalist propaganda existed from the earliest date.

2. *motto*] Horace, II *Epistles*, i, 63: 'Sometimes the general public judge correctly.'

3. *Moliere, as we are told by Monsieur Boileau*] A famous anecdote in Boileau's *Réflexions sur Longin*, I.

4. *Ben. Jonson used to say*] Nowhere earlier noted in print.

5. *Sir Philip Sidney in his Discourse of Poetry*] An *Apologie for Poetrie* (1595; frequently reprinted with *Arcadia*).

6. *a Rule, That an Heroick Poem should be founded upon some important Precept of Morality*] That art should serve a moral, didactic purpose is a commonplace of neo-classic critical theory; Addison is here, however, using passages from one particular influential work, René le Bossu's *Traité du Poème Épique* (1675; translated into English, 1695), which applies the idea to Homer and Virgil with great certainty: Le Bossu also employs the erroneous history of the Greek states in his argument.

7. *Valerius Flaccus and Statius*] Valerius Flaccus (d. *c.*90), author of eight books of an incomplete epic poem, *Argonautica*. P. P. Statius (*c.*45–*c.*96), author of the *Thebaid* (92) in twelve books.

8. *Tum sic exspirans, &c.*] Aeneid, XI, 820 ff.; the verse translations here and following are from Dryden's *Aeneis*.

9. *Vicisti, & victum tendere palmas / Ausonii videre*] Aeneid, XII, 936–7.

10. *At vero . . .*] Aeneid, X, 821–3.

S74

1. *motto*] Virgil, Aeneid, IV, 88: 'The works are suspended, broken off.'

2. *Audiet pugnas . . .*] Horace, I *Odes*, ii, 23–4: 'Made fewer by the sins of their fathers, they shall hear of battles.'

3. *Vocat ingenti Clamore . . . remugit*] Virgil, *Georgics*, III, 43–5: 'With a mighty noise Cithaeron calls, and the hounds of Taygetus and Epidaurus,

tamer of horses; and the call re-doubled by the sounding groves echoes back.'

4. *Adversi campo apparent . . . Tiberim Fabarimque bibunt*] Aeneid, XI, 605–6; VII, 682–4, 712–15: 'They come forth against them on the plain, and draw back their hands and level the points of their quivering lances [. . .] The men of steep Praeneste, and of Juno's fields at Gabina, and of the chilly Anio and those who live among Hernican rocks sopping with streams [. . .] those who dwell in the Rosean country near Velinus, who subdue the crags of rugged Tetrica and Mount Serverus, Casperia and Foruli, the river Himella, and drink the waters of Tiber and Fabaris.'

5. *Turnus ut antevolans . . .*] Aeneid, IX, 47, 269–70: 'Turnus, who had rushed forward in front of his lagging column . . . You saw the horse and armour of Turnus as he passed, all in gold . . .'

6. *Has inter voces . . . quâ pulsa manu*] Aeneid, XII, 318–20: 'Amid these shouts, amid words like these, see! a whistling arrow winged its way towards him, shot by what hand, no one knows . . .'

7. *Cadit . . . aliter visum est*] Aeneid, II, 426–8: 'Next Rhipeus fell, the one man among all the Teucrians who was most upright and steadfastly just (the gods have another view of things) . . .'

8. *that Passage ridiculed in Hudibras*] I, iii, 94–6: 'And being down still laid about;/ As Widdrington in doleful Dumps/ Is said to fight upon his Stumps.'

9. *Non pudet . . . Non sumus —?*] Aeneid, XII, 229–31: 'For shame, O Rutulians, for so many men like these shall we place one man on the spot; are we not equal in numbers and courage?'

S85

1. *Broadsides and 'The Two Children in the Wood'*] A broadside was a single sheet of paper printed on one side only. From the earliest days of printing it was the means of wide dissemination of proclamations, news and other material in prose, verse or pictures, or a mixture of all three. The verses found in such publications are topical or versions of traditional pieces, usually meant to be sung to a well-known tune specified in the heading: up to 1640, ballads form the most numerous class of titles registered by printers and booksellers in the *Stationers'* (Company) *Register*, the earliest form of copyright. Pepys was one of the most notable collectors of these ephemeral sheets. 'The Two Child n in the Wood', also known as 'The Babes in the Wood', was a popular broadside crime story, which was registered in 1595 as 'The Norfolk Gentleman, his Will and Testament, and how he committed the keeping of his children to his own brother, who dealt most wretchedly by them, and how God punished him

for it'. The ballad is to be sung to *Rogero*, which Gay uses in *The Beggar's Opera*, I, with the words 'Oh, ponder well! be not severe'; Gay's song picks up the first line of the broadside, 'Now ponder well you Parents dear/ These words which I shall write'. The defiant last paragraph of this essay perhaps indicates some demur among the readership at Addison's enthusiasm for ballads in *S*70 and *S*74.

  2. *motto*] Horace, *Ars Poetica*, 319–22: 'Sometimes a play that has a few brilliant passages showing a true appreciation of character, even if it lacks grace and has little depth or artistry, will catch the fancy of an audience and keep its attention more firmly than verse which lacks substance but is filled with fine-sounding trifles' (T. S. Dorsch).

  3. *the Custom of the Mahometans*] Cf. *Letters Writ by a Turkish Spy* (10th ed., London, 1734), VI, Book I, letter 7, pp. 25–6: 'Either of us would have accounted it an irregular Negligence, if we had seen a Piece of *Paper* on the Ground, and had not stoop'd to take it up, with Reverence wiping off the Dirt, and kissing the *Tabula Rasa*, on which Men used write the *Name* of GOD. As if it were not an equal Argument of Respect to secure from Profanation, Sticks, Stones, Rags, or any thing where-on 'twere possible to engross or print the *All-Mysterious* Character . . .'

  4. *a Poem of an Eminent Author on a Victory*] Addison's poem *The Campaign* (1704), written to celebrate Marlborough's victory at Blenheim, made him well-known to the men in power and politically acceptable.

  5. *a Page of Mr. Baxter under a Christmas Pye*] Richard Baxter (1615 to 8 December 1691), puritan preacher and voluminous religious writer.

  6. *Me fabulosæ Vulture . . . Texere . . .*] Horace, III *Odes*, iv, 9–13: 'In my days of childhood, on trackless Vultur beyond the borders of Apulia, once when I was tired of playing and overcome with sleep, the fabled doves covered me over with newly-fallen leaves.'

  7. *the late Lord Dorset*] Charles Sackville (1643–1706), Sixth Earl of Dorset. Nothing further is known of his ballad collection.

  8. *Moliere's Thoughts on this Subject*] Le Misanthrope, I, ii, 401–4: 'The versification is not rich, and the style is old-fashioned. But don't you see that this is infinitely better than such gewgaw stuff as good sense would scorn. And that pure artless nature is speaking here.' Alceste quotes an old song and comments on it.

*The Pleasures of the Imagination] The twelve essays *S*409 and *S*411 to *S*421 have been grouped under this title. *S*409 is apparently specially written for *The Spectator* and forms an introduction to the kind of aesthetic theory Addison develops in the following pieces. The series of papers *S*411 to *S*421 represents a revised version of a treatise which he had

apparently drafted some time before, and perhaps is deploying now because of the pressure on him for *Spectator* material. Substantial parts of the original treatise survive in Addison's hand, with additions, alterations and corrections in another script, in a notebook now in the Houghton Library at Harvard. This material was published in *Some Portions of Essays contributed to the Spectator by Mr. Joseph Addison* (Glasgow, 1864), edited by J. Dykes Campbell, who at that time owned the manuscript. The phrase used for the title of this series was apparently originated by Sir William Temple in the Preface to his *Observations upon the United Provinces of the Netherlands* (1673; often reprinted). In one of his typically suggestive asides, Sir William contrasts 'the Pleasures of the Sense', short-lived, dependent on availability of physical resources and appetites, with 'the Pleasures of the Imagination', which 'heighten and refine the very Pleasures of the Sense, so they are of longer Extent and longer Duration'. Addison follows Temple's lead, and the authority and vast circulation of the *Spectator* papers gave an important nudge to the contemporary trend towards psychologizing aesthetics and literary criticism. There is good reason for Addison's establishing at the outset some doctrine of taste as an inner, personal configuration of ideas and feelings. The influential series also made the phrase the hall-mark of Addison's criticism, and at least partly led to other important works later in the century, such as Mark Akenside's poem *The Pleasures of Imagination* (1746; many editions: translated into French, 1759; German, 1757; Italian, 1764).

S409

   1. *motto*] Lucretius, *De Rerum Natura*, I, 934 (adapted): 'To grace each subject with enduring wit.'

   2. *Gratian very often recommends the fine Taste*] Balthasar Gracián (1601–58), s.j., Spanish critic and moralist; the reference is to his *Agudeza y arte de ingenio* (1648; translated into English, 1681), in which he discusses with examples *conceptismo* or mannerist literary principles; the taste Gracián is talking about is *cultismo*, the taste for conceits in prose and verse; Addison is developing a rather different train of thought, in a piece which became one of the most important documents in English literary criticism of the eighteenth century.

   3. *Rome in the Reign of Augustus . . . Greece about the Age of Socrates . . . [France under Louis XIV] . . .*] Accepted classical ages, with which by implication contemporary England is to be compared; see T 130. For Boileau and Le Bossu see S70, *n* 3 and *n* 6, p. 545. André Dacier (1651–1722) translated Aristotle's *Poetics* and other texts for the Dauphin's

education; his wife Anne (1654–1720) translated Homer and other Greek writers and wrote much-used commentaries on them.

4. *few of the Criticks besides Longinus*] 'Longinus', *On the Sublime*, a Greek text of about the middle of the first century A.D., available in several English translations, and one of the formative critical works of the century.

5. *an Essay upon Wit*] Spectators 56–60, 63, S61, S62 (pp. 341 ff).

6. *I afterwards gave an Instance*] S70, S74 (pp. 350 ff.); *Spectator* 75.

7. *I have likewise examined the Works of the greatest Poet . . .*] Milton; see pp. 412 ff and *n**, p. 554.

S411

1. *motto*] Lucretius, *De Rerum Natura*, I, 926–8: 'I pioneer through pathless tracts of the [Muses'] Pierian realm where no foot has ever trod before; what a joy to come on virgin springs and drink their waters.'

2. *the Fancy and the Imagination . . . the Notion of these two Words*] In using the terms as more or less interchangeable, Addison is the prisoner of his own psychological doctrine based on Locke (hence his *primary* and *secondary* pleasures), uniting imagination/fancy to a simplistic notion of the processing of sense-impressions; and also narrowing psychological states to 'pleasure' and 'pain'. So, Hobbes describes imagination as 'decaying sense' (*Leviathan*, 1651, chapter II). Later, when the impulse to psychologize the theory of literary criticism had proceeded so far as to demand a more elaborate and carefully thought-out psychology, distinctions were drawn between imagination (a powerful, active, profound force) and fancy (a more limited activity): Coleridge is an important thinker in this development.

3. *Sir Francis Bacon in his Essay upon Health*] 'Of Regiment of Health': '. . . Avoid . . . Subtill and Knottie inquisitions . . . Entertain . . . Studies that fill the Mind with Splendid and Illustrious Objects, as Histories, Fables and Contemplations of Nature.'

S412

1. *motto*] Martial, *Epigrams*, IV, lxxxii, 8: 'The task, suitably broken up, grows shorter.'

2. *Scit thalamo servare fidem . . . patriisque coloribus ardet*] The Latin verses are by Addison and occur in the Harvard MS in his own hand. In the 1744 12mo edition of the collected *Spectators* they are translated by the lines inserted in the text within square brackets.

S413

1. *motto*] Ovid, *Metamorphoses*, IV, 287: 'The Cause is secret, but the Effect is known' (Addison).

2. *Things would make but a poor Appearance to the Eye*] Not everybody took such a favourable view of the power and effects of the imagination: cf. Swift, *A Tale of a Tub* (1704 etc.), 'A Digression on Madness': 'But when a Man's Fancy gets *astride* on his Reason, when Imagination is at Cuffs with the Senses, and common Understanding as well as common Sense is kickt out of Doors . . . How fade and insipid do all Objects accost us that are not convey'd in the Vehicle of *Delusion?* How shrunk is every-thing, as it appears in the Glass of Nature?'

S414

1. *motto*] Horace, *Ars Poetica*, 410–11: 'Each needs the other's help, and they enter into a friendly pact.'

2. *Scriptorum chorus omnis*] Horace, II *Epistles*, ii, 77: 'The whole chorus of writers hates the town and yearns for the sacred grove.'

3. *Hìc Secura quies . . . sub arbore somni*] Virgil, *Georgics*, II, 467–70: 'Here is quiet without care and a life that is innocent of fraud, rich in various treasures; here is repose in broad acres, caves, living lakes and cool vales, the lowing of cattle, and soft sleep beneath the trees.'

4. *The prettiest Landskip I ever saw . . .*] This sounds like the image projected by a *camera obscura*. On 12 June 1710, von Uffenbach visited the Royal Observatory at Greenwich and mentions, on either side of ☿ Flamsteed's observatory balcony, 'two "camerae obscurae" which are here uncommonly pleasant on account of the charming prospect [i.e. the layout of the park] and the great traffic on the Thames' (*London in 1710*, p. 23).

5. *our English Gardens are not so entertaining to the Fancy as those in France and Italy*] This is an interesting early attack on the English formal garden, which in some measure showed the influence of William III's Dutch taste. Addison's comments and suggestions foreshadow the later developments in garden design of the English eighteenth century.

6. *[the Chinese] have a Word*] Sir William Temple's essay 'Upon the Gardens of Epicurus' in *Miscellanea: the second part* (1690, etc.) is the influential source of a contrast asserted between European formal gardens and the 'irregularity' of the Chinese, their idea of beauty without order that strikes the eye at first sight. For this quality he presents the reader with a 'chinese' word 'sharawadgi', not otherwise known.

7. *Evergreens, and the like Moveable Plants*] The evergreens then used on terraces, such as oranges and some of the new exotic conifers, being tender (or thought to be so) were grown in tubs and moved outside in the summer; in the winter they were kept in heated 'green-houses'.

S415

1. *motto*] Virgil, *Georgics*, II, 155: 'Add to this all the cities, the effort of men's toil.'

2. *we find the Antients . . . infinitely superior to the Moderns*] The information about ancient buildings in this essay is chiefly drawn from Herodotus, *History*, and Diodorus Siculus, *Library of History*.

3. *Slime they used . . .*] Genesis, xi, 3.

4. *Lysippus's Statues of Alexander . . . the Proposal of Phidias*] Plutarch, 'Life of Alexander', IV, i, and lxxii; the proposal was made by Stasicrates.

5. *an Observation . . . in Monsieur Freart's Parallel*] Roland Freart, *Parallèle de l'architecture antique et de la moderne* (1650). Addison gives an almost verbatim extract from John Evelyn's translation of this work (1664), chapter II, 'Of Dorique Order'.

6. *Look upon the Rainbow*] Ecclesiasticus xliii, 11.

S416

1. *motto*] Lucretius, *De rerum Natura*, IV, 750: 'In so far as a vision perceived by the mind closely resembles one seen by the eyes.'

2. *as I have before observed*] S413, p. 375.

S417

1. *motto*] Horace, IV *Odes*, iii, 1–4, 10–12: 'The man, Melpomene, whose birth you once favoured with a benign look shall never be made a famous boxer with any Isthmian training, nor shall any impetuous horse etc. But the waters that flow through fruitful Tibur and the dense foliage of the groves shall make him famous by Aeolian song.'

2. *A Cartesian . . . in the following Manner*] René Descartes, *Les Passions et l'Âme* (1649), art. xxi (English translation, 1650; pp. 18–19): '[Imaginations] proceed from nothing but this, that the spirits being agitated severall wayes, and meeting the traces of divers impressions preceding them in the brain, they take their course at haphazard through some certain pores, rather than others. Such are the illusions of our dreames, and those dotages we are often troubled with waking, when our thought carelessly roames without applying it selfe to any thing of its own' (D. F. Bond).

3. Ἦ καὶ κυανέῃσιν . . . Ὄλυμπον' *Iliad*, I, 528–20: 'Zeus, as he finished, bowed his sable brows. The ambrosial locks rolled forward from the immortal head of the King and high Olympus shook' (E. V. Rieu).

4. *Dixit . . . patuit Dea*] *Aeneid*, I, 402–5: 'So saying, she turned away and her neck glowed red; the divine tresses on her head breathed a

heavenly fragrance; her vesture swept down to her feet, and in her walk the goddess was made manifest.'

5. . . . *lumenque juventæ . . . honores*] *Aeneid*, I, 590–91: 'And shed on him the radiant light of youth, and the sparkle of joyful eyes.'

S418

1. *motto*] Virgil, *Eclogues*, III, 89: 'And brambles yield myrrh.'

2. *Informe cadaver . . . extinctos faucibus ignes*] Virgil, *Aeneid*, VIII, 264–7: 'And the mis-shapen carcase is dragged forward. Men cannot assuage their spirits by gazing on the terrible eyes, the monstrous visage and shaggy bristling chest, and the throat with its fire extinguished.'

S419

1. *motto*] Horace, II *Epistles*, ii, 140: 'A delusion most gratifying to the mind.'

2. *This Mr. Dryden calls the Fairy way of Writing*] In the Dedication (to the Marquess of Halifax) of *King Arthur* (1691): 'that Fairy kind of Writing which depends only upon the Force of Imagination.'

3. *Sylvis deducti caveant . . . versibus . . .*] Horace, *Ars Poetica*, 244–6: 'If you are going to bring woodland fauns on to the stage, in my opinion you shouldn't allow them to speak as though they were bred in the city centre; don't let them be too youthfully bold in their lines.'

4. *Mr. Bays in the Rehearsal*] The Duke of Buckingham, *The Rehearsal* (1663; 1671), V, i: 'Did you ever hear any people in clouds speak plain? They must be all for flights of fancy . . . When once you tie up spirits and people in clouds to speak plain, you spoil all.'

5. *Hunger and Envy in Ovid, of Fame in Virgil, and of Sin and Death in Milton*] Examples of allegorical figures: *Metamorphoses*, II, 768–82; *Aeneid*, IV, 173–88: *Paradise Lost*, X. In *Spectator* 357, however, one of the series on Milton's great poem, Addison judges these 'beautiful extended Allegorics' to be 'not agreeable to the Nature of an Heroick Poem'.

S420

1. *motto*] Horace, *Ars Poetica*, 100 (adapted): 'They lead the souls of the audience where they will.'

2. *the Fancy . . . feels in it self a kind of Chasm . . . a more sensible Bulk*] This is the view of Fancy/Imagination as being closely related to the mental processing of sense impressions. For the romantics, the imaginative faculty was to be far more powerful, active and independent.

S 421

1. *motto*] Ovid, *Metamorphoses*, IV, 294–5: 'He sought fresh Fountains on a foreign Soil. / The Pleasure lessen'd the attending Toil' (Addison).

2. *Eumenidum . . . in limine Diræ*] Virgil, *Aeneid*, IV, 469–73: 'Even as the distracted Pentheus sees the troop of Furies, and twin suns, and Thebes shows herself double to him: or Agamemnonian Orestes driven frantic flees across the stage pursued by his mother brandishing torches and black serpents, sees the avenging Fates blocking the doorway.'

S 65

1. *Etherege's The Man of Mode*] Sir George Etherege's popular piece *The Man of Mode: or, Sir Fopling Flutter* (licensed 3 June 1676), one of the greatest Restoration comedies, had been given at Drury Lane the month before this paper, on 20 April. Steele's attack on this play is both a journalist's theatre piece and an important document in the history of the change of taste of the English audience. Etherege's piece is not an 'exemplary comedy' of the kind that Steele wants, and was at this time writing in his 'sentimental' play *The Conscious Lovers* (acted 1722). In an essay, *A Defence of Sir Fopling Flutter*, timed to appear just before Steele's own comedy appeared, the old critic John ◊ Dennis sought to refute this paper which had appeared so many years before. He advanced a neo-Aristotelian theory of the genre of comedy which suggests the two best justifications of Etherege's brilliant play: that it is true to the life at the court of Charles II; and that the viewer is not to identify himself with Dorimant, since the aim is to caution the audience: 'Comedy is an Imitation of the very worst of men.' Dennis asserts that '*Dorim[a]nt* is a young courtier, haughty, vain and prone to Anger, amorous, false and inconstant. He debauches *Loveit*, and betrays her; loves *Belinda*, and as soon as he enjoys her is false to her.' Thus ridicule is the most powerful principle of the comedy (*Dennis's Critical Works*, ed. N. Hooker, ii, 241–50). Dennis may have had the better of the argument, but Steele correctly gauged the movement in the taste of the Town, and his kind of comedy rose to a long period of supremacy on the stage. Steele succeeds in denigrating the theatre of the past age (see *S* 2, *n* 3, p. 525).

2. *motto*] Horace, I *Satires*, x, 90–91: 'Demetrius and Tigellius, I bid you snivel in the ranks of your female followers.'

3. *an Over-grown Jade . . . she is some awkward, ill-fashioned, Country Toad . . . I'll Uncase you . . .* etc.] All from the opening scene.

4. *that she is so pleased*] III, iii.

5. *In what struggle*] IV, i.

6. *She has more Wit*] I, i.

7. *I Think, says she, I might*} III, i.
8. *one of his Companions*} Bellair.

S290

1. *Ambrose ◊ Philip's The Distress'd Mother*} See S555, *n* 5, p. 527.
2. *motto*} Horace, *Ars Poetica*, 97; 'Renounce their rant and bombastic words.'
3. *a Stroke of Self-pity*} III, i; the scene between Orestes, played by Powell, and Pylades.

*From the series of papers on Paradise Lost} In this series, Addison wrote eighteen Saturday essays (which by design are devoted to graver subjects for Sunday reading). Of these, four are printed here; they set out the general lines of his treatment. He was not the first critic to praise Milton's great work. John ◊ Dennis in his *The Advancement and Reformation of Poetry* (1701) had placed Milton before the ancient poets for sublime, truly religious passages. Addison's extensive, professional, systematic critique of the poem as a whole, with quotations, placed it prominently before the eighteenth-century reader, in a persuasive and widely distributed reading. This influential reading formed English taste for a long period; it stresses the classical side to Milton's complex masterpiece, which is undoubtedly there, in theory and practice. At the same time it discounts other aspects, in particular the rhetoric and plenitude linking it with earlier, Renaissance poetic achievements like Ariosto's *Orlando Furioso* (1516–32) and Tasso's *Gerusalemme Liberata* (1581), as well as the idiosyncratic even bizarre power of Milton's learning, or the political and religious thought that place the great poem firmly in the context of the mid-seventeenth-century struggles in the English state. The bloc of essays was revised and reprinted as *Notes upon the Twelve Books of Paradise Lost written by Mr. Addison* (1719); this was in turn translated into French (1721, etc.) and as part of a critical controversy with nationalist overtones into German (1740). Addison carefully, if in a low key, confronts unfavourable judgements made of *Paradise Lost* by the rigid application of the Aristotelian rules of epic poetry (see S267, *n* 3, below).

S267

1. *the rules of epic poetry: the fable and the action*} Addison makes unacknowledged use of French neo-classic critics, including Dacier's translation of Aristotle's *Poetics*, with comments. In particular, he follows Le Bossu's formulation of *fable* as 'a Discourse invented to form Men's Manners by Instructions disguis'd under the Allegories of one Single

Action' (see S70, n 6, p. 545), and the same critic's notion of the unity, integrity, importance and duration of the *action*.

2. *motto*] Propertius, *Elegies*, II, xxxiv, 65: 'Give place to him, writers of Greece and Rome.'

3. *Whether Milton's Paradise Lost may be called an Heroick Poem*] 'His subject is not that of an heroic poem, properly so-called. His design is the losing of our happiness; this event is not prosperous, like that of all other epic works; his heavenly machines are many, and his human persons are but two' (Dryden, *A Discourse concerning . . . satire*, 1693; in *Critical Essays*, ed. G. Watson, ii, 84).

4. *as Horace has observed*] Ars Poetica, 146–52.

5. *Aristotle himself allows*] Poetics, xxvi.

6. *as Aristotle describes it*] Poetics, xxv.

7. *the Book of Games . . . Virgil's Simile of a Top*] Aeneid, V; Iliad, XXIII . . . Aeneid, VII, 378–84.

8. *Aristotle . . . explains by the following Similitude*] Poetics, vii.

9. *Episodes . . . and the Machinery of Gods*] Aristotle, Poetics, xvii.

10. *the Space of Time, which is taken up by the Action of those Poems*] e.g. Dryden, 'Discourse concerning . . . Satire': 'Homer has limited . . . his actions to forty-eight natural days . . .'; 'A Parallel Betwixt Painting and Poetry', 1695: '. . . but whether Virgil's action was comprehended in a year or somewhat more, is not determined by Bossu'.

S273

1. *motto*] Horace, *Ars Poetica*, 156: 'Make an accurate note of behaviour.'

2. *a Person, who had lived thrice the Age of Man*] Nestor in the *Iliad* (I, 247–65).

3. *Fortemque Gyan*] Aeneid, I, 222.

4. *the Persons of Sin and Death*] See S419, n 5, p. 552.

5. *Fame as an Actress in the Aeneid*] IV, 173–97: 'Immediately Rumour [Fame] runs through the great cities of Libya; Rumour, than whom no one is quicker to do mischief; she thrives on restlessness' etc.

6. *Mock-Heroic Poems . . . the Dispensary and the Lutrin*] Sir Samuel Garth's *The Dispensary: a poem* (1699, etc.) – see T105, n 5; Nicholas Boileau, *Le Lutrin* (The Pulpit), 1674; 1681.

7. *Ulysses in Homer's Odyssey is very much admired by Aristotle*] Poetics, xvii, xxiv.

8. *an admirable Observation out of Aristotle*] Poetics, ii, slightly misquoted. Aristotle says that good men should not be shown falling into adversity,

since this excites neither our pity nor terror, but merely shocks or disgusts us.

S 291

1. *motto*] Horace, *Ars Poetica*, 351–2: 'Where there are plenty of fine passages shining in a poem, I won't take exception to a few blemishes which the poet has incautiously let by, or which his fallible human nature has not guarded against.'

2. *the French Authors*] See S 409, *n* 3, p. 548.

3. *Mr. Dryden . . . Errors, like Straws*] Dryden, *All for Love*, Prologue, 25–6.

4. *Tully observes . . . verbum ardens*] Cicero, *Ad Marcum Brutum Orator*, viii.

5. *observe with Longinus*] *On the Sublime*, xxxvi.

6. *a Story out of Boccalini*] Troiano Boccalini's two centuries of satirical *Ragguagli di Parnaso* were published in 1612 and 1613; translated into English, 1656, 1669 etc. A version titled *Advices from Parnassus* (1706) was corrected by ♢ Hughes. Addison's story is the last piece of the first century.

S 297

1. *motto*] Horace, I *Satires*, vi, 66–7: 'Just as otherwise perfectly good-looking bodies have moles.'

2. *Simple or Implex*] Poetics, x; *implex* is borrowed from Dacier's French translation.

3. *a former Paper*] S 40, p. 322.

4. *a beautiful Passage of the tenth Book*] *Paradise Lost*, X, 504 ff.

5. *and likewise by the Vision*] *Paradise Lost*, XII, 325 ff.

6. *Mr. Dryden's Reflection*] Dedication of the *Aeneis*, 1697; in *Critical Essays*, ed. Watson, ii, 233.

7. *Sin and Death . . . the Lymbo of Vanity*] *Paradise Lost*, II, 648–889; *Paradise Lost*, III, 444–97.

8. *It is finely observed by Aristotle*] Poetics, xxiv.

9. *Tully tells us*] Cicero, *De Amicitia* (*On Friendship*), I, iv.

10. *that Passage of the Tenth Book*] *Aeneid*, X, 501–5.

11. *[Lucan's] Diverticula, as Scaliger calls them*] For Lucan, see T 81, *n* 7, p. 514; the remark is in J. C. Scaliger's *Poetices*, iii, 25; the reference is to *Pharsalia*, II, 1–15.

12. *these very Digressions*] *Paradise Lost*, III, 1–55; IV, 750–70; IV, 312–20; V, 404–33.

13. *the small Infantry*] *Paradise Lost*, I, 575–6.

14. *Seneca's Objection*] Annaeus Seneca the elder (*c.* 54 B.C.–A.D. 39),

Controversies, VII, iv, 8 (adapted): (speaking of Calvus who set himself against Cicero as an orator) 'His style is stiff; it has nothing gentle or smooth in it.'

15. *a Kind of Jingle in his Words*] See S61, 'Punning', p. 341.

16. *the following Passages*] *Paradise Lost*, IX, 11; V, 868–9; I, 642; IV, 181.

17. *Aristotle himself . . . in his Rhetorick*] *Rhetoric*, III, ix.

18. *Mr. Dryden could translate . . . Milton makes use*] Dryden's *Aeneis*, III, 526–7.

S3

1. *The Bank of England: a vision*] The Bank of England had been founded in 1694, and was at this time renting the Grocers' Hall at the east end of Poultry for its offices. Addison's essay in this number is overtly political. The Bank, though not yet the sole channel of government finance, was the most important credit-raising institution in the City, because of its very powerful board of directors. It was the organization of the monied men *par excellence*, men like Sir Andrew Freeport. As Harley came to power in 1710, the directors of the Bank sent a deputation to try to pressure the Queen into retaining Godolphin as Lord Treasurer. The argument made against changing the ministry was the damage to public credit, with a suggestion that the Tory landed interest, which had triumphed in the General Election and was represented in *The Spectator* by Sir Roger de Coverley, was Jacobite. The bogey of Jacobitism, with the fears of a repudiation of the huge public debts contracted since 1688 for the struggle against France, was a common Whig preoccupation.

2. *motto*] Lucretius, *De Rerum Natura*, IV, 962–5: 'Whatever employment has the strongest hold on our interest, or has filled our waking hours so as to engage the mind's attention, that is what seems most often to keep us occupied in sleep' (R. E. Latham).

3. *the Genius of a Common-Wealth and a Young Man . . . a Spunge*] The republican spirit (the ghost of the seventeenth-century Commonwealth) and the Pretender (Jacobitism) both threaten to sponge clean the slate of the country's debts to (anti-Jacobite) investors in the public funds and wipe out the °Act of Settlement.

4. *in the Rehearsal*] The last act; Bayes (Dryden) arranges for the moon, the earth and the sun to dance the hay and show the eclipses.

5. *Et neque jam color*] Ovid, *Metamorphoses*, III, 491–3 (adapted): '[Her] complexion with its rosy flush faded away; gone was [her] vigour and strength and the beauties which had lately charmed [his] eye. Nothing remained of [her] body.'

6. *which Homer tells us*] Odyssey, X, 19.

7. *little Piles of notched Sticks*] The notched wooden tallies which were split down the middle to give both the creditor and the Treasury evidence of debt to the Exchequer.

8. *a Person whom I had never seen*] George Augustus, the electoral Prince of Hanover, who became George I. He had been created Duke of Cambridge in the English peerage, and the Whigs were campaigning for him to be invited over to take his seat in the Lords. The Queen would not countenance the idea, and the Whig suggestion was thus a constant double embarrassment to Harley and his colleagues.

*S*50

1. *The Indian kings in London*] The four Iroquois sachems, known as the Indian kings, had been brought to London in 1710 as part of the political bid by the Massachusetts colonial government for the Queen's aid in military operations against the French in Canada and their Indian allies. Spending five weeks of sight-seeing in London, during which they had an audience of Queen Anne on 19 April, the sachems aroused great journalistic interest. Steele, with only a touch of irony, presented them as examples of the noble savage to conclude a paragraph in *Tatler* 171 (Saturday, 13 May 1710) on honour and title. The Indians were accommodated at the Two Crowns and Cushions, King Street, Covent Garden, by Thomas Arne, the upholsterer and father of the composer. On the morning of the day after the present essay appeared, Swift wrote: 'The Spectator is written by Steele, with Addison's help: 'tis often very pretty. Yesterday it was made of a noble Hint I gave him long ago for his Tatler, about an Indian supposed to write his Travels into England. I repent he ever had it. I intended to have written a book on that subject. I believe he has spent it all in one paper, and all the under-hints there are mine too; but I never see him or Addison' (*Journal to Stella*). Swift's 'hint' and this essay are early examples of an effective European form of satire that became quite popular in the eighteenth century, namely, the European observers themselves observed at home: cf. Montesquieu's *Lettres Persanes* and Goldsmith's *The Man in Black*.

2. *motto*] Juvenal, *Satires*, XIV, 321: 'Nature never says one thing and Wisdom another.'

3. *little black Spots*] Patches; this was a favourite subject of contemporary social satire: e.g. *S*81, p. 440.

S 69

1. *The Royal Exchange*] A large two-storeyed structure built in 1669
round a great courtyard. It lay on the north side of Cornhill, backing on
to Threadneedle Street. In the middle of the quadrangle stood a statue by
Grinling Gibbons of Charles II as a laurel-wreathed Roman emperor;
another casting of this piece may be seen in Centre Court of Chelsea
Hospital. The Royal Exchange building itself housed a series of shops and
boutiques on both floors and was embellished with arches containing
statues of English monarchs by Caius Gabriel Cibber, father of Colley. In
the ground-floor arcade different groups of merchants had their places of
forgathering. The place was also a fashionable lounging place; destroyed
by fire in 1838, it was replaced by the present Royal Exchange building.
Von Uffenbach visited it on 10 June 1710, 'in order to speak with the
merchants', describing it as 'not so large as that at Amsterdam, but much
more massive and elegant' (*London in 1710*, p. 15).

2. *motto*] Virgil, *Georgics*, I, 54–61: 'Here cornfields, there grapevines
yield most abundantly; elsewhere fruitful trees shoot up and grass
flourishes unbidden. Do you not see how Timolus sends us the perfumes
of saffron, India ivory, the gentle Sabaeans their frankincense; but the
naked Chalybes send us iron, Pontus rank beaver-oil, Epirus prize-winning
mares for the Olympics? Nature imposed these laws and everlasting
covenants on certain lands.'

3. *the old Philosopher*] Diogenes the Cynic, according to Diogenes
Laertius, *Lives and Opinions of the Philosophers*, vi, 63, who called himself
cosmopolitan; Cicero, *Tusculan Disputations*, V, 37, gives the reply to
Socrates.

4. *remitted me some Mony to Grand Cairo*] See *S* 1, p. 198.

S 81

1. *motto*] Statius, *Thebaid*, II, 128–9 (adapted): 'As when the tigress
hears the clamour of the hunters, spots rise on her skin.'

2. *the Hay-Market*] For the Haymarket Theatre, see *T* 12, *n* 3, p. 509.

3. *Party-Signals*] An earlier joke of the same kind is found in Swift's
Examiner, no. 31, 8 March 1711: 'as the *Zealots* among the *Jews* bound the
law about their Foreheads and Wrists, and Hems of their Garments; so
the Women among us have got the distinguishing Marks of Party in their
Muffs, their Fans, and their Furbelows. The Whig Ladies put on their
Patches in a different Manner from the Tories. They have made *Schisms* in
the *Play-House*, and each have their particular Sides at the Opera . . .'

4. *as Mr. Cowley has imitated . . . the Motto of this Paper*] Cowley,
Davideis, III, 403–4, changed to a female reference; in a note, Cowley

gives the quotation from Statius used as the motto to this paper.

5. *a Sentence in . . . Pericles*] Thucydides, *History of the Peloponnesian War*, II, 45.

S125

1. *motto*] Virgil, *Aeneid*, VI, 832-3: 'Nay, children, do not harden your hearts to warfare like that, nor turn upon her own heart the over-powering force of your own country.'

2. *St. Anne's Lane*] In the City, north of Cheapside and west of Aldersgate in St Martin-le-Grand.

3. *Plutarch says very finely*] Plutarch, *Moralia*, ii: 'How one shall be helped by Enemies', 'Life of Pericles', near the end etc.

4. *that great Rule*] Luke vi, 27.

S174

1. *motto*] Virgil, *Eclogues*, VII, 69: 'So much I can recall, Thyrsis struggled, but in vain.'

2. *the old Roman Fable*] e.g. Livy, *History*, II, xxxii; a commonplace of contemporary economic argument.

3. *Carthaginian Faith*] *Punica fides*, i.e. treachery; a proverbial phrase no better based than such xenophobic abuse generally is.

4. *to purchase a Room for his Picture . . . the Maid of Honour*] See S109, p. 224.

S232

1. *The economics of charity*] This paper is signed 'X' in the folio half-sheets, 'Z' in the 8vo collected *Spectators* and left unsigned in the 12mo volumes. Though 'Z' is used for some of the contributions assigned to John ♢ Hughes, there is no sure external evidence for the authorship of this number. Some editors have assigned it to Hughes, others to Henry ♢ Martyn on account of the subject matter.

2. *motto*] Sallust, *Bellum Catilinae*, liv: 'Never offering presents he won glory.'

3. *Sir William Petty has given Examples . . . One of them*] Sir William Petty, 'Concerning the Growth of the City of London', 1683; reprinted in his *Essays in Political Arithmetic*.

4. *every Parish is taxed to the Maintenance of their own Poor*] Elizabethan legislation established the system of every parish in England raising money by a Poor Rate for the relief of indigence; the Act of Settlement of the Poor of 1662 empowered a parish to send back to the parish of which he or she was a native anyone who was liable to be a charge on the rates.

All such Poor Law legislation attempted to exact work from the poor in return for relief.

5. *that famous Song . . . The merry Beggars*] The editor is unable to identify specifically a song called *The Merry Beggars* which has the two opening lines given by Addison. 'Hang Sorrow and cast away Care' occurs in several seventeenth-century catch books with music by William Lawes, but apparently without the second line. Sets of verses opening with 'Hang Sorrow . . .' were common enough to make the phrase an alternative title for the very popular tune, 'Old Sir Simon'. *The Merry Beggars* is a rather unspecific element in song titles; it is associated with other elements such as *The Jovial Crew*, and in that form provides the title for Richard Brome's comedy of 1641.

6. *I was hungry*] Matthew xxv, 42–3.

S 384

1. *A bold stroke in the party war*] Steele blatantly disregards earlier declarations that *The Spectator* would not be a party paper. This number is a direct contribution to an eddy of political controversy. William ◊ Fleetwood was appointed by the House of Lords to preach before them on the Fast Day, Wednesday, 16 January 1712. This was at the height of the crisis in the upper house over the ministry's peace policy, just after Oxford had been forced to ask the Queen to create the twelve 'Utrecht' peers to give him a majority. The ministry, fearing a public attack, prevented the Lords from meeting to hear the sermon; Fleetwood immediately published his discourse, in which he strongly urged the continuation of the war. On 14 May, Fleetwood published his volume of four sermons on: the death of Queen Mary, 1694; the death of the Duke of Gloucester, Anne's surviving son, 1700; the death of William III, 1701; and the commemoration in 1703 of the 'Queen's accession. A second edition appeared twelve days later. Public interest lay, not in the four servile old sermons, but in a provocative nine-page Preface, written for the new publication. This political pamphlet argues that the Whigs are the guardians of the Revolution Settlement, and that under the new administration the settlement is in danger from crypto-Jacobites. The Tory majority in the Commons secured an order for the volume to be burned in Parliament Yard by the hangman. A considerable pamphlet scuffle took place. Such was the piece to which Steele gave even greater circulation in his periodical: 'the *Spectator* has conveyed above 14,000 of them into other People's Hands' (Fleetwood to Bishop Burnet, 17 June 1712; in his *A Compleat Collection of Sermons* . . . (1737), p. vi).

2. *motto*] The sickly, two-year-old Dauphin, who survived to succeed

as Louis XV, was the great-grandson of the seventy-three-year-old Louis
XIV. Louis' only son had died in 1711, and in February 1712 his
grandson, the Duke of Burgundy, the Duke's wife and their eldest son
had all died of a fever. The Chevalier de St George was the 'un-dress' title
assumed by the Old °Pretender, the son of James II. Hans Kaspar von
Bothmer, a Hanoverian courtier and diplomat, was the Elector's envoy in
London from 1711. Abel Roper's unguardedly Jacobite news paragraph in
his *Post-Boy* attracted much journalistic attack and attention, including
rumours of his arrest.

   3. *two most excellent Princes*] Queen Mary and William III.

   4. *the Duke of Gloucester's Death*] Princess (later Queen) Anne's son
(1689–July 1700); his death ended any possibility of a continuation of the
Stuart dynasty.

   5. *settling the Succession*] By the °Act of Settlement.

   6. *the Queen's Accession*] William III died on 8 September 1702.

   7. *a name and a Praise*] Zephaniah iii, 20.

S445

   1. *The Stamp Act*] At the Restoration, censorship of the press was
provided for by the Licensing Act of 1662. When this lapsed in 1694,
there was a printing free-for-all governed only by the uncertain rules of
the common law of libel and sporadic government action under treason
statutes and other miscellaneous provisions. There were frequent calls for
censorship legislation, but too many politicians, both in and out of office,
saw a free appeal outside Parliament to the public at large as advantageous.
When Harley's peace policy provoked fierce attack in periodicals and
pamphlets, pressure grew strong for a more restrictive law of libel. The
Queen's message to the Houses of Parliament on 17 January 1712 drew
attention to 'How great License is taken in publishing false and scandalous
Libels, such as are a Reproach to any Government'. The Commons were
slow in bringing forward a Bill they promised, but it was finally introduced
on 10 June, only to die in the Committee stage. On the same day,
however, the ministry adopted a suggestion of Bolingbroke's and had a
clause added to the Supply Bill (10 Anne cap. 10); this Bill levied duties
on a variety of products and the ministry included a half-penny tax on all
newspapers and pamphlets printed on a half-sheet or less, and a penny on
a whole-sheet and not more, together with a shilling for each advertisement
carried in an issue. The Act came into force on 1 August. It was meant to
disable the finances of ephemeral publications, though for a time it
remained rather ineffective through bad drafting. This system of financial
censorship, though with different levels of impost, was in force until the

final abolition of the Stamp Tax on newspapers in 1855. Each paper bore a red printed stamp to show that the tax had been paid. Stamped paper was purchased through the Stamp Office. Swift wrote on 7 August: 'Do you know that Grub Street is dead and gone last week; No more Ghosts or Murders now for Love or Money . . . The Observator is fallen . . . the Examiner is deadly sick, the Spectator keeps up and doubles its price' (*Journal to Stella*).

2. *motto*] Martial, *Epigrams*, I, cxvii, 18: 'Do I hear you say "You're not worth so much?" Lupercus, you've got sense' (James Michie).

3. *Mr. Baxter's Death*] For Richard Baxter, see S85, *n* 5, p. 547.

4. *Five or Six Pounds a-Day*] At ½d a paper, this would indicate (£1 = 480 half-pennies) a circulation of 2,400 or 2,880.

S11

1. *motto*] Juvenal, *Satires*, II, 63: 'The doves are censured while the crows are spared.'

2. *the celebrated Story of the Ephesian Matron*] She went into the tomb with the body of her husband, intending to die of weeping, but after fasting for five days she was offered a share of his supper by a soldier who was guarding several crucified corpses exposed to public view. She became his mistress, even giving him her husband's corpse to replace that of one of the executed malefactors which relatives had removed for burial. The story is told in Petronius's *Satyricon*, part II, and as 'La matrone d'Ephèse' was re-told by La Fontaine and printed with his Twelfth Book of *Fables*.

3. *the Fable of the Lion and the Man*] Aesop, *Fables*, no. 219; also La Fontaine, *Fables*, iii, no. 10.

4. *Ligon's Account of Barbadoes*] Richard Ligon, *A True and Exact History of the Island of Barbadoes* (1657; 1673). Ligon's paragraph is simply a story of ingratitude. Yarico, with 'small breasts with the nipples of a porphyrie colour', was a slave who had borne a child to one of the Christian servants in the colony before she aids and falls in love with 'a young man' attacked by the Indians. Steele supplies the name °*Inkle*, the seduction and the character of the young merchant. He had inherited an estate in Barbados from his first wife.

S159

1. *the vision of Mirzah*] Addison describes this as 'the first Vision', presumably intending a series, but no other followed. The piece stands on its own as one of the best-known of the *Spectator* papers. *Mirza* or *Mirzah* (based on a Persian word), as a title of honour meaning 'son of a prince', is found in the pages of Sir John Chardin's *Travels into Persia and the East*

Indies (1686). D. F. Bond notes that in the French edition of Chardin's *Voyages* (Amsterdam, 1711, viii, 220–3), the account of the Pont de Barbouc in Ispahan gives details parallel with touches in Addison's allegory; two folding plates accompanying the text reinforce this suggestion.

2. *motto*] Virgil, *Aeneid*, II, 604–6: 'All the cloud that now hangs over your eyes and obscures mortal vision with damp encircling mist, I shall rip away.'

S264

1. *motto*] Horace, I *Epistles*, xviii, 103: 'A sequestered path, and the noiseless tenor of your days.'

2. *Irus*] Irus is a beggar of Ithaca in the *Odyssey* (VIII, 1 and 55), a hanger-on of Penelope's suitors; from him comes the proverb 'Irus pauperior' (poorer than Irus).

3. *in Lily's Grammar how sweetly Bacchus and Apollo run in a Verse*] The ancient collaborative grammar, dating from the reign of Henry VIII and passing under the authorship of William Lily, was still in use at this time in one form or another. The section on the genders of nouns has for its first rule: 'Propria quae maribus tribuuntur, mascula dicas:/ Ut sunt divorum: Mars, Bacchus, Apollo . . .' etc.

4. *Richard Estcourt*] had advertised in *Spectators* 260, 261 and 263 the opening on 1 January of his Bumper Tavern in St James's Street, Covent Garden, selling '°neat, natural Wines, fresh and in Perfection; being bought of Brooke and Hellier' to be sold by 'his old Servant trusty Anthony' who had so often adorned the English and Irish theatres.

S543

1. *motto*] Ovid, *Metamorphoses*, II, 13–14: 'Though not alike, consenting parts agree,/ Fashion'd with similar variety.'

2. *Galen was converted by his Dissection*] Greek physician (*c.*A.D. 129–?199). His extensive medical writings formed (with the teaching of Hippocrates) the basis of orthodox medicine and medical teaching into and beyond the Renaissance. He is the leading ancient anatomist, whose comparative work based on the dissection of animals is outstanding in grasp.

3. *Creation*] Sir Richard Blackmore's *Creation: A Philosophical Poem* in seven books (1712; several editions) was published by Buckley and Tonson: see *T*3, *n* 2, pp. 506–7.

S 385

1. *motto*] Ovid, *Tristia*, I, iii, 66: 'Hearts joined with love as strong as Theseus'.'

2. *Patroclus . . . Achates*] In the *Iliad* and *Aeneid*.

3. *Atticus . . . an exact Account of all his Affairs*] Budgell is drawing on Bayle's *Dictionary*, article 'Atticus'; at the end of the second paragraph he has put the references to Cornelius Nepos in the wrong order.

Appendix

1. *Swift . . . Verses on the Shower in Town and the Description of the Morning*] *T* 238 and *T* 9.

2. *Mr. Twisden*] Heneage ◇ Twisden's monument is in the north aisle.

3. *The Epistle from Mr. Downes the Prompter*] John ◇ Downes.

4. *one Gentleman*] Addison.

5. *The same Hand writ*] *Tatler* 153, *T* 18, *Tatlers* 42 and 220.

6. *Raillery in Behalf of . . . Mr. Hoadley*] Under the guise of referring to Martin Powell, the puppeteer, Steele (*Tatlers* 44 and 50) satirized Offspring Blackall, Bishop of Exeter. The Bishop held extreme views on the Divine Rights of Kings and Passive Obedience which, it was suggested, would reduce the subject to a puppet. The Rev. Benjamin Hoadley was at the same time controverting his ecclesiastical superior in more orthodox fashion.

7. *Dr. Smalridge . . . Dr. Atterbury*] High-church Tories. George ◇ Smalridge is favourably characterized in *Tatlers* 72 and 114. *Tatler* 66 includes an encomium on Francis ◇ Atterbury as a preacher.

8. *Dr. South*] See *S* 106, *n* 2, p. 527.

Biographical Index
of Contemporaries Mentioned in the Essays

The symbol ◊ preceding a name in the Introduction and Notes refers the reader to an entry in this Index: e.g. Thomas ◊ Betterton.

ALBERGOTTI, Francesco Zanobi Filippo (Florence, 1654–Paris, 1717). Naturalized Frenchman; Lieutenant-General, 1702. During the War of the Spanish Succession, he took an important part in the fighting in Italy. In Flanders, he served at Malplaquet, 1709, and he defended Douai in 1710.

ATTERBURY, Dr Francis (1662–1732). An active and eloquent Tory ecclesiastical politician; Dean of Carlisle; afterwards Bishop of Rochester and Dean of Westminster, 1713.

AUGUSTUS II ('the Strong'). Friedrich August I, hereditary Elector of Saxony, King of Poland (1697–1733); in exile 1706–9 as a result of his defeat by ◊ Charles XII of Sweden, who supported Louis XIV.

BARRY, Mrs Elizabeth (1658–1713). Coached and promoted by her lover, the Earl of Rochester, she became an outstanding tragic and comic actress (*T*1, *n* 5, p. 506).

BERNARD, Samuel (Paris, 1651–1739). Banker; principal financial adviser to Louis XIV, without holding office, raising the vast sums necessary for fighting the War of the Spanish Succession. In 1708, he refused Louis further advances, but relented and went spectacularly bankrupt in 1709, though he recovered.

BETTERTON, Thomas (*c*.1635–1710). Leading actor and actor-manager, playwright and adapter of Shakespeare. The principal actor of Davenant's Duke's Company, he took over Drury Lane Theatre in 1682 and ran the United Company. In 1695 he seceded with an actors' company and played in Lincoln's Inn Fields for a decade (*T*1, *n* 5, p. 505; *T*4, *n* 1, p. 507).

BICKERSTAFF, John (d.*c*.1724). Actor with a wide range of roles though specializing in comic parts. He was one of the seven actor 'managers' at Drury Lane in 1709–10 and was involved in the disorders there.

BIGNALL (BICKNELL or 'pretty Mrs BIGNELL'), ?Margaret (*c.*1695–May 1723). A popular comic actress whose dancing was admired by Steele (*Spectator* 370).

BONONCINI (BUONONCINI), Giovanni Battista (Modena, 1670–Vienna, 1747). Composer mainly of operas, the youngest of a famous family of Italian musicians. He was popular in London and for a time rivalled Handel.

BOUFFLERS, Louis François, Duc de (1644–1711). Marshal of France, 1693. A resourceful and formidable opponent of Marlborough, he defended Lille, 1708, and assumed command at Malplaquet, August 1709.

BOYER, Abel (1667–1729). Journalist and writer of contemporary history, particularly the most useful and thorough *Political State of Great Britain*, which appeared in monthly parts and yearly collections from 1711 as far as his death and a decade beyond. He wrote in the Whig interest.

BOYLE, Henry (*c.*1677–1725). Dedicatee of vol. III of the collected *Spectators*. A court Whig, he was Chancellor of the Exchequer 1701–8. He replaced Harley as Secretary of State for the Northern Department when the latter's resignation was forced in 1708 by Godolphin and Marlborough. Boyle was dismissed in 1710 when Harley's peace administration came to power.

BRACEGIRDLE, Anne (*c.*1673–1748). The adopted daughter of ◊ Betterton and his wife, she was one of the most popular actresses of the age, with a fine singing voice. She excelled in both tragic and comic parts (written for her by Congreve in all his comedies), and retired from the stage in 1707.

BUCKLEY, Samuel (d. 1741). Leading printer and bookseller, publisher of *The Spectator*. Possessing considerable learning and journalistic skill himself, he printed and published *The Monthly Register* and the first English daily paper, *The °Daily Courant*. His shop was first at Amen Corner and then at the Dolphin in Little Britain.

BUDGELL, Eustace (1686–1737). Miscellaneous writer. His mother was Addison's cousin and he became a protégé of Addison, who took him to Ireland as a clerk in his office. Budgell acted as an assistant to Addison in writing *The Spectator*, contributing twenty-nine papers on varied topics to the first series, including four papers on education.

BULLOCK, William (?1657–?1740). A comic actor who exploited his great height and a foolish expression; often paired with the small ◊ Norris.

CADOGAN, William (1675–1726). Major-General; promoted Lieutenant-General, January 1709. A close friend of ◊ Marlborough's and one of
his principal staff officers, he was seriously wounded at the siege of Mons.
He resigned his offices in 1712, when his chief was dismissed; re-instated
on the accession of George I.

CAREY, William (1685–1757). A member of Addison's circle; B.A.,
New College, Oxford, 1708; Whig office-holder and later M.P. He is
mentioned in Steele's Acknowledgements, S555. No specific piece(s) in
the *Spectator* series may on external evidence be attributed to him.
(Identified by D. F. Bond, *Spectator*, I, pp. liii–liv.)

CASSINI, Giovanni Domenico, see S552, *n* 5, p. 537.

CHARLES XII(1686–1718). King of Sweden from 1697. A rash and
formidable soldier, he waged unremitting war against Denmark, Norway,
Russia and their allies, placing himself on the side of Louis XIV. Charles
was seriously defeated by Peter the Great at Poltava in the Ukraine, 1709.
He fled to Turkey where he remained a prisoner until 1715.

CORRELLI, Arcangelo (1653–1713). Italian violinist and composer.

COWPER, William Cowper (*c*.1665–1723). Baron, 1706. A leading
Whig, he was Lord Keeper then Lord Chancellor from 1707 to 1710,
when he lost office with the fall of Godolphin and the Whigs. He became
Lord Chancellor again on the accession of George I.

DAWKS, Ichabod (1661–1730). Printer and news-writer who ran °*Ichabod
Dawks' Letter*.

DENNIS, John (1657–1734). Critic and dramatist, political pamphleteer
in the Whig interest. His critical work is in general treated with
(?contemptuous) silence in *The Tatler* and *The Spectator*, except for a few
satirical allusions, but he was at his best, at this time, undoubtedly the
leading neo-classical theoretician in London. He became soured, cantan-
kerous and eccentric and his behaviour attracted the mockery of Pope and
others. His most important work is *The Grounds of Criticism in Poetry*
(1704; reprinted in ed. Hooker, *Critical Works of John Dennis*, New York,
1911, and in ed. Durham, *Critical Essays: 1700–1725*, Yale U.P., 1915),
the sketch for a longer work which failed to attract subscribers.

D'HARCOURT, Henri (1654–1718). Duc, 1700; Marshal of France,
employed by Louis XIV as ambassador to Spain.

DOGGETT, Thomas (*c*.1670–1721). An Irish comedian specializing in low-life characters acted with close realistic observation. He was briefly one of the managers of the Haymarket Theatre (1709–10) and later of Drury Lane. He founded Doggett's prize-race for Thames watermen, still run.

DOWNES, John (fl. 1661–1719). Failing in 1661 through stage fright as an actor, he was prompter for the Duke's Company and for the United and Betterton's companies. This experience gave him the information which he too tersely put together as *Roscius Anglicanus* (1708), one of the few primary sources for the history of the Restoration stage.

D'URFEY, Thomas (1653–1723). Dramatist and popular song-writer. A friend of Charles II and James II, he was a prolific writer; his thirty plays show more theatrical ingenuity and originality than he is commonly given credit for. He had a keen eye for the developing interests of 'the Town'.

DYER, John (d. 6 September 1713). Jacobite news-writer who published °*Dyer's Letter* until his death.

EUGÈNE (François Eugène) of Savoy, Prince (1663–1736). Born in Paris and educated at the court of Louis XIV, he took service with his relative the Emperor Leopold I against the Turks; Field Marshal, 1696. He commanded Imperial forces in the War of the Spanish Succession and was Marlborough's partner in the victory at Blenheim, 1704. Thereafter the two commanders worked together, e.g. at Oudenarde, 1708. On Marlborough's fall in 1712, Eugène visited London and was fêted by the Whigs as part of their defiant pro-war opposition to the peace policy of the Harley (Oxford) administration.

EUSDEN, the Rev. Laurence (1688–1730). Poetaster who attached himself to the Whigs; poet laureate, 1718. One of the 'nucleus of nobodies' in Pope's *Dunciad* and further abused by the satirist as a 'Parson, much be-mus'd in Beer'. Apart from guesses or tradition naming him as the writer of letters in *Spectators* 54, 78 and 87, there is no hard evidence for assigning any particular piece(s) or paper(s) to him.

FLAMSTEED, the Rev. John, see *S*552, *n* 5, p. 537.

FLEETWOOD, William (1650–1723). A popular preacher at St Dunstan's-in-the-West, he became a royal chaplain to William III and Queen Anne, as well as a Canon of Windsor. Although he was a Whig, with low-church views, the Queen liked his pulpit style and advanced him to the see of St Asaph, 1708. He was an active member of the opposition in the Lords to

Harley's peace policy, taking part in the printing of the 'protests' entered in the upper House against pro-administration votes.

GALWAY, Henri de Massue (1648–1720), Marquis de Ruvigny, Viscount, 1692 and Earl of, 1697. Huguenot refugee who entered the service of William III and fought in Ireland; a brave and experienced General, he held command of the allied armies in Spain and Portugal, but was decisively defeated at the battle of Almanza, April 1707. His conduct became the focus of Tory attacks on the war.

GODOLPHIN, Sidney Godolphin (1645–1712), First Earl of. Held office under Charles II, James II and William III, an expert in Treasury affairs. He became Lord Treasurer in 1700 and, holding this office under Anne, was the financial and political member of the duumvirate with Marlborough that waged the war against Louis XIV on England's part. He was dismissed in August 1710 on the defeat by Harley of the Whigs, whom he had been forced to admit to his administration in return for parliamentary support.

GRANT, Roger (d. 1724). 'Oculist and Operator in Extraordinary to Her Majesty' (*Gazette*, 28 September 1710). He was alleged to be illiterate and was doubtless a more-or-less skilful and self-taught °coucher. See *T*55, *n* 1, pp. 511–12.

HALLEY, Edmund, see *S*552, *n* 5, p. 537.

HOADLY, Benjamin (1676–1761). Religious controversialist. At this time, as rector of St Peter-le-Poor, Broad Street, he was attacking ♢ Atterbury on various theological points, and making his mark as a low-church polemicist of Revolution principles and the religious champion of the Whigs. On the accession of George I, he became a royal chaplain and, by continuing his career as a latitudinarian writer, Bishop of Bangor, 1715; of Hereford, 1721; of Salisbury, 1723; of Winchester, 1734.

HUGH[E]S, John (1677–1720). Miscellaneous writer. His *Poems on Several Occasions: with some select Essays in Prose* appeared posthumously in two volumes (1735), edited by his brother-in-law, William Duncombe; based on the latter's 'Introduction' when not in conflict with other information, the following assignments of *Tatler* and *Spectator* essays are generally made to Hughes: complete papers; *Tatler* 113; *Spectators* 210, 302, 375, 525, 541, 554; together with letters in *Spectators* 33, 53, 66, 104, 220, 230, 252.

INCE, Richard (d. 1758). Of Christ Church, Oxford, and the Middle

Temple, barrister and Whig office-holder. He contributed to the *Spectator* (according to Steele in *S*555), but his pieces or hints are not as yet definitely identified.

KIDNEY, Humphry. The waiter at the St James's Coffee-house, frequently mentioned in *The Tatler*, and in *Spectator* 104.

LINTOT[T], (Barnaby) Bernard (1675–1736). Bookseller, whose shop at the Cross Keys, between the Temple Gates, was a meeting place for writers. He published some poems by Dryden and works by ◊ Pope, Gay, Farquhar and ◊ Parnell. He had a period of strained relationship with Pope, who put him in the *Dunciad*.

MARLBOROUGH, John Churchill (1650–1722), First Duke of; Prince of Mindelheim in the Empire, 1704. Appointed Captain General, 1702; commander-in-chief of the allied armies in Flanders and ambassador extraordinary and plenipotentiary to the allied powers. A brilliant general and organizer, he was the military half of the duumvirate with ◊ Godolphin that led the English part of the war against Louis XIV. He became through his financial dealings a major target of Tory opposition to the war. After the defeat by Harley in 1710 of the Whigs who had forced themselves into the administration, and who were strongly supported by his wife, both he and the Duchess (once the Queen's favourite) were dismissed from all their offices at the end of 1711. In 1713, they went into exile. The Duke was re-instated on the accession of George I. Marlborough was the dedicatee of vol. IV of the collected *Spectators*.

MARTYN, Henry (d. 1721). Whig economist and office-holder after 1714. He collaborated in *The British Merchant, or Commerce preserv'd* (thrice-weekly, 1 August 1713 to 30 July 1714), published to attack Bolingbroke's commercial treaty with France, parallel with the political treaty of the Peace of Utrecht, voted out in the Commons, 18 June 1713. It is reasonable to suppose that Martyn was responsible for, or gave assistance with, *S*232 ('The economics of charity'), as well as the letters in *Spectators* 180 and 200 on 'political arithmetic'.

MAYNWARING, Arthur (1668–1712). Whig politician and clever controversialist. He acted as secretary and political confidant to Sarah, Duchess of Marlborough, and became an M.P., commissioner of the customs and auditor of the imprests. He was the dedicatee of volume I of the collected *Tatlers*, and a member of the Whig political and literary group, the Kit-Cat Club.

MILLS, John, the elder (d. 1736). A leading actor in ◊ Betterton's company at Drury Lane; his wife also acted in the company.

MORPHEW, John (fl. 1706–20). A leading bookseller and publisher near Stationers' Hall. His list included newsheets such as *The Country-Gentleman's Courant*, of which the first number was given free as an advertisement, and the *Monthly Miscellany*; his pamphlets included Swift's *Predictions for the Year 1708* (◊ Partridge). He was the printer of *The Tatler*.

NORRIS, Henry (1665–?1720). A short, comic actor, often paired with the tall William ◊ Bullock. Norris made a hit as Dicky in Farquhar's *Constant Couple, or A Trip to the Jubilee*, hence his nickname 'Jubilee Dicky'.

PARNELL, the Rev. Thomas (1679–1718). Poet, later Archdeacon of Clogher in Ireland. He contributed two allegorical dream visions, the first in (Steele's) *Spectator* 460, the second in (Addison's) *Spectator* 501. He was a friend of ◊ Swift's and a member of the Tory Scriblerus Club, but remained on good terms with Steele and Addison. Pope brought out a carefully edited posthumous selection of his work, *Poems on Several Occasions* (1722), which contains the two pieces mentioned above.

PARTRIDGE, John (1644–1715). First a shoe-maker then a writer of astrological publications, chiefly his yearly almanac, *Merlinus Liberatus*, from 1680. In March 1708, John ◊ Morphew published Swift's *Predictions for the Year 1708*, 'By Isaac Bickerstaff Esq.', in which Partridge's death is foretold 'upon the 29th of *March* next, about Eleven at Night, of a raging Feaver'. On 30 March Morphew published Swift's April Fool piece, *The Accomplishment of the first of Mr. Bickerstaff's Predictions*, giving a detailed account of Partridge's end. Partridge protested in his almanac for 1709 that he was still alive and Swift countered with *A Vindication of Isaac Bickerstaff Esq.*, proving that the 'philomath' was indeed dead.

PINKETHMAN (PENKETHMAN), William (?–1725), known as 'Pinkey'. A very well-known comic actor, droll and showman. As well as appearing regularly in the repertoire at Drury Lane, he had booths at °May Fair and Bartholomew Fair. The year after opening his summer theatre at Greenwich, in 1710 he was running *The Pantheon*, a show in Covent Garden with a hundred figures of the heathen Gods. He is an interesting show-business entrepreneur who often attracted the sneers of patrons of the legitimate stage (*Tatler* 189).

POPE, Alexander (1688–1744). Mentioned in *S*555 as a contributor to the *Spectator*. Clear attributions, because he later printed the material in his works, are: *Spectators* 378 ('Messiah', a poem); 527 (verses translated from Ovid); 406 (letter); 575 (letter). A probable attribution suggested by G. W. Sherburn is *Spectator* 457 (letter), and therefore also *Spectator* 427 (letter), since the former is 'by the same hand').

POWELL, George (?1658–December 1714). One of the chief actors at Drury Lane. Less restrained in style than ◊ Betterton, he was judged to have a tendency to 'ranting' (S40), as were Cibber and Wilks later. Powell was a touchy leader of actors' protests.

POWELL, Martin (d. 1729). Puppeteer and showman. A cripple, he performed in Bath and elsewhere before establishing in 1710 his Punch's Theatre, first at the top of St Martin's Lane, then in 'the Little Piazza, Covent Garden' (*Spectator* 14). His marionette theatre included satire on the opera, the legitimate stage and contemporary events.

READ, Sir William (d. 1715). Oculist and operator in ordinary to Queen Anne and George I. Knighted in 1705 for treating servicemen, he was another self-taught °coucher, like Roger ◊ Grant, who practised in the Strand at York Buildings. Something of a quack, he made a fortune.

RICH, Christopher (c. 1658–1714). A lawyer by trade, he bought himself into the management of Drury Lane Theatre before 1690. A bully, none too scrupulous and avaricious, he ran the theatre strictly as a business and soon alienated many of the players, who seceded under the leadership of ◊ Betterton. By 1706, Rich was making money at Drury Lane with popular but 'low' entertainments, °rope-dancers and the like. He was beaten in a fight for Drury Lane, remodelled the house in Lincoln's Inn Fields, but died before it could be opened. He was succeeded by his son.

RUSSELL, Edward (1652–1727). Admiral and victor of °La Hogue, May 1692; created First Earl of Orford. One of the five Whig Lords of the Junto and leader of an important group of M.P.s.

SMALRIDGE, Dr George (1663–1719). A Tory and even a Jacobite, but not a violent party man. A friend of ◊ Atterbury, he was a Canon of Christ Church, Oxford, and succeeded Atterbury as Dean of Carlisle, 1711; Dean of Christ Church, 1713; Bishop of Bristol, 1714.

SOMERS (of Evesham), John Somers (1681–1716), First Baron. Acknowledged leader of the Whig Junto lords. A brilliant lawyer, he was Solicitor-General, Attorney-General, Lord Keeper and finally (1697–1700) Lord Chancellor; Lord President of the Council, 1708, dismissed 1710; dedicatee of vol. I of the collected *Spectators*.

SOUTH, the Rev. Robert, D.D. (1636–1716). Rector of Islip, Oxon., and prebendary of Westminster. He refused the see of Rochester, 1713. He was a popular Restoration preacher noted for his wit. His sermons were published in various collections of several volumes from 1679 until well into the eighteenth century.

SUNDERLAND, Charles Spencer (1674–1722), succeeded in 1703 as Third Earl of. One of the Whig Lords of the Junto, he married in 1701 Anne Churchill, second daughter of ◊ Marlborough. When the Whigs forced themselves into the Godolphin–Marlborough administration in 1706, he became Secretary of State for the Southern Department, retaining Addison as his secretary. He was disliked by the Queen, and was dismissed in June 1710, as Harley came to power.

SWIFT, Jonathan (1667–1742). Swift was in London in 1701, 1707–9, 1710–14, on leave from his Irish church preferments. Acting as an ecclesiastical agent of the Church of Ireland, he was also trying to make an English career for himself by his brilliant writing talent. His witty *jeux d'esprit* against John ◊ Partridge, the astrologer, offered the name and character of Isaac Bickerstaff, borrowed by Steele to write *The Tatler*. One side of Swift's writing is close to the wit and freedom of the *Tatler* and *Spectator* essays. He was a friend of Steele's, and Addison had a close relationship with him, inscribing a large-paper presentation-copy of his *Travels in Italy* (1705): 'To Dr. Jonathan Swift, the most Agreeable Companion The Truest Friend and the Greatest Genius of his Age.' When Swift became in 1710 the chief political writer for the Harley ministry and the Tories, Steele and Addison supported the fallen Whigs, and 'the rage of party' drove them apart. Many years afterwards, Swift claimed several *Tatlers* and *Spectators*, either as completely his, or based on his hints, of which there are printed here: *T*9 (part), *T*230, *T*238 and *S*50 (see *T*81, *n* 1, p. 513; *T*249, *n* 1, p. 524).

SWINEY (SWINNY), Owen (c. 1675–1754). An Irishman, he was one of the group that ran the Haymarket Theatre from 1706 to 1711. He was able to translate and prepare the books for English productions of Italian operas.

TASWELL (incorrectly called CASWELL in *T*55), Dr William. Rector of St Mary's parish church, Newington; King's Scholar at Westminster; student at Christ Church, Oxford, 1670.

TICKELL, Thomas (1686–1740). Poet and protégé of Addison, who made him Under-Secretary of State in Ireland. He helped Addison to bring out the second series of *Spectators* (1714) and edited Addison's posthumous work (1721) with a good Elegy. In the first series his only contribution definitely established is the set of verses 'To the supposed Author of the *Spectator*' which appears in (Steele's) *Spectator* 532.

TOOKE, Junior, Ben(jamin) (*d*. 1723). Bookseller and printer at the Middle Temple Gateway, Fleet Street; publisher of the London °*Gazette* from 1711 and of various works by Swift.

TORCY, Jean Baptiste Colbert (1665–1746), Marquis de. Louis XIV's Secretary of State for Foreign Affairs; directed the French side of the negotiations leading to the Peace of Utrecht, 1713.

TOWNSHEND, Charles Townshend (1775–1738), Second Viscount. Whig politician and ambassador at The Hague, 1705–11. He signed the Barrier Treaty with the Dutch, an important act to further the continuation of the war, and for this he was in 1712 censured by the Tory majority in the Commons.

TWISDEN (TWYSDEN), Heneage (1680–1709), son of Sir William Twysden Bart., of Royden Hall, East Peckham, Kent. Captain in Sir Richard Temple's foot regiment and aide-de-camp to the Duke of Argyle, he was killed at the battle of Mons.

VANBRUGH, Sir John (1664–1726). Architect, dramatist and theatrical impresario. He built the elaborate Haymarket Theatre, opened 1705 (see *T*12, *n* 3, p. 509). He was the architect of Blenheim Palace, the vast house built by parliamentary grant on the royal manor of Woodstock, near Oxford, and voted to Marlborough.

VENDOSME (VENDÔME), Louis-Joseph (1654–1727). Marshal of France. He took command in Flanders after the disaster of Ramillies 1705, and lost the battle of Oudenarde, July 1708.

VERBRUGGEN, Susanna *née* Perceval (1667–1703). An admired comic actress who specialized in hoydens and minxes. She married the actor William Mountfort; when he was murdered in 1692 by Captain Hill and Lord Mohun, she married another player, Jack Verbruggen.

VILLARS, Claude Louis Hector, Duc de (1653–1734). Marshal of France; probably the most formidable of Marlborough's opponents. The latter worsted him, however, in one of his most brilliant series of manoeuvres, the penetration in 1711 of Villars' boastfully named 'ne plus ultra' lines, constructed as a last defence of France.

WHARTON, Thomas Wharton (1648–1715), 2nd baron; Earl of, 1706, and Marquis of, 1715. One of the Whig Lords of the Junto. His personal reputation was appalling, but 'honest Tom' was an able politician and parliamentarian with a large income which he spent on accumulating votes. Lord Lieutenant of Ireland, 1708, he was dismissed when the Tories came to office in 1710. Dedicatee of vol. V of the collected *Spectators*.

WILKS, Robert (1670–1732), actor and manager. His performance as Sir Harry Wildair in Farquhar's *The Constant Couple, or A trip to the Jubilee* was famous but he had a wide range.

WOOD, Lt-General Cornelius (1636–1712). Served in Ireland under William III; made Major-General by Marlborough after Blenheim, 1704; Lt-General of the Horse, 1707, following distinguished conduct at Ramillies, 1706.

WYCHERLEY, William (1640–1716). Dramatist. His first comedy, *Love in a Wood, or St. James's Park* was acted in 1671. He is best-known for *The Country Wife* (1675) and *The Plain Dealer* (1676), savage critiques of a licentious society, which were by Steele's day falling into disfavour as the trend of public taste went against 'indecency' on the stage in favour of the comedy of feeling.

ZINZENDORF, Philip Louis (1672–1742). Count; Austrian diplomat and Chancellor of the Holy Roman Empire.

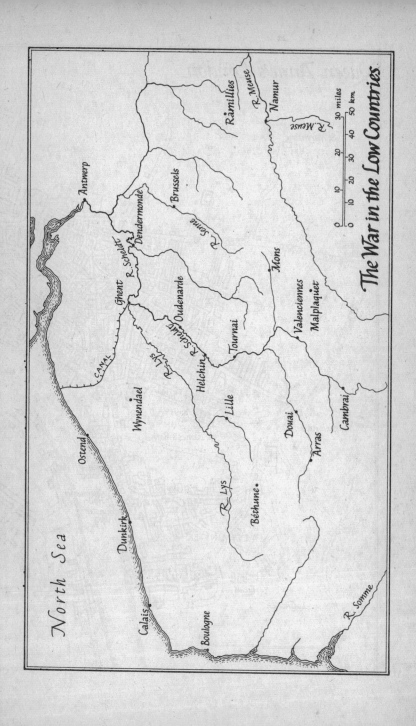

The War in the Low Countries

North Sea

Antwerp
Ostend
Dunkirk
Calais
Boulogne
Wynendael
Ghent
R. Schelt
Dendermonde
Brussels
Senne
Ramillies
R. Meuse
Namur
R. Meuse
Mons
Valenciennes
Malplaquet
Oudenarde
R. Schelde
Helchin
Tournai
R. LYS
Lille
R. Lys
Béthune
Douai
Arras
Cambrai
R. Somme
CANAL

0   10   20   30 miles
0   10   20   30   40   50 km.

Queen Anne's London

St Marylebone

Tyburn Gibbet

TYBURN ROAD   OXFORD ST

St Giles-in-the-Fields

Bloomsbury Sq.

HIGH ST

Lincoln's Inn Fields

Golden Sq!

TYBURN LANE

ST MARTIN'S LANE

KING ST

LONG ACRE

DRURY LANE

RUSSEL ST

Covent Garden

Somerset House

PICCADILLY

HAY MARKET

STRAND

Knightsbridge

PALL MALL

Charing Cross

River

St James's Palace

St James's Park

WHITEHALL

Privy Stairs

Westminster Hall

Westminster Abbey

WESTMINSTER

Tothill Fields

to Chelsea

0   ½ mile

0   ½ km

Gray's Inn
Red Lion Sq.
HOLBORN
CHANCERY LA
FETTER LA
FLEET ST
Ludgate
The Temple
Temple Stairs

Charterhouse
St Bartholomew
West Sm field
Newgate
Aldersgate
St Paul's Cathedral
CHEAPSIDE

Cripplegate
Moorfields
Moorgate
Bishopsgate
THREADNEEDLE
CORNHILL
LOMBARD
GRACECHURCH ST
LEADENHALL ST
Aldgate

T h a m e s
CITY
BANKSIDE
London Bridge
Billinggate
EAST CHEAP
THAMES
TOWER ST
Tower of London

SOUTHWARK

BERMONDSEY

Glossary of Words and Phrases

The symbol ° in the text, preceding a word or phrase, indicates an entry in the following pages (e.g. °scowrer; °rolling in the publick stocks)

abstracted Abstruse, rarefied, difficult.

account Reckoning in one's favour, benefit.

Act of Naturalization A very contentious Act for Naturalizing Foreign Protestants received the Royal Assent on 23 March 1709; it was meant to accommodate refugees from the dominions of Louis XIV and his allies but was later repealed by the Tories. (°Palatines.)

Act of Settlement An Act passed in 1701 by the English Parliament which settled the English crown, after descendants (if any) of William III and Princess Anne, on the Electress of Hanover and her descendants.

Act of Toleration An Act passed in 1689, the best William III could manage against Anglican rigour. It abolished no penal statute, but allowed 'dissenters' who believed in the Trinity to meet in their own, unlocked places of worship, and under restriction to have their own preachers and teachers.

Act of Uniformity An Act passed in 1662, part of the series of restrictive Acts known as the 'Clarendon Code'. By oaths and subscriptions it excluded a large section of believers from communion in the Church of England and was the basic law that turned them into 'dissenters', disadvantaged and denied political power.

act upon consignment . . . answer readily what their correspondents draw Transact business on written authority . . . meet in ready cash what such signatures require; cash cheques.

amuse Divert attention, mislead, cheat.

antanaclasis (a figure in rhetoric) Repeating a word in a different or opposite sense.

apparently Visibly.

artist Craftsman.

astragal (in architecture) A moulding of semicircular section at the top or bottom of a column.

Baeotians (Boeotians) The inhabitants of the country north-west of Attica, proverbial among the rest of the Greeks for their stupidity.

band-box Cardboard box, for °bands, collars, millinery, etc.

bands Two ornamental strips of cloth hanging from the neck band of a shirt to finish off the top front like the modern tie.

bell-man Town crier (and night watchman).

biters Hoaxers.

blind Italian character Smudgy italics.

blots In backgammon, exposed pieces in danger of being taken; likewise, plays making pieces vulnerable.

board-wages Payments made to servants who keep themselves in food and drink.

boxes The compartments boarded off in the public coffee-room of an inn, or a tavern.

break Go bankrupt.

bred by hand Not breast-fed.

breeches and pumps Light dress with pull-on shoes for exercise or dancing, the traditional garb for duelling: '*Sir Oliver Cockwood*: Death, and Hell, and Furies! I will have my pumps and long sword' (Sir George Etherege, *She Would If She Could*, 1688, IV, i).

brims Marginal rims.

broke Bankrupt, went bankrupt.

bubble (verb and noun) Dupe.

bugles and bredes Tubular beads (for ornamenting clothes) and braids.

bully Ponce, ruffian.

burridge in the glass (borage) Sprigs of this plant were used in cordials and cups.

Burton ale Ale skilfully brewed at Burton-on-Trent using the hard water there, and highly prized.

buy as hard Bargain as keenly.

campaign-whig (campaign wig) Plain, close-fitting, travelling wig.

carbonadoed Literally, of meat, scored across and broiled on the coals; figuratively, 'roasted'.

cardmatches Thin pieces of pasteboard dipped in sulphur.

carmen Draymen, cart drivers.

carminitive Wind-expelling (medicine).

Cartesians Students of the mathematics, physics and philosophy of René Descartes (1596–1650), whose method of systematic doubt was widely held to be irreligious, or at least, with justification, hostile to contemporary religious teaching.

cast, been cast Thrown, over-thrown, defeated.

casting a figure Casting a horoscope.

caudle or sack posset A warm, sweet, spiced drink, milk or thin gruel mixed with wine (°sack).

chamber-practice Private legal consultation as distinct from pleading in the courts.

'Change Alley Exchange Alley was a small street opposite the Royal Exchange, running from Cornhill south to Lombard Street, in which were situated Garraway's and Jonathan's, two coffee-houses frequented by merchants and moneyed men.

character (of print) Type, letter.

chariot A light, four-wheeled carriage, with only two back seats.

chronogram Group of words within which certain distinguished letters express by their numerical value a date.

circumforaneous Moving from market to market, itinerant.

cits (citizens) Merchants, tradesmen, shopkeepers from the business end of London.

clinch A play on words, a pun.

cloath Cloth; woollen, winter-weight.

clock of a stocking Pattern worked, normally in silk, on the side of a stocking.

close hunks Close-fisted, old miser.

collar round her neck Orthopaedic device to induce erect carriage; the collar and back-board.

commoner Member of the House of Commons.

compassionate (verb) To feel sympathy with, to commiserate with; (adj.) demanding sympathy, pitiful.

conjurer Magician, astrologer.

conscience Consciousness.

conundrum Pun, play on words.

coral and bells Polished coral beads with silver balls, toys for teething infants.

couched Removed a cataract by pushing down the clouded lens of the eye with a knife or a needle until it rested below the axis of vision.

country put Country bumpkin.

Courant °*Daily Courant*.

Court of Requests A court of record for dealing with petitions to the crown.

couzenage (cozenage) Cheating, fraud.

crack Crazy bent; a person thus obsessed.

critick Critique, criticism.

crown A five-shilling piece; 25p.

cunning man A man possessing esoteric (magical) powers, knowledge and skill, often a 'healer'; a °conjurer.

cupping In general, drawing blood, a common medical treatment of the time; specifically, by making incisions through the skin and applying a cup which exerted suction after it had been heated.

cutting Swaggering.

Daily Courant The first English daily newspaper, which ran from 11 March 1702 to 27 September 1714, printed by Samuel Buckley, who also published *The Spectator.*

dentelli (in architecture) The small blocks, arranged like a row of teeth, underneath the lowest moulding of the cornice in several of the classical orders.

devoted Consecrated, doomed.

distemper Discomposure.

divisions running upon the same ground Descants or variations on the same theme.

Don Diegoed Cheated.

'Drawcansir Blustering braggart, after the character in the Duke of Buckingham's comedy *The Rehearsal*, first acted at the Theatre Royal, Vere Street, 1 December 1671.

Dyer's Letter A weekly newsletter published by John ◊ Dyer in a type-face resembling handwriting, much read by Tory country gentlemen like Sir Roger de Coverly (*Spectator* 127).

ecliptick, ecliptic The apparent orbit of the sun, which forms the great circle of the celestial sphere, so called because eclipses happen when the moon is on, or near, this line.

efficient cause The Aristotelian metaphysics which Addison employs offered a four-fold discussion of causality, employing the terms: (a) *material cause*, or the stuff out of which a thing is made; (b) *formal cause*, or the essence of that thing; (c) *efficient cause* (Addison also calls this the *occasional cause* or the *necessary cause*), or the impetus or immediate instrument by which a thing is produced; (d) *final cause*, or the aim or idea of the change.

elah The highest note (la) in Guido's highest (E) hexachord; the name was preserved in later verbal descriptions of notes; a very high note.

electuaries medicinal powders mixed with honey, jam or syrup.

English-Post A paper edited by N. Crouch, no. 1 14 October 1700. It seems to have discontinued publication on 19 May 1708, with no. 1191.

enormous Away from the norm, outrageous, disorderly, wicked.

ens rationis A term of scholastic philosophy; an entity of being created by the mind.

enthusiasm in religion Extreme religious fervour; belief in special, personal communication with God.

equipage Following, retinue.

erudition Training, cultivation.

eugh Yew.

Exchange Alley See *'Change Alley*.

exercises School or college work; particularly, translation into or out of Latin at school, disputations at university.

factors Doers; (commission) agents.

final cause See *efficient cause*.

flint bottles Bottles of the best, clearest, most lustrous glass made with ground flint in the mix.

flustered Tipsy, confused with drink.

forrester A half-wild thing; a free spirit.

Fox-hall Fauxhall or Vauxhall.

frize (frieze) Coarse woollen cloth, often with a nap on one side only.

fruz (frizz) A row, or hair-piece of crisp curls.

furniture Accessories, knick-knacks.

Game Act The Game Laws were designed to restrict the right of killing or catching game to landowners. The basic qualifications were £100 p.a. from a freehold estate, £150 p.a. from 99-year leases, being the son of an esquire etc. (22 and 23 Charles II, c.25, the principal Act). See D. Hay, 'Poaching and Game Laws on Cannock Chase', in D. Hay et al., *Albion's Fatal Tree: Crime and Society in Eighteenth-Century England* (1975; Peregrine Books, 1977). See *S* 122.

gamut The full range of notes in music.

garlands Anthologies or miscellanies of songs and verse, from the common form of chap-book titles such as *Robin Hood's Garland*.

Gazette The London Gazette, the weekly (from late June 1709 twice-weekly) official government newspaper (also published in a French edition); Steele wrote it from 1707 until he lost the place, worth £300 a year, in October 1710. Each number contained on average 1,650 words of text.

gentile (genteel) At this time, well-bred, polished, obliging.

gigg Jig.

glasses Optical instruments with lenses, telescopes, ? microscopes.

go-carts Baby-walkers.

gola or cymatium (gula) In architecture, the moulding of a cornice, the section of which is convex and concave.

go upon the town Become a prostitute.

grand elixir An essence or drug capable of prolonging life indefinitely.

grimace A movement of the facial muscles to indicate recognition etc.; not at this time necessarily pejorative.

Guelfes and Gibbelines (Guelphs and Ghibellines) The (Hohenstaufen) Imperial party and the anti-Imperialists that fought over Italy in the Holy Roman Empire from the eleventh to the fourteenth centuries.

hacks Drivers of hackney-carriages; survives in America as a word for taxi drivers.

half-pike Spontoon or short halberd carried by infantry officers.

hanging out of false colours Displaying false flags at sea.

hasped in my bar, hasped up Confined, locked up.

hazard Game of dice with arbitrary rules.

high-change The peak trading time in the Royal Exchange.

hipps Hypochondriacs, people in depression or low spirits without real cause.

Hockley-in-the-Hole A lawless district near Newington Green, the location of a bear-garden.

horary question The answer to which is found by consulting an astrological figure of the heavens for the relevant moment.

Humble-down Homildon, a mile north of Wooler in Glendale, one of the six wards of Northumberland.

humourists Persons who indulge their whims or caprices (humours); faddists.

hung beef Beef cured by drying in the air.

husbandman A frugal, prudent man.

hussars Skirmishers or light cavalry, independent and fierce.

hypps See *hipps*.

Ichabod Dawks' Letter A weekly newsletter published by Ichabod ◊ Dawks in a type-face resembling handwriting; it ran from 23 June 1690 to 22 December 1716, and had a blank space for subscribers' own correspondence from London.

inkle Linen tape, or the yarn for making this.

Jack (1) Jacobite.

jack (2) Pike (fish).

jetteaus Jets of water from fountains or pipes, or such ornamental engines themselves (Fr. *jet d'eau*; It. *getto d'acqua*).

jetting Protruding.

John Sly's Best Tobacco: 'Mr Sly, Haberdasher [and tobacconist] at the Corner of Devereux Court in the Strand . . .' (advertisement in *Spectator* 187).

Knights of the Shire Members of Parliament for a county.

labours Suffers from a defect.

ladder-dancers Balancers who performed on the tops of ladders.

La Hogue (or Barfleur) A decisive sea battle, 19–25 May 1692, in which the English fleet under Admiral Russell destroyed enough French warships to prevent an invasion force accompanied by James II from attempting a landing in England.

lanistae (Latin) Trainers of gladiators, fencing masters.

law is open 'Wherefore if Demetrius and the craftsmen which are with him, have a matter against any man, the law is open, and there are deputies: let them implead one another' (Acts xix, 38).

League An alliance of nobles formed in France under the house of Guise in 1576, to prevent the protestant Henry of Navarre acceding to the throne; when he did so, as Henry IV, he became a catholic.

Leda's egg Leda, daughter of Thestios, was impregnated by Zeus in the form of a swan; the egg she produced gave birth to Helen of Troy.

lettice (*lattice*) The wooden grating common on the windows of inns and ale-houses; the 'red lattice' was a popular sign.

licentiates Medical practitioners who have received a licence to practice from the Royal College of Physicians; junior doctors.

light Link, torch carried in the streets at night; the man who carries a link.

limbeck A vessel for distillation (alembic).

lipograms Pieces of writing in which all words containing a certain letter or letters are omitted.

loggerheads Contentions.

Long-lane A street with an open market for old clothes; it was an eastward extension of Barbican, from the north end of Aldersgate Street to West Smithfield.

Lydian King Midas, of the legendary golden touch, King of Phrygia (part of Lydia).

lyrick Song-writer, lyric poet.

machines Stage machinery.

made Trained.

manes (Latin) (Deified) spirits of the dead.

mansion house Dwelling house, residence.

marked at Pointed to, as by a hunting dog (a pointer).

May-Fair Under a charter granted by James II in 1689, a fair held yearly for the first fortnight in May in the Brookfield, to the north of the west end of Piccadilly: 'In pity to the emptying Town/Some God May-Fair invented . . .' It was abolished in 1709 on the usual grounds of the encouragement of idleness, dissipation, profligacy. Though briefly revived under George I, it no doubt succumbed to the development of the area for high-class, fashionable housing.

Mercure Gallant The monthly *Mercure Galant* was a prototype of *The Tatler* and *The Spectator* begun in 1672 by Donneau de Visé and run as a gentlemanly literary miscellany, which sought contributions but did not pay for them; it also appeared in yearly collected volumes.

Merry-Andrew A mountebank's assistant.

methoughts Methought; erroneous parallel with *methinks*.

midnight magistrate The watchman.

Million Lottery A public lottery authorized by Parliament in 1709–10 to raise £1,000,000 towards the cost of the war; all tickets, including 31 blanks, were loans to the government.

mobb (mob: from Latin *mobile vulgus*, the excitable) Crowd.

morrions (morions) Helmets without visors, worn on the crown of the head.

mother Hysteria.

mum A kind of beer.

murrain Cattle plague, pestilence in general.

neat Port, neat wine Pure unadulterated wine from Oporto; at this time a table wine, not fortified with brandy. The protection offered by the Methuen Treaty with Portugal, 1703, and the war with France were helping it to replace French wine, but its success in the market made it of even more uncertain quality, and it was frequently adulterated to attempt to give it a uniform colour, taste and strength.

necessary cause See *efficient cause*.

newly come upon the town Recently taken to prostitution.

new philosophy The observation-based study of the Royal Society with its attendant theories and attempted quantifications; the speculations of thinkers like Descartes (°Cartesians) and Isaac Newton.

nightcap-wigs Close-fitting wigs with short tails, resembling night caps.

night-gowns Dressing-gowns.

nostrum Patent medicine, quack remedy.

novelists News-writers, journalists.

N.S. New Style; the date according to the reformed Gregorian calendar used in continental Europe at this time, eleven days behind the old Julian calendar used in England or Old Style (°O.S.).

Numps Fool, dolt; a jocular address.

occasional cause See *efficient cause*.

oeconomy (economy) Order, (good) organization.

officious Ready to do kindness, eager to serve, attentive.

on every post in town The many posts in the streets of London, supporting over-hanging buildings and signs or marking the road, were used for the public display of advertisements such as the title-pages of new books, lampoons etc. 'Mean Time on every Pissing-Post/Paste up this

Recreant's Name,/So that each Pisser-by shall read,/And piss against the same' (Pope, *Duke upon Duke: an excellent new ballad*, 1720).

ordinary A public eating-house where a meal was regularly offered at a fixed price, so, a five-penny ordinary, a twelve-penny ordinary.

ordonnance Systematic arrangement, plan of composition.

O.S. Date according to the old Julian calendar still used in England, at this time eleven days in front of the Gregorian calendar used in continental Europe, or New Style (°N.S.).

out-set Out-lay, investment.

pair of new globes Two spheres: the *terrestial globe* showing the geographical configuration of the earth's surface; the *celestial globe* showing the heavenly bodies.

Palatines Protestant refugees from the Rhenish Palatinate (Bavaria), encouraged to settle in England in 1709; the 'poor Palatines' soon posed a severe economic and social problem.

paranomasia (paronomasia) Play on words which sound alike, pun.

partizan A spear or halberd carried by an infantryman in the sixteenth and seventeeth centuries; a soldier who carries such a weapon.

Philippick Islands ?The Philippines and perhaps the Moluccas (or Spice Islands).

Phizz Physiognomy, face.

pip Lose, or be a loser; cf. the modern phrase 'pipped at the post'.

plenipos Plenipotentiaries, ambassadors.

ploce A rhetorical figure employing the repetition of a word in some special or altered sense, or for emphasis.

point of war A phrase repeated on a trumpet as a signal.

porpusses Porpoises.

Post-Boy The leading Tory newspaper, thrice weekly, conducted by Abel Roper.

Post-Man A Whig paper, thrice weekly, conducted at this time by Jean de Fonvive, a Huguenot journalist.

pozz Positive.

Present State of England Angliae Notitia (from 1708 *Magnae Britanniae Notitia*), *or The Present State of England (Great Britain)*, a year book from 1669, first by Edward Chamberlayne, then by his son John, containing lists of peers, Members of Parliament, office-holders, a gazetteer, government income and expenditure etc.

pretend To profess or claim.

Pretender The son of the deposed James II.

prisoner at discretion Prisoner at the will of the jailor.

problematical Hypothetical.

Projector A promoter, a schemer; often in a bad sense, a cheat.

pure Capital, splendid.

purle (purl) Infusion of bitter herbs (wormwood etc.) in beer.

purlues (purlieus) The outlying parts, the ramifications of anything; may be used with an abstract noun.

push-pin A children's game using pins, like tiddly-winks.

putt (put) Bumpkin, fool, 'buffer'.

quail pipe A pipe or call to lure quail into firing range.

questions and commands A children's game in which one participant is chosen 'king' to command the forfeits incurred by failing to answer the questions.

quick Lively.

quorum (Latin) 'Of whom', from the formula specifying certain specially qualified Justices of the Peace, whose presence was needed for a properly constituted sitting of the Bench; or, more loosely, the Justices of the Peace of a district.

ramage de la ville (Fr. *ramage* = warbling, bird song) City warbling, town chorus.

rank of mankind The ordinary mass of humanity.

receipt Formula, prescription, recipe.

red letters Used in church calendars to indicate saints' days and festivals.

Reformers of Manners Members of the groups which were formed and flourished in the 1690s; a widely read *Account of the Societies for Reformation of Manners in England and Ireland* was published by Josiah Woodward in 1698 and frequently reprinted.

refreshment Re-hash; something warmed-up again.

relievo A work of art in relief, i.e. parts of it raised from a plane surface.

rep Reputation.

repartee (verb) To retort, to make a smart reply.

revival of letters The literary aspect of the Renaissance.

Ring The circular drive in Hyde Park, frequented by promenaders and those wishing to display their carriages and horses; a place to see and be seen.

rings (mourning) It was common to bequeath rings to legatees as mementoes.

Road of Scheveling The roadstead or anchorage at the fishing port of Scheveningen, near The Hague.

rolling in the publick stocks Investing heavily in government loans; may be connected with 'rolling in money'.

rope-dancers Dancers and balancers on tight- and slack-ropes.

round-house Guard-house and lock-up, from which the watch went out on their rounds.

sack (Fr. *sec*, dry) White wine imported from Spain and the Canaries.

St John Street A street running north from West Smithfield to Sadler's Wells.

Save the pass Get through a narrow place first.

scamperer A vandal who decamps after committing damage.

scowrer (scourer) Roisterer, one who scours the streets breaking windows etc.

sentences Maxims, opinions weightily or pointedly expressed.

sham-prize Spurious prize.

shoots flying Shoots birds on the wing, at this time a relatively recent practice among sportsmen, becoming increasingly common as a sign of skill.

shower of consequence Shower which had great consequences or effects.

side-boxes The seating in the theatres was arranged on four levels: '. . . the Pit is sunk below the Stage . . . Then, the Boxes are built round, and raised to a Level with the Scene, in deference to the Ladies, because, That large Portion of Wit laid out in raising Pruriences and Protuberancies, is observed to run much upon a Line [to the ladies in the front boxes facing the stage], and ever in a circle [to the men in the side-boxes] . . . the middle Region [of the first gallery] . . . a fourth Place, called *the Twelve-Penny Gallery* . . .' Swift, *A Tale of A Tub* (1704), Introduction. Any ladies in the side-boxes were usurpers.

simplex munditiis (Horace, *Odes*, I, v, 5) Natural elegance.

sippet Croûton; small piece of toast or fried bread in soup or for dipping in gravy.

smoaky Shrewd, suspicious.

sophisters Students: in Cambridge, second year; in Trinity College, Dublin, third or fourth year.

Spanish Snuff; plain Spanish was the cheapest, and cost 4s to 6s a pound.

squirred Skimmed.

staggered Bewildered, perplexed.

staked himself Impaled himself on a stake while jumping.

stand of the stairs Landing.

stone-horse Stallion.

story History.

stuff Woollen fabric, summer-weight.

Supplement To *The °Post Boy*.

taken up Apprehended, arrested.

tansy Pudding or egg dish flavoured with the juice of Tansy, *Tanacetum vulgare*.

tar-jacket Seaman's jacket made of tarred canvas.

taw A game played with large fancy marbles.

temper Temperament; also, mental composure under trials.

Temple See *Templers*.

Templers (Templars) Literally, persons with chambers in the Inner or Middle Temple, two of the Inns of Court, the London organizations of barristers; more generally, any residents of any of the Inns and particularly those, usually gentlemen's sons, studying the law there, traditionally supporters of the theatre, literary periodicals etc.

ten yard land A yardland (*virgata terrae*, virgate) was a rather elastic measurement of 20 to 30 acres; so, 200 to 300 acres.

titles The inscriptions round the rim of a coin.

Tividale Teviotdale.

toyman A man who keeps a gift shop, selling trinkets, knick-knacks.

Toyshop A gift shop.

traces Paths, tracks.

tract Track.

trepidation An oscillating movement of the heavenly bodies, specifically a movement introduced into Ptolemy's model of the heavens to account for observations really caused by movements of the earth's axis.

tucked cravats Pleated, lace neck-cloths.

tucker A lace ruff round the top of a woman's stays or corset.

turned Adapted or 'cut out for' some activity.

undertakers Managers, contractors, suppliers.

urinal A glass vessel holding urine for medical inspection.

vapours Literally, exhalations developed within the body, believed to cause several disorders, especially hysteria, depression etc.; more generally such disorders themselves.

Virtuoso A connoisseur; often in a bad sense, one skilled in trifles.

vowel'd (in a game) Played against unfairly (a form of *fouled*).

waiters Attendants, often of superior rank, not necessarily at table.

westerly wind Interrupts the news by preventing the paquet boats from the Low Countries from making English ports.

Wheels Condemned men were bound, spreadeagled, to the spokes of horizontal wheels and destroyed by breaking their bones, broken on the wheel (e.g. in France); in Otway's *Venice Preserved*, V, a scene opens to discover '*a Scaffold and a Wheel prepar'd for the executing of* Pierre . . .'

whitepot A dish of milk, flour, eggs, spices.

white witch A person who uses magical powers for beneficent purposes.

winyard (whinyard; whinger) A short sword or knife.

wrought-bed Embroidered bed (cover, hangings etc.).

884 9866